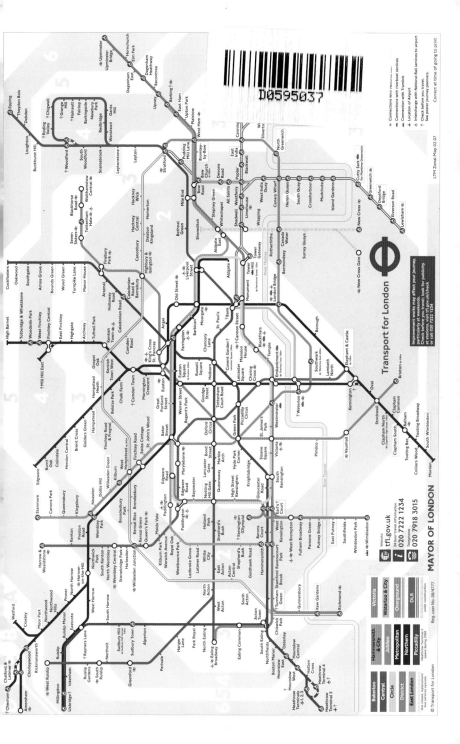

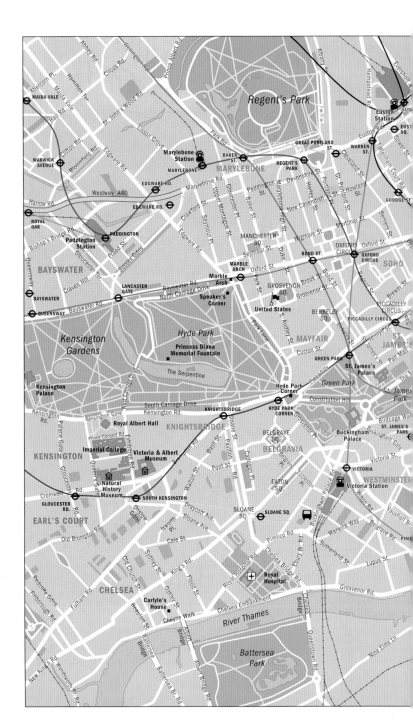

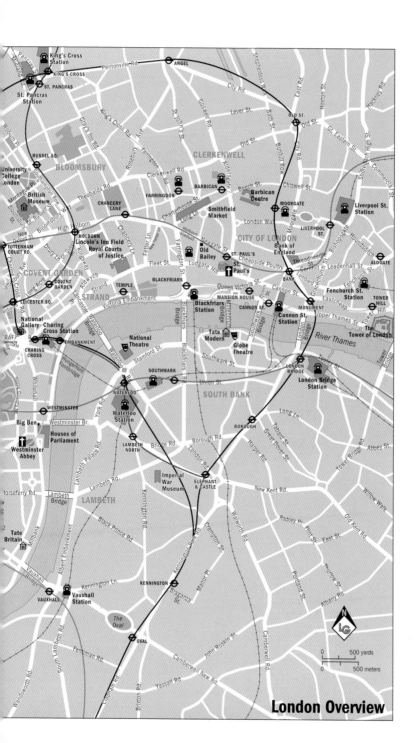

London Overview

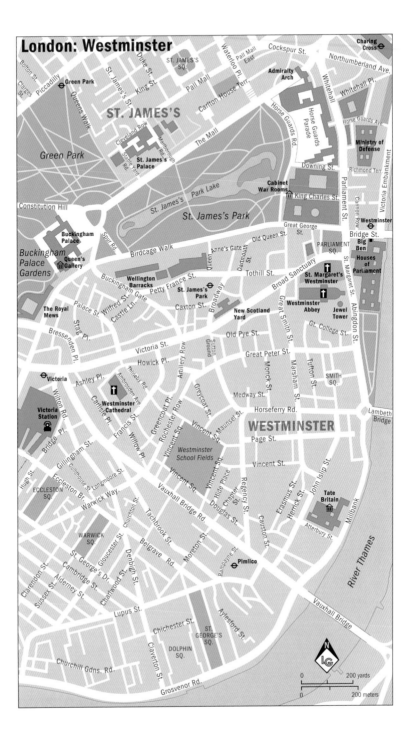

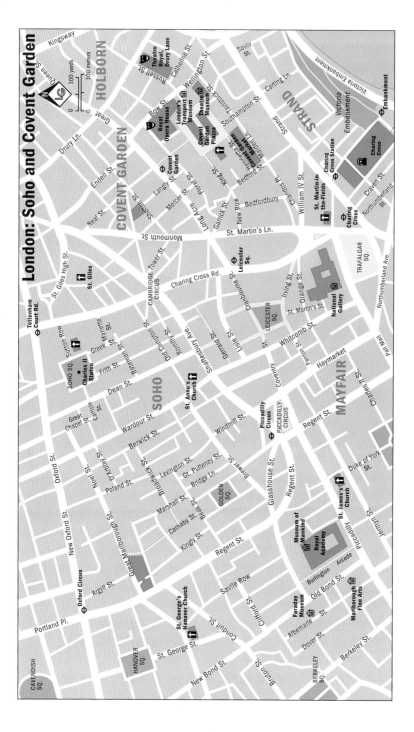

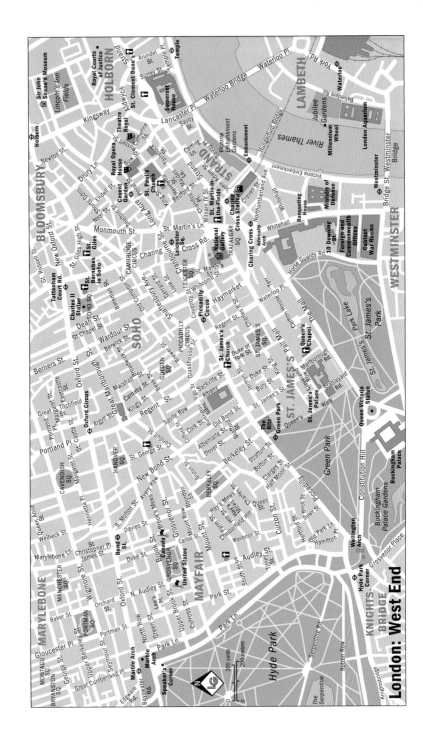

London: West End

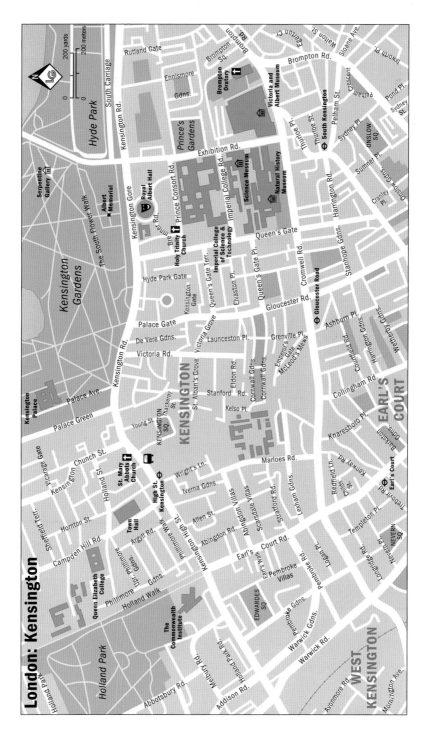

London: Notting Hill and Bayswater

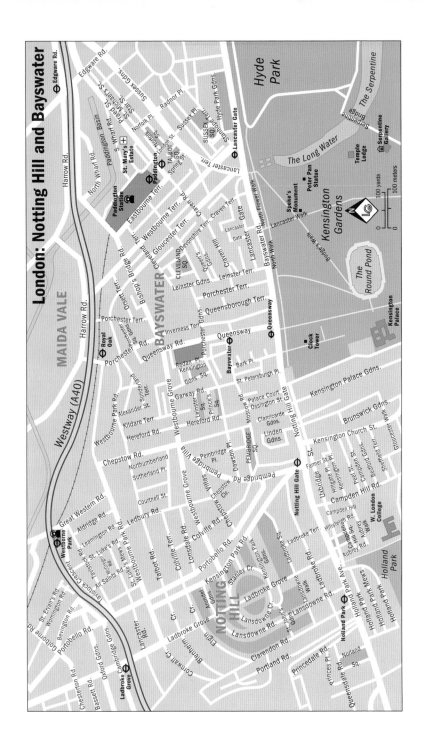

LET'S GO

■ PAGES PACKED WITH ESSENTIAL INFORMATION

"Value-packed, unbeatable, accurate, and comprehensive."

—The Los Angeles Times

"The guides are aimed not only at young budget travelers but at the independent traveler; a sort of streetwise cookbook for traveling alone."

—The New York Times

"Unbeatable; good sight-seeing advice; up-to-date info on restaurants, hotels, and inns; a commitment to money-saving travel; and a wry style that brightens nearly every page."

—The Washington Post

■ THE BEST TRAVEL BARGAINS IN YOUR BUDGET

"All the dirt, dirt cheap."

—People

"Let's Go follows the creed that you don't have to toss your life's savings to the wind to travel—unless you want to."

—The Salt Lake Tribune

■ REAL ADVICE FOR REAL EXPERIENCES

"The writers seem to have experienced every rooster-packed bus and lunar-surfaced mattress about which they write."

—The New York Times

"[Let's Go's] devoted updaters really walk the walk (and thumb the ride, and trek the trail). Learn how to fish, haggle, find work—anywhere."

—Food & Wine

"A world-wise traveling companion—always ready with friendly advice and helpful hints, all sprinkled with a bit of wit."

—The Philadelphia Inquirer

■ A GUIDE WITH A SPIRIT AND A SOCIAL CONSCIENCE

"Lighthearted and sophisticated, informative and fun to read. [Let's Go] helps the novice traveler navigate like a knowledgeable old hand."

—Atlanta Journal-Constitution

"The serious mission at the book's core reveals itself in exhortations to respect the culture and the environment—and, if possible, to visit as a volunteer, a student, or a teacher rather than a tourist."

—San Francisco Chronicle

LET'S GO PUBLICATIONS

TRAVEL GUIDES

Australia 9th edition
Austria & Switzerland 12th edition
Brazil 1st edition
Britain 2008
California 10th edition
Central America 9th edition
Chile 2nd edition
China 5th edition
Costa Rica 3rd edition
Eastern Europe 13th edition
Ecuador 1st edition
Egypt 2nd edition
Europe 2008
France 2008
Germany 13th edition
Greece 9th edition
Hawaii 4th edition
India & Nepal 8th edition
Ireland 13th edition
Israel 4th edition
Italy 2008
Japan 1st edition
Mexico 22nd edition
New Zealand 8th edition
Peru 1st edition
Puerto Rico 3rd edition
Southeast Asia 9th edition
Spain & Portugal 2008
Thailand 3rd edition
USA 24th edition
Vietnam 2nd edition
Western Europe 2008

ROADTRIP GUIDE

Roadtripping USA 2nd edition

ADVENTURE GUIDES

Alaska 1st edition
Pacific Northwest 1st edition
Southwest USA 3rd edition

CITY GUIDES

Amsterdam 5th edition
Barcelona 3rd edition
Boston 4th edition
London 16th edition
New York City 16th edition
Paris 14th edition
Rome 12th edition
San Francisco 4th edition
Washington, D.C. 13th edition

POCKET CITY GUIDES

Amsterdam
Berlin
Boston
Chicago
London
New York City
Paris
San Francisco
Venice
Washington, D.C.

LET'S GO

LONDON

R. DEREK WETZEL EDITOR

RESEARCHER-WRITERS
ELSA Ó RIAIN
ALISSA K. VALIANTE

DREW DAVIS MAP EDITOR
VICTORIA NORELID MANAGING EDITOR

ST. MARTIN'S PRESS ⚟ NEW YORK

HELPING LET'S GO. If you want to share your discoveries, suggestions, or corrections, please drop us a line. We read every piece of correspondence, whether a postcard, a 10-page email, or a coconut. **Address mail to:**

Let's Go: London
67 Mount Auburn St.
Cambridge, MA 02138
USA

Visit Let's Go at **http://www.letsgo.com,** or send email to:

feedback@letsgo.com
Subject: "Let's Go: London"

In addition to the invaluable travel advice our readers share with us, many are kind enough to offer their services as researchers or editors. Unfortunately, our charter enables us to employ only currently enrolled Harvard students.

HOW TO USE THIS BOOK

COVERAGE LAYOUT. Here it is: all of the magnificence and excitement of London in your hands. But how to begin your journey through the city? *Let's Go: London* arranges chapters with the essentials to travel first; recreation and merriment second: **Accommodations, Food, Sights, Museums, Entertainment, Shopping, Nightlife,** and **Daytrips.** Listings are organized by neighborhood in the above chapters, except for **Entertainment,** in which they are organized by type of entertainment. *Let's Go* organizes London's neighborhoods roughly from east to west. The coverage progresses in a snake-like fashion westward so that adjacent neighborhoods' coverage appear next to one another in the book. Refer to the Table of Contents as well as the neighborhood map on p. 356 to navigate the neighborhoods.

TRANSPORTATION INFO. *Let's Go* lists the nearest **Tube** station to most establishments. **Buses** are an equally effective way to get around, and are included when relevant. The book also lists the closest **Night Buses** for most Accommodations and Nightlife listings; refer to the Night Bus map (p. 352) for a quick reference. The **Essentials** chapter (p. 17) has extensive transportation information, while the **Map Appendix** (p. 348) has detailed maps to help you navigate London's byways.

COVERING THE BASICS. The first chapter, **Discover London** (p. 1), outlines each neighborhood and offers **Suggested Itineraries** for a day in the city. The **Essentials** chapter (p. 17) contains information on planning a budget, getting around the city, and other useful tips for traveling in London. The **Practical Information** chapter (p. 95) details local services including tourist offices, financial services, and emergency information. Take some time to peruse the **Life and Times** chapter (p. 55), which includes a brief history of the city along with a cultural overview of London. For study abroad, volunteer, and work options in London, look no further than **Beyond Tourism** (p. 81). The **Appendix** (p. 345) has climate information, measurement conversions, and a language phrasebook.

FEATURE ARTICLES. Two contributors with unique regional insight wrote articles for *Let's Go: London.* Fulbright Scholar Thomas Sleigh discusses Britain's multi-faceted relations with the US and the EU (p. 75). Harvard graduate and London native Olivia Brown shares her experience volunteering in a London pre-natal ward (p. 89).

PRICE DIVERSITY. Our researchers list establishments in order of value from best to worst, with absolute favorites denoted by the *Let's Go* thumbs-up (🖑). Since the cheapest price does not always mean the best value, we have incorporated a system of price ranges for food and accommodations (see p. XI).

PHONE CODES AND TELEPHONE NUMBERS. Phone numbers in text are preceded by the ☎ icon. See p. 44 of the **Essentials** chapter for detailed information regarding phone codes in London. Regional codes are listed beside appropriate regions in the **Daytrips** chapter.

A NOTE TO OUR READERS. The information for this book was gathered by *Let's Go* researchers from May through August of 2007. Each listing is based on one researcher's opinion, formed during his or her visit at a particular time. Those traveling at other times may have different experiences since prices, dates, hours, and conditions are always subject to change. You are urged to check the facts presented in this book beforehand to avoid inconvenience and surprises.

CONTENTS

RESEARCHER-WRITERS

Elsa Ó Riain   *Chelsea, The South Bank, South London, The City of London, Bloomsbury, Marylebone, Knightsbridge and Belgravia, North London, Kensington and Earl's Court*

Elsa took her researching experience from *Let's Go: Australia 2007* and hit the streets of London with a purpose. The Ireland native brought a worldly flavor to her London writing, boldly sampling foreign dishes and getting the lowdown on uncharted clubs. Not even torrential flooding could keep her from uncovering London's secrets—and its best Guinness on tap. Trust us, she knows what she's talking about.

Alissa Valiante   *West London, Bayswater, Notting Hill, West End, Westminster, East London, Holborn, Clerkenwell, North London*

A one-time resident of London, Alissa used her knowledge to her advantage, tracking down essential details by getting to know the Londoners who make the city tick. She shared the city with friends and other Let's Go researchers, enjoying the Wimbledon grounds and East London's allure. Whether it was scouring the Taste festival for the best eats or talking her way up to rooftop gardens, Alissa always brought the party.

CONTRIBUTING WRITERS

Ravi Ramchandani   *Researcher-Writer, Let's Go: Europe*

Patrick McKiernan   *Editor, Let's Go: Britain*

Jen Rugani   *Associate Editor, Let's Go: Britain*

Thomas Sleigh studied Political Science at Cambridge University (1997-2000). He was a Fulbright Scholar at Harvard University (2003-04) and now works in London.

Olivia Brown is a senior at Harvard University studying history. She has lived in London since she was 9 months old, and has also lived in Cuba, Ecuador and New York. She was a Researcher-Writer for *Let's Go: Paris 2007*.

ACKNOWLEDGMENTS

DEREK THANKS: Alissa, thank you for your incredible street spirit and absolute tirelessness—you constantly outdid yourself, and your phone calls made my week! Elsa, thanks for always being on point and putting up with my incessant tasks and questions and constantly turning in truly solid work, not to mention awesome souvenirs!

Victoria, thank you for your amazing support in all things LG and all things life. This book is as much a fruition of your efforts as anyone else's, and I consider myself fortunate (and more learned) for having worked with you this summer.

Drew, thanks for always being on point with maps and always making time to help. Awkward pod love: Nathaniel, thanks for inspiring me to always do better, and for your incredible edits. RaNo, you were always there, in sickness and in health. Thanks for making funny faces at me.

Thanks to everyone in the office who made the summer in Cambridge truly sweet: you are too many to list here, but you know who you are. Woo woo!

Finally, thanks to my family, to whom I owe everything. Mom, Dad, Kurtis, Cameron, Olivia, Grammy, and everyone else: I love you and cherish your unending support.

DREW THANKS: Thanks to the RWs for all of their hard work and crazy attention to detail. Thanks to Mr. Let's Go for being such a laid-back Editor. Thanks to Mapland for techno dance parties, 2hr. lunches, and brownie floorplans. Thanks to 7-11 for allowing me to buy 40 oz. of Coke for under $1.00. And thanks to Mom and Dad for the weekends in Rhode Island.

Editor
R. Derek Wetzel
Managing Editor
Victoria Norelid
Map Editor
Drew Davis
Typesetter
Jansen A.S. Thurmer
Photographers
Lance Bellers, Les Chatfield, D. Jonathan Dawid, Tom Edwards, Paul Friel, William Helsen, Colin Gregory Palmer, Lori Walter

LET'S GO

Publishing Director
Jennifer Q. Wong
Editor-in-Chief
Silvia Gonzalez Killingsworth
Production Manager
Victoria Esquivel-Korsiak
Cartography Manager
Thomas MacDonald Barron
Editorial Managers
Anne Bensson, Calina Ciobanu, Rachel Nolan
Financial Manager
Sara Culver
Business and Marketing Manager
Julie Vodhanel
Personnel Manager
Victoria Norelid
Production Associate
Jansen A. S. Thurmer
Director of E-Commerce & IT
Patrick Carroll
Website Manager
Kathryne A. Bevilacqua
Office Coordinators
Juan L. Peña, Bradley J. Jones

Director of Advertising Sales
Hunter McDonald
Senior Advertising Associate
Daniel Lee

President
William Hauser
General Managers
Bob Rombauer, Jim McKellar

X

PRICE RANGES

LONDON

Our researchers list establishments in order of value from best to worst; our favorites are denoted by the Let's Go thumbs-up (🖐). However, because the best value is not always the cheapest price, we have also incorporated a system of price ranges, based on a rough expectation of what you'll spend. For **accommodations,** we base our range on the cheapest price for which a single traveler can stay for one night. For **restaurants** and other dining establishments, we estimate the average amount a traveler will spend. The table tells you what you'll typically find in London at the corresponding price range, but keep in mind that no system can allow for every individual establishment's quirks. In other words: expect anything.

ACCOMMODATIONS	RANGE	WHAT YOU'RE LIKELY TO FIND
❶	under £25	Dorm rooms, or hostels with dorm-style rooms. Expect bunk beds and a communal bath; you may have to provide or rent towels and sheets.
❷	£25-40	Upper-end hostels or lower-end pensions. You may have a private bathroom, or there may be a sink in your room and a communal shower in the hall.
❸	£41-55	A small room with a private bath, probably in a budget hotel or pension. Should have decent amenities, such as phone and TV. Breakfast may be included in the price of the room.
❹	£56-75	Similar to 3, but may have more amenities or be in a more centrally located area.
❺	above £75	Large hotels or upscale chains. A splurge for budget travelers, but everyone deserves to go fancy once in a while.
FOOD	RANGE	WHAT YOU'RE LIKELY TO FIND
❶	under £6	Mostly street-corner stands, pizza places, snack bars, or sandwich stores. Besides pub sandwiches, rarely a sit-down meal.
❷	£6-10	Pub grub, fish 'n' chips, and cheap ethnic eateries. Could be a sit-down meal or takeaway.
❸	£11-15	Mid-priced entrees. Fancier pubs and higher quality ethnic food; most Indian places start in this range. You'll probably have a waiter or waitress, so the tip will bump you up a few pounds. For advice on tipping in London, see p. 24.
❹	£16-20	As in 3, higher prices are probably related to better service. Includes somewhat fancy restaurants and high-end pubs.
❺	above £20	Elegant restaurants with serious gourmet. You'll probably need to wear something other than sandals and a T-shirt.

DISCOVER LONDON

Beyond the blinding lights of Oxford and Piccadilly Circuses, London is just as much a working and living city as it is a tourist destination. Comprised of 32 boroughs along with the City, London is often described as more of a conglomerate of villages than a unified city. While this understates the pride Londoners take in their city as a whole, it is true that locals are strongly attached to their neighborhoods. Each area's heritage and traditions are alive and evolving, from the City of London's 2000-year-old association with trade to the West End's ever-changing theatre scene. Thanks to the feisty independence and diversity of each area, the London "buzz" is continually on the move—every few years a previously disregarded neighborhood explodes into cultural prominence. Most recently, South London has come to prominence with the cultural rebirth of the South Bank and the thumping nightlife of a recharged Brixton. No matter which neighborhood you start your journey in, Londoners of all creeds invite visitors to take part. Wander between cultures in London's diverse neighborhoods or take part in a political rally in Trafalgar Square. Each day in London brings something new, so get ready for adventures and prepare to love the city in all its splendor.

FACTS AND FIGURES

POPULATION: 7,421,600.

LAND MASS: 1577 sq. km, 30% of which is outdoor parks—147 registered parks and gardens and 8 royal parks.

LANGUAGE: English is the primary language, but over 300 languages are spoken.

RELIGION: 58% Christian (compared to 72% nationally), 16% no religion.

ETHNICITY: 71% classify themselves as white; 13% Indian, Bangladeshi, or Pakistani; 7% African; 5% Caribbean; 3% mixed race; and 1% Chinese.

STUDENTS: Home to over 350,000 students of higher education.

GDP: London produces 20% of the UK's Gross Domestic Product.

TOURISM: 13.8 million tourists visit London each year.

SITES: Home to four World Heritage Sites (Westminster Palace, Westminster Abbey, and St. Margaret's Church; Tower of London; Maritime Greenwich; and Royal Botanical Gardens, Kew) and 17 national museums.

WORKFORCE: Of 3.4 million people, 750,000 commute from outlying areas. Average salary for manual jobs is £21K for men, £19K for women; for non-manual jobs, £42K/39.6K.

POVERTY: 7.6% unemployment rate (5.5% nationally); 48% of children in inner London live in poverty (30% nationally); roughly 60,500 homeless households.

SOCIAL CARE: London boroughs look after over 11,000 children, support more than 34,000 adults in residential and nursing homes, and spend £5 billion annually on education.

WHEN TO GO

London's popularity as a top tourist destination makes it wise to plan around high season (June-Aug.). Spring or autumn (Apr.-May and Sept.-Oct.) are more appealing times to visit; the weather is still reasonable and flights are cheaper. If rainy weather doesn't bother you, the low season (Nov.-Mar.) is most economical.

NEIGHBORHOOD OVERVIEWS

The book organizes neighborhoods roughly from east to west, starting with the City of London and East London and moving in a snake-like manner westward, so that adjacent neighborhoods are next to one another in the book. Look at the London overview map (p. 372) to familiarize yourself with the city's layout and refer to the map thumbnails throughout the book for location reminders.

SEE MAP, p. 349

THE CITY OF LONDON

The City is where London began—indeed, for most of its history, the City *was* London. Even though urban sprawl has pushed the border of London outward, the City remains as tightly knit as ever, with its own mayor, separate jurisdiction, and sway over even the Queen, who must ask permission of the Lord Mayor before entering. One of the most important financial centers in Europe, the City employs a quarter of a million people during the day, but, not surprisingly, little happens here outside office hours—come evening, the City is almost completely empty. The majority of restaurants and pubs are aimed squarely at the millions of tourists who outnumber the pigeons at St. Paul's Cathedral and storm the Tower of London. The architectural mix of old and new—from the stately Bank of England to the futuristic Lloyd's of London building—makes the City a conglomerate of all the different eras of London's history. You'll find no better place to explore London's historic roots, from Romans to royals, all within one dense, bustling area. *(Within the compact City, walking is easy. Of the numerous Tube stations, ⊖Bank and St. Paul's are within easy reach of most sights; ⊖Tower Hill is useful for destinations farther east. Buses: Dozens of routes pass through the City; those from the West End and Holborn arrive along Ludgate Hill and Holborn Viaduct, while Liverpool St. station is the terminus for buses arriving from North London.)*

EAST LONDON

At Aldgate, the fabulous wealth of the City of London abruptly gives way to the historically impoverished East End, the heart of East London. In the past, cheap land and the nearby docks made this area a natural site for immigration, including waves of Huguenots, Jews, and, more recently, Bangladeshis. Today the site of extensive urban regeneration, the East End is at the center of new growth. Independent artists and designers are colonizing one of the last affordable areas in central London; they sell their wares at the Spitalfields Sunday Market or showcase them at the well-known Whitechapel Art Gallery and White Cube showrooms. In contrast with the East End and Whitechapel's bohemia, the Docklands is mostly a financial center. Since the late 1980s, this vast district of skyscrapers has been busy building itself up from an abandoned port into a minimetropolis. Enormous towers of steel and glass are surging skyward in record time. Greenwich, an area that was once the favorite residence of Queen Elizabeth, is home to a variety of sights documenting its maritime past. *(Much of East London is central; you're unlikely to get beyond Zone 2. The East End area is well served by the Tube. ⊖Old St. is best for Hoxton and Shoreditch while Aldgate East and Liverpool St. are nearest the Whitechapel sights; ⊖Shoreditch is also convenient, though only open M-F 7-10:30am and 3:30-8:30pm, Su 7am-3pm. Farther east, newly extended Tube lines serve Canary Wharf and Wapping. The Docklands Light Railway (DLR) will take you all the way to Greenwich. Travelcards valid. Buses are useful for getting from the City to the East End, but for distances farther east, the Tube and DLR are quicker. Use caution and stick to main roads when walking at night.)*

SEE MAP, p. 364

CLERKENWELL

Though lacking the historical heft of neighboring Holborn and the City of London, Clerkenwell still offers a refreshing local taste. A medieval monastic center until Henry VIII closed the priory of St. John, Clerkenwell became home to London's top craftspeople. During Queen Victoria's reign, it devolved into Dickensian slums, but since then Clerkenwell has experienced a revitalization, with trendy, acclaimed bars and clubs lining the streets in Farringdon. A stroll through tiny, cobblestoned Exmouth Market or the small and winding streets around Smithfield Market reveal Italian, Turkish, and Spanish restaurants as well as sidewalk cafes perfect for spending an afternoon people-watching. *(Walking is the best way to get around Clerkenwell. Everything is in walking distance of ⊖Farringdon; southern and eastern parts can be reached from ⊖Barbican, western parts can be reached by Chancery Ln., and northern parts can be reached by Angel. Buses: routes on Clerkenwell Rd. and Rosebery Ave. Night Buses: Rosebery Ave.)*

SEE MAP, p. 364

HOLBORN

Holborn was the first part of the city settled by Saxons—"Aldwych," on the western edge of Holborn, is Anglo-Saxon for "old port." Formally associated with religious righteousness, Holborn has dynamically modernized, now the home of many offices of law and journalism. The Royal Courts of Justice are housed in an enormous Gothic structure that sits right in the middle of a main thoroughfare. East of the courts, Fleet Street leads visitors to the winding lanes of the Temple and charms of St. Bride's Church. After hours, the nightlife is centered on Holborn's many historic pubs dotting the corners and catering to the opinionated patrons who pack in after work. The Courtauld Galleries, perhaps one of the most overlooked collections in London, lie within Somerset House, and both the building itself and the museum are worth an extended visit. *(Holborn is walkable—compact and easy to navigate. ⊖Holborn or Farringdon; or ⊖Chancery Ln. and Temple, both closed Su. Buses: High Holborn, Kinsway St., and Fleet St. Night Buses: Theobalds Rd., Kinsway St., and Fleet St.)*

SEE MAP, pp. 370-371

THE SOUTH BANK

Just across the Thames from the City, but lacking the business suits and the briefcases, the South Bank has long been the center of London's entertainment industry. In Shakespeare's time it was renowned for its theatres, cock-fighting, bull-baiting, and gentlemanly diversions of lesser repute. Dominated by wharves and warehouses in the 19th and early 20th centuries, the devastation of WWII forced the South Bank to rebuild—an opportunity for the neighborhood to reassert its fun-loving heritage. Now, the "Millennium Mile" stretches from the twirling London Eye in the west to the swanky restaurants of Butlers Wharf in the east, passing by the cultural powerhouses of the Festival Hall, Hayward Gallery, National Theatre, Tate Modern, and Shakespeare's Globe Theatre. *(Served by a series of Tube stops along the Thames, as well as the central train station of Waterloo, South Bank attractions are easily accessible, and a number of boardwalks and paths make the South Bank very pedestrian-friendly. The closest station to the South Bank Centre is across the river at ⊖Embankment; take the Hungerford Foot Bridge. Use ⊖Waterloo for*

TOP 10 WAYS TO LOSE £10

While hardly anything in London can be considered inexpensive—and you will be hard-pressed to spend a day or evening out for free—£10 seems just about right. You'll be surprised with how much you can do for so little (relatively speaking):

1. Let it all hang out at the **Big Chill Bar** (pints £3; p. 260), then dance into the early morning at down-to-earth **Herbal**, where cover is rarely over £7 (p. 261).

2. Immerse yourself in everything Churchillian, from signature cigars to one-piece velvet suits, at the new and highly interactive **Churchill Museum** (£10; p. 202).

3. Throw on a Hawaiian shirt and head to **22 Below.** Sip on an oversized fresh-fruit martini (£7) and critique new material at Monday's **Old Rope Comedy Night.** Cover is £3 (p. 268).

4. Enjoy classical music bliss at the **Proms** (£4, awkward date and corsage optional; p. 222). End the evening with a round of pints from £6 at **The Troubadour** (p. 281).

5. Partake in a two-course gourmet lunch at **Hoxton Apprentice** (£10; see p. 122) and spend the afternoon perusing East London's ultrahip **Whitechapel, White Cube,** and **Victoria Miro** art galleries, where admission is free (p. 195).

inland attractions, Southwark for Bankside, and London Bridge for Borough and Butlers Wharf.)

SOUTH LONDON

Spanning a large area south of the Thames, South London includes everything from the hopping nightlife of Brixton to the sleepy village of Dulwich. Historically maligned for being "dodgy," areas of South London have now become hot spots for hip and happening youngsters looking for upscale dining and all-night parties. The former swanky suburb of Brixton has been thoroughly urbanized, showcasing the charm of its Afro-Caribbean-flavored market. Stockwell and Vauxhall each offer pubs galore, while Dulwich and Forest Hill have quiet streets, green lawns, and offbeat museums for those looking for a relaxed day outside of the urban bustle. Clapham is experiencing a boom in nightlife and culture that makes a visit well worth while. No longer an area to be avoided, South London has become quite the opposite: a must-see for anyone visiting the city. *(⊖Stockwell and Brixton for the Brixton neighborhood; ⊖Clapham and Clapham North for the Clapham neighborhood. For access to some areas, overland rail service from Victoria, Waterloo, and London Bridge is necessary. Buses: from Brixton, #P4 will take you to all the Dulwich sites. Bus #345 from South Kensington, #333 from Elephant and Castle, and #2 from Baker St. also serve Brixton. Night Bus #N2, 3, 35, 133, and 159 all run between London and Brixton.)*

SEE MAP, p. 368

WESTMINSTER

Westminster, with its postcard-friendly spires and lush parks, often feels like the heart of the old British Empire. It is, after all, home to both the Houses of Parliament and the Queen herself—convenient for die-hard sightseers who want to cram all of the biggest sights into one day. But away from the bureaucracy of Whitehall and the Gothic grandeur of the Abbey, Westminster is a surprisingly down-to-earth district—thousands of workers make Victoria the busiest Tube station, and Happy hour always finds Westminster's pubs crowded. South of Victoria, Pimlico is a residential district with row after row of B&Bs. Still, with its proximity to Soho, the West End, and Knightsbridge, many travelers use Westminster as a home base. True history buffs will find the easy distance to sights unbeatable, but those looking to chow down or party late into the night should cruise elsewhere. *(Getting here is not a problem. ⊖Victoria, to the west, doubles as a train station and the nearby London terminus for most long-distance coach services. ⊖Westminster places you near most sights; use ⊖St. James's Park for Buckingham Palace and Pimlico for most accommodations and Tate Britain. Buses: numerous buses swirl around Parliament Sq. before going up Whitehall to Trafalgar Sq., down Victoria St. to Victoria, along the Embankment to Pimlico, or across the river into Lambeth.)*

THE WEST END

SEE MAP, p. 356

If Westminster is the heart of historical London, then the West End is at the center of, well, just about everything else. The biggest, brightest, and boldest (though not always best) of London nightlife, theatre, shopping, and eating can all be found within this tough-to-define district, wedged between royal regalia to the south and financial powerhouses to the northeast.

See a world-renowned musical at one of over 30 major theatres in the area, head to Chinatown for some dim sum, and window-shop on Oxford Street, London's premier monument to commercialism for the past 150 years and the most popular shopping district in the UK. If it's nightlife you're craving, the awe-inspiring collection of bars and clubs in Soho will keep you busy through the wee hours of morning. Stroll around the gay nightlife nexus of Old Compton Street or mingle with street performers in Covent Garden.

And if none of this sounds like your cup of tea, you can always cruise the posh streets of Mayfair and St. James's, which offer a distinctly different flavor than the West End's more touristed areas do. Citizens of the West End's upper class emerge from their mansions to prowl the designer boutiques that line Bond Street or to attend a political (and cigar) forum at one of the local gentlemen's clubs. Whichever lifestyle strikes your fancy, spend a little time in central Trafalgar Square to bask in the glory of Britain's greatest days. *(The Tube is best for getting in and out of the West End: ⊖Charing Cross for Trafalgar Sq.; Oxford Circus and Bond St. for Oxford St. and northern Mayfair; Green Park for southern Mayfair; Oxford Circus and Tottenham Court Rd. for Soho; and Piccadilly Circus, Covent Garden, and Leicester Sq. for Covent Garden, Chinatown, and southern Soho. Buses are a quicker way to get around. Many routes head from Trafalgar Sq. to the Strand, Piccadilly, and Charing Cross Rd.; more bus lines converge at Oxford Circus, where they proceed south down Regent St. to Piccadilly Circus, west up Oxford St. to Marble Arch, and east to Tottenham Court Rd. Piccadilly Circus, Oxford Circus, and Trafalgar Sq. are all major hubs for the Night Bus network. In many cases, however, walking is the fastest and most eye-pleasing way to explore the West End.)*

6. Share some liquid courage with your four closest friends at **Thirst** (£10 bottles of wine daily 5-7pm; p. 271). Then, express your inner ABBA at the **Karaoke Box.** From 6-11pm, 5-person boxes are £15 per hr. (p. 272). Afterward, head to the stage door of the **Prince of Wales** theatre to sing a number with the cast of *Mamma Mia!*

7. Don your fake pearls and faux fur and delight in a front-row diva experience at the **Royal Opera House.** Day-of tickets go for £10 through Travelex Mondays (p. 221). If you can't get a ticket to an evening performance, attend one of their free lunchtime concerts on Mondays at 1pm and spend the leftover £10 shopping in **Covent Garden.**

8. Grab an early Friday dinner for two at **Cafe in the Crypt** for £10 (p. 132). Then, test your pop culture knowledge across the street at the **National Portrait Gallery** while tapping your feet to free live jazz (p. 205).

9. Catch a commonfolk cricket match at the **Oval** (£10) and spend the afternoon doing the wave—and trying to figure out how one actually plays cricket. (p. 227).

10. At the gym. (Well, what did you think we'd say?) Take a community yoga class at **Triyoga** (£6) to build up your energy for your long-awaited trip to London; afterward, refresh yourself with an organic, post-*asana* snack for £4 (p. 99).

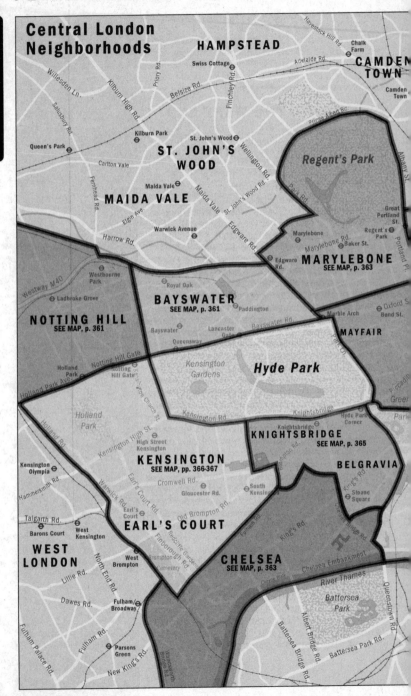

Central London Neighborhoods

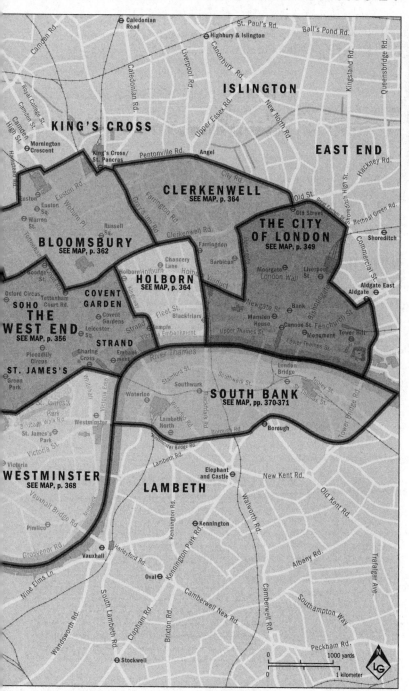

SEE MAP, p. 362

BLOOMSBURY

Noted for its literary connections and garden squares dating from the 17th and 18th centuries, Bloomsbury is home to some of London's finest attractions. The neighborhood boasts the British Museum and British Library, along with numerous colleges, the most famous being the University of London and University College London. This decidedly intellectual atmosphere fostered the influential early-20th-century Bloomsbury Group, whose great thinkers and writers—including T. S. Eliot, E. M. Forster, and Virginia Woolf—are largely responsible for London's unfaltering artistic and literary relevance. The torch of academia continues to burn strongly in Bloomsbury, which also has much to offer the visitor, including the budget traveler's mecca—affordable accommodations within walking distance of the center of the city. *(Though fairly large, Bloomsbury is easy to walk around.* ⊖*King's Cross is the system's biggest interchange but not the most convenient, while Goodge St. and Russell Sq. are most central for the sights.* ⊖*Euston, Euston Sq., and Warren St. hit the northern border. Buses: a number of one-way streets make bus routes confusing; most run north to south, either between Warren St. and Tottenham Court Rd. stations (along Gower St. heading south, along Tottenham Court Rd. heading north) or between Euston and Holborn along Southampton Pl. Night Buses: Tottenham Court Rd., Gower St., and New Oxford St.)*

NORTH LONDON

From the crowded stalls of the Camden Markets to the natural tranquility of Hampstead Heath, North London's attractions appeal to travelers and residents of all leanings. What we call "North London" is actually a conglomerate of several distinct neighborhoods, united simply by their positions north of central London. Once hotbeds of London's counter-culture movement, Camden Town and Islington are now home to more posh restaurants than punks and more espressos than mohawks. But don't let that fool you—tucked away among the world-class eateries and designer boutiques are still some of the best underground music venues in town. Hampstead and Highgate retain the feel of small villages, removed from the bustle of downtown. They are the gateways to the sprawling Hampstead Heath, a luscious green oasis in the middle of the city. St. John's Wood and Maida Vale are wealthy residential extensions of Marylebone and Bayswater and can be perfect for a short-term getaway. *(Most individual neighborhoods are walkable once you are there. Note that north of* ⊖*Euston is Zone 2, while Highgate and Golders Green are Zone 3. You can always get off in Zone 2 and take a bus. Buses are essential for getting to some locations. Take advantage of the bus and area maps in Tube stations and at bus stops to help you find your way.)*

SEE MAP, p. 369

MARYLEBONE AND REGENT'S PARK

Marylebone is defined by its eclectic borders. Adjacent to academic Bloomsbury in the east, beautiful Portland Place stands as an architectural wonder. To the west, Edgware Road houses London's largest Lebanese population and boasts many Middle Eastern eateries, shops, and markets. To the south, the West End's Oxford Street is a shopaholic's paradise. Similarly chain-oriented, Marylebone Road runs parallel, while the Marylebone High Street area is filled with trendy shops, cafes, and restaurants on its way from Marylebone Rd. to Oxford St. Rounding out the northern border of Marylebone, Regent's Park is a giant, popular stretch of greenery and flower gardens, surrounded by elegant Regency terraces. Much more than London's biggest football practice ground, the park is home to a multitude of sights, including the must-see Gardens of St. John's Lodge, and is a wonderful place of respite from the commotion of Marylebone's bustling street life. *(*⊖*Baker St. is con-*

venient for Marylebone's northern sights; Bond St. covers the south. There are 2 entirely separate Edgware Rd. stations; fortunately, they're across the street from one another. Buses are the best way to get across Marylebone. 10 bus routes link north and south via Baker St. heading south and Gloucester Pl. heading north, while 7 more lie along Edgware Rd. Night Buses abound along Marylebone Rd., Gloucester Pl., Baker St., Oxford St., and Edgware Rd.)

SEE MAP, p. 361

BAYSWATER

With a plum position nestled between Notting Hill, Marylebone, and Hyde Park, Bayswater is full of affordable accommodations with easy access to public transportation. These make for a great home base from which to see the more exciting sights in London's other neighborhoods. The main drags of Westbourne Grove and Queensway are frequented mostly by teenage mall-hoppers. Off these beaten paths, rows and rows of Georgian mansions, most of which have been renovated into hostels, line the quiet streets. While wandering the neighborhood, make sure to check street signs, since the area can look exactly the same from one street to the next. The lawns of Hyde Park are just steps away, and nearby Paddington Station acts as a gateway to Britain and beyond. *(The longest stretch of walking you'll have to do is along pleasant fringes of Kensington Gardens and Hyde Park. ⊖Bayswater for the west; ⊖Paddington and Lancaster Gate for the east. Note that there are 2 separate Paddington Tube stations: the Hammersmith & City line runs from above-ground tracks in the Paddington train station; the other lines run from a station underground. Buses: plenty of routes converge at Paddington from the West End and Knightsbridge. Night Buses: Bayswater Rd. and Westbourne Grove.)*

SEE MAP, p. 361

NOTTING HILL

The enclave of Notting Hill is a popular neighborhood for many reasons. Its position within walking distance to the hustle and bustle of Oxford St. is tempered by leafy streets and gardens. The mix of affluent, fashionable mansions, diverse ethnic culture, and a youthful, artsy vibe provides something for everyone. Class and style take precedence in Notting Hill, which also has an exciting annual carnival in August. Portobello Road is home to an ever-bustling market, and the quiet, winding lanes around it are ideal for a stroll after exploring streets full of shops and cafes. *(Getting to Notting Hill is easy; getting around is slightly less so. ⊖Notting Hill Gate serves the south, while Ladbroke Grove deposits you further north, by Portobello Rd. Bus #52 runs from Ladbroke Grove down to the Gate and Kensington Park Rd. From the West End, #12 and 94 will get you to Notting Hill Gate, while a handful of buses make the trip from High St. Kensington.)*

SEE MAP, pp. 366-367

KENSINGTON AND EARL'S COURT

The former stomping ground of Princess Diana, Kensington is divided into two distinct areas. To the west is the posh consumer mecca of Kensington High Street, to the east the awe-inspiring museums and colleges of South Kensington's "Albertopolis," including the Victoria and Albert, Natural History, and Natural Science Museums. The presence of 2000 French schoolchildren at the local *lycée* gives parts of South Kensington a distinctly continental feel, enhanced by numerous quality, cheap restaurants. Both High St. and South Kensington have a smattering of budget accommodations, but neither can compare with the options in the "Kangaroo Valley" area of Earl's Court, to the southwest. In the

1960s and 70s, Earl's Court was the destination of Aussie backpackers and home to London's gay population, but today others have caught on to its combination of cheap accommodations and good transportation links. *(One of central London's larger neighborhoods, public transportation is necessary to get around. Tube stations are helpfully named: ⊖High St. Kensington for High St., South Kensington for the South Kensington museums, and Earl's Court for Earl's Court. Buses: numerous buses run on High St. Kensington before climbing up Kensington Church St. to Notting Hill; to get to South Kensington, take #49 or 70.)*

SEE MAP, p. 365

KNIGHTSBRIDGE AND BELGRAVIA

Knightsbridge and Belgravia are both wildly expensive. Their locations come at such a price that even millionaire penthouse owners have sold their property to foreign embassies and consulates—the only ones who can afford the land anymore. Not surprisingly, the primary draw for tourists is the excellent window shopping. Knightsbridge is home to two of shopping's biggest names: famed department stores Harrods and Harvey Nichols, which exude an air of superiority. Belgravia, which occupies the region east of Sloane St., is an expanse of grand 19th-century mansions occupied by the aforementioned millionaires and embassies. *(⊖Knightsbridge is near all the shops; most of the hotels in Belgravia are accessible from Victoria, while the north end of the neighborhood, near the park, is closest to ⊖Hyde Park Corner. Buses: numerous routes converge on Hyde Park Corner, Sloane St., and Brompton Rd. Night Buses: hubs at Hyde Park Corner and Knightsbridge.)*

SEE MAP, p. 363

CHELSEA

Chelsea would still like to be considered London's artistic bohemia, a notion stemming from the 1960s and 70s, when King's Road was the stoop of "Swinging London," and home to some of the Rolling Stones along with other seminal rockers. This background makes Chelsea less stuffy than nearby Knightsbridge and Kensington, but, now stifled by a surfeit of wealth, today's neighborhood is a bit more staid than it might have been 40 years ago. Vintage boutiques selling electric-blue frocks remain from Chelsea's glory days and are a welcome break from run of the mill high-street shopping. *(Since most of Chelsea exists along King's Rd., it is pretty walkable. ⊖Sloane Sq. to the east and South Kensington to the north will put you within reasonable distance of most attractions. Most buses run from Sloane Sq. down King's Rd. on their way from Knightsbridge or Victoria. Night Buses: Sloane Sq. and King's Rd.)*

WEST LONDON

West London stretches for miles along the Thames before petering out in the valley's hills. The river changes track so often and so sharply that it is difficult to distinguish between the north and south banks, and communities have developed almost in isolation from their neighbors. Shepherd's Bush, one of these relatively autonomous districts, distinguishes itself with a number of well-known concert and theatre venues. Hammersmith bridges the gap between the shopping malls around the Tube station and the pleasant parks and pubs along the Thames. To the north, White City is home to the world-famous BBC. The Kew Gardens offer peaceful walks and isolation not far from the bustle of the city. Historically, the western reaches of the Thames were fashionable spots for country retreats, and the river still winds through the grounds of stately homes and former palaces. *(West London is huge, but most sights are easy to get to; the District Line on the Tube goes to most sights. Buses are invaluable for getting to some of the more obscure sights and efficient for traveling between West London neighborhoods. A riverboat can be a relaxing way to get to Kew Gardens.)*

✎ LET'S GO PICKS

BEST PLACE TO PARTY AND THEN CONFESS YOUR SINS THE NEXT MORNING: Mass (p. 266), located in a church basement, has all your bases covered.

BEST OVERPRICED SIGHT: The Tower of London (p. 148) may be over £10, but, of the big-name sights, it provides the most bang for your buck.

BEST WAY TO SEE A SIGHT FOR FREE: Attending the Evensong service at **St. Paul's Cathedral** (p. 145) gets you into the building, although you won't be able to see the crypt.

BEST VIEW/STAIRS RATIO: Monument (p. 150) in the City provides an amazing view, plus a certificate of achievement for getting to the top.

BEST PLACE TO ESCAPE STREET HUSTLE AND HASSLE: Relax in **Regent's Park's** rose gardens (p. 183) or duck through the secluded passageway into **The Temple** (p. 156).

BEST PLACE TO ESCAPE THE RAIN: Strike back with a quality fightin' brolly from **James Smith & Sons** (p. 249).

BEST PLACE TO CHILL OUT: The Absolut Icebar (p. 268) keeps their drinks—and everything else in the bar—on ice.

BEST SPORT THAT NOBODY UNDERSTANDS: Viewing a **cricket match** (p. 227) is a great way to spend a relaxing, bewildering afternoon.

BEST PLACE TO SEE THOSE GUARDS WITH FUNNY HATS: The Queen's Life Guard presides over Buckingham Palace (p. 166) and changes guard every afternoon.

BEST PLACE FOR A PINT: Clerkenwell's **Jerusalem Tavern** (p. 262) or Holborn's **Ye Olde Cheshire Cheese** (p. 263).

BEST WWII THROWBACK: The Cabinet War Rooms (p. 202) are a remarkable preservation of Churchill and Co.'s headquarters and memorabilia.

BEST GAY LIFE: Old Compton St. area's **The Edge** (p. 273) may be the nightlife niche, while Bloomsbury's **Gay's the Word** (p. 249) is the daytime spot (for reading and reference).

BEST WEST END MUSICAL: Les Misérables (p. 230) for an old standard; **Billy Elliot** or **Mary Poppins** (p. 230) for a newbie.

BEST PLACE TO BE SCHOLARLY: Buy a book at **Sotheran's of Sackville St.** (p. 243) and then head to Bloomsbury to garner vibes from past resident Virginia Woolf and current residents at the **University College London** (p. 179).

BEST LIVE JAZZ: Ronnie Scott's (p. 223) has long hosted the best names in jazz, with a great house band to boot.

BEST PLACE TO PIG OUT: The **Taste festival** (p. 136) has the best of London's cuisine in an all-you-can eat bonanza.

BEST ROMANTIC PICNIC (PLEASE DON'T PIG OUT): Regent's Park (p. 183) has plenty of lush, secluded greenery.

DISCOVER

A DAY IN LONDON ON £0

10AM
Ask to take your (free) B&B full English breakfast to go and eat it in **Hyde** (p. 185) or **Regent's Park** (p. 183); anything you don't eat now, save for later–it's going to be a long day.

11AM
If you must window shop, do it early before the crowds kick in. Oxford St. is overrun at all times of the day, so stick to **Regent Street** (p. 243).

11:30AM
For intellectual stimulation, peruse the collection at the **National Portrait Gallery** (p. 205) and learn a bit of British history; sprint through the **National Gallery** (p 203) to build up your appetite for lunch.

1:30PM
Duck out of the concert a few minutes early in order to get to the **Courtauld Galleries** at **Somerset House** (p. 196) before 2pm (free M 10am-2pm).

3PM
Pick up fixings for a late lunch at a corner supermarket (Tesco Metro on Strand, just before Aldwych) and have a picnic in the **Middle Temple Gardens** (p. 156).

4PM
Although the **Tate Modern** (p. 198) is the third museum of the day, it brings a change of pace. You can also take a quick nap on one of their leather couches.

5PM
Take the **Millennium Bridge** across the Thames to **St. Paul's Cathedral** (p. 145). The Evensong service won't allow you to see the crypt, but will get you into the building and massive nave for free.

6PM
Time to let loose: forget free, and head to dinner, to the theatre, and to a pub or club.

LONDON IN FILM

Meander around **St. Paul's Cathedral** (p. 145), where Mary Poppins sang to cartoon birds many years ago. None of us can sing and dance like Julie Andrews, but you can try.

Descend to **King's Cross Station** (p. 179) and see *Harry Potter's* Platform 9 3/4–it's really just the column between Platforms 9 and 10, but it is the location from the books and films. Just don't run too fast into the pillar, unless you're really a wizard on your way to Hogwarts.

19th-century **Spitalfields** (p. 240), was recreated in the 2001 film *From Hell*. Johnny Depp searched for Jack the Ripper in the film, but you can browse the market in comfort.

Walk across **Westminster Bridge** (p. 164), where Cillian Murphy first witnessed a desolate, zombified London in *28 Days Later*. The city is decidedly more upbeat today than it was in the film.

Swing through the **Globe Theatre** (p. 158), a recreation of Shakespeare's famous playhouse featured in *Shakespeare in Love*. The building is a faithfully detailed reproduction of the original, so you'll feel like you are in your own film (or play).

Take a tour of the **Houses of Parliament** (p. 168), where Martine McCutcheon fell for Prime Minister Hugh Grant in *Love Actually*.

Westminster Abbey (p. 164) wouldn't permit *The Da Vinci Code* to be filmed on-site, but you can explore and discover all of its secrets yourself.

PUB CRAWL

6:00PM

Start off your night at **Dog and Duck** (p. 270), the oldest (and smallest) pub in Soho. The spirit of George Orwell presides over this pub, his former stomping grounds.

7:30PM

By now you're feeling like a rock star and ready to belt out your favorite tune at **Cousin Jill's Karaoke Lounge**. Frequented by visitors and locals alike, this is a great place to show off (or embarass yourself) and wrap up your pub crawl--or gear up for a night at the club.

8:30PM

Continue the night with some Irish pride at **The Toucan** (p. 270). If the weather is nice you can take out your Guiness and enjoy it in nearby Soho Park.

START

6:45PM

Enjoy a beer with the after-work crowd at **Jrink**, a popular destination for locals. You might even catch an up-and-coming local band.

9:30PM

After a bit of a walk, you need a cold one to relax. Another great spot for locals, the **Old Coffee House** (p. 270) offers a cozy atmosphere and good conversation (or eavesdropping).

FINISH

10:30PM

For a nice change in pace from the local pubs, enjoy a fine cocktail at **Cecconi's**. The drink list is extensive, if a bit pricey, but every night out has a splurge or two.

11:15PM

Bundle up and head downstairs to the **Absolut Ice Bar** (p. 268), where everything from the bar to the seats to the glasses themselves are frozen. You won't find a colder drink in town.

You'd rather be traveling.

LET'S GO
BUDGET TRAVEL GUIDES
www.letsgo.com

ESSENTIALS

PLANNING YOUR TRIP

ENTRANCE REQUIREMENTS
Passport (see p. 18). Required of non-EU citizens.
Visa (see p. 19). Required of non-EU citizens for stays over 6 months.
Work Permit (see p. 19). Required of non-European Economic Area citizens.

EMBASSIES AND CONSULATES

BRITISH CONSULAR SERVICES ABROAD

For addresses of British embassies in countries not listed here and for up-to-date information on entry requirements, consult the **Foreign and Commonwealth Office** (general inquiries ☎7008 1500; www.fco.gov.uk) or your local telephone directory. Some large cities have a local British consulate that can handle most of the same functions as an embassy.

Australia: Commonwealth Ave., Yarralumla, ACT 2600 (☎61 026 270 6666; bhc.brit-aus.net). Consular Section (UK passports and visas), Piccadilly House, 39 Brindabella Circuit, Brindabella Business Park, Canberra Airport, Canberra ACT 2609 (☎61 1902 941 555). **Consulates-General** in Brisbane, Melbourne, Perth, and Sydney; Consulate in Adelaide.

Canada: 80 Elgin St., Ottawa, ON K1P 5K7 (☎613-237-1530; www.britainincan-ada.org). **Consulate-General,** 777 Bay St., Ste. 2800, Toronto, ON M5G 2G2 (☎416-593-1290). Other Consulates-General in Montreal and Vancouver; Honorary Consuls in Quebec City, St. John's, and Winnipeg.

Ireland: 29 Merrion Rd., Ballsbridge, Dublin 4 (☎353 01 205 3700; www.britishembassy.ie).

New Zealand: 44 Hill St., Thorndon, Wellington 6011 (☎64 04 924 2888; www.brit-ain.org.nz); mail to P.O. Box 1812, Wellington 6140. **Consulate-General:** 151 Queen St., Auckland (☎64 09 303 2973); mail to Private Bag 92014, Auckland.

US: 3100 Massachusetts Ave. NW, Washington, D.C. 20008 (☎202-588-7800; www.britainusa.com). **Consulate-General:** 845 Third Ave., New York, NY 10022 (☎212-745-0200). Other Consulates-General in Atlanta, Boston, Chicago, Houston, Los Angeles, and San Francisco. Consulates in Dallas, Denver, Miami, and Seattle.

CONSULAR SERVICES IN LONDON

Australia: Australia House, Strand (☎7379 4334; www.australia.org.uk). ⊖Temple. Open M-F 9am-5pm.

Canada: MacDonald House, 1 Grosvenor Sq. (☎7258 6600; www.london.gc.ca). ⊖Bond St. or Charing Cross. Open M-F 9am-5pm.

Ireland: 17 Grosvenor Pl. (☎7235 2171). ⊖Hyde Park Corner. Open M-F 9:30am-1pm and 2:15-5pm.

New Zealand: New Zealand House, 80 The Haymarket (☎7930 8422; www.nzembassy.com). ⊖Piccadilly Circus. Open M-F 9am-5pm.

US: 24 Grosvenor Sq. (☎7499 9000; www.usembassy.org.uk). ⊖Bond St. or Marble Arch. Open M-F 8:30am-5:30pm.

TOURIST OFFICES

London is represented abroad by the **British Tourist Authority** (**BTA;** www.visit-britain.com) and in the UK by the **London Tourist Board** (www.visitlondon.com). Visit the London Tourist Board website for a list of local tourist offices. BTA offices abroad supply advance tickets to major attractions and travel passes as well as information on how to get to Britain, where to stay, and what to do. They also sell the **Great British Heritage Pass,** which grants entrance to almost 600 sights around Britain (4 days £28, 7 days £39, 15 days £52, 1 month £70). There are BTA offices in:

Australia: Level 16, Gateway, 1 Macquarie Place, Sydney, NSW 2000 (☎61 029 377 4400).

Canada: 5915 Airport Rd., Ste. 120, Mississauga, ONT L4V 1T1 (☎905-405-1840).

Ireland: 18-19 College Green, Dublin 2 (☎353 01 670 8000).

New Zealand: Dilworth Building, 3rd fl., Auckland 1 (☎64 09 303 1446).

US: 551 Fifth Ave., 7th fl., New York, NY 10176 (☎ 212-986-2200). Also in Chicago (☎800-462-2748).

HEY, I'M A COMPUTER! New computer kiosks on street corners have lots of tourist information that they're robotically dying to give you. They offer BBC news, free outgoing email, maps, and weather reports.

DOCUMENTS AND FORMALITIES

PASSPORTS

REQUIREMENTS

Citizens of Australia, Canada, New Zealand, and the US need valid passports to enter the UK and re-enter their home countries. EU citizens should carry their passports, though they may not be checked. Britain does not allow entrance if the holder's passport expires in under six months. Returning home with an expired passport is illegal and may result in a fine.

NEW PASSPORTS

Citizens of Australia, Canada, New Zealand, and the US can apply for a passport at any passport office or at selected post offices and courts of law. Citizens of these countries may also download passport applications from the official website of their country's government or passport office. Any new passport or renewal applications must be filed well in advance of the departure date, though most passport offices offer rush services for a very steep fee. Note, however, that "rushed" passports still take up to two weeks to arrive.

PASSPORT MAINTENANCE

Photocopy the page of your passport with your photo, as well as your visas, traveler's check serial numbers, and any other important documents. Carry one set of copies in a safe place, apart from the originals, and leave another set at home. Consulates also recommend that you carry an expired passport or an official copy of your birth certificate in a part of your baggage separate from other documents.

If you lose your passport, immediately notify the local police and your government's nearest embassy or consulate. To expedite its replacement, you must show ID and proof of citizenship; it also helps to know all information previously recorded in the passport. In some cases, a replacement may take weeks to process, and it may be valid only for a limited time. Any visas stamped in your old passport will be irretrievably lost. In an emergency, ask for immediate temporary traveling papers that will permit you to re-enter your home country.

ONE EUROPE. European unity has come a long way since 1958, when the European Economic Community (EEC) was created to promote European solidarity and cooperation. Since then, the EEC has become the European Union (EU), a mighty political, legal, and economic institution. On May 1, 2004, ten Southern, Central, and Eastern European countries— Cyprus, the Czech Republic, Estonia, Hungary, Latvia, Lithuania, Malta, Poland, Slovakia, and Slovenia—were admitted to the EU, joining 15 other member states: Austria, Belgium, Denmark, Finland, France, Germany, Greece, Ireland, Italy, Luxembourg, the Netherlands, Portugal, Spain, Sweden, and the UK. On January 1, 2007, Bulgaria and Romania were admitted.

What does this have to do with the average non-EU tourist? The EU's policy of **freedom of movement** means that border controls between the first 15 member states (minus Ireland and the UK, but plus Norway and Iceland) have been abolished, and visa policies harmonized. Under this treaty, formally known as the **Schengen Agreement,** you're still required to carry a passport (or government-issued ID card for EU citizens) when crossing an internal border, but once you've been admitted into one country, you're free to travel to other participating states. On June 5, 2005, Switzerland ratified the treaty but has yet to implement it. The 8 of the newest member states of the EU are anticipated to implement the policy in October of 2007. Britain and Ireland have also formed a **common travel area,** abolishing passport controls between the UK and the Republic of Ireland.

VISAS AND WORK PERMITS

VISAS

Citizens of Australia, Canada, New Zealand, and the US do not need a visa for stays of up to six months. European Economic Area (EEA)—which includes all EU nations, Iceland, Liechtenstein, and Norway—and Swiss citizens do not need a visa to enter Britain; neither do citizens of Israel, Japan, Malaysia, Mexico, Singapore, and some Eastern European, Caribbean, and Pacific countries. Citizens of most other countries must have a visa to enter Britain. If you are uncertain, contact your embassy or complete an online inquiry at www.ukvisas.gov.uk.

Citizens of Australia, Canada, New Zealand, and the US staying longer than six months must purchase a visa from the British consulate in their home country. Tourist visas cost £36. Visas come in all shapes and depend on why you plan on coming to the UK—tourism, work, longer-term stays, marriage—and from where you are coming—the EU, Commonwealth countries, non-visa countries (including Australia, Canada, New Zealand, and the US), or none of the above. US citizens can take advantage of the **Center for International Business and Travel (CIBT;** ☎800-929-2428; www.cibt.com), which secures visas for travel for a variable service charge. If you need a **visa extension** while in the UK, contact the **Home Office, Border and Immigration Agency** (☎0114 207 4074; www.ind.homeoffice.gov.uk).

Double-check entrance requirements at the nearest UK embassy or consulate (listed under **British Consular Services Abroad,** p. 17) for up-to-date info before departure. US citizens can also consult travel.state.gov.

WORK PERMITS

Citizens of Australia, Canada, New Zealand, and the US need a work permit to work in the UK. EU citizens staying over three months must apply for a residence permit after their arrival in the UK. For details about long-term visas and work, study, and residence permits, see **Beyond Tourism** (p. 81).

IDENTIFICATION

When you travel, always carry at least two forms of identification, including a photo ID; a passport and either a driver's license or birth certificate is usually an adequate combination. Never carry all of your IDs together; split them up in case of theft or loss and keep photocopies of them in your luggage and at home.

STUDENT, TEACHER, AND YOUTH IDENTIFICATION

The **International Student Identity Card (ISIC)**, the most widely accepted form of student ID, provides discounts on some sights, accommodations, food, and transportation; access to a 24hr. emergency helpline; and insurance benefits for US cardholders (see **Insurance**, p. 28). Applicants must be full-time secondary or post-secondary school students at least 12 years of age. Because of the proliferation of fake ISICs, some services (particularly airlines) may require additional proof of student identity.

The **International Teacher Identity Card (ITIC)** offers teachers the same insurance coverage as the ISIC and limited discounts. For travelers who are under 26 years of age but are not students, the **International Youth Travel Card (IYTC)** also offers many of the same benefits as the ISIC.

Each of these identity cards costs US$22 or equivalent. ISICs and ITICs are valid until the new year. However, if the card is purchased between September and December, it is valid until the beginning of the following new year. IYTCs are valid for one year from the date of issue. To learn more about ISICs, ITICs, and IYTCs, try www.myisic.com. Many student travel agencies (see p. 30) issue the cards; for a list of issuing agencies or more information, see the **International Student Travel Confederation (ISTC)** website (www.istc.org).

The **International Student Exchange Card (ISE Card)** is a similar identification card available to students, faculty, and youths aged 12 to 26. The card provides discounts, medical benefits, access to a 24hr. emergency helpline, and the ability to purchase student airfares. An ISE Card costs US$25; call ☎800-255-8000 for more info or visit www.isecard.com.

CUSTOMS

Her Majesty's Revenue and Customs (www.hmrc.gov.uk) controls customs. Travelers from outside the EU may bring up to £145 worth of non-personal goods unintended for sale (such as gifts) into the UK, with special strictures for cigarettes, alcohol, and perfume. Upon entering the UK, you must declare items beyond the allowance and pay duty. Note that goods and gifts purchased at duty-free shops abroad are not exempt from duty or sales tax; "duty-free" merely means that you need not pay a tax in the country of purchase. Upon returning home, likewise, you must declare all articles acquired abroad and pay a duty on the value of articles in excess of your home country's allowance. If bringing valuables from home, consider registering them with customs before traveling abroad. Be sure to keep receipts. If you're returning to a non-EU country, you can claim back any **Value Added Tax** paid (see **Taxes,** p. 24).

MONEY

CURRENCY AND EXCHANGE

The currency chart below is based on August 2007 exchange rates between pounds sterling and Australian dollars (AUS$), Canadian dollars (CDN$), European Union euro (EUR€), New Zealand dollars (NZ$), and US dollars (US$).

Check the currency converter on websites like www.xe.com or www.bloomberg.com, or a large newspaper for the latest exchange rates.

POUND (£)		
AUS$1 = £0.42		£1 = AUS$2.39
CDN$1 = £0.47		£1 = CDN$2.13
EUR€1 = £0.68		£1 = EUR€1.47
NZ$1 = £0.36		£1 = NZ$2.74
US$1 = £0.50		£1 = US$2.00

As a general rule, it's cheaper to convert money in the UK than at home. While currency exchange will probably be available in your arrival airport, it's wise to bring enough foreign currency to last for the first 24 to 72hr. of your trip.

When changing money abroad, try to go only to banks or exchange bureaus that have at most a 5% margin between their buy and sell prices. Since you lose money with every transaction, **convert large sums** (unless the currency is depreciating rapidly) but **no more than you'll need.**

If you use traveler's checks or bills, carry some in small denominations (the equivalent of US$50 or less) for times when you are forced to exchange money at disadvantageous rates; also bring a range of denominations since charges may be levied per check cashed. Store your money in a variety of forms; ideally, at any given time you will be carrying some cash, some traveler's checks, and an ATM and/or credit card. All travelers should also consider carrying some US dollars (about US$50 worth), which are sometimes preferred by local tellers. For listings of exchange bureaus, see **Practical Information** (p. 95).

TRAVELER'S CHECKS

Traveler's checks are one of the safest and least troublesome means of carrying funds. American Express and Visa are the most recognized brands. Many banks and agencies sell them for a small commission. Check issuers provide refunds for lost or stolen checks, and many provide services such as toll-free refund hotlines, emergency message services, and assistance with lost or stolen credit cards or passports. Ask about toll-free refund hotlines and refund center locations when purchasing checks. Traveler's checks are readily accepted in London.

American Express: Checks available with commission at select banks, at all AmEx offices, and online (www.americanexpress.com; US residents only). AmEx cardholders can also purchase checks by phone (☎800-721-9768). Checks available in Australian, British, Canadian, European, Japanese, and US currencies. AmEx also offers the Travelers Cheque Card, a prepaid reloadable card. Cheques for Two can be signed by either of 2 people traveling together. For purchase locations or more information, contact AmEx's service centers: in Australia ☎61 800 688 022, in New Zealand 64 50 855 5358, in the UK 0800 587 6023, in the US and Canada 800-221-7282; elsewhere, call the US collect at 801-964-6665.

Travelex: Thomas Cook MasterCard and Interpayment Visa traveler's checks available. For information about Thomas Cook MasterCard in Canada and the US, call ☎800-223-7373, in the UK 0800 622 101; elsewhere, call the UK collect at +44 1733 318 950. For information about Interpayment Visa in the US and Canada, call ☎800-732-1322, in the UK 0800 515 884; elsewhere, call the UK collect at +44 1733 318 949. For more information, visit www.travelex.com.

Visa: Checks available (generally with commission) at banks worldwide. For the location of the nearest office, call the Visa Travelers Cheque Global Refund and Assistance Center: in the UK ☎0800 895 078, in the US 800-227-6811; elsewhere, call the UK collect at +44 2079 378 091. Checks available in British, Canadian, European, Japanese, and US currencies, among others. Visa also offers TravelMoney, a prepaid debit card that can be reloaded online or by phone. For more information on Visa travel services, see www.usa.visa.com/personal/using_visa/travel_with_visa.html.

CREDIT, DEBIT, AND ATM CARDS

Where they are accepted, credit cards often offer superior exchange rates—up to 5% better than the retail rate used by banks and other currency exchange establishments. Credit cards may also offer services such as insurance or emergency help and are sometimes required to reserve hotel rooms or rental cars. **MasterCard** and **Visa** are the most frequently accepted; **American Express** cards work at some businesses and ATMs as well as at AmEx offices and major airports. If you intend to use your credit card extensively in London, alert your card issuer before leaving; otherwise, they could block your card for "suspicious activity."

The use of **ATM cards** is widespread in the UK. Depending on the system that your home bank uses, you can most likely access your personal bank account from abroad. ATMs get the same wholesale exchange rate as credit cards, but there is often a limit on the amount of money you can withdraw per day (usually around US$500). There is typically also a surcharge of US$1-5 per withdrawal. Other ATM functions (including checking your balance, transferring funds, etc.) may not be accessible, depending on what kind of ATM card you have.

ATM CHARGES. Certain banks, like Barclay's, may not charge a fee for withdrawals by non-customers. Even though your bank at home may charge you, at least you don't have to get charged twice. Go inside and ask a teller before using the ATM.

Debit cards are as convenient as credit cards. A debit card can be used wherever its associated credit card company (usually MasterCard or Visa) is accepted. Debit cards often also function as ATM cards and can be used to withdraw cash from associated banks and ATMs throughout London.

The two major international money networks are **MasterCard/Maestro/Cirrus** (for ATM locations in London ☎ 800-424-7787 or www.mastercard.com) and **Visa/PLUS** (for ATM locations in London ☎ 800-843-7587 or www.visa.com). Most ATMs charge a transaction fee that is paid to the bank that owns the ATM.

PINS AND ATMS. To use a cash or credit card to withdraw money from a cash machine (ATM) in Europe, you must have a 4-digit **Personal Identification Number (PIN).** If your PIN is longer than 4 digits, ask your bank whether you can just use the first four, or if you'll need a new one. **Credit cards** don't usually come with PINs, so if you intend to hit up ATMs in Europe with a credit card to get cash advances, call your credit card company before leaving to request one. Travelers with alphabetic, rather than numerical, PINs may also be thrown off by the lack of letters on European cash machines. The following are the corresponding numbers to use: 1=QZ; 2=ABC; 3=DEF; 4=GHI; 5=JKL; 6=MNO; 7=PRS; 8=TUV; and 9=WXY. Note that if you mistakenly punch the wrong code into the machine 3 times, it will swallow your card for good.

GETTING MONEY FROM HOME

If you run out of money while traveling, the easiest and cheapest solution is to have someone back home make a deposit to your bank account. Failing that, consider one of the following options.

WIRING MONEY

It is possible to arrange a **bank money transfer,** which means asking a bank back home to wire money to a bank in London. This is the cheapest way to transfer cash, but it's also the slowest, usually taking several days or more. Note that some banks may only release your funds in pounds, potentially sticking you with a poor exchange rate; inquire about this in advance. Money transfer services like **Western Union** are faster and more convenient than bank transfers—but also much pricier. Western Union has many locations worldwide. To find one, visit www.westernunion.com, or call ☎ 61 800 173 833 in Australia, 800-325-6000 in Canada and the US, and 0800 833 833 in the UK. To wire money using a credit card (Discover, MasterCard, or Visa), call in Canada and the US ☎ 800-325-6000, or in the UK 0800 833 833. Money transfer services are also available to **American Express** cardholders and at selected **Thomas Cook** offices.

US STATE DEPARTMENT (US CITIZENS ONLY)

In serious emergencies only, the US State Department will forward money within hours to the nearest consular office, which will then disburse it according to instructions for a US$30 fee. If you wish to use this service, you must contact the Overseas Citizens Service division of the US State Department (☎ 202-501-4444, toll-free 888-407-4747).

COSTS

Budget travel in London can be a challenge, but the cost of your trip will vary considerably depending on where you go, how you travel, and where you stay. The most significant expenses will probably be your round-trip **airfare** to London (see **Getting to London: By Plane,** p. 30). Before you go, spend some time calculating a reasonable daily **budget.**

STAYING ON A BUDGET

To give you a general idea, a bare-bones day in London (sleeping in hostels/guest houses, buying food at supermarkets) would cost about £20 (US$37); a slightly more comfortable day (sleeping in hostels/guest houses and the occasional budget hotel, eating one meal per day at a restaurant, going out at night) would cost £30 (US$55); and for a luxurious day, the sky's the limit. Don't forget to factor in emergency reserve funds (at least £100) when planning how much money you'll need.

TIPS FOR SAVING MONEY

Some simpler ways include searching out opportunities for free entertainment, splitting accommodation and food costs with trustworthy fellow travelers, and buying food in supermarkets rather than eating out. Bring a **sleepsack** to save on sheet charges in hostels, and do your **laundry** in the sink (unless you're explicitly prohibited from doing so). Museums often have certain days once a month or once a week when admission is free; plan accordingly. If you are eligible, consider getting an ISIC or an IYTC (p. 20); many sights and museums offer reduced admission to students and youths. For getting around quickly, bikes are the most economical option. Renting a bike is cheaper than renting a moped or scooter. Don't forget about walking, though; you can learn a lot about a city by seeing it on foot. Drinking at bars and clubs quickly becomes expensive. It's cheaper to buy alcohol at a supermarket and imbibe before going out. That said, don't go overboard. Though staying within your budget is important, don't do so at the expense of your health or a great travel experience.

 I DO CONCEDE... Many theatres and attractions in London offer discounts for "concessions." Concessions can include senior citizens, students, persons with disabilities, children, pregnant women, and others. There is no rule for which are included, so if you see concessions in a listing, your best bet is to call ahead and ask the establishment whom they include in their concessions.

TIPPING AND BARGAINING

Tips in restaurants are often included in the bill (sometimes as a service charge). If gratuity is not included, you should tip your server about 15%. Taxi drivers should receive a 10-15% tip, and bellhops and chambermaids usually expect somewhere between £1-3. Never tip bartenders, even in pubs. If you're at an outdoor market, bargaining is sometimes acceptable.

 GROUNDED. Know your lingo! The "ground floor" in the UK is at street level; the "first floor" is one floor above, or what many travelers would call the "second floor." You don't want to get lost searching for the men's department.

TAXES

Both Britain and Ireland have a 17.5% **Value Added Tax (VAT),** a sales tax applied to everything but food, books, medicine, and children's clothing. The tax is included in the amount indicated on the price tag—no extra expenses should be added at the register. The prices stated in *Let's Go* include VAT. Upon exiting Britain, non-EU citizens can reclaim VAT (minus an administrative fee) through the Retail Export Scheme. You can obtain refunds only for goods you take out of the country—not for services rendered in the UK. Participating shops display a "Tax Free Shopping" sign and may have a purchase minimum of £50-100 before they offer refunds. To claim a refund, fill out the form you are given in the shop and present it with the goods and receipts at customs upon departure (look for the Tax Free Refund desk). At peak times, this process can take as long as an hour. You can receive your refund directly at most airports. To obtain the refund by check or by credit card, send the form (stamped by customs) back in the envelope provided. You must leave the country within three months of your purchase in order to claim a refund, and you must apply before leaving the UK.

PACKING

Pack lightly: Lay out only what you think you absolutely need. Then pack half the clothes and twice the money. The **Travelite FAQ** (www.travelite.org) is a good resource for tips on traveling light. The online **Universal Packing List** (http://upl.codeq.info) will generate a customized list of suggested items based on your trip length, the expected climate, your planned activities, and other factors.

Luggage: Although suitcases are fine, be sure that you can carry your luggage up and down stairs, as steep staircases are unavoidable at most Tube stops and in many B&Bs and hostels. A smaller daypack can be useful for daytrips out of the city.

Clothing: A rain jacket is essential year-round. Londoners generally dress conservatively and darkly—a pair of black trousers will help you blend in. Be sure to pack some semi-dressy pants and shoes, especially if you plan to go clubbing: many clubs ban jeans and sneakers. Flip-flops are must-haves for grubby hostel showers.

Converters and Adapters: In London, electricity is 230V AC, enough to fry any 120V North American appliance. 220/240V electrical appliances won't work with a 120V current, either. Americans and Canadians should buy an adapter (which changes the shape of the plug; US$5) and a converter (which changes the voltage; US$10-30). Don't make the mistake of using only an adapter (unless appliance instructions explicitly state otherwise). Australians and New Zealanders (who use 230V at home) won't need a converter but will need a set of adapters to use anything electrical. For more on all things adaptable, check out http://kropla.com/electric.htm.

First-Aid Kit: For a basic first-aid kit, pack bandages, a pain reliever, antibiotic cream, a thermometer, a multifunction pocketknife, tweezers, a decongestant, a motion-sickness remedy, a diarrhea or upset-stomach medication (Pepto Bismol® or Imodium®), an anti-histamine, sunscreen, insect repellent, and burn ointment.

Film: Consider bringing along enough film for your entire trip and developing it at home since this process is expensive in London. Despite disclaimers, airport-security X-rays can fog film, so buy a lead-lined pouch at a camera store or ask security to hand-inspect it. Always pack film in your carry-on luggage, since higher-intensity X-rays are used on checked luggage.

Toiletries: You'll easily find all the toiletries you need in London, but they are likely to be more expensive than at home, especially contact lens solution. Bring your glasses and a copy of your prescription in case you need emergency replacements.

Important Documents: Don't forget your passport, traveler's checks, ATM and/or credit cards, adequate ID, and photocopies of all of the aforementioned in case these documents are lost or stolen. Check that you have any of the following that apply to you: driver's license; hostel membership card; ISIC (p. 20); travel insurance forms (p. 28).

SAFETY AND HEALTH

GENERAL ADVICE

In any type of crisis situation, the most important thing to do is to **stay calm.** Your country's embassy in London (p. 17) is usually your best resource when things go wrong; registering with that embassy upon arrival in London is often a good idea. The government offices listed in the **Travel Advisories** box (p. 27) can provide information on the services they offer in case of emergencies abroad.

LOCAL LAWS AND POLICE

Police officers (bobbies) are stationed throughout the city and are more than willing to give directions or to help in an emergency situation. **In an emergency, dial ☎999 (or ☎112 from cell phones).** While the **Metropolitan Police** (New Scotland Yard, Broadway; ☎7230 1212; www.met.police.uk) oversees most of the city, the **City of London Police** (37 Wood St.; ☎7601 2455 www.cityoflondonpolice.uk) has jurisdiction over the City.

DRUGS AND ALCOHOL

The legal **drinking age** in the UK is complicated. Technically, it's legal for anyone to drink alcohol in private, but there are many regulations regarding who can buy or sell it. To buy alcohol in a **shop,** you have to be at least 18; it's illegal to buy alcohol on behalf of an underage person. Eighteen is also the normal drinking age in bars and pubs, but you can drink in a pub with food at 16 or even at 14 in a restaurant. While you need to look *really* young before anyone will demand ID, punishments are severe. **Smoking** is simpler—you have to be 16 or older to purchase cigarettes.

Drugs are a more serious offense, and you could be jailed or deported if convicted. Be especially wary in nightclubs. If you need to take a drug for **medical reasons,** check that it is legal in the UK and always carry a prescription or note from your doctor. **Cannabis** in the UK is a Class C drug, meaning that carrying a small amount is not always an arrest-worthy offense.

SPECIFIC CONCERNS

VIOLENT CRIME

By American and most European standards, violent crime in London is rare. While Hackney, Tottenham, and parts of South and East London are some of London's dodgier neighborhoods, they also hold some of the city's best nightlife—take extra care after dark around **King's Cross,** the **East End,** and **Brixton.**

THEFT

When it comes to theft (especially pickpocketing or bag snatching), travelers need to be careful in London. Don't put a wallet in your back pocket and don't keep all your valuables (money and important documents) in one place. If you carry a handbag, buy a sturdy one with a secure clasp and wear it crosswise with the clasp against you. Use a money belt and keep a small cash reserve ($40 or so) somewhere well protected and hidden.

RACISM

London traditionally prides itself on being an exceptionally tolerant city. However, no city is perfect, and the ethnic tensions since the 1950s have taken their toll. While overall London is color-blind, in **South London,** tensions are worst between black immigrants and poor whites; there's also friction within the black community between West Indians and Africans. In **East London,** racism sometimes targets South Asians. These trouble spots aside, races mix in London to a greater extent than in most cities. Among second-generation immigrants, there's little cultural distinction.

TERRORISM

As a world leader, London has been a target of local and global terrorism. Until their 1997 cease-fire, IRA bombers intermittently attacked London; their goal was to pressure the British government into negotiations with the political group Sinn Féin over the UK's control of Northern Ireland. Since the September 11, 2001 attacks on the US, authorities in London have been on alert for possible attacks, given the UK's close relation with the US.

On July 7, 2005, a series of bombs exploded, three in Tube cars and one on a city bus, killing roughly 50 people and wounding hundreds more. The explosions came one day after the announcement of London's successful bid for the 2012 Olympics and in the midst of the G8 summit (a meeting of eight of the world's most industrialized nations). Al-Qaeda eventually claimed responsibility for the attacks and several individuals were tried and sentenced to prison terms in the UK. Further bomb scares occurred in June of 2007, when three car bombs were discovered in different parts of London. None were detonated and nobody was harmed, and the investigation into these attacks is ongoing.

More information on international and domestic terrorism and the UK's response is available from the Foreign and Commonwealth Office (☎7270 1500; www.fco.gov.uk), the Prime Minister's office website (www.pm.gov.uk), and the Metropolitan Police (☎7230 1212; www.met.police.uk). The box on **travel advisories** (p. 27) lists offices and websites to consult to obtain the most up-to-date list of your home country's government's advisories about travel.

PERSONAL SAFETY

EXPLORING AND TRAVELING

To avoid unwanted attention, try to blend in as much as possible. Familiarize yourself with your surroundings before setting out, and carry yourself with confidence. Check maps in shops and restaurants rather than on the street. If you are traveling alone, be sure someone at home knows your itinerary and never admit that you're by yourself. When walking at night, stick to busy, well-lit streets and avoid dark alleyways. If you ever feel uncomfortable, leave the area as quickly and directly as you can.

TRAVEL ADVISORIES. The following government offices provide travel information and advisories by telephone, or via the web:

Australian Department of Foreign Affairs and Trade: ☎ 61 1300 555 135; www.dfat.gov.au.

Canadian Department of Foreign Affairs and International Trade (DFAIT): Call ☎ 800-267-8376; www.dfait-maeci.gc.ca. Call for their free booklet, *Bon Voyage...But.*

New Zealand Ministry of Foreign Affairs: ☎ 64 44 398 000; www.safe-travel.govt.nz.

United Kingdom Foreign and Commonwealth Office: ☎ 7008 1500; www.fco.gov.uk.

US Department of State: ☎ 202-501-4444; http://travel.state.gov. Visit the website to read *A Safe Trip Abroad.*

There is no sure-fire way to avoid all the threatening situations you might encounter while traveling, but a good **self-defense course** will give you concrete ways to react to unwanted advances. **Impact, Prepare, and Model Mugging** can refer you to local self-defense courses in the US. Visit the website at www.modelmugging.org for a list of nearby chapters.

POSSESSIONS AND VALUABLES

As in any metropolitan center, there are a few steps you can take to minimize the financial risk associated with traveling. First, **bring as little with you as possible.** Second, buy a few combination **padlocks** to secure your belongings either in your pack or in a hostel or train station locker. Third, carry as little cash as possible. Keep your traveler's checks and ATM/credit cards in a **money belt**—not a "fanny pack"—along with your passport and ID cards. Fourth, **keep a small cash reserve separate from your primary stash.** This should be about £25 sewn into or stored in the depths of your pack, along with your traveler's check numbers and important photocopies.

Con artists are not hugely prevalent in London, but incidences of pickpocketing and street theft at tourist destinations and on public transportation do happen. **Never let your passport and your bags out of your sight.** Also, be alert in public telephone booths. If you must say your calling card number, do so very quietly; if you punch it in, make sure no one can look over your shoulder.

If you will be traveling with electronic devices, such as a laptop computer or a PDA, check whether your homeowner's insurance covers loss, theft, or damage when you travel. If not, you might consider purchasing a low-cost separate insurance policy. For US citizens, **Safeware** (☎ 800-800-1492; www.safeware.com) specializes in covering computers and charges $90 for 90-day comprehensive international travel coverage up to $4000.

PRE-DEPARTURE HEALTH

In your **passport,** write the names the people to be contacted in case of a medical emergency; also list any allergies or medical conditions. Matching a prescription to a foreign equivalent is not always easy, safe, or possible, so if you take prescription drugs, consider carrying up-to-date, legible prescriptions or a statement from your doctor stating the medication's trade name, manufacturer, chemical name, and dosage. While traveling, be sure to keep all medication with you in your carry-on luggage. For tips on packing a basic **first-aid kit** and other health essentials, see p. 29.

ESSENTIALS

IMMUNIZATIONS AND PRECAUTIONS

Travelers over two years of age should make sure that the following vaccines are up to date: MMR (for measles, mumps, and rubella); DTaP or Td (for diphtheria, tetanus, and pertussis); IPV (for polio); Hib (for *Haemophilus influenzae* B); and HepB (for Hepatitis B). For recommendations on immunizations and prophylaxis, consult the **Centers for Disease Control and Prevention** (**CDC;** see p. 29) in the US or the equivalent in your home country and check with a doctor.

INSURANCE

Travel insurance covers four basic areas: medical/health problems, property loss, trip cancellation/interruption, and emergency evacuation. Though regular insurance policies sometimes extend to travel-related accidents, you may consider purchasing separate travel insurance if the cost of potential trip cancellation, interruption, or emergency medical evacuation is greater than you can absorb. Prices for travel insurance purchased separately generally run about US$50 per week for full coverage, while trip cancellation/interruption may be purchased separately at a rate of US$3-5 per day, depending on length of stay.

Medical insurance (especially university policies) often covers costs incurred abroad; check with your provider. **US Medicare** does not cover foreign travel. **Canadian** provincial health insurance plans increasingly do not cover foreign travel; check with the provincial Ministry of Health or Health Plan Headquarters for details. **Australians** traveling in the UK are entitled to many of the services that they would receive at home as part of the Reciprocal Health Care Agreement. **Homeowner's insurance** (or your family's coverage) often covers theft during travel and loss of travel documents (passport, plane ticket, railpass, etc.) up to US$500.

ISIC and **ITIC** (p. 20) provide basic insurance benefits to US cardholders, including US$100 per day of in-hospital sickness for up to 100 days and US$10,000 of accident-related medical reimbursement. **American Express** (☎800-338-1670) grants most cardholders automatic collision and theft insurance on rental cars paid for with the card.

USEFUL ORGANIZATIONS AND PUBLICATIONS

The CDC (☎877-FYI-TRIP; www.cdc.gov/travel) maintains an international travelers' hotline and an informative website. The CDC's comprehensive booklet *Health Information for International Travel* (The Yellow Book), a biannual rundown of disease, immunization, and general health advice, is free online. Consult your home country's appropriate government agency for consular information sheets on health, entry requirements, and other issues for various countries (see the listings in the box on **Travel Advisories,** p. 27). For quick information on health and other travel warnings, call the **Overseas Citizens Services** (M-F 8am-8pm ☎888-407-4747, from overseas 202-501-4444) or contact a passport agency, embassy, or consulate abroad. For information on medical evacuation services and travel insurance firms, consult the US government's website at http://travel.state.gov/travel/abroad_health.html or the **British Foreign and Commonwealth Office** (www.fco.gov.uk). For general health info, contact the **American Red Cross** (☎800-564-1234; www.redcross.org).

STAYING HEALTHY

Common sense is the simplest prescription for good health while you travel. Drink lots of fluids to prevent dehydration and wear sturdy, broken-in shoes and clean socks.

ONCE IN LONDON

FOOD- AND WATER-BORNE DISEASES

While concern over **bovine spongiform encephalopathy (BSE)**, better known as **mad cow disease**, and **foot and mouth disease (FMD)** has subsided over the past few years, as in any city, there is always a risk of food poisoning due to lack of cleanliness. Always wash fruits and vegetables bought at supermarkets, booths, and street markets. Make sure that red meat is completely cooked. Traveler's diarrhea results from drinking contaminated water or eating uncooked and contaminated foods. Symptoms include nausea, bloating, and urgency. Try quick-energy, non-sugary foods with protein and carbohydrates to keep your strength up. Over-the-counter anti-diarrheals (e.g., Imodium) may counteract the problem.

 CLEAN KITCHENS. The mark of a clean restaurant kitchen is often how clean its bathroom is. Take a trip to the loo before ordering.

OTHER INFECTIOUS DISEASES

AIDS and HIV: For detailed information on Acquired Immune Deficiency Syndrome (AIDS) in London, call the US CDC's 24hr. hotline at ☎800-232-4636 or contact the Joint United Nations Programme on HIV/AIDS (UNAIDS) 20 Ave. Appia, CH-1211 Geneva 27, Switzerland (☎+41 22 791 3666; fax 22 791 4187; www.unaids.org).

Hepatitis B: A viral infection of the liver transmitted via blood or other bodily fluids. Symptoms, which may not surface until years after infection, include jaundice, appetite loss, fever, and joint pain. It is transmitted through unprotected sex and unclean needles. A 3-shot vaccination sequence is recommended for sexually active travelers and anyone planning to seek medical treatment abroad; it must begin 6 months before traveling.

Hepatitis C: Like Hepatitis B, but the mode of transmission differs. IV drug users, those with occupational exposure to blood, hemodialysis patients, and recipients of blood transfusions are at highest risk, but the disease can also be spread through sexual contact or sharing items like razors and toothbrushes. No symptoms are usually exhibited. Untreated Hepatitis C can lead to liver failure.

Sexually transmitted infections (STIs): Gonorrhea, chlamydia, genital warts, syphilis, herpes, and other STIs are easier to catch than HIV and can be just as deadly. Hepatitis B and C can also be transmitted sexually. Though condoms may protect you from some STIs, oral or even tactile contact can lead to transmission. If you think you may have contracted an STI, see a doctor immediately.

OTHER HEALTH CONCERNS

MEDICAL CARE ON THE ROAD

Medical care in the UK is either part of the government-run **National Health Service** or is privately administered; doctors and hospitals often work for both NHS and private firms. EU citizens, citizens of many Commonwealth countries, and full-time students at British universities are eligible for free treatment from NHS. Many US health insurance plans (not Medicare) will cover emergency treatment abroad in private clinics, but you may be asked to pay up front and then apply for a reimbursement to your insurer. If you're unsure whether you have medical coverage in the UK, it's best to buy travel insurance (p. 28) before you leave. For a list of local hospitals and clinics in London, see **Practical Information** (p. 95).

If you are concerned about obtaining medical assistance while traveling, you may wish to employ special support services. The MedPass from **GlobalCare, Inc.,** 6875 Shiloh Rd. East, Alpharetta, GA 30005, USA (☎800-860-1111; www.globalcare.net), provides 24hr. international medical assistance, support, and evacuation resources. The **International Association for Medical Assistance to Travelers** (IAMAT; US ☎ 716-754-4883, Canada 519-836-0102; www.iamat.org) has free membership, lists English-speaking doctors worldwide, and has detailed info on immunization requirements and sanitation. If your regular **insurance** policy does not cover travel abroad, you may wish to purchase additional coverage (p. 28).

Those with medical conditions (such as diabetes, allergies to antibiotics, epilepsy, or heart conditions) may want to obtain a **MedicAlert** membership (US$40 per year), which includes, among other things, a stainless steel ID tag and a 24hr. collect-call number. Contact the MedicAlert Foundation International, 2323 Colorado Ave., Turlock, CA 95382, USA (☎ 888-633-4298, outside US ☎ 209-668-3333; www.medicalert.org).

WOMEN'S HEALTH
Tampons, pads, and **contraceptive devices** are widely available, though your favorite brand may not be stocked—bring extras of anything you can't live without. **Abortion** is legal in the UK, subject to the consent of two doctors who must agree that each woman seeking an abortion complies with the wording of the original 1967 act legalizing abortion. For a list of women's and sexual health clinics, see **Practical Information** (p. 95).

GETTING TO LONDON

BY PLANE

When it comes to airfare, a little effort can save you a bundle. Courier fares are the cheapest for those whose plans are flexible enough to deal with the restrictions. Tickets sold by consolidators and standby seating are also good deals, but last-minute specials, airfare wars, and charter flights often beat these fares. The key is to hunt around, be flexible, and ask about discounts. Students, seniors, and those under 26 should never pay full price for a ticket.

AIRFARES
Airfares to London peak between June and mid-September; holidays are also expensive. The cheapest times to travel are November to after New Year's Day and mid-February to the end of March. Midweek (M-Th morning) round-trip flights run US$40-50 cheaper than weekend flights, but they are generally more crowded and less likely to permit frequent-flier upgrades. Not fixing a return date ("open return") or arriving in and departing from different cities ("open jaw") can be pricier than round-trip flights. Patching one-way flights together is the most expensive way to travel. Flights to London Heathrow, rather than to the other airports, tend to be cheapest.

If London is only one stop on a more extensive globe-hop, consider a round-the-world (RTW) ticket. Tickets usually include at least five stops and are valid for about a year; prices range US$1200-5000. Try **Northwest Airlines/KLM** (☎ 800-225-2525; www.nwa.com) or **Star Alliance,** a consortium of 16 airlines including United Airlines (www.staralliance.com).

BUDGET AND STUDENT TRAVEL AGENCIES
While knowledgeable agents specializing in flights to London can make your life easy and help you save, they may not spend the time to find you the lowest possible fare—they get paid on commission. Travelers holding **ISICs** and **IYTCs** (p. 20)

qualify for discounts from student travel agencies. Most flights from budget agencies are on major airlines, but in peak season some may sell seats on chartered aircraft. For travel agencies in London, see **Practical Information** (p. 96).

STA Travel, 920 Westwood Blvd., Los Angeles, CA 90036, USA (24hr. reservations and info ☎800-781-4040; www.sta-travel.com). A student and youth travel organization with over 150 offices worldwide (check their website for a complete list), including US offices in Boston, Chicago, Los Angeles, New York, Seattle, San Francisco, and D.C. Ticket booking, travel insurance, railpasses, and more. Offices are located throughout Australia (☎61 134 STA), New Zealand (☎64 800 474 400), and the UK (☎08701 230 0040).

Travel CUTS (Canadian Universities Travel Services Limited), 187 College St., Toronto, ON M5T 1P7, Canada (☎800-592-2887; www.travelcuts.com). Offices across Canada and the US including Los Angeles, New York, Seattle, and San Francisco. Also includes information and program links for working and volunteering abroad.

USIT, 19-21 Aston Quay, Dublin 2, Ireland (☎353 01 602 1904; www.usit.ie), Ireland's leading student/budget travel agency has 20 offices throughout Northern Ireland and the Republic of Ireland. Offers programs to work, study, and volunteer worldwide.

FLIGHT PLANNING ON THE INTERNET. The Internet may be the budget traveler's dream when it comes to finding and booking bargain fares, but the array of options can be overwhelming. Many airline sites offer special last-minute deals on the Web. Some good websites for these are www.cheap-flights.com and www.travelpage.com.

STA (www.sta-travel.com) and **StudentUniverse** (www.studentuniverse.com) provide quotes on student tickets, while **Orbitz** (www.orbitz.com), **Expedia** (www.expedia.com), and **Travelocity** (www.travelocity.com) offer full travel services. **Opodo** (www.opodo.com) is a pan-European company. **Priceline** (www.priceline.com) lets you specify a price and obligates you to buy any ticket that meets or beats it. **Hotwire** (www.hotwire.com) offers bargain fares but won't reveal the airline or flight times until you buy. Other sites that compile deals include www.bestfares.com, www.flights.com, www.lowest-fare.com, www.onetravel.com, and www.travelzoo.com.

SideStep (www.sidestep.com) and **Booking Buddy** (www.bookingbuddy.com) let you enter your trip information once and search multiple sites.

An indispensable resource on the Internet is the **Air Traveler's Handbook** (www.faqs.org/faqs/travel/air/handbook), a comprehensive listing of links to everything you need to know before you board a plane.

COMMERCIAL AIRLINES

The commercial airlines' lowest regular offer is the **APEX** (Advance Purchase Excursion) fare, which provides confirmed reservations and allows "open jaw" tickets. Generally, reservations must be made seven to 21 days ahead of departure, with seven- to 14-day minimum-stay and up to 90-day maximum-stay restrictions. These fares carry hefty cancellation and change penalties (fees rise in summer). Book peak-season APEX fares early. Use **Expedia** (www.expedia.com) or **Travelocity** (www.travelocity.com) to get an idea of the lowest published fares, then use the resources outlined above to try to beat those fares. Low-season fares should be appreciably cheaper than the high-season (mid-June to Aug.) ones listed here.

TRAVELING FROM NORTH AMERICA

Basic round-trip fares to London range from roughly US$400-600. Standard commercial carriers like **American** (☎800-433-7300; www.aa.com), **United** (☎800-538-

ESSENTIALS

2929; www.ual.com), and **Northwest** (☎ 800-225-2525; www.nwa.com) will probably offer the most convenient flights, but they may not be the cheapest. Check **Lufthansa** (☎ 800-399-5838; www.lufthansa.com), **British Airways** (☎ 800-247-9297; www.britishairways.com), **Air France** (☎ 800-237-2747; www.airfrance.us), and **Alitalia** (☎ 800-223-5730; www.alitaliausa.com) for cheap tickets from destinations throughout the US to all over Europe. You might find a better deal on one of the following airlines, if any of their limited departure points is convenient for you.

Icelandair: ☎ 800-223-5500; www.icelandair.com. Stopovers in Iceland for no extra cost on most trans-Atlantic flights. For last-minute offers, subscribe to their email.

Finnair: ☎ 800-950-5000; www.finnair.com. Cheap round-trips from San Francisco, New York, and Toronto to London; connections throughout Europe.

TRAVELING FROM EUROPE

Travelers from Ireland and the continent can take advantage of the numerous no-frills budget airlines criss-crossing Europe. By only taking direct bookings, flying between lesser-known airports, and cutting back on free drinks, food, and sometimes baggage allowances, this new breed of carrier offers regular services at prices often lower than trains and ferries, let alone commercial airlines. The **Air Travel Advisory Bureau** in London (☎ 08707 370 021; www.atab.co.uk) provides referrals to travel agencies and consolidators that offer discounted airfares out of the UK. **Cheapflights** (www.cheapflights.co.uk) publishes airfare bargains.

Ryanair: Ireland ☎ 353 0818 303 030, UK 08712 460 000; www.ryanair.com. From London to destinations throughout Europe.

easyJet: UK ☎ 08712 442 366; www.easyjet.com. From London to Athens, Barcelona, Madrid, Nice, Palma, and Zurich (UK£72-141).

Aer Lingus: Ireland ☎ 353 0818 365 000; From London to many Ireland airports along with other worldwide destinations.

bmibaby: UK ☎ 0870 126 6726; www.bmibaby.com. Departures from throughout the UK, but best fares typically found from regional airports outside of London. London to Nice (UK£70) and Amsterdam (UK£60).

KLM: UK ☎ 08705 074 074; www.klm.com. Cheap round-trip tickets from London to Amsterdam, Brussels, Frankfurt, Düsseldorf, Milan, Paris, and Rome.

TRAVELING FROM AUSTRALIA AND NEW ZEALAND

Air New Zealand: New Zealand ☎ 64 800 73 70 00; www.airnz.co.nz. Auckland to London, around NZ$2800.

Qantas Air: Australia ☎ 61 13 11 31, New Zealand 64 800 101 500; www.qantas.com.au. Flights from Australia and New Zealand to London for around AUS$2000.

Singapore Air: Australia ☎ 61 13 10 11, New Zealand 64 800 808 909; www.singaporeair.com. Flies from Auckland, Christchurch, Melbourne, Perth, and Sydney to London.

AIR COURIER FLIGHTS

Those who travel light should consider courier flights. Couriers help transport cargo on international flights by using their checked luggage space for freight. Generally, couriers must travel with carry-ons only and deal with complex flight restrictions. Most flights are round-trip only, with short fixed-length stays (usually one week) and a limit of one ticket per issue. Generally, you must be over 18 (in some cases 21). In summer, the most popular destinations usually require an advance reservation of about two weeks (you can usually book up to two months ahead). Super-discounted fares are common for last-minute flights (three to 14 days ahead).

Travelers from **North America, the UK, Australia,** and **New Zealand** can book flights through the **International Association of Air Travel Couriers** (IAATC; ☎515-292-2458; www.courier.org), or **Courier Travel** (www.couriertravel.org). Travelers **only within North America** can go through **Air Courier Association** (☎877-303-4258; www.aircourier.org).

STANDBY FLIGHTS

Traveling standby requires considerable flexibility in arrival and departure dates and cities. Companies dealing in standby flights sell vouchers rather than tickets, along with the promise to get you to your destination (or near your destination) within a certain window of time (typically 1-5 days). You call in before your specific window of time to hear your flight options and the probability that you will be able to board each flight. You can then show up at the appropriate airport at the appropriate time, present your voucher, and board if space is available. Vouchers can usually be bought for both one-way and round-trip travel. You may receive a monetary refund only if every available flight within your date range is full; if you opt not to take an available (but perhaps less convenient) flight, you can only get credit toward future travel. Carefully read agreements with any company offering standby flights since tricky fine print can leave you in the lurch. To check on a company's service record in the US, contact the **Better Business Bureau** (☎703-276-0100; www.bbb.org). It is difficult to receive refunds, and clients' vouchers will not be honored when an airline fails to receive payment in time.

TICKET CONSOLIDATORS

Ticket consolidators, or "bucket shops," buy unsold tickets in bulk from commercial airlines and sell them at discounted rates. The best place to look is in the Sunday travel section of any major newspaper (such as *The New York Times*), where many bucket shops place tiny ads. Call quickly; availability is typically limited. Not all bucket shops are reliable, so insist on a receipt that gives full details of restrictions, refunds, and tickets, and pay by credit card (in spite of the 2-5% fee) so you can stop payment if you never receive your tickets. For more info, see www.travel-library.com/air-travel/consolidators.html.

NOW Voyager, 315 W. 49th St. Plaza Arcade, New York, NY 10019, USA (☎212-459-1616; www.nowvoyagertravel.com) arranges discounted flights, mostly from New York, to London. When traveling from the US and Canada, other consolidators worth trying are **Rebel** (☎800-732-3588; www.rebeltours.com) and **Cheap Tickets** (www.cheaptickets.com). Yet more consolidators on the web include **Flights.com** (www.flights.com) and **TravelHUB** (www.travelhub.com). Keep in mind that these are just suggestions to get you started in your research; *Let's Go* does not endorse any of these agencies. Be cautious and research companies before you hand over your credit card number.

CHARTER FLIGHTS

A tour operator contracts charter flights with an airline to fly extra loads of passengers during peak season. Charter flights fly less frequently than major airlines, make refunds particularly difficult, and are almost always fully booked. Schedules and itineraries may also change or be cancelled at the last moment (as late as 48hr. before the trip, and without a full refund), and check-in, boarding, and baggage claim are often much slower. However, they are often cheaper.

Discount clubs and fare brokers offer members savings on last-minute charter and tour deals. Study contracts closely—you don't want to end up with an unwanted overnight layover. **Travelers Advantage** (☎877-259-2691; www.travelersadvantage.com; US$90 annual fee includes discounts and cheap flight directories) specializes in European travel and tour packages.

BY CHUNNEL

Traversing 27 mi. under the sea, the Chunnel is undoubtedly the fastest and most convenient route from England to France.

BY TRAIN. Eurostar, Eurostar House, Waterloo Station, London SE1 8SE (UK ☎08705 186 186; www.eurostar.com) runs frequent trains between London and the continent. Ten to 28 trains per day run to 100 destinations including Paris (4hr., US$75-400, 2nd-class), Disneyland Paris, Brussels, Lille, and Calais. Book online, at major rail stations in the UK, or at the Eurostar office.

BY CAR. Eurotunnel, Customer Relations, P.O. Box 2000, Folkestone, Kent CT18 8XY (☎08705 353 535; www.eurotunnel.co.uk), shuttles cars and passengers between Kent and Nord-Pas-de-Calais. Round-trip fares for vehicle and all passengers range from £223-253. Same-day return costs £19-34 on top of the fare, two- to five-day return for a car £123-183. Book online or via phone.

GETTING INTO LONDON

THE AIRPORTS

HEATHROW

Heathrow (☎087 0000 0123; www.baa.co.uk/main/airports/heathrow), 15min. from central London, is just what you'd expect from one of the world's busiest international airports. Airlines and destinations are divvied up among its four terminals as listed below, with a few exceptions—if in doubt, check with the airline.

Terminal 1: Domestic flights and British Airways's European destinations, except for flights to Amsterdam and Paris. Also British Airways flights to Tokyo, Hong Kong, Johannesburg, San Francisco, and Los Angeles.

Terminal 2: All non-British Airways flights to Europe with the exception of Air Malta and KLM; British Airways flights to Basel.

Terminal 3: Intercontinental flights, except British Airways, Qantas, and Sri Lankan Airlines; British Airways flights to Miami.

Terminal 4: British Airways intercontinental flights and services to Amsterdam and Paris; Air Malta; KLM; Qantas; Sri Lankan Airlines; and any other flights that won't squeeze into terminals 1, 2, or 3.

TRANSPORTATION TO AND FROM CENTRAL LONDON

UNDERGROUND. The cheapest and best way to get to London, Heathrow's two Tube stations form a loop on the end of the Piccadilly Line. Trains stop first at **Heathrow Terminal 4** and then at **Heathrow Terminals 1, 2,** and **3** (both Zone 6) before swinging back toward central London. For those with heavy luggage, note that stairs are prevalent in most Tube stations. (☎08453 309 880; www.thetube.com. 50-70min. from central London, every 4-5min. Cost around £5, depending on where you are going.)

TRAIN. The **Heathrow Express** provides a speedy but expensive connection from Heathrow to Paddington station. An added bonus is check-in facilities at Paddington. (☎08456 001 515; www.heathrowexpress.co.uk., daily every 15min. 5:10am-

11:40pm. Railpasses and Travelcards not valid. £14, round-trip £26; children £6.50/ 12.50; £2 extra if bought on the train. Ask about day returns, student discounts, and group specials. AmEx/MC/V.) The new **Heathrow Connect** is a cheaper alternative to the Express, with direct routes from Paddington, Ealing Broadway, West Ealing, Hanwell, Southall, and Hayes to Terminals 1, 2, and 3. For Terminal 4, take the first Heathrow Express train. (☎08456 786 975; www.heathrowconnect.com. Daily every 30min. 5:30am-midnight. Railcards accepted. £9.50 to Paddington.)

BUS. While cheaper than trains, buses take longer and can end up in traffic. The **National Express** runs between Heathrow and Victoria Coach Station. (☎08705 808 080; www.nationalexpress.com. 40-85min., approx. every 20min. 5:35am-9:35pm Heathrow-Victoria, 7:15am-11:30pm Victoria-Heathrow. Railpasses and Travelcards not valid. From £8; ages 3-15 half price. AmEx/MC/V.)

TAXI. Metered fares to central London are unlikely to be under £50, and journey times are never under one hour.

 CARTING YOUR LUGGAGE. The walk from Heathrow's international terminals to the Tube can be quite long. Take advantage of the free luggage carts, which can be pushed most of the way.

GATWICK

Gatwick (☎08700 002 468; www.baa.co.uk) is much farther from London—30 minutes south of London—but numerous swift and affordable train services make it easy to get to. Transport facilities are concentrated in the **South Terminal;** a free monorail shuttle connects the South Terminal to the newer **North Terminal,** which has better shops and restaurants.

TRANSPORTATION TO AND FROM CENTRAL LONDON

TRAIN. The **Gatwick Express** runs non-stop service to Victoria station. (☎08456 001 515; www.gatwickexpress.com. 30-35min., daily every 15 min. 5am-11:45pm. £13, round-trip £24; ages 5-15 £6/11.75; tickets available for purchase on the train.) Additionally, **Thameslink** commuter trains head regularly to King's Cross, stopping in London Bridge and Blackfriars. Beware that Thameslink stations typically have lots of stairs. (☎08457 484 950; www.thameslink.co.uk. 50min., daily every 30min., £10.)

BUSES, SHUTTLES, AND TAXIS—OH MY. Road service is slow and unpredictable. National Express's **Airbus A5** takes roughly 1½hr. to travel to Victoria bus station but can also be much longer with a wait at Brighton. (Contact details same as for Heathrow. Daily every hr. 4:50am to 10:15pm from Gatwick, 7am-11:30pm from Victoria. From £6.20.) You should never take a **taxi** from Gatwick to London; the trip will take over an hour and cost at least £90. If you have heavy bags, take the train to Victoria and catch a taxi from there.

STANSTED

In Essex, 30 mi. north of London, Stansted (☎08700 000 303; www.baa.co.uk/main/airports/stansted) is a hub for many discount airlines.

TRANSPORTATION TO AND FROM CENTRAL LONDON

The train station is below the terminal building. The **Stansted Express** offers frequent service to Liverpool St. Station. (☎08457 484 950; www.stanstedexpress.co.uk. 45min.; daily every 15-30min. 6am-midnight from Stansted, 5am-11pm from Liverpool Street. £14.50, round-trip £24; children 5-15 £7.25/12.) The 24hr.

National Express Airbus A6 runs every 15min. to Victoria station. The 24hr. **A9** runs every 30min. to East London. (Contact same as for Heathrow. 1¼-1¾hr. From £8.)

LUTON

Luton (☎01582 405 100; www.london-luton.co.uk) serves mostly charter flights and no-frills budget airlines.

TRANSPORTATION TO AND FROM CENTRAL LONDON

The **Thameslink** train line links Gatwick to King's Cross and continues north to Luton. (Contact same as Gatwick. 30-40min.; every 30min. M-Sa 3:20am-1am, Su less frequently 6am-11:15pm. £10.40.) **Green Line 757** buses run to the West End and Victoria. (☎08706 087 261; www.greenline.co.uk. 1-1¾hr.; 3 per hr. 8am-6pm, 2 per hr. 6-11pm, 1 per hr. 11pm-8am. £9, round-trip £12.50; ages 5-15 £5.50/8.)

LONDON CITY AIRPORT

Built over the former Royal Docks in Docklands, it was once the heart of London's trading empire. Today, the main export is pin-striped business men (☎7646 0088; www.londoncityairport.com).

TRANSPORTATION TO AND FROM CENTRAL LONDON

Every 10min., **shuttles** make the 30min. run to Liverpool St. via Canary Wharf, or the 5min. run to Canning Town on the Jubilee Line. (To and from Liverpool St. via Canary Wharf: M-F 6:55am-9:20pm, Sa 6:45am-1:15pm, Su 11:56am-9:20pm; £3.50 to Canary Wharf, £6:50 to Liverpool St. To and from Canning Town: M-F 6am-9:30pm, Sa 6am-1pm, Su 12:13am-9:13pm; £3.) Bus **#69** also runs to Canning Town, while the **#473** stops at Silvertown rail station. (Both approx. every 10min., daily 6am-midnight, £1.)

TRAIN AND BUS STATIONS

London has nine mainline train stations, where a number of privatized companies run through. For impartial advice, call **National Rail Enquiries** (24hr. ☎08457 484 950). International services are dominated by **Eurolines,** which offers regular links to all major European cities. (☎08705 143 219; www.eurolines.co.uk.) **Victoria Coach Station,** Buckingham Palace Rd., is the hub of Britain's long-distance bus network. **National Express** is the largest operator of intercity services. (☎0870 580 8080; www.nationalexpress.com.) Much of the area around London is served by **Green Line** coaches, which leave from the Eccleston Bridge mall behind Victoria station. Purchase tickets from the driver. (☎08706 087 261; www.greenline.co.uk.)

GETTING AROUND LONDON

BY PUBLIC TRANSPORTATION

Local gripes aside, London's public transportation under the **Transport of London** (☎7222 1234; www.tfl.gov.uk) is remarkably efficient—and it's getting better. London's mayor, Ken Livingstone, is the man who first introduced Travelcards in the 1980s, and scarcely a week goes by without new talk about making travel in London easier and cheaper. New fares are generally introduced in January. Free maps of the Undergound network and of bus routes are available at Tube stations and Transport for London information centers.

TRAVEL PASSES

You're almost bound to save money by investing in one of London's travel passes, based on the zone system (p. 38). You probably won't need a pass past Zone 2. Passes can be purchased at Tube, DLR, and commuter rail stations. Avoid **ticket touts** hawking second-hand One-Day Travelcards, LT Cards, and Bus Passes; there's no guarantee the ticket will work, and it's illegal.

All children under 16 travel free on buses and trams in Greater London. On the Tube, all children under the age of five travel for free; children 5-10 are now free when accompanied by an adult; children 11-15 usually get half-price fares. To qualify for child fares, teenagers 14-15 must display a **child-rate Photocard** when purchasing tickets and traveling on public transportation. To qualify for half-price fares, full-time students at London universities must obtain a **Student Photocard.** These can often be a pain to get (you must send away for them), but the discounts can be worth it. Ask your London university about the Student Discount Scheme.

ZONES. The public-transport network is divided into a series of concentric zones; ticket prices depend on the zones passed during a journey. To confuse matters, there are two different zoning systems. The **Tube, rail,** and **Docklands Light Railway (DLR)** network operates on a system of six zones, with Zone 1 the most central. **Buses** reduce this to four zones. Bus Zones 1, 2, and 3 are the same as for the Tube, and Bus Zone 4 equates to Tube Zones 4, 5, and 6.

DAY TRAVELCARDS. Day Travelcards are valid for bus, Tube, DLR, and commuter rail services for one day. There are two types of Day Travelcards: **Peak** cards (all day) and **Off-Peak** cards (M-F after 9:30am, Sa-Su all day). Both Peak and Off-Peak Travelcards are valid until 4:30am the morning after the printed expiration date. Fares are subject to change; see www.tfl.gov.uk.

THREE-DAY TRAVELCARD. These have the same application as day Travelcard. Fares are subject to change; see www.tfl.gov.uk.

FAMILY TRAVELCARDS. These are for one or two adults and one to four children traveling together. When the only child is under five, a child fare must be paid; otherwise children under five go free. Each member must hold a Family Travelcard and must travel together. See www.tfl.gov.uk for fares.

SEASON TICKETS. Weekly, monthly, and annual Travelcards can be bought at any time and are valid for seven days, one month, or one year, respectively, from the date of purchase. A matching **Photocard** is required, free from Tube stations with an ID photo. See www.tfl.gov.uk for fares.

OYSTER CARD. Most long-term Londoners hold an Oyster Card, a plastic card which allows you to touch and go on Tube station entrances and on buses. Oyster Cards can act either as a normal Travelcard (week or month) or as a "Pre-Pay," with discounted adult fares. "Day Capping" promises that you will never pay more in a single day than you would with a Travelcard, and the Transportation for London Board continually introduces new and convenient ways to manage your account over the phone or online. Be sure to register your card—if it's lost or stolen, you'll be able to recover pre-paid funds to your account that way.

THE WORLD IS YOUR OYSTER. Don't forget to return your Oyster Card at the end of your time in London to receive your £3 deposit back.

THE UNDERGROUND

Universally known as "the Tube," the Underground provides a fast and convenient way of getting around London. Within Zone 1, use the Tube only for longer journeys; adjacent stations are so close together that walking or taking a bus makes more sense. You can save money on Tube fare with Travelcards or Oyster Cards (p. 37).

 GETTING HOME. The Tube closes around midnight, so planning transportation home is important. *Let's Go* includes local Night Bus routes for most nightlife listings—excluding pubs, which mostly close around 11pm. Coordinate the best Night Bus route by matching route numbers in nightlife listings with route numbers in accommodation listings. If you don't find a perfect fit, head toward a major transportation hub (Trafalgar Sq., Oxford Circus, Liverpool St., or Victoria) for a transfer.

CARNET. A carnet is a book of 10 singles, available only for a Tube journey starting and finishing in Zone 1; they cannot be used as extensions, nor can you purchase extensions for them. Each ticket must be validated at the station before you use it; failure to do so counts as fare evasion. Purchasing a carnet is cheaper than buying individual singles, but unless you plan to do a lot of walking, a Travelcard is definitely better. See www.tfl.gov.uk.

NAVIGATING THE SYSTEM. Color-coding makes navigating the 12 lines a breeze. Platforms are labeled by line name and general direction. If you are traveling on one of the lines that splits into two or more branches, check the platform indicators or the front of the train. Unless you want to be run down by a commuter in full stride, stand to the right on escalators.

HOURS OF OPERATION. The Tube runs daily from approximately 5:30am to midnight, giving clubbers that extra incentive to party till dawn. The exact time of the first and last train from each station should be posted in the ticket hall; check if you think you'll be taking the Tube any time after 11:30pm. Trains run less frequently early mornings, late nights, and Sundays.

TICKETS. You can buy tickets from ticket counters or machines in all stations. Tickets must be bought at the start of a journey and are valid only for the day of purchase (including round-trip tickets, but excluding carnets). **Keep your ticket for the entire journey;** it will be checked on the way out and may be checked at any time. There's a **£20 on-the-spot fine** for traveling without a valid ticket.

 In addition to the destination announced on the front of the train, many Tube stations also post arrival time and destination for upcoming trains, and those on the train conflict; **Tube officials recommend always following what is posted on the train.** This is especially important when heading to Heathrow on the Piccadilly line, as sometimes the screen conflicts with the actual arrival time and destination of the upcoming train.

BUSES

Only tourists use the Tube for short trips in central London—chances are you'll spend half as long walking underground as it would take to get to your destination. If it's only a couple of Tube stops, or if it involves more than one change, taking a bus (or even walking) will likely get you there faster. Bus riders can save money with Travelcards (p. 37).

NAVIGATING THE SYSTEM. Excellent signs make the bus system easy to use even for those with no local knowledge. Most stops display a map of local routes and nearby stops together with a key to help you find the bus and stop you need. Officially, bus stops come in two varieties: regular and request. Supposedly, buses must stop at regular stops (red logo on white background), but only pull up at request stops (white on red) if someone rings the bell, or someone at the bus stop indicates to the driver with an outstretched arm. In reality, it's safest to ring/indicate at all stops. On the older, open-platform "Routemaster" buses, you're free to jump on and off the moving vehicle at your own risk.

 I FOUGHT THE LAW... While it may seem easy to hop on or off of a bus or subway without paying, ticket officials perform random checks on passengers that can result in a £20 fine.

HOURS OF OPERATION. Buses run approximately 5:30am to midnight; a reduced network of **Night Buses** (p. 39) fills in the gap. During the day, double-deckers generally run every 10-15min., while single-decker "Hoppers" should arrive every 5-8min. It's not uncommon to wait 30min. only to have three buses arrive in a row.

NIGHT BUSES. Because the Tube closes around midnight, Night Buses are a necessary form of nighttime transportation (taxis can get quite pricey). Night Bus route numbers are prefixed with an N; they typically operate the same route as their daytime equivalents, but occasionally start and finish at different points. Buses that run 24hr. have no N in front. Most Night Buses operate every 30-60min. from midnight to 5:30am.

TICKETS. Bus and Night Bus fares are the same: £1.20, children 11-15 40p, children under 11 free; discounts on Oyster pre-pay. All tickets are good for traveling across the network and can be purchased at roadside machines or on the bus. Older buses still use conductors, who make the rounds between stops to collect fares. Keep your ticket until you get off the bus; otherwise you may face a £5 on-the-spot fine.

 TIGHTENING IT UP. In an effort to curb the city's environmentally harmful output, London is introducing a "low emissions zone" near the Financial District beginning in February 2008, primarily affecting lorries, trucks, and buses.

DOCKLANDS LIGHT RAILWAY

The toy-like driverless cabs of this elevated railway provide a vital link in the transport network of East London operated by the Transport for London authorities. Obvious physical differences aside, the network is basically an extension of the Tube, with the same tickets and pricing structure; within the validity of a given ticket, you can transfer from Tube to DLR at no charge. Travelers visiting both Greenwich and Docklands in one day should inquire about **Rail and Sail** tickets. For costumer service, call ☎7363 9700 (M-F 8:30am-5:30pm); for the Docklands travel hotline, call ☎7918 4000 (24hr.).

SUBURBAN RAILWAYS

In the suburbs, London's commuter rail network is almost as extensive as the Tube. In much of South and East London, this is the only option. Services are run by a range of companies: **Thameslink** heads north-south from Clerkenwell and the City of London; **Silverlink** runs east-west from Docklands to Richmond via Islington and Hampstead; and **WAGN** trains run from Liverpool St. to Hackney. Trains can cut journey times thanks to direct cross-town links—Silverlink takes 25min. from Hampstead to Kew versus one hour by Tube. Trains run less frequently than the Tube (generally every 20-30min.), but service often continues later into the night. For journeys combining rail travel with Tube and DLR, you can buy a single ticket valid for the entire trip. Travelcards are also valid on most suburban railways, but not on intercity lines that happen to make a few local stops. For schedule and fare information, visit www.railtrack.co.uk.

COMMUTER BOATS

The Thames, once London's major transportation artery, is now used primarily for pleasure cruises. A small number of regularly scheduled commuter boats still ply the river. There are three routes in operation: **Chelsea Harbour to Embankment via Cadogan** (near Tate Britain), operated by Riverside Launches (☎ 7352 5888; M-F 6:30am-7:10pm; £4, round-trip £8); **Savoy to Masthouse Terrace via Canary Wharf,** operated by Thames Clippers (☎ 7977 6892; M-F 6:25am-9pm, occasionally during the weekend; £2.50, round-trip £3.80, ages 5-15 £1.25/1.90); and **Hilton Docklands to Canary Wharf,** also operated by Thames Clippers (daily 6:25am-11:05pm; £2.50, round-trip £3.80, ages 5-15 £1.25/1.90). For detailed timetables of departure times for all boats, visit www.tfl.gov.uk/river. Holders of a valid Travelcard receive a 30% discount on most boat fares.

BY TAXI

LICENSED TAXICABS

Black cabs are very expensive, since driving a London taxi is skilled work. An approximate cost per hour in central London is £25-30. Taxis are obliged to take passengers on trips from just one block up to 12 mi., but longer journeys are at their discretion. If going outside the city, it's best to negotiate a fare in advance. A **10% tip** is expected. For all private hire licensing inquiries, call ☎ 08456 027 000. For listings of companies, see **Practical Information** (p. 95).

 Be wary of unlicensed minicab drivers, especially at night. According to Transport for London (TfL), eleven sexual assaults a month occur in unlicensed mincabs and they have been linked to other illegal activities. Take a licensed minicab, Night Bus, or black cab. All licensed vehicles should display a TfL license prominently; to confirm that an operator is licensed, visit www.tfl.gov.uk/pco.

BY CAR

Driving in central London is daunting. Various thoroughfares are off-limits to private vehicles during the week, on-street parking is almost non-existent, and off-street parking is hideously expensive—not to mention the labyrinth of one-way streets. In addition, driving in central London requires payment of a **Congestion Charge**. Cars are only useful for trips to the outer suburbs and nearby towns—that said, the extensive rail and bus networks can get you most everywhere with no need for a car.

If you plan to drive in Britain, you must be over 18 years old and have a valid driver's license. An **International Driving Permit (IDP)** is also advisable. Your IDP, valid for one year, must be issued in your home country before you depart. An application for an IDP usually requires one or two photos, a current local license, an additional form of identification, and a fee. To apply, contact your home country's automobile association. Be careful when purchasing an IDP online or anywhere other than your home automobile association. Many vendors sell permits of questionable legitimacy for higher prices.

Most credit cards cover standard **insurance.** If you rent, lease, or borrow a car, you will need a **Green Card** or an **International Insurance Certificate,** to certify that you have liability insurance and that it applies abroad. Green Cards can be obtained at rental agencies, car dealers (for those leasing cars), some travel agents, and some border crossings.

CAR RENTAL

Budget (reservations ☎08701 539 170, customer service 01344 668 833; www.budget.co.uk). Locations include Heathrow Airport (☎02088 978 095), open 6am-11pm; Gatwick Airport (☎8700 104 068), open 24hr.; and numerous London branches. Must be 25+.

easycar.com (☎09063 333 333; www.easycar.com). Internet-only rentals. 25 London locations, in addition to all airports. Must be 21+, holding a UK/EU driver's license for at least 1 year. From £7 per day, plus £5 preparation fee.

BY BICYCLE

London is a great city for bicycling. You'll be able to cover a lot more ground than you would on foot and still see the sights you'd miss traveling underground. Always be aware of traffic and ride with proper protection.

BICYCLE RENTAL

London Bicycle Tour Company, 1A Gabriel's Wharf, off 56 Upper Ground (☎7928 6838; www.londonbicycle.com). ⊖Blackfriars or Waterloo. Organizes bicycle tours of the city. Bikes and in-line skates £3 per hr. £16 for first 24hr., £8 per day thereafter. Credit card deposit. Open Apr.-Oct. daily 10am-6pm; call ahead Nov.-Mar. AmEx/MC/V.

London Cycling Campaign, 2 Newhams Row 30 (☎7928 7220; www.lcc.org.uk). ⊖London Bridge. Works to improve the cyclists' lot in London. They also organize group rides and sell a series of maps detailing cycle routes in London. Open M-F 10am-5pm.

Scootabout, 1-3 Leeke St. (☎7833 4607). ⊖King's Cross. Moped and scooter rentals. Riders must be experienced. 21+ only, with International Driving Permit. Rates include insurance coverage and vary with age. 50-125cc bikes £23 per day; 2-day min. Credit card deposit. Helmets occasionally available (£2); inquire when booking. Open M-F 9am-6pm, Sa 9am-1pm. MC/V.

TOP 10 WAYS TO SAVE IN LONDON

1. Make your base on the outskirts of the town, where restaurants and accommodations tend to be cheaper and less touristed.

2. If you have a choice, try walking or taking the bus instead of the Tube, which tends to be more expensive.

3. Buy food at markets (esp. open-air markets) and grocery stores instead of restaurants.

4. You can get into many shows on the cheap with matinee tickets or by waiting for standby seats.

5. Take advantage of flyers and coupons (in weekly papers or from promoters) that will allow you to bypass cover charges at clubs.

6. London's major museums are free, other museums and sights offer free or reduced admission on certain days.

7. Book a university dorm room during summer or winter break instead of a hostel room.

8. Find free Internet access in libraries and tourist offices.

9. Takeaway your meal and have a picnic instead of sitting down; food is often cheaper this way.

10. Forgo expensive museum tours and do some sleuthing yourself; it's more rewarding!

BY FOOT

London's public transport is quick, but footing it around the city will offer you experiences and sights you would miss otherwise. Since London does not have a neat grid system, a good map is key to successful walking. The pocket-sized ▓**London A-Z** (Geographer's A-Z Map Company, £5.95), available at most newsstands, is very useful. A far bigger menace to most foreigners than going mapless is the fact that Britons drive on the left—remember to **look both ways when crossing the road.**

BY THUMB

 Let's Go never recommends hitchhiking as a safe means of transportation, and none of the information presented here is intended to do so.

Let's Go strongly urges you to consider the risks before you choose to hitchhike. Hitching means entrusting your life to a stranger and risking assault, sexual harassment, theft, and unsafe driving.

GETTING AROUND BRITAIN

BY TRAIN

Railpasses covering specific regions are sometimes available from local train stations and may include bus and ferry travel. Prices and schedules often change; find up-to-date information from **National Rail Inquiries** (☎08457 484 950) or online at **Railtrack** (www.railtrack.co.uk).

BRITRAIL PASSES. If you plan to travel a great deal on trains within Britain, the **BritRail Pass** can be a good buy. Eurail passes are not valid in Britain, but there is often a discount on BritRail passes if you purchase the two simultaneously. **BritRail** passes are only available outside Britain; **you must buy them before traveling to Britain.** They allow unlimited train travel in England, Wales, and Scotland, regardless of which company is operating the trains, but they do not work in Northern Ireland or on Eurostar. Travelers under 26 should ask for a **youth pass** for a 25% discount on standard and first classes; **seniors** (over 60) should ask for a 15% discount on first class only. **Children** 5-15 can travel free with each adult pass as long as you ask for the **Family Pass** (free). All children under the age of 5 travel free. The **Party Discount** gets the 3rd through 9th travelers in a party a 50% discount on their railpasses. Check with BritRail (US ☎866-BRITRAIL/274-8724; www.britrail.net) or one of the distributors for details on other passes.

BRITRAIL DISTRIBUTORS. The distributors listed below will either sell you passes directly or tell you where to buy passes. Also ask at travel agencies.

Australia: Rail Plus, Level 4, 10-16 Queen Street, Melbourne, VIC 3000, Australia (☎61 03 9642 8644; www.railplus.com.au). **Concorde International Travel** (Rail Tickets), 403 George St., Sydney, NSW 2000 (☎61 02 9244 2222; www.concorde.com.au).

Ireland: usit NOW, 19-21 Aston Quay, O'Connell Bridge, Dublin 2 (☎353 01 602 1600).

New Zealand: Holiday Shoppe, Gullivers Holiday Rep: Holiday Shoppe, 5th fl. 66 Wyndham St:, Auckland (☎64 800 80 84 80; www.holidayshoppe.co.nz), with locations throughout New Zealand.

US and Canada: Rail Europe, 44 South Broadway, White Plains, NY 10601 (US ☎877-257-2887, Canada 800-361-7245; www.raileurope.com), is the North American distributor for BritRail. Or try **Rail Pass Express** (☎800-RAILPASS/724-5727; www.railpass.com/new).

RAIL DISCOUNT CARDS. Unlike BritRail passes, these can be purchased in the UK. Passes are valid for one year and generally offer 30% off standard fares (ages 16-25 and over 60, full-time students and families £20; people with disabilities £14). Visit the **Railcards** website (www.railcard.co.uk) for details.

KEEPING IN TOUCH

BY EMAIL AND INTERNET

Almost anywhere you walk in central London, you will be able to spot an Internet cafe. Though in some places it's possible to forge a remote link with your home server, in most cases this is a much slower option than taking advantage of free web-based email accounts (e.g., www.gmail.com and www.hotmail.com). For listings of **Internet cafes** and **libraries,** see **Practical Information** (p. 100).

Increasingly, travelers find that taking their **laptop computers** on the road with them can be a convenient option for staying connected. Laptop users can call an Internet service provider via a modem using long-distance phone cards specifically intended for such calls. They may also find Internet cafes that allow them to connect their laptops to the Internet. Travelers with wireless-enabled computers may be able to take advantage of an increasing number of Internet "hot spots" (many cafes in London), where they can get online for free or for a small fee. Newer computers can detect these hot spots automatically; otherwise, websites like www.jiwire.com, www.wi-fihotspotlist.com, and www.locfinder.net can help you find them.

 WARY WI-FI. Wireless hot spots make Internet access possible in public and remote places. Unfortunately, they also pose **security risks.** Hot spots are public, open networks that use unencrypted, unsecured connections. They are susceptible to hacks and "packet sniffing"—ways of stealing passwords and other private information. To prevent problems, disable ad hoc mode, turn off file sharing, turn off network discovery, encrypt your email, turn on your firewall, beware of phony networks, and watch for over-the-shoulder creeps. Ask the establishment whose wireless you're using for the name of the network so you know you're on the right one. If you are in the vicinity of a hot spot and do not plan to access the Internet, turn off your wireless adapter completely.

BY TELEPHONE

CALLING HOME FROM LONDON

You can usually make **direct international calls** from pay phones, but if you aren't using a phone card, you may need to feed the machine regularly. **Prepaid phone**

cards are a common and relatively inexpensive means of calling abroad. Each one comes with a Personal Identification Number (PIN) and a toll-free access number. You call the access number and then follow the directions for dialing your PIN. To purchase prepaid phone cards, check online for the best rates; www.calling-cards.com is a good place to start. Online providers generally send your access number and PIN via email, with no actual "card" involved.

PLACING INTERNATIONAL CALLS. To call London from home or to call home from London, dial:

1. The **international dialing prefix.** To call from **Australia,** dial 0011; **Canada** or the **US,** 011; **Ireland, New Zealand,** or the **UK,** 00.
2. The **country code** of the country you want to call. To call **Australia,** dial 61; **Canada** or the **US,** 1; **Ireland,** 353; **New Zealand,** 64; the **UK,** 44.
3. The **city/area code.** If the first digit is a zero (e.g., 020 for London), omit the zero when calling from abroad (e.g., dial 20 from Canada to reach London).
4. The **local number.**

PREPAID CALLING CARDS. Prepaid calling cards are sold in newsstands and post offices. Be sure to check **rates** and **connection charges** before you buy. If you're planning to make one long call, go for the card with the cheapest rate; for lots of short calls, look for a low connection charge. Before settling on a calling card plan, be sure to research your options in order to pick the one that best fits both your needs and your destination.

BILLED CALLING CARDS. These calling cards must be set up in your home country before you leave: contact your telephone provider. In the USA, AT&T, MCI, and Sprint all offer their own versions. From the UK, simply dial the free access number and your account code: you'll then be able to either make a direct-dial call home or reach an operator, who'll make the connection for you. Once a month, the bill will be sent home—make sure someone's around to pay it! The disadvantages of these cards is that rates are usually high, and they're only good for calling their home country. You can make calls to other countries, but you'll be charged the rate for calling home *plus* the rate from home to the other country.

COMPANY	TO OBTAIN A CARD:	TO CALL ABROAD:
AT&T (US)	www.att.com	0800 89 00 11 or 0500 89 00 11
Canada Direct	800-561-8868; www.infocanadadirect.com	0800 559 3141 or 0800 096 0634
MCI (US)	800-777-5000; www.minutepass.com	0800 279 5088
Telecom New Zealand Direct	www.telecom.co.nz	0800 899 776
Telstra Australia	www.telstra.com	0800 783 0021

CALLING WITHIN LONDON

London's phone codes have changed four times in the last two decades, so you may encounter some out-of-date numbers while in London. Here's the low-down on how to convert the old numbers to the new ones. Starting in the late 1980s, London had two phone codes, 071 and 081. In the 90s, these were changed to **0171** and

0181. To convert these old seven-digit numbers to the new eight-digit number, prefix 7 (if it was an 0171 number) or 8 (for 0181) to the start of the old number.

PHONE NUMBERS. London's phone code is **020;** within this area, all numbers are 8 digits long. **All telephone numbers given in this book are area code 020 unless otherwise specified.** Other UK codes: **0800** and **0808** numbers are free; **0845** numbers are charged at the local rate; **0870** numbers are charged at the national (long-distance) rate; numbers starting with **09** are premium rate (charging from £1-1.50 per min.); numbers starting with **07** are mobile phones, costing around 30p per min. from a landline (more from a pay phone).

ESSENTIALS

CELLULAR PHONES

Cell phones are ubiquitous in Britain; competitive, low prices and the variety of calling plans make them accessible even for short-term, low-budget travelers. For most visitors to Britain, a **pay-as-you-go plan** is the most attractive option. Once you arrive, pick up an eligible mobile (from £30) and recharge, or **top up,** with a card purchased at a grocery store, high-street shop, on the Internet, or by phone. **Incoming calls and text messages are always free.**

The international standard for cell phones is **Global System for Mobile Communication (GSM).** To make and receive calls in London you will need a **GSM-compatible phone** and a **SIM (Subscriber Identity Module) card,** a country-specific, thumbnail-sized chip that gives you a local phone number and plugs you into the local network. For more information on GSM phones, check out www.telestial.com, www.orange.co.uk, www.roadpost.com, or www.planetomni.com. Companies like **Cellular Abroad** (www.cellularabroad.com) rent cell phones that work in a variety of destinations around the world, providing a simpler option than picking up a phone in-country.

SERVICE PROVIDERS

Many of the providers below also have their own stores.

Carphone Warehouse (sales advice ☎0870 087 0870; www.carphonewarehouse.com). Dozens of branches, including: 220 Tottenham Court Rd. (☎08701 682 319; ⊖Tottenham Court Rd. or Goodge St.); 49 Oxford St. (☎08701 682 792; ⊖Tottenham Court Rd.), and 434 Strand (☎08701 682 033; ⊖Charing Cross or Embankment). Sells all of the below providers. Most stores open M-Sa 9am-7pm, Su 10am-5pm.

Mobile Phone Boutique, 100 N. Circular Rd. (☎8208 4198). One of many unlocking service stores. Also rents mobile phones for as low as £1 per day.

Rent-a-Mobile (☎7353 7705; www.rent-mobile-phone.com). Rents mobile phones for £1 per day, with a £7 delivery fee.

GSM PHONES. Just having a GSM phone doesn't mean you're necessarily good to go when you travel abroad. The majority of GSM phones sold in the US operate on a different **frequency** (1900) than international phones (900/1800) and will not work abroad. Tri-band phones work on all three frequencies (900/1800/1900) and will operate through most of the world. Additionally, some GSM phones are **SIM-locked** and will only accept SIM cards from a single carrier. You'll need a **SIM-unlocked** phone to use a SIM card from a local carrier when you travel.

TIME DIFFERENCES

The UK is on **Greenwich Mean Time (GMT).** New York (USA) is 5hr. behind, Vancouver (CAN) and San Francisco (USA) are 8hr. behind, Sydney (AUS) is 10hr. ahead, and Aukland (NZ) is 11hr. ahead.

4AM	5AM	6AM	7AM	8AM	NOON	10PM
Vancouver Seattle San Francisco Los Angeles	Denver	Chicago	New York Toronto	New Brunswick	**LONDON**	Sydney Canberra Melbourne

BY MAIL

SENDING MAIL HOME FROM BRITAIN

Airmail is the best way to send mail home from Britain. Just write "Par Avion—By Airmail" on the top left corner of your envelope or swing by any post office and get a free Airmail label. **Aerogrammes,** printed sheets that fold into envelopes and travel via airmail, are also available at post offices. For priority shipping, ask for **Airsure;** it costs £4.20 on top of the actual postage, but your letter will get on the next available flight. If Airsure is not available to the country to which you wish to ship, ask for **International Signed For** instead; for £3.50, your package will be signed for on delivery. **Surface mail** is the cheapest and slowest way to send mail, taking one to three months to cross the Atlantic and two to four to cross the Pacific.

Britain's **Royal Mail** (☎08457 740 740; www.royalmail.co.uk) is perhaps the best in the world and has taken great care to standardize its rates around the world; use the Royal Mail Postal Calculator (www.royalmail.com) to check rates. From Britain, postcards cost 21p domestically, 42p to send to Europe, and 47p to the rest of the world; airmail letters (up to 100g) are 24p domestically, 48p within Europe, and 78p elsewhere. These are 2nd-class mail rates and take two to three business days to arrive. Next-day delivery is also available for higher prices. International 2nd-class rates are as follows: packages up to 500g cost £5.72 and take five business days to travel around the world including to Australia, Canada, New Zealand, and the US. Packages up to 2kg cost £20.72 and take five days for the same countries. For listings of post offices, see **Practical Information** (p. 101).

SENDING MAIL TO BRITAIN

To ensure timely delivery, mark envelopes "Par Avion—By Airmail." In addition to the standard postage system, **Federal Express** (Canada and US ☎800-463-3339, Australia 13 26 10, Ireland 1800 535 800, New Zealand 0800 733 339, UK 0845 607 0809; www.fedex.com) handles express mail services to London; they can get a letter from New York to London in two days for US$35.

There are several ways to pick up letters sent to you by friends and relatives while you are abroad. Mail can be sent via **poste restante** (general delivery) to almost any city or town in the United Kingdom with a post office. Address *poste restante* letters like so:

POSTE RESTANTE,
[Post office name],
[Post office street address],
LONDON [Post office postcode],
UNITED KINGDOM
Hold for: [Name of Recipient].

The mail will go to a special desk in the central post o.ffice if you don't specify a post office by street address or postal code. Bring your passport (or other photo ID) for pickup.

SPECIFIC CONCERNS

SUSTAINABLE TRAVEL

As the number of travelers on the road continues to rise, the detrimental effect they can have on natural environments becomes an increasing concern. With this in mind, *Let's Go* promotes the philosophy of **sustainable travel.** Through a sensitivity to issues of ecology and sustainability, today's travelers can be a powerful force in preserving and restoring the places they visit.

Ecotourism, a rising trend in sustainable travel, focuses on the conservation of natural habitats and uses them to build up the economy without exploitation or overdevelopment. Travelers can make a difference by doing advance research and by supporting establishments that pay attention to their impact on their natural surroundings and strive to be environmentally friendly. For information on how to become involved with environmentalism in London, see **Beyond Tourism** (p. 82).

> **ECOTOURISM RESOURCES.** For more information on environmentally responsible tourism, contact one of the organizations below:
> **Conservation International,** 2011 Crystal Dr., Ste. 500, Arlington, VA 22202, USA (☎800-406-2306 or 703-341-2400; www.conservation.org).
> **Green Globe,** Green Globe vof, Verbenalaan 1, 2111 ZL Aerdenhout, the Netherlands (☎31 23 544 0306; www.greenglobe.com).
> **International Ecotourism Society,** 1333 H St. NW, Ste. 300E, Washington, D.C. 20005, USA (☎202-347-9203; www.ecotourism.org).
> **United Nations Environment Program (UNEP),** 39-43 Quai André Citroën, 75739 Paris Cedex 15, France (☎33 1 44 37 14 50; www.uneptie.org/pc/tourism).

RESPONSIBLE TRAVEL

London is filled with open-air historical sites. While many of the oldest testaments to its history (stemming from AD 43) are now in museums, others lie directly in your path—from cobblestone streets to Christopher Wren architecture. The last piece of the London wall, from AD 200, stands in the City of London unprotected and unmonitored. Tourists' good will is all that protects these beautiful public sites from harm.

The impact of tourist pounds on London should not be underestimated. The choices you make during your trip can have potent effects on local communities—for better or for worse. Travelers who care about the destinations and environments they explore should become aware of the social, cultural, and political implications of the choices they make when they travel. Simple decisions like buying local products instead of globally available products and paying a fair price can have a strong, positive effect on the community. An excellent resource for general information on community-based travel is *The Good Alternative Travel Guide* (UK£10), a project of **Tourism Concern** (☎7133 3330; www.tourismconcern.org.uk).

TRAVELING ALONE

There are many benefits to traveling alone, including independence and greater interaction with locals. On the other hand, any solo traveler is a more vulnerable target of harassment and street theft. As a lone traveler, try not to stand out as a tourist, look confident, and be especially careful in deserted or very crowded areas. Stay away from areas that are not well-lit. If questioned, never admit that you are traveling alone. Maintain regular contact with someone at home who knows your itinerary and always research your destination before traveling. For more tips, pick up *Traveling Solo* by Eleanor Berman (Globe Pequot Press; US$18), visit www.travelaloneandloveit.com, or subscribe to **Connecting: Solo Travel Network,** 689 Park Rd., Unit 6, Gibsons, BC V0N 1V7, Canada (☎ 800-557-1757; www.cstn.org; membership US$30-55).

GLBT TRAVELERS

London is widely recognized as one of the gay capitals of the world. **Soho,** particularly around Old Compton St., is London's gay nexus, though gay bars and pubs can be found throughout the city; *Let's Go* has included numerous rainbow-toting cafes, bars, and nightclubs in neighborhood listings. Newspaper resources include *The Pink Paper* (free), available from newsagents; *Gay Times* (£3), which covers political issues; and *Diva* (£2.25), a monthly lesbian lifestyle magazine with an excellent mix of features and good listings. *Boyz* (www.boyz.co.uk) is the main gay listings and lifestyle magazine for London (free from gay bars and clubs), while *Gingerbeer* offers the lesbian lowdown (www.gingerbeer.co.uk). **Out and About** (www.planetout.com) offers a weekly newsletter addressing gay travel concerns, and the online newspaper **365gay** also has a travel section (www.365gay.com/travel/travelchannel.htm). Listed below are contact organizations, mail-order bookstores, and publishers that offer materials addressing some specific concerns.

GLBT RESOURCES

GAY to Z (www.gaytoz.co.uk). Online and printed directory of gay-friendly resources and businesses throughout Britain.

Gay London (www.gaylondon.co.uk). Online community for gays and lesbians.

Gingerbeer (www.gingerbeer.co.uk). Lesbian and bisexual women web portal for London, with listings of clubs, bars, restaurants, and community resources.

London Lesbian and Gay Switchboard (☎ 7837 7324; www.llgs.org.uk). 24hr. helpline and information resource.

WOMEN TRAVELERS

Women exploring on their own inevitably face some additional safety concerns, but it's easy to be adventurous without taking undue risks. If you are concerned, consider staying in hostels which offer single rooms that lock from the inside or in religious organizations with single-sex rooms. Stick to centrally located accommodations and avoid solitary late-night treks or metro rides.

Always **carry extra cash** for a phone call, bus, or taxi. Hitchhiking is never safe for lone women or even for two women traveling together. Look as if you know where you're going and approach older women or couples for directions if you're lost or uncomfortable.

FURTHER READING: GLBT.
Spartacus International 2007 Gay Guide. Bruno Gmunder Verlag (US$22).
Ferrari Guides' Gay Travel A to Z, Ferrari Guides' Men's Travel in Your Pocket, Ferrari Guides' Women's Travel in Your Pocket, and *Ferrari Guides' Inn Places.* Ferrari Publications (US$16-20).
Time Out Gay and Lesbian London, Time Out Publishing (US$15).
Gay London, Will McLoughlin, Peter Jones, Ian Martin, and Andrew Wyllie, Ellipsis London (US$12).
The Gay Vacation Guide: The Best Trips and How to Plan Them, Mark Chesnut. Kensington Books (US$15).
Transgender London: London and the Third Sex, by Claudia Andrei, Glitter Books (US$18).

Generally, the less you look like a tourist, the better off you'll be. Dress conservatively, especially in rural areas. Wearing a conspicuous **wedding band** sometimes helps to prevent unwanted advances.

Your best answer to verbal harassment is no answer at all; feigning deafness, sitting motionless, and staring straight ahead at nothing in particular will usually do the trick. The extremely persistent can sometimes be dissuaded by a firm, loud, and very public "Go away!" Don't hesitate to seek out a police officer or a passerby if you are being harassed. Memorize London's emergency numbers (p. 100) in places you visit, and consider carrying a whistle on your keychain. A self-defense course will both prepare you for a potential attack and raise your level of awareness of your surroundings (see **Personal Safety,** p. 26).

TRAVELERS WITH DISABILITIES

Traveling by public transport in London with a disability is getting easier. While the Underground is almost exclusively accessible via numerous stairs and can be extremely crowded during peak travel times, new stations are beginning to incorporate lifts: Jubilee line trains are wheelchair-accessible at all new stations between Westminster and Stratford. The Docklands Light Railway has lifts, escalators, and/or ramps at every station, and all platforms are level with the train for free-step access; there is also a designated wheelchair area on each train. The National Rail website (www.nationalrail.co.uk) provides general information for travelers with disabilities as well as assistance phone numbers for individual rail companies. All buses, except for routes 9 and 15, have wheelchair-accessible ramps and designated spaces for riding while on board. The wheelchair-accessible Stationlink buses follow a similar route to the Circle Line; routes 205 and 705 travel from Paddington, Euston, St. Pancras, and King's Cross to Liverpool St., London Bridge, Waterloo, and Victoria. All black taxis are wheelchair-accessible. Those with disabilities should inform airlines and hotels of their specific disabilities when making reservations. When in doubt, call ahead to restaurants, museums, and other facilities to find out if they are wheelchair-accessible. Guide dog owners must have their dog fulfill a six month quarantine before entering the UK with the animal, see http://www.nfb-nagdu.org/laws/uk/pets.html for full details.

The London Tourist Board's *London For All* leaflet, available at London Visitors Centres (p. 95), includes information on disabled access in London. *Access in London,* by Gordon Couch (Quiller Press; US$12) is an in-depth guide to accommodations, transport, and general accessibility in London. The London

Tourist Board has information on programs and events specifically for disabled people (http://na.visitlondon.com/city_guide/disabled).

USEFUL ORGANIZATIONS

Access Abroad, www.umabroad.umn.edu/access. A website devoted to making study abroad available to students with disabilities. The site is maintained by Disability Services and the Learning Abroad Center, University of Minnesota, University Gateway, Ste. 180, 200 Oak St. SE, Minneapolis, MN 55455, USA (☎612-626-7379).

Accessible Journeys, 35 W. Sellers Ave., Ridley Park, PA 19078, USA (☎800-846-4537; www.disabilitytravel.com). Designs tours for wheelchair users and slow walkers. The site has tips and forums for all travelers.

Artsline, 54 Chalton St. (☎7388 2227; www.artsline.org.uk). ⊖Euston. Information on access to entertainment venues for disabled people.

The Guided Tour Inc., 7900 Old York Rd., Ste. 114B, Elkins Park, PA 19027, USA (☎800-783-5841; www.guidedtour.com). Organizes travel programs for persons with developmental and physical challenges in the UK.

Magic (www.magicdeaf.org.uk). Association of 14 museums in London that runs events and facilities for deaf and hard-of-hearing visitors.

Royal Association for Disability and Rehabilitation, 12 City Forum, 250 City Rd. (☎7250 3222; www.radar.org.uk). ⊖Old St. Umbrella organization for disabled volunteer groups. Info and links for resources throughout the city.

Society for Accessible Travel and Hospitality (SATH), 347 5th Ave., Ste. 605, New York, NY 10016, USA (☎212-447-7284; www.sath.org). Publishes free online travel information and reviews of past trips and highlights through the OPEN WORLD link on their website. Annual membership US$49, students and seniors US$29.

Transport for London: Access and Mobility, (☎0845 300 7000, Tube access 7941 4600, bus access 7918 4300; www.tfl.co.uk). Can provide information on public transportation accessibility within the city.

MINORITY TRAVELERS

Minority travelers in London should have few problems—London is as multiracial and tolerant as cities come. The **Commission for Racial Equality (CRE),** St. Dunstan's House, 201-211 Borough High St., London SE1 1GZ (☎7939 0000; www.cre.gov.uk), offers a wide variety of publications on diversity and race relations and can provide advice to minority travelers who encounter harassment or discrimination.

DIETARY CONCERNS

In a country battered by foot-and-mouth disease and besieged by mad cows, it's not surprising that one in five Brits under age 25 is vegetarian. For more information about vegetarian travel, contact **The Vegetarian Society of the UK** (☎0161 925 2000; www.vegsoc.org). Browse www.vegdining.com, www.happycow.net, www.vegetariansabroad.com, or the travel section of **The Vegetarian Resource Group's** website (www.vrg.org/travel). In your local bookstore, pick up *The Vegetarian Traveler: Where to Stay if You're Vegetarian, Vegan and Environmentally Sensitive,* by Jed and Susan Civic (Larson Publications; US$16), or *Vegetarians London,* by Alex Bourke (Vegetarian Guides Ltd.; US$11).

ESSENTIALS

In addition to satisfying the vegetarian's appetite, the popular *bhel poori* and Buddhist restaurants are also a boon to **kosher** travelers, since they offer religiously exacting standards and a complete absence of meat products. Jews with a taste for meat or who prefer to eat in rabbi-certified establishments can find a number of places in North London, particularly **Golders Green** (p. 134). For more information, check out the *Jewish Travel Guide*, edited by Michael Zaidner (Vallentine Mitchell; US$18). Travelers who eat **halal** will have little trouble eating well in London, as long as they have a good appetite for North Indian, Turkish, and Middle-Eastern food. Marylebone and Bayswater have the highest concentration of Lebanese restaurants and Islington the most Turkish. Indian restaurants are fairly ubiquitous (though not all are *halal*), and the **East End** is known for its large Bangladeshi community. Travelers looking for *halal* restaurants may find www.zabihah.com a useful resource.

OTHER RESOURCES

USEFUL PUBLICATIONS

Time Out (☎ 7813 3000; www.timeout.com). The absolute best weekly guide to what's going on in London. The magazine is sold at every newsstand in the city, and the website is a virtual hub for the latest on dining, entertainment, and discounts.

Atlas London A-Z, Hunter Publishing, 2004 (US$19). Comprehensive street atlas.

Brit-Think, Ameri-Think: A Transatlantic Survival Guide, Jane Walmsley and Gray Golliffe. Penguin Books, 2003 (US$14). Differences in attitudes and aspirations on pets, sports, humor, consumerism, sex, death, religion, and other topics.

Culture Shock! London at Your Door, Orin Hargraves. Graphic Arts Center Publishing, 2001 (US$14).

Living and Working in London, Dan Finlay. Survival Books, 2004 (US$22). Practical information on everyday life.

Secret London: Exploring the Hidden City, With Original Walks and Unusual Places to Visit, Andrew Duncan. Interlink Publishing Group, 2003 (US$18). Includes over 20 mi. of walking tours.

WORLD WIDE WEB

Almost every aspect of budget travel is accessible via the web. In 10min. at the keyboard, you can make a hostel reservation, get advice on travel hot spots from other travelers, or find out how much a Night Bus trip into the City costs. Listed here are some regional and travel-related sites to start off your surfing; other relevant websites are listed throughout the book. Because website turnover is high, use search engines (such as www.google.com) to strike out on your own.

 WWW.LETSGO.COM. Our website features extensive content from our guides; a community forum where travelers can connect with each other, ask questions or advice, and share stories and tips; and expanded resources to help you plan your trip. Visit us to browse by destination, find information about ordering our titles, and sign up for our e-newsletter!

THE ART OF TRAVEL

BootsnAll.com: www.bootsnall.com. Numerous resources for independent travelers, from planning your trip to reporting on it when you get back.

Travel Intelligence: www.travelintelligence.net. A large collection of travel writing by distinguished travel writers.

Travel Library: www.travel-library.com. A fantastic set of links for general information and personal travelogues.

World Hum: www.worldhum.com. An independently produced collection of "travel dispatches from a shrinking planet."

INFORMATION ON LONDON

Britannia: www.britannia.com. Information on UK travel, British history, and British life.

London Tourist Board: www.londontouristboard.com. Info for visitors, including addresses of London Visitors Centres.

LondonTown: www.londontown.com. Tourist info, special offers, and maps, specializing in entertainment and nightlife.

Transport For London: www.tfl.gov.uk. Comprehensive info on public transportation in London, including ticket prices, maps, and current service reports.

Visit London: www.visitlondon.com. The British Tourist Association website. Plenty of useful info about visiting Britain and London.

ESSENTIALS

LIFE AND TIMES

When a man is tired of London, he is tired of life; for there is in London all that life can afford.
    —Samuel Johnson, 1777

Though London has experienced a long and tumultuous history, it has always emerged from its struggles as a pioneering and vibrant city. Throughout the years, London has been at the forefront of the world's political, cultural, and literary movements, and each series of change leaves its mark on this continuously evolving city. Whether fighting off barbarian invaders, resisting the Great Plague (or Great Fire), or rebuilding after the Blitz of World War II, London has remained a strong, resilient part of the world. This fortitude manifests itself today in London's incredible ethnic and cultural diversity, its countless museums and theatres, and its exciting nightlife. It is hard to say what the London of tomorrow will be like, but, based on its past, one would expect a strong, diverse city with citizens who expect their voices to be heard.

HISTORY

ROMANS TO NORMANS (AD 43-1042)

LONDON BRIDGE, TAKE ONE

London was originally known as Londinium, with its **Roman foundations** in AD 43. Commercially minded **Aulus Plautius** converted an area of marsh and farmsteads into a focal point of trade, building a bridge across the Thames. Placed at the lowest navigable point on the river, the crossing became the center of an excellent network of Roman roads and a mercantile mecca.

AD 43
Romans bridge the Thames and create Londinium.

By the AD 2nd century, London boasted a forum four times the size of Trafalgar Square and a population of 45,000 drawn from all over the Roman Empire. However, the trip up and down the Thames was not completely smooth sailing for the Romans. In AD 60, **Queen Boudicca** from the nearby Iceni tribe made waves by marching on Londinium, massacring its inhabitants and razing the settlement. Boudicca didn't destroy London on a lark—she was retaliating against the Romans' brutal attack on her and her family. **Boudicca's Rebellion** marks the first in a line of great destructions and fires in London.

AD 60
Boudicca's Rebellion destroys much of the city.

In AD 200, the Romans built the London Wall around the city, one of the largest fortifications ever constructed by the Romans and part of a long list of defensive measures against centralized, tribal power. In an effort to enforce stability over a potentially warring Britannia, Rome divided the region into two districts, Inferior and Superior. Rome divided Britannia again in AD 288, this time into four provinces, London became the capital of Maxima Caesariensis, and a mint was founded in the city, solidifying its position as a commercial and financial center.

AD 200
London reigns superior as the capital of Britannia Superior.

AD 288
Mint established in London—inflation of the pound begins.

EXIT THE ROMANS, ENTER THE ANGLOS AND SAXONS

In decline due to barbarian invasions elsewhere in the Empire, the Romans withdrew from Britannia in AD 410, leaving London little more than a backwater settlement. By the mid-5th century, Anglos and Saxons had overrun southern Britain and begun ethnically cleansing their new home of its Celtic inhabitants. Although religious wars like this one tend to be bloody affairs, the arrival of Christianity did benefit London as a political institution. The consecration of its first bishop saw the rise of **St. Paul's Cathedral,** begun in AD 604, as well as financial prosperity; in the 640s, a trading settlement emerged west of the city in what is today the Strand and Charing Cross.

Unsurprisingly, London's prosperity brought unwelcome attention: 9th-century **Vikings** went from mere raiders (first invading London in AD 842, then burning it to the ground in AD 851) to conquerors, occupying the city in AD 871. It took **Alfred the Great** 15 years to retake the city. Even so, Danes still controlled half of England and intermittent war continued for over a century. Weakened Saxon leadership brought the Danes back for more in 1013—**King Æthelred the Unready** fled to Normandy.

AD 604
St. Paul's built (but will soon be destroyed).

AD 842
Viking raiders ransack the city.

AD 851
Vikings come back for more.

LONDON BRIDGE, TAKE II

An old Norse saga tells the tale of Æthelred's return at the Battle of London Bridge: reinforced by his ally, 19-year-old Norwegian Olaf, the king hitched ropes between his fleet and the bridge supports and rowed away. The supports gave way, the Danes fell into the Thames, and the ditty "London Bridge is Falling Down" was born. When Æthelred died in 1016, the kingdom passed (peacefully) back to a Dane, **Canute,** who made London the capital of an empire encompassing present-day England, Denmark, and Norway.

THE MIDDLE AGES (1042-1485)

STORMY WEATHER, AS LONDON WILL HAVE

Canute's successors held onto England until 1042, when Æthelred's son **St. Edward the Confessor** became king. London owes its status as capital to Edward, who restricted Royal Councils to meeting at only a few major centers (Gloucester and Winchester were the other two). After all, Edward wanted to live near his favorite new church, the West Minster. **Westminster** has been home to the English government ever since. Edward's death in 1066 set the scene for the most famous battle in English history. **William of Normandy** claimed that Edward—who grew up in Normandy and was half-Norman—had promised him the throne. **Harold,** Earl of Wessex, disagreed, as did the Royal Council, who appointed him king. The difference was resolved on October 14, 1066, at Hastings. By sunset Harold was dead, and William (now known as William the Conqueror) had a new kingdom.

1066
William I conquers Britain and is crowned king; London is granted charter.

LIFE AND TIMES

THE TOWER OF LONDON

A foreign invader, William lived up to his title of Conqueror. In 1067, construction began on the **Tower of London** (p. 148) as the center of intimidation—the sight of future beheadings and prison terms. At the same time, Norman kings, desperate to finance their wars abroad, made numerous concessions to London. The City of London was incorporated in 1191, granting the city a measure of self-governance and independence from the crown. The first mayor, **Henry FitzAilwyn,** was elected in 1193. The Lord Mayor still presides over the 680 acres of the City; even today, the Queen may not enter the City without the mayor's permission. Wide-ranging reactions to **King John's** abuse of power led to the signing of the **Magna Carta** in 1215. This famous document included many provisions distributing power to the people and is considered a fundamental predecessor to the US Constitution and Bill of Rights.

WAR, PLAGUE, DECEPTION, OH MY!

In the 14th century, London suffered one of the biggest disasters in human history. Rats carrying the plague scurried inland from ships overseas. The resulting **Black Death** claimed the lives of 30,000 Londoners—about half the city's total population. Thousands more died in the later outbreaks of 1361, 1369, and 1375. In 1381 came the **Peasants' Revolt.** Incensed by a new poll tax, 60,000 men marched on London, destroyed the Savoy Palace, and burned legal records in **The Temple** (p. 156). After the peasants occupied the Tower, the 14-year-old **Richard II** agreed to meet their leader **Wat Tyler** at Smithfield. During a heated discussion, the mayor of London killed Tyler with a dagger. Richard rode calmly forward and informed the peasants that he would grant all their demands if only they would return peacefully to their homes. Incredibly, the crowd believed him. As soon as he was safe, Richard had the ringleaders executed and withdrew his promises of better conditions.

After Richard II, a succession of Henrys (IV, V, and VI), saw the transition from foreign rulers to native speakers; **Henry V** was the first ruler since the Conquest to speak English as his first language. While Henry V proved to be one of England's most capable kings, his son,**Henry VI,** led England into the quagmire known as the **Wars of the Roses.** Tired of Henry's ambivalent leadership, London's merchants gave full backing to the financially astute **Edward IV,** whose shared interest in business led the merchants to overlook his equal interest in their wives. **Henry VII** finally put an end to the Wars of the Roses by defeating **Richard III** in 1487, initiating the Tudor dynasty.

TUDORS AND STUARTS (1485-1685)

LOVE, MARRIAGE, REFORMATION

The Tudor Age is probably best known for its drama—made into many a Hollywood movie—beginning with **Henry VIII** and his

1067
Tower of London is built.

1215
Magna Carta is signed.

1348
Rats conquer Britain. Black Death kills 30,000.

1381
14-year-old Richard II gets an early start as a ruthless ruler.

1455-1485
Henry VI wages the Wars of the Roses.

LIFE AND TIMES

1534
Henry VIII renounces the Catholic Church and names himself head of the Anglican Church.

1550s
Bloody Mary earns her name, burning 200 Protestant martyrs at Smithfield.

1558
Elizabeth I is crowned.

1599
James Burbage builds The Globe. Drama reigns supreme.

Late 16th century
Shakespeare rises to literary dominance.

1625
Charles I becomes king.

renouncement of the Catholic Church in 1534. The formation of the Anglican Church resulted in part from Henry's infidelities and the refusal of the Pope to grant him an annulment from **Catherine of Aragon**. This was the beginning of the Reformation that would continue for centuries, resulting in many Protestant denominations and a considerable weakening of the Catholic Church. However, the Tudor dynasty is also notable for its focus on London as a capital for the everyday citizen. During the 16th century London's population quadrupled to 200,000, mostly a result of emigration from rural areas and Henry's dissolution of the monasteries in 1536. Many of the new arrivals found employment with Henry's numerous building projects, including palaces at **Hampton Court, Whitehall** (p. 172), and **St. James's** (p. 174), all of which were financed by plunder from the Catholic Church. Other newcomers built the equally luxurious houses that line the Strand between the City and Westminster, including **Somerset House** (p. 196), built for the Duke of Somerset in 1547.

Henry's only son, **Edward VI**, reigned just six years before dying in 1553 at the age of 15. He was succeeded by his Catholic half-sister **Mary I**, who earned the nickname "Bloody Mary" for her campaign against the Anglican church. She burned over 200 people at the stake for heresy between 1553 and 1558.

When Mary died in 1558, **Elizabeth I**, daughter of Henry VIII and Anne Boleyn, inherited the throne—but she avoided her father's marital woes. Indeed, her refusal to marry earned her the title "The Virgin Queen." During Elizabeth's reign, explorers Sir Francis Drake and Sir Walter Raleigh expanded the English empire's geographic horizons, while dramatists **William Shakespeare, Christopher Marlowe,** and **Ben Jonson** stretched the seams of its literature. At first, plays were performed in the courtyards of London inns with audiences packed into the galleries. Eventually, the city authorities sent the actors packing over the river to Southwark, where **James Burbage** constructed London's first custom-built playhouse, first named The Theatre and later renamed **The Globe** (p. 158), in 1599.

CIVILITY AND CIVIL WAR

Elizabeth's refusal to take a husband led to the end of the Tudor dynasty. Her cousin, James VI of Scotland, a Stuart, inherited the throne in 1603, becoming **James I** of England. If London loved Elizabeth, it only tolerated James. Closing himself up in Whitehall, James replied to the people's desire to see his face with the retort, "Then I will pull down my breeches and they shall also see my arse." Nevertheless, James was not wholly uncaring of the fate of Londoners. He gave his backing to an ambitious project to supply London with fresh drinking water via hollowed-out wooden pipes from a new reservoir in Clerkenwell. Such improvements were all the more necessary as London continued its unchecked expansion. The city increasingly spilled beyond the walls and into the future **West End**—better west than east, as prevailing winds carried the stench and pollution of the growing metropolis eastward.

James's autocratic tendencies meant that his passing in 1625 was little mourned. Affairs did not improve under his son, **Charles I**. With the nation beset by military defeat abroad and religious dissent at home, tensions between Charles I and the House of Commons degenerated into the 1642 **English Civil War,** an armed conflict between the Royalists (supporters of the monarchy) and Parliamentarians (supporters of Parliament). London's support for Parliament sealed the King's fate: without the city's money and manpower, his chance of victory was slim. The king was tried for treason in Westminster Hall, spent his last night in **St. James's Palace** (p. 174), and was executed on the lawn of the Banqueting House on January 25, 1649. **Oliver Cromwell** was soon elected by the Parliament as the Lord Protector of the Commonwealth of England.

Though Cromwell's firm hand restored the health of the Puritan-dominated **Commonwealth,** Parliament proved to be as repressive and unpopular as the king it replaced. Not content with simply outlawing theatre and most other forms of entertainment, it went as far as banning music in churches and even, in 1652, abolishing Christmas—Cromwell claimed that the holiday was a Catholic superstition.

The Commonwealth didn't last long. In 1660, **Charles II** returned from exile in the Netherlands to a rapturous welcome. Among those accompanying him on his return was **Samuel Pepys,** whose diary of 1660s London provides an invaluable account of this tumultuous time. Even though his reign was eventually dubbed **The Restoration,** Charles II and the rest of the Stuart line (his brother, **James II**) would fare almost as poorly as his predecessors did, beginning with the **Great Plague** in 1665, in which more than 75,000 Londoners perished. Worse disaster followed: early in the morning of September 2, 1666, fire broke out in a bakery on Pudding Lane. When the **Great Fire** was finally extinguished, 80% of London lay in ruins, including 80 churches, 13,000 homes, St. Paul's, the Guildhall, and virtually every other building of note save the Tower.

The city now faced the huge task of rebuilding. Several visionary figures emerged in response to the fire and helped redesign the face of London. Christopher Wren submitted his magnificent plan for the **St. Paul's Cathedral** in 1673. It underwent many alterations at the hands of the clergy, and Wren eventually had to compromise and scale down his design to build the cathedral, now a tourist mainstay. The fire itself was commemorated by Wren's simple **Monument** (p. 150), a 202 ft. column situated 202 ft. from the spot where the fire broke out. Upon Charles II's death in 1685, **James II** came to the throne. During his short reign, the City gained its full autonomy. However, he was no more popular than his Stuart predecessors, entrenched in the political battle in the British Isles between his own Catholicism and England's Protestantism and between the divine right of the crown and the political rights of Parliament.

THE ENLIGHTENED CITY (1685-1783)

A GLORIOUS REVOLUTION

The Parliamentary overthrow of James II in 1688 was considered both a "bloodless" and "glorious" revolution. Under the new lead-

LIFE AND TIMES

1649
Charles I is beheaded and Commonwealth is declared; Cromwell reigns.

1660
The Restoration begins with the return of Charles II.

1666
The Great Fire destroys the city.

1675-1710
Wren rebuilds St. Paul's Cathedral.

1688
The Glorious Revolution—William and Mary bloodlessly replace James II.

ership of the Dutch **William and Mary,** London gradually supplanted Amsterdam as the linchpin of international trade, an achievement greatly aided by the 1694 founding of the **Bank of England** (p. 193) on the model of the Bank of Amsterdam. Other future financial behemoths had less obvious beginnings: **Lloyd's of London** (p. 149), the world's oldest insurance company, started out in Edward Lloyd's coffee shop, a popular resting spot for sea captains.

On the accession of William, Parliament fixed the line of succession to ensure that no Catholic would ever sit on the throne again. Because of this, in 1714 the crown passed to a German prince who spoke no English: **George I,** the first of the House of Hanover. By this time, however, most of the business of government was handled by the man who invented the role of prime minister, **Robert Walpole.**

ANARCHY IN THE UK

When **George III** came to the throne in 1760, Britain gained its first English-speaking king in 70 years. The **British Museum** opened its doors in 1759 and the city eagerly followed the well-publicized doings of **Samuel Johnson,** famed wit and author of the charmingly idiosyncratic *Dictionary* (1755). Together with his good friend and painter **Sir Joshua Reynolds,** Johnson founded **The Club** in 1764, an exclusive institution whose members included historian **Edward Gibbon,** economist **Adam Smith,** and writer **James Boswell.** Later Boswell wrote *Life of Johnson,* providing a vivid portrait of the great man and his era. Reynolds was also the prime mover behind the 1768 foundation of the **Royal Academy of Arts** (p. 205), whose early members included favorite royal painters like **Thomas Gainsborough.**

In the latter part of the 18th century, London began to take on many of the characteristics of the present-day city. As the focus of life shifted westward, **Oxford Street** became the capital's main shopping artery, tempting customers with new-fangled ideas like window displays and fixed prices. In 1750, London Bridge—until then the sole crossing over the Thames—acquired a neighbor, **Westminster Bridge,** which in 1802 inspired poet **William Wordsworth's** tribute to the beauty of the sleeping city, "Composed upon Westminster Bridge."

With the trappings of a modern city, London also acquired modern problems, not least among them a massive increase in crime. Much of this has been attributed to the widening gulf between rich and poor, but there was another cause: cheap liquor. **Gin,** invented in the Netherlands in the 17th century, was so cheap and plentiful that by the 1730s consumption had risen to an average of two pints per week for every man, woman, and child in the city—memorably illustrated in **William Hogarth's** allegorical prints, *Gin Lane* and *Beer Street.* In 1751, Parliament passed the **Gin Act,** imposing government regulation of the sale of alcohol; as a result, mortality rates dropped dramatically. In the same year, magistrate and novelist **Henry Fielding,** together with his brother John, established the **Bow Street Runners,** a band of volunteer "thief-takers" which evolved into the Metropolitan Police. Even so, crime was still prevalent enough that in the 1770s the prime minister, the Lord Mayor, and even the Prince of Wales were all robbed in broad daylight.

LIFE AND TIMES

1760
George III gains the throne.

1764
Samuel Johnson founds a secret club, inspiring countless children to do the same.

1751
Parliament passes Gin Act; tonic sales plummet.

Chaos broke out in 1780, when Parliament proposed lifting the law prohibiting Catholics from buying and inheriting property. Following Member of Parliament (MP) Lord George Gordon's "No Popery" demonstration were the **Gordon Riots,** during which a mob of 30,000 attacked Irish workers and achieved general anarchy before being quelled by the army.

1780
The Gordon Riots result in almost 300 deaths.

FROM REGENCY TO EMPIRE (1783-1901)

BREAKING DOWN, BUILDING UP

There could be no mistaking the Prince of Wales (the future **George IV**) for his staid father. From the moment he turned 21 in 1783, the prince was known for his flamboyant opposition of his father's ministers and an utter disregard for convention. Although **George III** had overcome an earlier bout of madness in 1788 (subject of the play and film, *The Madness of King George III*), he descended into permanent insanity in 1811, and his son assumed power as the **Prince Regent.**

1811
George III goes nuts; his son steps up.

Unpopular as a wastrel concerned more with his appearance than the state of the country, George IV's obsession with self-aggrandizement nevertheless brought important benefits to London. Inspired by the changes wrought by Napoleon in Paris, he dreamt of creating a processional way leading from Marylebone Park to his residence at Carlton House. **John Nash** was chosen to transform this vision into reality. Nash's work covered the city, including the grand **Nash Terraces**, the great sweep of **Regent's Street** leading up to **Piccadilly Circus** (p. 176), and the Carlton House. Alas, this work was in vain: when the Prince Regent finally became king in 1820 he abruptly ordered Carlton House demolished and commissioned Nash to remodel **Buckingham Palace** (p. 166) for his future residence.

1820
Carlton House is built—then demolished.

THE VICTORIAN ERA

By the time the 18-year-old **Queen Victoria** ascended the throne in 1837, London was already at the heart of the largest empire the world had ever seen. Inspired by Admiral Nelson's 1805 victory over the French at the Battle of Trafalgar, work on **Trafalgar Square** began in 1839 with Nelson's Column. On top of global expansion, the city's population increased by almost a million during every decade of Victoria's 64-year reign. The Industrial Revolution drove both the population and the size of the city into rapid growth. London's first **railway** opened in 1836, connecting London Bridge to the then-distant suburb of Greenwich. Pressure on the capital's roads was relieved in 1863 with the inauguration of the **Metropolitan Line,** the world's first underground railway. Together with horse-drawn trams, the railways made commuting possible for the first time: once-rural villages like Islington and Hampstead were rapidly engulfed by the voracious city.

1839
Trafalgar Square is built.

Victorian architects reacted to the rush of modernization with a return to the past. **Charles Barry's** enormous and ornate **Houses of Parliament** (p. 168) characterizes the retrospective

LIFE AND TIMES

1856
Big Ben is put up; Londoners no longer have an excuse to be late for work.

neo-Gothic architecture popular at the time. This period also signified a reversion to Puritan sexual repression and a sense of public morality. Victorian influences still pervade literature, architecture, and fine art today.

FROM LABOR TO LABOUR

Many Victorian artistic movements were deeply influenced by the work of visionary poet and artist **William Blake,** who as early as 1804 had written about the "dark satanic mills" spawned by the Industrial Revolution. Working and living conditions for the majority of the capital's inhabitants were appalling, with health care and sanitation almost non-existent. **Child labor** was unregu-

1858
London stinks.

lated until 1886, **cholera** raged until the **Great Stink** of 1858 forced Parliament to reform the city's sewers, and air pollution was such that in 1879 the capital was shrouded in smog for the entire winter. **Jack the Ripper** stalked the city in 1888, preying on women of the night and evading identification to this day.

This was the London that inspired **Charles Dickens** to write such urban reformist literature as *Oliver Twist,* and saw **Karl**

1864
Karl Marx leads the proletariat, eventually fathering the Independent Labour Party.

Marx lead the proto-communist First International, founded in London in 1864. Even so, it was not until the last third of the century that significant progress was made: the three **Reform Acts,** in 1832, 1867, and 1884, extended the vote to most of London's working men—although even after each, much of London remained disenfranchised due to property qualifications. In 1870, the **Education Act** provided schooling for all children, rich and poor. In 1878, the **University College London** became the first British educational establishment to admit women. Organized labor also made headway. In 1889, Marx's daughter Eleanor led gas workers in a strike which won recognition for the eight-hour day, while in 1893 the working classes found a political voice with the establishment of the **Independent Labour Party.**

THE 20TH CENTURY

FROM WEALTH TO HEALTH

1895
Oscar Wilde stands trial and receives conviction of "gross indecency."

Although **Edward VII** did not succeed his mother until 1901, Victorian morality had already begun to crumble during the "naughty nineties," when two Irish-born Londoners, taboo-breaking **George Bernard Shaw** and flamboyant **Oscar Wilde,** thrilled theatre goers and shocked the authorities. Female voices also increasingly emerged on the scene. **Emmeline Pankhurst** started the Woman's Social and Political Union to win the vote for women, a struggle that lasted until 1928. The stunts that she and her suffragettes pulled were meat and drink to the tabloid press, a

1896
Daily Mail launches.

medium born with the launching of the **Daily Mail** in 1896 which rapidly became London's main source of news.

The changes wrought on London by steam power in the previous century were furthered by the advent of electricity and petroleum power. By the outbreak of **World War I** in 1914, London was one of the most modern, urban cities in the world. Clean, electrically powered underground trains took Londoners to new department stores like **Selfridges** (opened 1909) and **Harrods,** which moved to its present site in 1905 (opened 1853). Numerous **West End** theatres and cinemas became the center of the London entertainment scene and new telephone booths all over town set a distinct tableau of a picturesque London.

LONDON GOES TO WAR

Londoners greeted WWI with jubilant confidence, and recruiting stations were besieged by eager young men. The horror of modern warfare was soon brought home, though, when in 1915 the first German air raid on London occurred. When the war ended in 1918, almost one million British soldiers were dead. As the boom brought on by the wartime economy came to an end, unemployment rose, and in 1926 the 10-day **General Strike** brought the nation to a standstill amid fears of revolution. In the end, however, the main beneficiary of the strike was the radio. The paralysis of Fleet St. made the nation dependent on the new **BBC** for news.

WWI's end assured many years of calm. Pacifism soon turned into fascism, both in London and around the world. Oswald Mosley, who had served in the House of Commons successively as a Conservative, an Independent, and a Labourite, founded the British Union of Fascists in 1932. Hostile demonstrations by Mosley and his followers in the Jewish part of East London were not taken lightly by the rest of London.

London suffered from the **Great Depression** almost as much as the United States did. As the population peaked (8.6 million in 1939), employment plummeted and production waned. When **World War II** broke out in 1939, London was ill-prepared: the thousands of gas masks issued in expectation of German chemical attacks were useless against the incendiary devices of **The Blitz.** Starting September 7th, 1940, London suffered 57 consecutive days of bombing; regular raids continued until 1941. The bombing resumed toward the end of the war with rockets fired from Nazi-occupied Europe. **Winston Churchill** spent much of his war time in London, where he would later spend his final days after retiring from the prime ministry. By the end of the war, London had suffered destruction on a scale unseen since the Great Fire of 1666. Over 30,000 Londoners lost their lives, with over 50,000 more injured. While the all-night vigils of volunteer firefighters saved St. Paul's, the same could not be said for the House of Commons, Buckingham Palace, or most of the East End. Over 130,000 houses were damaged beyond repair, and a third of the City of London was flattened.

PATCHING AND THATCHERING

With the rebuilding of the city came a general feeling of renewal and optimism. The **National Health Service** was born in 1946. London hosted the 1948 **Olympics,** showcasing a regenerated city, and the **Festival of Britain** in 1951 helped drive confidence upward. Britain crowned **Queen Elizabeth II** in 1953, ushering in a new age of leadership. Home to thousands of European exiles and American troops during the war, postwar London transformed itself from hide-bound capital of

1915
Zeppelins begin bombing London. (The band came later.)

1930s-1940s
The Great Depression hits London. Most people aren't happy about it.

1940-1941
London gets Blitzed.

1948
The Olympics come to London.

LIFE AND TIMES

empire to cosmopolitan city of the world. **Carnaby Street** and the **King's Road** became the twin foci of a London peopled by progressives, hipsters, and bohemians. The **Rolling Stones** battled for supremacy with the **Beatles,** and **The Who** chronicled the fights between scooter-riding "mods" and quiff-toting "rockers." Somewhat belatedly, in 1966 *Time* magazine announced that London "swings, it is the scene."

Swinging London died with the oil shocks of the 1970s. Unemployment rose as conflict between unions and the government escalated. In 1979, Britons elected their first female Prime Minister, **Margaret Thatcher,** commonly (and unaffectionately) nicknamed the "Iron Lady." A polarizing figure in British politics even today, Thatcher's program of economic liberalization, combined with a return to "Victorian values" in everyday life, brought her into direct conflict with the overwhelmingly Labour-dominated **Greater London Council** (GLC) and its charismatic leader **Ken Livingstone.** Thatcher's solution was to abolish the GLC, depriving London of its sole unified administrative structure and devolving power to the 32 boroughs. Thatcher's monetarist program called for deregulation, tax cuts, greater use of supply-side policies, and a rigorous control of the money supply in order to keep inflation low. Upon her entering office, income taxes were cut immediately and offset by an increase in the value added tax (VAT), representing an important shift from direct to indirect taxation. However, the tax rate in the top-earning bracket was cut significantly more than in the medium-earning bracket, leading critics to highlight a preference for the rich. On the streets, Thatcher's government was marked by the **Brixton and Toxteth Riots** of 1981. These were largely brought on by reactions to the "sus" law, which allowed British police to stop and search anyone on suspicion alone. The riots resulted in dozens of injuries and much property damage, but few deaths.

Divisions among Conservative MPs were highlighted toward the end of the 1980s when the question of Britain's economic and political relationship with Europe arose. Thatcher rejected any form of political and economic integration with Europe, striking the wrong note with many of her colleagues. In November 1990, following a high-profile resignation from the House of Commons leader Geoffrey House, former cabinet member Michael Heseltine stood against the prime minister in the Conservative Party leadership ballot. Barely surviving the first round and persuaded that a 2nd attempt would result in a humiliating defeat, Margaret Thatcher "retired" on November 22, 1990. Nevertheless, the Conservatives were elected to another term in 1992. But following a deeper recession, an increased rate of homelessness, and bombings, the city was ready for a change.

INTO THE FUTURE

Tony Blair was elected Prime Minister in 1997, bringing Labour into power after 18 consecutive years of Conservative rule. Blair's stated priorities on coming into office were "education, education, education." Elected to a 2nd term in 2001, the new govern-

1979
Margaret Thatcher comes to power.

1981
Brixton riots rage, later inspiring The Clash.

1990
Thatcher retires.

1997
Tony Blair elected Prime Minister.

ment poured millions into a plan to make London the "Capital of the Millennium." Gilbert Scott's 1930s Bankside power station reopened in 2000 as the **Tate Modern** (p. 198). If Norman Foster's reputation suffered when his **Millennium Bridge** was closed for safety reasons after three days, it recovered with his ambitious reworking of the Great Court at the British Museum.

2000
Tate Modern opens.

London regained a unified voice with the election of maverick Ken Livingstone as its first-ever directly elected mayor in 2000. Relationships with Westminster soured even before Livingstone took office when Blair tried to prevent Livingstone from winning the Labour nomination. Undaunted, Livingstone stood as an independent and won by a landslide. He was re-elected for his 2nd term on June 10, 2004.

Blair maintained a controversial position on the war in Iraq until his resignation on June 27, 2007. He joined US President George W. Bush in calling for the overthrow of Saddam Hussein's regime before the invasion of Iraq began. Political analysts remarked that any positive aspects of Blair's legacy as Prime Minister would be overshadowed by his actions regarding Iraq, though only time will tell.

2002
Blair supports allied invasion of Iraq; controversy ensues.

Blair's detractors also pointed to the Prime Minister's stance on the **euro.** Blair's long-time position on the euro—that Britain will convert to the currency when the economy is ready—was seen as an equivocation and a political tool. In June 2005, Blair declined to hold a referendum on the ratification of the European Union (EU) constitution, again isolating Britain from the continent. Britain's participation in the EU continues to be a heated issue, and the British people remain, as ever, distrustful of integration with the rest of Europe. In June 2007 Blair stepped down and was succeeded by **Gordon Brown,** who continues to lead Britain under the blessing of the Labour Party.

2007
Blair steps down; Gordon Brown becomes Prime Minister.

LIFE AND TIMES

LONDON TODAY

PEOPLE

SIZE

London is a city of 7.5 million people—13 million including those who live just outside the boundaries of **Greater London**—making it the most populous city in Europe. Even so, London's enormous size—over 30 mi. from east to west, covering some 650 sq. mi. (1584 sq. km)—has less to do with its population than with the English aversion to apartments: the majority of homes are single-family houses, each with its own patch of garden. The apartments that do exist in central London are hardly affordable anyway. Kensington and Chelsea are the most densely populated neighborhoods, followed shortly by Islington, in North London. Add to this a dislike of city-wide planning and a strong sense of community, and you're left with a sprawling metropolis composed of proudly distinct neighborhoods.

ETHNIC COMPOSITION

Londoners defy typification. Although London's roots are mainly white Anglo-Saxon, today one in three Londoners belongs to an ethnic minority, comprising the largest non-white population of any European city. Approximately 300 languages are spoken within the city; English is a secondary language to over 33% of primary school children. The majority of Londoners identify themselves as Christian, although the remaining three million residents include Muslims, Hindus, Buddhists, Jews, and Sikhs.

RELIGIOUS REFUGEES

London's origins as a port and center of trade mean that it has always been home to a number of small foreign communities. The first large-scale immigration to London occurred in the 17th century, as religious wars sent Protestants from all over Europe seeking refuge in England: 1685 saw the arrival of 30,000 French **Huguenots.** Although Edward I expelled **Jews** from London and Britain in 1292, a number of Spanish and Portuguese Jews fleeing the Inquisition arrived in London via Amsterdam during Charles I's reign in the mid-17th century. A new wave of persecution in the 19th century brought 20,000 Russian and Polish Jews, many of whom believed they had arrived in America. Overall, Jews were not treated as well as the Huguenots. The sheer number of immigrants (Jewish and otherwise) at the turn of the 20th century prompted the first **Alien Act** (1905), which restricted immigration. With the rise of fascism in the 1930s, the Jewish population swelled with fleeing Germans and Austrians. Meanwhile, Oswald Mosley's British Union of Fascists instilled fear in London Jews. After WWII, communist rule sent hundreds of thousands of Central and Eastern Europeans spilling into England, including 250,000 Polish refugees.

COLLAPSE OF THE EMPIRE

Nineteenth-century British imperialism and the eventual post-war collapse of the British Empire brought a new type of immigrant: the imperial subject. These immigrants were taught to think of Britain as the "mother country"—or at least as a source of economic opportunity unheard of at home. Those who immigrated to London imagined that they were simply shifting locales, rather than supplanting the old for the new. A trip to the British Museum underscores the mind-set that London and Britain do not have finite borders—the history of London would be incomplete without a global history. London's inhabitants now include 250,000 **Irish** and 60,000 **Chinese**, along with 300,000 **West Indians** and 500,000 **Asians.** More recently, political upheaval in Britain's former colonies has sent a new wave of refugees to London, including some 160,000 **West Africans.**

While ethnic ghettos are rare in London, many neighborhoods are grouped by nationality and provide residents with the sights, smells, and sounds (if not the sunshine) of their former homeland. **South Asians,** London's largest ethnic group, are also the most fragmented. Sikhs from **Punjab** congregate in **Ealing**. The **East End** is the center of the **Bengali** community. **Pakistanis** prefer **Walthamstow.** London's black population is divided into two main groups: those of **Caribbean** origin, whose cultural focus is in **Brixton,** and 160,000 **Africans,** mostly West African in origin, who tend to settle in **West London.** Though few of London's ethnic Chinese actually live there, they still pack **Soho's** Chinatown on weekends to shop and eat—though today, they are often outnumbered by tourists. From the Saudis to Lebanese refugees, **Arabs** congregate on **Edgware Road.** Many other ethnic groups are harder to spot. The majority of the strong **Jewish** community leads secular lives in **Golders Green.** A large number of **Cypriot Greeks** gather around **Camden Town.**

GLBT LIFE

From the **Pride Parade** to the **Gay and Lesbian Film Festival** to the city's myriad GLBT clubs, London has come a long way from deeming homosexuality a "gross indecency," as it did at Oscar Wilde's trial at the end of the 19th century. Now London is one of the gay capitals of the world with a vibrant and active GLBT community.

Despite its growing progressivism and artistic intellectualism—assemblies like the Bloomsbury Group encouraged sexual liberation—London has also seen its fair share of backlash. In the conservative era following WWII, social reformers like Sir Bernard Law Montgomery were less keen on free-flowing sexuality and sought to rid London of homosexuality. Prosecution of homosexual acts increased in the 1940s and 50s. Police raids and arrests, though, only spurred streamlined activism in the 1960s and 70s; the 1967 **Sexual Offences Act** decriminalized homosexual acts for people over age 18. In 1979, the nightclub **Heaven** opened in Charing Cross and soon became the largest gay disco in Europe (it still runs today, although it no longer holds the same hype as decades ago). While the election of Margaret Thatcher in 1979 hindered gay and lesbian activism in the city, activists continue to be inspired. The infamous **Clause 28,** passed in 1988, prohibited the promotion or teaching of homosexuality in state schools; it led to **Sir Ian McKellen** coming out in a BBC radio interview and the formation of the **Stonewall Group,** Britain's first gay and lesbian rights organization. Clause 28 was repealed in 2003. Ironically, Thatcher's radical free-market and individualist politics contributed to the rise of **Soho** as London's largest gay area, with vociferous commercial consumerism and reactionary politics in the face of the growing global AIDS crisis.

Increased attention to GLBT matters has made homosexuals targets of violence. In 1999, a bomb exploded in the Admiral Duncan bar on **Old Compton Street,** killing two and injuring 80. Responses to the bombing included huge investment in Soho to build a definable area for London's GLBT community—Soho is currently considered the home of GLBT life. Sitting only blocks from Covent Garden, Piccadilly Circus, and Trafalgar Square, Old Compton St. and Soho figure prominently in the public eye and in London culture. But GLBT life is not restricted by borders— GLBT people, nightlife, culture, and activism infuse the entire city.

GOVERNMENT AND POLITICS

NATIONAL GOVERNMENT

Britain has become one of the world's most stable constitutional monarchies without the aid of a single constitution. A combination of parliamentary legislation, common law, and convention composes the flexible system of British government. Since the 1700s, the monarch has had a purely symbolic role. Real political power resides with **Parliament,** consisting of the **House of Commons,** with its elected Members of Parliament (MPs), and the **House of Lords.** Power has shifted from the Lords to the Commons over time. Reforms in 1999 removed the majority of hereditary peers from the House of Lords, replacing them with Life Peers, appointed by the **prime minister** to serve for life. Parliament holds supreme legislative power and may change or even directly contradict its previous laws. All members of the executive branch, which includes the prime minister and the **Cabinet,** are also MPs. This fusing of legislative and executive functions, called the "efficient secret" of the British government, ensures the quick passage of the majority party's programs into bills. The prime minister is never elected to the post directly; rather, he or she wins a local constituency. The head of the ruling party is the prime minister. From an elegant roost on **10 Downing Street,** the prime minister chooses a Cabinet, whose members head the government's departments and present a cohesive platform to the public. Political parties keep their MPs in line on most votes in Parliament and provide a pool of talent and support for the smooth functioning of the executive. Roughly, the **Labour** party, currently in power, is center-left; the **Conservatives,** or Tories, are center-right; and the smaller, feisty **Liberal Democrat** party is left. The parties, though, do not translate directly

LIFE AND TIMES

into American politics. Labour supported the war in Iraq, which the Conservatives opposed, and support of gay marriage and abortion rights are widespread.

LOCAL GOVERNMENT

Local government may be even trickier than the national government, if that is possible. London gained the right to self-government in 1193, when Henry FitzAilwyn became the first mayor. But as London has grown beyond its original boundaries of the City of London, creating government that is both localized and solidified has been quite the task; nothing has been permanent.

Since London's 32 boroughs were created in 1965, power has constantly shifted between the boroughs themselves and the GLC, which was created in the same year to look after local interests. When Ken Livingstone took over the GLC in the early 1980s in his pursuit of a Labour-focused government, it was easy to predict a rift between local authority and national government—a Labour versus Conservative battle at its finest. Margaret Thatcher promptly abolished the GLC in 1986, leaving London the only major capital in the world without a self-governing body. Although the boroughs did their best to proceed without falling into anarchy—they appointed a transport minister and a Cabinet sub-committee and created **London First,** a business-led organization focused on maintaining London as a world city—nobody was altogether happy without Livingstone leading the way. The Labour victory in 1997 represented a shift from right to left and brought not only Tony Blair to the scene, but also a new version of London city authority in the **Greater London Authority (GLA).** Livingstone became the first-ever popularly elected mayor in 2000, alongside his 25-member GLA.

The City of London is a completely separate institution, run not by conventional local authority but by the **Corporation of London.** The Corporation is headed by the **Lord Mayor**, currently John Stuttard.

CULTURE

FOOD

PUB GRUB

It's impossible to visit London and not go to a pub—almost anywhere you go, you'll be within a few blocks of one. And, for a proper sit-down meal without a high bill, pubs offer a glimmer of hope. Far more than mere drinking establishments, most pubs offer a range of hot and cold fare during the day and also often in the evening. For around £6 you can lunch on traditional English fare like bangers and mash or steak and kidney pie. Of course, no trip to London is complete without the traditional **fish 'n' chips.** "Pub grub" may be cheap, but be warned that it isn't always fresh. Meals may be left under hot lamps for hours or microwaved from frozen. Find a pub where locals eat, and keep away from the tourist trail. More yuppified gastropubs place a higher priority on fresh, original dishes—although higher prices often reflect the change.

ETHNIC TASTES

Many of the best budget meals can be found in the variety of ethnic restaurants the city has to offer. **Indian** food, at the top of the list, is recognized as Britain's unofficial national cuisine. When Prince Charles was asked to describe the archetypal British meal, he chose the classic Anglo-Indian hybrid chicken tikka masala. **Turkish** cooks are also experts at cooking up low-budget feasts, while some of the cheapest and tastiest sit-down dinners in town are **Chinese.** Recently, **Japanese** cuisine has shed its upmarket image with a proliferation of noodle bars—**Wagamama** most notable among them.

DRINKING AND DANCING

PUBS

Sir William Harcourt, a 19th-century MP, believed that English history was made in the pubs as much as in the Houses of Parliament. The routine inspired by the pub is considerable; to stop in at lunchtime and after work is not uncommon. Brits rapidly develop affinities for neighborhood establishments, becoming loyal to their locals, and pubs tend to cater to their regulars and develop a particular character. Local dens are almost invariably your best bet over bigger or more touristy locales. The drinking age is a weakly enforced 18, but you need be only 14 to enter a pub.

Every pub keeps a range of different beers on tap and has dozens more in bottles. There are four basic types of beer: lagers, stouts, bitters, and cask ales. **Lagers** are light, gassy beers with little substance (by UK standards)—most American beers are lagers. **Stouts** are dark and heavy; Guinness is the best-known stout, and one of the darkest. **Bitters** lie in the middle—they are rich and full-bodied with very little gas. Bitters are served at slightly below room temperature, and are normally hand-pulled from casks in the cellar. **Cask ales,** a particular type of bitter, are pulled from large hand pumps and have no gas. Two good ones are from ■**Fuller's Brewery** and ■**Young's Brewery.** A pint is always less expensive than mixed drinks.

All pubs have a fully stocked bar in addition to their beer taps. **Cider** is an alcoholic drink, about as strong as beer. A **martini** in Britain is not a cocktail—it's just a glass of vermouth. **Lemonade** in Britain is a carbonated drink similar to ginger ale. Lemonade and beer can be mixed to form a **shandy**. Whatever your favorite drink, be sure to give something different a try in London—you just might like it.

BARS AND CLUBS

A night of clubbing will usually start at one of London's countless bars, which can be packed well before Happy hour. Londoners have been known to find a table and stick there all night. At the same time, London's bars offer a huge range of styles and ambiences. An explosion of **DJ bars** has invaded the previously forgotten zone between pubs and clubs, offering stylish surroundings and top-flight DJs, with plentiful lounging space and a wide selection of bottled lagers. Often incorporating both restaurants and dance floors, they are designed as one-stop night spots. They tend to close earlier than clubs, usually between midnight and 2am, so you'll need to move on to a "real" nightclub for late-night or early-morning action.

London clubs often fall into one of two categories: those for **dancing** and those for **lounging.** In the former, **dress codes** are generally relaxed; it's not uncommon to find clubbers dressed in nothing fancier than jeans, a stylish T-shirt, and trainers (sneakers), although pulling on a pair of "proper" shoes is a good idea (many clubs allow jeans but not sneakers). As the night goes on, clubbers end up wearing less and less. At lounging clubs, however, dress is crucial, and what's expected depends very much on the scene. Black and slinky is a generally good bet. Clubs often enforce stricter dress codes on weekends, when bouncers can be choosier. The exception to dress code rules are theme nights, especially at retro clubs—you're unlikely to get in unless you look like an extra from *Saturday Night Fever*. If a bouncer says it's "members and regulars only," he thinks you're not up to scratch.

Planning is important for the discriminating clubber. Look before you leap, and especially before you drink. Locals frequent the clubs of **South London** and **Brixton,** where you can dance the night away or chill with your pint in comfort. For popular clubs, it's worth learning the names of the DJs (not to mention the type of music) just to prove to the bouncer that you're part of the scene. Look in local papers (*Time Out* is a particularly good resource) or ask around at your hostel for specific events and DJs. Also, go a little early to the popular night spots. Just because there's no queue outside doesn't mean there won't be one later. Working out how to

The Chronicle

IN RECENT NEWS

COUNTDOWN TO 2012

While Britain's armchair athletes are second-to-none, the country has never been known for its high concentration of world-champion sports stars—David Beckham aside. Football fans may argue to the contrary, and they have a right to do so given the large niche the British-born sport has carved in London culture, but lest they forget, it's been over 60 years since a local won Wimbledon (tennis) and 40 since they last won the World Cup (football) in 1966. The return of the Ashes trophy in the Cricket World Championships in 2005 was a welcome boost to Britain's loyal sports fans.

Come 2012, though, London will be the only city to have hosted the summer Olympics three times (previously in 1908 and 1948). It was difficult to ignore their highly publicized and glamorous Olympic bid, complete with personal pleas from Nelson Mandela and "Back the Bid" subway upholstery. With only four years to go, London is gearing up for the games, which are to be held July 27 to August 12, 2012.

While some residents are concerned over the possibility of gentrification in Stratford (a historically distressed segment of East London where the Olympic Village and the center of athletic events will take place) others look forward to the transformation the city will see over the years leading up to the games. Plans include:

get home afterward is also crucial; remember that the **Tube and regular buses stop shortly after midnight,** and after 1am black cabs are like gold dust. In the unlikely event that there is no convenient Night Bus home, some clubbers order minicabs (unlicensed taxicabs). Although it's technically illegal for minicabs to ply for hire, whispered calls of "taxi, taxi" or honking horns signal their presence outside clubs and in nightlife-heavy neighborhoods. However, there is no guarantee that the driver is reputable or even insured. Be careful with these cabs and only use them if you have no other option. Agree on a price before you get in, and **never ride alone.** The best option is to take a minute or two to **look at the Night Bus map before you leave home** so you know how to get back.

MEDIA

NEWSPAPERS
Although newspaper circulation has been dropping in the UK for the last 40 years, print media is still a major source of news for Londoners. *The Times* is London's leading periodical, distributed to a readership throughout the UK. *The Guardian*, formerly *The Manchester Guardian*, is a popular alternative. *The Standard* was joined in 1999 by the daily *Metro*, free in Tube stations Monday to Friday (though they're usually all gone by 9am).

MAGAZINES
News magazines are generally published weekly and provide a more in-depth examination of issues than the papers, often with a strong political slant. *The Economist* is the most respected and apolitical of the bunch. Political hacks get their kicks from the New Labour *New Statesman* and the Tory *Spectator*. For a less reverent approach, *Private Eye* walks a fine line between hilarity and libel.

BROADCAST MEDIA
The **BBC** was at the helm during the radio boom, delivering the breaking news from the WWI front. It continues to be a radio mainstay for news and now commands the lion's share of Britain's television audience as well. Its two main television channels, BBC1 and BBC2, are publicly funded and offer a steady dose of news along with Britain's unique comedies and other programs. Classics like *Monty Python's Flying Circus* and *Mr. Bean* made BBC television the must-see network it is today. The BBC Studios (p. 190) was the first building designed specifically for television broadcasting. Its commercial competitor, **ITV**, carries British programs and American imports alike.

SPORTS

Londoners have always been mad about sports. They hosted the 1908 and 1948 **Olympics** and will host again in 2012—a deserving win, as during the bid process, the city was loaded with Olympic-themed memorabilia, a huge video screen in Trafalgar Square, and reupholstered Tube cars. London also boasts a number of **crew** races and hosts one of the world's most participated-in marathons, the **London Marathon.** Held every April, the London Marathon sees over 30,000 runners complete the grueling 26.2 mi. course from Greenwich, in southeast London, to the final stretch just outside Buckingham Palace.

All sports pale in comparison to **football**—don't call it soccer unless you're looking for trouble. London's fans, endearingly referred to as hooligans, are notoriously loud, belligerent, and otherwise fanatical about their teams. From August to May, thousands turn out every weekend to see the top London clubs: **Arsenal, Chelsea, West Ham,** and **Tottenham Hotspur, or** "Spurs" for short (p. 226). Historically, London clubs have not performed as fiercely as those from the Northwest—Liverpool and Manchester United. Recently, both Arsenal (in Highbury) and Chelsea (in Fulham) have been considered two of the **Premier League's** "Big Three." Chelsea won the League twice between 2004 and 2006, while Manchester United reclaimed the title in the 2006-2007 season. London's clubs have also made strong showings in the **UEFA Champions League,** a tournament that includes the best club teams throughout Europe.

Rugby is London's other main winter sport, allegedly created when an inspired (or confused) Rugby School—one of England's oldest and most prestigious public schools—student picked up a regular football and ran it into the goal. Rugby is far more popular in the north than it is in the city. Rugby is divided into two slightly-differing species, Rugby League and Rugby Union. Union rules the roost in London: **Wasps, Harlequins,** and **Saracens** are the top London teams (p. 227). More than football, rugby is a game of international rivalries: even those with no team affiliation follow the ups and downs of England at the international matches at Twickenham.

In the spring, when the rugby fields are little more than expanses of mud, national attention turns to **cricket.** A game, according to Lord Mancroft, a 20th century British political figure, "which the English have invented in order to give themselves some conception of eternity," cricket is the ideal way to spend long summer days. For non-Commonwealth visitors who have no understanding of the game, cricket can seem baffling. Either find someone with a lot of time

Building a 500-acre site (including the Olympic Village) in Stratford, 7min. from central London.

Revitalizing already existing facilities in locations where events will take place: triathlon in Hyde Park, equestrian in Greenwich Park, gymnastics at the Millennium Dome, football at Wembley, and tennis at Wimbledon.

Improving city transportation, enough to shuttle 240,000 people to the Village each hour via Tube, train, and bus; the new Olympic Javelin line will run from King's Cross St. Pancras.

Producing a low-carbon and zero-waste Games.

Transforming the Lea Valley into one of the largest urban parks created in Europe in the past 150 years, stretching 20 mi. from the Hertfordshire countryside to the tidal estuary of the Thames; post-Games, it will provide facilities for community use, as well as being a wildlife preserve.

Creating 12,000 new jobs and 9000 new homes (half to be designated as affordable housing) in East London.

70,000 volunteers will be needed to put these plans into effect and to work during the Games. For information on how you can volunteer, see www.volunteer2012.com.

to explain it to you or just give up and play along. In a bid to attract younger viewers, one-day matches have been introduced, with risk-taking players dressed in gaudy colors, but purists denounce the new version. Cricket does, however, get a lot of press attention. During the summer there are matches nearly every day at the famous **Lord's Cricket Grounds** and the **Oval,** in south London (p. 227). "Test matches" last up to five days with lunch and tea breaks—naturally.

London also boasts the world's biggest **tennis** tournament, **Wimbledon.** For three weeks starting at the end of June, thousands of fans from around the world descend on the lawn at Wimbledon to see the best men and women in tennis battle for the Cup. Good luck getting in, though; it's one of the toughest tickets in sports. Check out p. 227 for some tricks that could potentially land you a seat at the tournament.

THE ARTS

LITERATURE

London runs the gamut in its literary fame, from **Shakespeare** to **Helen Fielding** (*Bridget Jones's Diary*) and **J.K. Rowling** (*Harry Potter*). The mark of great London literature, though, is not how quickly it is made into a Hollywood blockbuster. London is home to some of the world's greatest and most influential writers, in addition to being the setting of many works of literature. After all, Waterstones, the bookstore chain, is almost as ubiquitous in London as Starbucks is in the US.

OLDIES BUT GOODIES

Geoffrey Chaucer's *Canterbury Tales* may read like a foreign language in Old English, but it put London on the literary map when written in the late 14th century. The Bard himself lived in London, writing the plays and poetry that helped to define modern English. Shakespeare's influence and legacy continue to shape the character of London—one needs only to visit the countless theatres and playhouses in the city to see proof. **Edmund Spencer's** glorification of England and Elizabeth I in *The Faerie Queene* (1590) earned him favor at court, while his contemporary **John Donne** wrote metaphysical poetry and penned erotic verse on the side. Playwright **Christopher Marlowe** lost his life in a pub brawl, but not before he produced plays of temptation and damnation, including *Tamburlaine* (circa 1587).

The Puritans in London in the late sixteenth and early seventeenth centuries cranked out a huge volume of beautiful literature, including **John Milton's** epic *Paradise Lost* (1667) and **John Bunyan's** *Pilgrim's Progress* (1678). **Samuel Pepys** is most remembered for his diary entries documenting the Great Fire (1666). In 1719, **Daniel Defoe** inaugurated the era of the English novel with his popular island-bound *Robinson Crusoe*, following with *Moll Flanders* in 1722. Poets **John Keats,** who wrote *Ode to a Grecian Urn* in 1819 after a trip to the British Museum, and **William Wordsworth,** who wrote *London* in 1802, spoke of—you guessed it—London in verse.

HOW NOVEL

In the Victorian period, poverty and social change spawned the sentimental novels of **Charles Dickens;** *Oliver Twist* (1838) and *David Copperfield* (1849) draw on the bleakness of his childhood and portray the harsh living conditions of working-class Londoners. At the same time, **Sir Arthur Conan Doyle's** *Sherlock Holmes* mysteries brought intrigue and affability to London streets. Although born in Dublin, Oscar Wilde was central to London literary culture; he wrote *The Picture of Dorian Gray* (1891), as well as plenty of material for the city's newspapers.

The 20th century was a time for reflection. "On or about December 1910," wrote **Virginia Woolf,** "human nature changed." Woolf, a key member of the Bloomsbury Group, was among the ground-breaking practitioners of **Modernism** (1910-1930). Breaking from Victorian molds, works like *Mrs. Dalloway* (1925) and *To the Lighthouse* (1927) not only revolutionized literary forms, but also contemplated issues of gender and sexuality.

After the World Wars, many of London's literary figures expressed the horrors of fascism in their works. George Orwell's *1984* (1949) became one of the 20th century's seminal works of literature. Aldous Huxley also spent time in London while formulating his own distopian vision, *Brave New World* (1932).

Londoner J.K. Rowling's wild, unparalleled success with the *Harry Potter* series is worth noting—by some reports the billionaire writer is richer than Queen Elizabeth II. The great writers of tomorrow study at the many schools in and around London, carrying on an English tradition in which London continues to play a most central role.

THEATRE

Theatre permeates every aspect of London life and history. A timeline of the city reads like a theatrical resume through the ages, where playwrights and their plays define a particular decade or even an entire century. Shakespeare may have well been king to Elizabeth I's queen, as his works very often dealt with the characters and issues of her reign. Today, advertisements of West End musicals plaster the Tube as thickly as pigeons do Trafalgar Square.

If Shakespeare embodies pre-20th-century theatre, than **Sir Laurence Olivier** is his contemporary peer. Olivier's stage breakthrough was in 1930 in *Private Lives*, and then in 1935 in *Romeo and Juliet*, also starring **Sir John Gielgud.** Before going on to win an Emmy, a Grammy, an Oscar, and a Tony Award in the US, Gielgud began his career as a student at the **Royal Academy of Dramatic Arts,** founded in London in 1904 by **Sir Herbert Beerbohm Tree.**

Now the theatrical tradition of Shakespeare is carried on by venues like the Globe Theatre (p. 232), while the West End features a new musical every week, it seems. Name a world-famous musical—you can see it in the West End. There are plenty of non-musical shows to take in as well. Check out the Theatre section on p. 227 for the scoop on all of London's fabulous theatre.

MUSIC

CLASSICAL

In the middle ages, traveling minstrels sang narrative folk ballads in the courts of the rich. During the Renaissance, London's ears were tuned to cathedral anthems, psalms, and madrigals. The **English Madrigal School** was founded in 1588, led by **Thomas Morley. Henry Purcell** (1659-1695) created instrumental music for Shakespeare's plays and London's first opera, *Dido and Aeneas*, in the Baroque period. Today's audiences are familiar with the operettas of **W.S. Gilbert** (1836-1911) and **Arthur Sullivan** (1842-1900). Although the pair was rumored to hate each other, they managed to produce comic operas that survive today in the realm of musical theatre; their *Mikado*, mocking the English obsession with the East, premiered in London in 1885. The **London Symphony Orchestra,** which currently performs at the **Barbican Centre,** emerged on the scene in 1904.

TALKIN' BOUT MY GENERATION

In the 1960s, London took the R&B sounds coming from across the Atlantic and infused them with raw rock 'n' roll power, birthing a new era in modern music. The city fostered some of the biggest bands and recordings in rock history, topped by the untouchable **Beatles.** At **Abbey Road Studios,** the Beatles recorded classic albums like *Revolver, Sgt. Pepper's Lonely Hearts Club Band*, and *Abbey Road*. Indeed, the latter's famous cover featured the band striding across Abbey Road, a nostalgic destination today. A force of equal importance, the **Rolling Stones** formed in London when Mick Jagger and Keith Richards met at primary school and eventually spearheaded the **British Invasion.** The third of the 60s rock powerhouses was **The Who,** led by Pete Townshend and fierce drummer Keith Moon. In addition to their innovative and ground-breaking albums like *My Generation, Tommy*, and *Quadrophenia*, The Who continually stunned audiences with uncompromising live concerts.

Brixton-born **David Bowie** introduced the world to glam-rock with albums like *Ziggy Stardust* and *Hunky Dory*. **Queen** also formed in London in 1970, bringing majestic guitar arrangements and operatic harmonies to rock, befitting their royal name. **The Police** infused the New Wave movement with a punk edge and unparalleled virtuosity in the 70s and 80s. **The Clash** held no punches with regard to their London roots, penning classics like "London Calling" and "Guns of Brixton." Sid Vicious and the **Sex Pistols** maintained a perpetually brash and controversial image, best known for their sarcastically titled "God Save the Queen."

LONDON CONTINUES TO ROCK

In the late 1980s, the focus of British music swung north to Manchester before landing back in London in the mid-1990s as groups like **Blur** and **Pulp** fought it out with Manchester-boys-come-south **Oasis.** Meanwhile, musical standards became as manufactured as the lawns of St. James's Park with the carefully crafted appeal of pop. Of course, some fared better than others. **George Michael** succeeded in turning his time with **Wham!** into a solo career, and **Elton John's** career has successfully spanned four decades. Of course, no 90s overview is complete without a shout-out to the **Spice Girls,** who at least served their time: the four girls were put into a house and made to like each other before they began "making music." **Coldplay** has ascended to international popularity with albums like *Parachutes* and *X&Y*.

Rap and hip hop have also caught on in the UK in recent years, London being an obvious urban hub of music. Artists like **Roots Manuva** and **The Streets** bring a distinctly British flavor to the rhymes and beats of hip hop. As in the US, British authorities have blamed rap for violence and intolerance in the city, even though London is still among the safest European cities.

CONTEMPORARY ART

London's premier art space is known as the **Tate** (p. 198). This group of museums actually includes the Tate Modern, the Tate Britain, the Tate Liverpool, and the Tate St. Ives. Galleries like the Tate Modern include collections of art from various historical periods, organized not by artist but by theme. The Tate Modern is also in the midst of a £215 million expansion, to be completed in time for the 2012

brits and yanks: the real story

Bob Kagan wrote that Americans are from Venus and Europeans from Mars. From the late 1990s onwards, popular opinion in Britain has suggested that it must choose between its "special relationship" with the United States and its made for a closer relationship between the two nations.

Political personalities have also helped bring the US and Britain closer. Prime Minister Harold Macmillan and President John F. Kennedy were said to get along well despite their age difference. The young President, in 1963, confided in the elder statesman that he got nasty headaches if he went too long without a woman, to which Macmillan replied that he

"Britain must draw upon its shared history with the United States and its geopolitical proximity to the EU..."

role as a central part of the European Union. However, this is a false dichotomy. Instead, Britain must draw upon its shared history with the US and its geopolitical proximity to the EU to plot a careful course between them, acting as both power broker and keystone.

British-US links stretch back to the landing of the Mayflower in Plymouth, Massachusetts in 1620, and have been marked by many highs and lows. The War of Independence (American Revolution) was the obvious low point, and Britain's occasional support for Confederate forces in the Civil War set the tone for a hundred years of sour relations. Imposing coastal defenses on the Eastern seaboard, many manned through the 19th century, exposed the suspicion with which the US regarded its one-time partner across the Atlantic. Yet, with so many shared ideologies, family links, and cross-Atlantic business capital and financing, the relationship was bound to improve. Most vital to rebuilding the friendship was US support for Britain in both World Wars. Since 1945, the relationship could hardly have been better: a shared nuclear program in the 1950s helped the UK to achieve nuclear-power status, and joint military actions through NATO membership and bilateral arrangements have all

would rather have the headaches. Some differences, then, remained! Prime Minister Margaret Thatcher and President Ronald Reagan got along famously, with the Prime Minister backing the President in his drive to end the Cold War and the President giving Thatcher diplomatic and logistical support in the 1982 Falklands War. Most recently, Prime Minister Tony Blair struck up an extremely close relationship with President Clinton, his ideological soulmate,

"From the "War on Terror" to the "War on Poverty," Britain often stands at odds between both its allies and friends."

both pursuing the new politics of the "Third Way" together. Of considerable surprise to many in his left-wing Party, Blair also formed a very close relationship with President Bush, with whom, as most people believed, he shared few political beliefs.

Where Britain's relation to the US is considered "special"—based on good personal friendships—the nation's relation to the EU is, at best, uneasy. Due to hundreds of years of realist tradition in international relations which pit nations against one another in a constantly shifting game of diplomacy and war, by the start of the 20th century almost no single state in Europe trusted another. Britain's self-perception as a superior nation was summed up in a headline in *The Times of London* regarding relations between Britain and France: "Fog on the Channel:

continent cut off." Yet the horrors of war have, above all else, molded British relations with Europe. WWII cast disputes previously taken seriously between the Allied nations into irrelevance. Now, despite historical separation and more recent disagreeable events, Britain continues to share its WWII history with other European nations. Children in the UK are

"Britain continues to share its WWII history with other European nations."

taught from a young age, as are many of their European counterparts, about the unity with which their ancestors fought the Axis powers in that "greatest generation."

Politically, Britain has arrived fashionably late to the European scene. French President Charles de Gaulle, who was sheltered along the Thames during WWII, twice vetoed British membership to the European Economic Community due to the fear that they might be a "Trojan Horse" for American political interests. Since joining in 1975, Britain has been a reluctant member of the EU. Extremely anti-European PM Margaret Thatcher riled many EU states by demanding a rebate for the British financial contribution to the organization. Since 1997, despite ten years under its pro-EU Prime Minister Tony Blair, Britain has not joined the Single European Currency.

Recently, the war in Iraq has driven an even larger wedge between Europe and America. Britain, as the face of international support for the war alongside the US, clashed with French President Jacques Chirac, who became the face of international opposition of military action. In response to a 2004 declaration by Kofi Annan, the Secretary General of the UN, that the invasion of Iraq was "illegal," several anti-war pressure groups wanted to try Blair for war crimes at the International Criminal Court. Bush could not be tried, since the US is not a signatory on the court's statute. While a trial is unlikely to occur, such stress—from the continent and from within Britain—testifies at least in part to diminishing support for British leaders subsequent to growing ties between Britain and the US. From the "War on Terror" (including international response after the bombings on the London Tube in July 2005 and the more recently discovered car bombs in the summer of 2007) to the "War on Poverty" (including discussions of debt forgiveness in Africa at the 2005 G8 summit), Britain often stands at odds between both its American and European allies and friends.

After Kagan made his Mars and Venus comments, German Foreign Minister Joschka Fischer responded that Europeans are the "children of Mars," and being born to the God of War—forged in two World Wars—makes them more critical of war than

"Britain will remain a critical friend to both the US and Europe."

American counterparts. Despite these differences, and perhaps because of them, Britain will remain a critical friend to both the US and Europe. The idea that Britain must somehow choose between the two is false—faced with the problems of international conflict, global hunger relief, and escalating environmental issues, the country (and the world at large) has no choice but to fully utilize all of its diverse relationships.

Thomas Sleigh studied political science at Cambridge University from 1997 to 2000. He was a Fulbright Scholar to Harvard University (2003-04) where he taught a class on American Foreign Policy. He now works in London.

Olympics. Contrasting with these tourist-minded galleries are independently funded spaces. In 1992, a group of young artists appropriately dubbed the **Young British Artists** caught the eye of wealthy art collector Charles Saatchi, who began featuring their avant-garde, often unusual work in his gallery. The group's envelope-pushing quickly became the standard of London's art scene in the 90s. The group's star is **Damien Hirst**, whose *The Physical Impossibility of Death in the Mind of Someone Living* features a tiger shark immersed in formaldehyde. At the beginning of the 21st century, the Young British Artists broke away from Saatchi and started to be featured in the Tate Modern and the Tate Britain. Now with so many galleries in the city, London is the art fan's ideal destination.

DANCE

While many Londoners feel perfectly comfortable shaking their booty on the dance floor (and in front of their mirror at home, a la *Billy Elliot*), the stage is a whole different can of worms. London, though, houses a vibrant dance community: musical theatre in the West End, **Sadler's Wells** (p. 221) in North London, and the **Laban Centre for Movement and Dance** (p. 88) in East London.

For those inspired to put on their own dancing shoes, head to the Laban Centre and a variety of other studios (p. 88). You can also look for the **Dance Umbrella** festival each June. This festival brings contemporary dance to the forefront of London's culture with its multitude of events and performances. For more traditional dance fans, London has many ballet companies and performances, including the Royal Opera House (p. 88).

FILM

London may be one of the most filmed locations in the world, but its own film industry pales in comparison to the city's other art forms, namely theatre. The British film industry, in fact, began as an extension of the stage. British films of the early 1900s tended to be technologically crude; many were nothing more than recordings of stage plays, often with the same sets and actors. American companies moved in during the mid-20s, and home production withered.

Alexander Korda spearheaded a minor cinematic resurgence in the 1930s. Originally from Hungary, Korda founded **London Films** in 1932 and turned it into one of the finest studios in the world. London Films produced a slew of lavish flicks, including *Things to Come*, *The Scarlet Pimpernel*, and *The Private Life of Henry VIII*, a brilliant and successful film that made **Charles Laughton** a star. **Ealing Studios** claims to be the oldest film studio in the world. Held at the Will Baker Studios site from 1896 and re-opened as Ealing in 1931 it is known for its array of genres: documentary-like war films include *Went the Day Well* and *San Demetrio, London*. A string of comedies between 1948 and 1955, though, became the studio's hallmark: *Whisky Galore!*, *Passport to Pimlico*, *The Titfield Thunderbolt*, and *The Ladykillers*. The BBC bought the studio in 1955.

A post-WWII boom saw British studios expand, only to slump in the 1960s with the rise of television. While the major studios shriveled, independent production expanded with the aid of American expats like John Houston and Stanley Kubrick. If not known for the films that come out of this era, at least some of today's biggest stars were born in London in the 1960s: **Minnie Driver, Hugh Grant, Emma Thompson, Emily Watson,** and **Guy Ritchie.**

A lack of government support has left the independent industry largely high and dry. But London actors and directors have flourished in Hollywood, as has London as a setting of Hollywood films. Driver starred in South Kensington native **Andrew Lloyd Webber's** *Phantom of the Opera*, and Webber's *Jesus Christ Superstar* and *Evita* have been adapted to screen. Writer **Ian Fleming's** *Chitty Chitty Bang Bang* became a movie in 1968 (and a West End musical in 2002), but he is better known for *James Bond*. Of the six actors to play Bond, only one is from London: **Roger Moore.**

LIFE AND TIMES

ADDITIONAL RESOURCES

HELPFUL WEBSITES

BBC: www.bbc.co.uk. Major source of news for Britain and London. Also has information on London history and culture.

London Theatre Guide: www.londontheatre.co.uk. Reviews, listings, tickets, chatrooms, and theatre seating plans.

London Dance: www.londondance.com. Listings, features, directory, and news.

Times Online: www.timesonline.co.uk. Online newspaper.

Time Out London: www.timeout.com/london. Online newspaper with up-to-date entertainment and nightlife information.

GREAT BOOKS

The London Encyclopedia: The Most Comprehensive Book on London Ever Published, by Christopher Hibbert (1993). The title says it all: over 100 experts contributed to this book on all things London.

Secret London: Exploring the Hidden City, With Original Walks And Unusual Places to Visit, by Andrew Duncan (2006). Uncovers the lesser-known bits of London for the traveler eager to explore.

Down and Out in Paris and London, by George Orwell (1933). A quasi-fictional account of Orwell's days as a tramp in the two cities. London makes up the latter half of the book, but the Paris bits aren't bad themselves.

2008-09 HOLIDAYS AND FESTIVALS

HOLIDAY OR FESTIVAL	2008	2009
New Year's Day	January 1	January 1
London International Boat Show (www.schroder-slondonboatshow.com)	January 11-20	TBA
London Mimefest (www.mimefest.co.uk)	January 13-28	TBA
London Art Fair (www.londonartfair.co.uk)	January 16-20	TBA
Chinese New Year Festival (www.chinatown-online.co.uk)	February 8	January 27
Great Spitalfields Pancake Day Race	February 5	February 24
Ash Wednesday	February 6	February 25
Ideal Home Show (www.idealhomeshow.co.uk)	March 15-April 6	TBA
St. Patrick's Day Festival (www.london.gov.uk/stpatricksday)	March 15	March 21
Head of the River Race (www.horr.co.uk)	March 15	March 21
Oxford and Cambridge Boat Race (www.the-boatrace.org)	March 29	TBA
Gay and Lesbian Film Festival (www.llgff.org.uk)	early April	early April
Good Friday	March 21	April 10
Easter Sunday	March 23	April 12
Queen's Birthday	April 21	April 21
London Marathon (www.london-marathon.co.uk)	April 13	TBA
Shakespeare's Birthday Celebration at the Globe	TBA	TBA

Covent Garden May Fayre and Puppet Festival (www.alternativearts.co.uk)	Early May	TBA
Royal Windsor Horse Show (www.royal-windsor-horse-show.co.uk)	May 8-11	TBA
Chelsea Flower Show (www.rhs.org.uk)	End of May	TBA
Beating the Retreat	June	TBA
Architecture Week (www.architectureweek.org.uk)	mid-June	mid-June
Royal Ascot (www.ascot.co.uk)	end of June	TBA
Wimbledon Lawn Tennis Championship (www.wimbledon.org)	late June-early July	late June-early July
City of London Festival (www.colf.org)	late June-July	late June-July
Coin Street Festival (www.coinstreetfestival.org)	June-August	June-August
Royal Academy Summer Exhibition (www.royalacademy.org.uk)	June-August	June-August
London Pride (www.pridelondon.ca)	July	July
Greenwich and Docklands International Festival (www.festival.org)	July	July
Soho Festival (www.thesohosociety.org.uk)	mid-July	TBA
BBC Promenade Concerts (Proms) (www.bbc.co.uk/proms)	July-September	July-September
Respect Festival (www.respectfestival.org.uk)	mid-July	TBA
Jazz on the Streets Midsummer Festival (www.jazzonthestreets.co.uk)	late July	late July
Great British Beer Festival (www.gbbf.org)	early August	early August
Notting Hill Carnival (www.lnhc.org.uk)	late August	late August
London Fashion Week (www.londonfashionweek.co.uk)	mid-September	mid-September
London Open House (www.londonopenhouse.org)	mid-September	mid-September
Brick Lane Festival (www.bricklanefestival.com)	early September	early September
Thames Festival (www.thamesfestival.org)	mid-September	mid-September
Dance Umbrella (www.danceumbrella.co.uk)	September-November	September-November
Trafalgar Day Parade	mid-October	TBA
London Film Festival (www.lff.org.uk)	mid-October to early November	mid-October to early November
Guy Fawkes (Bonfire Night)	November 5	November 5
Lord Mayor's Show (www.lordmayorsshow.org)	November 10	TBA
Remembrance Sunday	November 12	November 11
State Opening of Parliament (www.parliament.co.uk)	mid-November to early December	mid-November to early December
Christmas Day	December 25	December 25
Boxing Day	December 26	December 26
New Year's Eve	December 31	December 31

LIFE AND TIMES

BEYOND TOURISM

A PHILOSOPHY FOR TRAVELERS

BEYOND TOURISM HIGHLIGHTS

CONSERVE the environment with one of Britain's many volunteer organizations (p. 81).

CAMPAIGN with one of Britain's political parties (p. 83).

HELP young homeless in the streets with Alone in London (p. 84).

MASTER the fine points of theatre and dance in the West End (p. 88).

London offers innumerable experiences for the traveler passing through, but it also has scads of opportunities for those looking to spend more time in the city. These can give you chance to understand London more intimately and sometimes defray the considerable costs that come with the territory. With this Beyond Tourism chapter, *Let's Go* hopes to promote a better understanding of London and to provide suggestions for those who want to get more than a photo album out of their travels.

There are several options for those who seek to participate in Beyond Tourism activities. Opportunities for **volunteerism** abound with both local and international organizations. **Studying** in a new environment can be enlightening, whether through direct enrollment in a local university or in an independent research project. **Working** is a great way to immerse yourself in local culture while financing your travels.

As a **volunteer** in London, you can participate in projects from working with environmental nonprofit organizations to helping deliver global disaster relief, either on a short-term basis or as the main component of your trip. Later in this chapter, we recommend organizations that can help you find the opportunities that best suit your interests, whether you're looking to get involved for a day or for a year.

Studying at a college abroad is another option. London's universities are among the finest in the world—just ask any of the 54 Nobel Laureates who either studied or worked at the **University of London.** Students interested in literature, the sciences, politics, the arts, or any other field can find a program to suit them in London.

Many travelers structure their trips by the **work** available to them along the way, ranging from odd jobs on the go to full-time, long-term stints in cities.

VOLUNTEERING

Volunteering can be a powerful and fulfilling experience, especially when combined with the thrill of traveling in a new place. Opportunities in London include (but are not limited to) environmental advocacy, political campaigning or activism, global relief groups, work with elderly and disabled people, and intra-London poverty relief groups.

Most people who volunteer in London do so on a short-term basis at organizations that make use of drop-in or once-a-week volunteers. A good place to begin your search for openings in London is at **www.volunteerabroad.com,** which allows you to search specifically within the city. Also try **www.do-it.org.uk.** Another useful engine for broadening your search is **www.idealist.org.** For listings within London, try **www.voluntarywork.org.uk.**

Those looking for longer, more intensive volunteer opportunities usually choose to go through a parent organization that takes care of logistical details and often provides a group environment and support system—for a fee. There are two main types of organizations—religious and non-sectarian—although there are rarely restrictions on participation for either.

WHY PAY MONEY TO VOLUNTEER? Many volunteers are surprised to learn that some organizations require large fees or "donations." While this may seem ridiculous at first glance, such fees often keep the organization afloat, in addition to covering airfare, room, board, and administrative expenses for the volunteers. (Other organizations must rely on private donations and government subsidies.) If you're concerned about how a program spends its fees, request an annual report or finance account. A reputable organization won't refuse to inform you of how volunteer money is spent. Pay-to-volunteer programs might be a good idea for young travelers who are looking for more support and structure (such as pre-arranged transportation and housing), or anyone who would rather not deal with the uncertainty implicit in creating a volunteer experience from scratch.

ENVIRONMENTALISM

As an urban center, London does not have as many sprawling fields teeming with wildlife as, for instance, the UK Lakes District does. However, the city is full of environmentally conscious people who actively work to preserve greenery in the UK and the rest of the world.

British Trust for Conservation Volunteers (BTCV), c/o 80 York Way, King's Cross, London N1 9AG (☎ 7278 4294; www.btcv.org). The largest practical conservation organization in Britain, helping over 130,000 volunteers take hands-on action. Sponsors community and school programs, training for employment, and regular sessions of conservation activities through Green Gym.

Friends of the Earth, 26-28 Underwood St., London N1 7JQ (☎ 7490 1555; www.foe.co.uk). Circulates news events and networks with local groups. Also works on the world's water problem and on creative ideas for sustainable development.

Greenpeace UK, Canonbury Villas, London N1 2PN (☎ 7865 8100; www.greenpeace.org.uk). Active in a wide range of regional campaigns against forest logging, toxic chemicals and nuclear waste, and the war in Iraq. Also advocates for renewable energy. Contact the London central office for calendar and volunteer openings.

Sustain, 94 White Lion St., London N1 9PF (☎ 7837 1228; www.sustainweb.org). Launched in 1999 as a merger of the National Food Alliance and the Sustainable Agriculture Food and Environment (SAFE) Alliance, Sustain relies on volunteers to maintain a network of over 100 organizations committed to safe food production.

INTERNATIONAL HUMAN RIGHTS

London is locally and globally conscious of human rights, home to the headquarters of a number of the world's largest NGOs and aid organizations. The

BEYOND TOURISM

issues that appear to plague only developing world countries have an impact on London as well; for instance, a number of slaves are illegally brought into London each year from around the world. Organizations often need volunteers for local administration and events, and many offer long-term internships.

Amnesty International, The Human Rights Action Centre, 17-25 New Inn Yard, London EC2A 3EA (☎7033 1500; www.amnesty.org.uk). Campaigns against torture, child soldiers, and violence against women. Advocates arms control and international justice.

Anti-Slavery International, Thomas Clarkson House, The Stableyard, Broomgrove Rd., London SW9 9TL (☎7501 8920; www.antislavery.org). The world's oldest international human rights organization, Anti-Slavery works at the local, national, and international level to stop slavery today. They lobby governments, conduct research, and educate the public. Office volunteer and internship positions.

Minority Rights Group, 54 Commercial St., London E1 6LT (☎7422 4200; www.minorityrights.org). Works to secure rights of ethnic, religious, and linguistic minorities, and indigenous peoples worldwide.

Save the Children, 1 St. John's Ln., London EC1M 4AR (☎7012 6400; www.savethe-children.org.uk). Dedicated to issues of health, education, human rights, and protection for children around the world. Volunteer for fund raising, local events and campaigns.

Survival International, 6 Charterhouse Buildings, London EC1M 7ET (☎7687 8700; www.survival-international.org). Works for minority rights in education, advocacy, and campaigns. Volunteers welcome in all department offices, including press, publications, research and campaigns, and outreach and administration.

POLITICAL ACTIVISM

For the politically minded, London is the ideal place to get involved in third-party activism or get on board with party campaigning. Your best bet is to contact the party directly to ask what kinds of tasks are needed. Often volunteers are recruited for clerical support, fund raising, and publicity. Usually no fee is required to participate, though you may be solicited to contribute to "the cause."

The Labour Party, 39 Victoria St., London SW1H 0HA (☎0845 850 0588; www.labour-inlondon.org.uk). Currently Her Majesty's government, Labour is led by Prime Minister Gordon Brown. Originally founded by the Labour Movement, the center-left party continues to advocate increased social services, although recently it has been criticized by leftist groups for its moderate stances. They support the war in Iraq.

The Conservative Party, 30 Millbank, London SW1P 4DP (☎7222 9000; www.conservative-party.org.uk). The oldest political party in the world, the Tories hold sway over the moderate right, locking horns with Labour over social and fiscal spending for a decade. They oppose the war in Iraq.

Liberal Democrats, 4 Cowley St., London SW1P 3NB (☎7222 7999; www.lib-dems.org.uk). Britain's 3rd largest political party, the Liberal Democrats advocate changing the voting system for a "fairer distribution of power," scrapping student fees for university, and providing free care for the elderly. They oppose the war in Iraq.

Communist Party of Britain, 23 Coombe Rd., London CR0 1BD (☎8686 1659; www.communist-party.org.uk). Advocating unabashed socialism since 1920, the Communist Party remains opposed to the so-called right-wing tactics of the Labour Party.

The Green Party of England and Wales, 1a Waterlow Rd., London N19 5NJ (☎7272 4474; www.greenparty.org.uk). Aiming for a "just and sustainable society," this ecologically minded leftist party advises volunteers to mail an application to the Green Party Volunteer Manager.

B E Y O N D   T O U R I S M

Trade Justice Movement (secretariat ☎7404 0530; www.tradejusticemove-ment.org.uk). An umbrella organization for numerous British, Scottish, and Welsh charity organizations dedicated to fighting world poverty and promoting fair trade. Political campaigns often address the UK's position in the WTO. Website provides links to member organizations, including Save the Children, Action Aid, and the World Development Movement. Volunteer positions, when available, are usually at the Fair Trade Foundation offices in central London.

ELDERLY AND DISABLED PEOPLE

While London is a popular young person's destination, many elderly and disabled people also call the city home. Volunteers may spend a single day in a nursing home, or forge a unique longer-term bond with a hospice-care patient.

Help the Hospices, 34-44 Britannia St., London WC1X 9JG (☎7520 8200; www.helpthehospices.org.uk). Hospice care aims to give the best quality of care at the end of life. Help the Hospices is connected to 220 individual centers. See website for information on local hospices.

Kith and Kids, The Irish Centre, Pretoria Rd., London N17 8DX (☎8801 7432; www.kithandkids.org.uk). Help disabled youth during community outings, at summer camp, and with sports and arts activities.

Shape, 356 Holloway Rd., London N7 6PA (☎7619 6160; www.shapearts.org.uk). Enables access to the arts for elderly and disabled people. Volunteer opportunities include administration, press and marketing, finance, and event and show planning. You can volunteer for as little as a few hours.

Skill, National Bureau for Students with Disabilities, 18-20 Crucifix Ln., London SE1 3JW (☎7450 0620; www.skill.org.uk). Promotes opportunities for people with any disability in learning and employment. Helps disabled people volunteer in the community.

URBAN ISSUES

Large economic disparities exist within London. Listed below are some organizations that work on urban issues like youth homelessness in London.

Alone in London, 188 King's Cross Rd., London WC1X 9DE (☎7278 4224 for volunteering; www.als.org.uk). Committed to the young homeless. Volunteer posts are 3-6 months. Application required.

Crisis Skylight, 66 Commercial St., London E1 6LT (☎0870 011 3335; www.crisis.org.uk). Provides a range of workshops and creative activities for the homeless. Application required.

Community Service Volunteers (CSV), 237 Pentonville Rd., London N1 9NJ (☎7278 6601; www.csv.org.uk). Offers both full- (4-12 months) and part-time volunteer positions, including teaching citizenship courses and supporting troubled youth and the homeless. See website for fee details and to download an application.

Detainee Support and Health Unit, 54 Camberwell Rd., London SE5 0EN (www.langlinks.org.uk). Provides help and support to those detained under the Immigration act by helping those released from detention and providing assistance to those being deported. Aims to develop bilingual abilities in London's many immigrants.

The Food Chain, 202-208 New North Rd., London N1 7BJ (☎7354 0333; www.food-chain.org.uk). Aims to ensure that those living with HIV in the UK have access to food and good nutrition to help regain their health and stay well.

Oxfam, John Smith Dr., Cowley, Oxford OX4 2JY (☎0870 333 2700; www.oxfam.co.uk). The UK's largest secular organization supporting the poor; contact Oxfam for your nearest regional office. Download an application online.

The Salvation Army UK Headquarters, 33-35 Kings Exchange, Tileyard Rd., London N7 9AH (☎7619 6100; www.salvationarmy.org.uk). A Christian organization that provides emergency aid and social services, including youth programs and family tracing.

The Simon Community, 89-93 Fonthill Rd., London N4 3JH (☎7561 8270; www.simoncommunity.org.uk). Supports the homeless, working on the streets to deliver a better quality of life.

Thames Reach Bondway, 122-126 Backchurch Ln., London E1 1ND (☎7702 4260; www.thamesreachbondway.com). Conducts street work, documents stories, and provides community support for the homeless. 1-day and administrative positions available. See website for details and application.

Time Bank, 1 London Bridge, London SE1 9BG (☎0845 456 1668 for volunteering; www.timebank.org.uk). A national campaign places volunteers with organizations dealing with a wide variety of issues, from art to music to dance to education. See website for long list of partner organizations.

STUDYING

Study abroad programs consist of college-level classes, often for credit. In order to choose a program that best fits your needs, research as much as you can before making your decision—determine costs and duration, as well as what kind of students participate in the program and what sort of accommodations are provided.

VISA INFORMATION. You will need a visa to study in the UK if you are a **visa national** (see www.ukvisas.gov.uk for details), are stateless, hold a non-traditional travel document, or hold a passport not recognized by the UK. To obtain a student visa, you must provide proof of admittance to a course of study and financial support. **Non-visa nationals** (citizens of Australia, Canada, New Zealand, and the US) only need a visa if they are staying longer than 6 months. In order to gain entry clearance, non-visa nationals must provide proof of student status and continue to provide documentation while traveling in and out of London (so remember to keep that documentation with your passport). **Prospective students** can travel to the UK for up to 6 months as long as they show that they intend to enroll in a university, can pay for their studies and support themselves, and intend to leave the UK once they finish their studies or once their permission to stay ends (if a visa cannot be obtained). **EEA citizens** (27 member countries of the EU, plus Iceland, Liechtenstein, and Norway) and Swiss nationals have the right to free movement and residence in the UK.

Many American students choose London as their study-abroad destination in order to avoid a language barrier; a number of American universities even have direct-enroll programs in London universities—Tufts University, for instance, has its own subset at University College London. Studying with other foreign students may be less of an immersive experience than studying with Londoners, so choose your program of study carefully.

In an urban environment, most student accommodations exist as dorms or flats—homestays are rare. Most university housing is not centralized around a

ANYONE FOR TEA?

Perhaps the most quintessential British pastime, taking tea, has a colorful and unusual history. In fact, Britain lagged behind most countries in their discovery of tea, something they have been trying to make up for ever since by consuming enormous quantities of the Indian import.

Tea was first introduced into England in the 17th century by Catherine of Braganza, the wife of King Charles II. It is believed she enjoyed tea as a child in Portugal and so asked for it to be brought to Britain for her consumption. The fashion soon spread, and London's coffee houses added tea to their menus. It's popularity grew drastically, so much so that tavern owners noticed a steep decline in gin and ale sales, while the government turned a quick profit by taxing all imports. Despite the taxes, tea had become London's favored drink by 1750.

Tea has remained a way of life since then and continues to be consumed en masse by all Brits. The most popular form of tea consumption is afternoon tea, which is said to have been introduced by Anna, the 7th Duchess of Bedford, in the early 19th century. Seemingly the Duchess was looking for something to fill her afternoons between lunch and dinner. Little did she realize what the consequences of her boredom would be!

main campus as it may be in other countries. Even if you're offered dorm housing, it may be a 45-minute Tube ride away from early-morning class, so plan accordingly.

UNIVERSITIES

With dozens of institutions from the sprawling colleges of the University of London to the vast collections of the British Library, you can study almost any subject at any level in London. It's not surprising that every year thousands of international students choose to make London their academic home away from home. Even if you didn't come to study, taking evening courses—whether in medieval architecture or jazz dance—can be a great way to broaden your horizons and meet similarly minded people. For a comprehensive list of part-time and evening classes, the annual **Floodlight** directory lists over 40,000 courses in Greater London (www.floodlight.co.uk, also available at newsstands). You can also search **www.studyabroad.com** for various semester-abroad programs that meet your criteria, including your desired location and focus of study. The following is a list of organizations that can help place students in university programs abroad (often through University of London colleges) or have their own branch in London.

AMERICAN PROGRAMS

American Institute for Foreign Study, College Division, River Plaza, 9 West Broad St., Stamford, CT 06902, USA (☎800-727-2437; www.aifsabroad.com). Organizes programs for high school and college study in universities in London, including the American International University in London.

Arcadia University for Education Abroad, 450 S. Easton Rd., Glenside, PA 19038, USA (☎866-927-2234; www.arcadia.edu/cea). Operates both study and internship programs in London. Includes term-time and summer programs. Costs range from $1560 (summer) to $33,000 (full-year).

Council on International Educational Exchange (CIEE), 7 Custom House St., 3rd fl., Portland, ME 01401, USA (☎800-407-8839; www.ciee.org/study). Sponsors work, volunteer, academic, and internship programs in London.

Intern Exchange International (IEI), 2606 Bridgewood Circle, Boca Raton, FL 33434, USA (☎561-477-2434; www.internexchange.com). Accepts high school students (aged 16-18 years) from US and Canada for various career internships in business, the professions, and the arts in London for a summer. Combined with an exploration of the sights and culture of England. $6945 plus airfare.

Institute for Study Abroad, Butler University, 1100 W. 42nd St., Suite 305, Indianapolis, IN 46208, USA (☎800-858-0229; www.ifsa-butler.org). Runs both study and internship programs. Includes term-time and summer programs. Costs range from $3000 (summer) to $30,000 (full-year).

International Association for the Exchange of Students for Technical Experience (IAESTE), 10400 Little Patuxent Pkwy., Suite 250, Columbia, MD 21044, USA (☎410-997-2200; www.iaeste.org). Offers 8- to 12-week internships in London for college students who have completed 2 years of technical study. $25-450 application fee, depending on experience.

LONDON PROGRAMS

Combined, the **University of London** and the **London Institute** encompass the vast majority of London's universities and colleges, though there are also numerous independent specialist institutions. Many offer **special programs** for international students on **exchange visits, semesters abroad,** and **summer schools.**

Enrolling for a **degree course**—meaning that you plan on attaining your final degree from a London school—rather than a semester- or year-long program can often present problems to those raised in a different system. UK universities will want to see evidence that you have attained the same educational standard as British 18-year-olds, either by passing the British A-level exams or a recognized equivalent such as the International Baccalaureate; EU credentials are generally admissible. Americans may have problems, since SAT scores and high-school diplomas are not normally accepted; frequently, Americans must have completed a year of college in the US before being considered equivalent to European high-school graduates. High marks on a number of Advanced Placement exams may, however, do the trick. The **British Council** (www.britishcouncil.org) can often arrange for people to take British exams in their home countries. The Council also runs **EducationUK** (www.educationuk.org), a slick website explaining the British education system.

Fees for degree programs for non-EU students depend on the subject and school, from around £8500 per year for humanities to £18,000 for medicine. This is always more expensive than what UK students pay: both UK natives and EU residents pay up to £3070 per year. In addition, you need approximately £5500-8000 per year for accommodation and living expenses. The British Council website listed above also offers resources to help fund study in the UK. Below is a list of unique universities and programs offered in London.

The London Institute, International Development Office, University of the Arts London, 65 Davies St., London W1K 5DA (☎7514 7605; www.linst.ac.uk). Five of London's best-known art and design schools, including Central St. Martins College, Chelsea College of Art, and the London College of Fashion.

Universities and Colleges Admissions Services (UCAS), P.O. Box 28, Cheltenham, Gloucestershire GL52 3LZ (☎0870 112 2211; www.ucas.ac.uk). The centralized admissions service for all undergraduate degree courses in the UK. Also provides impartial information to international students on the application process.

The University of London, Senate House, Malet St., London WC1E 7HO (☎7862 8000; www.lon.ac.uk), is an umbrella organization uniting the vast majority of London's academic institutions, with 19 constituent universities and colleges. A few of the best are listed below.

King's College London, Study Abroad Office, James Clerk Maxwell Building, 57 Waterloo Rd., London SE1 8WA (☎7848 6522 for international liaison; www.kcl.ac.uk). One of the largest

University of London colleges. Affiliates normally must have completed 2 years of university at time of admission to King's. Special study-abroad programs in association with the Royal Academy of Dramatic Arts (RADA) and Globe Enterprises, where students take English courses at King's and theatre courses at RADA or the Globe.

London School of Economics, Undergraduate Admissions, London School of Economics, Houghton St., London WC2A 2AS (☎7405 7686; www.lse.ac.uk). Year-long courses for international students. Focuses on political science and economics.

School of Oriental and African Studies (SOAS), Thornbaugh St., Russell Sq., London WC1H 0XG (☎7637 2388; www.soas.ac.uk). A college of the University of London. The only UK school to specialize in the study of Asia, Africa, and the Near and Middle East.

University College London, Gower St., London WC1E 6BT (☎7679 2000; www.ucl.ac.uk). The biggest of University of London's schools (and one of the UK's top universities), with a complete academic curriculum. Special programs are offered for international affiliate students on semester or 1-year leaves from their home universities; affiliates normally must have completed 2 years of university at time of admission to UCL. **Slade School of Fine Arts** (p. 88) is also run through UCL.

ARTS AND PERFORMANCE

It is no surprise that London's West End is one of the most successful theatre and performing arts destinations in the world. Although "real" actors may quibble with the abundance of flashy musicals and jazz hands, London houses an astonishing array of talent. There are plenty of programs for those looking to hone their craft or to become a star. Many of London's elite **art, music, drama,** and **dance** academies supplement their income by offering part-time and summer courses to motivated amateurs. Typically there are no admissions requirements (though some courses fill up quickly), but you will rarely receive any recognition other than a certificate of attendance for the work you put in. Always check whether you'll be taught by the same master artists who teach the colleges' regular offerings.

Central St. Martins College of Art and Design, Southampton Row, London WC1B 4AP (☎7514 7015; www.csm.linst.ac.uk). Dozens of evening courses throughout the year, as well as a comprehensive summer program covering all aspects of fine art, graphic design, fashion, and film.

Courtauld Institute, Somerset House, Strand, London WC2R 0RN (☎7848 2777; www.courtauld.ac.uk). 12-week summer courses in art history. Courses include gallery visits, focusing on the Courtauld's own impressive collections. Also offers undergraduate degree program in Art History and a year-long Master's program in Art History and Art Restoration. Tuition for summer courses starts at £400.

Laban Centre for Contemporary Dance, Creekside, London SE8 3DZ (☎8691 8600; www.laban.org). Dance classes from ballet to contemporary dance to jazz offered for all ages and levels. £475 for a 2-week summer intensive course.

Royal Academy of Dramatic Arts (RADA), 62-64 Gower St., London WC1E 6ED; 18-22 Chenies St., London WC1E 7EX (for both ☎7636 7076; www.rada.org). The alma mater of Ralph Fiennes, Kenneth Branagh, and Anthony Hopkins offers 4- and 8-week summer courses in acting, technical production, and script writing. Applicants must be at least 18; no experience required. Around £2500 per 4 weeks. See website for course offerings and to download application.

Royal Opera House (Royal Opera and **Royal Ballet),** ROH Education, Royal Opera House, Covent Garden, London WC2E 9DD (☎7212 9410; www.royalopera.org). Classes in performance art for all ages. Classes from £120-170.

Slade School of Fine Art, part of University College London, Gower St., London WC1E 6BT (☎7679 7772; www.ucl.ac.uk/slade). A range of general and specialized art courses over the summer, between £290 and £2700 for 1-10 weeks.

life in the ward

The first time I entered Chelsea and Westminster hospital, I was 15, visiting a friend who had just fallen ill. Standing outside, overwhelmed by the size of the hospital, I couldn't imagine working there every day. Inside, the hospital offered a different impression, however; most of the nurses and doctors

In the UK, there is not a significant emphasis on volunteer work in the school system; much more emphasis is placed on academic performance and achievement. The volunteer landscape is improving, however, and for anybody in the UK, donating time in any capacity is very worthwhile and rewarding. Opportunities are increasingly available, and there is certainly no shortage of people and organizations looking for help.

"I felt a sense of responsibility and duty in the absence of the doctors."

seemed content working there, in a sense comforted by their patients and work. I returned two years later invigorated and excited, ready to volunteer.

I chose a station in the post-natal ward, which meant changing a lot of nappies (diapers) and spending my Wednesday nights surrounded by cute little babies. My orders were simple: assist the nurses as they saw fit. On my first day, I was informed by some very tired and frustrated nurses that my sole duty was to change bed sheets for every new mother that came in from the delivery ward. However, after a few short weeks I was showing first-time mothers how to bathe their babies, changing diapers, and monitoring the babies'

I volunteered directly through the Chelsea and Westminster Volunteer Office, but there are many ways to get involved in hospital volunteering. A large hospital in Central London such as Chelsea and Westminster has hundreds of volunteers working on any given day, so anyone can find a position suitable for them. For those interested in HIV/AIDS relief, St. Stephen's Volunteers (ststephensvolunteers.org.uk) is a very well-established group which works specifically with HIV/AIDS patients in

"I developed real connections with the patients who passed through the post-natal ward."

health. I saw the doctors on duty only once or twice a shift, as they whirled through with quick rounds before disappearing off to their other duties—I felt a sense of responsibility and duty in the absence of the doctors.

Volunteering in the hospital was an eye-opener for me. I developed real connections with the patients who passed through the post-natal ward and learned more than I could ever imagine about birth and how to care for newborn babies. Even as a Londoner I felt it gave me a whole new perspective; anybody, native or foreigner, would benefit from donating their time to a hospital.

the hospital. The hospital also runs an arts project called "Hospital Arts," the aim of which is to improve the "healing environment" of the hospital by offering patients performances and exhibitions. Whichever department you choose, you will be fulfilled by spending time in a London hospital, and you will have the chance to develop a bond with the city and its inhabitants that you would never experience as a tourist.

Olivia Brown is a senior at Harvard University studying history. She has lived in London since she was 9 months old, and has also lived in Cuba, Ecuador and New York. She was a Researcher-Writer for Let's Go: Paris 2007.

A DIFFERENT PATH

WORKING

As with volunteering, work opportunities tend to fall into two categories. Some travelers want long-term jobs that allow them to integrate into a community, while others seek out short-term jobs to finance the next leg of their travels. Long-term jobs in London range across almost all fields. For short-term work, **bartending** or **waiting tables** is popular, as are **hostel jobs** and **secretarial work.**

Local papers are good resources for want ads. Working abroad often requires a special work visa; see the box below for information about obtaining one.

VISA INFORMATION. The **Foreign and Commonwealth Office's (FCO)** Joint Entry Clearance Unit (www.ukvisas.gov.uk) has info on visa and work permit requirements and downloadable application forms; also see **workpermit.com** (☎7842 0800). Information for visitors already in the UK is also available from the **Home Office Immigration and Nationality Directorate** (☎0114 207 4074; www.ind.homeoffice.gov.uk). The **Immigration Advisory Service,** County House, 190 Great Dover St., London, SE1 4YB (☎7357 6917; www.iasuk.org), is an independent charity providing free advice and assistance to UK visa applicants.

YOUR RIGHTS. The **minimum wage** varies with age and length of employment. People aged 18 to 21 may not be paid less than £4.60 per hr.; otherwise the rate is £5.52. **Full-time workers** may not be forced to work over 48hr. per week, 13hr. per day, or six days per week. They are also entitled to four weeks of paid vacation per year. **Part-time workers** are now entitled to many of the benefits an employer must accord full-time employees, including paid vacation on a pro-rated basis. For more information, including details of **maternity leave** and **anti-discrimination laws,** visit **www.direct.gov.co.uk.**

COMMONWEALTH CITIZENS. Commonwealth citizens ages 17-30 are eligible for a **working holidaymaker visa,** allowing them to stay and work in the UK for up to two years provided that employment is "incidental to your holiday"—no more than 12 months of that two-year period. Commonwealth nationals who have at least one **UK-born grandparent** (including Ireland, if born before March 31, 1922) are eligible for a **UK Ancestry Visa,** which gives the right to reside and work in the UK for an initial period of four years. Canadian citizens should also refer to the **Student Work Abroad Programme** (www.swap.ca), which has 40 offices in Canada administered by the Canadian Universities Travel Service. This program is similar to the BUNAC program available to US citizens (p. 90).

US STUDENTS. In general, US citizens are required to have a work permit (p. 19) to work in the UK. However, American citizens who are full-time students and are over 18 can apply for a special permit from the **British Universities North America Club (BUNAC),** P.O. Box 430, Southbury, CT 06488, which allows them to work **up to six months** (US ☎203-264-0901, UK 020 7251 3472; www.bunac.org.uk). BUNAC also offers limited assistance in finding housing and employment, and organizes regular social events. You will need to enter the UK within one semester of graduation and have at least £1000 on entry. BUNAC also has a very helpful bulletin board in their London office, 16 Bowling Green Ln. (☎7251 3472), with housing and job postings.

WORK PERMITS AND WORK VISAS. If you do not fall into one of the above categories, you will need a work permit in order to work in the UK. If you require a visa to travel to the UK, you will also need a work visa. You must already have a job set up in the UK before obtaining a work permit, which can only be applied for through your employer. For further information, consult **www.workpermits.gov.uk.**

LONG-TERM WORK

If you're planning on spending a substantial amount of time (more than 3 months) working in London, search for a job well in advance. Although often only available to college students, **internships** are a good way to segue into working abroad; even if they are un- or underpaid, many say the experience is well worth it. Be wary of advertisements for companies claiming to be able get you a job abroad for a fee—often the same listings are available online or in newspapers. Some reputable organizations include:

Council Exchanges, 3 Copley Pl., 2nd fl., Boston, MA 02116, USA (☎617-247-0350). Charges US$300-475 for arranging short-term working authorizations (generally valid for 3-6 months) and provides extensive information on different job opportunities.

International Exchange Programs (IEP), Level 3, 333 George St., Sydney NSW 2000, Australia (☎+61 02 9299 0400; www.iep.org.au); P.O. Box 1786, Shortland St., Auckland 1010, New Zealand (☎+64 0800 443 769; www.iep.co.nz). Helps Aussies and Kiwis who have working holidaymaker visas find employment, lodging, and friends. AUS$215/NZ$495 fee.

Tate, 7 Hanover Sq., London, W1S 1HQ (☎7408 0424; www.tate.co.uk). Arranges secretarial placements for foreigners in London.

TEACHING

Teaching jobs abroad are rarely well-paid. Volunteering as a teacher in lieu of getting paid is a popular option; in this case, teachers often receive some sort of daily stipend to help with living expenses. In almost all cases, you must have at least a bachelor's degree to be a full-fledged teacher, although college undergraduates can often get summer positions teaching or tutoring. The British school system is comprised of state (public, government-funded), public (independent, privately funded), and international (often for children of expatriates in the UK) schools, as well as universities. Applications to teach at state schools must be made through the local government; public and international schools must be applied to individually. University positions are typically only available through fellowship or exchange programs. Placement agencies are often a good way to find teaching jobs in Britain; vacancies are also

GIVING BACK

EATING FOR A CAUSE

Sampling London's mos renowned cuisine generally comes at a price, but two new res taurants have found a unique wa to ensure that your hard-earne dollars also help a good cause.

Fifteen—the latest creation o chef-of-the-moment Jamie Oliver—was first profiled in Channel 4's reality show "Jamie's Kitchen." The restaurant provides training oppo tunities for young people facing homelessness and drug problems Many "graduates" of the restauran go on to work in other gourme establishments. The menu feature Mediterranean food with an Italia influence—pricey but delicious. Fo a big splurge, try the three-course lunch *menu* for £25.

Hoxton Apprentice is a affordable do-good gourmet expe rience in London's trendy Eas End. The restaurant provide front- and back-of-the-house apprenticeships for disadvan taged youth. A swanky setting and well-made pan-European staple make it well worth a visit. The lo prices (two-course express lunc £10, dinners £8-13) certainly d not mean lesser quality.

Fifteen: Westland Place. ☎133(*1515; www.fifteenrestaurant.com* ⊖*Old St. Open daily noon-4:30pn and 6:30-11:30pm. Hoxtor Apprentice: 16 Hoxton Sq.* ⊖*Ol St.* ☎*7749 2828; www.hoxtonaյ prentice.com. Open Tu-Sa noon 11pm, Su noon-10:30pm.*

listed in major newspapers. An alternative is to make contacts directly with schools or just to try your luck once you get there. If you are going to try the latter, the best time of the year is several weeks before the start of the school year. The following organizations may help in your search.

Independent Schools Council, 30 Orange St., London WC2H 7HH (☎7766 7070; www.iscis.uk.net). Lists British independent schools and further information on teaching opportunities.

International Schools Services (ISS), 15 Roszel Rd., Box 5910, Princeton, NJ 08543-5910, USA (☎609-452-0990; www.iss.edu). Candidates should have experience teaching or with international affairs. 2-year commitment expected.

European Council of International Schools, 21B Lavant St., Petersfield, Hampshire GU32 3EL (☎1730 268 244; www.ecis.org). Provides contact details for British international schools, as well as placement opportunities.

AU PAIR WORK

Au pairs are typically women (although sometimes men), aged 18-27, who work as live-in nannies, caring for children and doing light housework in exchange for room, board, and a small spending allowance or stipend. One perk of the job is that it allows you to get to know London without the high expenses of traveling. Drawbacks, however, can include mediocre pay and long hours. Weekly allowances for au pairs in London run between £60 and £80. Much of the au pair experience depends on the family with whom you are placed. Visit **www.au-pair.org** for information about working as an au pair and help finding positions. The agencies below are also a good place to look for employment.

InterExchange, 161 Sixth Ave., New York, NY 10013, USA (☎800-287-2477; www.interexchange.org).

Childcare International, Ltd., Trafalgar House, Grenville Pl., London NW7 3SA (☎8906 3116; www.childint.co.uk).

SHORT-TERM WORK

Traveling for long periods of time can get expensive; therefore, many travelers try their hand at odd jobs for a few weeks at a time to help finance another month or two of touring. A good place for foreigners to get their start is by checking newspapers such as *The Guardian, The Times,* and *The Evening Standard.* Other good (and free!) employment-specific publications include *TNT Magazine UK,* which appears every Monday, and *Metro,* found in blue bins at Tube stations. The jobs published may vary by day. Most often, these short-term jobs are found by word of mouth or simply by talking to the owner of a hostel or restaurant. Due to the high turnover in the tourism industry, many places are eager for help, even if it is only temporary.

HOTEL AND CATERING. There's no shortage of jobs in London waiting tables, tending bars, or working in kitchen and cleaning positions. These jobs may not pay well, even for long hours of work. Also, tipping is not as customary in the UK as in other countries; many restaurants include the gratuity in the check. Another popular option is to work several hours per day at a **hostel** in exchange for free or discounted room and/or board.

SECRETARIAL WORK. If you can type like a demon, then temping can be a good way to pay the bills. Temps are temporary secretaries on short-term placements (from as little as one day to a few weeks); you'll need to register with a temping agency that will match available positions to your skills. Check out **www.letstemp.co.uk** for referrals to temping agencies.

FURTHER READING ON BEYOND TOURISM.

Alternatives to the Peace Corps: A Guide of Global Volunteer Opportunities, by Paul Backhurst. Food First Books, 2005 (US$12).

The Back Door Guide to Short-Term Job Adventures: Internships, Summer Jobs, Seasonal Work, Volunteer Vacations, and Transitions Abroad, by Michael Landes. Ten Speed Press, 2005 (US$22).

Green Volunteers: The World Guide to Voluntary Work in Nature Conservation, ed. Fabio Ausenda. Universe, 2007 (US$15).

How to Get a Job in Europe, by Cheryl Matherly and Robert Sanborn. Planning Communications, 2003 (US$23).

How to Live Your Dream of Volunteering Overseas, by Joseph Collins, Stefano DeZerega, and Zahara Heckscher. Penguin Books, 2002 (US$20).

International Job Finder: Where the Jobs Are Worldwide, by Daniel Lauber and Kraig Rice. Planning Communications, 2002 (US$20).

Live and Work Abroad: A Guide for Modern Nomads, by Huw Francis and Michelyne Callan. Vacation-Work Publications, 2001 (US$16).

Living and Working in London: A Survival Handbook, 2nd Edition, by Dan Finlay. Survival Books, 2004 (US$22).

Overseas Summer Jobs 2002. Peterson's Guides and Vacation Work, 2002 (US$18).

Volunteer Vacations: Short-Term Adventures That Will Benefit You and Others, by Doug Cutchins, Anne Geissinger, and Bill McMillon. Chicago Review Press, 2006 (US$18).

Work Abroad: The Complete Guide to Finding a Job Overseas, by Clayton Hubbs. Transitions Abroad Publishing, 2002 (US$16).

Work Your Way Around the World, by Susan Griffith. Vacation-Work Publications, 2007 (US$22).

PRACTICAL INFORMATION

TOURIST AND FINANCIAL SERVICES

TOURIST INFORMATION

Britain Visitor Centre, 1 Regent St. (www.visitbritain.com). ⊖Oxford Circus. Run by British Tourist Association. Open M 9:30am-6:30pm, Tu-F 9am-6:30pm, Sa-Su 10am-4pm.

City Information Centre, St. Paul's Churchyard (☎7606 3030; www.cityoflondon.gov.uk). ⊖St. Paul's. Open Easter-Sept. daily 9:30am-5pm; Oct.-Easter M-F 9:30am-5pm, Sa 9:30am-12:30pm.

Greenwich, 2 Cutty Sark Gardens (☎1120 8854 8888; www.greenwich.gov.uk). ⊖Cutty Sark. Open daily 10am-5pm.

London Information Centre, 1 Leicester Pl. (☎7930 6769; www.londontown.com or www.londoninformationcentre.com). ⊖Leicester Sq. Next to Leicester Sq.'s ½-price ticket booth. Advises about events and directions and can also book hotels with negotiated rates. Open M-F 8am-midnight, Sa-Su 9am-6pm.

 TIC-ED OFF. In London (and throughout the UK), Tourist Information Centre is often abbreviated to TIC. If you encounter the acronym in this book, that's what it stands for.

ORGANIZED TOURS

The Big Bus Company, 35-37 Grosvenor Gardens (☎7233 7797; www.bigbus.co.uk). ⊖Victoria. Choice of live commentary in English or recorded in 8 languages. Multiple routes, with buses every 5-15min. 1hr walking tours and Thames mini-cruise included. Also books fast-track entry tickets to many attractions. Buses start at central office, as well as at hubs throughout the city. Tickets valid 24hr. from 1st use. £20, children £8. £2 discount on adult ticket when purchased online. AmEx/MC/V.

London Bicycle Tour Company, 1a Gabriel's Wharf (☎7928 6838; www.londonbicycle.com). ⊖Waterloo or Southwark. Leisurely paced tours designed to keep actual biking to a minimum. "East Tour" (Sa 2pm) encompasses the City, Docklands, and the East End, while "Royal West Tour" (Su 2pm) takes you to the South Bank, Chelsea, Kensington, and the West End. Both 9 mi., 3½hr. Tours leave from the LBTC store. Book in advance. £17.

London Duck Tours, 55 York Rd. (☎7928 3132; www.londonducktours.co.uk). ⊖Waterloo or Westminster. Duck Tours' amphibious fleet follows a 70min. nonstop road tour with a splash into the Thames for a 30min. cruise. Tours depart County Hall, opposite the London Eye. £17.50, concessions £14, children £12, families £53.

Original London Sightseeing Tour (☎8877 1722; www.theoriginaltour.com). 4 different routes, with buses every 20min. Also books fast-track entry tickets to many attractions. Tickets valid 24hr. £19, children under 16 £11, families £72. £1 discount with online booking. £10 discount for family package.

Original London Walks (☎7624 3978, recorded info 7624 9255; www.walks.com). The biggest walking tour company, with the most variety. Weekly program runs themed walks, from "Haunted London" to "Slice of India." Also offers guided visits to larger museums. Most walks last 2hr. £6, concessions £5, children under 16 free.

BUDGET TRAVEL AGENCIES

Times CTS International, 71 Oxford St. (☎7447 5000). ⊖Tottenham Court Rd. Special fares for teachers and youth under 26. Open M-F 10am-6pm, Sa 10am-1pm. AmEx/MC/V.

STA Travel, (☎0870 1600 599; www.statravel.co.uk). 14 London branches; largest at 85 Shaftesbury Ave. (☎7432 7474). ⊖Piccadilly Circus. Open M-W and F 11am-7pm, Th 11am-8pm, Sa 11am-6pm. Other branches at 11 Goodge St.; 86 Old Brompton Rd.; 117 Euston Rd.; London School of Economics, East Building.

Travel CUTS, 295A Regent St. (☎7255 1944; www.travelcuts.com). ⊖Oxford Circus. 2nd location at International Student House, 209 Portland St. (☎7436 0459). Open M-W and F 9am-6pm, Th 9am-7pm, Sa 11am-4pm.

CURRENCY EXCHANGE

American Express, (☎0895 456 6524; www.americanexpress.com). Locations include:

84 Kensington High St. (☎7795 6703). ⊖High St. Kensington. Open M-Sa 9am-5:30pm.

30-31 Haymarket (☎7484 9610). ⊖Piccadilly Circus. Open M-F 9am-7pm, Sa 9am-6pm, Su 10am-5pm.

Terminals 3 and 4 Heathrow (☎8897 0134). ⊖Heathrow. 9 locations throughout Terminals 3 and 4. Open daily 5:30am-10pm.

7 Wilton Rd. (☎7630 6365). ⊖Victoria. Open M-Sa 9am-5:30pm.

156A Southampton Row (☎7837 4416). ⊖Holborn. Open M-F 9am-5:30pm, Sa 9am-5pm.

Thomas Cook, (☎0870 750 5711; www.thomascook.com). For traveler's check refunds, call ☎0800 587 623.

TRANSPORT INFORMATION

Transport for London (☎7222 1234; www.tfl.gov.uk/tfl). Manages London Underground, buses, DLR, River Services, Victoria Coach Station, and London Transport Museum. See website for journey planner, maps, and travel information.

Taxis: The listings below refer to licensed taxicabs ("black cabs"). All operate throughout London and charge the same rates.

Taxi One-Number (☎0818 718 710; www.onenumbertaxis.com). Licensed taxi cabs from 1 of the 6 radio taxi circuits. Wheelchair-accessible.

Computer Cab (payment by credit card ☎7432 1432, cash 7908 0207; www.computercab.co.uk).

Dial-a-Cab (payment by credit card ☎7426 3420, cash 7253 5000; www.dialacab.co.uk).

Minicabs: Private companies, not under Transport for London regulations. See p. 40 for a warning on minicabs.

Lady Cabs (☎7254 3501). Providing **female drivers,** but not limited to women passengers. Pickup in North London only. Open M-F 8am-10pm, Sa 9am-10pm, Su 10am-10pm.

Liberty Cars, 330 Old St. (☎0800 600 006; www.liberty-cars.com). Licensed by Public Carriage Office and Transport for London. Shoreditch-based cab service catering to **gays and lesbians.** 24hr. pickup anywhere in London. Central London to airports: Heathrow £35, Gatwick/Stansted/Luton £50; £10 more from airport to central London.

London Radio Cars (☎8905 0000 or 8204 4444). Large, well-run service with 24hr. pickup anywhere in London. To central London from airports: Heathrow £17, Gatwick £43, Luton £22, Stansted £36.

LOCAL SERVICES

CHEMISTS/PHARMACIES

Most chemists keep standard store hours (M-Sa 9:30am-5:30pm); one "duty" chemist in each neighborhood will also open on Sunday, though hours may be limited. Late-night and 24hr. pharmacies are extremely rare.

Bliss, 5-6 Marble Arch (☎7723 6116). ✆Marble Arch. Open daily 9am-midnight.

Zafash Pharmacy, 233 Old Brompton Rd. (☎7373 2798). ✆Earl's Court. Open 24hr. AmEx/MC/V.

HAIRCUTS FOR POCKET CHANGE. If your coif (and your wallet) have seen better days, head to the Toni & Guy Academy (☎7836 0606) or the Vidal Sassoon School (☎7318 5205) to lend your head for training purposes. A decent cut could cost as little as £5. Then again, so could a multi-colored mullet. It's wise to be specific.

LEGAL RESOURCES

Embassies may provide legal advice and services to foreign citizens under arrest (see **Essentials,** p. 17)

Citizen's Advice Bureaux (www.citizensadvice.org.uk). Independent nationwide network of offices gives free advice on legal and consumer issues. London bureaus include Holborn Library, 32-38 Theobalds Rd. (☎0845 120 2965; ✆Holborn); Town Hall, Kings Rd. (☎0870 122 2313; ✆South Kensington). Opening hours limited, appointments often necessary; call ahead.

Community Legal Service (☎0845 345 4345; www.clsdirect.org.uk). Government-run online advice and directory of legal advisors.

Release, 388 Old St. (☎7729 9904, helpline 0845 4500 215; www.release.org.uk). ✆Old St. Advice and information on drugs, law, and human rights.

LIBRARIES

Visitors are allowed to use libraries for reference but will not be able to borrow materials. Below is a select list for those in Westminster borough; see www.westminster.gov.uk/libraries for a complete list. Contact ☎7641 1300 for all libraries.

Charing Cross, 4 Charing Cross Rd. ✆Charing Cross. Open M 9:30am-8pm, Tu and Th-F 9:30am-7pm, W 10am-7pm, Sa 10:30am-2pm, Su 11am-5pm.

Maida Vale, Sutherland Ave. ✆Warwick Ave. or Maida Vale. Open M 9:30am-8pm, Tu and Th-F 9:30am-7pm, W 10am-7pm, Sa 9:30am-5pm.

Marylebone, 109-117 Marylebone Rd. ✆Marylebone or Baker St. Open M-Tu and Th-F 9:30am-8pm, W 10am-8pm, Sa 9:30am-5pm, Su 1:30-5pm.

Mayfair, 25 South Audley St. ✆Green Park. Open M-F 11am-7pm, Sa 10:30am-2pm.

Paddington, Porchester Rd. ✆Royal Oak or Bayswater. Open M and Th-F 9:30am-10pm, Tu 9:30am-9pm, W 10am-9pm, Sa 9:30am-5pm, Su 11am-5pm.

Pimlico, Rampayne St. ✆Pimlico. Open M 9:30am-8pm, Tu and Th-F 9:30am-7pm, W 10am-7pm, Sa 9:30am-5pm, Su 1:30-5pm.

Victoria, 160 Buckingham Palace Rd. ✆Victoria. Open M 9:30am-8pm, Tu and Th-F 9:30am-7pm, W 10am-7pm, Sa 9:30am-5pm.

LOST PROPERTY

Transport for London Lost Property Office, 200 Baker St., NW1 5RZ (☎08453 309 882; www.tfl.gov.uk/contact/871.aspx). ✆Baker St. Items left on London Underground, buses, DLR, Victoria Coach Station, and London taxis forwarded to the above address. Call first. Web queries also available at www.tfl.gov.uk/tfl/contact/lostproperty/default.asp. Open M-F 8:30am-4pm.

SUPERMARKETS

Marks and Spencer, flagship at 458 Oxford St. (Oxford St. store ☎7935 7954, corporate 08453 021 234; www.marksandspencer.com). ✆Marble Arch. Other locations include:

PRACTICAL INFO

JUST SAY OM...

Too many gray London days or silent Tube rides could put even Richard Simmons in a rut. Don't despair! The next time big-city woes have got you down, take comfort in knowing that plenty of Londoners are willing and able to turn your bad mood into a business opportunity. You'll have your inner calm back in no time flat with a visit to one of these heavenly holistic hotspots.

Perfect your downward dog at **Triyoga** with some of Europe's top instructors (and more than a few celebrities). They offer workshops in many different disciplines and methods. Yoga and pilates classes start at around £9, and a half-price "community" yoga class is offered daily.

The **Sanctuary Day Spa** offers a different type of relax and escapism. One of their most popular treatments is what is referred to as "dry flotation," in which you are completely dry but floating in a warm water capsule, simultaneously soothed by aromatherapy oils and relaxing music (£39). Several types of relaxing and invigorating massages (£39-65) are also offered.

Triyoga: 6 Erskine Rd. ☎ 7483 3344; www.triyoga.co.uk. ⊖Chalk Farm. Smaller location at 2 Neal's Yard; ⊖Covent Garden. Open M-F 7:15am-5:30pm. Sanctuary: (12 Floral St. ☎0770 3350; www.thesanctuary.co.uk. ⊖Covent Garden.)

Oxford St. Pantheon, 173 Oxford St. (☎7437 7722; ⊖Oxford Circus), and 107-115 Long Acre (☎7240 9549; ⊖Covent Garden). Hundreds of locations around London, selling food and clothing. AmEx/MC/V.

Sainsbury's (☎08453 012 020; www.sainsburys.co.uk). 2 central locations: 3-11 Southampton St. (⊖Covent Garden) and 113-117 Oxford St. (⊖Oxford Circus). Traditionally a supermarket, but some of the larger stores also have furniture, clothes, toys, and even car insurance. Some open 24hr. MC/V.

Tesco (☎08457 225 533; www.tesco.com). 100s of locations throughout London. Tesco Express offers foods and limited groceries; Tesco Metro caters to urban areas; and behemoth Tesco Superstores are a maze of groceries and non-food items. Basic budget food that won't thrill but will satisfy. Some open 24hr. MC/V.

RECREATIONAL ACTIVITIES

HEALTH AND FITNESS

London has hundreds of fitness clubs. Search Yellow Pages under "Health Clubs and Fitness" or online.

Barbican YMCA, 2 Fann St. (☎7628 0697). ⊖Barbican. Weights, Nautilus machines, treadmills, and bikes. Non-members £5 per session. Membership £55 per year, £27 for 3 months, plus £3.50 per use. Open M-F 7am-9:30pm, Sa-Su 10am-6pm.

Central YMCA Club, 112 Great Russell St. (☎7343 1700). ⊖Tottenham Court Rd. This may be the world's oldest YMCA, but you'll never guess from this club's modern interior and state-of-the-art exercise equipment. Facilities include 25m pool, cardio machines, weights, and badminton courts. Extensive schedule of exercise classes. Day pass £10, 1-week pass £45. 3-month short-term memberships available.

Chelsea Sports Centre, Chelsea Manor St. (☎7352 6985). ⊖Sloane Sq. or South Kensington. Pool, gym, tennis, ping pong, volleyball, basketball, football, and badminton. Numerous yoga, pilates, and body conditioning classes. £3 drop-in pool use; £4.20 aerobic classes; £5.30 yoga and pilates classes; 1hr. intro course (non-members £20) required for use of weights and cardio machines. Call for other prices. Open M-F 6:30am-10pm, Sa 8am-8pm, Su and holidays 8am-10pm.

Fitness First (☎01202 845 125; www.fitnessfirst.co.uk). The largest health club operator in the UK and Europe, with over 40 locations in London, including Bloomsbury (☎7833 1887), Liverpool St. (☎7247 5511), and Shepherd's Bush (☎8743 4444). Offers NUS student and budget plans with 3-month min. membership.

Kensington Leisure Centre, Walmer Rd. (☎ 7727 9747). ⊖Ladbroke Grove. In Notting Hill, despite the name. Pool, sauna, weights, badminton, and squash, plus aerobics, self-defense, and scuba-diving classes. Open M-F 6:30am-10pm, Sa-Su 8am-8pm.

Paris Gym, 73 Goding St. (☎ 7735 8989; www.parisgym.com). ⊖Vauxhall. The only exclusively gay men's gym in the city. 1 day £7, 1 week £22, 1 month £55. Open M-F 7am-11pm, Sa 10am-10pm, Su 10am-8pm.

Soho Gyms (☎ 7284 3433; www.sohogyms.com). Fitness center chain with locations in Bayswater, Camden Town, Clapham Common, Covent Garden, and Earl's Court. 1-month membership from £55. No joining fees or contracts.

DANCE

DanceWorks, 16 Balderton St. (☎ 7629 6183; www.danceworks.net), in **Mayfair.** ⊖Bond St. 168 dance, fitness, martial arts and yoga classes each week. £4-12 per class, plus day membership fee (£2-5). Open M-F 8:30am-10pm, Sa-Su 9am-6pm.

Laban Centre for Dance, Creekside (☎ 8691 8600; www.laban.org), in **East London.** DLR: Cutty Sark. Adult evening classes in African dance, ballet, contemporary, jazz, pilates, and yoga. Call or check website for availability and schedules. Open Tu-Th 6:30-8pm, Sa 9am-12:15pm.

Marylebone Dance Studio, 12 Lisson Grove (☎ 7258 0767; www.m-dancestudio.co.uk), in **Marylebone.** ⊖Marylebone. Classes in ballet, contemporary, Bollywood, capoeira, "Streetz," and Pilates. £6-10 per class. Open M 6:30am-10pm, Tu 5am-9pm, W and F 6am-8:30pm, Th 6:30am-9pm, Sa 9am-5:15pm, Su 10:30am-4:30pm.

Pineapple Dance Studio, 7 Langley St. (☎ 7836 4004; www.pineapple.uk.com), in **Covent Garden.** ⊖Covent Garden or Leicester Sq. Classes in ballet, hip hop, jazz, martial arts, pilates, pole dancing, tap, yoga, and more. £5-8 per class, plus day membership fee (£2-4). Open M-F 9am-10pm, Sa 9am-6:30pm, Su 10am-6pm.

Triyoga, 6 Erskine Road (☎ 7483 3344; www.triyoga.co.uk), in **North London.** ⊖Chalk Farm. Smaller location at 2 Neal's Yard, in **Covent Garden** (⊖Covent Garden). One of the most well-known and well-respected yoga and pilates studios in Europe, with over 100 classes per week. Everything from "Saturday Night Yoga Fever" to prenatal yoga. Community yoga and pilates start at just £8.50 per visit. Regular classes £12. Students receive up to 20% off all off-peak classes. Daily community class at 50% off regular price. Mats available for use.

SWIMMING

Parliament Hill, Hampstead Heath (p. 182), in **North London.**

Serpentine Lido, Hyde Park (p. 185), in **Kensington and Earl's Court.**

TENNIS

Holland Park (sports reception ☎ 7361 3003; www.quadronservices.co.uk), in **Kensington and Earl's Court.** ⊖Kensington High St. Courts toward the southern end of the park. Tennis classes, along with female-only and mixed leagues. Free.

Regent's Park Tennis Centre (☎ 7262 3474), in **Marylebone.** ⊖Regent's Park. On the southeast side of the park. Courts open year-round. 1hr. non-member court use £7-9; 1 day advance reservations recommended.

OTHER

Horseback Riding, Hyde Park Stables (☎ 7723 2813; www.hydeparkstables.com), in **Kensington and Earl's Court.** ⊖Lancaster Gate. Group, semi-private, and private lessons for children and adults. Open M-F 7:15am-5pm, Sa-Su 9am-5pm. £42-70 per hr.

PRACTICAL INFO

Ice Skating, Somerset House, Strand (www.somerset-house.org.uk/icerink), in **Holborn.** ⊖Charing Cross or Temple. Outdoors courtyard rink. Daytime (10am-5:15pm) £9.50, evening (from 6:30pm) £11, children under 13 £6. Open daily Dec.-Jan. 10am-10pm.

EMERGENCY AND COMMUNICATIONS

CRISIS LINES

NHS Direct (☎0845 4647; www.nhsdirect.nhs.uk). Confidential nurse advice and health info. Open 24hr.

Rights of Women (legal advice ☎7251 6577, sexual violence legal advice 7251 8887; www.rightsofwomen.org.uk). Confidential advice on divorce and relationship breakdown, children and contact issues, domestic violence, sexual violence, discrimination, and lesbian parenting. Open Tu-Th 2-4pm and 7-9pm, F noon-2pm.

Samaritans (☎0845 790 9090, central London branch ☎7734 2800; www.samaritans.org/~cls). Emotional support for depression and those contemplating suicide. Open 24hr.

Victim Support (☎0845 303 0900; www.victimsupportline.org.uk). Emotional help and legal advice for crime victims. Open M-F 9am-9pm, Sa-Su 9am-7pm.

EMERGENCY SERVICES

In an emergency, dial ☎999 from any land phone or ☎112 from a mobile phone.

City of London Police, 37 Wood St. (☎7601 2222; www.cityoflondon.police.uk). ⊖Barbican. Jurisdiction only over the City of London.

Metropolitan Police, New Scotland Yard, Broadway (see website for division phone numbers; www.met.police.uk). ⊖Victoria. There is at least 1 police station in each of the 32 boroughs open 24hr. (☎7230 1212 to find the nearest station.)

Belgravia, 202-206 Buckingham Palace Rd. (☎7730 1212). ⊖Victoria. Open daily 7am-10pm.

Brixton, 367 Brixton Rd. (☎7326 1212). ⊖Brixton. Open 24hr.

Charing Cross, Agar St. (☎7240 1212). ⊖Charing Cross. Open 24hr.

Chelsea, 2 Lucan Pl. (☎7376 1212). ⊖South Kensington. Open 24hr.

Holborn, 10 Lambs Conduit St. (☎7404 1212). ⊖Holborn. Open 24hr.

Islington, 2 Tolpuddle St. (☎7704 1212). ⊖Angel. Open 24hr.

Kensington, 72-74 Earl's Ct. Rd. (☎7376 1212). ⊖High St. Kensington. Open 24hr.

Marylebone, 1-9 Seymour St. (☎7486 1212). ⊖Marble Arch. Open 24hr.

Notting Hill, 99-101 Ladbroke Grove (☎7221 1212). ⊖Holland Park. Open 24hr.

INTERNET ACCESS

Independent cyber cafes are on almost every business street in London. If you're paying more than £2 per hr., you're paying too much.

easyInternet cafes (☎7241 9000; www.easyeverything.com). 8 Greater London locations, including: 112-114 Camden High St. (⊖Camden Town); 9-16 Tottenham Court Rd. (⊖Tottenham Court Rd.); 456/459 Strand (⊖Charing Cross); 358 Oxford St. (⊖Bond St.); 160-166 Kensington High St. (⊖High St. Kensington). Prices vary with demand, from £1 per 15min. during busy times; usually around £1.60 per hr. Min. 50p-£1. Hours vary by store.

MEDICAL SERVICES

Hospitals: For urgent care, go to one of the 24hr. **Accident and Emergency** departments listed below. You may need to pay for prescriptions. For non-urgent care, or to see a specialist, you will need a referral from a primary-care doctor.

Charing Cross Hospital, Fulham Palace Rd. (main reception ☎8846 1234 or 8383 0088), entrance on St. Dunstan's Rd. ⊖Hammersmith, or Bus #220 or 295. No medical advice given over phone.

Chelsea and Westminster Hospital, 369 Fulham Rd. (main reception ☎8746 8000). ⊖South Kensington, then Bus #14 or 414; or Bus #C3, 11, 22, 211, 295, 328.

Royal Free, Pond St. (☎7794 0500). ⊖Belsize Park or Rail: Hampstead Heath.

St. Mary's, Praed St. (☎7886 6666). ⊖Paddington or Edgware.

St. Thomas's, Lambeth Palace Rd. (☎7188 7188). ⊖Waterloo.

University College London Hospital, Accident and Emergency Department at Cecil Fleming House on Grafton Way (☎0845 155 500). ⊖Warren St. or Euston Sq.

Whittington, Magdala Avenue (☎7272 3070). ⊖Archway.

Dental Care:

Dental Accident and Emergency, Guy's Hospital, 23 fl., Guy's Tower, St. Thomas St. (☎7188 7188 or 7188 9282). ⊖London Bridge. Adults treated until patient quota is reached (usually M-F 9-11am), children M-F 9am-noon and 2-4pm. Sa-Su and holidays use paying services at Emergency Dental Clinic (ground fl.). Open Sa-Su and holidays 9am-6pm.

24hr. Emergency Dental Treatment, 78 Dalling Rd., Hammersmith or 102 Baker St. (☎8748 9365).

Clinics:

Ambrose King Centre, Royal London Hospital, Whitechapel Rd. (☎7377 7306). ⊖Whitechapel. Provides services and advice on STIs, HIV testing and counseling, emergency contraception, sexual assault, and family planning for persons under age 25. Hepatitis clinic for men who have sex with men Th 6-8pm; no appointment necessary. Open M and Th 8:30am-4pm, Tu 8:30am-3pm and 4pm-6pm, W 11:30am-4pm, F 8:30am-3pm.

Jefferiss Centre for Sexual Health, St. Mary's Hospital, Praed St. (☎7886 1697; www.st-marys.nhs.uk). ⊖Paddington. HIV testing. Sexual health screening and treatment. Open for walk-ins M-Tu and Th 8:45am-6:15pm, W 11:45am-6:15pm, F 8:45am-1:15pm.

The Well Women Centre, Marie Stopes House, 108 Whitfield St. (☎08453 008 090; www.mari-estopes.org.uk). ⊖Warren St. Offers advice on and performs abortion, contraception, and health screening.

West London Center for Sexual Health, Charing Cross Hospital, Fulham Palace Rd. (appointments ☎0845 811 6699, info 8846 1579). ⊖Baron's Court or Hammersmith. NHS-run sexual and women's health clinic. By appointment only. Appointments fill up 3-7 days in advance. Non-UK citizens seen directly as long as they call for an appointment. Open M-Tu and Th 9am-5pm, W 1-7pm, F 9am-noon. Tu clinic 5:30-7:30pm for men who have sex with men; W clinic 1:30-7pm for women who have sex with women; walk-in clinic for patients under 20 M and Th 3-5pm, last patient accepted at 4:30pm.

POSTAL SERVICES

There are hundreds of post offices throughout London. To find the one closest to you, call ☎08457 223 344 or see www.postoffice.co.uk. Most branches are open Monday through Friday 9am-6pm.

Bloomsbury, 54-56 Great Portland St. ⊖Great Portland St. Open M and W-F 9am-6pm, Tu 9:30am-6pm, Sa 9am-12:30pm.

Marylebone, 111 Baker St. ⊖Baker St. Open M and W-F 9am-5:30pm, Tu 9:30am-5:30pm, Sa 9am-12:30pm.

Mayfair, 43-44 Albermarle St. ⊖Green Park. Open M and W-F 9am-6pm, Tu 9:30am-6pm.

Soho, 1-5 Poland St. ⊖Oxford Circus. Open M and W-F 9am-6pm, Tu 9:30am-6pm, Sa 9am-12:30pm.

Trafalgar Square, 24-28 William IV St. ⊖Charing Cross. Open M and W-F 8:30am-6:30pm, Tu 9:15am-6:30pm, Sa 9am-5:30pm.

ACCOMMODATIONS

London's short-term living and real estate alike are notoriously expensive. However, with a little bit of searching and a lot of planning, it is possible to find rooms that are both comfortable and affordable—although you will usually be somewhat separated from the heart of the action. Bloomsbury is by far the budget traveler's best option. In a close second, Kensington and Earl's Court have a number of mid-range, high-quality digs, while Bayswater has less expensive options that are also a step down in quality. Below are some starting points for accommodations across a variety of price ranges and comfort levels. Specific listings appear later in the chapter organized by neighborhood.

HOSTELS

Many hostels are laid out dorm-style, often with large single-sex rooms and bunk beds, although private rooms that sleep two to four are becoming more common. While hostels often offer a number of amenities—kitchens, bike or moped rentals, storage areas, transportation to airports, breakfast and other meals, laundry facilities, and Internet access—there can be drawbacks: some hostels close during certain daytime "lockout" hours, have a curfew, don't accept reservations, impose a maximum stay, or, less frequently, require that you do chores. In London, a dorm bed in a hostel will average around £18 and a private room around £30-40.

A HOSTELER'S BILL OF RIGHTS. There are certain standard features that we do not include in our hostel listings. Unless we state otherwise, you can expect that every hostel has no lockout, no curfew, a kitchen, free hot showers, some system of secure luggage storage, and no key deposit.

HOSTELLING INTERNATIONAL

Joining the youth hostel association in your own country automatically grants you membership privileges in **Hostelling International (HI)**, a federation of national hosteling associations. Non-HI members may be allowed to stay in some hostels, but will have to pay extra to do so. HI hostels are scattered throughout London and are typically less expensive than private hostels. HI's umbrella organization's website (www.hihostels.com) lists the web addresses and phone numbers of all national associations. Other comprehensive hosteling websites include www.hostels.com and www.hostelplanet.com.

Most HI hostels also honor **guest memberships**—you'll get a blank card with space for six validation stamps. Each night you'll pay a nonmember supplement (one-sixth the membership fee) and earn one guest stamp; get six stamps and you're a member. A new membership benefit is the **FreeNites** program, which allows hostelers to gain points toward free rooms. Most student travel agencies (see p. 30) sell HI cards.

BOOKING HOSTELS ONLINE. One of the easiest ways to ensure you've got a bed for the night is by reserving online. Click to the **Hostelworld** booking engine through **www.letsgo.com,** and you'll have access to bargain accommodations from Argentina to Zimbabwe with no added commission.

BED AND BREAKFASTS (B&BS)

For a cozy alternative to impersonal hotel rooms, B&Bs (private homes with rooms available to travelers) range from the acceptable to the sublime. B&B owners sometimes go out of their way to be accommodating, giving personalized tours or offering home-cooked meals. Some B&Bs, however, do not provide private bathrooms, and most do not provide phones. London also offers B&B-style accommodations—hotels that offer much of the intimacy of privately owned B&Bs (Bloomsbury has many of these).

The British tourist boards operate a B&B **rating system,** using a scale of one to five diamonds. Rated accommodations are part of the tourist board's booking system, but it costs money to be rated and some perfectly good B&Bs choose not to participate.

Any number of websites provide listings for B&Bs; check out **Bed & Breakfast Inns Online** (www.bbonline.com), **InnFinder** (www.inncrawler.com), **InnSite** (www.innsite.com), **BedandBreakfast.com** (www.bedandbreakfast.com), or **Pamela Lanier's Bed & Breakfast Guide Online** (www.lanierbb.com).

OTHER TYPES OF ACCOMMODATIONS

YMCAS AND YWCAS

Young Men's Christian Association (YMCA) and **Young Women's Christian Association (YWCA)** lodgings are usually cheaper than a hotel but more expensive than a hostel. Not all locations offer lodging. Many YMCAs accept women and families; some will not lodge those under 18 without parental permission.

World Alliance of YMCAs, 12 Clos Belmont, 1208 Geneva, Switzerland (☎+41 22 849 5100; www.ymca.int). Maintains listings of Ys worldwide. 9 listings in London, many of which offer accommodations.

HOTELS, GUESTHOUSES, AND PENSIONS

Hotel singles in London cost about £44 (US$80) per night, doubles £61 (US$110). You'll typically share a hall bathroom; a private bathroom will cost extra, as may hot showers. Some hotels offer "full pension" (all meals) and "half pension" (no lunch). Smaller **guesthouses** and **pensions** are often cheaper than hotels. If you make **reservations** in writing, indicate your night of arrival and the number of nights you plan to stay. The hotel will send you a confirmation and may request payment for the first night. It is often easiest to make reservations over the phone or on the Internet with a credit card.

UNIVERSITY DORMS

Many colleges and universities open their residence halls to travelers when school is not in session; some do so even during term time. Getting a room may take a couple of phone calls and require advanced planning, but rates tend to be low, and many offer free local calls and Internet access.

City University Finsbury Residences, see p. 107.

IES Chelsea Pointe, see p. 116.

King's College Conference and Vacation Bureau (☎7848 1700; www.kcl.ac.uk). Accommodations in the halls of King's College, mostly located on the South Bank. Rooms available July to mid-Sept.

London School of Economics (☎7955 7575; www.lse.ac.uk/collections/vacations). Central information site for 6 halls throughout central London. Most halls have rooms available July to mid-Sept.; some available year-round.See p. p. 108 for information on their largest hall, **the LSE Bankside House.**

Rosebery Hall, see p. p. 107.

University College London Residential Services (www.ucl.ac.uk/residences). Website contains description and contact information for 8 halls, mostly around Bloomsbury. Rooms available Apr. and mid-June to mid-Sept.

University of London Accommodations Office, Senate House, Room B, Malet St. (☎7862 8880; www.housing.lon.ac.uk). ⊖Russell Sq. Keeps a list of summer room and apartment vacancies. See "Hall Vacation List" on website for list of residence halls to contact directly. In-person services available only during vacations to students with valid IDs. Calls answered M and W-F 10am-5pm, Tu 11am-5pm.

University of Westminster (☎7911 5000; www.wmin.ac.uk/comserv). 7 halls throughout central London. Rooms available mid-June to mid-Sept. Singles from £20. See p. p. 112.

HOME EXCHANGES AND HOSPITALITY CLUBS

Home exchange offers the traveler various types of homes (houses, apartments, condominiums, villas, even castles in some cases), plus the opportunity to live like a native and cut down on accommodation fees. For more information, contact HomeExchange.com, P.O. Box 787, Hermosa Beach, CA 90254, USA (☎800-877-8723; www.homeexchange.com), or Intervac International Home Exchange (www.intervac.com).

Hospitality clubs link their members with individuals or families abroad who are willing to host travelers for free or for a small fee to promote cultural exchange and general good karma. In exchange, members usually must be willing to host travelers in their own homes; a small membership fee may also be required. **GlobalFreeloaders.com** (www.globalfreeloaders.com) and **The Hospitality Club** (www.hospitalityclub.org) are good places to start. **Servas** (www.servas.org) is a more formal, established peace-based organization, and requires a fee and an interview to join. An Internet search will find many similar organizations, some of which cater to special interests (e.g., women, GLBT travelers, or members of certain professions). As always, use common sense when planning to stay with someone you do not know.

LONG-TERM ACCOMMODATIONS

Travelers planning to stay in London for extended periods of time may find it most cost-effective to rent a **flat.** Rents range drastically, depending on where you are in the city (central London is much more expensive than North, South, East, and West London). When deciding how much you can afford, don't forget to figure in **transportation costs.** If you work in central London but live in the suburbs, transportation could add £30-50 to your monthly expenses. The best way to find a flat is to search the web: **Gum Tree** (www.gumtree.com), **craigslist** (www.london.craigslist.org), **Move Flat** (www.moveflat.com), **Loot** (www.loot.com; also available in print). **UK Flatshare** (www.flatshare.com/uk-flat-share) has an extensive listing of available apartments and rooms for sublet.

Local taxes are a factor that shouldn't be ignored when choosing a place to live. In England, **council tax** is levied on each "dwelling," with the amount owed being set by the local council and dependent on the market price of the dwelling. In rented flats the tenant is generally liable to pay the tax, though if the landlord lives on the premises, he or she is normally liable. If everyone in the dwelling is a full-time student or earns less than a certain amount, it may be exempt from council tax; this exemption must be applied for. If your dwelling is liable for council tax, expect to pay around £600 per year for a small flat.

All tenants have certain **rights.** For example, the landlord has certain responsibilities for keeping the accommodation in habitable condition and paying for necessary repairs; it's also illegal for landlords to threaten or harass tenants. Note that terms set out in the **tenancy agreement** cannot override rights laid out by law. Oral agreements have the force of law but are hard to enforce; it's best to get a signed document.

ACCOMMODATION AGENCIES

Accommodation Outlet, 32 Old Compton St. (☎7287 4244; www.outlet.co.uk). ⊖Piccadilly Circus or Leicester Sq. Organizes short- and long-term vacation accommodations in Soho and Covent Garden. Double bedrooms from £40, with private bath £70. Studio apartments from £75 per night, 1-bedroom from £100, 2-bedroom from £120, 3-bedroom from £150. Office open M-F 10am-6pm, Sa noon-5pm. Up to 30% discount for long stays. AmEx/MC/V.

ACCOMMODATIONS BY PRICE

UNDER £25 (PRICE ICON ❶)	
▨Ashlee House(110)	BLOOM
▨The Generator(109)	BLOOM
Hyde Park Hostel(113)	BAY
International Student House(112)	M/RP
Pickwick Hall Int'l Backpackers(111)	BLOOM
Quest Hostel(113)	BAY
St. Christopher's Inn(111)(117)	NL, WL
YHA Earl's Court(115)	KEN/EC
▨YHA Holland House(114)	KEN/EC
▨YHA Oxford Street(109)	WEND

£25-40 (PRICE ICON ❷)	
Astor's Museum Hostel(110)	BLOOM
Carr-Saunders Hall(111)	BLOOM
▨City University Finsbury (107)	CLERK
Commonwealth Hall(111)	BLOOM
Euro Hotel(117)	WL
Kensington Gardens Hotel(113)	BAY
LSE Bankside House(108)	SB
Rosebery Hall(107)	CLERK
University of Westminster Halls(112)	M/RP
Windsor Guest House(117)	WL
YHA St. Pancras International(110)	BLOOM

£41-55 (PRICE ICON ❸)	
Admiral Hotel(113)	BAY
Alexander Hotel(109)	WEMIN
Balmoral House Hotel(113)	BAY
Dalmacia Hotel(117)	WL
easyHotel(109)	WEMIN

Garden Court Hotel(113)	BAY
▨The Gate Hotel(114)	NH
▨George Hotel(110)	BLOOM
Georgian House Hotel(108)	WEMIN
Grenville House Hotel(107)	HOL
Guilford House Hotel(107)	HOL
Hotel Orlando(117)	WL
IES Chelsea Pointe(116)	CHEL
▨Kandara Guesthouse(111)	NL
The Langland Hotel(110)	BLOOM
▨Luna Simone Hotel(108)	WEMIN
Melbourne House(108)	WEMIN
▨Morgan House(116)	K/B
Mowbray Court Hotel(115)	KEN/EC
▨Oxford Hotel(115)	KEN/EC
Philbeach Hotel(115)	KEN/EC
▨Star Hotel(116)	WL
▨Vicarage Hotel(114)	KEN/EC
Westminster House Hotel(116)	K/B

£56-75 (PRICE ICON ❹)	
Hampstead Village Guest House(112)	NL
Hart House Hotel(112)	M/RP
James House Hotel(116)	K/B
▨Jenkins Hotel(110)	BLOOM
Lincoln House Hotel(112)	M/RP
▨Portobello Gold Rooms(114)	NH
Thanet Hotel(110)	BLOOM

OVER £75 (PRICE ICON ❺)	
Amsterdam Hotel(115)	KEN/EC

NEIGHBORHOOD ABBREVIATIONS: BAY Bayswater **BLOOM** Bloomsbury **CHEL** Chelsea **CITY** The City of London **CLERK** Clerkenwell **HOL** Holborn **KEN/EC** Kensington and Earl's Court **K/B** Knightsbridge and Belgravia **M/RP** Marylebone and Regent's Park **NH** Notting Hill **SB** The South Bank **WEND** The West End **WEMIN** Westminster **NL** North London **SL** South London **EL** East London **WL** West London

ACCOMMODATIONS

ACCOMMODATIONS BY NEIGHBORHOOD

CLERKENWELL

Clerkenwell boasts two smashing bargains in its inexpensive university dormitories (only open during the summer and Christmas holidays). For affordable hotels and B&Bs, look to nearby Bloomsbury and the King's Cross area.

SEE MAP, p. 364

■ **City University Finsbury Residences,** 15 Bastwick St. (☎7040 8811; www.city.ac.uk/ems/accomm/fins.html). ⊖Barbican. Night Bus #N35 and N55 stop at the corner of Old St. and Goswell Rd. A 1970s tower block is simple but sufficient for a budget stay in central London. The rooms are within walking distance of City sights, Islington restaurants, and Clerkenwell nightlife. Singles in the main building have shared shower, toilet, kitchen access, and a laundry room. Early reservations recommended. Open early June to early Sept. Wheelchair-accessible. Singles £21. MC/V. ❷

Rosebery Hall, 90 Rosebery Ave. (☎7955 7575; www.lse.ac.uk/collections/vacations). ⊖Angel. Night Bus #N19, N38, 341. Exit left from the Tube, cross the road, and take the 2nd right on Rosebery Ave. Ring bell to enter. A quick walk from Exmouth Market, the 2 LSE student residence buildings surround a sunken garden. Rooms in the newer block are more spacious, with wheelchair-accessible baths. Pool tables in the common rooms. TV lounge, laundry, and bar. Online request form available. Open mid-Aug. to Sept. and mid-Dec. to early Jan. Singles from £31; doubles £50, with bath £60; triples £62. ❷

HOLBORN

Located near all the major sights in the City of London, Holborn's location is ideal, but the few rooms that are available are likely to fill up fast.

SEE MAP, p. 364

Guilford House Hotel, 6 Guilford St. (☎7430 2504; www.guilfordhotel.co.uk). ⊖Russell Sq. or Chancery Ln. Night Bus #N19, N35, N38, N43, N55, N243 all stop at the corner of Gray's Inn Rd. and Theobald's Rd. Situated near the sights of Holborn and the City, this mid-range hotel offers immaculate quarters and a number of welcome conveniences. Rooms all come with small shower, kettle, TV, hair dryer, and telephone. Continental breakfast included. Reception 24hr. Check-in after noon. Check-out 11am. Reserve 2 weeks in advance for June-Aug. 36hr. cancellation policy. Singles £54; doubles £69; triples £89; quads £99; family room £110. Pay on arrival. AmEx/MC/V. ❸

Grenville House Hotel, 4 Guilford St. (☎7430 2504; www.grenvillehotel.co.uk). ⊖Russell Sq. or Chancery Ln. Night Bus #N19, N35, N38, N43, N55, N243 all stop at the corner of Gray's Inn Rd. and Theobald's Rd. Affiliated with the Guilford House, its next-door neighbor offers the same amenities in equally equipped, well-priced rooms. Rooms all come with small shower, kettle, TV, hair dryer, and telephone. Continental breakfast included. Reception 24hr. Check-in after noon. Check-out 11am. Reserve 2 weeks in advance for June-Aug. 36hr. cancellation policy. Singles £54; doubles £69; triples £89; quads £99; family room £110. Pay on arrival. AmEx/MC/V. ❸

ACCOMMODATIONS

THE SOUTH BANK

What it lacks in bar-hopping nightlife the South Bank makes up for in accessibility; the lively central neighborhoods of the City, West End, and Westminster are all a stone's throw away, just across a bridge.

SEE MAP, pp. 370-371

LSE Bankside House, 24 Sumner St. (☎7107 5750; www.lse.ac.uk/vacations). ⊖Southwark or London Bridge. Night Bus #N381, N343. The largest of the London School of Economics's student halls, facing the Tate Modern. 3 wings sleep over 800 and offer more privacy than the average dorm. Facilities include elevator, laundry, TV lounge, game room, restaurant, and bar. English breakfast £3.50. Wheelchair-accessible. Open from the last week of June to mid-Sept. Singles (shared bath between 2 rooms) £38, with private bath £48; doubles with bath £67; triples with bath £86; quads with bath £95. MC/V. ❷

WESTMINSTER

Pimlico, south of Victoria Station, is a grid-like district of late Georgian and early Victorian terraces housing dozens of cream-colored B&Bs. Very few have elevators, so if stairs are a problem, be sure to request a ground-floor room. Quiet and more residential, Pimlico does not compare to Bayswater or Bloomsbury for a social backpacking atmosphere. While ultra-residential Pimlico itself has little to offer the visitor,

SEE MAP, p. 368

Westminster Abbey, Parliament, the Tate Britain, and Buckingham Palace are close by, and Victoria's transportation links put the rest of London within easy reach.

■ **Luna Simone Hotel,** 47-49 Belgrave Rd. (☎7834 5897; www.lunasimonehotel.com). ⊖Victoria or Pimlico. Night Bus #N2, 24, N36. Sparkling and spacious showers, modern decor, and a staff that takes a keen interest in its guests make this hotel the pick of the neighborhood. Large yellow rooms with desk, TV, phone, kettle, and hair dryer. Singles without bath are cramped. Full English breakfast included. Free Internet access. Reserve at least 2 weeks in advance. 48hr. cancellation policy £10; if less than 48hr. notice 1 night's charge. Singles £40, with bath £60; doubles with bath £90; triples with bath £110; quads with bath £130. 10-20% discount in low season. MC/V. ❸

Melbourne House, 79 Belgrave Rd. (☎7828 3516; www.melbournehousehotel.co.uk). ⊖Pimlico. Night Bus #N2, 24, N36. This newly renovated hotel offers clean and basic rooms in a quiet atmosphere. For a little more spice, plan in advance and reserve the basement double, complete with spacious bathtub for 2. Singles, doubles, triples with bath (3 twin beds), and 2-room quads (1 double bed and 2 twins). Continental breakfast included. Free Internet access. Reception 7am-midnight. Reserve at least 2 weeks in advance; 48hr. cancellation policy. Singles £39, with bath £80; doubles with bath £90; triples with bath £115; quad with bath £130. Substantial discounts for week-long stays or for large groups. MC/V. ❸

Georgian House Hotel, 35-39 St. George's Dr. (☎7834 1438; www.georgianhouse-hotel.co.uk). ⊖Victoria. Night Bus #N2, N11, 24, N36. This historic hotel has many of the amenities you might expect from somewhere fancier. All rooms have TV, phone, hair dryer, and kettle. Seven "basic" rooms on the 4th fl. may lack private bathrooms, but the rock-bottom prices more than make up for it. English breakfast included. Internet access. Concierge service. Reserve 1 month in advance for summer months, Sa-Su, and student rooms. Basic singles £30; doubles £45; triples £68; quads £79. Singles £50/with bath £70; doubles £70/99; triples £90/129; quads £105/140. Sale rates (often in peak travel season) are £15-40 lower than regular prices. Call or check website for current deals. MC/V. ❸

Alexander Hotel, 13 Belgrave Rd. (☎ 7834 9738; www.alexanderhotel.co.uk). ⊖Victoria. Night Bus #N2, N11, 24, N36. Good-sized, eclectically furnished rooms with solid oak dressers and comfy beds. Satellite TV. Some singles are very small. A plastic suit of armor (nicknamed Sir Fry-a-Lot) keeps order in the sunny and pleasant breakfast room. Breakfast included 7:30-9:30am. Reception 7:30am-11:30pm. Singles £50; doubles £70; triples from £90; quads and quints £120. AmEx/MC/V. ❸

easyHotel, 36-40 Belgrave Rd. (www.easyhotel.com). ⊖Victoria. Night Bus #N2, N11, 24, N36. Additional locations in South Kensington and Earl's Court. Living up to the "no frills" reputation of the brand, the bright orange-and-gray rooms are sparse (with only a bed, small trash can, and mounted flat screen TV) but decently sized and spotless. Doubles start at £25. AmEx/MC/V. ❸

THE WEST END

Unless you have tons of money, accommodations in the West End are scarce; unless you book months in advance, you won't find a bed here. You may get lucky on short-term notice, but don't count on it. If you want to be close to the action of Soho, don't forget that many Bloomsbury accommodations are a short walk away and probably cheaper.

SEE MAP, p. 356

▨ **YHA Oxford Street (HI),** 14 Noel St. (☎ 7734 1618; www.yha.org.uk). ⊖Oxford Circus. Night Bus: More than 10 Night Buses run along Oxford St., including #N7, N8, and N207. Small, clean, sunny rooms with limited facilities but an unbeatable location for nightlife. Some double rooms have bunk beds, sink, mirror, and wardrobe; others have single beds and wardrobes. Toilets and showers off the hallways. Spacious and comfy TV and smoking lounge. Towels £3.50. Internet terminal and Wi-Fi available. A well-equipped kitchen is also available. Travelcards sold at reception. Reserve at least 2 weeks in advance. May-Sept. 3- to 4-bed dorms £25, under 18 £20.50; 2-bed dorms £27. Oct.-Mar. £23.50/19/25.50. MC/V. ❶

BLOOMSBURY

Bloomsbury's quiet squares and Georgian terraces are home to an endless and varied assortment of accommodations. An abundance of quasi-affordable B&Bs line leafy **Cartwright Gardens, Bedford Place, Gower Street,** and **Montague Street.** During the summer, depopulated university halls dot the area around **UCL.** While King's Cross can no longer be considered "dodgy" due to a massive redevelopment project, it is best to avoid dark side streets at night.

SEE MAP, p. 362

▨ **The Generator,** Compton Pl. (☎ 7388 7666; www.generatorhostels.com), off 37 Tavistock Pl. ⊖Russell Sq. or King's Cross St. Pancras. Night Bus #N19, N35, N38, N41, N55, N91, N243. At this ultimate party hostel, you might be greeted by the "Welcome Host" with a complimentary beer and a grin. Mixed-sex dorms (all-female available), a hopping bar (6pm-2am), cheap pints (6-9pm, £1), dinner specials, nightly entertainment, and well-equipped common rooms make this one of the best places to meet fellow travelers. All rooms have sinks; private doubles have tables and chairs. Continental breakfast included. Lockers (bring your own lock), free towels and linens, laundry, kitchen, cash machine, and an in-house travel shop that sells Tube and train tickets. Internet 50p per 7min. Reception 24hr. Reserve 1 week in advance for Sa-Su. Online booking. Credit card required with reservation. 12- to 14-bed dorms M-W and Su £12.50, Th-Sa £17.50; singles £30/35; doubles with 2 twin beds £40/44; triples £54/60; quads £60/68. Discounts for long stays. Under 18 not allowed unless part of a family group. MC/V. ❶

■ **Ashlee House,** 261-265 Gray's Inn Rd. (☎7833 9400; www.ashleehouse.co.uk). ⊖King's Cross St. Pancras. Night Bus #N10, N63, N73, N91, 390. A friendly, "designer" budget accommodation fit for the most discerning of backpackers. Retro-themed rooms and common areas make it feel more like a trendy lounge bar than a low-priced place to crash. Mixed-sex (all-female available) dorms are rather small but bright, while private rooms include table, sink, and kettle. Luggage room, safe, laundry, and kitchen. Brand-new bathrooms. Small elevator and TV room. Continental breakfast included. Linens included; towels £1. Internet £1 per hr. 2-week max. stay. Reception 24hr. 16-bed dorms £9-18; 8- to 10-bed £11-20; 4- to 6-bed £13-22; singles £37; doubles £50. MC/V. ●

■ **Jenkins Hotel,** 45 Cartwright Gardens (☎7387 2067; www.jenkinshotel.demon.co.uk), entry on Barton Pl. ⊖Euston or King's Cross St. Pancras. Night Bus #N10, N73, N91, 390. A small, friendly hotel with plenty of quirky fun. Taller folks should avoid the low-ceilinged basement (although it boasts the nicest bathroom). All rooms are well decorated and spotless. Rooms have TV, kettle, phone, fridge, hair dryer, and safe. Free access to the tennis courts in Cartwright Gardens. English breakfast included. Reserve 1-2 months in advance for summer; 24hr. cancellation policy. Singles £52, with bath £72; doubles with bath (some with tub) £89; triples with bath £105. MC/V. ●

■ **George Hotel,** 58-60 Cartwright Gardens (☎7387 8777; www.georgehotel.com). ⊖Russell Sq. Night Bus #N10, N73, N91, 390. Meticulous rooms with satellite TV, radio, kettle, phone, alarm clock, and sink, plus hair dryer and iron on request. The forward-facing rooms on the 1st fl. are the best, with high ceilings and tall windows. English breakfast included. Free Internet. Reserve 3 weeks in advance for summer; 48hr. cancellation policy. Singles £50, with shower £75; doubles £68.50/75, with bath £89; triples £79/89/99; basic quad £89. Discount for stays over 4 days. MC/V. ●

Astor's Museum Hostel, 27 Montague St. (☎7580 5360; www.astorhotels.com). ⊖Tottenham Court Rd., Russell Sq., or Goodge St. Night Bus #N19, N35, N38, N41, N55, N91, N243. This backpackers' hostel is bare-bones but friendly. High-maintenance types and anyone over 35 need not apply. Seriously—you'll be asked for proof of age. Communal kitchen and free DVDs available to watch in downstairs lounge. English breakfast and linens included. Bring your own towel or buy one in a pinch (£5). Reservations recommended. 12-bed dorms £19; 10-bed £20; 8-bed £21; 6-bed £23; private double £66. AmEx/MC/V. ●

YHA St. Pancras International, 79-81 Euston Rd. (☎0870 770 6044; stpancras@yha.org.uk). ⊖King's Cross St. Pancras. Night Bus #N10, N73, N91, 390. Opposite the British Library. Caters to families and older adults. Family bunk rooms, single-sex dorms, basic doubles, and premium doubles (with bath and TV) are sparkling new. English breakfast included. Lockers (bring your own lock). Linens included. Laundry, kitchen, and elevators. Internet £1 per 15min. 10-day max. stay. Reserve dorms 1 week in advance for Sa-Su or summer, 2 weeks for doubles. Dorms £26.50, under 18 £22.50; doubles £60, with bath £65. £3 discount with ISIC or NUS card. Non-HI members add £3 per night. MC/V. ●

Thanet Hotel, 8 Bedford Pl., Russell Sq. (☎7636 2869; www.thanethotel.co.uk). ⊖Russell Sq. or Holborn. Night Bus #N19, N35, N38, N41, N55, N91, N243. A homey B&B. Some rooms have been recently refurbished and modernized with fireplaces and big mirrors, though even the "old" rooms are perfectly bright and comfortable. Request a room with a view of the garden. All rooms with bath, TV, radio, hair dryer, kettle, and phone. Breakfast included. Reserve 1 month in advance. Singles £76; doubles £100; triples £112; quads £120. AmEx/MC/V. ●

The Langland Hotel, 29-31 Gower St. (☎7636 5801; www.langlandhotel.com). ⊖Goodge St. Night Bus #N5, N10, N20, 24, N29, N73, 134, N253, N279, 390. A comfortable B&B that distinguishes itself with lower rates. Staff keeps the large rooms spotless. Lounge with satellite TV. Recently refurbished rooms have TV, kettle, and fan. English breakfast included. Reserve room away from street to avoid noise.

48hr. cancellation policy. Singles from £45; doubles from £55, with bath £65; triples from £60/75; quads from £75. Discounts in winter and for longer stays, students, and advance booking. AmEx/MC/V. ❸

Pickwick Hall International Backpackers, 7 Bedford Pl. (☎7323 4958; www.pickwickhall.co.uk). ✪Russell Sq. or Holborn. Night Bus #N7, N91. Small, simple rooms are clean and include mini-fridge and microwave. Continental breakfast included. Lockers (bring your own lock). Linens included. Coin laundry, kitchen, TV lounge, and Internet available. Reception approx. 8am-10pm. Book 2-3 days in advance, 3 weeks in advance for July-Aug. Singles £35, with bath £55; doubles £46/62; triples £63/69; quads £84/92. MC/V. ❷

Commonwealth Hall, 1-11 Cartwright Gardens (☎7121 7000; www.lon.ac.uk/services/students/halls1/halls2/vacrates.asp). ✪Russell Sq. Night Bus #N10, N73, N91, 390. Post-WWII block residential hall. 425 nicely sized, recently refurbished student singles with telephones. A good value, especially with English breakfast included and the garden. Fridge and microwave on each floor. Elevators and cafeteria. Access to tennis/squash courts for a fee. Dinner included. Open mid-Mar. to late Apr. and mid-June to mid-Sept. Reserve at least 3 months in advance for July-Aug. Walk-ins only accommodated M-F 9am-5pm. Singles from £28. AmEx/MC/V. ❷

Carr-Saunders Hall, 18-24 Fitzroy St. (☎7955 7575; www.lse.ac.uk/vacations). ✪Warren St. Night Bus #N7, N8, N10, 25, N55, N73, N98, 176, N207, 390. Old student residential hall. Rooms are large and include sink and phone. TV lounge, game room, and elevator to all floors, including the panoramic roof terrace. English breakfast included. Internet access. Reserve 6-8 weeks in advance for July-Aug., but check for openings any time. Open late Mar.-late Apr. and late June-late Sept. 30% deposit required. Singles from £30; doubles from £48, with bath from £52. Discounts for stays over 5 weeks. MC/V. ❷

NORTH LONDON

CAMDEN TOWN, KING'S CROSS, AND ISLINGTON

Home to a few cheap options, North London can be a good home for budget travelers. Affordable accommodations tend to be in more residential and suburban areas, however, and will require getting in and out of central London via public transportation for an additional cost.

▨ **Kandara Guesthouse,** 68 Ockendon Rd. (☎7226 5721; www.kandara.co.uk). From ✪Angel, take Bus #38, 56, 73, 341 to the Ockendon Rd. stop. Night Bus #N38, N73, 341. Far from the Tube but with ample access to downtown. Sparkling clean rooms and a friendly, bustling atmosphere that still offers plenty of privacy. 11 rooms with 5 communal baths. Hair dryer and iron on request. Breakfast included. Reserve well in advance; call for family quad. 1-night deposit required with reservation; 1-week cancellation notice or loss of deposit. Singles £44-54; doubles £59-71; triples £69-82. MC/V. ❸

St. Christopher's Inn, 48-50 Camden High St. (☎7388 1012; www.st-christophers.co.uk). ✪Mornington Crescent. Night Bus #N5, N20, N253. The reception in Belushi's Bar downstairs serves as a fitting entrance to this party-friendly backpacker hostel. Nicknamed the "hostel with attitude," St. Christopher's gets you started right with 10% off all food and drinks at the bar. Location is perfect for hitting the Camden Town bars and Clerkenwell clubs. The rooms are surprisingly fresh, cheerful, and spacious. Most have private bath; if not, common showers are close by. Continental breakfast and linens included. Luggage room, safety deposit boxes, lockers, laundry, and common rooms. Internet access. Reception 24hr. 10-bed dorms from £9.50; 8-bed £17; 6-bed £18; doubles £24. Discount with online booking. ❶

HAMPSTEAD, HIGHGATE, AND GOLDERS GREEN

A highly residential area on the border between Tube Zones 2 and 3, Hampstead, Highgate, and Golders Green is a good place to get away from the urban landscape of central London. Stay here if you are looking for a quiet, removed experience.

Hampstead Village Guest House, 2 Kemplay Rd. (☎7435 8679; www.hampsteadguesthouse.com). ⊖Hampstead. Night Bus #N5. Hidden on a side street off Hampstead High St., this well-maintained Victorian house has 8 good-sized rooms with a touch of old-fashioned elegance. All rooms have TV, fridge, phone, iron, and kettle. Studio apartment, in a converted garage, sleeps 5 and has a small kitchen. English breakfast £7. Reservations essential. Singles £50-60, with bath £70; doubles £75-90; studio £95 for 1 person, £125 for 2, £145 for 3, £160 for 4, £170 for 5. ❹

MARYLEBONE AND REGENT'S PARK

Marylebone's proximity to the West End means that, while there are plenty of accommodations, they tend to be beyond the price range of the average budget traveler. There are a number of attractive B&Bs, but don't expect the deals you'll find in Bloomsbury or Bayswater. Here, you're paying to be in walking distance of Oxford St., the proximity of which makes up for basic accommodations. The area's student rooms are a good deal.

SEE MAP, p. 369

International Student House, 229 Great Portland St. (☎7631 8310; www.ish.org.uk). ⊖Great Portland St. Night Bus #N18. Large and institutional-feeling dorm. Good selection of rooms during summer, limited options during school year (mainly dorms, triples, and quads). Most rooms have desk, sink, phone, and fridge; some have private bath. Bar, nightclub, cafeteria, fitness center (£6 per day), and cinema (Su only). Continental breakfast included except for dorms (£2.30); English breakfast £3. Laundry. Internet £2 per hr. £20 key deposit. Some rooms wheelchair-accessible. 3-week max. stay. Advance booking recommended. Dorms £12; singles £34; doubles £52; triples £62; quads £76. 10% discount on singles, doubles, and triples with ISIC. MC/V. ❶

University of Westminster Halls, 35 Marylebone Rd. (☎7911 5181; www.wmin.ac.uk/comserv). ⊖Baker St. Night Bus #N18. Typical student singles: not much character, but convenient. Students only. Laundry, kitchen, lounges, and shared baths. 1-week advance booking recommended; occasional last-minute availability. Available early June to mid-Sept. Singles from £27, under 26 from £23. MC/V. ❷

Lincoln House Hotel, 33 Gloucester Pl. (☎7486 7630; www.lincoln-house-hotel.co.uk). ⊖Marble Arch. Night Bus #6, N7, N15, 23, N36, N74, 94, N98. Only a 5min. walk from Oxford St. and Marble Arch, Lincoln House is within easy reach of the Tube, buses, and Hyde Park. Friendly staff, accommodating management, and small conveniences contribute to a pleasant experience. Navy-themed decor; rooms are clean and basic. All have phone, TV, kettle, fridge, private toilet, and shower. Some rooms wheelchair-accessible. Singles £59-79; doubles £89-109; triples £119-129; quads £135-139. Discounts on multi-night stays through website. AmEx/MC/V. ❹

Hart House Hotel, 51 Gloucester Pl. (☎7935 2288; www.harthouse.co.uk). ⊖Marble Arch. Night Bus #6, N7, N15, 23, N36, N74, 94, N98. A Revolution-era home for French nobility, this recently remodeled hotel is now a bright and cheerful place to spend the night—if you can afford it. Better for a group's budget, this small hotel has simple but comfortable rooms, all with private bath. Recipient of the "Sparkling Diamond" award, it is also squeaky clean. Full English breakfast and taxes included in rates. Online booking available. Singles £85; doubles £125; triples £145; quads £175. AmEx/MC/V. ❹

BAYSWATER

Flanked by the twin attractions of expansive Hyde Park and posh Notting Hill, Bayswater offers a great location along with an abundance of budget-friendly accommodations. Almost every side street is lined with converted Victorian houses offering rooms. The greatest variety of rooms, and all the cheaper hostels, can be found around **Queensway;** try **Inverness Terrace, Kensington Square Gardens,** and **Leinster Square.** On the other side of Bayswater, the area around **Paddington** is convenient for travelers arriving on the Heathrow Express: **Sussex Gardens** is lined with affordable B&Bs, while slightly cheaper hotels surround the Tube station.

SEE MAP, p. 361

 SCALING THE HEIGHTS. Most accommodations in Bayswater are converted townhouses that have long and narrow staircases. Those who have trouble with stairs may want to consider staying elsewhere.

Quest Hostel, 45 Queensborough Terr. (☎ 7229 7782; www.astorhostels.com). ⊖Queensway. Night Bus #N15, 94, 148. A chummy staff operates this simple backpacker hostel with a whiteboard welcoming new check-ins by name. Mostly mixed-sex dorms (1 female-only room); nearly all have bath. Otherwise, facilities on every other fl. Kitchen available. Continental breakfast, lockers, and linen included. Laundry, luggage storage, free Wi-Fi. 4- to 9-bed dorms £18-23; doubles £30. MC/V. ●

Hyde Park Hostel, 2-6 Inverness Terr. (☎ 7229 5101; www.astorhostels.com). ⊖Queensway. Night Bus #N15, 94, 148. There's nothing fancy about the tightly bunked dorms, but with 260 beds and a veritable theme park of diversions, this colorful and backpacker-friendly hostel is entertaining if nothing else. Jungle-themed basement bar and dance space hosts DJs and parties (open W-Su 8pm-3am). Kitchen, laundry, TV lounge, secure luggage room. Continental breakfast and linens included. Internet access 50p per 30min. Reception 24hr. Reserve 2 weeks in advance for summer. 24hr. cancellation policy. Online booking with 10% non-refundable deposit. 4- to 18-bed dorms £11-18; twins £25; weekly rates available from £81-95 per person. Ages 16-35 only. MC/V. ●

Admiral Hotel, 143 Sussex Gardens (☎7723 7309; www.admiral-hotel.com). ⊖Paddington. Night Bus #N15, 94, 148. Beautifully kept B&B with a sleek bar adding an unexpected but modern touch. Recently redecorated rooms with bath, hair dryer, satellite TV, and kettle. No smoking. English breakfast included. Free Wi-Fi. 4-day cancellation policy. Singles £40-50; doubles £58-75; triples £75-90; quads £88-110; quints £100-130. Ask about winter and long-stay discounts. MC/V. ❸

Balmoral House Hotel, 156 Sussex Gardens (☎7723 7445; www.balmoralhousehotel.co.uk). ⊖Paddington. Night Bus #N15, 94, 148. Convenient location close to the Tube station. Well-kept rooms have smallish bathroom, satellite TV, kettle, and hairdryer. English breakfast included. Singles £50; doubles £75; triples £90; quads £104; family suites for 5 £120. 5% surcharge for MC/V. ❸

Garden Court Hotel, 30-31 Kensington Gardens Sq. (☎ 7229 2553; www.gardencourthotel.co.uk). ⊖Bayswater. Night Bus #N15, 94, 148. Newly refurbished rooms with crisp, attractive decor vary in size. Elevator. All rooms have sink, flat screen TV, hair dryer, and phone; some with full bath. Many have beautifully restored crown molding and fireplaces. Access to the patio garden. Buffet breakfast included. Strict 14-day cancellation policy. Singles £47, with bath £72; doubles £75/115; triples £90/150; family quads £100/170. MC/V. ❸

Kensington Gardens Hotel, 9 Kensington Gardens Sq. (☎7221 7790; www.kensingtongardenshotel.co.uk). ⊖Bayswater. Night Bus #N15, 94, 148. Well-equipped rooms with kettle, TV, phone, mini-bar, fan, and hair dryer on demand. All rooms are similarly sized, so singles feel the most spacious. All rooms have shower; singles share 3 hall toilets. Continental breakfast included; English breakfast £6.50. Reception 24hr. 48hr. cancellation policy. Prices depend on days of the week and vacancies. Singles from £80; doubles from £120; triples from £160. AmEx/MC/V. ❺

NOTTING HILL

Although a lovely residential neighborhood, Notting Hill is not home to budget accommodations. Try nearby Bayswater for better deals.

SEE MAP, p. 361

▧ **The Gate Hotel,** 6 Portobello Rd. (☎7221 0707; www.gatehotel.co.uk). ⊖Notting Hill Gate. Night Bus #N52. The friendly staff make staying here a pleasure. A great base for Notting Hill and West End excursions and a short walk from markets down the road. Clean, relatively spacious, and a good deal for the area. Rooms have bath, TV/DVD, desk, mini-fridge, and phone. Continental breakfast included, served in-room. 48hr. cancellation policy. Singles £55-70; doubles £75-90; triples £90-110. AmEx/MC/V. ❹

▧ **Portobello Gold Rooms,** 97 Portobello Rd. (☎7460 4910; www.portobellogold.com). ⊖Notting Hill Gate. Night Bus #N52. Upstairs from its namesake pub is a simple but well-maintained selection of 6 decent-sized rooms, all ensuite with TV and phone. For larger groups, the family apartment may be ideal: though a bit pricey, it spans 2 fl. and includes a kitchen, gardened private roof terrace, and mosaic-tiled bath. Continental breakfast included. Twins and doubles £70 when booking online, £80 in person; apartment for 4 £170, each additional person £5. Discounts available for stays of a week or longer. AmEx/MC/V. ❹

KENSINGTON AND EARL'S COURT

For such an upscale neighborhood, Kensington is not entirely devoid of affordable accommodations—mid-priced B&Bs sit just a few blocks away from the mansions. The area is pretty large, however, and a Kensington address doesn't necessarily put you within walking distance of the main sights and shops. Decidedly less exclusive Earl's Court remains popular with backpackers and budget travelers who don't mind staying a step away from all the action.

SEE MAP, pp. 366-367

▧ **Vicarage Hotel,** 10 Vicarage Gate (☎7229 4030; www.londonvicaragehotel.com). ⊖High St. Kensington. Night Bus #27, N28, N31, N52. Walking on Kensington Church St. from Kensington High St., you'll see 2 streets marked Vicarage Gate; take the 2nd on your right. Immaculately maintained Victorian house with ornate hallways, TV lounge, and charming bedrooms; all rooms have solid wood furnishings, kettle, and hair dryer. Rooms with private bath have TV. Full English breakfast included. Best to reserve 2 months in advance with 1 night's deposit; personal checks accepted for deposit with at least 2 months notice. Singles £50, with private bathroom £85; doubles £85/110; triples £105/140; quads £112/155. MC/V. ❸

▧ **YHA Holland House,** Holland Walk (☎7937 0748; www.hihostels.com). ⊖High St. Kensington or Holland Park. Night Bus #27, 94, 148. A picturesque location makes this one of the better hostels in the city. In the middle of Holland Park, ½ of the rooms are in a gorgeous 17th-century mansion and overlooking a large flowery courtyard. Standard 12- to 20-bed single-sex dorms are less alluring (some bunks are 3-tiered), but a cleaner facility would be hard to find. Caters mostly to younger student groups. Internet access 50p per 7min. TV room, laundry, kitchen. Full English breakfast included; 3-course set dinners £5.50. Reception 24hr. Book 2-3 weeks in advance for summer, although there are frequent last-minute vacancies. Dorms £21.50, under 18 £16.50. £3 discount with student ID. AmEx/MC/V. ❶

Oxford Hotel, 24 Penywern Rd. (☎7370 1161; www.the-oxford-hotel.com). ⊖Earl's Court. Night Bus #N31, N74, N97. Fun fact: Sir William Ramsey, the physicist who discovered helium, once lived in a section of this hotel—guests would often hear high-pitched voices coming from his room. Mid-size, bright rooms, all with shower and some with full bath. Minimal but generally high-quality furnishings: comfortable bed, TV, kettle, and safe. Rooms in the annex down the road of comparable quality. Continental breakfast included. Reception 24hr. Reserve 2-3 weeks in advance for June. Singles with shower £45, with bath £58; doubles £65/75; triples with bath £83; quads £92/100; quints £120. MC/V. ❸

YHA Earl's Court, 38 Bolton Gardens (☎7373 7083; www.hihostels.com). ⊖Earl's Court. Night Bus #N31, N74, N97. Sprawling Victorian townhouse considerably better-equipped than most YHAs. Bright, tidy, 4- to 10-bed single-sex dorms have wooden bunks, lockers (bring your own lock), and sink. Features a small garden, spacious communal kitchen, 2 TV lounges, and luggage storage. Breakfast included only for private rooms; otherwise £4. Linens included. Coin laundry and Internet access available. 2-week max stay. 24hr. cancellation policy; £5 cancellation charge. Book private rooms at least 24hr. in advance. Dorms £19.50, under 18 £17.20; doubles £60; quads £82. £3 added charge per night for non-members. MC/V. ❶

Mowbray Court Hotel, 28-32 Penywern Rd. (☎7373 8285; www.mowbraycourthotel.co.uk). ⊖Earl's Court. Night Bus #N31, N74, N97. Large B&B with elevator, lounge, and bar. Room size ranges from small to enormous. All have TV, trouser press, hair dryer, safe, fluffy comforter, phone, and large bath. Continental breakfast included. Reception 24hr. Reserve 1 week in advance. 24hr. cancellation policy. Singles £45, with bath £55; doubles £60/69; triples £72/84; quads £88/96; quints £110/120; 6-bed rooms £125/132. AmEx/MC/V. ❸

Amsterdam Hotel, 7 Trebovir Rd. (☎7370 5084, within UK 0800 279 9132; www.amsterdam-hotel.com). ⊖Earl's Court. Night Bus #N31, N74, N94. An elegant splurge. Choose between rooms and suites, with enough variety to suit a range of needs. All rooms with bath, TV, kettle, and phone. Elevator to all floors. Continental breakfast included. Free Wi-Fi. 48hr. cancellation policy. Wheelchair-accessible. Singles £82; standard doubles £92, executives £105; triples £120/132. Studio suites £110; doubles £115; triples £150; 2-bedroom £185. AmEx/MC/V. ❺

Philbeach Hotel, 30-31 Philbeach Gardens (☎7373 1244; www.philbeachhotel.freeserve.co.uk). ⊖Earl's Court. Night Bus #N31, N74, N97. The decomposing awning outside suggests that this gay and lesbian B&B (London's largest) has seen better days. Rooms vary greatly: "budget singles" are very basic (phone and sink), while 1 double with private bath features a cast-iron bed frame, desk, and full bay window. Rooms include TV, phone, kettle, and sink. Garden out back. Continental breakfast included, served in the Thai restaurant downstairs. Free Wi-Fi as well as an Internet kiosk. Reserve 1-2 weeks in advance; 48hr. cancellation policy. Budget singles £35; standards £50, with bath £59; doubles £63/81; triples £81/95. 10% discount with online booking. AmEx/MC/V. ❸

KNIGHTSBRIDGE AND BELGRAVIA

Belgravia's B&Bs are concentrated on **Ebury Street,** a fairly busy road as close to Victoria and Sloane Square as it is to Belgravia proper. That's not a disadvantage—on the contrary, with Westminster's sights and Chelsea's shops within walking distance, you'd be hard-pressed to do better. We've listed three of Ebury's best, but if none of these is available, chances are you'll find a vacancy in a comparable establishment somewhere else on the street.

SEE MAP, p. 365

■ **Morgan House,** 120 Ebury St. (☎7730 2384; www.morganhouse.co.uk). ⊖Victoria. A touch of pizzazz makes this B&B a neighborhood standout. Mid-sized, stylish rooms, many with fireplaces, all with TV, kettle, and phone for incoming calls (pay phone downstairs). English breakfast included. Reserve 2-3 months in advance. 48hr. cancellation policy. Singles with sink £52; doubles with sink £72, with bath £92; triples £92/112; quads (1 double bed and 1 set of bunk beds) with bath £132. MC/V. ❸

Westminster House Hotel, 96 Ebury St. (☎7730 4302; www.westminsterhousehotel.co.uk). ⊖Victoria. With charming and well-decorated rooms paired with a prime location and friendly staff, Westminster makes for an excellent home base. 12 mid-sized rooms have TV, tea trays, coffee, and hot chocolate; except for 1 single, all have private bath. Full English breakfast included and rumored to be among the best in London. Reserve well in advance. 48hr. cancellation policy. Single £50, with bath £60; doubles £75/90; triples with bath £110; quads with bath £120. AmEx/MC/V. ❸

James House Hotel, 108 Ebury St. (☎7730 5880; www.eburybedandbreakfast.co.uk). ⊖Victoria or Sloane Sq. Sparkling, mid-sized rooms and tidy hallways. Bright breakfast room overlooking the garden. All rooms with TV, kettle, hair dryer, and fan. No smoking. English breakfast included. Reserve with 1-night deposit; 10% non-refundable, the rest refundable with 2-week notice. Singles £55; doubles £75; triples £95; family room (1 double and 2 bunks for children under 12) £130. AmEx/MC/V. ❹

CHELSEA

Mostly a residential area, Chelsea is not known for its abundance of budget accommodations. However, those who dream of calling Chelsea their home—if only for one night—have one great option.

SEE MAP, p. 363

IES Chelsea Pointe, (☎7808 9200; www.iesreshall.com), corner of Manresa Rd. and King's Rd., entrance on Manresa Rd. ⊖Sloane Sq., then Bus #11, 19, 22, 319; ⊖South Kensington, then Bus #49. Night Bus #N11, N19, N22. Brand-new university residence hall offers clean and spacious dorm rooms year-round. In the heart of trendy Chelsea, these prices are unheard of. All rooms have bath, data ports (free, unlimited Internet if you bring a computer), phone, and access to a kitchen, laundry services, and 5 TV/DVD lounges. Reservations recommended. 72hr. cancellation policy. 20 rooms wheelchair-accessible. More availability during summer and winter school breaks. Singles £285 per week; doubles £375 per week. AmEx/MC/V. ❸

DAYTRIPPING IN CHELSEA. Given the lack of affordable beds in Chelsea, day tripping from the City is a smart idea. Hop on the Tube and spend the day shopping, walking around the numerous parks and gardens, or sipping lattes on the busy King's Road. Stay for a pint or two, but a Tube trip back to base before closing will be kinder to your wallet than most hotels in the area.

WEST LONDON

Relative proximity to Notting Hill and Hyde Park, along with affordable prices and good transportation, make **Shepherd's Bush** popular with budget travelers (especially Australians). There are plenty of B&Bs and small, independent hotels to choose from.

■ **Star Hotel,** 97-99 Shepherd's Bush Rd. (☎7603 2755; www.star-hotel.net). ⊖Hammersmith. Night Bus #9, 10, 11, 24. A family-run B&B. Rooms are clean, bright, and relatively spacious; all have TV, kettle, hair dryer, and large bath. Full English breakfast included, served in a sky-lit dining area. Book 1-2 months in advance for July-Aug. and

Easter. 72hr. cancellation policy. Singles £42; doubles £50-60; triples £69-75; quads £84-95. Stays over 2 nights receive a substantial discount. 3% surcharge for MC/V. ❸

St. Christopher's Inn, 13-15 Shepherd's Bush Green. (☎8735 0270; www.st-christophers.co.uk). ⊖Shepherd's Bush. Night Bus #N72 or N97. This crowded hangout is perfect for social backpackers. Basic rooms with bunk beds (linens provided) and sinks. A 24hr. downstairs lounge can be reserved for parties and has ping pong and pool tables, TV, comfy couches, and Internet access. With the attached bar and restaurant (Belushi's, see p. 143), there is no shortage of nightly entertainment. Breakfast included. Laundry facilities. Office safe for valuables. Airport pickup available (see website for details). 8-bed dorms £16-23, 6-bed dorms £17-24, 4-bed dorms £18.50-28; doubles £50. MC/V. ❶

Euro Hotel, 31 Shepherd's Bush Rd. (☎7603 4721; www.euro-hotel.co.uk). ⊖Shepherd's Bush. Located 2 blocks from Shepherd's Bush Green, this hotel offers spacious, *ensuite* rooms with free Wi-Fi and satellite TV for up to 6 people. Reception 24hr. Doubles £65; quads £85; 4-6 person rooms £95. Discounts offered for stays of 4 nights or more. MC/V. ❷

Hotel Orlando, 83 Shepherd's Bush Rd. (☎/fax 7603 4890; www.hotelorlando.co.uk). ⊖Shepherd's Bush. Night Bus #N220. Clean, pleasant rooms are decent-sized, with TV, phone, and bath; most have mini-fridge. English breakfast included. Clean towels provided daily. Pay in advance. 5-day cancellation policy. Singles (some with double beds) £45; doubles £58; triples £78; quads £98. AmEx/MC/V. ❸

Dalmacia Hotel, 71 Shepherd's Bush Rd. (☎7603 2887; www.dalmacia.co.uk). ⊖Shepherd's Bush. Nirvana's pre-stardom accommodation of choice, this B&B is slightly more expensive than others up the road. Niceties like toiletries, decent-sized bathrooms, and in-room safes may be worth the extra pounds—if you can tolerate the no visitors policy and unconventional bed configurations ("double" beds are actually twins pushed together). All rooms include kettle, TV, and hair dryer. Singles £49; doubles £69; triples £81. Discounts depending on season. MC/V. ❸

Windsor Guest House, 43 Shepherd's Bush Rd. (☎7603 2116; www.windsorghs.co.uk). ⊖Shepherd's Bush. Small, unpretentious, family-run B&B catering to tourists and working people. English breakfast included. Reserve 1-2 months ahead for summer. Singles £40; doubles £60; triples £75. Cash only. ❷

FOOD

While insiders have known London as a hot spot for inventive, internationally influenced cuisine for years, it has taken a little while to spread the word to tourists that Great Britain is more than just bangers and mash. London's thriving and enormously diverse food scene is fueled by its growing ethnic communities, many of which use their culinary traditions to maintain ties to their own culture while introducing others to their cuisine. Head to Whitechapel for the region's best Baltic food, to Chinatown for traditional dim sum, to South Kensington for French pastries, and to Edgware Rd. for a stunning assortment of Lebanese Shawarma. As London continues to become more diverse, the assortment and fusion of the dizzying number of food styles will most likely keep growing. That said, it would be a shame to come to the home of proper afternoon tea and fish 'n' chips and deny yourself these delicious and long-standing British traditions. The moral of the story: try everything.

 CHECK, PLEASE. In most restaurants, it's considered rude for the waiter to give a patron their bill, since it implies they should hurry and give up the table. If you would like to pay, you will most likely have to ask for the check.

FOOD BY TYPE

ASIAN

Aki(126)	HOL ❶
▨ Busaba Eathai(130)	WEND ❷
▨ The Drunken Monkey(123)	EL ❷
▨ Golden Dragon(130)	WEND ❷
Gyoza(127)	SL ❶
▨ Jenny Lo's Teahouse(141)	K/B ❷
itsu(131)	WEND ❸
▨ Mandalay(137)	M/RP ❶
▨ New Culture Revolution(135)	NL ❶
Noodle Noodle(129)	WEMIN ❷
Phật Phúc(142)	CHEL ❷
Royal China(137)	M/RP ❸
Satay Bar(127)	SL ❷
Soba Noodle Bar(132)	WEND ❷
Wagamama(134)	BLOOM ❷
▨ Yelo(122)	EL ❷

CAFE (SANDWICHES AND SNACKS)

Al Bar/Cafe(125)	CLERK ❶
Bar Italia(131)	WEND ❶
Belushi's(143)	WL ❷
Bar Italia(131)	WEND ❷
▨ Café 1001(122)	EL ❶
Cafe 180(126)	HOL ❶
▨ Cafe in the Crypt(132)	WEND ❶
Candid Cafe(135)	NL ❶
Carrot Cafe(126)	HOL ❶
Carlton Coffee House(131)	WEND ❶

▨ Chelsea Bun(142)	CHEL ❷
The Clerkenwell Kitchen(124)	CLERK ❷
Futures(121)	CITY ❶
Gloriette(141)	K/B ❷
The Island Café(127)	SB ❶
Lazy Daisy Café(139)	NH ❶
Mange(128)	WEMIN ❶
▨ Neal's Yard Salad Bar(132)	WEND ❶
▨ Newens Maids of Honor(143)	WL ❶
The Orangery(141)	KEN/EC ❷
Organic Cafe(122)	EL ❷
Raison d'Être(140)	KEN/EC ❶
Relish(129)	WEMIN ❶
Richoux(130)	WE ❹
Spianata & Co.(122)	CITY ❶
Tom's Delicatessen(139)	NH ❷
Woolley's(125)	HOL ❶

CARIBBEAN

Cubana(127)	SB ❷
▨ Mango Room(134)	NL ❷
Mr. Jerk(131)	WEND ❷

COFFEE AND BAKERY

Beigel Bake(123)	EL ❶
Carmelli Bakery(136)	NL ❶
Hummus Bros.(131)	WEND ❶
Coffee @(123)	EL ❶
The Grain Shop(139)	NH ❶
Lisboa Patisserie(139)	NH ❶

My Old Dutch(142)   CHEL ❷
Poilâne(142)   K/B ❶
The Tea and Coffee Plant(139)   NH ❶

CREPES
▨ La Crêperie de Hampstead(136)   NL ❶

EASTERN EUROPEAN
L'Autre(130)   WEND ❸
▨ Bloom's(136)   NL ❷
Daquise(141)   KEN/EC ❷
Patio(143)   WL ❸
Trojka(135)   NL ❷

FRENCH
Bleeding Heart(125)   HOL ❺
La Brasserie(141)   KEN/EC ❸
Gordon Ramsay(142)   CHEL ❺
▨ Le Mercury(135)   NL ❷
Savoir Faire(134)   BLOOM ❷

GREEK/MEDITERRANEAN
Aphrodite Taverna(138)   BAY ❸
The Real Greek(123)   EL ❷
Sofra(125)(129)   CLERK, WEND ❷

ICE CREAM AND GELATO
▨ La Bottega del Gelato(138)   BAY ❶
Marine Ices(136)   NL ❶
▨ Scoop(132)   WEND ❶

INDIAN
▨ Aladin(123)   EL ❷
▨ Café Spice Namaste(121)   CITY ❸
Chutney Raj(126)   HOL ❷
Diwana Bhel Poori House(134)   BLOOM ❷
Durbar Tandoori(138)   BAY ❷
Khan's Restaurant(138)   BAY ❷
▨ Masala Zone(130)   WEND ❷
Shish(123)   EL ❷
Sweet and Spicy(123)   EL ❷
▨ Utsav(140)   KEN/EC ❷
Zaika(140)   KEN/EC ❺

ITALIAN/PIZZA
▨ Buona sera, at the Jam(142)   CHEL ❸
▨ Cantina del Ponte(126)   SB ❸
Carluccio's(129)   WEND ❷
Gourmet Pizza Co.(127)   SB ❷
▨ ICCo(133)   BLOOM ❶

Pizzeria Oregano(135)   NL ❷
▨ San Marco(128)   SL ❷
Strada(128)   SL ❸
Spighetta(137)   M/RP ❸

MIDDLE EASTERN
Afghan Kitchen(135)   NL ❶
▨ Gallipoli(134)   NL ❷
▨ Levantine(138)   BAY ❷
Manzara(139)   NH ❶
▨ Patogh(137)   M/RP ❷
Tas(126)   SB ❷

MODERN BRITISH
Babylon(141)   KEN/EC ❹
▨ Bleeding Heart Tavern(125)   HOL ❸
▨ The Golden Hind(137)   M/RP ❸
Hoxton Apprentice(122)   EL ❸
The Ivy(133)   WEND ❺
Metro(128)   SL ❸
Metro Bar & Grill(135)   NL ❸
▨ Newman Arms(133)   BLOOM ❷
St. John(124)   CLERK ❹
▨ Rock and Sole Plaice(132)   WEND ❷
SW9(127)   SL ❷
Tamarind(130)   WEND ❸
Tiles(128)   WEMIN ❸

MOROCCAN
Al Casbah(137)   NL ❸
Mo Tearoom(129)   WEND ❸
▨ Zagora(143)   WL ❷

SEAFOOD
▨ George's Portobello Fish Bar(138)   NH ❶
North Sea Fish Restaurant(134)   BLOOM ❸

SPANISH/LATIN AMERICAN
▨ Anexo(124)   CLERK ❷
L'Autre(130)   WEND ❸
Café Pacifico(133)   WEND ❸
Cuba Libre(135)   NL ❷
▨ Goya(128)(142)   K/B, WEMIN ❸
▨ Navarro's Tapas Bar(133)   BLOOM ❸

VEGETARIAN
Honest(128)   SL ❷
▨ The Gate(143)   WL ❸
The Greenery(124)   CLERK ❶
The Place Below(121)   CITY ❶

NEIGHBORHOOD ABBREVIATIONS: BAY Bayswater **BLOOM** Bloomsbury **CHEL** Chelsea **CITY** The City of London **CLERK** Clerkenwell **HOL** Holborn **KEN/EC** Kensington and Earl's Court **K/B** Knightsbridge and Belgravia **M/RP** Marylebone and Regent's Park **NH** Notting Hill **SB** The South Bank **WEND** The West End **WEMIN** Westminster **NL** North London **SL** South London **EL** East London **WL** West London

FOOD BY NEIGHBORHOOD

THE CITY OF LONDON

With hardly any residents and almost none of the City's workforce sticking around for supper, it's not surprising that the vast majority of City eateries open only for weekday breakfast and lunch—it's nearly impossi-

SEE MAP, p. 349

ble to find a decent dinner here, although most pubs are open and serve food well into the evenings. If you can't decide what to eat, the alleyways of **Leadenhall Market** pack in numerous mid-range chain restaurants, cafes, and pubs.

■ **CafeSpice Namaste,** 16 Prescot St. (☎7488 9242; www.cafespice.co.uk). ⊖Tower Hill or DLR: Tower Gateway. While somewhat out of the way, Spice is well worth the trek. Bright, festive decoration brings an exotic feel to this old Victorian warehouse, and the outdoor courtyard seating is a plus. The extensive menu of Goan and Parsi specialties helpfully explains each dish. Meat mains are on the pricey side (from £14.25), but vegetarian dishes (from £4.75) are affordable, especially for an establishment of this quality. A varied wine list and excellent but expensive desserts complete the experience. Open M-F noon-3pm and 6:15-10:30pm, Sa 6:30-10:30pm. AmEx/MC/V. ❸

Futures, 8 Botolph Alley (☎7623 4529; www.futures-vta.net), between Botolph Ln. and Lovat Ln. ⊖Monument. London's workforce besieges this tiny takeaway joint during lunch; come before noon to take advantage of the place. Variety of vegetarian soups (from £2.50), salads (from £2.20), and hot dishes (from £5.20) all change weekly. For breakfast you'll find a wide variety of pastries (from 85p) or porridges and cereals (from £1.35). Wheelchair-accessible. Open M-F 8-10am and 11:30am-2:30pm. ❶

The Place Below (☎7329 0789; www.theplacebelow.co.uk), on Cheapside, in the basement of St. Mary-le-Bow Church. ⊖St. Paul's or Mansion House. Climb down the winding steps from the foyer of St. Mary-le-Bow, and you'll find yourself in a fantastic vegetarian restaurant. Be prepared to wait at lunchtime and count on taking your food with you. Fresh, elaborate sandwiches (from £4.50), yummy porridge (£1.70), and a constantly changing menu of tasty mains (from £6).

ON THE MENU

FISH 'N' CHIPS

While any city can take batter-dipped fish and potatoes, fry them up and call it a meal, only London could take such a dish, in all of its greasy, newspaper glory, and reinvent it as the new upper-class favorite. The Queen and commonfolk alike now enjoy this tartar-sauced dish.

Fish 'n' chips is considered by many to be the quintessential British meal. Its popularity began centuries ago, for the simple reasons that its two main ingredients (fish and potatoes) were cheap, readily available, and filling. While its popularity has waxed and waned throughout the years, its status as a traditional favorite has never truly disappeared. However, it is only recently that Londoners have embraced the sinfully delicious comfort food and turned it into a chic throwback. You can now find the dish on the menu at high-end restaurants and opening posh new places devoted to its renewed status.

Whether you're in a gritty local pub or a swanky upscale restaurant, you're likely to find fish 'n' chips on the menu. While some places may try to serve the dish on fancy china with unnecessary garnishes, the best way to enjoy a fish 'n' chips meal is the way it was intended to be enjoyed, newspaper wrapping and all.

There are also pastries (from £1.35) and plenty of hot drinks as well as the daily health bowl, a concoction of various healthful foods (from £4.50). Open M-F 7:30am-3pm. ❶

Spianata & Co., 73a Watling St. (☎7236 3666; www.spianata.com). ⊖Mansion House. This sandwich shop is light on seating but heavy on organic treats; try the salads (from £3). The name, however, comes from the wide, flat sandwiches (from £2.50) served on Italian *spianata* bread and made on the premises. Daily offerings include classic mozzarella and tomato or slightly more elaborate shrimp and roasted pepper. Wheelchair-accessible. Open M-F 7:30am-3:30pm. ❶

 FOOD FOR POCKET CHANGE. Pub grub is often the cheapest way to eat in London without having to cook for yourself. Head to one of the **pubs** recommended by *Let's Go*, listed in the **Nightlife** chapter (p. 257). **Supermarkets,** listed in the **Practical Information** chapter (p. 97), are also a decent option.

EAST LONDON

WHITECHAPEL AND THE EAST END

Long considered a hot spot for Asian food, **Brick Lane** is one of the most mouth-watering destinations in London. With competition among over 100 restaurants in the area, the food is inexpensive and good. Aspiring chefs can stock up on spices at a number of food stores as well as on organic produce from **Spitalfields Market** (p. 240). Here, the Edwardian hall is teeming with creatively decorated international food stalls offering everything from goulash to guacamole. Most hot food stalls open only on Sundays and for lunch on weekdays, but the multitude of stalls selling fresh produce is open whenever the market is. With so many choices, it's best to leave some room for a second or third course.

Hoxton and **Shoreditch** are the places to go for haute cuisine in the area's bars and drinking haunts. A growing number of trendy restaurants lining Hoxton Sq. and Shoreditch High St. also offer excellent pre-club fuel, and Kingsland Rd. boasts a treasure trove of affordable Vietnamese eateries. *(⊖Old St., ⊖Shoreditch, or a 10min. walk from ⊖Aldgate East or ⊖Liverpool St.)*

Café 1001, 91 Brick Lane, Dray Walk (☎7247 9679; www.cafe1001.co.uk), in an alley just off Brick Ln. ⊖Aldgate East. Bring your sketch pad or laptop to this artists' den; you're likely to pass a whole afternoon rather than just grab a quick bite. Dreadlocked 20-somethings lounge around the spacious upstairs or the numerous tables outside while staff dole out homemade food straight from casserole dishes downstairs. Freshly baked cakes (£2 per slice), premade salads (£3), and sandwiches (£2.50) will satiate any craving. Selections of wine and beer (£2-4). Outdoor barbecue weather permitting. Nightly DJs or live bands 7pm-close, W live jazz. Open M-W and Su 7am-11:30pm, Th-Sa 7pm-midnight. ❶

Yelo, 8-9 Hoxton Sq. (☎7729 4626; www.yelothai.com). ⊖Old St. The hipper cousin of traditional Thai restaurants, this popular eatery serves up old standbys in a comfortable and laid-back space. Pad thai, curry, and stir-fry (£5) make for familiar fare, but the industrial lighting, exposed brick, and house music shake things up. Eat outside overlooking the square in summer or make new friends at the indoor communal benches. For a more formal affair, call to book a "proper" table downstairs. Wheelchair-accessible. Takeaway and delivery available. Open daily noon-3pm and 6-11pm. ❶

Organic Cafe, 12-14 Greenwich Church St. (☎8465 5577). DLR: Cutty Sark. One of the few non-chain restaurants lining the high street, with daily specials including squash and coconut soup (£3.75). Sandwiches and salads (£3-4.60). Breakfast all day (£3-4). Smoothies, teas, coffees, and homemade cakes from £1.50. Open M-F 8:30am-6:30pm, Sa-Su 8am-7pm. ❷

Hoxton Apprentice, 16 Hoxton Sq. (☎7749 2828). ⊖Old St. Try one of the mains like stuffed chicken breast (£13) or try a tasty starter like mushroom brioche, smoked haddock with avocado puree, or ceviche (from £5). 2-course Express Lunch £10. Su brunch noon-6pm. Open Tu-Sa noon-11pm, Su noon-10:30pm. MC/V. ❸

Aladin, 132 Brick Ln. (☎7247 8210). ⊖Aldgate East. Serving up Pakistani, Bangladeshi, and Indian food, Aladin stands out among Brick Lane's overwhelming Balti options. Friendly service, plenty of vegetarian options, and BYO wine and beer make this an appealing choice for the masses. Mains £4-8.50; 3-course lunch *menu* £6. Daily lunch special noon-4:30pm. Open M-Th and Su noon-11:30pm, F-Sa noon-midnight. ❷

The Real Greek, 14-15 Hoxton Market (☎7739 8212; www.therealgreek.com). ⊖Old St. Somewhat hidden except for its cobalt blue doors, this Mediterranean restaurant serves a large variety of hot and cold *mezze* dishes such as grilled octopus and stuffed grape leaves (£3.25-5.75). Several dining rooms with chandeliers and large windows facing onto the square accommodate a large crowd. Open M-Sa noon-11pm. ❷

The Drunken Monkey, 222 Shoreditch High St. (☎7392 9606; www.thedrunkenmonkey.co.uk). ⊖Liverpool St. A far cry from the typical tableclothed Chinese affair, this dim sum restaurant-bar is hipper than most Shanghai nightclubs. Spacious wooden tables, dozens of low-hanging oriental lamps, and DJs spinning Tu-Su attract a young crowd. Large lounge area in the front with smaller, more intimate dining rooms in the back. Rice and noodle dishes £3-6; small dim sum plates £2.50-4.50. Takeaway available. Happy hour drinks from £4.50; M-F 5-7pm, Sa 6-8pm, Su noon-11pm. Open M-F noon-midnight, Sa 6pm-midnight, Su noon-11pm. AmEx/MC/V. ❷

Beigel Bake, 159 Brick Ln. (☎1729 0616). ⊖Aldgate East. In the former heart of Jewish London, this tiny, traditional bakery is a perfect fix for post-club pastry cravings. Overflowing baskets of challah bread, bagels, and sweets line the back walls, and customers can peek in the open kitchen for a glimpse of the master bakers. Efficient counter staff keeps the line moving quickly. Low prices (bagels 18p) draw crowds at all hours. All items under £1.50. Takeaway or eat at the standing-room-only counter. Open 24hr. ❶

Shish, 313-319 Old St. (☎7749 0990; www.shish.com). ⊖Old St. Not to be confused with Sh! (the women's erotic emporium around the corner), this popular restaurant serves up Silk Road spice. Hot and cold *mezze* dishes, including chicken pandana, tabbouleh, and red and green falafel (£4-5) complement a range of kebabs (£7-8.50). Large lounge downstairs with cushions and detailed metal tables is great for a drink. Brunch Sa-Su 10:30am-4pm. Wheelchair-accessible. Open M-F 11am-midnight, Sa 10:30am-midnight, Su 10:30am-11pm. MC/V. ❷

Sweet and Spicy, 40 Brick Ln. (☎7247 1081). ⊖Aldgate East. Faded pictures of scantily clad wrestlers and decor reminiscent of a roadside rest stop won't inspire, but the authentic food is a good option for quick bite. Order inexpensive vegetarian and meat-based curries at the counter (£3-6.50) or takeaway the food for an even cheaper feast. Open daily 8am-11pm. ❷

Coffee @, 154 Brick Ln. (☎7247 6735). ⊖Aldgate East. Other locations at Goswell Rd. and Bermondsey St. Small and cozy cafe that sells organic, fair trade coffees and teas (£1.20), frappes, and smoothies (£2.80). Selection of premade sandwiches and pasta salads from £3. Eclectic decorations such as light fixtures made from paper cups and a rusted pipe-lined bar add a bit of flair. Wi-Fi available. Open 7am-8pm daily. ❶

CLERKENWELL

There's no shortage of fine dining in Clerkenwell, and even the most expensive restaurants offer some affordable sustenance. A weekday crowd enjoys leisurely lunches and after-work snacks but deserts Clerkenwell during the weekend. For a bite on the run or ingredients for a picnic lunch, there are many sandwich bars south of Farringdon station or along **Clerkenwell Green** or **St. John Street.** You'll also find inexpensive snack bars, pubs, and Chinese takeaways on

SEE MAP, p. 364

FOOD

UP ON THE ROOF

While London has an enormous amount of space devoted to greenery on the ground, there has been a recent influx of gardens on the city's rooftops. While the entrance fee for gardens atop luxury hotels or private clubs is often steep, there are a growing number of cheaper options. **Spring Gardens** in Trafalgar Sq. is seven stories high and overlooks one of London's most historic and architecturally stunning areas. It is popular for after-work cocktails on the terrace or at the Rockwell Bar inside. The Babylon restaurant at the **Kensington Roof Gardens**, with its tropical-themed, 6000 sq. m gardens, complete with pink flamingoes and mandarin ducks wandering the grounds, is a worthwhile splurge. The gardens were constructed in the late 1930s, which means that all of the trees have matured naturally.

London's highest public park is planned for the top of **20 Fenchurch Street** in the City, 37 stories (155m) from ground level. While many roof gardens are private, 20 Fenchurch will be free to the public upon its opening in 2011. In addition to gardens and viewing spaces, it will also house cafes and restaurants.

(Spring Gardens ☎ 7870 2900; www.thetrafalgar.com. £25-32 includes roof access, drinks, and a meal. Kensington Roof Gardens ☎ 7937 7994; www.virgin.com/limitededition. Access is free, but meals are expensive. Call ahead.)

West Smithfield just south of the market. For a proper sit-down meal, your best bet is either **Charterhouse Street** or **Exmouth Market**, a pedestrian street north of Clerkenwell Rd. flanked on both sides by all manner of eateries, offering everything from tasty tapas to falafel to lo mein. Although perhaps not as renowned as its fine dining options, Clerkenwell **pubs** are some of London's oldest and most unique (p. 262). From eccentric decor to rare and flavorful ales, Clerkenwell offers great pub options for those in the mood for something less formal than the area's posh restaurants.

Anexo, 61 Turnmill St. (☎ 7250 3401; www.anexo.co.uk). ⊖Farringdon. Funky and laid-back, this Spanish restaurant and bar serves up tasty Iberian dishes in a colorful tiled interior. The large menu offers authentic paella (£7.50-9), fajitas (£7.50-11.50), and tapas (from £3.50) as well as a lunch special that's hard to beat (£6 for 2 courses, £8 for 3 courses). Extensive drink menu. Takeaway available. Wheelchair-accessible. Happy hour M-Sa 5-7pm. Open M-F 10am-11pm, Sa 6-11pm, Su 4:30-11pm. Bar open 11am-2am. AmEx/MC/V. ❷

St. John, 26 St. John St. (☎ 7251 0848; www.stjohnrestaurant.com). ⊖Farringdon. Unusual dishes here reward the adventurous eater. Not a choice destination for vegetarians. Menu changes daily; meals include veal heart and celeriac (£6.80) and roast bone marrow (£7). Bakery at the back of the bar churns out delicious loaves of bread (£2.50). Drinks £8-12. Open M-F noon-3pm and 6-11pm, Sa 6-11pm. Bar open M-F 11am-11pm, Sa 6-11pm. AmEx/MC/V. ❸

The Clerkenwell Kitchen, 31 Clerkenwell Close (☎ 7101 9959; www.theclerkenwellkitchen.co.uk). ⊖Farringdon. Slightly hidden cafe is worth the search to find. Opened to promote the idea of sustainable food production. Almost all of their dishes use organic and local ingredients. From one of the tables inside, you can watch your food made fresh in the large, open kitchen. If the weather is nice, grab a muffin or pastry (£1.40) and head outside to the spacious, enclosed terrace. Specials such as spinach, onion, and feta tart (£7) change daily. Open M-F 8am-5pm. MC/V. ❷

The Greenery, 5 Cowcross St. (☎ 7490 4870). ⊖Farringdon. For the vegetarian or health fanatic in your party, this tiny, spotless restaurant and juice bar is a bit of leafy heaven and a standout from the other sidewalk cafes in the area. Salads starting at £2, savories (lasagna, pizza, quiche) from £2.10, and jacket potatoes from £1.50 make for delicious, cheap lunches. Packed sandwiches from £2. Vitamin-enriched smoothies from £2.30. Expect long queues during lunch. There are only a few tables in this busy shop; takeaway your organic goodies. Open M-F 7am-5pm. ❶

Curved Angel, 53 Clerkenwell Close (☎7251 6311), by St. James Church. ⊖Farringdon. More than just a coffee shop. Stop in for maps of the Clerkenwell Historic Trail and plan your route over coffee (£1) and a huge brownie (£1) or relax with a stuffed *panino* (£3.40) and one of the many free newspapers dotting the end tables. Local artisans' novelty wares sit on display atop the many shelves. Open M-F 8am-8pm, Sa-Su 8am-5pm. MC/V. ❶

Al's Bar/Cafe, 11-13 Exmouth Market (☎7837 4821). ⊖Angel or Farringdon. A favorite hangout for journalists from nearby *Guardian, Face,* and *Arena* newspapers. Red-lit with a basement club. With comfortable leather lounge chairs and windows all around, Al's is a prime spot to relax with coffee (£1.20-2) and people-watch. Outdoor seating in good weather. Sandwiches and salads from £1.50. Daily pasta specials £7. All-day weekend breakfast (from £3.75). DJs visit W-Su. Open M 8am-11pm, Tu-F 8am-2am, Sa 9am-2am, Su 9am-11pm. Kitchen closes at 10pm. AmEx/MC/V. ❶

Sofra, 21 Exmouth Market (☎7833 1111). ⊖Angel. Enjoy Mediterranean food at reasonable prices. Outdoor seating in warmer weather. Meal deals such as their "7 hot, 7 cold" starters (£10 per person). Set *menus* start at £8. Traditional dishes such as lamb *kofte* (£7.50) and a variety of pastas. Free Wi-Fi. Open daily noon-11:30pm. MC/V. ❷

 CONTINENTAL CAFES. Exmouth Market is as close as London gets to the sidewalk cafes of continental Europe. A stroll down this street and tea at any one of its many cafes are great rewards after a full day of sightseeing.

HOLBORN

In the 18th century, there was one tavern in Holborn for every five homes; although the ratio has since diminished, pubs still occupy many a street corner. You don't have to look hard to find cozy enclaves of smoke-blackened wood, traditional fare, and hand-pulled ales. Catering heavily to the after-work crowd from Fleet St. and surrounding areas, they are best for a pint or bite between sightseeing or simply a relaxed bit of traditional London.

SEE MAP, p. 364

For those hungry but not up for pub grub, affordable eateries line the alleys around **Red Lion Street** and **Theobald's Road,** and small cafes cater to the shoppers at **Leather Lane Market.** Whatever your cuisine, if it's in a box or a bag, take it over to **Lincoln's Inn Fields** or **Gray's Inn** for a fair-weather picnic.

▨ **Bleeding Heart Tavern,** corner of Greville St. and Bleeding Heart Yard (☎7404 0333). ⊖Farringdon. Highlights include the roast suckling pig with delicately spiced apple slices (£12), classic beer-battered fish (£10), and chocolate honey pot dessert (£4.50). Extraordinarily good service and fine ale round out your dining experience. Open M-F 7-10:30am, noon-2:30pm, 6-10:30pm. Upstairs pub open M-F 11:30am-11pm. AmEx/MC/V. ❸

Bleeding Heart Bistro and Restaurant, Bleeding Heart Yard (bistro ☎7242 8238, restaurant 7242 2056). ⊖Farringdon. Around the corner from the Tavern (follow the signs). The Parisian cousins of the Bleeding Heart Tavern, this duo ranks among London's finest French cuisine, boasting "one of the finest wine lists in the world." Tucked behind the Tavern, it feels miles away from the hustle and bustle of the surrounding streets. The Bistro features molasses salmon (£8), risotto with greens (£12), and a la carte mains (£8-16). Mains at the restaurant £16-22. Weather permitting, eat outdoors and enjoy the quiet cobblestone courtyard. Outdoor seating wheelchair-accessible. Bistro and restaurant open M-F noon-2:30pm and 6-10:30pm. AmEx/MC/V. Bistro ❹/ Restaurant ❺

Woolley's, 33 Theobald's Rd. (☎7405 3028; www.woolleys.co.uk). Rear entrance on Lamb's Conduit Passage. ⊖Holborn. Narrow takeaway joint in 2 parts: salads (£2-4), savories (£2-4), and jacket potatoes (£2.50-3.50) dished out from the Theobald's Rd.

F O O D

side while the Lamb's Conduit side supplies fresh sandwiches (£2-3) made to order. Daily specials like lentil coconut curry (£6) and duck and orange pate (£5). You can walk through to the Lamb's Conduit side and eat in the charming passage, which makes for great rush-hour people-watching. Open M-F 7:30am-3:30pm. MC/V. ❶

Chutney Raj, 137 Gray's Inn Rd. (☎7831 1149). ⊖Chancery Ln. The smaller size of this Indian and Bangladeshi restaurant belies the enormous menu and special offers for patrons. Traditional tandoori and Balti dishes from £6, plenty of vegetarian dishes, and over 10 varieties of curry (£5-9). Lunch special includes papadams, a starter, and a main course (daily noon-2:30pm; £6), and the similar "student offer" is a great deal (daily noon-2pm and 5:30-11:30pm; £5). Takeaway and delivery also available. Open M-Sa noon-2:30pm and 5:30-11:30pm, Su noon-2pm and 5:30-11pm. MC/V. ❷

Carrot Cafe, 185 Gray's Inn Rd. (☎7278 1417). ⊖Chancery Ln. Small cafe that serves fresh sandwiches like organic chicken and spinach, falafel, or tuna and black olive (from £2) as well as prepared hot foods like quiche (£2.50). Smoothies and fresh juices also available (£2-2.50). All coffee and teas are organic and fair trade. Open M-F 7am-3pm. MC/V. ❶

Cafe 180, 118 Gray's Inn Rd. (☎7916 1279). ⊖Chancery Ln. Spacious and with more sitting room than nearby cafes. 180's high ceilings, crown moldings, and tiny tables are reminscent of an old-fashioned ice cream parlor. Pop in for a filled bagel or croissant (£1.60) or a large cup of soup with a baguette (£1.50). Sandwiches and salads £1.20-£3.80. Takeaway also available. Open M-F 6:30am-4pm. MC/V. ❶

Aki, 182 Gray's Inn Rd. (☎7837 9281). ⊖ Chancery Ln. The bambooed warmth of this cozy Japanese restaurant is an appropriate setting for its traditional menu and dishes. Noodle dishes (from £5), meat dishes (£7-12), and sushi meals (from £5) are bargains. *Bento* box lunch from £5.20. Takeaway or eat in and enjoy the traditional Japanese decor. Wheelchair-accessible. Open M-F noon-2:30pm and 6-11pm, Sa 6-10:30pm. AmEx/MC/V. ❸

THE SOUTH BANK

Although the views of the Thames often outdo the quality of the food, the South Bank is perfect for a small snack or a riverbank picnic. Wharfside eateries are generally the priciest; consider buying food elsewhere and eating on one of the multitude of waterside benches. Numerous pavement eateries of **Gabriel's Wharf** (between the National Theatre and OXO Tower) are mostly cafeteria-style and almost indistinguishable from each other; tide yourself over with an ice cream and head across the river for more variety. Those who prefer to assemble their own meals can turn to the ▧**Borough Market,** where stalls lay out fresh gourmet cheeses, breads, fruits, and cured meats. *(Off Borough High St. www.boroughmarket.org.uk. ⊖London Bridge. Open Th 11am-5pm, F noon-6pm, Sa 9am-4pm, some stalls open daily; best on 3rd Sa of every month.)*

SEE MAP, pp. 370-371

▧ **Cantina del Ponte,** 36c Shad Thames, Butlers Wharf (☎7403 5403). ⊖Tower Hill or London Bridge. Wonderful riverside location by Tower Bridge, with slightly less of the tourist-trap feel of neighboring spots. The busy Mediterranean mural can't hold a candle to the views of the Thames, but given the quality of the classic Italian food, it's okay if you can't get a riverside seat. Lunch *menu* is a bargain at 2 courses for £10, 3 for £13.50 (available M-F noon-3pm). Pizzas from £5. Mains from £8.50. Wheelchair-accessible. Open M-Sa noon-3pm and 6-10:45pm, Su noon-3pm and 6-9:45pm. AmEx/MC/V. ❸

Tas, 33 The Cut (☎7928 1444; www.tasrestaurant.com). ⊖Southwark. Also at 72 Borough High St.; **Tas Cafe,** 76 Borough High; **Tas Pide,** 20-22 New Globe Walk (☎7928 3300). ⊖London Bridge. A dynamic group of stylish and affordable Turkish restaurants. Soups and baked dishes, many vegetarian, outshine the respectable kebabs. Mains from £7.35, 2-course *menus* from £8.75. Live music daily from 7:30pm. Wheelchair-accessible. Open M-Sa noon-11:30pm, Su noon-10:30pm. Dinner reservations recommended at Tas and Tas Pide. AmEx/MC/V. ❷

Cubana, 48 Lower Marsh (☎ 7928 8778; www.cubana.co.uk). ⊖Waterloo. Look for the giant salsa dancers on the walls. Food takes second place to the spicy mixed drinks (from £5, 2-pint jug £15). Sample some classic drinks like the "Sputnik" (Bacardi and Soviet Brandy). At lunch or Happy hour get 2 tapas for £6, a 2-course meal for £6, and 3 courses for £8. Try succulent mains like the *camarones criollo* (creole-style shrimp; £10). Happy hour M-Tu 5-6:30pm and 10pm-midnight, W-Sa 5-6:30pm; cocktails from £2.45. W-Sa nights salsa with live band. Cover F-Sa £5. Open M-Tu noon-midnight, W-Th noon-1am, F noon-3am, Sa 5pm-3am. Reservations recommended. AmEx/MC/V. ❷

Gourmet Pizza Co., Gabriel's Wharf, 56 Upper Ground (☎ 7928 3188). ⊖Southwark or Waterloo. Adventurous pizzeria with something for everyone. Pizzas with unexpected toppings, like Thai chicken (£9), eggplant (£8.25), and beetroot and blue cheese (£8). Appetizers £2-5. Also serves standard Italian pastas and salads. Friendly service, hearty portions. Wheelchair-accessible. Open M-Th noon-11:30pm, F-Sa noon-midnight, Su noon-11pm. Reservations recommended. AmEx/MC/V. ❷

The Island Cafe, 1 Flat Iron Sq. (☎ 7407 2224). ⊖Southwark. At the junction of Union St. and Southwark Bridge Rd. Sit amid the chaos indoors or take your grub to the back patio. One of the only places in the South Bank that serves lunch for under £4. Take-away breakfasts (from £1.80) and classic lunch-box-style sandwiches (from £1.70), from tuna with sweet corn and egg salad to classic brie. There's also a substantial list of hot lunch specials, most around £4. Wheelchair-accessible. Open daily 6am-4pm. ❶

SOUTH LONDON

The area south of the Thames, like so many other parts of London, benefits from a diverse selection of eateries offering cuisine from around the world. From traditional Indonesian to fish 'n' chips, South London has an upscale bistro or a take-away joint for any appetite. Come during market hours to the **Brixton Market** (p. 242) for traditional delights like curry goat or saltfish with ackee.

 GET YOUR VIEW ON. For the budget traveler, the South Bank provides two essential features: a plenitude of takeaway sandwich shops and delis and some of the most beautiful views in the city. Combine the two for a cheap meal served with a side of scenery.

BRIXTON

SW9, 11 Dorrell Pl. (☎ 7738 3116; www.sw9bar.com). ⊖Brixton. This stylish hangout, named after the once-dreaded Brixton postal code, offers plush couches and outdoor seating on a quiet, pedestrian street. Sip a mixed drink during Happy hour (M-F 4:30-7pm) or enjoy an amply portioned meal. Try a gourmet omelette for breakfast or lunch (£8.50); the venison and root-vegetable pie is a dinner favorite (£10). F-Sa live jazz music. Open M-Th 10am-11pm, F-Sa 10am-1am. MC/V. ❷

Gyoza, 426 Coldharbour Ln. (☎ 7274 1492). ⊖Brixton. Chinese food for the budget-conscious that doesn't skimp on taste. The large noodle soups (from £4) will satisfy any appetite, as will the Gyoza boxes (from £7). Takeaway available. Open M-Th noon-11pm, F-Sa noon-midnight, Su 3-11pm. MC/V. ❶

Satay Bar, 447 Coldharbour Ln. (☎ 7326 5001; www.sataybar.co.uk). ⊖Brixton. An Indonesian restaurant with an upscale look, specializing in—you guessed it—satay. Savory dishes include the *ayam panggang* (chicken in spicy coconut sauce; £6) and the vegetarian *gado gado* (bean curd; £5). Balinese masks and modern art watch over dining locals. Happy hour daily 5-8pm (mixed drinks from £4.25, carafes from £12). Open M-Th noon-3pm and 5pm-midnight, F noon-3pm and 5pm-1:30am, Sa 2pm-1:30am, Su 2-11:30pm. MC/V. ❷

Honest, 424 Coldharbour Ln. (☎7738 6161). ❻Brixton. Flip through an environmental magazine as you sip an espresso or munch on vegetarian, vegan, or gluten-free dishes. Start with an English breakfast (£7) and wash it down with fresh juice (from £2). Open M-Th 9am-5pm, F 9am-6pm, Sa 10am-6pm, Su 11am-5pm. MC/V. ❷

CLAPHAM

🔲 **San Marco,** 126 Clapham High St. (☎7622 0452). ❻Clapham North. The friendly staff at San Marco offers authentic Italian fare that will make you wonder if you've actually been transported to Italy. Pasta from £6.30, pizza from £6.50, and meat dishes from £9. Try the delicious baby spinach and toasted bacon salad (£6.30). Open daily 11:30am-11:30pm. MC/V. ❷

Metro, 9a Clapham Common Southside (☎7627 0632; www.metromotel.co.uk). ❻Clapham Common. This garden bar and restaurant oozes romance and sophistication. The delicious cuisine and candlelit atmosphere are a winning combination. Mains start at £11. Tasty and filling Sunday Roast £10. Open M-Tu 6-11pm, Sa noon-11pm, Su noon-10pm. MC/V. ❸

Strada, 102-104 Clapham High St. (☎7627 4847; www.strada.co.uk). ❻Clapham North. Another fine Italian option in Clapham. Tasty pastas start at £8; the pick of the lot is the risotto primavera (£9). Traditional Italian main courses, along with mouth-watering pizza (from £7). Open daily 11:30am-11pm. MC/V. ❸

WESTMINSTER

With one of London's highest concentrations of office workers, Westminster has no shortage of restaurants at every price range—at least for a weekday lunch. Sandwich shops, delicatessens, and takeaway shops rest on most corners. Come nighttime, it's a different story; restaurants raise their prices and sandwich bars close. Many places shut down entirely over the weekend. **Strutton Ground,** a short pedestrian road between Victoria and Great Peter St., has a variety of sandwich and salad bars and cheap Chinese buffets. South of Victoria, **Tachbrook Street** has a number of cheap eats, as well as a tiny but excellent food market (open M-Sa 9am-5pm). Pubs in the area also provide good dining options (p. 267).

SEE MAP, p. 368

🔲 **Goya,** 34 Lupus St. (☎7976 5309; www.goyarestaurant.co.uk). ❻Pimlico. Join the local clientele for a post-siesta meal. Mirrors, large windows, and bright wood give the sunny interior an elegant aura. In good weather, sit outside and enjoy the sun more directly. Generous, diverse tapas (mostly £4-7), including plenty of vegetarian options; 2-3 per person is more than enough. Special sangria £3; alcohol only served with food. Wheelchair-accessible. Open daily 11:30am-11:30pm. £10 min. for AmEx/MC/V. ❸

Tiles, 36 Buckingham Palace Rd. (☎7834 7761). ❻Victoria. Despite Tiles's proximity to Buckingham Palace, the ambience inside this wine bar and restaurant is more continental than British. With cozy wooden tables, faded Spanish-tile floor, and chalkboard menu, the upstairs has a casual, hole-in-the-wall feel. Downstairs is more formal, with exposed brick, candles, and secluded couches. Creative mains include honey-roasted duck (£11), goat cheese and pepper-stuffed chicken (£10), and fish-cakes with chips (£8.50). Wheelchair-accessible. Open M-F noon-11pm. Kitchen open noon-2:30pm and 5:30-10:30pm. AmEx/MC/V. ❸

Mange, 2 Greycoat Pl. (☎7263 5000; www.mange.co.uk). ❻St. James's Park or Victoria. Just around the corner from Strutton Ground, this popular lunchtime caterer is a perfect pit stop for upscale picnic fixings. A meticulously arranged deli case displays an ever-changing mix of prepared salads (£2). Soups (£1.80-2.25), sandwiches (£3-4), yogurt, fruit, and juices available for takeaway only. Several vegetarian options. Also an excellent spot for a quick, healthy breakfast. Open M-F 8am-5pm. £5 min. for MC/V. ❶

Relish, 8 John Islip St. (☎071 828 0628). ⊖Pimlico. A line of hungry office workers often spills out the door of this fresh lunch shop. Order tasty deli sandwiches (£2.40-3.70), baked potatoes (£2.50-4), salads, and plenty of vegetarian options. Come early for the best selection. Diners lucky enough to find a table can stay to enjoy the eclectic Beatles/ Europop music mix. Open M-Th 7:30am-3:30pm, F 7:30am-3pm. Cash only. ❶

Noodle Noodle, 18 Buckingham Palace Rd. (☎7931 9911; www.noodle-noo-dle.co.uk). ⊖Victoria. Additional location across from the Apollo Victoria Theatre on Vauxhall Bridge Rd. Tropically-colored walls and Lionel Richie's "Live and in Concert" over the speakers makes this Chinese restaurant a unique experience. Massive portions and tasty noodle and rice dishes make this a great place for a sightseeing break. Side dishes (£4) aren't a great deal, but the mains will feed you 3 times over (£5-7). 3-course special (£11) M-F 3-10pm, Sa noon-11pm. Takeaway available. Open daily noon-11pm. £10 min. for AmEx/MC/V. ❷

THE WEST END

MAYFAIR AND ST. JAMES'S

Food on **Oxford Street** itself is predictable and tourist-oriented, with mostly underwhelming fast-food and restaurant chains. Fortunately, sidestreets in the heart of Mayfair offer plenty of better food and wider selections, though

SEE MAP, p. 356

prices can still be a bit steep. Londoners have long kept quiet about the bustling **St. Christopher's Place,** reached by an alley opposite the Bond St. Tube station. Less picturesque but just as wallet-friendly, **Kingly Street,** between Regent St. and Carnaby St., is popular with local diners as well. One of the most pleasant places to eat and drink is in and around the winding cobblestone alleys of **Shepherd Market.**

Carluccio's, St. Christopher's Pl. (☎7935 5927; www.carluccios.com). ⊖Bond St. Fine Italian cooking in a pleasant and bustling environment. Short menu stocks many variations on pasta as well as a few meat dishes, plenty of appetizers, salads, and scrumptious desserts. Choose from shared tables on the ground floor, more formal indoor seating, or the open patio that spills into St. Christopher's Courtyard. *Antipasti* from £4.50, mains from £8.75. Carluccio's also has an on-site deli with Italian hams, gourmet pastas, and olive oils. Branches in Islington and the City, and delis all over London. Wheelchair-accessible patio. Open M-F 8am-11pm, Sa 9am-11pm, Su 9am-10:30pm. AmEx/MC/V. ❷

Mo Tearoom, 23 Heddon St. (☎7434 3999; www.momoresto.com). ⊖Piccadilly Circus or Oxford Circus. Restaurant, tea room, members-only bar, and bazaar all in one, Momo is an authentic slice of Marrakesh. For the hippest crowd and the cheapest prices, stick to the tea room. The interior is hung with traditional lanterns and decorated with Moroccan crafts, some of which are available for purchase. Carved chairs, floor cushions, and low tables add to the ambience. Mix and match tapas-style appetizers (£4-7.80) including the popular Harira and mini chicken tagine. Hookah is also available (£9). Wheelchair-accessible outside seating. Come early to avoid an evening wait. Open daily noon-midnight. AmEx/MC/V. ❸

Sofra, 18 Shepherd St. (☎7493 3320; www.sofra.co.uk), in Shepherd's Market. ⊖Hyde Park Corner or Green Park. Another location at 1 St. Christopher's Pl. One of the most popular restaurants in Shepherd's Market, Sofra offers fine Turkish cuisine at a reasonable price. Their most popular dish, the Mixed Grill, includes minced lamb and chicken on a skewer (£13.45). Vegetarian options are also plentiful. Try the Healthy Menu, a mix of 11 dishes (lunch £9, dinner £11) or the Summer *menu* (£10/12). Open daily noon-midnight. AmEx/MC/V. ❷

FOOD

Richoux, 41a South Audley St. (☎ 7629 5228; www.richoux.co.uk). ⊖Hyde Park Corner or Marble Arch. Another location at 172 Piccadilly (⊖Piccadilly Circus). Richoux is a fine spot for afternoon tea in sumptuous surroundings. A cafe, restaurant, and tea room, Richoux offers traditional English fare, but is best known for its tea service, which attracts an international crowd from nearby embassies. The cream tea, with scones, preserves, and hot chocolate, is a pricey £9, as is the traditional tea, with sandwiches and pastries (£16.50, £30 for two). A normal pot of tea, however, costs only £2.85. Open M-F 8am-11pm, Sa 8am-11:30pm, Su 9am-11pm. AmEx/MC/V. ❹

L'Autre, 5b Shepherd St. (☎ 7499 4680), in Shepherd's Market. ⊖Hyde Park Corner or Green Park. This charming and eccentric restaurant offers Mexican and Polish dishes served in a cozy Victorian dining room. Specializes in fresh, seasonal game. Try the roast quail with wild boar sausage (£14.50), or the authentic Mexican paella (£14). Open M-F noon-3pm and 6-11pm, Sa-Su 12:30-11pm. AmEx/MC/V. ❸

Tamarind, 20 Queen St. (☎ 7629 3561). ⊖Green Park. A sumptuous interior and classy look are evidence that Tamarind is far from cheap, but the food is worth its weight in gold. Vegetarian dishes start at £6, meat kebabs from £16.50. For the best deal, come for the *prix-fixe* lunch (2 courses £17, 3 £19, tasting menu £25). Reserve ahead. Open M-F noon-2:45pm and 6-11:30pm, Sa 6-11:30pm, Su noon-2:45pm and 6:30-10:30pm. AmEx/MC/V. ❸

 FOOD FOR POCKET CHANGE. Takeaway is cheaper than staying in for many lunch places. Save yourself a few quid by getting your grub to go.

SOHO

One of the best places in London to eat and drink, Soho has restaurants, cafes, and bars to suit every taste and budget. While Gerrard St. is considered **Chinatown's** heart, its eateries cater just as much to non-Chinese tourists. Those on Lisle St., one block south toward Leicester Sq., are often cheaper, less crowded, and more "authentic." **Little Italy** has pizza, pasta, and lots of garlic goodness on Frith St., as well as various late-night and 24hr. options. **Wardour Street** is a new hot spot for everything from vegetarian food to creperies and Asian cuisine. The southern side of Shaftesbury Ave., just north of Gerrard St., feeds hungry postclubbers. Midday, the outdoor cafes near Soho Sq. are perfect for lounging.

■ **Masala Zone,** 9 Marshall St. (☎ 7287 9966; www.realindianfood.com). ⊖Oxford Circus. Also in Islington at 80 Upper St. (☎ 7359 3399). Masala Zone oozes hipness with its softly lit interior and sunken dining room. The food is steeped in South Indian tradition, cooked in a kitchen visible from anywhere in the restaurant and loaded with *masala*. The menu has typical favorites (£6-8), as well as "street food," which is served in small bowls (£3.40-5.50). The speciality is *thalis*, platters that allow you to sample a variety of dishes (£7.50-11.50). Special dishes available for diabetics. *Menu* available before 6:30pm (from £8). Open M-F noon-2:45pm and 5:30-11pm, Sa 12:30-11pm, Su 12:30-3:30pm and 6-10:30pm. MC/V. ❷

■ **Busaba Eathai,** 106-110 Wardour St. (☎ 7255 8686). ⊖Tottenham Court Rd., Leicester Sq., or Piccadilly Circus. Incense, floating candles, and slick wooden paneling will make you feel like you're dining in a Buddhist temple. Large but tightly packed communal tables ensure a lively wait for the affordable, filling dishes. Students and locals line up for pad thai, curries, and wok creations (£6-8). Plenty of vegetarian options. No reservations. Open M-Th noon-11pm, F-Sa noon-11:30pm, Su noon-10pm. AmEx/MC/V. ❷

■ **Golden Dragon,** 28-29 Gerrard St. (☎ 1705 2503). ⊖Leicester Sq. The ritziest and best-known dim sum joint in Chinatown. Golden Dragon's 2 large red-and-gold rooms are packed on the weekends with families and couples taking in the cheery atmosphere and shoveling in the dumplings—from veggie staples to minced prawn and sugar cane

FOOD

treats (each dish £3-4). Regular dinner items £6-20. Dim sum £12.50-22.50. Open M-Th noon-11:30pm, F-Sa noon-midnight, Su 11am-11pm. Dim sum served M-Sa noon-5pm, Su 11am-5pm. AmEx/MC/V. ❸

Mr. Jerk, 189 Wardour St. (☎7287 2878; www.mrjerk.com). ⊖Tottenham Court Rd. Small and simple, this restaurant lets its fine Caribbean fare do the talking. Feast on the house specialties: jerk chicken (£7.50), Trinidadian *mutton roti* (£5), or several vegetarian options (£6-8). All mains come with a hearty portion of rice and peas. Add fried plantains (£1.30) or delicious baked mac 'n' cheese (£3). Extensive alcohol menu, including hard-to-find and imported liquors. Takeaway available. Open M-Sa 10am-11pm, Su noon-8pm. AmEx/MC/V. ❷

Hummus Bros., 88 Wardour St. (☎7734 1311; www.hbros.co.uk). ⊖Oxford Circus or Tottenham Court Rd. Small, bright space with red-lacquered cafeteria-style tables. The Bros., true to their name, offer variations on hummus; 2 sizes of this versatile dish are topped with everything from spiced chicken to salad and are served with warm pita bread (£3-5.20). Many vegetarian options. Environmentally friendly (completely carbon-neutral) with free Wi-Fi. Open M-W 11am-10pm, Th-F 11am-11pm, Sa noon-11pm, Su noon-10pm. AmEx/MC/V. ❶

Carlton Coffee House, 41 Broadwick St. (☎7437 3807). ⊖Oxford Circus or Tottenham Court Rd. Cozy tables for 2, an energetic staff, and catchy Italian music will get you moving for late-afternoon Soho sightseeing. Homemade soups (£1.80), basic pastas (£5), and made-to-order *panini* (£4-6). Locals congregate for some of the best coffee in town. Takeaway and delivery available. Bring your own wine (£2 uncorking fee) for a complete dining experience. Open M-F 7am-5:30pm, Sa 8:30am-6:30pm. MC/V. ❶

itsu, 103 Wardour St. (☎7479 4790, for delivery to Chelsea, Canary Wharf, and Hanover Sq. 7590 2404; www.itsu.co.uk). ⊖Oxford Circus, Piccadilly Circus, or Tottenham Court Rd. A genuinely groundbreaking eating experience amidst shiny retro decor. A steel monorail shuttles color-coded Asian fusion delights and traditional raw-fish plates (£3-4) right to your table; you simply lift off dishes that catch your eye (or taste buds). Everything from miso soup to shot glasses of chocolate and raspberry mousse sails by. Expect to spend about £12. Takeaway available. Open M-Th noon-11pm, F noon-midnight, Sa 12:30pm-midnight, Su 1-10pm. MC/V. ❸

Bar Italia, 22 Frith St. (☎7437 4520). ⊖Piccadilly Circus or Leicester Sq. This garlic-adorned 50s-style coffee bar is a Soho institution, nostalgically reviving hard-partying rock stars and their many imitators. Get your fix from espresso (£2), or munch on a post-club *panino* (£5-7) or pizza (£6-9.50). Waitresses don't need an

ON THE MENU

CORNISH PASTIES

Cornish pasties are everywhere in London. They line the shelves of supermarkets, make guest appearances in the hot food sections of delis, and are sold to intoxicated clubbers from late-night street stalls and takeaway joints. However, even the modern ubiquity of these tasty treats does not do justice to their importance in British history.

The story of the pasty begins in the Cornish tin mines of the 19th century. Miners' wives engineered the pasty as a food durable enough for long hours in the mines. Unlike today's potato-heavy imitations, the original Cornish pasty contained skirt steak, potato, swede, onion salt, and pepper—all enclosed by a protective chunky crust. By holding the pasty by its folded edge, miners were able to eat their lunch without ingesting the grime and arsenic of their surroundings. Legend also has it that the miners threw the crusts down the mine-shafts to appease the "knockers," mischievous goblins who lived deep below the surface.

When mining ended in Cornwall, the miners scattered, bringing their pasties with them. As a result, people all over the country enjoy these versatile meals. Travelers should beware, however, that the presence of carrots in store-bought pasties is a sign of inferior quality. Those seeking genuine pasties should stick to bakeries for the real deal.

occasion to dress in festive gear, and bartenders frequently sing along with whatever Europop music may be playing. Outdoor seating perfect for people-watching in good weather. Accepts euro. Open M-Th 7:30am-4:30am, F-Sa 7:30am-6am, Su 7:30am-3am. Alcohol served 10am-11pm. £10 min. for MC/V . ❷

Soba Noodle Bar, 38 Poland St. (☎017 1734 6400; www.soba.co.uk). ⊖Oxford Circus Also at 11/13 Soho St. (☎7827 7300). ⊖Tottenham Court Rd. Narrow noodle bar with a long communal table, bench seating, and walls covered with corrugated plastic. Close proximity to Tube stations makes it ideal for a meal on the go. Big bowls of noodles (from £6), rice plates (from £5.30), and lots of vegetarian options. Wheelchair-accessible. Happy hour (all mains £4.50) M-W 5:30-7pm, Sa noon-5pm, Su all day. Open M-F noon-3:30pm and 5:30-11pm, Sa noon-10pm, Su noon-9pm. AmEx/MC/V. ❷

Patisserie Valerie, 44 Old Compton St. (☎7437 3466; www.patisserie-valerie.co.uk). ⊖Piccadilly Circus or Leicester Sq. Branches at 27 Kensington Church St., 215 Brompton Rd., 8 Russell St., and 105 Marylebone High St. The excellent pastries are delicious, and the smell is an experience in itself. The variety of croissants (£1.20-1.50) is stiff competition for any French rival. The upstairs restaurant offers excellent English breakfasts and lunches. Cafe: cakes and pastries £2.30-4.50. Restaurant: mains £3-7. Open M-Tu 7:30am-8pm, W-Sa 7:30am-11pm, Su 9am-8pm. ❶

COVENT GARDEN AND THE STRAND

In spite of its trendiness—or perhaps because of it—Covent Garden is not known for its cuisine. The **Piazza** within has unremarkable tourist-oriented cafes and overpriced restaurants catering to theatre- and opera-goers, while sandwich bars and theme pubs prevail on side streets. Two exceptions are **Neal's Yard,** a small open courtyard that has evolved into a wholesome haven of vegetarian, vegan, and organic delights, and the side streets surrounding **Seven Dials.** Since the **Strand** is essentially one busy thoroughfare, it's not surprising that the majority of dining is mediocre at best. Head to **Craven Passage** and **Villiers Street,** between the Strand and Victoria Embankment, if you're looking to grab a bite in the area.

🏅 **Rock and Sole Plaice,** 47 Endell St. (☎7836 3785). ⊖Covent Garden. A street-side outdoor picnic area with overhead Christmas lights makes this one of London's most picturesque fish 'n' chips joints. A self-proclaimed "master fryer" (qualifications unclear) turns out tasty haddock, cod, halibut, and sole filets (all with chips) for £9-11. Specialties change daily but range from £4-6. Seating inside is tight, and there is a strong possibility you will share a table, since the restaurant gets packed throughout the mealtime rushes. Open M-Sa 11:30am-11:30pm, Su 11:30am-10pm. MC/V. ❷

🏅 **Cafe in the Crypt,** Duncannon St. (☎7839 4342). ⊖Embankment or Charing Cross. In the basement of St.-Martins-in-the-Fields Church, this spacious, exposed-brick cellar is a monastery gone modern. An excellent fresh salad bar (£6.75), freshly made sandwiches (£4), and hearty warm puddings (£3) served cafeteria-style make the Crypt a perfect break from Trafalgar sightseeing. Linger with a glass of wine (from £3) or stay for afternoon tea (£5). Jazz some W nights. Open M-W 8am-8pm, Th-Sa 8am-10:30pm, Su noon-6:30pm. £5 min. for AmEx/MC/V. ❶

🏅 **Scoop,** 40 Shorts Gardens (☎7240 7086; www.scoopgelato.com). ⊖Covent Garden. A bright orange storefront attracts passersby, but the creamy gelato and fresh sorbet—made each morning on the premises—keeps them coming back. Using only fresh ingredients—many imported from the owner's Tuscan homeland—flavors range from *pompelmo* (grapefruit) to *cioccolato al latte* (milk chocolate). Also sells an assortment of pastries, coffee, and tea. Cups and cones start at £2. Open daily 8am-11:30pm. MC/V. ❶

🏅 **Neal's Yard Salad Bar,** 1, 2, 8-10 Neal's Yard (☎7836 3233; www.nealsyardsalad-bar.co.uk). ⊖Covent Garden. Much more than just a salad bar, this 3-building complex of vegetarian and vegan fare is a great dining option. Choices include special salad mixes that change often (couscous, pepper, kidney beans, and spices £8), hearty soups (£5.50), and slices of homemade quiche (£4.50). If you're sticking around, battle the pigeons for table space in the colorful outdoor courtyard or linger in the vibrant upstairs sitting room. Look out for the motion-activated frog croaking as you step into the loo. Open daily 8am-9pm. Cash only. ●

Cafe Pacifico, 5 Langley St. (☎7379 7728; www.cafepacifico-laperla.com). ⊖Covent Garden. A rare touch of Cabo in Covent Garden, this Mexican cantina is the most authentic in town. Pacifico's standards and promotion of tequila have been recognized as one of the top 3 most authentic by the Tequila Regulatory Council of Mexico. Take a shopping break with chips and salsa (free with meal) and a cold Corona (£3); heartier lunch special (£6; £10 including 2 beers or a margarita) M-F noon-4:30pm. Dinner options include fajitas (£13-17), tostadas (£12-13), and enchiladas (£8-9). Open Tu-Sa noon-11:30pm, Su noon-10:30pm. AmEx/MC/V. ●

The Ivy, 1-5 West St. (☎7836 4751). ⊖Leicester Sq. "A table at the Ivy is one of the most sought-after pieces of furniture in London," or so goes the saying. The superb modern British food is mouth-watering enough to make the saying believable. Trademark shepherd's pie £14.50, hors d'oeuvres from £7.50. Dinner reservations require booking up to 3 months in advance, but lunch tables are much easier to come by and provide excellent views. Wheelchair-accessible. Open daily noon-3pm and 5:30pm-midnight. AmEx/MC/V. ●

 RESTAURANT SECURITY. Many restaurants have security clips underneath the tables to thwart would-be thieves. Attach your purse or backpack straps to them to ease your mind.

BLOOMSBURY

At the heart of London's student community, Bloomsbury is overflowing with top-notch budget food. Running parallel to Tottenham Court Rd., **Charlotte Street** is one of London's best-known culinary stretches, with fashionable restaurants in all price ranges. A string of extremely cheap vegetarian Indian eateries and sweet shops lines **Drummond Street**, near Euston. On the other side of Bloomsbury, bordering Holborn, **Sicilian Avenue**

SEE MAP, p. 362

has great sandwich and snack shops. **Euston Road, Museum Street,** and **Cosmo Place** boast particularly flavorful ethnic food. Of course, on a sunny day, the ideal meal only requires a bit of takeaway and a patch of grass on one of the numerous squares and gardens that dot the neighborhood.

▨ **ICCo (Italiano Coffee Company)**, 46 Goodge St. (☎7580 9688). ⊖Goodge St. A young student crowd usually fills the steel-tabled dining area. Light-years ahead of its competition, ICCo serves delicious 11 in. pizzas made to order from £3. Pre-packaged sandwiches and baguettes on fresh bread start at £1.50 (rolls 50p). Pasta from £2. Buy any hot drink before noon and get a free freshly baked croissant. Sandwiches and baguettes half-price after 4pm. Takeaway available. Pizzas available after noon. Open daily 7am-11pm. AmEx/MC/V. ●

▨ **Navarro's Tapas Bar**, 67 Charlotte St. (☎7637 7713; www.navarros.co.uk). ⊖Goodge St. Colorful, bustling tapas restaurant boasts tiled walls, brightly painted furniture, and flamenco music straight from Seville. The authenticity carries over to the excellent food—try the spicy fried potatoes (patatas bravas; £3.55). Tapas £3.50-11; 2-3 per person is plenty. £7.50 min. purchase. Open M-F noon-3pm and 6-10pm, Sa 6-10pm. AmEx/MC/V. ●

▨ **Newman Arms**, 23 Rathbone St., (☎7636 1127). ⊖Tottenham Court Rd. or Goodge St. A pub with a famous upstairs pie room and restaurant. Connoisseurs at 10 sought-

FOOD

after tables dig into homemade meat pies. Seasonal game fillings most popular; vegetarian and fish options available. Pie with potatoes and veggies on the side £9. Pints start at £3. Book in advance or face a hungry wait. Pub open M-F 11am-11pm. Restaurant open M-Th noon-3pm and 6-9pm, F noon-3pm. ❷

Savoir Faire, 42 New Oxford St. (☎ 7436 0707). ⊖Tottenham Court Rd. or Holborn. Cherubic murals and handwritten quotations cover the walls of this bistro. Sit at wooden tables and enjoy excellent seafood and continental standards like steak frites and salad (£12). 2-course vegetarian dinner £9. Popular brunch spot serving eggs Benedict and florentine (£7). Open M-Sa noon-4pm and 5-11:30pm, Su noon-10:30pm. AmEx/MC/V. ❷

Diwana Bhel Poori House, 121-123 Drummond St. (☎ 7387 5556; www.diwanarestaurant.com). ⊖Euston or Euston Sq. No frills here—just great, cheap South Indian vegetarian food and quiet, efficient service. Try the excellent all-you-can-eat lunch buffet (£6.50, served daily noon-2:30pm) or enjoy ample portions on the regular menu. Outside of buffet hours, *thali* set *menu* is a good deal (£6-9). Open daily noon-11:30pm. AmEx/MC/V. ❷

North Sea Fish Restaurant, 7-8 Leigh St. (☎ 7387 5892). ⊖Russell Sq. or King's Cross St. Pancras. Fish 'n' chips done right. The classy little restaurant, heavily populated by retired Brits, offers a boatload of fresh, tasty seafood dishes (£9-19) in a warm setting. For a younger scene—and much lower prices—order from the takeaway shop next door (cod fillets £4.30-6). Restaurant open M-Sa noon-2:30pm and 5:30-10:30pm. Takeaway M-Sa noon-2:30pm and 5-11pm. AmEx/MC/V. ❸

Wagamama, 40 Streatham St. (☎ 7323 9223; www.wagamama.com). ⊖Tottenham Court Rd. or Russell Sq. The original branch of the London noodle dynasty. A chain, but cheap and tasty dishes make it a suitable dining option. Cafeteria-style seating. Ramen from £7.15. Wide vegetarian selection. Open M-Sa noon-11pm, Su noon-10pm. ❷

NORTH LONDON

CAMDEN TOWN, KING'S CROSS, AND ISLINGTON

In Camden Town, the allure of the inexpensive food at market stalls may pull you away from the restaurant tables, but that would be a mistake. **Parkway,** running from the Tube toward Regent's Park, is home to several noodle bars, and **Inverness Street** also has some good cafes. In nearby Islington, **Upper Street** has over 100 restaurants, with close to 200 more in the surrounding area, ranging from Indian to Turkish to French to fish 'n' chips. For a taste of the ungentrified, pre-yuppie Islington, head to **Chapel Market,** just off Liverpool St. opposite the Angel Tube station. Here you can have an English meal with all the fixings for under £3 in any of the hole-in-the-wall restaurants that line the street. Just don't expect linen tablecloths.

▩ **Gallipoli,** 102 Upper St. (☎ 7359 0630), **Gallipoli Again,** 120 Upper St. (☎ 7359 1578), and **Gallipoli Bazaar,** 107 Upper St. (☎ 7226 5333). ⊖Angel. Three's usually a crowd, but not with this group of tasty Upper St. eateries. Dark walls, patterned tiles, and hanging lamps provide the background to spectacular Lebanese, North African, and Turkish delights like *iskender kebab* (grilled lamb with yogurt and marinated pita bread in secret sauce; £8.75) and the 2-course lunch (£7). After the success of the 1st restaurant, Gallipoli Again opened on the same block with the added bonus of an outdoor patio. Gallipoli Bazaar sits between the other 2 and serves up food, cocktails, and sheesha pipes in tearoom surroundings. Again and Bazaar wheelchair-accessible. Open M-Th 10:30am-11pm, F-Sa 10:30am-midnight, Su 10:30am-11pm. Reservations recommended F-Sa. MC/V. ❷

▩ **Mango Room,** 10-12 Kentish Town Rd. (☎ 7482 5065; www.mangoroom.co.uk). ⊖Camden Town. A neighborhood favorite in an area where few restaurants last more than a year. Decor includes funky paintings and orange walls. The small Caribbean menu features fish complemented with plenty of mango, avocado, and coconut sauces.

Mains from £10. Lunch from £6. A wide array of potent tropical drinks is served from the tiny bar, but only at night. Wheelchair-accessible. Open daily noon-midnight. Reservations recommended Sa-Su. MC/V. ❷

🖼 **New Culture Revolution,** 42 Duncan St. (☎ 7833 9083; www.newculturerevolution.co.uk). ⊖Angel. When this small restaurant first opened in 1994, it increased Londoners' appetite for East Asian food. The revolution refers to the wealth of healthful menu options. Huge portions of noodles and steaming soups can be ordered from a menu that champions meats and veggies, too. Choose from dumplings (£5), vegetable chow mein (£5.20), or chili and lemongrass seafood lo mein (from £6). Open daily noon-11pm. AmEx/MC/V. ❶

Le Mercury, 140a Upper St. (☎ 7354 4088). ⊖Angel. This sunny little corner restaurant offers delicious and delightfully presented French food at extremely affordable prices. The service is excellent, and the romantic ambience complete with dripping candles belies the price: dinner mains like *gateaux de poissons* and *poitrine du porc* are only £6.45. The appetizers and desserts are not to be missed. Wheelchair-accessible. Open daily noon-12:30am. Dinner reservations recommended. MC/V. ❷

Candid Cafe, 3 Torrens St. (☎ 7837 4237). ⊖Angel. Signs point to the door beneath the horse sculpture; go up 2 fl. to reach the cafe, part of the Candid Arts Trust. Quirky antique sofas and Victorian candlesticks decorate the room. The intellectual bohemian scene is ages away from the street-level bustle. Watercolors and sexually provocative paintings provide the perfect backdrop for, well, candid discussions. Baguette sandwiches from £3; other hot dishes £5.50-7. Open M-Sa noon-10pm, Su noon-5pm. ❶

Cuba Libre, 72 Upper St. (☎ 7354 9998). ⊖Angel. This colorful and spirited tapas restaurant has standard Latin dishes from various countries (the recipes here certainly aren't all Cuban). Music plays loudly, Che Guevara posters hang, and exuberant waiters tend to diners. The bar in the back has some dance space. Choose an appetizer and a main course for £10, or you can order tapas and eat outside (6 tapas for £15). Happy hour 5-8pm (2 for £2.50 among the 241 different mixed drinks). Wheelchair-accessible. Open M-Sa 10am-2am, Su 10:30am-10:30pm. MC/V. ❷

Pizzeria Oregano, 18-19 St. Alban's Pl. (☎ 7288 1123). ⊖Angel. 2 steps away but almost hidden from Upper St. and its trendy eateries. The cafeteria-style decor may leave something to be desired, but the pizzas (from £7) and mains (from £8) are top-notch. Open Tu-Th 5:30-11pm, F 5:30-11:30pm, Sa 12:30-11:30pm, Su 12:30-10pm. MC/V. ❷

Afghan Kitchen, 35 Islington Green (☎ 7359 8019). ⊖Angel. This tiny restaurant sits on a busy street, but the cool mint walls and simple decor feel serene. Enjoy the food while sitting on stools and wooden planks either communally downstairs or more privately upstairs. "Traditional Afghan home cooking" equals manageable portions of spicy meat and vegetarian dishes; most are £5-6.50. Sides £2-3.50, yummy baklava £1. Partially wheelchair-accessible. Open Tu-Sa noon-3:30pm and 5:30-11pm. Cash only. ❶

Trojka, 101 Regent's Park Rd. (☎ 7483 3765; www.trojka.co.uk). ⊖Camden Town. Part restaurant, part Russian tea room, the 3-horse trap of its name could refer to the Russian, Ukrainian, and Polish influences tugging on the menu. If your budget doesn't stretch to the *sevruga* caviar (£36), the lumpfish caviar makes for an affordable substitute (£9). *Pelmeni* (meat pastries; £7) are perfect for a light supper; otherwise coffees, teas, and homemade desserts are also served. 2-course lunch *menu* M-F £10, Sa-Su £8. Open daily 9am-10:30pm. MC/V. ❷

Metro Bar & Grill, 270 Upper St. (☎ 7226 1118; www.metrobargrill.com). ⊖Highbury and Islington. Metro considers itself the "height of barbecue," and it doesn't disappoint. Try the char-grilled Thai-style tuna steak if you're feeling adventurous or stick to the baby back ribs (£11) for a more traditional barbecue option. If you've got a sweet tooth, wash your meal down with a chocolate tulip full of berry mousse (£5.25). Open Tu-Th noon-2:30pm and 5-10pm, F noon-2:30pm and 5pm-midnight, Sa noon-midnight, Su 1-9:30pm. MC/V. ❸

FOOD

THE BIG SPLURGE

MMM, YUMMY

London brings together its passion for food and its growing reputation as a hot spot for inventive, international cuisine during a four-day festival appropriately titled **Taste of London.** Taste festivals occur all over the UK, but the feature event is the one held during the end of June in the capital.

Taking over the southern edge of Regent's Park, the Taste festival includes chefs representing approximately 50 gourmet restaurants from around the city, as well as food and drink companies who come to show off their products to eager consumers. Each restaurant prepares 3 signature dishes—typically a starter, main course, and dessert.

The official currency of the festival is crowns, available in packets of 20 which allow for more than enough tasting and testing. Free samples from over 100 companies who set up shop almost negate the need to buy anything and ensure that regardless of how many crowns you spend, you will not walk away hungry from this festival.

www.tasteoflondon.co.uk. ⊖*Regent's Park. Standard entry £21; premium entry £35, includes £20 worth of crowns; VIP entry £50 includes £20 worth of crowns, access to VIP lounge, and complimentary glass of champagne. Prices subject to change.*

Marine Ices, 8 Haverstock Hill (☎ 7482 9003). ⊖Chalk Farm. The Mansi family has been in charge at this *gelateria* and restaurant since 1930 and now supplies its superb *gelati* to 1500 restaurants in and around London. Single scoop £1.50; more elaborate concoctions start at £2.80. Italian standards from £5. *Gelateria* open M-Sa 10:30am-11pm, Su 11am-10pm. Restaurant open M-F noon-3pm and 6-11pm, Sa noon-11pm, Su noon-10pm. AmEx/MC/V. ❶

HAMPSTEAD, HIGHGATE, AND GOLDERS GREEN

Hampstead High Street has no shortage of eating opportunities for the area's wealthy residents; most of the places are fairly high-end but very good. The establishments know they have to maintain their quality to retain customers, so Hampstead is perfect for a culinary splurge. It's also a sugar lover's paradise, with countless bakeries and *patisseries*, offering inexpensive sweet and savory bites. For a cluster of cheap restaurants, head to **South End Road** near the Hampstead Heath train station. **Highgate** is short on eats; you'll mostly find pubs and convenience stores. Bakeries in the Jewish neighborhood **Golders Green** make some of the best challah in the city.

▧ **Le Crêperie de Hampstead,** 77 Hampstead High St. (www.hampsteadcreperie.com), the metal stand on the side of the King William IV statue. ⊖Hampstead. Don't let the slow-moving line deter you; these phenomenal crepes are worth the wait. Among many other varieties, try the favorite ham, egg, and cheese (£3.70) or the maple, walnut, and cream (£3). Open M-Th 11:45am-11pm, F-Su 11:45am-11:30pm. ❶

▧ **Carmelli Bakery,** 128 Golders Green Rd. (☎ 8455 2074). ⊖Golders Green (Zone 3). Carmelli's golden egg-glazed challah (from £1.50) is one of the best in London. With a pastry case filled to the brim with goodies large and small (starting around £1.50), it's hard to go wrong here. F afternoons are packed as people prepare for the Sabbath. Kosher. Parve available. Wheelchair-accessible. Hours vary, but generally open daily 6am-1am; Th and Sa 24hr. Cash only. ❶

▧ **Bloom's,** 130 Golders Green Rd. (☎ 8455 1338). ⊖Golders Green (Zone 3). The waiters' signature black bow ties have been an essential part of the experience since 1920. The takeaway shop in the front serves freshly made dishes like potato salad and sandwich fillers (from £4.50), and the sleek restaurant in back has traditional dishes like chopped liver sandwiches (£8.50) chicken *schnitzel* (£12.50). Jewish favorites like *gefilte* fish (£4.50) and *latkes* (£2) served as side orders. Kosher. Parve available. Wheelchair-accessible. Open M-Th and Su noon-11pm, F 11am-3pm. ❷

Al Casbah, 42 Hampstead High St. (☎7431 6356). ⊖Hampstead. Amid the percussive music and cushioned stools, the Moroccan chef cooks up an array of mixed grillades platters (from £12.50) and couscous dishes (from £12.50) large enough for 2. Lounge on the low couches with ornate pillows and, on warm days, people-watch through the enormous windows looking onto the sidewalk. Sa belly dancing. Open daily 9am-11pm. MC/V. ❸

MARYLEBONE AND REGENT'S PARK

Marylebone's culinary landscape is ever-changing. The many restaurants, delis, and bakeries clustered around Edgware Rd., including the Maroush food empire, serve up some of the best Middle Eastern food in London, while a growing number of fashionable sandwich bars and restaurants around Marylebone High St. cater to a crowd with a light appetite. Not known for its wealth of budget eateries, Marylebone can be a challenging place to find a cheap bite. But with a little hunting, (relative) deals abound.

SEE MAP, p. 369

🎏 **Mandalay,** 444 Edgware Rd. (☎7258 3696; www.mandalayway.com). ⊖Edgware Rd. 5min. walk north from the Tube. Looks ordinary, tastes extraordinary—one of the best meal deals around. With huge portions of wildly inexpensive food, this Burmese restaurant is justly plastered with awards. Less character than nearby Patogh, but cheaper. Lunch specials offer great value (curry and rice £3.90; 3 courses, including a banana fritter, £6). Ask for the full menu, which includes an explanation of Burmese cuisine. Mains, including sizeable vegetarian selection, £4-7.90. Open M-Sa noon-2:30pm and 6-10:30pm. Dinner reservations recommended. MC/V. ❶

🎏 **Patogh,** 8 Crawford Pl. (☎7262 4015). ⊖Edgware Rd. With just 10 tables (5 upstairs and 5 downstairs) and a cave-like interior, this tiny but charming Persian restaurant gives new meaning to "hole in the wall." Generous portions of sesame-seed flatbread (£2) and freshly prepared starters (£2.50-6) will whet your appetite; flame-grilled mains like *kebab koobideh* (minced lamb kebab) with bread, rice, or salad (£6-11) will feed you for days. Takeaway available. Open daily noon-midnight. ❷

🎏 **The Golden Hind,** 73 Marylebone Ln. (☎7486 3644). ⊖Baker St. or Bond St. Short of serving food on newspaper, this fish 'n' chips joint is as authentic as they come. Open since 1914, the no-nonsense "chippie" serves up fried cod and haddock (£3.40-£5.70) to a local clientele and travelers in on the secret. Chips (£1.30) and mushy peas (90p) round out the bare-bones menu. Takeaway available. Open M-F noon-3pm and 6-10pm, Sa 6-10pm. Reservations recommended after 7pm. AmEx/MC/V. ❷

Spighetta, 43 Blanford St. (☎7486 7340). ⊖Baker St. While not for pepperoni-and-sausage purists, this 2-story Sardinian restaurant offers creative wood-fired pizzas (£7-11), pastas (£7-14), and seafood dishes (£12-13) for more adventurous Italian tastes. Upbeat jazz music and linen tablecloths give a comfortable yet polished feel. Try the couscous soup with baby clams (£6.50) as a starter. Takeaway available. Lunch daily noon-3pm. Dinner M-Sa 6:30-11pm, Su 6:30-10:30pm. AmEx/MC/V. ❸

Royal China, 24-26 Baker St. (☎7487 4688; www.royalchinagroup.co.uk). ⊖Baker St. This upscale, sleek, and attractive branch of the micro-chain renowned for London's best dim sum straddles the line between faux and real elegance. Order from a menu rather than from a cart—what you lose in charm you gain in freshness. Service is variable, but food is reliable. Keep your eyes open—this restaurant is crawling with MPs and minor celebs. If you're with a group and looking to splurge, try the 5-course seafood *menu* (£38) or the standard and vegetarian versions (£30). Most entrees and dim sum £8-18. Open M-Th noon-11pm, F-Sa noon-11:30pm, Su 11am-10pm; dim sum served until 5pm. AmEx/MC/V. ❸

FOOD

BAYSWATER

Cheap and central, Bayswater was an immigrant destination after WWII and played a large role in developing Britain's taste buds beyond meat pie and spotted dick. Hummus, kebabs, and other Middle Eastern delights came to Londoners through Bayswater's large Arab population. **Westbourne Grove** and **Queensway** offer plenty of cheap Chinese, Indian, and Middle Eastern restaurants. A similar smattering of affordable flavors borders Paddington Station on **London Street.**

SEE MAP, p. 361

▓ **Levantine,** 26 London St. (☎ 7262 1111; www.levant.co.uk). ⊖Paddington. A seductive Lebanese restaurant that just wants to keep feeding you, amidst the faint aroma of incense and rose petals. Indulge in several Mezze offerings like falafel and homemade hummus (£4.75) or the affordable lunch *menu* (£6.95). Loads of vegetarian options. With featured nights of belly-dancing and *shisha* (water pipe) this is a trip worth making. Open daily noon-12:30am. MC/V. ❷

▓ **La Bottega del Gelato,** 127 Bayswater Rd. (☎ 7243 2443). ⊖Queensway. The handmade, creamy gelato is ideal after a hard day of sightseeing. Perfect to take on a stroll in the Kensington Gardens across the street; eat up as children stare at you with jealousy. 1-3 scoops £2-4. Open daily 11am-10pm. ❶

Aphrodite Taverna, 15 Hereford Rd. (☎ 7229 2206). ⊖Bayswater. The homey warmth is almost as striking as the zealously decorated walls. Fabulous menu is a grab bag of polysyllabic treats, like *dolmedes* (stuffed grape leaves; £8.50) or *keftedes* (Greek meatballs; £8.50). £1 cover is amply rewarded with baskets of freshly baked pita bread and other appetizers. **Cafe Aphrodite** next door offers some of Taverna's specialties at cheaper prices as well as a full sandwich menu (from £2.60). Restaurant open M-Sa noon-midnight. Cafe open daily 8am-5pm. AmEx/MC/V. Restaurant ❷/Cafe ❶

Durbar Tandoori, 24 Hereford St. (☎ 7727 1947; www.durbartandoori.co.uk). ⊖Bayswater. Enjoy the simple dining room and revel in the low-priced goodness of it all in one of London's more famous Indian restaurants. Good-sized portions and dishes from several regions throughout India. Veggie and meat mains from £5.25. Bargain takeaway lunch box £3.95. Chef's special dinner for 2 £22.95. Open M-Th and Sa-Su noon-2:30pm and daily 5:30-11:30pm. AmEx/MC/V. ❷

Khan's Restaurant, 13-15 Westbourne Grove (☎ 7727 5420; www.khanrestaurant.com). ⊖Bayswater. This family-run restaurant, with landscape murals and fauxpalm tree pillars, dishes up hearty portions of Indian favorites. Chicken tikka (£4.95) and fish curry (£5.55) are favorites from the extensive menu. Takeaway available. Open M-Th and Sa-Su noon-3pm and 6pm-midnight, F 6pm-midnight. AmEx/MC/V. ❷

NOTTING HILL

Dining options in Notting Hill basically come down to a choice between high-priced bistros and the inexpensive but excellent bites serving the market crowds around Portobello Rd., including produce and bakery stalls within the market itself. For the widest variety of food, hunt around at the southern end of the general market and under the Westway.

SEE MAP, p. 361

▓ **George's Portobello Fish Bar,** 329 Portobello Rd. (☎ 8969 7895). ⊖Ladbroke Grove. George opened up here in 1961, and though the little space has lived through various incarnations, the fish 'n' chips are still as good as ever: cod, rockfish, plaice, and skate come with a huge serving of chunky chips (from £7). Another specialty is the barbecue ribs (£7), whose secret recipe is closely guarded. Open M-F 11am-midnight, Sa 11am-9pm, Su noon-9:30pm. ❷

Lazy Daisy Cafe, 59a Portobello Rd. (☎7221 8417). ⊖Notting Hill Gate. Tucked into an alley, alongside a white washed church. Cheery cafe serves a healthful selection of salads and pastries, as well as some fancier breakfast concoctions. All-day breakfast, including a lazy fry-up (£6) and eggs florentine (£5). Lunches include quiche (£5) and a make-your-own panini option (£4.75). A wide range of periodicals and bin of toys keep customers of all ages happily occupied. Outdoor patio in summer months. Wheelchair-accessible. Open M-Sa 9am-5pm, Su noon-2:30pm. 70p surcharge with MC/V. ●

Kitchen and Pantry, 59a Portobello Rd. (☎7221 8417). ⊖Notting Hill Gate. Just off busy Portobello Rd., this bright but homey cafe attracts a more chilled-out crowd than the market-frenzied masses. The grass-green exterior gives way to bleached wooden floors, sliding glass windows, and wrap-around leather couches, which provide a great place to relax with a homemade crepe (£3) or quiche (£2.50). Wide selection of organic and fresh juices, coffee, and pre-packaged salads and sandwiches (£3). Free Wi-Fi. Open M-Sa 9am-5pm, Su noon-2:30pm. MC/V. ●

Tom's Delicatessen, 226 Westbourne Grove (☎7221 8818). ⊖Ladbroke Grove or Notting Hill Gate. Locals recommend this for a quick bite. Upstairs a bakery and cafe, downstairs a deli and mini-market with imported foods from around the world. Fills quickly during busy times, and the table-sharing policy means you might make a mealtime friend. Fresh cakes and pastries (from £1), takeaway portions of lasagna (£1.70), goat cheese pizza (£4), and paella (£3) are great for a picnic lunch. Full English breakfast (£9). Open M-F 8am-7:30pm, Sa-Su 8am-6:30pm. MC/V. ❷

Lisboa Patisserie, 57 Golborne Rd. (☎0181 8968 5242). ⊖Ladbroke Grove. This little bakery is packed all the time with Portuguese and Moroccan men talking football over coffee (80p). The decor is not much to look at, and it can get extremely hot in late afternoon, but you can always get your goodies to go. The broad selection of cakes and pastries, including wafer-thin biscuits (from 5p) and over-stuffed cream puffs (50p), is impossible to resist. Open M-Sa 8am-8pm, Su 8am-7pm. ●

The Hummingbird Bakery, 133 Portobello Rd. (☎7229 6446; www.hummingbirdbakery.com). ⊖Ladbroke Grove or Notting Hill Gate. 2nd location at 47 Old Brompton Rd. (☎7584 0055), in South Kensington. It's hard to ignore the cupcake-lined windows or the smell of buttercream and vanilla wafting onto the street. With flavors such as lavender, caramel heart, and red velvet with cream cheese frosting (their bestseller), the toughest decision will be which to try. Red velvet cupcakes £1.85, all others £1.55. Open Tu-Sa 10am-5:30pm, Su 11am-5pm. ●

The Grain Shop, 269a Portobello Rd. (☎7229 5571). ⊖Ladbroke Grove. The aromatic smells of this mini-bakery are irresistible, and the queue snakes onto Portobello Rd. at lunchtime. The organic breads and numerous vegetarian and vegan options draw in tourists and loyal locals alike. There's also a selection of homemade cakes and salads; mix as many dishes as you like in a takeaway box for £3.85-5. Breads and cakes baked on-site (from 80p). Open M-Sa 9am-6pm. MC/V. ●

Manzara, 24 Pembridge Rd. (☎7727 3062). ⊖Notting Hill Gate. Manzara's street-side cafe vibe belies the menu of Turkish delicacies. Besides standard kebabs, the cafe specializes in *pide* (rolled pizza-like pastries filled with various delicacies, from eggplant and spinach to pepperoni; takeaway £4.25, eat-in £6.45). You'll also find organic Welsh beef burgers (from £4), and a sandwich and wrap menu. Perfect for a filling bite on the way to the markets. Open M-Sa 8am-1am, Su 8am-11:30pm. ❷

The Tea and Coffee Plant, 180 Portobello Rd. (☎7221 8137). ⊖Ladbroke Grove. The rich smell of freshly ground coffee permeates this small but uncluttered shop, which offers a wide selection of coffees (from £1), teas (from 90p), and takeaway concoctions of organic chocolate, caramel, and nuts (from £3). All are fair-traded and organic. Chew on some beans before committing to a kilo (from £4), smell the tea varieties, or sip on a fresh espresso (80p). Mail order available. Open M-Sa 8:15am-6:30pm, Su 9:30am-5:30pm. MC/V. ●

FOOD

ON THE MENU

FULL ENGLISH BREAKFAST

f you're after more food than you can handle, there is little in ife more fulfilling than a **full English breakfast** (a.k.a. the 'fry-up") to start off your morning. Variations abound, but an English breakfast typically consists of fried eggs and bacon in double servings, plus fried toast and baked beans; a selection of side dishes may include pork sausages, liver, kidneys, black or white pudding (not actually pudding, but sausages of the blood and non-blood variety), grilled or ried tomato, and mushrooms, all of which is washed down with coffee or tea (or beer, if you're he hardy type).

Before spending those extra ew pounds for a chance at supposedly authentic English fare, note that while it may be traditionally English, very few British people actually eat a full English breakfast every morning; it's just oo heavy and unhealthy to stomach daily. Quicker and healthier options have increasingly displaced this delicious English specialty, exiling it mostly to hotels, B&Bs, and neighborhood haunts ike diners, where it's readily consumed by tourists and working men looking for an early-morning cholesterol fix. If your B&B, hostel, or hotel offers free English breakfast, by all means partake— f possible, save the leftovers for unch and dinner.

KENSINGTON AND EARL'S COURT

Kensington's uniform prettiness makes for a classy dining experience. The most attractive spot is **Kensington Court,** a short pedestrian street lined with budget and mid-range cafes, always popular on warm summer evenings. **Kensington High Street** is roughly split between overpriced yuppie hangouts and family-friendly pizzerias, while **Kensington Square's** environs provide decent sit-down options. **South Kensington** is a good bet; the area around the Tube station overflows with sandwich bars and cheap restaurants. On **Bute Street,** just opposite the Institut Francais's *lycée* (high school), you're as likely to hear French as English in the sidewalk cafes, *patisseries,* and continental delis full of delicious cheap eats. In Earl's Court, both Earl's Court Rd. and Old Brompton Rd. have a variety of affordable eateries, though they tend to be scruffier than their northern and eastern neighbors.

SEE MAP, pp. 366-367

🍴 **Utsav,** 17 Kensington High St. (☎ 7368 0022; www.utsav-restaurant.co.uk). ⊖High St. Kensington. An affordable and stylish Indian option. 4 regional chefs serve up artistically presented specialties from the north, south, east, and west. Try their creative twist on a vegetable *samosa* (£6) or the filling *masala dosa* (£7.50). The 2-course lunch *menu* (vegetarian £5, non-vegetarian £6) is a tasty steal. Open M-Sa 11am-11pm, Su 11am-10pm. AmEx/MC/V. ❷

🍴 **Raison d'Être,** 18 Bute St. (☎ 7584 5008). ⊖South Kensington. One of many small cafes on Bute St. catering to the local French community; eating here may not be your reason to live, but it will at least make for a nice afternoon. Offers a bewildering range of filled baguettes and focaccia (£2.50-5.50). *Salades composées* (£3.75-6.25) and various other light dishes (yogurt with fruit from £3.25) are all made to order and popular with a young crowd. After your meal, enjoy a divine *café au lait* under the canopy outside. Open M-F 8am-6pm, Sa 9:30am-4pm. Cash only. ❶

Zaika, 1 Kensington High St. (☎ 7795 6533; www.zaika-restaurant.co.uk). ⊖High St. Kensington. Eat like a maharaja at one of London's best Indian restaurants— definitely a splurge. Elegant copper decor, attentive service, and original, beautiful food served on silver platters are the height of gourmet dining. Excellent wine list. Starters £7-13. Mains £14-19. Try the coconut poached prawns (£17). Desserts £6-12. 4-course lunch *menu* £20; 4-course dinner *menu* £39, with wine £60. 2-course min. for dinner. Dress code: formal. Open M-Sa noon-2:45pm and 6-10:45pm; Su 6-9:45pm. Dinner reservations recommended. AmEx/MC/V. ❺

The Orangery, Kensington Palace (☎7376 0239). ⊖High St. Kensington. Built for Queen Anne's dinner parties and full of white, high-ceilinged stateliness, this airy Neo-classical building behind Kensington Palace is popular with a tourist-heavy clientele for light gourmet lunches (from £8) and set afternoon teas (from £7). Light breakfast £2-5. Open daily 10am-noon for breakfast, noon-3pm for lunch, 3-6pm for tea. MC/V. ❷

Babylon, Kensington Roof Gardens (☎7368 3993; www.roofgardens.com). ⊖High St. Kensington. 99 Kensington High St. entrance is on Derry St. There's nothing like a lofty perch to render an otherwise fine eatery quite special, and the recently refurbished Babylon benefits enormously from its location in the beautiful Roof Gardens, 7 stories above Kensington. Eat outside if you can and marvel at the view. A la carte starters £9.50-14.50. Mains £18-24. Best deal is the lunch *menu* (Sa noon-3pm; 2-course £16, 3-course £18). Open M-Sa noon-3pm and 7-11pm, Su noon-3pm. Reservations recommended. AmEx/MC/V. ❹

Daquise, 20 Thurloe St. (☎7589 6117). ⊖South Kensington. With the ultimate in comfort food, this quiet neighborhood diner serves up heavy Polish fare to a local crowd. Cheery yellow dining room is a perfect antidote to a rainy London day. Favorite dishes include potato pancakes (£10) or meatballs with mushroom sauce (£6). More adventurous types can try the chicken liver (£5.50). Open daily 11:30am-11pm. MC/V. ❷

La Brasserie, 272 Brompton Rd. (☎7581 3089). ⊖South Kensington. Bustling, cheerful French brasserie, famous for its oyster bar and renowned for its steak tartare. Serves large portions and usually buzzes with blazer-adorned locals. Mains from vegetarian pasta and cheese plates to hearty steak and poultry offerings (£10-20). Appetizers £4-9. Best value is the 2-course *menu* (M-F noon-7pm, £10). Breakfast and afternoon tea also available. Open M-Sa 8am-11pm, Su 9am-11pm. AmEx/MC/V. ❸

 BREAKFASTING. Take advantage if breakfast is offered at your hostel, B&B, or hotel. If not, check out the cafes listed at the beginning of this chapter (p. 119).

KNIGHTSBRIDGE AND BELGRAVIA

The usual steep prices may deceive you into thinking that **Knightsbridge** is not promising territory for affordable eats, but look closely and you'll reap some benefits. Within Harrods, the bakery and some stands in the awe-inspiring food halls approach affordable levels. **Beauchamp Place** (BEE-cham), off Old Brompton Rd., and the surrounding streets are lined with cafes, noodle bars, and sandwich bars. **Belgravia** is a bit tougher—there's little chance of get-

SEE MAP, p. 365

ting a sit-down meal at a restaurant for under £15. The mews behind **Grosvenor Place** cradle some popular pubs, and the gourmet delis and specialty food stores on **Elizabeth Street** will furnish a picnic basket fit for a prince. Some cheaper ethnic restaurants can be found on the side streets around **Sloane Square.**

▨ **Jenny Lo's Teahouse,** 14 Eccleston St. (☎7259 0399). ⊖Victoria. Right around the corner from Jenny's father's higher-end restaurant (Ken Lo is one of the most famous Cantonese chefs in the UK). The small modern interior here bustles on weekdays, but the delicious *cha shao* (pork noodle soup; £6.50) and the broad selection of Asian noodles, from Vietnamese to Beijing style (£6.50-8), make eating here well worth the wait. Vegetarian options abound. Takeaway and delivery available (min. £5 per person). Open M-F noon-3pm and 6-10pm, Sa 6-10pm. Cash only. ❷

Gloriette, 128 Brompton Rd. (☎7589 4750). ⊖Knightsbridge. This venerable *patisserie* offers meals and desserts in a bright cafe atmosphere. Eat next to the beautiful baked goods on the ground fl. or in the delicately ornate upper dining room. A few outside tables are available as well, but you'll have to cope with tailpipe exhaust. Leaf teas £2 per pot. Yummy cakes and pastries £2.60-3.60. Sandwiches £4.50-7.50. More sub-

FOOD

stantial fare includes a rich goulash soup with bread (£5) and 2- and 3-course *menu* (£10 and £12). Open M-F 7am-8pm, Sa 7am-8pm, Su 8am-7pm. AmEx/MC/V. ❷

Goya, 2 Eccleston Pl. (☎7730 4299). ⊖Victoria. London's most carefully prepared tapas (£2-7 per dish; order 2-3 per person) in a polished space. Outdoor seating if you want to brave the exhaust. Spanish mains (£10-18) include vegetarian and seafood options. Open daily 11:30am-11:30pm. AmEx/MC/V. ❸

Poilâne, 46 Elizabeth St. (☎7808 4910; www.poilane.fr). ⊖Victoria or Sloane Sq. Paris's most famous *boulangerie* brings freshly baked delights to Belgravia. The shop is *très petit* and only offers a selection of breads for takeaway service. Not the place for a full meal, but an excellent snack destination. Traditional sourdough country loaves cost £4 per kg, with special-occasion loaves sometimes more. Buttery *pain au chocolat* is only £1.10. Also stocks a selection of stone-ground flours. Open M-F 7:30am-7:30pm, Sa 7:30am-6pm. MC/V. ❶

CHELSEA

It's hard to walk more than 30 ft. without stumbling into a decent eatery on **King's Road.** The chic thoroughfare includes quality, affordable restaurants to suit a wide range of tastes with a particularly high concentration between Sydney St. and the **World's End** area. The **Chelsea Farmer's Market** and **Duke of York Square,** both just off King's Rd., are a good bet for stylish outdoor cafes.

SEE MAP, p. 363

🌆 **Buona Sera, at the Jam,** 289a King's Rd. (☎7352 8827). ⊖Sloane Sq., then Bus #19 or 319. With patented "bunk" tables stacked high into the air, the treetop-esque dining experience alone justifies a visit, and the mouth-watering Italian fare makes one practically mandatory. Waiters climb small wooden ladders to deliver sizeable pasta plates (£7.20-8.50) along with fish and steak dishes (£8-12). Enjoy, but don't drop your fork. Alcohol only served with food. Open M 6pm-midnight, Tu-F noon-3pm and 6pm-midnight, Sa-Su noon-midnight. Reservations recommended F-Sa. AmEx/MC/V. ❸

🌆 **Chelsea Bun,** 9a Limerston St. (☎7352 3635). ⊖Sloane Sq., then Bus #11 or 22. Spirited and casual Anglo-American diner that serves heaping portions of everything from the "Ultimate Breakfast" (eggs, pancakes, sausages, and french toast; £10.30) to Tijuana Benedict (eggs with chorizo sausage; £8). Extensive vegetarian and vegan options include faux sausages with a full English breakfast. Sandwiches, pasta, and burgers £2.80-8. No need to set the alarm clock: early-bird specials available M–F 7am-noon (£2.20-3.20) and breakfast (from £4) served until 6pm. £3.50 min. per person lunch, £5.50 dinner. Open M-Sa 7am-midnight, Su 9am-7pm. MC/V. ❸

Gordon Ramsay, 68 Royal Hospital Rd. (☎7352 4441 or 7592 1373; www.gordanramsay.com). ⊖Sloane Sq., then Bus #137 or 360. Founded by Gordon Ramsay—eccentric artist, former footballer, and current reality TV star—this restaurant serves up light and innovative French concoctions. The fare has been awarded 3 Michelin stars (only 2 other UK restaurants can match that), and Ramsay is widely considered to be the best chef in England. Lunch *menu* £40. Multi-course dinner £85-110. Open M-F noon-2:30pm and 6:30-11pm. Reserve 1 month in advance. AmEx/MC/V. ❺

Phát Phúc, The Courtyard at 250 King's Rd. (☎07832 199 738), entrance on Sydney St. ⊖Sloane Sq., then Bus #11, 19, 22, 319. Most giggly diners only eat here because of the witty name, but the courtyard seating and heaping portions of Vietnamese soup are more than just a gimmick. Choose from a selection of soups (£6), along with an appetizer and dessert of the day. Open daily noon-4pm. Cash only. ❷

My Old Dutch, 221 King's Rd. (☎7376 5650; www.myolddutch.com). ⊖Sloane Sq. One of 3 locations in London, My Old Dutch is a quiet place for lunch, dinner, and, most importantly, dessert. Dutch food has never tasted better, with scrumptious offerings like the amsterdammer (savory pancake with apple and smoked bacon; £8) and sweet pancakes with fruit and ice cream (£6-7.25). Open M-Sa 11am-11pm, Su 11am-10pm. MC/V.❷

WEST LONDON

The chain-dominated restaurants around **Turnham Green** are fine places for a reliable bite, while Goldhawk Rd. provides a wealth of cheap ethnic eateries in the **Shepherd's Bush** neighborhood. **Hammersmith** is famous for the riverside pubs along the Upper and Lower Malls, west of the bridge.

▨ **Zagora,** 38 Devonshire Rd. (☎8742 7922; www.zagora.co.uk). ⊖Turnham Green. From the Tube, walk south along Turnham Green Terr., turn right at Chiswick High Rd., then left onto Devonshire Rd. From the attentive service to the warm North African interior (complete with mosaic tabletops and embroidered pillows), Zagora is a world away from London. Moroccan cuisine is reasonably priced (mains £10-17) and generously portioned. Share several small dishes at £4-5 each. Desserts (£3.50) are worth every penny—the assortment of scrumptiously sticky baklava melts in your mouth. Menu (£10) 5-7pm. Wheelchair-accessible. Open daily 5-11pm. MC/V. ❸

▨ **The Gate,** 51 Queen Caroline St., 2nd fl. (☎8748 6932; www.gateveg.co.uk). ⊖Hammersmith. From the Tube, follow signs for Riverside Studios to Queen Caroline St., then follow the street towards the Thames. The restaurant is on the left, 2 blocks before the river. One of London's top spots for gourmet vegetarian fare, sitting above a church. Fresh flowers and plenty of natural light provide a welcoming yet elegant atmosphere, and the staff are attentive and knowledgeable about the different menu offerings. Starters £4-5. Mains £8-13.50. Extensive wine list. Reservations recommended for dinner. Outdoor seating in summer. Open M-F noon-2:45pm and 6-10:45pm, Sa 6-10:30pm. AmEx/MC/V. ❸

▨ **Newens Maids of Honor,** 288 Kew Rd. (☎8940 2752). ⊖Kew Gardens. Facing Kew Rd. from the Victoria Gate of Kew Gardens, cross the street and walk left for 5min. Sip tea with an extended pinky finger at this quirky and historical tea house. Waitresses in smock dresses serve pastries and piping hot drinks. Best for set tea (2:30-5:30pm, £6.85) served on proper china with all of the traditional fixtures, including scones with jam and clotted cream. Cheap lunch options include quiche and vegetarian pastries from £3. Open M 9:30am-1pm, Tu-F 9:30am-5:30pm, Sa 9am-5:30pm. MC/V. ❶

Belushi's, 13-15 Shepherd's Bush Green (☎8735 0270). ⊖Shepherd's Bush. Those craving a hearty burger and fries (£5.50-7) will not be disappointed at this backpacker's restaurant and bar, attached to St. Christopher's Inn (p. 111). The rather rowdy nighttime bar scene (complete with 24hr. webcam) is not for everyone, but meals have basic appeal, including outdoor BBQs (weather permitting) F 5pm. Daily 2-for-1 specials on meals. Those staying at the inn receive drink specials and a 10% discount on food. Open M-W 11am-11pm, Th-Sa 11am-midnight, Su noon-11pm. MC/V. ❷

Patio, 5 Goldhawk Rd. (☎8743 5194). ⊖Goldhawk Rd. You wouldn't notice this place if you walked by it, save for the windows crowded with proudly displayed starred reviews and awards. Inside it is a quirky establishment that looks just like grandma's living room, where servers are happy to guide you through the Eastern European menu. With the huge portions, you'll be stuffed, and leftovers will last for the next 3 days. Try one of the Polish dishes, such as stuffed pancakes with mushroom sauce, cucumber and avocado salad, or roast lamb (£3.50-12). Incredibly heavy 3-course menu includes an after-dinner vodka shot (£16). Wheelchair-accessible. Open M-Sa noon-3pm and 6pm-midnight, Su 6pm-midnight. AmEx/MC/V. ❸

FOOD

SIGHTS

If you seek London's history, you've come to the right place. The city's parks, churches, and palaces are the places that have come to define London for the millions who flock to the city every year. From the hints of the city's Roman past that poke through the ground at the London Wall to the reminders of the Blitz etched on the face of every church, London wears every period of its long history for the present to see; to walk from east to west is to watch the city unfold through time. Christopher Wren's work continues to marvel all around the City of London. Holborn's Fleet St. was long associated with the London press and the Royal Courts. Down in Westminster, you will hold court with the regents, royals, and ruffians who run this fair capital, and up in Bloomsbury you'll mingle with the students and youth who hold the future of London in their eager grasp.

Unlike London's museums, sights tend to be expensive. There is no reason to spend £30 on tourist trips to the Tower of London, St. Paul's Cathedral, and the London Eye, only to be left wondering what to do for the rest of your trip with just pocket change to spare. Be your own tour guide (with *Let's Go* in hand). From avant-garde architecture in Islington to the urban wilderness of Hampstead Heath, the best of London's sights are often those seen via excursions on foot. No matter what path you choose, whether you're strolling down small cobblestone streets or briskly marching down a modern thoroughfare, your exploration will be rewarded. There is no wrong turn.

THE CITY OF LONDON

The City of London (usually shortened to "the City") is the oldest part of London; all other districts are simply outlying villages. The most interesting sights, sounds, and smells are located within walking distance of each other in what is called the **"Square Mile."** Today, archaeology is pulling London's history out of the ground, and the ancient Roman roots of the City are becoming ever more visible. The City strikes a delicate balance between tradition and modernity;

SEE MAP, p. 349

400-year-old churches share sidewalks with modern office buildings. Above it all rises the stately dome of St. Paul's and the weathered battlements of the Tower of London, looking down at the millions of tourists who flock to them every year. The 39 churches and the labyrinthine alleyways that have survived the fires and wars are almost the only reminders of the time when this was the beating heart of London. All the same, London's history is never more prevalent or exciting than in the City.

ST. PAUL'S CATHEDRAL

St. Paul's Churchyard. ⊖St. Paul's. ☎7246 8350; www.stpauls.co.uk. Open M-Sa 8:30am-4pm; last admission 3:45pm. Dome and galleries open M-Sa 9:30am-4pm. Open for worship daily 7:15am-6pm. Partially wheelchair-accessible. Admission £9.50, concessions £8.50, children 7-16 £3.50; worshippers free. Group of 10 or more 50p discount per ticket. "Supertour" M-F 11, 11:30am, 1:30, 2pm; £3, concessions £2.50, children 7-16 £1; English only. Audio tours available in many languages daily 9am-3:30pm; £3.50, concessions £3.

Majestic St. Paul's remains a cornerstone of London's architectural and historical legacy—as well as an obvious tourist magnet. Architect Christopher Wren's masterpiece is the fifth cathedral to occupy the site; the original was built in AD 604. In 1668, after Old St. Paul's was swept away in the Great Fire, construction began on the current cathedral. The Church and architect were at odds from the start: when the bishops finally approved his third design, Wren started building. Sneakily, Wren had persuaded the King to let him make "necessary alterations" as work progressed, and the building that emerged in 1708 bore a close resemblance to Wren's second "Great Model" design, the architect's favorite.

 ST. PAUL'S FOR POCKET CHANGE. To gain access to the Cathedral's nave for free, attend an Evensong service (M-Sa 5pm, 45min.). Arrive at 4:50pm to be admitted to seats in the quire.

INTERIOR. The entrance leads to the nave, the largest space in the cathedral. The enormous memorial to the Duke of Wellington completely fills one of the arches. The nave leads to the second tallest freestanding dome in Europe (after St. Peter's in the Vatican), which seems even larger from inside, its height extended by the perspective of the paintings on the inner surface. The north transept functions as the **baptistry,** whose lid is so heavy that machinery is needed to lift it. The third version of William Holman Hunt's ethereal *The Light of the World* hangs opposite the font. The south transept holds the larger-than-life **Nelson Memorial,** hailing Britain's most famous naval hero. The stalls in the **quire** narrowly escaped a bomb during the Blitz, but the old altar did not. It was replaced by the current marble **high altar,** above which looms the fiery ceiling mosaic of *Christ Seated in Majesty.* The north quire aisle holds Henry Moore's *Mother and Child,* one of the church's best pieces of sculpture. The south quire aisle contains one of the only statues to survive from Old St. Paul's: a swaddled tomb effigy of **John Donne,** Dean of the Cathedral and famous poet. The monument to Donne almost didn't make it; burn marks can be seen at its base.

SCALING THE HEIGHTS. St. Paul's dome is built in three parts: an inner brick dome, visible from the inside of the cathedral; an outer timber structure; and, between the two, a brick cone that carries the weight of the lantern on top. The first stop is the narrow **Whispering Gallery,** reached by 259 shallow wood steps. None of the galleries are wheelchair-accessible, and the first climb is the only one that isn't steep, narrow, or slightly strenuous. Circling the base of the inner dome, the Whispering Gallery is a perfect resounding chamber: whisper into the wall, and your friend on the other side will hear you—or theoretically they could if everyone else weren't trying the same thing. Instead, admire the scenes from the life of St. Paul painted on the canopy. Continue trudging upward, conquering 119 steps to the Stone Gallery and 152 steps to the Golden Gallery at the base of the lantern. The view from the top is impressive, though an equally grand vista can be had for fewer steps from the top of the Monument (p. 150).

PLUMBING THE DEPTHS. The mosaic-floored crypt is bright and surprisingly welcoming. The sheer number of memorials, however, makes finding individual graves a bit difficult; on-hand volunteers have maps of all the headstones. The free "Key to the Crypt" brochure from the information desk is indispensable. The crypt is packed wall-to-wall with plaques and tombs of great Britons (and the occasional foreigner). Nelson's tributes are most grandiose and numerous, but radiating galleries filled with gravestones and tributes honor other military heroes. The collection features everything from Epstein's bust of T.E. Lawrence (of Arabia) to a plaque commemorating the casualties of the Gulf War. The neighboring chamber contains Wellington's massive tomb, and the rear of the crypt bears the graves of artists, including Sir William Blake, J.M.W. Turner, and Henry Moore. The graves are crowded around the starkly simple black slab concealing the body of Sir Christopher Wren. Inscribed on the wall above is his famous epitaph: *Lector, si monumentum requiris circumspice* ("Reader, if you seek his monument, look around").

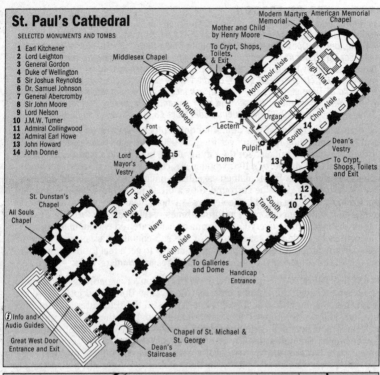

St. Paul's Cathedral

SELECTED MONUMENTS AND TOMBS

1 Earl Kitchener
2 Lord Leighton
3 General Gordon
4 Duke of Wellington
5 Sir Joshua Reynolds
6 Dr. Samuel Johnson
7 General Abercromby
8 Sir John Moore
9 Lord Nelson
10 J.M.W. Turner
11 Admiral Collingwood
12 Admiral Earl Howe
13 John Howard
14 John Donne

Modern Martyrs Memorial
American Memorial Chapel
Mother and Child by Henry Moore
To Crypt, Shops, Toilets, & Exit
Middlesex Chapel
North Choir Aisle
High Altar
North Transept
Quire
South Choir Aisle
Organ
Font
Lectern
Dean's Vestry
Lord Mayor's Vestry
Pulpit
To Crypt, Shops, Toilets and Exit
St. Dunstan's Chapel
Dome
All Souls Chapel
North Aisle
South Transept
Nave
South Aisle
To Galleries and Dome
Handicap Entrance
Info and Audio Guides
Great West Door Entrance and Exit
Chapel of St. Michael & St. George
Dean's Staircase

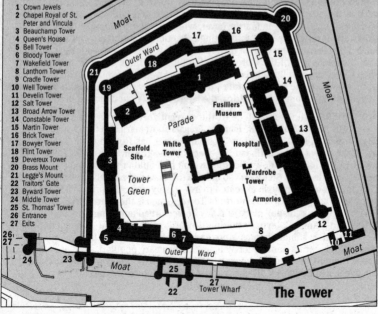

1 Crown Jewels
2 Chapel Royal of St. Peter and Vincula
3 Beauchamp Tower
4 Queen's House
5 Bell Tower
6 Bloody Tower
7 Wakefield Tower
8 Lanthorn Tower
9 Cradle Tower
10 Well Tower
11 Develin Tower
12 Salt Tower
13 Broad Arrow Tower
14 Constable Tower
15 Martin Tower
16 Brick Tower
17 Bowyer Tower
18 Flint Tower
19 Devereux Tower
20 Brass Mount
21 Legge's Mount
22 Traitors' Gate
23 Byward Tower
24 Middle Tower
25 St. Thomas' Tower
26 Entrance
27 Exits

Moat
Outer Ward
Fusiliers' Museum
Parade
Scaffold Site
White Tower
Hospital
Tower Green
Wardrobe Tower
Armories
Outer Ward
Tower Wharf
Moat

The Tower

■ THE TOWER OF LONDON

Tower Hill, next to Tower Bridge, within easy reach of the South Bank and the East End. ➍Tower Hill or DLR: Tower Gateway. ☎0870 751 5175, ticket sales 0870 756 6060; www.hrp.org.uk. Open Mar.-Oct. M 10am-6pm, Tu-Sa 9am-6pm, Su 10am-6pm; buildings close at 5:30pm, last entry 5pm; Nov.-Feb. all closing times 1hr. earlier. Tower Green open only by Yeoman tours, after 4:30pm, or for daily services. Admission £16, concessions £13, children 5-15 £9.50, children under 5 free, families of 5 £45. Tickets also sold at Tube stations; buy them in advance to avoid long queues at the door. Tours: "Yeoman Warders' Tours" meet near entrance; 1hr., every 30min. M and Su 10am-3:30pm, Tu-Sa 9:30am-3:30pm. Audio tours £3.50, concessions £2.50.

The turrets and towers of this multi-functional block—serving as palace, prison, royal mint, and living museum over the past 900 years—are impressive not only for their appearance but also for their integral role in England's history. Beginning with William the Conqueror's 1067 wooden structure and soon thereafter replaced with stone, the tower has remained essentially unchanged since medieval times. The whole castle used to be surrounded by a broad moat, but severe contamination led to its draining in 1843. "Beefeaters"—whose nickname may be a reference to their daily allowance of meat in former times—still guard the fortress, dressed in their distinctive blue everyday uniforms or elaborate red ceremonial uniforms. The fortress is divided into seven more or less self-contained areas, which can be visited in any order. An enjoyable and popular way to get a feel for the Tower is to join one of the animated and fairly theatrical ■Yeoman Warders' Tours.

CROSSING THE MOAT. Entering the Tower is no longer as perilous as it used to be; passing through the **Traitor's Gate,** as Queen Anne Boleyn did just before her death, was once a bad sign. Today, security is still tight: to enter after closing time, one still needs a top-secret password known only by the Yeoman and other high-ranking officials and changed daily since 1327. Once inside, St. Thomas's Tower begins the self-guided tour of the **Medieval Palace.** The rooms at first appear bare but are filled progressively with 13th-century decor and furniture. The **Wall Walk** is a series of eight towers that runs along the eastern wall, originally used to house guests and then adapted into a prison. Inscriptions scratched by inmates, including religious messages from persecuted Catholics, are still legible. At the end of the walk is **Martin Tower,** which traces the history of the British Crown and is now home to a fascinating collection of retired crowns; documentation is much better here than in the **Jewel House,** where the crown jewels are held. With the exception of the Coronation Spoon, everything dates from after 1660, when Oliver Cromwell melted down the original treasure. While you might be naturally drawn to the **Imperial State Crown,** don't miss the **Sceptre with the Cross,** topped with the First Star of Africa, the largest quality-cut diamond in the world.

TWO TOWERS. The centerpiece of the current fortress is **White Tower,** which begins with the ■Chapel of St. John the Evangelist. Remarkable for its quietly stunning simplicity, this 11th-century Norman chapel has Roman undertones and is one of the oldest and most beautiful spaces in the Tower. Don't miss Henry VIII's corset in the hall next door, without which he couldn't fit into his tournament armor. Outside, **Tower Green** isn't so much a tower as it is a lovely grassy area—not so lovely, though, for those executed there—reserved for the private beheading of very important guests. On the north of Tower Green is the **Chapel Royal of St. Peter ad Vincula,** the last resting place of many Tower Green unfortunates. Three queens of England—Anne Boleyn, Catherine Howard, and Lady Jane Grey—are buried here, as well as saints Thomas More and John Fisher. Across the green is **Bloody Tower,** which got its name after William Shakespeare popularized it. It is the site where Richard III allegedly imprisoned and murdered his young nephews, Richard, age 9, and Edward V, the 12-year-old rightful heir to the throne.

IN THE LIGHT OF DAY. The Tower's jurisdiction extends beyond its walls into the surrounding area, known as the **Liberty of the Tower.** Directly outside the walls is **Tower Hill,** the traditional site for public beheadings. The last execution was that of 80-year-old Lord Lovat, leader of the Jacobite rebellion, in 1747. Between the Tower and the Thames, the **Wharf** offers a view of Tower Bridge and Southwark. Ceremonial salutes are fired from the river bank here on royal birthdays and during state visits. One of the most popular ceremonies is the **Ceremony of the Keys.** This nightly locking-up ritual has been performed every night for over 700 years. At precisely 9:53pm, the Chief Warder locks the outer gates of the Tower before presenting the keys to the Governor amid much marching and salutation. *(For tickets, write at least 2 months in advance with the full names of those attending, a choice of at least 3 dates, and a stamped addressed envelope or international response coupon to: Ceremony of the Keys, Waterloo Block, HM Tower of London, EC3N 4AB. Free.)*

OTHER CITY OF LONDON SIGHTS

▨ ALL HALLOWS-BY-THE-TOWER. Nearly hidden by redevelopment projects and nearby office buildings, All Hallows bears its longevity with pride. Just inside the entrance on the left stands the oldest part of the church, a Saxon arch dating from AD 675. The main chapel has three parts: the right and left transepts date from the 13th and 14th centuries, respectively, and the central ceiling from the 20th. The undercroft museum is home to a diverse collection of Roman and Saxon artifacts, medieval art, and church record books from the time of the plague, all well worth a look. The spectacular Lady Chapel is home to a magnificent altarpiece dating from the 15th century and has been restored to look like it did when it was built in 1489. The stark cement arches and barred windows of the nave, rebuilt after the Blitz, give this church a mysterious and impressive dignity. *(Byward St. ⊖Tower Hill. ☎7481 2928; www.allhallowsbythetower.org.uk. Church open M-F 8:30am-5:45pm, Su 9:30am-5pm; crypt and museum open daily 10:30am-4pm. Free.)*

▨ GUILDHALL. This used to be the administrative center of the Corporation of London, but the Lord Mayor and his associates have since moved to more modern environs in the surrounding area in the City and on the South Bank. Before heading into the building itself, take a moment in the open stone **Guildhall Yard,** which is usually empty and feels strangely removed from the bustle of the City. Excavations in the 90s revealed the remains of a Roman amphitheatre below the Yard; its ruins are on display in the **Guildhall Art Gallery** (p. 194) on the Yard's eastern side. The towering Gothic building dates from 1440, though after repeated remodeling in the 17th and 18th centuries—not to mention almost complete reconstruction following the Great Fire and the Blitz—little of the original remains. Still, the hall maintains its style and skeleton; there are statues and gargoyles inside to preserve the Gothic image. The stained-glass windows bear the names of all Mayors and Lord Mayors of the Corporation, past and present—the builders must have foreseen the City's longevity, since there is still room for about 700 more. The downstairs crypt is only open by guided tour. Guildhall is more often than not closed for events, but arrive early and you might be able to pop in for a look. The **Guildhall Library,** in the 1970s annex and accessed via Aldermanbury or the Yard, specializes in the history of London. Its unparalleled collection of microfilm and books is a must for any serious history scholar, and the friendly librarians make the experience all the more pleasurable. It houses the **Guildhall Clockmaker's Museum** (p. 194) as well. *(Off Gresham St. Enter the Guildhall through the low, modern annex; entrance for library on Aldermanbury. ⊖St. Paul's, Moorgate, or Bank. Guildhall: ☎7606 3030, for occasional tour information 7606 3030, ext. 1463. Open May-Sept. daily 10am-5pm; Sept. weekends are open-house; Oct.-Apr. M-Sa 10am-5pm. Last admission 4:30pm. Free. Library ☎7332 1862. Open M-Sa 9:30am-5pm. Free.)*

SIGHTS

MONUMENT. The only non-ecclesiastical Wren building in the City, the Monument was built to commemorate the devastating Great Fire of 1666. Finished in 1677, the 202 ft. column stands 202 ft. from the bakery on Pudding Ln. where the fire first broke out. The colossal Monument can only be scaled by climbing the very narrow spiral staircase inside. The climb brings you close to the copper urn of flames that caps the pillar, a mythic reminder of the fire. The enclosed platform at the top, however, offers one of the best views of London, especially of the Tower Bridge. The brave who make the steep climb are rewarded with a certificate of completion on the way out—the best souvenir. *(Monument St. ⊖Monument. ☎ 7626 2717. Open daily 9:30am-5pm; last admission 4:40pm. £2.50, children £1. The Monument and the Tower Bridge Exhibition (p. 150) offer joint admission £7, concessions £5, children £3.50.)*

 EYE OF THE TIGER. When traveling, fitness tends to be difficult to maintain, and months of gym time are lost to pub grub and nights out on the town. Instead of joining a gym, why not try climbing the Monument—at 311 steps it'll get your heart racing, and the certificate will ease your guilt for days following.

TOWER BRIDGE. Not to be mistaken as its plainer sibling, London Bridge, Tower Bridge is the one you know from all the London-based movies. A relatively new construction—built in 1894—its impressive stature and bright blue suspension cables connect the banks of the Thames and rise above the many other bridges in the area. A marvel of engineering, the steam-powered lifting mechanism remained in use until 1973, when electric motors took over. Though clippers no longer sail into London very often, there's still enough large river traffic for the bridge to be lifted around 1000 times per year and five or six times per day in the summer. Call for the schedule or check the signs posted at each entrance. Historians and technophiles will appreciate the **Tower Bridge Exhibition,** which combines scenic 140 ft. glass-enclosed walkways with videos presenting a history of the bridge. *(Entrance to the Tower Bridge Exhibition is through the west side (upriver) of the North Tower. ⊖Tower Hill or London Bridge. ☎ 7403 3761, for lifting schedule 7940 3984; www.towerbridge.org.uk. Open daily Apr.-Sept. 10am-6:30pm, last entry 5:30pm; Oct.-Mar. 9:30am-6pm, last entry 5pm. Wheelchair-accessible. £6, concessions £4.50, children 5-16 £3.)*

ST. MARY-LE-BOW. Another Wren construction, St. Mary's is most famous for its Great Bell, which rang the City curfew and wake-up call daily from 1334 to 1874. True Cockneys must have been born within earshot of the bells. The gardens and the dark tower contrast with the strikingly modern interior. Gold-lined columns and a huge hanging crucifix dominate the room, which also contains the starkly simple altar and soundboard. The church had to be rebuilt almost completely after the Blitz, but the small 11th-century crypt, whose "bows" (arches) gave the church its epithet, survived. Since the 12th century, it has hosted the ecclesiastical Court of Arches, where the Archbishop of Canterbury swears in bishops. *(Cheapside, by Bow Ln. Access the crypt via stairs in the west courtyard. ⊖St. Paul's or Mansion House. ☎ 7248 5139; www.stmarylebow.co.uk. Open M-W 8:15am-6:30pm, Th 7:30am-6:30pm, F 8:15am-1:30pm. Occasional Th concerts 1:05pm. Free.)*

ST. STEPHEN WALBROOK. On the site of a 7th-century Saxon church, St. Stephen (built 1672-79) was Wren's personal favorite and boasts "the most perfectly proportioned interior in the world"; you can decide for yourself. The unexpected simplicity of the interior complements Henry Moore's stark freeform altar, dedicated in 1987. The church mixes classic columns and lines with Moore's ultra-modern circular structure. Honorary phones, donated by British Telecom, commemorate former rector Chad Varah, who founded the Samaritans—the UK's first crisis hotline—here in 1953. It's still in operation now as a national crisis line. *(39 Walbrook. ⊖Bank or Cannon St. ☎ 7606 3998. Open M-F 10am-4pm. Wheelchair-accessible. Free.)*

ORGAN MUSIC FOR POCKET CHANGE. For pipe music fans, St. Stephen Walbrook church provides free 1hr. organ concerts on Friday at 12:30pm.

ST. MARY WOOLNOTH. The dearth of lower windows is due to the lack of open space around the site at the time of its building (1716-27). Even so, the domed design and the semicircular windows up top fill the small church with light. The remarkable altarpiece and oak soundboard are particularly noteworthy. *(Junction of King William and Lombard St. ⊖Bank or Monument. ☎ 7626 9701. Open M-F 9:30am-4:30pm.)*

LLOYD'S OF LONDON. The most famous modern structure in the City looks like a towering postmodern factory but it is actually the home of the world's largest insurance market, built in 1986. With raw metal ducts, lifts, and chutes on the outside, it wears its heart (or at least its internal organs) on its sleeve. *(Leadenhall St. ⊖Bank. Wheelchair-accessible.)*

ST. DUNSTAN-IN-THE-EAST. Only the tower and outer walls remain of Wren's masterpiece. The Blitzed, mossy ruins have been converted into a stunning garden and peaceful picnic spot. Vines cover the Gothic-style walls, and a bubbling fountain surrounded by benches makes it an oasis in the City. *(St. Dunstan's Hill. ⊖Monument or Tower Hill. Wheelchair-accessible.)*

ST. MARGARET LOTHBURY. While rebuilding this church in 1689, Wren was obliged to follow the lines of the former church, despite its north wall being shorter than its south; the result is a roof that's charmingly off-kilter. The carved-wood screen was saved from another now-demolished City church. An abundance of stained glass makes St. Margaret unique. *(Lothbury. ⊖Bank. ☎ 7606 8330; www.stml.org.uk.)*

EAST LONDON

WHITECHAPEL AND THE EAST END

Although the boroughs of the East End and the City are neighbors on the map, the two areas are virtual opposites. The border is as clear as it was when Aldgate and Bishopsgate were actual gates in the wall separating the City from the poorer quarters to the east. The buttoned-up feeling of the City contrasts the artsy, diverse flavor of its neighbor. The oldest part of the East End, **Whitechapel,** is home to London's largest Bangladeshi community, as well as strong Pakistani and Afghani communities, as evidenced by the minaret of the **East London Mosque.** *(45 Fieldgate St., off Whitechapel. ⊖Aldgate East.)* Years ago the East was also home to the nucleus of London's sizable Jewish community. The old **Bevis Marks Synagogue** is the largest of the area synagogues, and tiny synagogues are nestled into alleys all over Whitechapel. *(Bevis Marks Rd. ⊖Aldgate.)* The best reasons to visit the East End are its markets, restaurants, and nightlife. Shoppers descend on **Spitalfields** (p. 240) each weekend in search of organic produce and high-quality crafts and clothing.

Brick Lane boasts a number of delicious ethnic eateries, and East London's bars and clubs comprise one of the best evening scenes in the city. A winding mass of curry houses, a few remaining Jewish bakeries, independent clothing boutiques, and popular nightlife destinations give Brick Lane a spicy atmosphere. The blending of cultures has not always gone smoothly, however: it was long the center of London's gang activity, and the Aldgate Tube station was one of the three targeted by suicide bombers in July of 2005. *(⊖Shoreditch open only at rush hour, ⊖Aldgate, ⊖Aldgate East, or ⊖Liverpool St.)*

While remnants of an industrial past remain, the neighborhoods of **Hoxton** and **Shoreditch** have recently become some of London's trendiest districts. In the 1990s, struggling artists, including Damien Hirst and Tracey Emin, saw potential in the

SIGHTS

neighborhood's cheap property and vacant warehouses, and Hoxton became the focus of an underground art scene. Eventually, word about the neighborhood spread, bringing an influx of artists from all over the world, followed by graphic and web designers. **Hoxton Square,** the compact center of the restaurant, gallery, and nightlife scene, emerged as the place to be. Many of the real artists have since fled to cheaper living, but the region still clings to its hip, independent past; stop by before lunchtime—when most people are still sleeping off the night before—to get the full "deserted slum" experience, or, better yet, around midnight when the area's denizens and their City neighbors are out on the town. (⊖*Old St. The center of the Hoxton and Shoreditch scene spreads out on either side of Old St. between the junction with Great Eastern St. and Kingsland Rd./Shoreditch High St.)*

CHRIST CHURCH SPITALFIELDS. Christ Church, the largest design by Christopher Wren's pupil, Nicholas Hawksmoor, stands proudly above its East End surroundings. A recently completed £7 million renovation has returned the church's stone facade to its former glory, and the inside is nicely outfitted with white crown moldings and marble pillars. *(Commercial St., opposite Spitalfields Market. ⊖Liverpool St.* ☎ *7247 7202. Worship held Su 10:30am; Communion the 1st and 3rd Su of each month at 8:30am. Church open M-F 10am-4pm, Su 1-4pm when not in use for functions.)*

 CHRIST CHURCH CONCERTS FOR POCKET CHANGE. Christ Church Spitalfields opens its doors for a series of excellent and mostly free concerts during the Spitalfields Festivals in both June and December. See www.spitalfieldsfestival.org.uk for upcoming dates and concert schedules.

DOCKLANDS

Skyscrapers, stores, and secretaries populate the busy Docklands area, distinguishing it from the churches and monuments of the surrounding areas. Until the 1960s, when the shipping industry began its permanent decline, this man-made jumble of floating docks was the commercial heart of the British Empire. The London Docklands Development Corporation (LDDC) was founded to revitalize the region in 1981, creating London's second financial district. Today, the Docklands is one of the largest commercial developments in Europe—a mix of high-tech office buildings covered with scrolling stock prices, countless shops and restaurants, and ultra-modern apartment complexes. Pressed for space, construction companies now set up makeshift offices on Thames barges. Undergoing constant growth, the area proudly broadcasts its status as a temple to consumerism.

CANARY WHARF. At 800 ft. high, the glass-paneled, pyramid-topped tower of 1 Canada Sq. is Britain's tallest building. In the past three years it has been joined by almost equally tall companions—HSBC, Barclays, and Citigroup—whose logos can be seen from miles away. The area surrounding the tower, including parks, malls, and restaurants, is commonly called Canary Wharf. The dockside plaza is lined with upscale corporate restaurants and bars; on a nice day they are a decent place for a drink or a bite to eat. *(⊖Canary Wharf, DLR: Canary Wharf or Heron Quays. Wheelchair-accessible.)*

GREENWICH

Maritime Greenwich, as it's officially known, has played many different roles over the last few centuries. It was built as a royal palace, but after the royal family vacated the premises, Greenwich became home to the Royal Navy until 1997. The Royal Observatory, on the Prime Meridian line, was originally founded to produce accurate star charts for navigation. The newly renovated O_2 Dome is a modern entertainment venue that hosts everything from concerts to museum exhibits. Greenwich's relaxed pace and interesting sights and museums make it a more-than-pleasant place to spend a day. *(DLR: Cutty Sark unless stated otherwise. The Green-wich Tourist Information Center, Pepys House, 2 Cutty Sark Gardens, offers tourist services as well as a slick exhibit on local history. ☎0870 608 2000. Guided walking tours leave the center daily at 12:15pm for the town and observatory and at 2:15pm for the Royal Naval College; £5, conces-sions £4, children under 14 free. Information Center open daily 10am-5pm.)*

Many people choose to make the hour-long boat trip from Westminster or Tower Hill to Greenwich; boats also run to the Thames Barrier. Travelcard holders get 33% off riverboat trips from a variety of companies. *(See Transport for London website for full details; www.tfl.gov.uk/gettingaround/1131.aspx.)* **City Cruises** oper-ates from Westminster Pier to Greenwich via the Tower of London. *(☎7740 0400; www.citycruises.com. Schedule changes constantly; call for times. Round-trip £9.40, all-day "rover" ticket £10; children £3.10/3.70).*

ROYAL OBSERVATORY GREENWICH. The climb to the peak of Greenwich Park is not for the lazy, but the view is well worth the trek; you can see all of the Dock-lands and Westminster on a clear day. The peak is home to the Royal Observatory, founded by Charles II in 1675 to accelerate the task of "finding the longitude" after one too many shipwrecks led to public outcry. Despite its importance, Charles decreed it must be built for under £500, so beams from ships and other construc-tion sites were brought in to offset costs. Even though the puzzle of longitude was eventually solved using seafaring clocks, Greenwich still plays an important role as the marker of hemispheres. The **Prime Meridian,** marked by a constantly photo-graphed red LED strip in the courtyard, is the axis along which the astronomers' telescopes swung. Stand with one foot in each hemisphere before ducking into **Flamsteed House,** a Christopher Wren creation originally designed as a living space for the Astronomer Royal and now home to famous clocks and old astronomical equipment. Next to the Meridian Building's telescope display you can climb the **Observatory Dome,** cunningly disguised as a freakishly large rust-colored onion, to see the cleverly named 28 in. Telescope, constructed in 1893. It's still the seventh-largest refracting lens in the world, and, although it was officially retired in 1971, it is still fully functional. *(At the top of Greenwich Park, a short but fairly steep climb from the National Maritime Museum; for an easier walk, take the Avenue from St. Mary's Gate at the top of King William Walk. Tram leaves from the back of the Museum every 30min. on the hr. ☎8858 4422; www.nmm.ac.uk. Open daily 10am-5pm; last admission 4:30pm. Summer open 10am-6pm; call to confirm. Daily guided tour leaves at 2:30pm in front of the Flamsteed House; free.)*

THE ROYAL NAVAL COLLEGE. On the site of Henry VIII's Palace of Placentia—where he and his daughters Mary and Elizabeth I were born—the Royal Naval Col-lege was built in 1696 as the Royal Hospital for Seamen, a naval retirement in the vein of the army's Royal Hospital in Chelsea (p. 190). However, the strict regime proved unpopular with former seamen, and in 1873 it was converted into the Royal Naval College. In 1998, the Navy packed its bags and the newly formed University of Greenwich stepped in, along with the famed **Trinity College of Music.** While most of the buildings are closed to the public, the grounds of the college—including the extravagant ◪**Painted Hall** that took Sir James Thornhill 19 years to complete—and the colorful **chapel** are free for wandering. While impressive, the college is more of a side trip from the observatory and National Maritime Museum than a main destination. The campus also has a Queen Mary Bar and King William Res-taurant below the chapel and Painted Hall, respectively. *(King William Walk. ☎8269 4747; www.greenwichfoundation.org.uk. Chapel and Painted Hall open daily 10am-5pm; chapel may close at 4:30pm for weddings. Su 11am worship service open to public. Free.)*

GREENWICH PARK. A former royal hunting ground, Greenwich Park is home to recreation and relaxation as young people and families come out in droves to sun-bathe, strike up football games, and picnic. The remains of a first-century Roman settlement and Saxon **tumuli** (burial mounds) are down the hill from the observatory. On the east side of the park is the **Queen Elizabeth Oak;** for centuries before its collapse, the tree marked the spot where Henry VIII frolicked with an 11-fingered Anne Boleyn. A new oak was planted in the spot as a replacement in 1992. The garden in the southeast corner of the park blends English garden and fairy tale, complete with a deer park. **The Children's Boating Pool** just behind the museum gives children a chance to unleash pent-up seafaring energy. While almost always crowded with families and young'uns, the park is best visited in the early to mid-morning. Start at the observatory and wander down toward the museums and riverside area for a walk and a bite to eat. *(Open daily 7am-dusk. Children's Boating Pool open June-Aug. daily 10:30am-5pm; Sept.-May Sa-Su 10:30am-5pm. 20min. paddle boat rental £2.50, children £1.50.)*

CUTTY SARK. The Cutty Sark was the fastest of the British tea-liners. Built in 1869, she made the round-trip voyage from China in only 120 days, carrying over a million pounds of tea. Retired from the sea in the 1930s, the deck and cabins have been partially restored to their 19th-century prime (complete with animatronic sailors). The hold houses an exhibit on the ship's history and a fascinating collection of figureheads. The upper deck has the officer's quarters—a far cry, comfortwise, from those of the crew. Due to a large-scale conservation project that began in 2006 and was set back by a large fire in the spring of 2007, the ship is closed to visitors until early 2009. A small shop is open but not worth the trip unless already in the area. *(King William Walk, by Greenwich Pier. ☎8858 3445; www.cuttysark.org.uk. Open daily 10am-5pm. Call for opening updates and details.)*

THAMES BARRIER. Around the next bend in the Thames from Greenwich stands the world's largest and strongest movable flood barrier, protecting London from the dangers of the tides. Constructed during the 1970s and (over-)hyped as "the eighth wonder of the world," the barrier spans 520m and consists of 10 separate movable steel gates. When raised, the main gates stand as high as a five-story building. Nobody's allowed on the barrier, of course, but you can see it from the Thames Barrier Information Centre, which houses a video, working model of the barrier, and history display. The best time to see the gates is when they are raised, although this happens as little as once a month. Call to verify times. *(Information Center: 1 Unity Way. ☎8305 4188. Centre open M-Sa Apr.-Sept. 10:30am-4pm; Oct.-Mar. 11am-3:30pm. Admission £2, concessions £1.50, children £1.)*

CLERKENWELL

The mercurial popularity of now-hip Clerkenwell coincides, appropriately enough, with the fluctuating role that alcohol has played in the local economy. Clerkenwell was founded as a monastic hamlet in the 12th century, but an influx of brewers and distilleries about 600 years later brought a slew of liquor-centric jobs to the area. The population boomed a bit too strongly, though, and Clerkenwell soon became the notorious slum detailed in Charles Dickens's *Oliver Twist.*

SEE MAP, p. 364

The area was heavily damaged during WWII and again by fire in the 1980s and 90s. Today, it is less chic than before but definitely more fun, with a lively population of young bars and nightclubs. Many of the neighborhood's historic buildings are beautiful from the outside but are inaccessible to tourists; instead, walking all or part of the **Clerkenwell Historic Trail** (maps available at the Curved Angel; p. 125) provides a wonderful history lesson as well as a great way to see the under-appreciated streets of Clerkenwell. *(All sights are closest to ⊖Farringdon unless otherwise stated.)*

ST. BARTHOLOMEW THE GREAT. Enter through a 13th-century arch to reach this gem of a Norman church, hidden between other buildings and houses. The

TAKE A HIKE. Many of the sights in Clerkenwell keep irregular and inconvenient hours. Instead of trying to coordinate your time to see these sights, embark on the Clerkenwell Historic Trail. You'll get a sense of the history, see the great architecture, and be able to spend your precious time at other, more educational sights.

peaceful elevated courtyard provides a close view of its unique and eccentric exterior as well as a lovely place to sit and relax. Inside, the current neck-stretching nave was just the chancel of the original 12th-century church, which once reached all the way to the street. William Hogarth was baptized in the 15th-century font, and at one time Benjamin Franklin worked as a printer's apprentice in the Lady Chapel. The tomb near the central altar is the resting place of Rahere, who in 1123 founded both the church and the neighboring **St. Bartholomew's Hospital.** *(Little Britain, off West Smithfield. ⊖Barbican. ☎7606 5171. Open M-F 8:30am-5pm, Sa 10:30am-4pm, Su 8:30am-8pm. £4, concessions £3.)*

ST. JOHN'S SQUARE. Bisected by the busy Clerkenwell Rd., St. John's Sq. occupies the site of the 12th-century **Priory of St. John,** former seat of the Knights Hospitallers. The Hospitallers (in full, the Order of the Hospital of St. John of Jerusalem) were founded in 1113 during the First Crusade to simultaneously tend to the sick and fight the heathens. What remains of their London seat is now in the hands of the British Order of St. John. Unaffiliated with the original Vatican order—which still exists—this Protestant organization founded their Ambulance Brigade in 1887 to provide first-aid service to the public.

Built in 1504 as the main entrance to the priory, **St. John's Gate** now arches grandly over the entrance to the square. The small museum on the ground floor mixes artifacts relating to the original priory and Knights Hospitallers, including everything from armor to table settings, with a "Time to Care" room detailing the order's modern-day exploits in bringing medical aid to the masses. Join a tour to see the upstairs council chamber and the priory church, which is otherwise closed to the public. *(St. John's Ln. ☎7324 4070; www.sja.org.uk/history. Open M-F 10am-5pm, Sa 10am-4pm. Tours Tu and F-Sa 11am and 2:30pm; £5, concessions £4. Call for group bookings. Free; requested donation £5.)*

On the other side of Clerkenwell Rd., cobblestones in St. John's Sq. mark the position of the original **Norman church.** The current building dates to the 16th century and lies at the end of a cloister garden. Two panels of the 1480 Weston Triptych stand on their original altar, but the real treasure of the church is the **crypt,** a remnant from the 12th-century priory and one of London's few surviving pieces of Norman architecture. Now it serves as a convenient place to sit and eat a meal while watching the business of the city whip by. *(Open only to tours of St. John's Gate, unless by special arrangement; see above.)*

CLERKENWELL GREEN. Not very green at all—actually just a wider-than-normal street—Clerkenwell Green boasts a few venerable historical associations. Wat Tyler rallied the Peasants' Revolt here in 1381, and Lenin published the Bolshevik newspaper *Iskra* from No. 37a, the Green's oldest building, built in 1737. It now houses the **Marx Memorial Library.** Across from this revolutionary hotbed, the **Old Sessions House,** built in 1782, was formerly the courthouse for the county of Middlesex—note the Middlesex arms on the portico. Reputedly haunted, it's now the enigmatic London Masonic Centre. *(Closed to the public.)* Overall, there's not too much to see on the Green, but many small, winding streets around it offer quaint cafes and places to relax.

THE CHARTERHOUSE. Originally a 14th-century Carthusian monastery, the Charterhouse and its walls were built around the communal grave of thousands of victims of the 1349 Black Death. In 1611, the corpses got some new company when Thomas Sutton bought the property and established a foundation for the education of 40 boys and the care of 80 impoverished old men. Charterhouse School rapidly established itself as one of the most prestigious (and expensive) schools in England. In 1872 the school moved to Surrey, leaving the complex to the (still penniless) pensioners. The weekly tour guides you through the grounds and into some of the buildings, including the Duke of Norfolk's Great Hall and the chapel with Sutton's ornate tomb. *(On the north side of Charterhouse Sq. ⊖Barbican. ☎7251 5002. Partially wheelchair-accessible. Open only for 1½hr. tours May-Aug. W 2:15pm. Book months in advance. £10.)*

HOLBORN

Holborn native Samuel Johnson once advised, "You must not be content with seeing Holborn's great streets and squares but must survey the innumerable little lanes and courts." The delights of Holborn are found in the unexpected, jewel-like gardens hidden by sprawling offices. From the tiny and winding lanes of the Temple to the enormous and ornate Royal Courts of Justice, Holborn is a neighborhood of contrasts, with the mod-

SEE MAP, p. 364

ern skyline of London's commercial present rising above the Gothic remains of the past. Only in the Courtauld Galleries in Somerset House (p. 196) could a Modigliani share a floor with a Botticelli.

Running through the center of Holborn is **Fleet Street.** Named for the (now underground) tributary that flows from Hampstead to the Thames, Fleet St. became synonymous with the London press in the 19th century, when it housed all of the major dailies. "Fleet Street" is still used to describe London-based newspapers and the famous facades, such as the *Daily Telegraph*'s startling Greek and Egyptian Revival building or the *Daily Express*'s manse of chrome and black glass. After a standoff with the printers in 1986, Rupert Murdoch moved all his papers (including *The Times*) to Wapping, Docklands and initiated a mass exodus. Today, Fleet St. is home to churches, coffee shops, and photocopying stores—the street's final nod to the printing industry.

■**THE TEMPLE.** The Temple is a complex of buildings that derives its name from the crusading Order of the Knights Templar, which embraced this site as its English seat in 1185. Today the Temple houses legal and parliamentary offices, but its charming network of gardens and its medieval church remain open to the enterprising visitor. Make sure to check out the **Inner Temple Gateway,** between 16 and 17 Fleet St., the 1681 fountain of **Fountain Court** (featured in Dickens's *Martin Chiz-zlewit*) and **Elm Court,** tucked behind the church, a tiny yet exquisite garden ringed by massive stone structures. *(Between Essex St. and Temple Ave.; church courtyard off Middle Temple Ln. ⊖Temple or Blackfriars. Free.)*

Temple Church is one of the finest surviving medieval round churches and London's first Gothic church, completed in 1185 on the model of Jerusalem's Church of the Holy Sepulchre. Intricately crafted stained-glass windows, towering ceilings, an original Norman doorway, and 10 armored effigies complete the impressive interior, although much of it was rebuilt after WWII bombings. Adjoining the round church is a rectangular Gothic choir, built in 1240, with 1682 altar screen by Christopher Wren. The church hosts frequent recitals and musical services, including weekly organ recitals. *(☎7353 3470. Hours vary depending on the week's services and are posted outside the door of the church for the coming week. Organ recitals W 1:15-1:45pm; no services Aug.-Sept.)*

The **Middle Temple** largely escaped the destruction of WWII and retains fine examples of 16th- and 17th-century architecture. In Middle Temple Hall (closed to the public), Elizabeth I saw Shakespeare act in the premiere of *Twelfth Night*, and his *Henry*

VI points to Middle Temple Garden as the origin of the red and white flowers that served as emblems throughout the War of the Roses. *(Open May-Sept. M-F noon-3pm.)*

ROYAL COURTS OF JUSTICE. This massive Neo-Gothic structure, designed in 1874 by G.E. Street, holds its own among the distinguished facades of Fleet St. Inside are 88 courtrooms, chambers for judges and court staff, and cells for defendants. The architecture is impressive, more akin to a castle than a courthouse. Exterior views from Carey St. are also quite amazing, and the Great Hall features Europe's largest mosaic floor. Skip the uninspired display of legal costume at the rear of the Great Hall and instead watch the real thing. The back bench of every courtroom is open to the public during trials unless the courtroom door says "In Chambers." The notice boards beside the Enquiry Desk in the Great Hall display a list of cases being tried. Otherwise, inquire at the Press Association office. *(Where the Strand becomes Fleet St.; rear entrance on Carey St. ⊖Temple or Chancery Ln. ☎7947 6000, tours 7947 7684. Open M-F 9am-4:30pm; cases are heard 10:30am-1pm and 2-4pm. Wheelchair-accessible. Be prepared to go through a security checkpoint with metal detector. Free. Tours £6.)*

ST. ETHELDREDA'S. The mid-13th-century Church of St. Etheldreda is the last remaining vestige of the Bishop of Ely's palace. St. Etheldreda's is now the only pre-Reformation Catholic church in the city, bought back from the Church of England in 1874 after centuries of rotating landlords (one bold but unsuccessful tenant tried to convert the building into a brewery in the mid-1700s). Inside, the surprisingly high ceiling swallows up the bustle of the streets, creating an island of calm in the midst of Holborn Circus. The self-described "ancient rector" is happy to explain the history of Ely Place. Creepily enough, the crypt houses a cafe serving light lunches for £3.50-5. *(In Ely Place. ☎7405 1061. Church open daily 7:30am-7pm. Free.)*

ST. BRIDE'S CHURCH. The unusual spire of Christopher Wren's 1675 church is the most imitated piece of architecture in the world: perhaps taking his cue from the church's name, a local baker used it as the model for the first multi-tiered wedding cake. Dubbed "the printers' cathedral" in 1531 when Wyken de Worde set up his press here, it has long been closely associated with nearby newspapermen. Check out the pews that are dedicated to reporters who have "lost their lives in search of the truth." Although the modern interior is disappointing, its underbelly is not: the crypt includes the baker's wife's wedding dress and bonnet, as well as the remains of a Roman pavement and ditch from about AD 180. This is the eighth church that has been built on this site, making it a place for Christian worship for 1500 years. *(St. Bride's Ave., just off Fleet St. ⊖Blackfriars. ☎7427 0133; www.stbrides.com. Open daily 8am-4:45pm. Lunchtime concerts and nighttime classical music; call for details. Free.)*

ST. CLEMENT DANES. Legend places this church over the tomb of Harold Harefoot, a Danish warlord who settled here in the 9th century. Its fame with Londoners derives from its opening role in the famous nursery rhyme (*Oranges and Lemons Say the Bells of St. Clement's*—and they still do, daily at 9am, noon, 3, 6pm). With a long history of destruction, it was rebuilt most notably by Christopher Wren in 1681 and again after German bombs destroyed the interior during the Blitz. Its interior has now been restored to its white-and-gold splendor. It is now the official church of the Royal Air Force. The church houses the RAF regimental standards and a small tribute to the American airmen who died in WWII (left of the inner doors). The quiet, simple crypt houses an eerie collection of 17th-century funeral monuments. *(At the eastern junction of Aldwych and Strand. ⊖Temple. ☎7242 8282. Open M-F 9am-4pm, Sa-Su 9:30am-3:30pm. Free.)*

ST. DUNSTAN-IN-THE-WEST. An early Victorian church crammed between Fleet St. facades, St. Dunstan is most notable for its 1641 clock, whose bells are struck every 15min. by a pair of hammer-wielding musclemen (figurines) representing the mythical giant guardians of London, Gog and Magog. The statue of Elizabeth I adorning the porch was saved from the 16th-century Lud Gate that stood nearby. The church today is a model of ecumenical worship—seven separate and lavish chapels house seven different faiths. While inside, note the elaborate wood altar screen of the Eastern Orthodox chapel and take a peek at the plaque in memory of "The Honest Solicitor," that rarest inhabitant of Fleet St. The church offers free lunchtime recitals; check website for details. *(186a Fleet St. ⊖Temple or Chancery Ln. ☎7405 1929; www.stdunstaninthewest.org. Open Tu 11am-3pm. Free.)*

GRAY'S INN. Housing a picnic-perfect garden with plenty of green space and benches to relax, Gray's Inn is a great place to while away an afternoon. Francis Bacon maintained chambers here and purportedly designed the sprawling, lovely walks. With an appropriately colored facade on Gray's Inn Rd., the inn itself does not inspire joy from the outside—Dickens dubbed it "that stronghold of melancholy"—but inside, it's actually quite pleasant. Though the hall (on the left as you pass through the Gray's Inn Rd. entrance) is closed to the public, its small chapel, with original 16th-century stained glass, is open on weekdays. Its plain and modern interior is not worth the trip alone. *(Between Theobald's Rd., Jockey's Fields, High Holborn, and Gray's Inn Rd.; the entrances along Gray's Inn Rd. are not marked—look for the "Private Road" signs. ⊖Chancery Ln. or Holborn. Chapel open M-F 10am-6pm. Gardens open M-F noon-2:30pm.)*

ELY PLACE. Step through the gates separating Ely Place from Holborn Circus, and you'll no longer be in London. In the 13th century, the Bishop of Ely built a palace here (later appropriated by Henry VIII). Though the palace is long gone, by a constitutional quirk the street remains outside the jurisdiction of local government (and police). Next to Ely Place, Hatton Garden (actually a street) is the center of Britain's gem trade, with dozens of diamond merchants. *(⊖Chancery Ln. From the Tube, walk east along High Holborn onto Charterhouse St. and then make an immediate left through the gates.)*

THE SOUTH BANK

During the Middle Ages, the South Bank was outside the jurisdiction of the City authorities, and thus, all manner of illicit attractions sprouted in "the Borough" at the southern end of London Bridge. Bankside soon became the city's entertainment center. After the English Civil War, the South Bank's fortunes turned to the sea, as wharves groaned under the weight of cargoes from across the Empire. By the time shipping moved elsewhere in the late

SEE MAP, pp. 370-371

1950s, the seeds of regeneration had been sown. From the 1951 Festival of Britain sprang the Royal Festival Hall, the nucleus of the South Bank Centre and heart of the new South Bank. The National Theatre followed 20 years later, and development has continued at such a pace that the South Bank is now once more the heart of the London art scene, with a visitor-friendly conglomeration of art galleries, theatres, and music halls, each with their own bit of history.

■ **SHAKESPEARE'S GLOBE THEATRE.** This incarnation of the Globe is faithful to the original, thatch roof and all. The original burned down in 1613 after a 14-year run as the Bard's preferred playhouse. Today's reconstruction had its first full season in 1997 and now stands as the cornerstone of the International Shakespeare Globe Centre. The informative exhibit inside covers the theatre's history and includes displays on costumes and customs of the theatre, as well as information on other prominent playwrights of Shakespeare's era. There's also an interactive display where you get to trade lines with recorded Globe actors. Try to arrive in time for a tour of the theatre itself. Tours that run during a matinee skip the Globe but are the only way to gain admission to the neighboring **Rose Theatre,** where both Shakespeare and Christopher Marlowe performed. For info on performances, see p. 232. *(Bankside, close to Bankside pier.* ✆*Southwark or London Bridge.* ☎ *7902 1400; www.shakespeares-globe.org. Open daily Apr.-Sept. 9am-noon (exhibit and tours) and 12:30-5pm (exhibit only); Oct.-Apr. 10am-5pm (exhibit and tours). Wheelchair-accessible. £9, concessions £7.50, children 5-15 £6.50, families of 5 £20.)*

■ **SOUTHWARK CATHEDRAL.** A site of worship since AD 606, the cathedral has undergone numerous transformations in the last 1400 years. The majestic main chapel is full of historical connections. Shakespeare's brother Edmund is buried here, and a rare stained-glass window depicts characters from Shakespearean plays. In the rear of the nave, there are four smaller chapels; the northernmost Chapel of St. Andrew is specifically dedicated to those living with and dying from HIV and AIDS. In 2001, a new conference center and cafe were opened on the grounds by Nelson Mandela as part of the millennium celebrations. Near the center, the **archaeological gallery** is actually a small excavation revealing a 1st-century Roman road along with Saxon, Norman, and 18th-century remains. Various treasures from the cathedral's face-lifts are on display; don't miss the medieval wooden decorations, including a frightening depiction of the devil swallowing Judas. *(Montague Close.* ✆ *London Bridge.* ☎ *7367 6700; www.southwark.anglican.org/cathedral. Open M-F 8am-6pm, Sa-Su 9am-6pm. Wheelchair-accessible. Admission free, suggested donation £4. Groups are asked to book in advance; group rates available. Audio tours £5; concessions £4, children 5-15 £2.50. Camera permit £2; video permit £5.)*

LONDON EYE. Also known as the Millennium Wheel, at 135m (430 ft.) the British Airways London Eye is the biggest observational wheel in the world, taller than St. Paul's Cathedral and visible for miles around. The lines are about a millennium long, so don't come in the middle of the day or you'll be there forever. The elliptical glass "pods" give uninterrupted views from the top of each 30min. revolution. On clear days, you can see Windsor in the west, though eastward views are blocked by skyscrapers farther down the river. *(Jubilee Gardens, between County Hall and the Festival Hall.* ✆*Waterloo.* ☎ *087 990 8883; www.ba-londoneye.com. Open daily Oct.-May 10am-8pm, June-Sept. 10am-9pm. Wheelchair-accessible. Buy tickets from box office at the corner of County Hall before joining the queue at the Eye. Advance booking recommended, but check the weather. £14.50, concessions £11, children under 16 £7.25.)*

LOCAL LEGEND

GOING GLOBAL

Shakespeare's Globe Theatre (the first) burned down in 1613 as a result of sound effects gone awry. On one fateful day, a small cannon was set off in the attic gallery as part of the play *Henry VIII.* Unfortunately, the staff apparently didn't think about the large, thick ring of straw that made up the roof, which quickly caught fire.

While a replica of the theatre stands on the site of the original—and patrons continue a tradition of standing room only—the new Globe is, in some ways, a far cry from the old. Groundlings, as commoners who would stand in front of the stage were called, would pay one penny to come see the show (around 10% of their weekly salary). We can only guess as to the lack of comfort in the pit: the alleged capacity was close to 3000. Bathroom services were unheard of, largely because exiting the theatre would mean that not only would you lose your spot, but you might also have to pay to re-enter. The solution—groundlings relieved themselves on the spot... talk about getting to know your neighbor. The higher classes who purchased seats were allowed to use the stairwells as restrooms, a luxury of which the common man could only dream. So while you enjoy the show today, appreciate the modern WCs.

GET HIGH FOR FREE. If paying £20 for the London Eye seems a bit steep for a bird's-eye view of the city, climb the tower at the Tate Modern (p. 198), which gives a similar view for free.

GABRIEL'S WHARF AND OXO TOWER. One of the more colorful additions to the South Bank, **Gabriel's Wharf** is a craftsy market-like area where little shops and restaurants stretch from the water down into the surrounding streets. A few steps away is the Art Deco **OXO Tower,** built by a company that once supplied instant beef stock to the entire British Empire. OXO Tower is famous for its clever subversion of rules prohibiting advertising on buildings: the windows subtly spell out "OXO." The Tower is now enveloped in the brick mass of the **OXO Tower Wharf,** full of tiny boutiques and workshops run by some of London's most innovative young designers. A free public viewing gallery on the eighth floor provides prime views over the South Bank area and connects to a bar and restaurant. *(Between Upper Ground and the Thames. ⊖Blackfriars, Southwark, or Waterloo. Wheelchair-accessible.)*

HMS BELFAST. This enormous cruiser was one of the most powerful ships in the world when launched in 1938. The *Belfast* led the British landing at Normandy on D-Day and supported UN forces in Korea before retiring in 1965. In 1971, she went on display as part of the Imperial War Museum and still holds her regal floating spot on the Thames, boasting a prodigious mid-river view. Children will love clambering over the decks and aiming the 40mm anti-aircraft guns at dive-bombing seagulls. A climb down the narrow steps shows the inner-workings of the carrier. You can tour the kitchens and operations room, where waxworks and sound recordings recreate the sinking of the German battleship *Scharnhorst* in 1943. The steep staircases and ladders from deck to deck add to the realism but make exploring the boat a physical challenge. On-deck benches are pleasant resting spots. *(At the end of Morgans Ln., off Tooley St.; also accessible via the Queen's Walk. ⊖London Bridge. ☎7940 6300; www.iwm.org.uk. Open daily Mar.-Oct. 10am-6pm; Nov.-Feb. 10am-5pm. Last admission 45min. before closing. £10, concessions £6.15, children under 16 free.)*

BUTLERS WHARF. Just east of Tower Bridge, Butlers Wharf is one of the best places to take in the view. The narrow cobblestone streets are a stark contrast to the broad boardwalks along the water. During the 1970s Butlers Wharf became home to London's largest artist colonies. The party ended in 1980, when developers moved in. Today, the wharf is lined with various shops and restaurants, which certainly make good use of their waterside location. *(⊖London Bridge.)*

LONDON AQUARIUM. As aquariums go, this is a small fish in a big pond, but it's the only one in London. The main attractions are dual three-story ocean tanks—one holds Atlantic fish and the other Pacific fish, including sharks. Children can pet rays and fish at the two petting tanks, if they don't mind getting wet. *(County Hall, Westminster Bridge Rd. ⊖Westminster or Waterloo. ☎7967 8000; www.londonaquarium.co.uk. Open daily 10am-6pm, in Aug. until 7pm; last admission 5pm. Wheelchair-accessible. £13.25, concessions £11.25, children under 14 £9.75, families of 4 £44.)*

DALÍ UNIVERSE. With over 500 works of art, this gallery earns its grandiose name. The entrance is a bizarre, blacked-out tunnel with cutout images of the artist and quotations designed to exhibit the artist's notorious and fabulous craziness. Almost all the works in this collection are multiple-run prints, castings, or reproductions. There are a few originals. Only real Dalí enthusiasts will find it worth it. However, if famous melting watches and lithographs are your thing, you won't be disappointed. Don't miss Dalí's custom-designed sofa shaped like Mae

West's lips, although you can't sit on it. A smaller but better set of Dalís are viewable for free in the Tate Modern (p. 198). *(Riverside Building, County Hall. ⊖Waterloo. ☎0870 744 7485; www.daliuniverse.com. Open daily 10am-6:30pm, last entry 5:30pm. Wheelchair-accessible. £12, concessions £10, families £30. Audio tours £2.50. AmEx/MC/V.)*

SOUTH LONDON

Initially, **Brixton** was just another South London railway suburb—actually a rather prosperous one, to which the once-grand houses along Electric Ave. and Electric Ln. (the first streets in South London with electric lighting) attest. Beginning in 1948, a steady stream of Caribbean immigrants made Brixton the heart of London's West Indian community, and simmering racial tensions erupted with major riots in 1981, 1985, and 1995. The flames have quelled, however, and Brixton is developing into a fashionable area for young artists and students, aided by the rise of an impressive club scene. A stroll through the area highlights the unique qualities of a town in flux: Afro-Caribbean markets, trendy new cafes, and increasing numbers of chain stores share street space. You can see the best of old Brixton early in the day, when **Brixton Market** is in full swing, and the best of new Brixton late at night, when young Brixtonians pile out of work and into the clubs and bars.

A short bus or train ride from Brixton, **Dulwich** could hardly offer a greater contrast; not much has changed in this old-money mecca in about four centuries. South London's snobbiest suburb, Dulwich bumbled along as an unremarkable country village until 1605, when Elizabethan actor Edward Alleyn bought a local manor. Wealth and sprawling estates soon followed. His legacy lives on in the College of God's Gift, established according to his will for the education of 12 poor children. The original **Old College** buildings, including the chapel where Alleyn is buried, still stand close to Dulwich Picture Gallery (p. 200). **Dulwich College,** now with 1600 very wealthy pupils, has since moved south to a palatial 19th-century site on College Rd. The college still profits from its private stretch of College Rd., south of the common: its **toll gate** is the last in London. *(Rail: North or West Dulwich.)*

BROCKWELL PARK. This massive stretch of rolling grass sprinkled with leafy trees is perfect for joggers, unleashed dogs, and those looking to get away from the crowded London streets. Just past the gated entrance is the popular **Brockwell Lido,** a 1930s outdoor swimming pool often described as "London's beach." The park also boasts tennis courts, a children's playground, miles of walking paths, a BMX track, and a small cafe at its summit (water £1, sandwiches from £2), from which you can catch a glimpse of the London Eye. *(The park is situated between Tulse Hill and Dulwich Rd.; from ⊖ Brixton, turn left out of the station, bear left at the fork onto Effra Rd., walk about 10min. then turn left again onto Brixton Water Lane. The entrance is on the right. www.brockwellpark.com. Open daily 7:30am-dusk.)*

CLAPHAM COMMON. The Common is comprised of over 200 acres of grassland shaped in a triangle and situated between Clapham, Battersea, and Balham. Apart from usual park offerings, the Common boasts three ponds, two of which play host to fishing. The Common's most notable feature is its 100-year-old bandstand, which has played host to numerous open-air concerts and festivals. *(The Common is situated between Clapham Common North Side Rd. and Clapham Common South Side Rd.; from ⊖Clapham North, turn left out of the station and walk about 10min. down Clapham High St.)*

 At night the Common is not very well lit and should not be traversed alone. Unless you're with a friend, take the streets around it instead.

Time: 8-9hr.

Distance: 2½ mi. (4km)

When To Go: Start early morning

Start: ⊖Tower Hill

Finish: ⊖Westminster

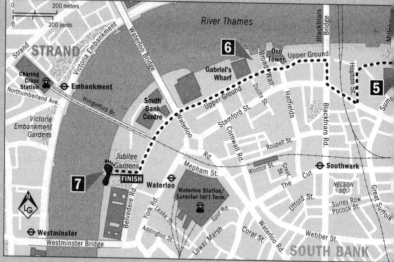

THE MILLENNIUM MILE

A stroll along the South Bank is a trip through history and back again. Across the river you will pass the timeless monuments of London's past, like the Tower of London and St. Paul's Cathedral, while next to you the round glass sphere of City Hall and the converted power facility of the Tate provide a stark and modern contrast. Whether it's a search for Shakespeare and Picasso that brings you to the South Bank, or just a hankering for a nice walk, you will find yourself rewarded.

1. TOWER OF LONDON. Begin your trek to the Tower **early** to avoid the crowds. Tours given by the Yeomen Warders meet every 1½hr. near the entrance. Listen as they expertly recount tales of royal conspiracy, treason, and murder. See the **White Tower,** once a fortress and residence of kings. Shiver at the executioner's stone on the tower green and pay your respects at the Chapel of St. Peter ad Vinculum, holding the remains of three queens. First, get the dirt on the gemstones at **Martin Tower,** then wait in line to see the **Crown Jewels.** The jewels include such glittering lovelies as the First Star of Africa, the largest cut diamond in the world (p. 148). Time: 2hr.

2. TOWER BRIDGE. An engineering wonder that puts its plainer sibling, the London Bridge, to shame. Marvel at its beauty, but skip the Tower Bridge Experience tour. Better yet, call in advance to inquire what times the Tower drawbridge is lifted (p. 150). Time: no need to stop walking; take in the mechanics as you head to the next sight.

3. DESIGN MUSEUM. On Butler's Wharf, let the Design Museum introduce you to the latest innovations in contemporary design. See what's to come in the forward-looking Review Gallery or hone in on individual designers and products in the Temporary Gallery (see p. 199). From the museum, walk along the **Queen's Walk.** To your left you will find the **HMS Belfast,** which was launched in 1938 and led the landing for D-Day, 1944 (p. 160). Time: 1hr.

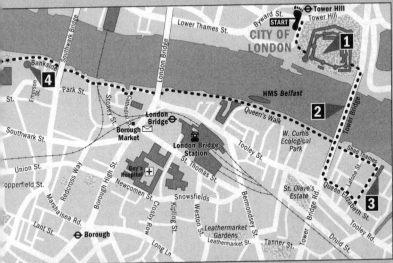

4. SHAKESPEARE'S GLOBE THEATRE. Take your time at this beautiful recreation of The Bard's most famous theatre. Excellent exhibits demonstrate how Shakespearean actors dressed and the secrets of stage effects, and tell of the painstaking process of rebuilding the theatre almost 400 years after the original burned down (p. 158). You might be able to catch a matinee performance if you time your visit right. Call in advance for tour and show times. Time: 1hr. for tour; 3hr. for performance.

5. TATE MODERN. It's hard to imagine anything casting a shadow over the Globe Theatre, but the massive former Bankside Power Station does just that. One of the world's premier Modern art museums, the Tate promises a new spin on well-known favorites and works by emerging British artists. Be sure to catch one of the informative docent tours and don't forget to check out the rotating installation in the Turbine Room (p. 198). Time: 2hr.

6. GABRIEL'S WHARF. Check out the cafes, bars, and boutiques of colorful Gabriel's Wharf. If you missed the top floor of the Tate Modern, go to the public viewing gallery on the eighth floor of the **OXO Tower Wharf** (p. 160). On your way to the London Eye, stop by the **South Bank Centre.** Established as a primary cultural center in 1951, it now exhibits a range of music from Philharmonic extravaganzas to low-key jazz. You may even catch one of the free lunchtime or afternoon events. Call in advance for dates and times (p. 222). Time: 1½hr. for schmoozing and dinner.

7. LONDON EYE. Once known as the Millennium Wheel, the London Eye shed its maiden name at the first possible chance. The Eye has firmly established itself as one of London's top attractions, popular with locals and tourists alike. It offers amazing 360° views from its glass pods; you may be able to see all of London lit up at sunset. Book in advance to minimize queue time, and be sure to check the weather (p. 159). Time: 1hr.

RICHARD III— INNOCENT OR GUILTY?

The villain of one of William Shakespeare's best known plays was based on a real figure—King Richard III. Whether he was a villain or not in real life remains unproven. Some believe Richard was responsible for the deaths of his two nephews in the Tower of London in 1483. One of his nephews, 12-year-old Edward V, was the rightful heir to the throne, and was due to be crowned at the Tower before he and his 10-year-old brother mysteriously disappeared.

In 1674 two child-sized skeletons, believed to be the remains of the boys, were found in the Tower during renovations. Unfortunately for the curious, no forensic examination is possible since the remains of the boys were later buried in the protected Westminister Abbey. Therefore, the mystery of the heir's fate after he and his brother entered the gates of the Tower of London will continue.

Many believe Richard was guilty of murder, but others believe he was framed. One such group, the Richard III Society, believe that Richard is innocent of any wrongdoing and consider it their mission to clear his name. For more information on this historical tale, visit the Tower of London (see p. 148), which houses a special exhibit on the tale in the Bloody Tower.

WESTMINSTER

SEE MAP, p. 368

Responsible for the images that grace most London postcards, Westminster is a goldmine of historical sights. Big Ben, the Houses of Parliament, Westminster Abbey, Buckingham Palace, and more all fall within the confines of this age-old neighborhood, a necessary stop for all new visitors to the city. With so many choices, many of which require a good chunk of time, it can be difficult to decide what to visit and what to leave out. Don't feel as though you need to hit them all; just take your time and enjoy what you can.

■ WESTMINSTER ABBEY

Parliament Sq. Access Old Monastery, Cloister, and Garden from Dean's Yard, behind the Abbey. ⊖Westminster. Abbey ☎7654 4900, Chapter House 7222 5152; www.westminster-abbey.org. No photography. Abbey open M-Tu and Th-F 9:30am-3:45pm, W 9:30am-7pm, Sa 9:30am-1:45pm, Su open for services only. Museum open daily 10:30am-4pm. Partially wheelchair-accessible. Abbey and Museum £10, students and children 11-17 £7, families of 4 £24. Services free. 1½hr. tours £5 Apr.-Oct. M-F 10, 10:30, 11am, 2, 2:30pm, Sa 10, 10:30, 11am; Oct.-Mar. M-F 10:30, 11am, 2, 2:30pm, Sa 10:30, 11am. Audio tours £4 available M-F 9:30am-3pm, Sa 9:30am-1pm. AmEx/MC/V.

Originally founded as a Benedictine monastery, Westminster Abbey has evolved to become a house of kings and queens both living and dead. On December 28, 1065, St. Edward the Confessor, last Saxon King of England, was buried in the Abbey in his still-unfinished Abbey Church of the West Monastery. Almost exactly a year later, on Christmas Day, the Abbey saw the coronation of William the Conqueror. Even before it was completed, the Abbey's twin traditions as the birthplace and final resting place of royalty had been established. Little remains of St. Edward's Abbey: Henry III's 13th-century Gothic reworking created most of the grand structure you see today. In 1540, Henry VIII dissolved the monasteries, expelling the monks and seizing control of the Abbey. Fortunately, Henry's respect for his royal forbearers outweighed his vindictiveness against Catholicism, so Westminster escaped destruction and desecration. Much of the monastic artwork has been lost over time, but the structure and the vaulted Gothic architecture remain beautifully preserved. The Abbey became a "Royal Peculiar" under the direct control of Henry VIII. Under this ambiguous status, the Abbey has since become a ceremo-

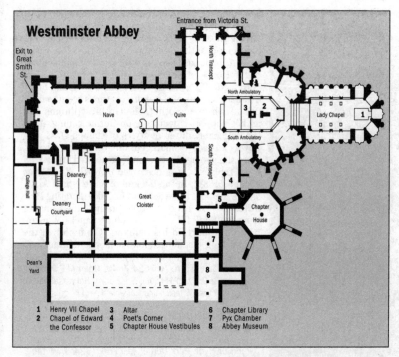

Westminster Abbey

Entrance from Victoria St.

Exit to
Great
Smith
St.

North Transept

Nave

Quire

North Ambulatory

3 2

Lady Chapel 1

South Ambulatory

Deanery

College Hall

South Transept

Deanery
Courtyard

Great
Cloister

4

5

Chapter
House

6

Dean's
Yard

7

8

1	Henry VII Chapel	3	Altar	6	Chapter Library
2	Chapel of Edward the Confessor	4	Poet's Corner	7	Pyx Chamber
		5	Chapter House Vestibules	8	Abbey Museum

nial center for the nation. Every ruler since William I has been coronated here, and many have been married here as well. The Abbey is also a place for royal funerals. The varied uses and styles in the Abbey have combined to make an intriguing and often strange mix of statues, tombs, and plaques.

Of the many Brits buried and commemorated inside the Abbey, highlights include statesmen (and women) Henry VII, Bloody Mary, and Elizabeth I; scholars and artists in the "Poet's Corner" (honored with plaques, but not buried there) include Geoffrey Chaucer, the Brontë sisters, Jane Austen, George Handel, and Shakespeare. Next door to the Abbey (through the cloisters), the lackluster **Abbey Museum** is housed in the Norman undercroft. The highlight of the collection is the array of fully dressed medieval royal funeral effigies, undergarments and all.

OLD MONASTERY, CLOISTERS, AND GARDENS. Formerly a major monastery, the Abbey complex still stretches far beyond the church itself, including gardens and other structures. A door off the east cloister leads to the octagonal **Chapter House,** the original meeting place of the House of Commons, whose 13th-century tiled floor is the best preserved in Europe. The faded but still exquisite frescoes of the Book of Revelations around the walls date from this period, as do the sculpture and floor tiles. The **Great Cloisters** hold yet more tombs and commemorative plaques. A passage running off the southeast corner leads to the idyllic flowering **Little Cloister** courtyard, from which another passage leads to the 900-year-old **College Gardens,** which are kept in immaculate condition. *(Chapter House open daily 10:30am-4pm. Cloisters open daily 8am-6pm. Garden open Apr.-Sept. Tu-Th 10am-6pm; Oct.-Mar. daily 10am-4pm. Free.)*

ST. MARGARET'S. Just north of the Abbey, this church enjoys a strange status: as a part of the Royal Peculiar, it is not under the jurisdiction of the diocese of

QUEEN'S GUARD

Let's Go got the scoop on a London icon. Corporal of Horse Simon Knowles is an 19-year veteran of the Queen's Guard.

LG: What sort of training did you undergo?

A: In addition to a year of basic military camp, which involves mainly training on tanks and armored cars, I was also trained as a gunner and radio operator. Then I joined the service regiment at 18 years of age.

LG: So it's not all glamor?

A: Not at all. That's a common misconception. After armored training, we go through mounted training on horseback in Windsor for six months where we learn the tools of horseback riding, beginning with bareback training. The final month is spent in London training in full state uniform.

LG: Do the horses ever act up?

A: Yes, but it's natural. During the Queen's Jubilee Parade, with three million people lining the Mall, to expect any animal to be fully relaxed is absurd. The horses rely on the rider to give them confidence. If the guard is riding the horses confidently and strongly, the horse will settle down.

LG: Your uniforms look pretty heavy. Are they comfortable?

A: They're not comfortable at all. They were designed way back in Queen Victoria's time, and the

England or even the archbishop of Canterbury. It was built for local residents by Abbey monks tired of having to share their own church with laymen and has been beautifully restored in the past few years. Since 1614, it has been the official worshipping place of the House of Commons—the first few pews are cordoned off for the Speaker, Black Rod, and other dignitaries. Parts of the church at times seem to be at odds with one another: the Gothic columns and arches support a decidedly un-Gothic ceiling. Also, the noticeably different styles of stained-glass windows can feel mismatched, but with good reason, since the geometric, gray-and-green-hued Piper Windows replaced those destroyed in WWII. The **Milton Window** (1888), in the back above the North Aisle, shows the poet (married here in 1608) dictating *Paradise Lost* to his daughters. Stained-glass images from the book fill the surrounding panels. Winston Churchill married his beloved "Clemmie" in the chapel. In the summer months, free lunchtime concerts are offered on a weekly basis: call to find out more information. (☎ *7654 4840. Open M-F 9:30am-3:45pm, Sa 9:30am-1:45pm, Su 2-5pm. Hours subject to change; call first. Wheelchair-accessible. Free.*)

◪ BUCKINGHAM PALACE

At the end of the Mall, between Westminster, Belgravia, and Mayfair. ⊖St. James's Park, Victoria, Green Park, or Hyde Park Corner. ☎ 7766 7324; www.the-royal-collection.com.

Originally built for the Dukes of Buckingham, Buckingham House was acquired by George III for his new wife, Queen Charlotte, in 1761. Charlotte gave birth to 14 of her 15 children at Buckingham House. George IV, the next sovereign, decided it wasn't nearly big enough to be a royal residence and commissioned John Nash to expand the existing building into a palace. Neither George IV nor his successor, William IV, ever lived in the palace; when the 1834 fire left Parliament without a home, William offered Buckingham. Three years later, however, Queen Victoria moved in, and it has been the royal residence ever since. The structure was too small for Victoria's rapidly growing family, a problem that was solved by removing Nash's Marble Arch (which now stands just north at Marble Arch) and building a fourth wall to enclose the courtyard.

THE STATE ROOMS. The Palace opens to visitors every August and September while the royals are off sunning themselves. Don't expect to find any insights into the Queen's personal life—the State Rooms are the only rooms on view, and they are used only for formal occasions, like entertaining visiting heads of state. Fortunately, they are also the most sumptuous in the Palace. After ascending the grand staircase, you can tour the chromatically labeled drawing rooms, bedecked in white, blue, and green. Look for the secret door concealed in one of the **White Drawing Room's** mirrors—the royals enter the state apartments through this door. You'll also see the **Throne Room** and the domed and glittering **Music Room.** The **Galleries** display many of the finest pieces in the Royal Collection, including works by Rembrandt, Rubens, Poussin, and Canaletto. Queen Elizabeth has graciously allowed commoners into the **Gardens,** home to rare flowers and birds—keep off the grass! *(Enter on Buckingham Palace Rd. Ticket office ☎ 7766 7324. Tickets also available at Buckingham Palace. Open late July to late Sept. daily 9:30am-6:30pm, last admission 4:15pm. £15, students £13.50, children 6-17 £8.50, under 5 free, families of 5 £69.50. Advance booking is recommended; required for disabled visitors. AmEx/MC/V.)*

THE ROYAL MEWS. The Mews wears many hats: it acts as a museum, stable, riding school, and working carriage house. The main attraction is the Queen's collection of coaches, including the "Glass Coach" used to carry royal brides (including Diana) to their weddings, and the State Coaches of Australia, Ireland, and Scotland. The biggest draw is the four-ton **Gold State Coach,** which can occasionally be seen tooling around the streets in the early morning on practice runs for major events. The attendants on guard throughout the self-guided tour are gold mines of royal information, full of tips on when and where to catch glimpses of Their Royal Highnesses. Visitors can meet the carriage horses themselves, each named by the Queen. Each horse has undergone years of training to withstand the distractions of crowds, street traffic, and gun salutes. Displays regarding more modern forms of transportation (the royal fleet of Rolls Royces) and the training and garments of the carriage men are an interesting contrast. Note that horses and carriages are liable to be absent without notice, and opening hours are subject to change. *(☎ 7766 7302. Open late July to late Sept. daily 10am-5pm, last admission 4:15pm; Mar.-July and late Sept. to late Oct. M-Th and Sa-Su 11am-4pm, last admission 3:15pm. Wheelchair-accessible. £7, seniors £6, children under 17 £4.50, families £18.50. AmEx/MC/V.)*

QUEENS GALLERY. "God Save the Queen" is the rallying cry at this gallery dedicated to temporary exhibitions of jaw-droppingly valuable items from the Royal Collection. Most recently, a showing of Renaissance and Baroque Italian works were on display until January 2008. Five exquisite rooms are full of various artifacts dedicated to extolling the glory of the sovereign in numerous art forms. The friendly

leather trousers and boots are very solid. The uniform weighs about 3 stone [about 45 lb.].

LG: How do you overcome the itches, sneezes, and bees?

A: Discipline is instilled in every British soldier during training. We know not to move a muscle while on parade no matter what the provocation or distraction—unless, of course, it is a security matter. But our helmets are akin to wearing a boiling kettle on your head; to relieve the pressure, sometimes we use the back of our sword blade to ease the back of the helmet forward.

LG: How do you make the time pass while on duty?

A: The days are long. At Whitehall the shift system is derived upon inspection in Barracks. Smarter men work on horseback in the boxes in shifts from 10am-4pm; less smart men work on foot from 7am-8pm. Some guys count the number of buses that drive past. Unofficially, there are lots of pretty girls around here, and we *are* allowed to move our eyeballs.

LG: What has been your funniest distraction attempt?

A: One day a taxi pulled up, and out hopped four Playboy bunnies, who then posed for a photo shoot right in front of us. You could call that a distraction if you like.

older guards can show you the finest pieces of the Royal Collection, with the exception of the State Rooms. The rooms in this opulent museum are monochromatic and designed to look like the interior of the palace; a grand staircase and green marble pillars welcome visitors into the first room. Free audio tours typically accompany exhibits. Once purchased, passes may be registered online for 12 months of unlimited access. (☎7766 7301. *Open daily 10am-5:30pm, last admission 4:30pm. Wheelchair-accessible. £8, concessions £7, families £22.*)

CHANGING OF THE GUARD. The Palace is protected by a detachment of Foot Guards in full dress uniform, complete with highly impractical bearskin hats. "Changing of the Guard" refers not to replacing the sentries but to the exchange of guard duty between different regiments. When they meet at the central gates of the palace, the officers of the regiments touch hands, symbolically exchanging keys, and the guard is officially changed. Often, musical troops provide an accompanying soundtrack. To witness the 40min. spectacle, show up well before 11:30am and stand in front of the palace in view of the morning guards or use the steps of the Victoria Memorial as a vantage point. The middle of the week is the least crowded. (☎7766 7324. *Apr. to late July daily, Aug.-Mar. every other day, excepting the Queen's absence, inclement weather, or pressing state functions. Free.*)

 CROWD CONTROL. If the crowds at Buckingham Palace are too much to bear, head to the Pall Mall side of St. James's Palace, where two guards keep watch and ceremoniously patrol the main entrance. You'll encounter fewer crowds taking in the spectacle.

THE HOUSES OF PARLIAMENT

Parliament Sq., in Westminster. Queue for both Houses forms at St. Stephen's entrance, between Old and New Palace Yards. ⊖Westminster. ☎08709 063 773; www.parliament.uk/visiting/visiting.cfm. "Line of Route" Tour: includes both Houses. UK residents can contact their MPs for tours year-round, generally M-W mornings and F. Foreign visitors may tour Aug.-Sept. Book online, by phone, or in person at Abingdon Green ticket office (open mid-July) across from Palace of Westminster. Open Aug. M-Tu and F-Sa 9:15am-4:30pm, W-Th 1:15-4:30pm; Sept. M and F-Sa 9:15am-4:30pm, Tu-Th 1:15-4:30pm. 75min. tours depart every few min. £12, students £8, families of 4 £30. MC/V.

The Palace of Westminster has been home to both the House of Lords and the House of Commons (together known as Parliament) since the 11th century, when Edward the Confessor established his court here. William the Conqueror added **Westminster Hall** in 1099—a wise move, since the rest of the Palace burned down in 1834. As a result, with the exception of Westminster Hall, everything you can see today has been added in the 19th and 20th centuries. Two architects were commissioned for the rebuilding project—Classicist Charles Barry and Gothic champion Augustus Pugin—and a masterful combination of architectural styles resulted from their clash of temperaments. The exterior of the Palace is mostly Gothic, and the interior rooms and halls have a Classic dimension. Access has been restricted since a bomb killed an MP in 1979, but visitors can see some of the inside on the way to the galleries.

BIG BEN AND VICTORIA TOWER. The clock tower standing guard on the northern side of the building is famously nicknamed Big Ben, after the robustly proportioned Benjamin Hall, a former Commissioner of Works. "Big Ben" actually refers only to the 14-ton bell that hangs inside the tower. The tower itself, Victoria Tower, was erected in 1834 to celebrate the emancipation of slaves in the British Empire. The tower contains copies of every Act of Parliament since 1497. A flag flown from the top indicates that Parliament is in session. When the Queen is in the building, a special royal banner is flown instead of the Union Jack.

TIP **WATERLOO VIEW.** One of the best places in the city to watch a sunset is on the Waterloo Bridge. With views of Parliament, Big Ben, the London Eye, and St. Paul's, there are few better places to soak in the city on a clear night.

DEBATING CHAMBERS. Visitors with enough patience or luck to make it inside the chambers can hear the occasional debate among members of both the House of Lords and the House of Commons—although the architecture of the palace is more worthwhile than the debates themselves. The chambers are accessed via **St. Stephen's Hall,** which leads to the octagonal **Central Lobby**—the best example of the Gothic and Classical coexistence. The walls have ornate mosaics from 1870 depicting the kingdom's patron saints, while the Gothic archways hold stone sculptures of monarchs perched over the doors.

Access to the **House of Lords** is through the Peers' Lobby, which smug MPs have bedecked with scenes of Charles I's downfall. The ostentatious chamber itself is dominated by the sovereign's **Throne of State** under an elaborate gold gilt canopy—only when the golden throne is occupied can the Commons and the Lords congregate. The Lord Chancellor presides over the Peers from the **Woolsack,** a large red cushion that is quite the unusual post for a government official. Next to him rests the nearly 6 ft. gold **Mace,** which is brought in to open the House each morning. The lords face each other from their red leather benches arranged around the room. *(Lords Information Office ☎ 7219 3107. Chamber open Oct.-July M-Tu 2:30-10:30pm, W 3-10pm, Th 11am-7:30pm. Wait for Lords generally shorter than for Commons, although it still may not be possible to enter until after the 40min. "question time" M-W 2:30pm, Th-F 11am. Limited number of UK residents permitted for "question time." Foreign visitors must apply several weeks in advance for "question time" tickets through their embassy in London, or wait until questions are finished for entrance. Arrive in afternoon to minimize waiting, which regularly exceeds 2hr.)*

The contrast between the Lords and the **House of Commons**—with simple green-backed benches under an intricate but comparatively plain wooden roof—is not entirely due to the difference in class; the Commons was destroyed by bombs in 1941, and rebuilding took place during a time of post-war austerity. The Speaker sits at the center-rear of the chamber, where he keeps order in the room. The government MPs sit to his right and the opposition to his left. However, with room for only 437 of the 635 MPs, things can get hectic when all are present. The front benches are reserved for government ministers and their opposition "shadows"; the Prime Minister and the Leader of the Opposition face off across their dispatch boxes. *(Commons Information Office ☎ 7219 4272. Chamber open Oct.-July M-Tu 2:30-10:30pm, W 11:30am-7:30pm, Th 10:30am-6:30pm, occasionally F 9:30am-3pm. Hours subject to change.)*

OTHER WESTMINSTER SIGHTS

■ **ST. JAMES'S PARK AND GREEN PARK.** The streets leading up to Buckingham Palace are flanked by two sprawling expanses of greenery: St. James's Park and Green Park. In the middle of St. James's Park is the placid **St. James's Park Lake,** where you can catch glimpses of the pelicans that call it home—the lake and the grassy area surrounding it comprise an official waterfowl preserve. In the back corner, closest to the Palace, is a children's playground in memory of Princess Diana. Across the Mall, the lush Green Park is the creation of Charles II; it connects Westminster and St. James's. "Constitution Hill" refers not to the King's interest in political theory but to his daily exercises. If you sit on one of the lawn chairs scattered enticingly around both parks, an attendant will magically materialize and demand money. Alternatively, act like a local and bring a blanket for a picnic, at no charge. *(The Mall. ⊖ St. James's Park or Green Park. Open daily 5am-midnight. Lawn chairs available, weather permitting, Mar.-Oct. 10am-6pm; June-Aug. 10am-10pm £2 for 2hr., student deal £30*

SIGHTS

Time: could be as long as 15hr.

Distance: 1¾ mi. (2.7km)

When To Go: Early morning

Start: Westminster Abbey

Finish: The Houses of Parliament

A walk through Westminster, London's historical heartland, simply has no rival. By following the ci
cumference of St. James's Park, this tour covers the great traditions and monuments of near
1000 years of British history, from Westminster Abbey to the artistic jewels of the National Galle
to the seat of modern British politics. Don't necessarily expect to finish this tour in one day: ma
of the sights and museums included here could stand a full day of your attention all by themselve

1. WESTMINSTER ABBEY. Avoid the crowds by arriving early at medieval Westminster Abbe
As the place of royal coronations and burials since 1065, the Abbey immortalizes past monarchs
the impressive Royal Tombs. Along with the departed literati and musicians in the Poet's Corne
the Abbey also shelters the remains of Winston Churchill. Explore the monastery and gardens, b
if you plan to see the Changing of the Guard on the same morning, limit yourself to approximate
1hr. before heading to Buckingham Palace. Either make the 15min. walk there or take the Tub
from Westminster to St. James's Park. Time:1-2hr.

2. BUCKINGHAM PALACE. First occupied by Queen Victoria in 1832, the Palace continues
house the royal family. During Aug. and Sept., the State Rooms, the Throne Room, the White Drawi
room, the magnificent Galleries, and the beautifully manicured Gardens are open for tours. Call
advance for tickets. The Changing of the Guard outside Buckingham Palace takes place at 11:30a
arrive by 10:30am to gain a clear view. The ceremony takes place daily April to late July, every oth
day from August to March, provided the Queen is in residence, it's not raining too hard, and there a
no pressing state functions. After the Palace, take a stroll down the Mall, following the same rou
the Queen takes on her way to open Parliament. To your right, St. James's Park offers a pleasant si
for a snack. To your left is St. James's Palace. Approaching the end of the Mall, pass through Adm
ralty Arch and into Trafalgar Square. Time: 2-3hr. (if you include a leisurely stroll through the park)

3. TRAFALGAR SQUARE. Designed by John Nash, London's largest square serves as a forum f
public rallies and protest movements, not to mention controversial art. On December 31, the squa
hosts the City's largest New Year's Eve celebration (p. 173). All proceedings are soberly observed by sta
ues of Lord Nelson (perched on his column), George IV, Charles I, and George Washington. The easte
"Fourth Plinth" is reserved for rotating contemporary sculpture installations. It recently featured a Wor
Cup-inspired wax figure of David Beckham. Time: 30min. for people-watching.

4. NATIONAL GALLERY. Considering the thousands of works on display, it's hard to believe that th
gallery was founded with only 38 pictures. Depending on your interests, spend anywhere from 1hr. to th
remainder of the day savoring European masterpieces from the Middle Ages to the close of the 18th ce
tury. The Gallery, organized chronologically into four wings, contains gems from the Italian Renaissanc
the Dutch and Spanish Golden Ages, and the French Impressionist period, and finishes with a rotatir
exhibit on a single artist. To use your time most efficiently, design your own tour at the electronic statior
Hungry? The expensive restaurant atop the National Portrait Gallery provides spectacular views of th
city, while Cafe in the Crypt, across the street in St. Martin-in-the-Fields offers an affordable, slightly me
eval dining experience (p. 132 for Cafe; p. 177 for St. Martin). After lunch, walk south along Whiteha
where you will pass a long stretch of imposing Ministry building facades. Time: 3-5hr.

5. LIFE GUARDS. Stop by and wave hello to the two mounted soldiers guarding the shortcut
the Mall and St. James Park. Don't expect a response, though; it will take much more than a wav
We've saved you the trouble (and possible jail time) by interviewing one of the Queen's Life Guard
for you (p. 166). (Technically, the term "the Queen's Guard" only refers to those at Buckingham Pa
ace and St. James's Palace.) Time: 15min.

6. 10 DOWNING STREET. The former residence of Churchill, Thatcher, and all the other Britis
prime ministers, today 10 Downing Street is home to Prime Minister Gordon Brown. You'll have t

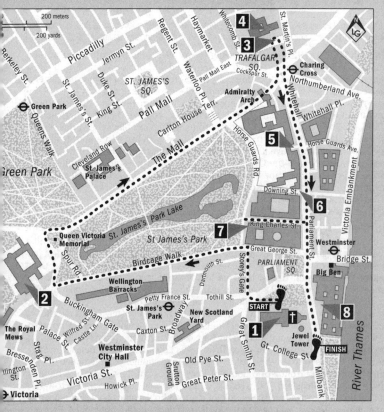

...eek at Downing Street from the gated entrance just off Whitehall; don't expect any up-close-...d-personal encounters. You might be able to see the Prime Minister going in or out for ...ork, though. Time: after 10min. of craning your neck trying to see Mr. Brown, you'll realize ...at he probably isn't going to show.

CABINET WAR ROOMS AND CHURCHILL MUSEUM. From 1938 to 1944, Winston ...hurchill ran the British war effort from these converted coal cellars. The new Churchill ...useum is the first major museum dedicated solely to Britain's beloved war hero, and the ...djoining Cabinet War Rooms have been perfectly restored to their wartime appearance, right ...wn to the paperclips. Highlights include "Churchill's personal loo," a small room containing ...e top-secret transatlantic hotline. Time: 2hr.

THE PALACE OF WESTMINSTER. The palace is also known as The Houses of Parlia-...ent. Containing both the House of Lords and the House of Commons, Westminster Palace has ...en at the heart of English governance since the 11th century. MPs in transit can be spotted ...m the New Palace Yard, while the Old Palace Yard was formerly a site for executions. Look ...ove to see the famous Clock Tower. Big Ben, the 14-ton bell inside the tower, still chimes ...the hour. Entering Parliament without a hefty wait is about as likely as private tea with ...e Prime Minister, but try if you must by heading to the St. Stephen's entrance. From ...gust to October, call in advance to arrange tours and to find out about debate ...es. Time: waiting to get inside could take all day; once inside, 1-2hr.

for the season. Last rental 2hr. before close. Summer walks in the park some M 1-2pm, including tour of Guard's Palace and Victoria Tower Gardens. Book in advance by calling ☎ 7930 1793.)

WESTMINSTER CATHEDRAL. Following Henry VIII's divorce from the Catholic Church, London's Catholic community remained without a cathedral until 1884 when the Church purchased a derelict prison on the site of a former monastery. The Neo-Byzantine church looks somewhat like a fortress and is now one of London's great religious landmarks. Construction began in 1895, but the architect's plan outran available funds. By 1903, when work stopped, the interior remained unfinished. The result, however, is extraordinary. The four blackened brick domes still await mosaic inlay. The front altar is covered with an ornate marble canopy called a *baldachino;* above it hangs an imposing 10m cross. The brightness of the mosaics contrasts with the Colosseum-style marble arches and balconies. A lift carries visitors up the striped 273 ft. bell tower for an all-encompassing view of Westminster, the river, and Kensington. *(Cathedral Piazza, off Victoria St. ⊖Victoria. ☎ 7798 9055; www.westminstercathedral.org.uk. Open daily 8am-7pm. Free; suggested donation £2. Bell tower open daily 9:30am-12:30pm and 1-5pm. Organ recitals Su 4:45pm.)*

WHITEHALL. Whitehall refers to the stretch of road connecting Trafalgar Sq. with Parliament Sq. and is synonymous with the British civil service. From 1532 until a devastating fire in 1698, it was the home of the monarchy and one of the grandest palaces in Europe, of which very little remains. Toward the north end of Whitehall, **Great Scotland Yard** marks the former headquarters of the Metropolitan Police. Nearer Parliament Sq., heavily guarded steel gates mark the entrance to **Downing Street.** In 1735, No. 10 was made the official residence of the First Lord of the Treasury, a position that soon became permanently identified with the Prime Minister. The Chancellor of the Exchequer traditionally resides at No. 11 and the Parliamentary Chief Whip at No. 12. When Tony Blair's family was too big for No. 10, he switched with Gordon Brown, a move that proved convenient when Brown was appointed Prime Minister in 2007. The street is closed to visitors, but if you wait long enough you might see the PM going to or coming from work. South of Downing St., in the middle of Whitehall, Edward Lutyen's **Cenotaph** (1919) stands, a tall and proud commemoration to WWI's dead. Many of the islands in the middle of the road hold statues honoring monarchs and military heroes, a testament to the avenue's identity as the center of civil service. *(Between Trafalgar Sq. and Parliament Sq. ⊖Westminster, Embankment, or Charing Cross.)*

LIFE GUARDS. The most photographed men in the area, the Queen's Life Guards, hold court in the center of Whitehall. Two mounted soldiers of the Household Cavalry, in shining breastplates and plumed helmets, guard a shortcut to The Mall and St. James's Park. While anyone can walk through, only those with a special ivory pass issued by the Queen may drive past the gates. The guards are posted from Monday to Saturday at 11am and Sunday at 10am, until a dismount for inspection daily at 4pm—a 200-year-old tradition broken only by WWII. Beyond the Neoclassical building is the pebbly expanse of **Horse Guards Parade,** where the Queen ceremonially sizes up her troops during the Trooping of the Colour ceremony on the second Saturday in June. *(Whitehall. ⊖Westminster, Embankment, or Charing Cross.)*

PARLIAMENT SQUARE. Conspiracy theorists will notice that this square, a center for anti-government protests over the last 250 years, is one of the few parks in the city without pedestrian access. Set in the middle of a busy traffic thoroughfare, would-be protesters must dodge traffic in all directions to reach this scruffy patch of grass. Until recently, anti-war activists displayed huge, eye-catching placards to passing motorists here, but a law instated in August 2005 has prohibited all "unauthorized" protests. The law was designed to remove a single anti-war protester, Brian Haw, who spent an impressive four years in the square despite several attempts to evict him. Despite the law, it's still not unusual to find protesters camped out in support of their cause. If you make it to the square, you will see statues of Parliamentary greats, as well as a huge cast of honest Abe Lincoln across the road behind the square. *(Across the street from Parliament and Westminster Abbey.* ⊖*Westminster.)*

VICTORIA TOWER GARDENS. South of the Palace of Westminster and overlooking the Thames, the open lawn and magnificent backdrop make the gardens a favorite spot for MPs, tourists, professionals, and TV crews running political features. For similar reasons, it's a first-rate picnic venue. Check out the superb cast of Rodin's *Burghers of Calais* and the memorial to suffragette Emmeline Pankhurst, which stands just inside the northwest gate. On the opposite side from the Palace, a tiny, slightly out-of-place Neo-Gothic gazebo commemorates the 1834 abolition of slavery on British territory. *(Millbank.* ⊖*Westminster. Open daily until dusk. Wheelchair-accessible.)*

THE WEST END

MAYFAIR AND ST. JAMES'S

SEE MAP, p. 356

The designer boutiques and prestigious gentlemen's clubs of Mayfair and St. James's are inaccessible to most budget-minded tourists, but the streets are perfect for afternoon strolls and window shopping. From the small alleys of Shepherd's Market to the stately vista of Waterloo Place, Mayfair and St. James's are home to some of London's most impressive views, as well as some of the best people watching.

■**TRAFALGAR SQUARE.** In 1820, John Nash laid out the first plans for Trafalgar, but it took almost 50 years for London's largest traffic roundabout to take on its current appearance. Nelson's Column arrived in 1843, and in 1867 the larger-than-life lions were enthroned at the base. The square is named in commemoration of the victory over Napoleon's navy at Trafalgar, considered England's greatest naval hour. From the Chartist rallies of 1848 to the anti-apartheid vigils held outside South Africa House to London's largest protest over the war in Iraq in 2003, Trafalgar has traditionally been a site for public rallies and protest movements. It is currently a favorite gathering place for Londoners. The masses congregate here on New Year's Eve to ring in midnight with the chimes of Big Ben, breaking the ice in the frozen fountains before the clock strikes midnight as an annual tradition. Every December since the end of WWII, the square has hosted a giant Christmas tree, provided by Norway as thanks for British assistance against the Nazis.

The 51m granite **Nelson's Column** towering over the square was, until recently, one of the world's tallest displays of decades-old pigeon droppings. Now, thanks to a cleanup sponsored by the Mayor, this monument to naval hero Lord Nelson sparkles once again. The four relief panels at the column's base were cast from captured French and Spanish cannons and commemorate Nelson's victories at Cape St. Vincent, Copenhagen, the Nile, and Trafalgar.

Nelson is not the only national hero to preside over the square. To prove that the English are not sore losers, **George Washington** keeps watch in the east corner. Upon leaving England, Washington vowed never to set foot on English soil again, so the small plot of soil underneath his statue was brought over from the US. The statue of **George IV** in the northeastern corner was originally intended to top the Marble Arch but never made it. A sculpture of William IV was supposed to reign over the eastern corner, but was never built due to funding problems. Since 1999, modern pieces have occupied the corner, such as a World-Cup inspired wax figure of David Beckham. It now features a modern sculpture by Marc Quinn, unveiled in 2005. South of the square, a rare equestrian monument to **Charles I** stands on the site of the original Charing Cross. The statue escaped Cromwell's wrath when John Rivett bought it

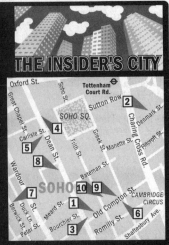

THE INSIDER'S CITY

PEOPLE-WATCHING IN SOHO

Soho is often hailed as the center of the West End experience—and for good reason. It's the beating heart of London nightlife, and the daylife isn't so bad either. No other neighborhood has quite the same level of excitement and acceptance of the devil-may-care attitude. Here is how we recommend you do it:

1 You've woken up mid-morning like a true Soho-er. Head to one of the many cafes on Old Compton Street for a latte and snack. Most have window-bar seating, so you can watch people scurrying to work as you lazily drink your tea.

2 Denmark Street has a huge concentration of guitar stores. Wander around checking out the great selection of sheet music, instruments, and the people who play them.

3 Soho has plenty of cutting edge shops and bookstores. For something to adorn your coffee table, start at Soho Books.

"for scrap" and did a roaring trade in souvenirs supposedly made from the figure. It was, in fact, hidden and later sold at a tidy profit to Charles II who re-erected it in 1633. (⊖ *Charing Cross or Leicester Sq.*)

CARLTON HOUSE TERRACE AND WATERLOO PLACE. Sweeping down from Piccadilly Circus, Regent St. comes to an abrupt halt at **Waterloo Place;** steps lead to the Mall. Regent St. was built to be a triumphal route leading to the Prince Regent's residence at Carlton House, but by the time it was finished, the prince had become King George IV, moved on to Buckingham Palace, and had his old house pulled down. The aging royal architect John Nash was recommissioned to build something quickly on the site; the result was **Carlton House Terrace,** a pair of imposing classical buildings that dominate the north side of the Mall and currently house the Institute of Contemporary Arts. Between the two Carlton House Terrace buildings, a statue of King Edward VII is dwarfed by a vast column topped with the "Grand Old" Duke of York, who docked his men's salaries in order to pay for the monument. The column's great height led many of the Duke's contemporaries to joke that he should climb it in order to flee his equally imposing debts. Despite the jokes, the sweep of Waterloo Place is stately and impressive. (⊖ *Piccadilly Circus.*)

ST. JAMES'S PALACE. Built in 1536 over the remains of a leper hospital, St. James's is London's only remaining purpose-built palace; even Buckingham Palace was a rough-and-ready conversion of a Duke's house. Ever since Henry VIII chose St. James's Palace to be the site of the royal court—foreign ambassadors to Britain are still officially called "Ambassadors to the Court of St. James"—this has been London's most aristocratic address. Current occupants include Prince Charles; the late Queen Mum lived in neighboring Clarence House. The massive gateway on St. James's St. is one of the few surviving remnants of the original edifice; outside, a pair of bearskin-hatted guards stomp and turn in perfect unison. As the official home of the Crown, royal proclamations are issued every Friday from the balcony in the interior Friary Court, which is also where the accession of a new monarch is first announced. However, the only part of the Palace usually accessible is the **Chapel Royal,** open for Sunday services from October to Easter at 8:30 and 11:15am. From Easter to July, services are held in **Queen's Chapel,** across Marlborough Rd. from the Palace, which was built in the 17th century for the marriage of then-prince Charles I. (⊖ *Green Park.*)

ST. JAMES'S CHURCH, PICCADILLY. Poet William Blake was baptized in this church, the exterior of which is now darkened from the soot of London's mills. The current structure is largely a post-WWII reconstruction of what Wren considered his greatest parish church; the original wooden flowers, garlands, and cherubs by master carver Grinling Gibbons escaped the Blitz. The churchyard is home to a tourist-oriented craft market which sells antiques on Tuesdays, as well as a cafe. *(Enter at 197 Piccadilly or on Jermyn St. ⊖Piccadilly Circus or Green Park. ☎7734 4511; www.st-james-piccadilly.org. Church open M-Sa 9am-6:30pm, Su 1-4:30pm. Market open Tu 8am-6pm, W-Sa 10am-6pm. Cafe open M-F 7am-7:30pm, Sa 9am-7:30pm, Su 9am-6:30pm. Church admission free.)*

SHEPHERD MARKET. This pedestrian area on the southern border of St. James's occupies the site of the original May Fair that gave the neighborhood its name. In 1706, the infamously raucous fair was closed until Edward Shepherd developed the area as a market later in the century. Today the 18th-century buildings house pubs, restaurants, shops, and art galleries. *(⊖Hyde Park Corner or Green Park.)*

GROSVENOR SQUARE. One of the largest squares in central London, Grosvenor has gradually evolved into a North American diplomatic enclave, alongside its more popular role as a warm-weather picnic spot. John Adams lived at No. 9 while serving as the first US ambassador to England in 1785. A century and a half later, Eisenhower established his wartime headquarters at No. 20. The eastern end of the square houses a memorial to the victims of September 11. *(⊖Bond St. or Marble Arch.)*

SPENCER HOUSE. At the end of a quiet, unassuming street near St. James's Palace lies the entrance to one of the finest 18th-century townhouses left in London. The home was built by the first Earl Spencer, ancestor of Princess Diana. The Spencer family kept the house as their London residence until 1926, after which it was used by the British intelligence service. Many of the finest rooms have been recently restored and opened to the public only on Sundays. Though the required tour is a bit long and overly detailed, the interiors are stunning and provide an excellent glimpse into 18th-century society as well as the early history of the Spencer family. *(Enter at 27 St. James Place. ⊖Green Park. ☎7514 1958; Open Su 10:30am-5:30pm. £9, students £7.)*

SOHO

Soho is a place to be experienced, not toured. A rainbow-hued extravaganza of trendy bars, cafes, and restaurants, Soho is many things to many people. A concentration of gay-owned restaurants and bars has

4 Head to Dean St.'s Tesco, (2-4 Dean Street) for picnic fixings. Then plant yourself in Soho Square. As the afternoon goes on, the lawn will fill with people, from street performers to corporate suits post-work.

5 A pint at Nellie Dean (89 Dean Street) will put you in the thick of things. Grab your pint and stand among everyone on the corner.

6 Cafe Boheme (15 Old Compton Street) or Boheme Kitchen and Bar (19 Old Compton Street) are the best places to park for people-watching with their cozy one-sided tables facing the street.

7 Bar hop like the locals and find one of the many hidden spots. Akbar (77 Dean St.) does it right.

8 To round out your experience, head to G-A-Y Bar (30 Old Compton Street). Despite the name (and obvious clientele emphasis), all orientations should feel comfortable rocking out to pop in this video-screen-plastered venue.

9 After you've drunk and danced your way to oblivion, finish off the night with a stop at Bar Italia (22 Firth St.), open well into the wee hours. You can watch the trickle (then flood) of midnight patrons while pat yourself on the back for a job well done.

turned **Old Compton Street** into the heart of GLBT London, and a seemingly endless assortment of theatres and clubs around **Theatreland** keeps night owls of any persuasion entertained. The south end of **Berwick Street**, a remnant of Soho's seedy past, is now the nexus of the area's sex trade, and the cafes around **Dean Street** are steeped in literary and musical history. Media types and celebrities regularly descend on the area, along with throngs of tourists looking for a wild night out.

CHINATOWN. It wasn't until the 1950s that immigrants from Hong Kong started moving en masse to these few blocks just north of Leicester Square. Pedestrian-heavy **Gerrard Street,** with scroll-worked dragon gates and pagoda-capped phone booths, is the self-proclaimed center of this tiny slice of Canton. Grittier **Lisle Street,** one block to the south, has more authenticity and induces less claustrophobia, with numerous specialty markets, bookshops, and craft stores to complement the food. Chinatown is most exciting during the **Mid-Autumn Festival** at the end of September and the raucous **Chinese New Year Festival** in February. *(Between Leicester Sq., Shaftesbury Ave., and Charing Cross Rd. ⊖Leicester Sq. or Piccadilly Circus.)*

SOHO SQUARE. First laid out in 1681, Soho Square is a rather scruffy patch of greenery popular with picnickers. Its removed location makes the square more hospitable and much less trafficked than its big brother, Leicester. If you're lucky, you might bump into Paul McCartney, whose business headquarters are at No. 1—crane your neck for a view of his first-floor office. Two monuments to Soho's cosmopolitan past border the square: London's only French **Protestant Church,** founded in 1550, and **St. Patrick's Catholic Church,** long the focal point of Soho's Irish and Italian communities. The petite, strange-looking mock-Tudor building at the center of the square is actually a Victorian garden shed that was never removed. *(⊖Tottenham Court Rd. Park open daily 10am-dusk.)*

PICCADILLY CIRCUS. Piccadilly Circus is made up of four of the West End's major arteries (Piccadilly, Regent St., Shaftesbury Ave., and the Haymarket). The square's atmosphere constantly fluctuates between excitement and chaos. In the middle of all the glitz and neon stands the famous **Statue of Eros.** Dedicated to the Victorian philanthropist Lord Shaftesbury, Eros was actually meant to be an "Angel of Christian Charity," but the aluminum figure has never been known as such. The archer originally pointed his bow and arrow down Shaftesbury Ave., but recent restoration work has put his aim significantly off. *(⊖Piccadilly Circus.)*

LEICESTER SQUARE. Lined with tour buses, clubs, and fast-food restaurants, Leicester Square is a place that probably is more frequented by tourists than by Londoners. Amusements in the entertainment hub range from London's largest cinemas to the **Swiss Centre** glockenspiel, whose renditions of anything from pop songs to Beethoven's *Moonlight Sonata* are amusing, even if not quite in-tune. Get a henna tattoo, sit for a caricature, or humor the rants of innumerable street preachers. *(Glockenspiel rings M-F at noon, 6, 7, 8pm; Sa-Su noon, 2, 4, 5, 6, 7, 8pm. ⊖Piccadilly Circus or Leicester Sq.)*

SWEPT OFF YOUR FEET. If you'd rather not explore Soho on foot, flag down a pedicab driver to cart you around. Rickshaws congregate at various points around the West End, but the most popular pickup spot is the corner of Firth St. and Old Compton St. Short spins around Soho £2.50-3 per person; longer trips £5 per person per mi. 2 full-sized people per rickshaw. Agree on a price before you go. M-Th and Su 6pm-1am, F-Sa 6pm-4am.

COVENT GARDEN AND THE STRAND

The name is misleading: come to shop or to stroll, but don't come looking for greenery—the main area is a cobblestoned **piazza**. An area popular with both tourists and locals, Covent Garden retains its charm even as its shops become more mainstream. On the very spot where Samuel Pepys saw the first "Punch and Judy" show in England 350 years ago, street performers entertain the hordes who flock here year-round, rain or shine. It's hard to imagine that for centuries this was London's main vegetable market (begun in medieval times, when it was just another "convent garden"). It was only in 1974 that the traders transferred to more spacious premises south of the river.

Simply known as the **Strand,** this busy road is perhaps the oldest in London, pre-dating the Romans. Originally a riverside track, shifting watercourses and Victorian engineering dried it out. Now, several narrow passageways lead down to the Thames. As the main thoroughfare between Westminster and the City, it remains as busy as ever. The only reminders of the many palaces that once made it London's top address are in nearby street names: **Villiers Street** recalls George Villiers, while **Essex Street** honors Elizabeth I's favorite, Robert Devereux, Earl of Essex.

 THIS WAY, PLEASE. Since Covent Garden is an extremely popular destination in the city, its Tube station can be overcrowded during peak hours. An alternate route goes through Holborn or Leicester Sq., with signs posted to direct diverted travelers.

ST. MARTIN-IN-THE-FIELDS. The fourth church to stand here, James Gibbs's 1726 creation is instantly recognizable: the rectangular portico building supporting a soaring steeple made it the model for countless Georgian churches in Ireland and America. The front of the church sports Corinthian columns and George I's coat of arms. He was the church's first warden, and it is still the Queen's parish church; look for the royal box above and to the left of the altar. Handel and Mozart both performed here, and the church hosts frequent concerts (p. 223). In order to support the cost of keeping the church open, there is a tourist-oriented **daily market** outside as well as a surprisingly extensive and delicious **cafe,** bookshop, and art gallery in the crypt. The popular **London Brass Rubbing Centre** also is housed in undercroft, where you can create charcoal and pastel impressions of medieval brass plates to take home. *(St. Martin's Ln., northeast corner of Trafalgar Sq.; crypt entrance on Duncannon St. ⊖ Leicester Sq. or Charing Cross. ☎ 7766 1100; www.smitf.org. Call or visit website for hours and further information.)*

ROYAL OPERA HOUSE. The physical house is home to the prestigious **Royal Opera, Royal Ballet,** and **ROH Orchestra.** The piazza's boutique-lined colonnade is now the rear of the ROH's rehearsal studios and workshops. The public can wander the ornate lobby of the original 1858 theatre and see previews of next season's performances on a screen near the box office. The enormous, glass-roofed **Hamlyn Hall** is also open to the public. From the Hamlyn Hall, take the escalator to reach the **terrace** overlooking the piazza, with a bird's-eye view of the streets below. With occasional cheap concession tickets and free lunchtime concerts on some Monday afternoons, ROH is better attended for a performance than for a tour. *(Enter on Bow St. or through the northeast corner of the piazza. ⊖ Covent Garden. ☎ 7304 4000; www.royaloperahouse.org. Opera house, cafe, and restaurant open M-Sa 10am-3:30pm. Box office open M-Sa 10am-8pm. 75-90min. backstage tours M-F 10:30am, 12:30, 2:30pm; Sa 10:30, 11:30am, 12:30, 1:30pm except during daytime performances; reservations recommended. Wheelchair-accessible. Tours £8, students £7. AmEx/MC/V.)*

ST. PAUL'S. Not to be confused with St. Paul's Cathedral, this 1633 Inigo Jones church is now the sole remnant of the original square. Shortage of funds begot its simplicity: the Earl of Bedford instructed the architect to make it "not much better than a barn." Known as "the actors' church" for its long association with nearby theatres, the interior is festooned with plaques commemorating the achievements of Boris Karloff, Vivien Leigh, and Charlie Chaplin. Musical lovers take note: W.S. Gilbert (of Gilbert and Sullivan) was baptized here, and George Bernard Shaw set the opening of *Pygmalion* (later known as *My Fair Lady*) under St. Paul's front portico. To enter the church, first pass through the peaceful churchyard, where award-winning gardens provide a welcome shelter from the bustle of the surrounding streets. *(On Covent Garden Piazza; enter via the Piazza, King St., Henrietta St., or Bedford St. ⊖Covent Garden. ☎ 7836 5221; www.actorschurch.org. Open M-F 8:30am-5:30pm. Morning services Su 11am. Evensong 2nd Su of month 4pm. Free.)*

THEATRE ROYAL, DRURY LANE. Cramped seating and nosebleed-inducing balcony views hint at the theatre's age—it was built in 1812. Today, it remains one of London's most popular theatres. Most recently, the Royal installed the stage adaptation of *Lord of the Rings* as its signature production. Join one of the actor-led backstage tours and you'll discover gems of Drury Lane lore, including the corpse and dagger found bricked up in the Royal's wall in the 19th century. *(Entrance on Catherine St. ⊖Covent Garden. ☎ 7850 8791, box office 08708 901 109, tours 7240 5357. Wheelchair-accessible. Tours M-W and F 2:15, 4:15pm, Th and Sa 10:15, 11:45am. £8.50, concessions £6.50. MC/V.)*

CHARING CROSS. The tiered Gothic monument standing outside Charing Cross was the last of the 12 crosses erected by Edward I in 1290 to mark the passage of his wife's funeral cortege (the cross itself is actually named "Eleanor's Cross"). The original was destroyed by Oliver Cromwell in 1647, and the current monument is a 19th-century replica. Deceptively, it's not in the correct place—the original stood on the spot now occupied by Charles I's statue in Trafalgar Square. The cross's odd placement in front of a major transportation hub is better explained when it is revealed as the point from which all road distances to and from the city are measured. *(⊖Charing Cross.)*

SAVOY. Considered the "fairest manor in all England," John of Gaunt's great Palace of Savoy was destroyed by rampaging peasants in 1381. Five hundred years later, the D'Oyly Carte Opera Company took its chances and moved into the new **Savoy Theatre,** the first in the world to be lit entirely by electricity. Managed by César Ritz, it was every bit as decadent as the Palace that once stood on the site. Don't be afraid to wander into the Savoy's grand foyer, second only to the Ritz in popularity for afternoon tea (although not as good a value). Be careful as you cross the Savoy driveway—this short, narrow road is the only street in the UK where people drive on the right, a historical relic meant to ensure that chauffeured women riding behind their drivers (on the right) could exit cars easily onto the sidewalk. *(⊖Charing Cross, then walk 5min. east on south side of the Strand.)*

SEVEN DIALS. The radial configuration of six streets is a rare surviving example of 16th-century town planning. Thomas Neale commissioned the central pillar in 1694, with one sundial facing each street; the seventh dial is the column itself. The original column was pulled down in 1773 to rid the area of the "undesirables" who congregated around it. A replica, erected in 1989, attracts all types, including those just trying to avoid the oncoming traffic. It tells the correct time to within 10 seconds—if you can figure out how to read it. *(Intersection of Monmouth, Earlham, and Mercer St. ⊖Covent Garden or Leicester Sq.)*

CLEOPATRA'S NEEDLE. The oldest monument in London, this Egyptian obelisk was first erected at Heliopolis in 1475 BC, making it some 1400 years older than

Cleo herself. The Turkish Viceroy of Egypt presented it to Britain in 1819 in recognition of their help in booting Napoleon out of Africa, but it wasn't shipped until 1877. The ship sank en route, but a salvage operation recovered the obelisk. It was finally re-erected in 1879. Underneath the foundation is a Victorian time capsule containing a railway guide, numerous Bibles, and pictures of the 12 prettiest British women of the day. The scars at the needle's base and on the sphinx were left by the first-ever bomb raid on London, by German Zeppelins in 1917. *(North bank of the Thames between Hungerford and Waterloo Bridges. ⊖Charing Cross or Temple.)*

BLOOMSBURY

Home to both University College—London's first university—and the British Museum, Bloomsbury has long been the stomping ground of eggheads and aspiring intellectuals. Farther down, **Bedford Square** is the only London square to retain all of its original Georgian buildings. Nowadays, the student landscape around **Gower Street** is liberally dotted with tourists, though the area's high concentration of academic and artistic institutions maintains its cerebral air. The

SEE MAP, p. 362

scads of leafy green squares and gardens are perfect for contemplation (or dozing). The area around **King's Cross** and **St. Pancras** is barely considered part of Bloomsbury (acting as the borderline to North London), but it is home to the British Library.

BRITISH LIBRARY. Castigated during its long construction by traditionalists for being too modern and by modernists for being too traditional, the new British Library building (opened in 1998) now impresses all doubters with its stunning interior. The heart of the library is underground, with 12 million books on 200 mi. of shelving; the above-ground brick building is home to cavernous reading rooms and an engrossing 🗹**Museum** (p. 209). Displayed in a glass cube toward the rear of the building, the 65,000 volumes of the King's Library were collected by George III and bequeathed to the nation in 1823 by his less bookish son, George IV. The sunken plaza out front offers a series of free concerts and events, although the integrated restaurant, cafes, and coffee bars are overpriced. *(96 Euston Rd. ⊖Euston Sq. or King's Cross St. Pancras. ☎7412 7332; www.bl.uk. Open M 9:30am-6pm, Tu 9:30am-8pm, W-F 9:30am-6pm, Sa 9:30am-5pm, Su 11am-5pm. Tours of public areas M, W, F 3pm; Sa 10:30am and 3pm. Tours including one of the reading rooms Su and bank holidays 11:30am and 3pm. Reservations recommended. Wheelchair-accessible. To use reading rooms, bring 2 forms of ID—1 with a signature and 1 with a home address. Free. Tours £8, concessions £6.50. Audio tours £3.50, concessions £2.50.)*

UNIVERSITY COLLEGE LONDON. Established in 1828 to provide an education to those rejected from Oxford and Cambridge, UCL was the first in Britain to ignore gender, race, creed, and politics in admissions. A co-founder and key advisor of the college, social philosopher Jeremy Bentham, still watches over his old haunts—his body has sat on display in the South Cloister since 1850 (wax head and all). Less dramatic, but certainly livelier, the squares and greens of the grounds make for good people-watching. At the southern end of Malet Street, the sight of UCL's massive central administrative building, **Senate House,** would quash the spirits of any student radical; during WWII it housed the BBC propaganda unit. George Orwell, who was employed by this so-called "Ministry of Information," used his experience there as the model for the Ministry of Truth in *1984*. *(Main entrance on Gower St. South Cloister entrance through the courtyard. ⊖Euston. ☎7679 2000; www.ucl.ac.uk. Quadrangle gates close at midnight; access to Jeremy Bentham ends at 6pm. Wheelchair-accessible. Free.)*

ST. PANCRAS STATION. Most visitors assume that the low concourse west of Midland Rd. is a railway station, and the soaring Gothic spires to the east are the

British Library. In fact, the opposite is true: this Victorian extravaganza is the facade of St. Pancras Station, whose massive 1868 train shed was once the largest undivided indoor area in the world. *(Euston Rd. just west of the King's Cross St. Pancras Tube station. ⊖King's Cross St. Pancras.)*

CORAM'S FIELDS. Seven acres of old Foundling Hospital's grounds live on as a spectacular (and free) children's park. Kids of all ages will love the petting zoo and paddling pond, not to mention the special under-5 toilets; older kids will relish the high-tech playgrounds. *(93 Guilford St. ⊖Russell Sq. ☎7837 6138; www.coramsfields.org. Open summer 9am-7pm, winter 9am-dusk. No adults admitted without children. Free.)*

ST. GEORGE'S BLOOMSBURY. Time, the Blitz, and general disrepair have taken their toll on the facade of this 1730 Hawksmoor church, but a £1 million restoration project in 2007 brought it back to its former glory. The interior—the setting of Dickens's *Bloomsbury Christening*—offers an unusual flat ceiling undecorated except for a central plaster rose. The church's most unusual feature is its stepped spire, based on the ancient Mausoleum of Halikarnassos (one of the seven Wonders of the Ancient World—partly on display at the British Museum) and topped by a statue of George I. The restoration will also reintroduce the magnificent 10 ft. lions and unicorns that originally stood at George's feet. *(Bloomsbury Way. ⊖Russell Sq. ☎7405 3044; www.stgeorgesbloomsbury.org.uk. Open for worship only; call for details.)*

NORTH LONDON

CAMDEN TOWN, KING'S CROSS, AND ISLINGTON

As North London becomes increasingly affluent, those in search of a slice of tawdriness come to Camden Town. The central Camden area, between Camden Town and Chalk Farm, has thrown off attempts at gentrification thanks to the numerous **street markets**, now among London's most popular attractions.

ST. PANCRAS OLD CHURCH. The first church on this site was reputedly founded by Roman legionaries in AD 314 for early Christian worship and became the first parish in London. The present building, though, dates from the 13th century—some of the Norman masonry is visible on the north wall of the nave. The church is not tremendously available to tourists, but if you do get a peek, don't miss the 6th-century altar stone, rumored to have belonged to St. Augustine of Canterbury, and the unique and lofty pulpit. In the large and lovely churchyard is Sir John Soanes's mausoleum and the **Hardy Tree,** designed by a young Thomas Hardy long before he became a writer. It features hundreds of tightly clustered headstones that seem to spring from the roots of a weeping ash. *(St. Pancras Rd. ⊖Mornington Crescent. ☎7424 0724. Wheelchair-accessible. Prayer services M-F 9am. Mass M 9:30am, Tu 7pm, Su 9:30am. Free.)*

ST. JOHN'S WOOD AND MAIDA VALE

In Maida Vale, the cross section of three canals is known as **Little Venice**—although there is nothing too Italian about it. While not filled with an abundance of interesting sights, St. John's Wood and Maida Vale do pay homage to two uniquely British institutions: cricket and the Beatles.

LORD'S CRICKET GROUND. The most famous cricket ground in England, Lord's is home to the local Marylebone Cricket Club (MCC) and hosts most of London's international matches. To see the **Lord's Museum,** home to the **Ashes Urn** as well as to all the cricket-related memorabilia you could ever dream of, attend a match or

Otel.com

take a 1¾-hr. tour led by a senior club member. Included in the tours are the MCC members' Long Room, the ground, stands, and the striking space-age NatWest Media Centre. On game days, tours after 10am skip the Long Room and media center, though visitors get a discount on game tickets as compensation (no tours during international test matches). Games take place on most summer days. *(10min. walk from ⊖St. John's Wood. Enter at Grace Gate, on St. John's Wood Rd. ☎ 7432 1000; www.lords.org.uk. Tours daily Oct.-Mar. noon and 2pm; Apr.-Sept. 10am, noon, 2pm. Wheelchair-accessible. Tours £10, concessions £7, children under 16 £6, families £27.)*

ABBEY ROAD. There's something in the way Abbey Rd. moves; it's most famous for the zebra crossing at its start, where it comes together with Grove End Rd. The best way to stop traffic: a photo op crossing the street in Beatles stride. Stop to read the adulatory graffiti on the nearby street signs and walls—fans from all over the world have left marks here. Next to the crossing, the Abbey Road Studios (3 Abbey Rd.), where the Beatles made most of their recordings, are closed to the public but still in business. *(⊖St. John's Wood.)*

HAMPSTEAD, HIGHGATE, AND GOLDERS GREEN

Home to the sprawling Hampstead Heath, Hampstead and Highgate is a great destination for a green getaway from central London. Above Hampstead and Highgate in a little corner of North London, **Golders Green** is the center of the city's Jewish community, with many storefronts lettered in both English and Hebrew. **Golders Green Road** is the axis around which life here revolves; turn right from the station, and a few blocks down you'll start to see specialized shops, excellent kosher restaurants, and Hebrew bookstores. **Golders Hill Park**—a western extension of Hampstead Heath—is at the heart of the area.

■ **HAMPSTEAD HEATH.** Hampstead Heath is one of the last remaining traditional commons in England, open to all since at least 1312—thanks to the pluck of local residents, who, in the 19th century, successfully fought off attempts to develop it. Since Parliament declared in 1871 that the Heath should remain "forever open, unenclosed, and un-built-upon," it has grown from 336 to 804 acres. Its imposing size can be daunting, but just spending a few hours enjoying the expansive, meadow-like green can be a lovely break from the city. Unlike so many other London parks, the Heath is not comprised of manicured gardens and paths but rather wild, spontaneous growth tumbling over rolling pastures and forested groves—perfect for picnicking. Dirt paths through the Heath are not well marked; travel in groups to avoid getting lost. On public holidays in spring and summer, **funfairs** are held at South End Green and on the south side of Spaniards Rd. *(⊖Hampstead. Train: Hampstead Heath. Bus #210. Wheelchair-accessible. Open 24hr.)*

■ **HILL GARDEN.** Unless you're specifically on the lookout for this lovely secret garden, you're unlikely to find it. There are a few paths down from North End Way, between Golders Green and North Hampstead, but you may have to poke through the forest a bit if you miss the marked path. You'll know you're there when you see the exquisite, raised pergola (Italian arched walkway) guarding the gardens. The flowery walkway passes over the former kitchen gardens of Lord Leverhulme's (founder of Lever Soap) mansion. The walkway was built to connect the mansion to his pleasure gardens. The summer sunsets here are particularly magnificent. *(In Hampstead Heath; take North End Way to Inverforth Close. Open daily 8:30am-1hr. before sunset.)*

GOLDERS GREEN CREMATORIUM. Though visiting a crematorium may seem grim, don't let the Neo-Romanesque chapel buildings scare you. Behind them lie several acres of picturesque, beautifully maintained gardens. Expansive rosebush groves fill the northern side, where temporary floral arrangements pay tribute to loved ones recently lost. Paths wander through leafy groves, water gardens, and open lawns, providing a fitting and peaceful sanctuary. Each flower serves as a living grave for an individual and bears the names of the departed who were sprinkled there. Luminaries who came to rest here include T. S. Eliot, H. G. Wells, Peter Sellers, Bram Stoker, Anna Pavlova, and five prime ministers. Sigmund Freud's ashes, in his favorite Greek vase, are locked in the Ernest George Columbarium; ask an attendant to let you in on weekdays. *(From ⊖Golders Green, turn right out of the exit, follow Finchley Rd. under the bridge, and continue for 5min. before turning right on Hoope Ln. Entrance is on the right. ☎8455 2374. Wheelchair-accessible. Grounds open daily in summer 9am-6pm; in winter 9am-4pm. Chapel and Hall of Memory open daily 9am-4pm. Free.)*

PARLIAMENT HILL. Legend claims that Guy Fawkes and his accomplices planned to watch their destruction of Parliament from atop Parliament Hill in 1605, but things didn't work out that way. The hike to the top yields a panorama stretching to Westminster and beyond. At the foot of the hill, a series of ponds marks the final gasp of the River Westbourne before it vanishes under concrete on its way to the Thames. The brave can swim for free in the waters of the sex-segregated **bathing ponds,** where some bathers choose to go nude. *(The southeastern part of the Heath. Rail: Gospel Oak or Hampstead Heath.)*

FENTON HOUSE. Dating from 1686, this was one of the first houses built in Hampstead. Built by a master bricklayer, the house was owned by the Fenton family and other aristocrats until 1952 and is now a National Trust historical sight. The first two floors of the house are home to a delicate collection of china, porcelain, and needlework as well as a remarkable collection of early keyboard and stringed instruments that continues on the upper floors. These 17th- and 18th-century instruments are still played in the parlor during summertime concerts. The sprawling French garden provides a picturesque stroll and a prime relaxation spot; it also includes an intricate flower garden, orchard, greenhouse, and beehive with fresh honey occasionally for sale. On the last Sunday in September, the house hosts Apple Day, with tastings, products, and pies from the orchard (adults £2). Call ahead to schedule a time to try out the keyboard collection. *(Hampstead Grove. ⊖Hampstead. ☎ 7435 3471. Partially wheelchair-accessible. Open Mar. Sa-Su 2-5pm; Apr.-Oct. W-F 2-5pm, Sa-Su 11am-5pm. £5.20, children £2.60, families £12.50. Joint ticket with Two Willow Rd. (p. 182) £7. Garden only £2.)*

TWO WILLOW ROAD. Resembling an unimposing 1950s-style mini-block, Two Willow Road was actually built in 1939 as the avant-garde home of architect Ernö Goldfinger (Ian Fleming hated the design so much he named a James Bond villain after him). It stands apart quite visibly from the quaint Victorian facades that line the rest of the street. The inventive use of space means that secret cabinets and doors pop up everywhere. With clothes still in their dry-cleaning plastic sheaves, everything looks as if the family had just left. Family photos on the mantelpiece sit next to works of art by Max Ernst, Marchel Duchamp, and Goldfinger's wife, Ursula Blackwell. *(15min. walk from ⊖Hampstead. ☎7435 6166. Open Apr.-Oct. Th-F noon-5pm, Sa 11am-5pm. Timed ticket and 1hr. guided tours available Th-F at noon, 1, 2pm; Sa 11am, noon, 1, 2pm. £5, children £2.50, families £12.30; joint ticket with Fenton House £7.)*

KEATS HOUSE. In this house, the great Romantic poet John Keats produced some of his last and finest work, including "Ode to a Nightingale." The gardens are small but lovely, as is the house itself, though, unfortunately, little of the original furnishings remain. The current space is a sparse recreation of its 1820 appearance, distinguished only because of its literary inhabitant. Inside, copies of Keats's poems lie scattered about the well-kept rooms, together with Keats memorabilia and informative biographical displays. *(Keats Grove. ⊖Hampstead. ☎7435 2062; www.keat-*

shouse.org.uk. Partially wheelchair-accessible. Open Tu-Su Apr.-Nov. 1-5pm; Dec.-Mar. noon-4pm.
£3.50, under 16 free, concessions £1.75. Ticket valid for 1 year of unlimited visits.)

MARYLEBONE AND REGENT'S PARK

SEE MAP, p. 369

Containing London's most beautiful park right next to creepy wax idols and the home of a fictional sleuth, Marylebone and its sights may best be considered scattered. Regent's Park is the area's main attraction, offering both manicured flower gardens and open fields suitable for a quiet stroll and picnic, a game of football, or simply a diversion from the hyped attractions on the other side of the park's gate. Along the southern edge of the park lie the avoidable tourist bits: Madame Tussaud's and 221b Baker St. (the storied home of Marylebone's most famous fictional resident, Sherlock Holmes). The 18th-century architecture of Portland Place offers a more substantial and accurate piece of Marylebone history, and was once home to Elizabeth Barrett Browning, John Milton, and John Stuart Mill.

Once part of a major Roman route out of London, **Edgware Road** to the west is the contemporary center of London's largest Lebanese community. Although Edgware extends into North London, the most concentrated area of the road lies between Marble Arch and Marylebone Rd., marking Marylebone's eastern border. Lined with countless restaurants, shops, and grocery markets, the noisy thoroughfare is full of fantastic food and affordable hidden shops selling fake pashminas, clothing, and other trinkets. The number of hookah cafes rivals the number of Maroush restaurants, creating an interesting combined smell of smoke and kebab.

■ REGENT'S PARK. When Crown Architect John Nash designed Regent's Park, he envisioned a private residential development for the "wealthy and good." Fortunately for us commonfolk, Parliament opened the space to all in 1811, creating London's most popular and attractive recreational area. With 500 acres of jogging trails, football-scarred fields, and lush gardens, Regent's Park offers a range of not-to-be-missed sunny-day diversions.

Most of the park's top attractions and activities lie near the **Inner Circle,** a road that separates the regal, meticulously maintained ■**Queen Mary's Gardens** from the rest of the grounds. Within the Circle, the **Rose Garden** and the well-muscled **Triton Fountain** are worth a visit, and the well-received **Open-Air Theatre** (p. 232) in the northwest quadrant provides fabulous summer entertainment. The **Boating Lake** and the **Children's Boating Lake** lie around the Inner Circle, where rowboats and children's pedaloos share the water with frisky ducks that flock to the city's primary waterfowl breeding center. *(Open daily Apr.-Sept. 10:30am-5pm, July-Aug. closes later. Rowboats £4.50 for 30min., £6 for 1hr.; under 14 £3/4; £5 deposit. Discounts before 1pm. Under 16 with adult only. Pedaloos £3 for 20min. MC/V.)* The Regent's Park **Tennis Centre** on the southeast side of the park offers non-aquatic recreation activities. *(☎ 7486 4216. Open year-round. 1hr. non-member court use £7-9. 24hr. advance reservations.)* While the few villas in the park—**The Holme** and **St. John's Lodge**—are private residences for the unimaginably rich and are not available for public viewing, the formal ■**Gardens of St. John's Lodge,** on the northern edge of the Inner Circle, provide a peek into the backyard of one such mansion. A blaze of lavender accessible through an easy-to-miss gate near the Royal Parks office, the grounds are open to the public and look like something straight out of *The Secret Garden*—a well-known fact among wedding photographers. The **London Central Mosque** is also open to the public. If you're looking for a rewarding climb, head up **Primrose Hill,** just north of Regent's Park proper, for an impressive panoramic view of central London. Other landmarks in the park include the large red-brick complex of **Regent's College,** to the south of

Inner Circle, and neo-Georgian **Winfield House,** the private residence of the US ambassador. (⊖*Baker St., Regent's Park, Great Portland St., or Camden Town.* ☎*7486 7905, police 7706 7272; www.royalparks.org. Open daily 5am-dusk. Free.*)

 TO SIT OR NOT TO SIT. The oh-so-tempting desk chairs scattered through Regent's Park come with a price: £2 per 4hr. For a picturesque perch without a fee, head to the benches in the circular garden near the Inner Circle's eastern entrance.

LONDON ZOO. First opened in 1826, the London Zoo has a range of expansive and completely modern exhibits along with a few less current bars-and-cement enclosures. The very oldest buildings are now considered too small to house animals and instead test parents with an array of stuffed toys at exorbitant prices. Perennial zoo favorites include the itch-inducing corridors of **BUGS!** (complete with American cockroaches devouring a messy kitchen), the jungle-like **primate** house, and the **komodo dragon** exhibit. For up-close-and-personal interaction, head to the **Meet the Monkeys** exhibit, an enclosed area where guests and playful squirrel monkeys can mingle. Pick up a Daily Event Planner leaflet to catch all the free special displays and keeper talks. (*Main gate on Outer Circle, Regent's Park.* ⊖*Camden Town plus a 10-15min. walk guided by signs or a short ride on Bus #274.* ☎*7722 3333; www.zsl.org. Open daily Apr.-Oct. 10am-5:30pm; Nov.-Mar. 10am-4pm. Last admission 1hr. before closing. Wheelchair-accessible. Admission £14.50, children 3-15 £11, family of 4 £48.50, concessions £13. AmEx/MC/V.*)

MADAME TUSSAUD'S. It may be one of London's top tourist attractions, but Madame Tussaud's is by far the most undeserving round-the-block queue. For those unwilling to pass up a photo op with wax models of George Clooney and Tom Cruise, it is at least an indisputably unique 90min. experience. Dodging the flash trajectories of the other camera-happy visitors, you'll wonder how Michael Jackson can look so real, while poor Claudia Schiffer is straight out of *The Rocky Horror Picture Show.* No question, there's something innately fascinating about the eerie wax look-alikes on display, but you'll spend more time being jostled around the crowded space than enjoying the effigies. The basement **Chamber of Horrors** exhibit is a particularly gory detour, complete with the bloodied, guillotined wax heads of Marie Antionette and Louis XVI, along with plenty of violent torture scenes that are any school-trip leader's worst nightmare. The fun continues with **The Spirit of London,** an odd taxi-coaster ride through the city's history. Cap off your waxy adventure with a relaxing short film at the **Auditorium** (which was once the London Planetarium)—at the very least a break from the sensory overload that precedes it. Unless you enjoy spending hours waiting outside and paying exorbitant prices, make sure to book in advance, get together with at least nine others to use the group entrance, or come during off-peak hours (late afternoon). (*Marylebone Rd.* ⊖*Baker St.* ☎*0870 999 0293; www.madame-tussauds.com. Open Jan.-June and Sept.-Dec. M-F 9:30am-5:30pm, Sa-Su 9am-6pm; Jul.-Aug. daily 9am-6pm. Wheelchair-accessible. Prices depend on day of the week, entrance time, and season. Admission £14-23, under 16 £7-17. "Chamber Live" exhibit adds £2. Advance booking by phone or online £2 extra; groups of 10+ approx. £1.50 less per person. Call in advance to ensure. AmEx/MC/V.*)

PORTLAND PLACE. One of the most architecturally well-endowed streets in London, Portland Pl. was first laid out by Robert and James Adam in the 18th century. Today its attraction lies in the great variety of building styles on display. Design buffs will enjoy it, although others might not be overly dazzled. The street is the natural home for the Royal Institute of British Architects (RIBA), whose 1932 headquarters is the most imposing building on Portland Pl.—particularly at night, when the facade is lit an eye-catching pink. Parts of the building are open to the public, including three exhibition galleries, an impressive architecture bookshop, and a cafe/restaurant. *(66 Portland Pl. ⊖Oxford Circus or Regent's Park. ☎7580 5533; www.architecture.com. Exhibits open M and W-F 9:30am-5pm, Tu 9:30am-6:30pm. Wheelchair-accessible. Free.)* Guarding the entrance to Portland Pl. from Regent St., the curved facade of the Broadcasting Center is instantly recognizable to all Britons as the symbol of the BBC (and still the company's main center for radio production). On the facade is Eric Gill's sculpture of Shakespeare's *Prospero and Ariel*, together with the BBC motto, "Nation Shall Speak Peace Unto Nation." There is not much to see in All Souls Langham Place, originally designed by John Nash and heavily damaged by WWII bombing. *(☎7580 3522; www.allsouls.org. Open M-F 9:30am-6pm, Su 9am-6:30pm.)*

KENSINGTON AND EARL'S COURT

Nobody took much notice of Kensington before 1689. When newly crowned William III and Mary II decided to move into Kensington Palace following the Glorious Revolution of 1688, high society soon followed. Although today the area continues to be associated with the elite—from Queen Victoria's husband Albert (of **"Albertopolis"**) to Princess Di—Kensington is also a locale for the masses. Not to be outdone by self-congratulatory exhibitions of French arts and industry in Paris in 1849, Prince Albert proposed to hold

SEE MAP, pp. 366-367

a bigger and better "Exhibition of All Nations" in London. The Great Exhibition opened on May 1, 1851, in Hyde Park, housed in the Crystal Palace—a gigantic iron-and-glass structure 1848 ft. long, 408 ft. wide, and tall enough to enclose mature trees. By the time the exhibition was dismantled a year later, six million people had passed through it—as many as saw the Millennium Dome in 2000—and the organizers were left with a £200,000 profit. At Albert's suggestion, the money was used to buy 86 acres of land in South Kensington and to found institutions promoting British arts and sciences. Even he would be surprised at how his dream has blossomed; today, on this land stands not only the quartet of the Royal Albert Hall (p. 187), Victoria and Albert Museum (p. 213), Science Museum (p. 214), and Natural History Museum (p. 214) but also the Royal College of Music, the Royal College of Art, and the Imperial College of Science and Technology, all world-renowned institutions in their respective fields. He might also be surprised to learn that "Albertopolis" is also known as "Coleville" after Sir Henry Cole, the man who actually implemented all of Albert's ideas after the Prince's untimely death in 1861. Kensington is roughly bound by Hyde Park to the north, Exhibition Rd. to the east, Cromwell Rd. to the south, and Queen's Gate to the west. Use the South Kensington or High St. Kensington Tube stations.

Blending into the neighborhood's southwestern corner, Earl's Court is a grimier, character-rich district still known by its nickname—"Kangaroo Valley"—an 80s- era testament to its popularity with Australian expats. The site of London's original gay village, the area also boasts a decent gay nightlife scene, although Soho is the clear favorite.

HYDE PARK AND KENSINGTON GARDENS

Framed by Kensington Rd., Knightsbridge, Park Ln., and Bayswater Rd. ⊖Queensway, Lancaster Gate, Marble Arch, Hyde Park Corner, or High St. Kensington. ☎7298 2100; www.royalparks.org.uk. Park open daily 6am-dusk. Admission free. "Liberty Drive" rides available Tu-F 10am-5pm for seniors and the disabled; ☎077 6749 8096. A full program of music, performance, and children's activities takes place during the summer; see park notice boards for details.)

Surrounded by London's wealthiest neighborhoods, Hyde Park has served as the model for city parks around the world, including Central Park in New York and Paris's Bois de Boulogne. Henry VIII stole the land from Westminster Abbey in 1536, and James I opened it to the public in 1637—the first royal park to be the product of theft. During an outbreak of the plague in 1665, terrified inhabitants of the city once set up camp here for a year in an attempt at quarantine. It's still the largest public space in central London, and the expansive grounds are popular with tourists and locals (but no longer with plague-fearing campers). Warm days attract swarms of sunbathers, along with people tossing frisbees, cycling, in-line skating, playing football, and horseback riding. A number of cafes and restaurants make a full day in the park easy—try **The Dell**. (On the eastern side of the Serpentine; ⊖Hyde Park Corner. ☎7706 0464. Open daily in summer 9am-8pm; in winter 9am-4pm.) **The Lido Cafe** is another option. (On the southern side of the Serpentine. ⊖Hyde Park Corner. ☎7706 7098. Open daily in summer 9am-8pm; in winter 9am-4pm.) **Kensington Gardens**, contiguous with Hyde Park and originally part of it, was created in the late 17th century when William and Mary set up house in Kensington Palace.

THE SERPENTINE. It is officially known as the "Long Water West of the Serpentine Bridge," and that's just what it is. The long, snaking, 41-acre Serpentine was created in 1730 as decoration, but today it's actually used quite a bit: dog-paddling tourists, rowers, and pedal boaters make it London's busiest swimming hole. Nowhere near the water, its namesake **Serpentine Gallery** (p. 215) holds contemporary art. (⊖Hyde Park Corner. Boating: ☎7262 1330. Open Apr.-Sept. daily 10am-5pm or later in fine weather. £4 per person for 30min., £6 per hr.; children £1.50/2.50. Deposit may be required for large groups. Swimming at the Lido, south shore: ☎7706 3422. Open June to early Sept. daily 10am-5:30pm. Lockers and sun lounges available. £3.50, after 4pm £2.80; students £2.50/1.60; children 80p/60p; families £8. Gallery open daily 10am-5pm. Free.)

OTHER PARK SIGHTS. Running south of the Serpentine, the dirt horse track **Rotten Row** stretches west from Hyde Park Corner. The name is a corruption of Route du Roi, or King's Road, so named because this was the royal route from Kensington Palace to Whitehall. At the southern end of Hyde Park and into Kensington Gardens clusters a group of statues: the goddess **Diana fountain;** the "family of man"; a likeness of **Lord Byron;** tiny **Peter Pan;** and a fig-leafed **Achilles** dedicated to the Duke of Wellington. Dip your feet into the **Princess Diana Memorial Fountain** just south of the Serpentine or take the kids to the **Diana, Princess of Wales Memorial Playground,** in the northwest corner of Kensington Gardens. At the northeast corner of the park, near Marble Arch, you can see free speech in action as proselytizers, politicos, and various crazies dispense the fruits of their knowledge to bemused tourists at **Speaker's Corner** on Sundays, the only place in London where demonstrators can assemble without a permit.

Looking rather displaced by itself, **Marble Arch** was originally intended to be the front entrance to Buckingham Palace, but palace extensions and new roadways cut off Nash's 1828 monument, leaving it stranded forlornly on a traffic roundabout. The arch now stands close to the former site of the Tyburn gallows, London's main execution site until 1783. (Near the intersection of Park Ln., Oxford St., Edgware Rd., and Bayswater Rd. ⊖Marble Arch.)

OTHER KENSINGTON AND EARL'S COURT SIGHTS

KENSINGTON PALACE. In 1689, William and Mary commissioned Christopher Wren to remodel Nottingham House into a palace. Kensington remained the principal royal residence until George III decamped to Kew in 1760, but it is still in use—Princess Diana was the most famous recent inhabitant. Although the heart of the palace is closed to visitors, royalty fanatics can tour the Hanoverian **State**

Apartments, with *trompe l'oeil* paintings by William Kent. More impressive is the **Royal Ceremonial Dress Collection,** a magnificent spread of beautifully tailored and embroidered garments. For flashy decadence, look no further than the permanent display of Diana's evening gowns (why yes, that is the 1985 blue silk number in which she famously shimmied alongside John Travolta). Nothing is labeled, so you must submit to the audio tour. Those who love gowns, royalty, or both will be in heaven; others should skip it and instead wander through the palace grounds, set apart from the rest of Kensington Gardens. The gardens encompass Sir John Vanbrugh's grand 1704 **Orangery,** built for Queen Anne's dinner parties and now a popular setting for afternoon tea. *(On the western edge of Kensington Gardens; enter through the park. ⊖ High St. Kensington, Notting Hill Gate, or Queensway. ☎ 7937 9561; www.royalresidences.com. Open daily 10am-6pm, last admission 1hr. before closing. Wheelchair-accessible. £12, students £10, children 5-15 £6, families of 5 (no more than 2 people over 15) £33. Combo passes with Tower of London or Hampton Court available. MC/V.)*

HOLLAND PARK. Smaller and less frequented than Kensington Gardens, Holland Park probably makes for a better picnic spot or quiet stroll than its famous cousin. Set off from Kensington High St. and full of shady paths, the grounds also offer open fields, football pitches, a golf bunker, cricket nets, tennis courts, Japanese gardens, cafes, an open-air opera venue (Holland Park Theatre, p. 222), and an adventure playground for the young or young at heart. A number of organized sport leagues and yoga and pilates classes take place here as well. Just up the road at 99 Kensington High St., take an elevator to some more greenery at the famous Rooftop Gardens, a bizarre and dazzling few acres that offer great views of the whole neighborhood. *(Bordered by Kensington High St., Holland Walk, and Abbotsbury Rd. Enter at Commonwealth Institute. ⊖ High St. Kensington. ☎ 7471 9813, police 7441 9811, sport league and recreation info 7602 2226; Open daily 7:30am-dusk. Free.)*

LEIGHTON HOUSE. The home of painter Lord Fredric Leighton (1830-1896) is a perfect example of all that is endearing (and somewhat ridiculous) in Victorian tastes. Inspired by his trips to the Middle East, Leighton's home combines oriental pastiche, Neoclassicism, and English decor. The centerpiece is the Arab Hall, a Moorish extravaganza of tilework and mosaic complete with fountain and carpets— the walls bear one of Europe's best collections of medieval Arabian tile. The other rooms contain works by Leighton as well as other artists, including Millais, Tintoretto, and Edward Burne-Jones. *(12 Holland Park Rd. ⊖ High St. Kensington. ☎ 7602 3316; www.rbkc.gov.uk/leightonhousemuseum/general. Open M and W-Su 11am-5:30pm. £3, students £1, families £6.50. Free guided tours W-Th at 2:30pm. Audio tours £3. MC/V.)*

ROYAL ALBERT HALL. In contrast to the ornate Albert Memorial across the street, the classical Royal Albert Hall is one of the more restrained pieces of Victorian architecture, though certainly not in size. Intended as an all-purpose venue, guests at the 1871 opening immediately noticed one shortcoming of the hall's elliptical design: a booming echo that made it next to useless for musical concerts. Acoustic experts finally solved the problem in 1968, installing dozens of sound-absorbing discs suspended in a haphazard fashion from the dome. The hall has hosted Britain's first full-length indoor marathon, the first public display of electric lighting, and the world premiere of *Hiawatha.* It remains a versatile venue for everything from boxing matches to rock concerts, but it is best known as the seat of the Proms classical music festival. For more information on the Proms, see p. 222. *(Kensington Gore, just south of Kensington Gardens and the Albert Memorial. ⊖ High St. Kensington. ☎ 7589 8212; www.royalalberthall.com. Box office at Door 12 open daily 9am-9pm. 45min. tours M-Tu and F-Su 10am-3pm every 30min.; reserve space in advance by calling box office. £6, students £5.)*

ALBERT MEMORIAL. An ornate example of Victorian High Gothic style, this 1868 canopy by George Gilbert Scott recently underwent a 10-year, £11.2 million restoration project. Queen Victoria, devastated by her dear husband's death, decided to immortalize him in gigantic gold-plated detail. At Albert's blindingly gilded feet, friezes represent the Four Industries, the Four Sciences, and the Four Continents, themes seemingly chosen more for their symmetry than for their accuracy. Above, over-the-top ornamentation continues with a 180 ft. spire inlaid with semi-precious stones. Head across to the Royal Albert Hall for the best view of the monument in its full glory. *(Kensington Gore, on the edge of Kensington Gardens, just north of Royal Albert Hall. ⊖High St. Kensington. ☎7495 0916. 45min. tours first Su of month Mar.-Dec. 2 and 3pm. Wheelchair-accessible. Admission free. Tours £4.50, concessions £4.)*

KNIGHTSBRIDGE AND BELGRAVIA

It's hard to imagine that in the 18th century, **Knightsbridge,** currently home to London's most expensive stores, was a district known for its taverns and salesmen taking advantage of the area's position just outside the City of London's jurisdiction. Gentrification has merely pushed the highway robbery indoors—just take a look at the price tags in Harrods and Harvey Nichols.

SEE MAP, p. 365

Squeezed between Knightsbridge, Chelsea, and Westminster, the wedge-shaped district of **Belgravia** was catapulted to respectability by the presence of royalty. When George IV decided to make Buckingham Palace his official residence in the 1820s, developers were quick to build suitably grand buildings for aristocratic hangers-on nearby. **Belgrave Square,** the setting for *My Fair Lady,* is now so expensive that the aristocracy has had to sell out to foreign governments. The primary reason most travelers come here is to get their passports replaced.

APSLEY HOUSE. Named for Baron Apsley, the house later known as "No. 1, London" was bought in 1817 by the Duke of Wellington, whose heirs still occupy a modest suite on the top floor. The opulent house itself warrants a visit, but most come for Wellington's fine art collection, much of which was given to him by the crowned heads of Europe following the Battle of Waterloo. Most of the old masters hang in the **Waterloo Gallery,** where the duke held his annual Waterloo banquet around the stupendous silver centerpiece, which was donated by the Portuguese government; the centerpiece is now displayed in the dining room. In the basement gallery reside caricatures from Wellington's later political career. *(Hyde Park Corner. ⊖Hyde Park Corner. ☎7499 5676; www.english-heritage.org.uk/london. Open Apr.-Oct. Tu-Su 10am-5pm; Nov.-Mar. Tu-Su 10am-4pm. Wheelchair-accessible. £5.30, students £4, children 5-18 £2.70. Joint ticket with Wellington Arch £6.90/5.20/3.50. Audio tours free. MC/V.)*

WELLINGTON ARCH. Standing at the center of London's most infamous traffic intersection, the Wellington Arch was long ignored by tourists and Londoners alike. All that changed in April 2001, when the completion of a long restoration project revealed the interior to the public for the first time. Built in 1825, the Green Park Arch was meant to form part of a processional route to London, part of George IV's scheme to beautify the city. Beauty turned grotesque, however, when the newly re-christened "Wellington Arch" was encumbered by an embarrassingly large statue of the duke. The government immediately ordered the statue's removal but desisted when Wellington threatened to resign from the army. The figure was replaced in 1912 by the even bigger (though less offensive) Quadriga of Peace. Inside the Arch, exhibitions on the building's history and the changing nature of war memorials play second fiddle to the two observation platforms with a bird's-eye view of the Buckingham Palace gardens, Green Park, and Hyde Park. *(Hyde Park Corner. ⊖Hyde Park Corner. ☎7930 2726; www.english-heritage.org.uk/london.*

Open W-Su Apr.-Oct. 10am-5pm, Nov.-Mar. 10am-4pm. Wheelchair-accessible. £3.20, students with ISIC £2.40, children 5-16 £1.60. Joint tickets with Apsley House available. MC/V.)

BROMPTON ORATORY. On entering this church, properly called the Oratory of St. Philip Neri, you are transported back in time via ornate Baroque flourishes. London's second largest Catholic church, the Oratory was built from 1874-1884 and was deliberately designed with a nave wider than St. Paul's. The KGB considered one of the church's altars to be the best dead drop in London—until 1985, agents left microfilm and other documents behind a statue for other agents to retrieve. The church lives up to its reputation for music during its Solemn Masses, sung in Latin. *(Thurloe Pl., Brompton Rd.* ⊖*South Kensington.* ☎ *7808 0900; www.bromptonoratory.com. Open daily 7am-8pm, except during frequent short services. Solemn Mass Su 11am. Call ahead for wheelchair access. Free.)*

CHELSEA

As wealthy as neighboring Belgravia and Kensington, Chelsea boasts a riverside location and a strong artistic heritage. Henry VIII's right-hand man (and later victim) St. Thomas More was the first big-name resident in the 16th century, but it was in the 19th century that the neighborhood acquired its artistic reputation with the founding of the famous Chelsea Arts Club. **Cheyne** (CHAIN-ee) **Walk** has been home to J.M.W. Turner, George Eliot, Dante Gabriel

SEE MAP, p. 363

Rossetti, and more recently Mick Jagger (at No. 48). Oscar Wilde, John Singer Sargent, and James McNeill Whistler all lived on **Tite Street,** while Mark Twain, Henry James, and T.S. Eliot were also Chelsea residents at various times. Chelsea's other distinguishing aspect is military: the Chelsea Barracks, the Royal Hospital, and the National Army Museum all happen to be stationed in this affluent artistic paradise.

CARLYLE'S HOUSE. In his time, Thomas Carlyle, the so-called "Sage of Chelsea," was the most famous writer and historian in England. When he died in 1881, admirers purchased his house and established it as a national monument. The house and garden in which he entertained Dickens, Tennyson, and Ruskin are preserved more or less as they were during his life. *(24 Cheyne Row.* ⊖*Sloane Sq., then Bus #19 or 319.* ☎ *7352 7087. Open Apr.-Oct. W-F 2-5pm, Sa-Su 11am-5pm; last admission 4:30pm. £4.50, children 5-16 £2.30.)*

CHELSEA OLD CHURCH. The quiet, unspectacular interior of the post-WWII-restored Saxon church won't do much for the lay observer. It is historically appealing, though, and fortunately the bombs spared the southern chapel, where St. Thomas More worshipped in the 16th century. Henry VIII is reported to have married Jane Seymour here before the official wedding took place. Just down the street is **Crosby Hall,** a 15th-century hall that was More's residence in Bishopsgate before being moved, stone by stone, to its present position in 1910. *(2 Old Church St.* ⊖*Sloane Sq., then Bus #19 or 319.* ☎ *7795 1019; www.chelseaoldchurch.org.uk. Open Tu-Th 2-4pm. Services Su 8, 11am, 12:15pm. Call about occasional 6pm services.)*

CHELSEA PHYSIC GARDEN. Founded in 1673 to provide medicinal herbs to locals, the Physic Garden remains a carefully ordered living repository of useful, rare, or just plain interesting plants. It has also played an important historic role, serving as the staging post from which tea was introduced to India and cotton to America. Today, the garden is a quiet place for picnics, teas, and scenic walks. You can purchase flora on display. *(66 Royal Hospital Rd.; entrance on Swan Walk.* ⊖*Sloane Sq., then Bus #137.* ☎ *7352 5646; www.chelseaphysicgarden.co.uk. Open early Apr.-Oct. W noon-9pm, Th-F noon-6pm, Su noon-6pm; during Chelsea Flower Show (late May) and*

Chelsea Festival (mid-June) M-F noon-5pm. Tea served daily from 12:30pm, Su from noon. Call in advance for wheelchair access. £7, students and children under 16 £4.)

ROYAL HOSPITAL. The environs of the Royal Hospital—including a chapel, a small museum detailing the history of the hospital, and a retirement home—house the Chelsea Pensioners, who totter around the grounds as they have done since 1692. The main draw is the once ritzy **Ranelagh Gardens.** They're a quiet oasis for picnics and park-playing—except during the **Chelsea Flower Show** in late May, when the braying masses of the Royal Horticultural Society descend en masse. *(2 entrance gates on Royal Hospital Rd. ⊖Sloane Sq., then Bus #137. ☎7881 5200; www.chelsea-pensioners.co.uk. Museum, Great Hall, and Chapel open daily 10am-noon and 2-4pm; museum closed Su Oct.-Mar. Grounds open Nov.-Mar. M-Sa 10am-4:30pm, Su 2-4:30pm.; Apr. daily 10am-7:30pm, May-Aug. daily 10am-8:30pm, Sept. daily 10am-7pm, Oct. daily 10am-5pm. Wheelchair-accessible. Flower show: www.rhs.org.uk; tickets must be purchased well in advance. Admission to Royal Hospital free.)*

WEST LONDON

Few people agree about where the "official" boundaries of West London lie, and even fewer agree about West London's defining characteristics. Encompassing everything from the live entertainment venues and urban sprawl of **Hammersmith** to the suburban and chain-store-saturated **Chiswick,** West London is held together more by geography than personality. The region's most famous employer, the BBC, has its headquarters here, and the charming areas of Chiswick and **Kew** provide a welcome break from the noise of the City. **Shepherd's Bush,** undergoing a growth spurt of sorts, is an excellent place to head for a range of ethnic cuisines and pub grub. *(In Shepherd's Bush, ⊖Central Line is at the east end of the Green, while ⊖Hammersmith and ⊖City Line are far west of the Green on Uxbridge Rd. ⊖Central Line has greater proximity to most sights and hotels. Both Hammersmith stations are close to each other, but the Piccadilly and District Lines are more convenient for the bus station. ⊖Goldhawk Rd. is also convenient.)*

BBC TELEVISION CENTRE. This vast media complex, shaped like a giant question mark, is the hub of British entertainment. All of the BBC's domestic television and radio programs are developed and filmed here, as well as shows from other networks who prefer to use their sprawling facilities. The BBC is always looking for regular people to be part of ▨**live studio audiences** for its many news, comedy, and game-show programs. Some visitors appear on news programs, others on prime-time programming. For a more in-depth experience, take a fun 1½-2hr. backstage tour of the center, complete with peeks at a number of studios and hallway encounters with media celebs. *(Wood Ln. ⊖White City. ☎0870 603 0304; www.bbc.co.uk. Wheelchair-accessible with advance notice. Tours M-Sa 10, 10:20, 10:40am, 1:15, 1:30, 1:45, 3:30, 3:45, 4pm. Booking required. Min. age 10. £9.50, seniors £8.50, students and children £7. Studio audience: ☎0870 901 1227; www.bbc.co.uk/tickets. Free. MC/V.)*

WIMBLEDON LAWN TENNIS MUSEUM. The All England Lawn Tennis and Croquet Club—the proper name for the arena that hosts the Wimbledon tennis championships every summer—includes a brand new museum dedicated to the history of tennis. Visitors can peruse memorabilia displays and interactive video exhibits, including a peek inside an original locker room with a three-dimensional John McEnroe as host. Tours (2hr.) of the grounds are led by certified Blue Badge Guides and include stops in the Millennium Building and the iconic Centre Court. *(Church Rd. ⊖Southfields. From Tube station, take Bus #493, or cross street and walk south on Wimbledon Park Road. Visitors to the museum should enter through Gate 3. ☎8946 6131; www.wimbledon.org/museum. Museum open daily 10:30am-5pm, guided tours at noon, 1:30, 2:30pm. Museum only £8.50, students £7.50, children £4.75; museum and guided tour £14.50/£13/£11.)*

CHISWICK HOUSE. Both Chiswick House and its gardens were created by Richard Boyle, Third Lord Burlington (1694-1753), the first of many Englishmen to try to recreate Italy's Tuscan hillside in his backyard. Chiswick's elegant parties catering to the English elite are credited with kick-starting the aristocracy's obsession with Palladian architecture. The rooms upstairs still contain much of the original decorative work, from gilded ceilings to textured wall coverings. The beautiful **gardens** are as innovative as the home, the first example of the naturalistic design that came to be known as the 18th century naturalistic English style. The grounds are popular with local families and are perfect for picnics, with a pond, open grassy areas, statues, and lots of woodsy trails. *(Between the Great West Rd. and the Great Chertsey Rd. ☎8995 0508. ⊖Turnham Green. From the Tube, walk south on Turnham Green Terr., turn right on Chiswick High Rd., turn left on Duke's Ave. Walk for 10min., then take a right on Devonshire Passage and go through the pedestrian underpass at Great West Rd. House open Apr.-Oct. W-F and Su 10am-5pm, Sa 10am-2pm. £4.20, students £3.20, children over 5 £2.10. Gardens open daily 8am-dusk; free. Frequently closes early for functions; call in advance.)*

HOGARTH'S HOUSE. Sandwiched between the peaceful gardens of Chiswick House, a modern business complex, and the traffic-laden A4 motorway, the former country estate of noted British painter and engraver William Hogarth remains a quiet getaway inside walled premises. Hogarth was most famous for his wildly popular satirical works, many of which depicted stories of moral character and ranged from pleasantly humorous to uncomfortably gruesome. The lower two floors of the house and the small garden are open to visitors and offer a relaxed environment in which to learn about one of Britain's most prolific artists. *(Hogarth Lane ☎8994 6757; www.hounslow.info/hogarthshouse. ⊖Turnham Green. From the Tube, walk south on Turnham Green Terr., turn right on Chiswick High Rd., then left on Duke's Ave. Walk for 10 min., then take a right on Devonshire Passage and go through the pedestrian underpass. Open Apr.-Oct. Tu-F 1-5pm, Sa-Su 1-6pm; Nov.-Dec. and Feb.-Mar., Tu-F 1-4pm, Sa-Su 1-5pm. Free.)*

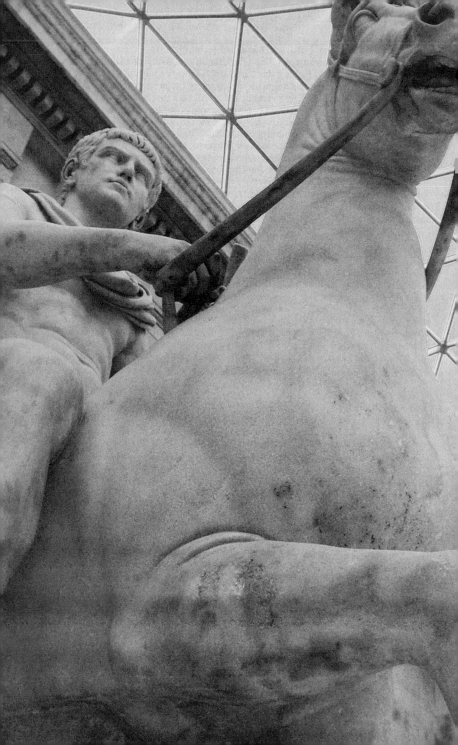

MUSEUMS

For centuries, rich Londoners have exhibited a penchant for collecting, and subsequent generations of Wallaces and Wellingtons enjoy putting the collections on display in order to keep the family name intact. Unfortunately, they also charge £5-10 in order to keep their estates intact. While not cheap, these galleries offer some of the best art in the city, and many do have certain hours of free or reduced admission. To rub elbows with buyers hoping to form private collections of their own, head to West End auction houses (including Christie's and Sotheby's) for a peek at old-fashioned and international greats, or to East End galleries (including Whitechapel and White Cube) for modern Britart and local up-and-comers. As long as you dress the part, nobody will know that you can't even afford the frame that most of the paintings come in, and you'll be able to see art that may end up in the National Gallery in a few decades.

If this sounds financially discouraging to you, fret not; London also has a substantial national collection, helped in large part by its position in the 18th and 19th centuries as the capital of an empire upon which the sun was said never to set. Touting collections of Syrian, Roman, and Egyptian ruins as authentically British in the British Museum and the V&A may be a dubious claim, but the collections are so impressive that art lovers, history buffs, and amateur ethnologists don't seem to care. Since 2002, museum lovers have had even more reason to celebrate London: admission to all major collections is ◼free indefinitely in celebration of the Queen's Golden Jubilee. (Note that most charge extra for temporary exhibits, which are often so popular that tickets must be booked in advance.) Touring London on a budget has never been easier.

THE CITY OF LONDON

Although St. Paul's and the Tower get all the attention, the City's museums are top-notch. The area's long-standing history makes a trip to a well-curated museum a must. They are a less crowded and cheaper alternative to the major sights.

SEE MAP, p. 349

◼ **MUSEUM OF LONDON.** Located in the southwest corner of the Barbican complex, the Museum of London resembles an industrial fortress from the outside. Inside, the engrossing collection traces the history of London from its Roman foundations to the present day, cleverly incorporating architectural history, including the adjacent ruins of the ancient **London Wall.** The **Roman Galleries** are particularly impressive, with a reconstructed dining room built over an original mosaic floor and a large collection of artifacts and sculptures. The **Anglo-Saxon** and **medieval** collections are small but excellent, including shields from the Norman invasion and an outstanding exhibit on Henry VIII's break from Catholicism. As a nice touch, a period-specific soundtrack accompanies each exhibit. The museum is worth a visit for the Cheapside Hoard alone, a 17th-century goldsmith's bounty uncovered in 1912, or for the Lord Mayor's State Coach, built in 1757 and dripping with gold carvings. *(London Wall. Enter through the Barbican or from Aldersgate; wheelchair-accessible via the elevator at Aldersgate entrance.* ❷ *St. Paul's or Barbican.* ☎ *08704 444 3851; www.museumoflondon.org.uk. Open M-Sa 10am-5:50pm, Su noon-5:50pm; last admission 5:30pm. Free. Audio tours £2. Frequent demonstrations, talks, and guided walks; some are free, others up to £10.)*

◼ **BANK OF ENGLAND MUSEUM.** The Bank itself is only available to those on business; to get to the museum, you will be shuttled by security attendants. The museum traces the history of the Bank from its foundation (1694) to the present day. Wax figures man a recreation of Sir John Soane's original Stock Office, while a display of banknotes includes a handwritten one for the sum of £1 million. At the center of the rotunda is a pyramid of gold bars; visitors are encouraged to try to pick one up. Different mini-displays showcase such varied things as the Bank's official silver and German firebomb casings. *(Threadneedle St. ⊖Bank. ☎7601 5545; www.bankofengland.co.uk. Open M-F 10am-5pm. Wheelchair-accessible. Free.)*

GUILDHALL ART GALLERY. Devoted to displaying the City's art collection, the walls are home to numerous portraits of former Lord Mayors. Downstairs is a fine collection of Victorian and pre-Raphaelite art that includes works by Stevens, Poynter, Rossetti, and Millais. The Copley Gallery on the first floor showcases John Singleton Copley's massive *The Defeat of the Floating Batteries*, commissioned by the government for popular appreciation. To get the full effect, it must be seen from the balcony on the third floor. While upstairs, check out the Allegory of London, seated with Athena, Pallas, Peace, and Plenty. The basement houses the ruins of a Roman amphitheatre. *(Guildhall Yard, off Gresham St. ⊖Moorgate or Bank. ☎7332 3700; www.guildhall-art-gallery.org.uk. Wheelchair-accessible. Open M-Sa 10am-5pm, last admission 4:30pm; Su noon-4pm, last admission 3:30pm. Free M-Th and Sa-Su 3:30-5pm, F 10am-5pm; M-Th and Sa-Su 10am-3:30pm £2.50, concessions £1, children under 16 free.)*

THE CLOCKMAKERS' MUSEUM. A one-room museum measuring the 500-year history of clockmakers through clocks, watches, chronometers, and sundials—you won't lose track of time at this museum. The display includes a watch that belonged to Mary Queen of Scots and the one worn by Sir Edmund Hillary when he climbed Everest. Impressive old grandfather clocks share space with pocket watches; the keeper of the clocks comes in weekly to wind them all by hand. *(Enter through Guildhall Yard on Aldermanbury. ⊖St. Paul's or Moorgate. ☎7332 1868; www.clockmakers.org. Open M-Sa 9:30am-4:30pm. Wheelchair-accessible. Free.)*

THE CITY OF LONDON GALLERIES

BARBICAN ART GALLERY. Housing British and international art and photography, Barbican exhibits change every few months and generally include a variety of media. Call in advance for the season's exhibit; previous themes have included "Folk Art" and "Colour After Klein." International pieces are showcased behind the concert hall on the first floor. *(Between London Wall, Beech St., Aldersgate, and Moorgate. ⊖Barbican or Moorgate. ☎7638 4141, box office 7638 8891; www.barbican.org.uk/gallery. Open M and W-Sa 11am-8pm, Tu 11am-6pm. Wheelchair-accessible. Rates vary—call box office for details.)*

EAST LONDON

WHITECHAPEL AND THE EAST END

Home to a bustling contemporary art scene, East London—particularly the East End—houses a number of museums. However, the art galleries are the true finds.

GEFFRYE MUSEUM. This tribute to English interior decorating through the ages will thrill your inner Martha Stewart. The setting—an elaborately restored terrace of a 17th-century almshouse—showcases a set of connecting rooms, each painstakingly recreating a specific period in interior design. Move through Elizabethan parlors, Victorian studies, and stark post-WWI sitting rooms. The obsessive attention to detail can be amusing: the radio in the "1990-2000" loft plays 1990s pop, and the table is strewn with glossy women's magazines. The downstairs space houses temporary exhibits and a design center for local artists' displays. The manicured backyard garden is lovely and can be admired from the popular glassed-in lunch cafe **At Home.** *(Kingsland Rd. ⊖Old St., then Bus #243 or 10min. walk along Old St. and left on Kingsland Rd. or ⊖Liverpool St. and Bus #149 or 242. ☎7739 9893; www.geffrye-museum.org.uk. Open Tu-Sa 10am-5pm; M, Su, bank holidays noon-5pm. Free. Cafe open 10am-4:45pm. Food £3-6.)*

MUSEUM OF CHILDHOOD. The place to be for under-fives or those wishing to reclaim their youth, this museum manages to please all ages. Colorful displays—housed in the original Victoria and Albert building—hold puzzles, toys, dolls, and furniture from hundreds of years ago. History of beloved toys such as Barbie® dolls and model cars accompany exhibits. Glass cases are interspersed with play areas where children can try out rocking horses, dress up in fabulous costumes, put on puppet shows, play games, and generally exhaust their parents. Organized story hours, dance and movement classes, and arts and crafts sessions are also part of the fun. *(Cambridge Heath Rd. ⊖Bethnal Green. ☎8983 5200; www.museumofchildhood.org.uk. Open M-Th and Sa-Su 10am-5:45pm. Free.)*

EAST LONDON GALLERIES

WHITECHAPEL ART GALLERY. Long the sole artistic beacon in a culturally and materially impoverished area, Whitechapel is now at the forefront of the buzzing art scene, displaying art from 19th-century Impressionist masterpieces to modern works. Founded in 1901, Whitechapel was one of the first publicly funded galleries in London. Since then, it has showcased art from Africa, India, and Latin America, and in the 1950s and 60s it was at the heart of the Pop Art movement. Its main drive is to exhibit artists who live and work in the East End, though as emerging artists move to other areas of the city, such exhibitions are becoming less relevant. Currently undergoing a large scale refurbishment, most of the gallery space is closed off to the public until early 2009, but small exhibits are still in rotation. Check website for details. *(Whitechapel High St. ⊖Aldgate East. ☎7522 7888; www.whitechapel.org. Open Tu-W and F-Su 11am-6pm, Th 11am-9pm. Wheelchair-accessible. Call for opening details. Free.)*

WHITE CUBE. One of the gems of Hoxton Sq., this stark white building has showcased some of the biggest names in international contemporary art. Housed in a former industrial building and opened in 2000, White Cube has an impressive list of alums, including Chuck Close and Damien Hirst. Although the Cube is small, many consider it to be the top modern art gallery in London and possibly Europe. They've shown almost every major British artist from the last few years and pride themselves on showing important up-and-coming talent. *(48 Hoxton Sq. ⊖Old St. ☎7930 5373; www.whitecube.com. Open Tu-Sa 10am-6pm. Sometimes closes for exhibit installation; call in advance. Wheelchair-accessible. Free.)*

VICTORIA MIRO. While the ex-warehouse feel is a bit intimidating, the excellent exhibits here are cleanly displayed. Buildings are connected by a small patio out back overlooking a tranquil lily pad pond. The gallery features works from young artists that often make the most of the sprawling warehouse area. Exhibits are less crowded than other museums on the area. *(16 Wharf Rd. ⊖Old St. or ⊖Angel. From Old St., take Exit 8 and walk north up City Rd. toward Angel, pass the 230 address block, then turn right after the Texaco Station; ring bell to enter. ☎7336 8109; www.victoria-miro.com. Open Tu-Sa 10am-6pm. Free.)*

GREENWICH

NATIONAL MARITIME MUSEUM. With around two million items in its possession, the NMM covers almost every aspect of seafaring history. Many of the galleries feel like a nautical theme park—for instance, the **Explorers** section recreates an Antarctic ice cave and a ship's foredeck. Exhibits change frequently and many are interactive, with videos and hands-on displays. The **Passengers** exhibit looks at the history of maritime travel and the conditions in which seafarers found themselves. **Our Ocean** exposes the potential consequences of pollution and global warming, including displays of harmful products to the environment and ways visitors can contribute to a solution. The pride of the naval displays, naturally, is the top-floor ▨ **Nelson Room,** which tells the stirring tale of Admiral Lord Nelson's life—inspiration for Nelson's column in Trafalgar Square. Starting with Nelson's induction into the Royal Navy as a 12-year-old midshipman, the cases chronicle his rise through the ranks, his brilliant naval victories, and his scandalous love affair with the married Lady Emma Hamilton. In the starkly lit center of the room, a glass case displays the uniform Nelson died in, the bullet hole still evident and the stockings stained with blood. *(Romney Rd. between the Royal Naval College and Greenwich Park. DLR: Cutty Sark. ☎8858 4422; www.nmm.ac.uk. Open daily mid-July to early Sept. 10am-6pm; early Sept. to mid-July 10am-5pm; last entry 30min. before closing. Free.)*

HOLBORN

Holborn's museums may not be as famous as the Tate Galleries, but they certainly deserve a visit. The collections at the Somerset House museums are top-notch, while the Hunterian Museum offers odd and interesting curiosities that are bound to intrigue any visitor.

SEE MAP, p. 364

▨ SOMERSET HOUSE

Strand, just east of Waterloo Bridge. ⊖Charing Cross or Temple. ☎7845 4600, events 7845 4670; www.somerset-house.org.uk. Courtyard open daily 7:30am-11pm. Galleries open daily 10am-6pm. Last admission 5:15pm. Tours 1st Sa of every month 1:30, 2:30, 3:45pm. Wheelchair-accessible. Ticket for 1 of the 3 collections £5, concessions £4, under 18 free; 2 collections £8/£7; 3 collections £12/11. MC/V.

Somerset House was London's first intentional office block. Originally home to the Royal Academy, the Royal Society, and the Navy Board, the elegant courtyard long induced a shiver of distaste in Londoners as the headquarters of the Inland Revenue. On sunny days, they face some competition from the spectacular view afforded by the **River Terrace** and its attractive but pricey outdoor cafe. In December and January, the central **Fountain Courtyard** is iced over to make an open-air rink while, in the summer months, frolicking toddlers splash through the cool fountain jets. Thursday evenings from mid-June to mid-July feature classical music concerts; in August there are open-air movie screenings. The annual Somerset House Concert Series features indie and pop bands outdoors.

THE COURTAULD INSTITUTE GALLERIES. The Courtauld's small but outstanding collection ranges from 14th-century Italian religious works to 20th-century abstracts. Not limited solely to paintings, the three floors of the Courtauld also house sculpture, decorative arts, prints, and drawings. Works are arranged by collector, not chronologically, so don't fret if you think you skipped a few hundred years. The Renaissance holdings feature a wide variety of pieces, including works from Ruben, Botticelli, and other renowned European artists. The undisputed gems of the collection, though, are from the Impressionist and Post-Impressionist periods: Manet's *A Bar at the Follies Bergères*, Van Gogh's *Self-Portrait with Bandaged Ear*, and an entire room devoted to Degas's bronzes, as well as works by Cézanne, Monet, Renoir, and Gauguin. Call to make sure pieces are not currently on loan to other institutions. *(☎7420 9400; www.courtauld.ac.uk. 1hr. tours held Sa 2:30pm. Wheelchair-accessible. Tours £6.50, concessions £6; M 10am-2pm free. Lunchtime talks free.)*

THE GILBERT COLLECTION. The Gilbert Collection of Decorative Arts opened in 2000 and houses some of the more exquisite non-paintings on display in any

COURTAULD FOR FREE. The collection at the Courtauld Galleries is remarkable and worth every penny of the entrance fee. But why pay if you don't have to? Go by on Mondays between 10am and 2pm and get in for free.

museum. The emphasis here is on incomparable craftsmanship and precious materials. The collection's approximately 1000 objects fall into three categories: mosaics, gold- and silver-work, and snuffboxes. Sir Arthur Gilbert's collection of the third is considered by many to be among the finest in the world, with over 200 pieces, including six made for Frederick the Great, each encrusted with diamonds, rubies, and emeralds. The collection of mosaics, inlaid onto otherwise bland objects of furniture and book coverings, is the most comprehensive ever formed. Be sure to spend time viewing the micromosaics carefully. To appreciate fully the craftsmanship of these pieces, you'll need to pick up a complimentary magnifying glass at the front desk (where you can also get a free audio tour). You can also access the King's Barge House from here, a reminder that the Thames once came all the way up to the walls of Somerset House. (☎ 7420 9400; www.gilbert-collection.org.uk. 1hr. tours held Sa 2:30pm. Wheelchair-accessible. Tours £6.50, concessions £6.)

THE HERMITAGE ROOMS. A unique chance to get a taste of the world-renowned Hermitage art museum without going to St. Petersburg, Russia. The five rooms in the south wing of the Somerset House have been recreated as smaller replicas of the Winter Palace in St. Petersburg, down to the door fittings and floor patterns, all of which were fashioned by Russian craftsmen. All of this recreated elegance almost overshadows the paintings on loan from the big brother in Russia, exchanged for new ones every six months to keep things fresh. Recent exhibits range from photographs of British settlers in Russia to modern porcelain pieces. In case you want to compare the museum to the real thing, the main room has a live webcast from the museum in Russia. (☎ 7485 4630; www.hermitagerooms.org.uk. Audio tours £1.)

OTHER HOLBORN MUSEUMS

▨ HUNTERIAN MUSEUM. Buried within the grandiose **Royal College of Surgeons,** this museum is not for the squeamish. John Hunter, considered the founder of modern surgery, had a keen interest in the anatomy of all living things, proven by his vast collection of both human and animal fetuses preserved in large glass jars. Only 3500 of his original 14,000 colorless pickled organs survived the Blitz, but that's enough to fill endless shelves. Galleries are devoted to subjects ranging from the ghastly history of surgical instruments to Hunter's personal art collection. Among the viscera are some genuine marvels, like the 7' 7" skeleton of the "Irish Giant." (35-43 Lincoln's Inn Fields. ⊖Holborn. Enter via the columned main entrance to the RCS building. ☎ 7869 6560; www.rcseng.ac.uk/services/museums. Open Tu-Sa 10am-5pm. Wheelchair-accessible. Free.)

SIR JOHN SOANE'S MUSEUM. Eccentric architect John Soane let his imagination run free when designing this intriguing, sometimes bewildering museum for his own collection of art and antiquities. Three separate homes in Lincoln's Field Rd. had to be joined together to accommodate the collection. The result is a somewhat incoherent but interesting maze of artifacts. Framed by endlessly mirrored walls, items range from the mummified corpse of Soane's wife's dog to an extraordinary sarcophagus of Seti I, for which Soane personally outbid the British Museum. In addition to the permanent collection, the museum holds five to six exhibitions a year in its limited gallery space. (13 Lincoln's Inn Fields. ⊖Holborn. ☎ 1405 2107. Open Tu-Sa 10am-5pm, 1st Tu of month also 6-9pm. Tours Sa. Tours £5, students free. Tickets sold from 11am. Free; £3 donation requested.)

THE SOUTH BANK

If Westminster and the City are London's historical and regal centers, then the South Bank is the aesthetic arts center, with one of the highest concentrations of interesting exhibits and museums in the world. Anchored by the gigantic Tate Modern, the area is home not only to top public contemporary art, but to private galleries, each with its own spin. Established masters hold court at the Hayward and promising newcomers at the Jerwood.

SEE MAP, pp. 370-371

■ TATE MODERN

Main entrance on Bankside, on the South Bank; 2nd entrance on Queen's Walk. ⊖Southwark or Blackfriars. From the Southwark Tube, turn left up Union, then left on Great Suffolk, then left on Holland. ☎7887 8000; www.tate.org.uk. Open M-Th and Su 10am-6pm, F-Sa 10am-10pm. Free; special exhibits can be up to £10. Free tours meet on the gallery concourses: Level 3 11am and noon, Level 5 2 and 3pm. Five types of audio tours include highlights, collection tour, architecture tour, children's tour, and the visually impaired tour; £2. Free talks M-F 1pm; meet at the concourse on the appropriate level. Wheelchair-accessible on Holland St.

Considered the second half of the national collection (the first portion held in the National Gallery), the Tate Modern is probably the most popular museum in London, as well as one of the most famous modern art museums in the world. From the outside, it doesn't look like much: the most striking aspect is Sir Giles Gilbert Scott's mammoth building, formerly the Bankside power station. Inside, though, the seventh floor has unblemished views of the Thames and the north and south of London, while **Turbine Hall** on the ground hall is now an open, immense atrium that dwarfs the installations it exhibits. The public galleries are on the third and fifth floors, divided into four themes. By grouping works thematically, the Tate has turned itself into a work of conceptual art. The collection is enormous while gallery space is limited—works rotate frequently. If you are dying to see a particular piece, head to the museum's computer station on the fifth floor to browse through the entire collection.

HIGHLIGHTS IN A HURRY: TATE MODERN. On-display collections at the Tate Modern are not enormous, and you should be able to get through all four sections within a few hours (although you could spend the whole day). Galleries not to be missed: Distinguished Voices and Expressionism in Material Gestures; Natural History in Poetry and Dream; Utopia and Abstraction in Idea and Object, and Roy Lichtenstein in States of Flux.

THIRD FLOOR. One of the four concept galleries, **Material Gestures** features postwar European and American painting and sculpture. The galleries within Material Gestures include artists such as Anish Kapoor, Claude Monet, and Douglas Gordon. Mark Rothko's famous Seagram Murals are also part of this richly filled area. On the other side of Level 3 is the **Poetry and Dream** gallery, which is devoted to Surrealism and related works. Highlights include works by Francis Bacon, Louise Bourgeois, and Francesca Woodman.

FIFTH FLOOR. Idea and Object houses a series of works related to minimalism and conceptual art. Main artists include Dan Flavin, Ellsworth Kelly, and Joseph Beuys. On the same level **States of Flux** features cubism, vorticism, and futurism alongside works that have a focus on change and modernity. Roy Lichtenstein, Steve McQueen, Dieter Roth, and Jonas Mekas are the chief artists on show.

OTHER SOUTH BANK MUSEUMS

■IMPERIAL WAR MUSEUM. Massive naval guns guard the entrance to the building, formerly the infamous lunatic asylum known as Bedlam. The best and most publicized display is on the third floor: the **Holocaust Exhibition** provides an honest and poignant look at all the events surrounding the tragedy. The **Large Exhibits Hall** features an impressive array of military hardware, from "Little Boy" (an atomic bomb of the type dropped on Hiroshima) to Montgomery's tank to a German V-2 rocket, all clearly labeled and carefully explained. The **cinema** shows a rotating schedule of historical documentaries. In the basement, the **Trench Experience** recreates the conditions of WWI, and the **Blitz Experience** details life on the home front in WWII. On the first floor, the remarkably high-tech **Secret War** is filled with gadgets and gizmos of espionage and a particularly gripping presentation of Operation NIMROD (the storming of a hostage-filled Iranian embassy in 1980 in London). On the fourth floor, **Crimes Against Humanity** is a sobering interactive display with a 30min. film at the back. *(Lambeth Rd., Lambeth. ⊖Lambeth North or Elephant & Castle. ☎7416 5320; www.iwm.org.uk. Open daily 10am-6pm. Admission free. Audio tours £3.50, concessions £3.)*

■DESIGN MUSEUM. Housed in an arrestingly white Art Deco riverfront building, this contemporary museum's installations fit right into the cool surroundings. Works cater mostly to the young, hip, and well dressed. You might find anything from avant-garde furniture pieces to galleries on big-name graphic designers. Everyone will enjoy the **Interaction Space** on the top floor, which includes a colorful variety of household items and a bay of **vintage video games** that inspired contemporary gaming. The **Museum Café** on the first floor—not to be confused with the much pricier **Blue Print Café** next door—serves an array of sweet treats as aesthetically pleasing as anything you'll find in the galleries. *(28 Shad Thames, Butlers Wharf. ⊖Tower Hill or London Bridge. ☎0870 833 9955; www.designmuseum.org. Open daily 10am-5:45pm, last entry 5:15pm. Wheelchair-accessible. £7, concessions £4.)*

FLORENCE NIGHTINGALE MUSEUM. On the grounds of St. Thomas's Hospital, where Florence Nightingale's first school of nursing opened in 1860, this one-floor tribute to the famous "Lady with the Lamp" is suitably reverent. Well-labeled displays chart Nightingale's life from childhood to posthumous renown using mostly personal effects and letters. *(St. Thomas's Hospital, 2 Lambeth Palace Rd. ⊖Waterloo or Westminster. Look for the ramp down to the museum near the corner of the hospital. ☎7620 0374; www.florence-nightingale.co.uk. Open*

THE BIG SPLURGE

SO MANY BOTTLES, SO LITTLE TIME

Vinopolis, the "City of Wine," is actually more like a universe. The masterminds of the attraction have created a tour of the world following the all-important thread of viticulture, which has become increasingly popular since the 2004 release of the wine-centric film *Sideways*. Learning to swish, gurgle, and spit is now a skill for the refined, not just one reserved for a trip to the dentist.

The tour starts with information about wine from Roman times, before heading to France, and everyone's favorite, Champagne. Around the world to Portugal, Germany, Chile, Argentina, and California, history is supplemented with samples. Ask one of the pros to pour a taste from the bottle of your choosing. You may even ask about their English selection—which isn't just wine from Tesco—and take your tour full circle.

The **Original Package** includes five tastes, a Bombay Sapphire gin cocktail, and the tour (£16). We recommend the **Ultimate Package** (£21), which will satisfy even the heartiest drinkers—it includes 9 tastings, topped off with two drinks of absinthe.

(Bank End, at the end of Clink St. ☎7940 8301; www.vinopolis.co.uk. ⊖London Bridge. Open M and Th-F noon-10pm, Sa 11am-9pm, Su noon-6pm. Last admission 2hr. before closing. Bookings recommended.)

M-F 10am-5pm, Sa-Su 10am-4:30pm; last entry 1hr. before closing. Wheelchair-accessible. £5.80, concessions £4.80, families of 4 £16. Free tours M-F 2 and 3pm. AmEx/MC/V.)

OLD OPERATING THEATRE AND HERB GARRET. Tucked into the loft of a 19th-century church, the theatre is the oldest restored operating theatre in the world. The surgeon's chair and restraining straps appear to await their next patient. A fearsome array of saws and knives are the core of the exhibit on surgical history, accompanied by plenty of amputation illustrations. The neighboring **herb garret** smells heavenly; it was used by the hospital apothecary to prepare medicines. A 1718 cure for venereal disease instructs the afflicted to ingest garden snails, cleansed and bruised. The multitude of frightful medical instruments, such as a trepanning drill, used to relieve headaches by boring a hole in the skull, elicit thanks for modern medicine. *(9a St. Thomas's St. ⊖London Bridge. ☎7188 2679; www.thegarret.org.uk. Open daily 10:30am-5pm; closed Dec. 15-Jan. 5. £5.25, concessions £4.25, children £3, families £13.)*

SOUTH BANK GALLERIES

BANKSIDE GALLERY. Run jointly by the Royal Watercolour Society and the Royal Society of Painter Printmakers, the gallery mostly displays members' works, but any type of media is liable to be shown. The exception (and best exhibit) is the annual Open Exhibition (held in late spring through July), when anyone can submit watercolors for inclusion. The wide range of works are all for sale and generally very good. There are also spring and autumn watercolor shows, as well as a yearly print show. *(48 Hopton St. ⊖Blackfriars. Entrance on Riverside Terr. ☎7928 7521; www.banksidegallery.com. Open daily 11am-6pm. Wheelchair-accessible. Free.)*

JERWOOD SPACE. Primarily a center for rehearsals of performing arts, the Jerwood Space gives promising young artists a leg up, most famously by hosting the prestigious Jerwood Painting Prize exhibition (early May to mid-June). Rotating exhibitions line the walls of this beautifully converted industrial space. *(171 Union St. ⊖Southwark or Borough. ☎7654 0171; www.jerwoodspace.co.uk. Open M-F 10am-5pm, Sa-Su 10am-3pm. Free.)*

HAYWARD GALLERY. Hiding next to the Royal Festival Hall, this stark concrete building is a distinctive maze of blocks, topped with a twisting red roof sculpture. Contemporary art dominates, with occasional forays into the early or mid-20th century. Two to three shows usually run concurrently. *(South Bank Centre. ⊖Waterloo, Embankment, or Temple. ☎0871 663 2501; www.hayward.org.uk. Call in advance, as the gallery closes between exhibits. Open M-Th and Su 10am-6pm, F-Sa 10am-10pm. £8, seniors £7, children 12-16 £4, children under 12 free, concessions £4.)*

SOUTH LONDON

Overshadowed by the fame of the museums on the nearby South Bank, South London's few but worthwhile galleries offer unique collections that are worth a peek. The Dulwich Picture Gallery houses old masters and Dutch treasures, while the Horniman Museum showcases African collectibles. Both provide engaging exhibits with ample elbow room, a claim no South Bank museum can make.

DULWICH PICTURE GALLERY. England's first public gallery is the unlikely legacy of Polish misfortune. In 1790, King Stanislaus Augustus of Poland decided to invest in a national art collection and commissioned two London dealers to buy the best pictures available. Unfortunately for the dealers (not to mention the Poles), the partition of Poland in 1795 left them with a full-blown, unpaid-for collection in hand. Rather than selling the works, they decided to put them on public display. The benefactors are buried in a domed mausoleum at the center of the gallery (designed by Sir John Sloane), and the high-ceilinged halls house a fine collection of old masters: mostly 17th- and 18th-century works from the Dutch, Spanish, Italian, French, and English schools of painting. Rubens, Veronese, and van Dyck feature prominently, while other Dutch masterpieces include Rembrandt's *Portrait of a Young Man*. (*Gallery Rd., Dulwich.* ⊖ *Brixton, then Bus #P4 to Picture Gallery stop. Rail: North Dulwich or West Dulwich. From West Dulwich station, turn right onto Thurlow Park Rd. and left onto Gallery Rd. and follow the signs for 15min.; from North Dulwich, turn left out of the station and walk 10min. through Dulwich Village to the Gallery.* ☎ *8693 5254; www.dulwich-picturegallery.org.uk. Open Tu-F 10am-5pm, Sa-Su 11am-5pm. Free tours Sa-Su 3pm. Wheelchair-accessible. Permanent collection £4, seniors £3, students and under 16 free. Exhibitions and permanent collection £8, seniors £7, students £4, children under 16 free.*)

HORNIMAN MUSEUM AND GARDENS. This eclectic and rather eccentric museum is devoted to the small and fascinating collection of 19th-century tea merchant Frederick Horniman, who was quite the world traveler. The African Worlds gallery displays a rich selection of over 6500 textile and costume items from African cultures of both past and present; ceremonial masks from Burkina Faso and Sierra Leone are dwarfed by the enormous Ijele, a Nigerian masquerade costume. The natural history collection features giant stuffed animals and skeletons, as well as several Egyptian sarcophagi. The neighboring hillside garden holds a tiny domestic zoo where crowing roosters and goats make their homes; the 16 acres of colorful flower beds are the perfect setting for a charming stroll. (*100 London Rd.* ⊖ *Brixton or Bus #P4 to the Horniman stop. Rail: Forest Hill. Exit the station, cross Dartmouth Rd., and follow A205 for 5min. until it becomes London Rd.* ☎ *8699 1872; www.horniman.ac.uk. Wheelchair-accessible. Open daily 10:30am-5:30pm. Gardens open M-Sa 7:30am-dusk, Su 8am-dusk. Free.*)

WESTMINSTER

Westminster is more of a sights neighborhood than a museums one. But history and political buffs who head down Whitehall to take a peek at Downing St. would be remiss to pass up the Cabinet War Rooms and the new Churchill Museum. Tate Britain may be slightly less hip than its Tate Modern counterpart, but it does host comprehensive themed exhibits that can be equally engrossing.

SEE MAP, p. 368

■ CABINET WAR ROOMS

Clive Steps, far end of King Charles St. ⊖ *Westminster.* ☎ *7930 6961; www.iwm.org.uk. Open daily 9:30am-6pm; last admission 5pm. £10, students £8, children under 16 free. MC/V.*

From 1939 to 1945, what started as a government coal storage basement transformed into the bomb-proof nerve center of a nation at war. For six tense years, Winston Churchill, his cabinet and generals, and dozens of support staff lived and worked in this dark, underground labyrinth while bombs wreaked havoc above. The day after the war ended in August 1945, the Cabinet War Rooms were abandoned, shut up, and left undisturbed for decades until their reopening in 1984 by Margaret Thatcher. Thanks to journals, testimonies, and photos, the space was able to be preserved and displayed almost exactly as it was in wartime. An indispensable free Churchillian-voiced audio tour talks you through the maze of rooms on show, supplemented by original recordings of Churchill's speeches and recreations that bring them to life. Highlights include "Churchill's personal loo"—a small room containing the top-secret transatlantic hotline—and the defense and map rooms that were in operation for six straight years, night and day. Details such as a general's secret sugar supply, scratchings on walls, and graffiti on maps make the experience that much more real. The clocks on display in Churchill's official meeting room read 4:58, the moment Churchill called the Cabinet's first official meeting, one day after a German air raid on London.

■ **CHURCHILL MUSEUM.** The adjoining museum, opened in February 2005, holds many of Churchill's WWII possessions, along with remnants from his lesser-known days as a journalist, prisoner of war, and amateur artist. Alternately somber and amusing, it provides an in-depth look at the man whom many consider to be one of history's greatest leaders. Wander through five highly interactive sections, all profiling a distinct phase in the former Prime Minister's life. In the hot pink **1874-1900** area, peruse Winnie's famously lackluster report cards and stop to read about his daring escape from South Africa. The red-hued **1900-1929** section features Churchill's first love letter to his beloved "Clemmie" and profiles his early days as an extremely liberal social reformer. Be sure to check out the many political cartoons—funnier if you can read German—scattered throughout the exhibit. The orange **Wilderness Years (1929-1940)** section profiles Churchill in his down-and-out days, with a hilarious interactive display of Churchill's witticisms and a computerized selection of Churchill's many amateur paintings. In the purple **1940-1945** section, visitors can immerse themselves in Churchill's wartime world. Hitler's anti-British propaganda, denouncing Churchill as "an utterly amoral repulsive creature," can also be seen here. Finally, the green **1945-1965** section, profiling Churchill's life as a statesmen and fashionista (he often donned one-piece zip-up velvet suits), explores his role in the Cold War and ends with a somber video of his funeral. The best part of the museum, a giant interactive timeline table that runs diagonally across the room, connects all five of the displays and is filled with sound bites, newspaper clippings, and historical information that puts Churchill's life in a wider context. Generate all kinds of disruptive effects by selecting from the many dates along the timeline. Be sure to check out August 6th, 1945, but be prepared to draw stares from surrounding visitors.

TIP | **SCENIC MUSEUM HOPPING.** Take the Tate Boat when traveling between Tate Modern and Tate Britain. The journey lasts 20min. and includes a stop at the London Eye. Book tickets at either Tate museum, the Bankside Pier, the London Eye, or online at www.tate.org.uk. Single adult trip £4, Transport for London Travelcard holders £2.75. Boats generally run 10am-5pm. Call ☎ 7887 8888 for more information.

OTHER WESTMINSTER MUSEUMS

TATE BRITAIN. Tate Britain is the foremost collection on British art but also includes pieces from foreign artists working in Britain and Brits working abroad from 1500 to the present. Of the four Tate Galleries in England, this is the original Tate, opened in 1897 to house Sir Henry Tate's collection of "modern" British art and later expanded to include a gift from famed British painter J.M.W. Turner. Turner's modest donation of 282 oils and 19,000 watercolors can make the museum feel like one big tribute to the man. Skip the prolific collection of hazy British landscapes in the **Clore Galleries** if you don't like his style. Much of the **second floor** houses the permanent collection, loosely tracing the chronology of art in Britain from 1500 to 2004. Three subdivisions, Historic, Modern, and Contemporary, house differently themed rooms such as "Modern Landscapes" and "Art and Victorian Society." These subdivisions also feature the fervent work of William Blake, as well as paintings by Pre-Raphaelites John Everett Millais, John Singer Sargent, and Frederic Lord Leighton. Other artists on display include John Constable, William Hogarth, Richard Long, Ben Nicholson, and David Hockney. Beloved works include Henry Moore's incredible *Recumbent Figure* sculpture and John Singer Sargent's colorful Victorian portraits. The bulk of modern British art is absent, having been transferred to the Tate Modern at Bankside in 1999 (p. 198), but that doesn't mean that what remains here is static or stodgy; one of the most recent exhibitions is an exact recreation of an anti-war protester's demonstration that was removed from Parliament Sq. The annual and always controversial ■ **Turner Prize** for contemporary visual art is still held here, the displays of which are worth a visit. Four contemporary British artists are nominated for the £40,000 prize; their short-listed works go on show from late October through late January. **Late at Tate Britain**, every Friday night, allows visitors an extended look at the museum's holdings. *(Millbank, near Vauxhall Bridge, in Westminster. ⊖Pimlico. Information ☎7887 8008, M-F exhibition booking 7887 8888; www.tate.org.uk. Open daily 10am-5:50pm, last admission 5pm. Wheelchair-accessible via Clore Wing. Free; special exhibitions £7-11. Audio tours free. Free tours: "Art from 1500-1800" 11am, "1800-1900" M-F noon; "Turner" M-F 2pm; "1900-2005" M-F 3pm; "1500-2005" Sa-Su noon, 3pm. Regular events include "Painting of the Month Lectures" (15min.) M 1:15pm and Sa 2:30pm; occasional "Friday Lectures" F 1pm.)*

HIGHLIGHTS IN A HURRY: TATE BRITAIN. Get a taste of Turner and his contemporaries in the second-story **Clore Galleries,** then head over to **Chris Ofili's upper room.** Stop by the second-story rooms dedicated to **John Constable** and experience the joys of prudent restraint in the **Victorian Galleries.** From October through late January, the restraints are cast aside with modern, often controversial art in the **Turner Prize** exhibition.

THE WEST END

MAYFAIR AND ST. JAMES'S

SEE MAP, p. 356

Auction houses and commercial galleries may outnumber museums in the West End, but Mayfair and St. James's is home to some of London's most recognizable art institutions: the National Gallery, its smaller (but just as worth-while) counterpart the National Portrait Gallery, and Christie's auction house. Mayfair is the center of London's art market—and despite its genteel aura, it's not all Old Masters and watercolors. **Cork Street,** running parallel to Old Bond St. between Clifford St. and Burlington Gardens, is lined with dozens of small commercial galleries specializing in contemporary art of all types. The auction houses give insight into what is being bought and sold in the upper-crust art world today.

◼ NATIONAL GALLERY

Main entrance (Portico Entrance) on north side of Trafalgar Sq. ⊖Charing Cross or Leicester Sq. ☎7747 2885; www.nationalgallery.org.uk. Wheelchair-accessible at Sainsbury Wing on Pall Mall East, Orange St., and Getty Entrance. Open M-Tu and Th-Su 10am-6pm, W 10am-9pm. Special exhibitions in the Sainsbury Wing occasionally open until 10pm. Free; some temporary exhibitions £5-10, seniors £4-8, students and ages 12-18 £2-5. 1hr. tours start at Sainsbury Wing information desk. Tours M-F and Su 11:30am and 2:30pm, Sa 11:30am, 12:30, 2:30, 3:30pm. Audio tours free, suggested donation £4. AmEx/MC/V for ticketed events.

The National Gallery was founded by an Act of Parliament in 1824, with 38 pictures displayed in a townhouse. Over the years it has become one of Britain's grandest museums. The Gallery has made numerous additions, the most recent (and controversial) being the massive, modern Sainsbury Wing—Prince Charles described an early version of the design as "a monstrous carbuncle on the face of a much-loved and elegant friend." The Sainsbury Wing holds almost all of the museum's large exhibitions as well as the restaurants and lecture halls. If you're pressed for time, head to **Art Start** in the Sainsbury Wing, where you can design and print out a personalized tour of the paintings you want to see. Themed audio tours and family routes are also available from the information desk.

SAINSBURY WING. The rooms of the gallery's newest extension house its oldest, most fragile paintings, dating from 1260 to 1510. Most of the works on display are reli-

HIGHLIGHTS IN A HURRY: NATIONAL GALLERY. Enter via the Sainsbury Wing. Pop up to **Room 56** on the 2nd fl. for a quick look at *The Arnolfini Portrait* by van Eyck and then head to **Rooms 23 and 24** in the North Wing. See how well Rembrandt aged by comparing his self portraits, then move to **Rooms 2 and 8** in the west wing and take a look at a collection of Renaissance works, including some of Leonardo's and Michelangelo's. Finally, wander through the Impressionist masterpieces in **Rooms 44** and **45.** Van Gogh's *Sunflowers* is a must-see in gloomy weather.

gious ones, with very few exceptions. The most famous of the devotional medieval paintings on display is the *Wilton Diptych*, a 14th-century altarpiece made by an unknown artist for (and featuring) Richard II (Room 53). The comprehensive early Renaissance collection features Botticelli's *Venus and Mars*—an early plea to make love, not war—and Piero della Francesca's ultra-famous *Baptism of Christ* (Rooms 58 and 66). One of the finest of the Sainsbury Wing's offerings, however, is van Eyck's 1434 masterpiece, *The Arnolfini Portrait*, hanging austerely in Room 56.

WEST WING. With paintings from 1510 to 1600, the West Wing is dominated by the Italian **High Renaissance,** both Roman and Venetian, as well as the first flowering of German and Flemish art. As you move through the rooms, the religious motifs give way to domestic and rural themes. Room 2 features one of the museum's most interesting works, the *Leonardo Cartoon*, a detailed preparatory drawing by Leonardo da Vinci for a never-executed painting. Other highlights include Leonardo's second *Virgin on the Rocks* and Parmigianino's nudes. Room 8 includes unfinished works by Michelangelo and a number of works by Raphael. Rooms 9 and 10 focus on northern Italy, with the latter dominated by Titian.

THE AMBASSADORS. While perusing Room 4 in the West Wing, you'll come across Hans Holbein's *The Ambassadors,* a work full of mystery and intrigue. At first glance the painting seems like a normal portrait of two men, until you notice the terribly skewed image of a human skull on the floor. The skull, signifying death, appears normal when viewed from the painting's left side. The various objects and decor surrounding Holbein's subjects have also been said to represent various religious theories and elements of discord. Just don't spend all day in front of the painting trying to decipher its mysteries—you'll miss out on the rest of the gallery!

NORTH WING. The North Wing spans the 17th century, with an exceptional display of Flemish and Spanish Renaissance works spread over 17 rooms. One of the museum's two Vermeers (the other is no longer on display) is one of only 34 in the world. Rooms 23 and 24 feature nine Rembrandts, including his *Self Portrait at the Age of 34* and *Self Portrait at the Age of 63*, painted the year he died. The massive Room 29 is dominated by Rubens's *Massacre of the Innocents* and his *Samson and Delilah*, along with dozens of his other works. Velàzquez's supersensuous and, at the time, highly controversial *The Toilet of Venus* is at odds with the rest of his mostly religious output on show in Room 30. Other Spanish masters Murillo and Zurbaran also have works hanging in the room.

EAST WING. Home to paintings dating from 1700 to 1900, the East Wing is the most crowded, housing the Impressionist galleries. The focus is primarily on Room 45, featuring one of Van Gogh's *Sunflowers*—which he originally hung in the guest room for his good friend Paul Gauguin, whose paintings are displayed nearby. Pissarro's landscapes and Cézanne's *Bathers* also are shown. Room 44 contains a brilliant set of paintings by Seurat as well as works by Manet, Monet, and Renoir. As a reminder that there was art on the English side of the Channel, Rooms 34 and 35 feature portraits by Reynolds and Gainsborough, as well as six luminescent Turners, including the stunning *The Fighting Temeraire.*

NATIONAL PORTRAIT GALLERY

St. Martin's Pl., at the start of Charing Cross Rd., Trafalgar Sq. ⊖Leicester Sq. or Charing Cross. ☎ 7312 2463; www.npg.org.uk. Wheelchair-accessible on Orange St. Open M-W and Sa-Su 10am-6pm, Th-F 10am-9pm. Free; some special exhibitions free, others up to £6. Audio tours £2. Lectures Tu 3pm free, but popular events require tickets, available from the information desk. Some evening talks Th 7pm free, others up to £3. Live music F 6:30pm free.

This artistic Who's Who in Britain began in 1856 and is now the place to see Britain's freshest new artwork as well as centuries-old portraiture. New facilities include the sleek Ondaatje Wing (completed in 2000) an IT Gallery with computers allowing you to search for pictures and print out a personalized tour, and a restaurant on the third floor offering an excellent view of Westminster—although the high prices (meals around £15) will limit most visitors to coffee.

> **HIGHLIGHTS IN A HURRY: NATIONAL PORTRAIT GALLERY.**
> Visit Henry VIII and Queen Elizabeth I in the **Tudor Galleries** before heading downstairs for a glimpse of Charles Dickens and the Brontë Sisters in **Early Victorian Arts.** Stare real royalty in the face at the **Sovereign Gallery,** then pass by pseudo-royalty in the **Balcony Gallery,** which houses portraits of Sir Elton John and Sir Paul McCartney. Put your British pop culture knowledge to the test in the ground fl. **Contemporary Galleries.**

SECOND FLOOR. To see the paintings in historical order, take the escalator from the reception hall in the Ondaatje Wing to the top floor. Pay your respects to Henry VIII in Room 1 and Shakespeare and Queen Elizabeth I in Room 2 before making your way to the Stuarts and Hanoverians. *Pride and Prejudice* enthusiasts should stop off in Room 18 and see the only known portrait of Jane Austen, not much bigger than a playing card, as well as portraits of the Romantics including Wordsworth, Coleridge, Byron, Keats, and others.

FIRST FLOOR. Explore the early Victorian arts in Room 24, including portraits of both Charles Dickens and all three Brontë sisters. The Brontës' portrait—crease lines and all—was discovered folded up on top of a dusty cupboard. The **Balcony Gallery** holds some of the gallery's most fun (and irreverent) works, including Andy Warhol's portrait of Elizabeth II and Sam Walsh's painting of Paul McCartney, jokingly titled *Mike's Brother*—Sam was friends with the slightly less-famous Mike McCartney.

GROUND FLOOR. Check out contemporary works in the 1990-present gallery, which boasts work by the young British artist Sam Taylor Wood and Turner Prize winners Gilbert & George. Enjoy their revealing self-portrait *In the Piss.*

OTHER MAYFAIR AND ST. JAMES'S MUSEUMS

■ **ROYAL ACADEMY OF ARTS.** Founded in 1768 with King George III's patronage, the Academy was designed to cultivate sculpture, painting, and architecture. Today the Academy shares courtyard space with the Royal Societies of Geology, Chemistry, Antiquaries, and Astronomy. The academics in charge are all accomplished artists or architects. The Summer Exhibition (June-Aug.), held every year since 1769, is open to any artist for submissions, providing an unparalleled range of contemporary art in every medium, much of which is available for purchase. On Friday nights, the museum stays open late with free jazz in the Friends Room after 6:30pm and candlelit suppers in the cafe. *(Burlington House, Piccadilly. ⊖Piccadilly Cir-*

cus or Green Park. ☎ *7300 8000; www.royalacademy.org.uk. Open M-Th and Sa-Su 10am-6pm, F 10am-10pm. Wheelchair-accessible. Free. Exhibits in the Main Galleries £7, students £5.)*

MAYFAIR AND ST. JAMES'S GALLERIES

INSTITUTE OF CONTEMPORARY ARTS (ICA). Housed in the grand Carlton House Terrace, the ICA is London's center for avant-garde art and hip contemporary artists. The artwork in the ICA does not shy away from the controversial, and showcases explorations of many contemporary issues. The ICA has a large ground-level and small upstairs gallery for temporary exhibits, an avant-garde cinema, a theatre, a trendy cafe, and a relaxed bar that hosts frequent club nights and gigs. *(The Mall.* ➌*Charing Cross or Piccadilly Circus* ☎ *7930 0493; www.ica.org.uk. Galleries open M-W and F-Su noon-7:30pm, Th noon-9pm. Cafe and bar open M noon-11pm, Tu-Sa noon-1am, Su noon-10:30pm. "Day membership," giving access to galleries, cafe, and bar M-F £2, concessions £1.50, Sa-Su £3, concessions £2. Cinema £8, M-F before 5pm £7; concessions £7/6.)*

> **ART FOR POCKET CHANGE.** The galleries and auction houses in May-fair and Soho are often free and showcase museum-quality work from famous artists—but without the lines you'll find at the big museums.

MAYFAIR AND ST. JAMES'S AUCTION HOUSES

CHRISTIE'S. Like a museum but more crowded and all for sale, Christie's is the best of the auction houses. The public can enter on days before an auction to peruse what's up for grabs. Lots range from busts of Greek gods to Monets to sports memorabilia. *(8 King St.* ➌*Green Park. There is a smaller branch at 85 Old Brompton St. in Kensington.* ☎ *7839 9060; www.christies.com. Open M-F 9am-5pm; call in advance for exact timings. Public viewings can close early for evening auctions. Wheelchair-accessible. Free. Catalogues from £10.)*

SOTHEBY'S. Before each auction, the items to be sold are displayed for viewing in the many interlocking galleries. Aristocratic Sotheby's is a busy place; auctions occur within days of each other. Each sale is accompanied by a glossy catalog (from £10); old catalogs are usually cheaper. *(34-35 New Bond St.* ➌*Bond St.* ☎ *7293 5000; www.sothebys.com. Open for viewing M-F 9am-4:30pm, Sa and occasional Su noon-4pm, call in advance for exact hours. Public viewings can close early for evening auctions. Wheelchair-accessible. Free.)*

GAGOSIAN GALLERY. A branch of the famed New York Gagosian, this gallery holds solo shows of famous artists like Willem de Kooning, Cy Twombly, and Jeff Koons. Sparse and spacious, the gallery space is completely visible from the street and contributes to an exciting stroll through Mayfair. It showcases contemporary and avant-garde art of every variety and material. Shows change monthly or every two months. *(17-19 Davies St.* ➌*Hyde Park Corner or Marble Arch.* ☎ *7493 3025; www.gagosian.com. Open Tu-Sa 10am-6pm. Free.)*

TIMOTHY TAYLOR GALLERY. Features exhibits based on individual artists or on common media or subjects. It recently brought in the largest collection of Andy Warhol's early drawings ever shown in Britain. *(21 Dering St./* ➌*Oxford Circus or Bond Street.* ☎ *7409 3344; www.timothytaylorgallery.com. Open M-F 10am-6pm, Sa 10am-1pm. Wheelchair-accessible. Free.)*

MARLBOROUGH FINE ARTS. This spacious gallery presents a variety of contemporary artists, including anything from sketches to mixed media, Lucian Freud to Frank Auerbach. *(6 Albermarle St.* ➌*Green Park.* ☎ *7629 5161; www.marlborough-finearts.com. Open M-F 10am-5:30pm, Sa 10am-12:30pm. Wheelchair-accessible. Free.)*

ROBERT SANDELSON. This small gallery, spread out over two floors, contains exhibits of big-time modern and contemporary artists like Damien Hirst, Tamara de Lempicka, Sam Francis, and Howard Hodgkin. (*5a Cork St.* ⊖*Bond St. or Green Park.* ☎ *7439 1001; www.robertsandelson.com. Open M-F 10am-6pm, Sa 11am-4pm. Free.*)

COVENT GARDEN AND THE STRAND

Covent Garden's museums are largely interactive, so get ready to get hands-on. You may be used to introspectively browsing fine art by now, but this is your chance to have a little fun.

LONDON'S TRANSPORT MUSEUM. From tram to Tube, learn about the glory and virtue of public transportation through mostly kid-oriented exhibits. Adults, too, will be engrossed by artifacts of the development of London's public transportation system over the last 200 years, including the earliest Tube maps and exhibits tracing London's growth as a metropolis. Actual antique and modern carriages, trams, buses, trains, and Tube cars invite curious little climbers. Wax models mine the coal that powered the first trams, and wax bus drivers collect passengers' "fare." Most of the interactive displays are conveniently located at kiddy level. The "Fast Forward" display explores the future of transport, from Sci-Fi hovercars to teleportation. (*Southeast corner of Covent Garden Piazza.* ⊖*Covent Garden.* ☎ *7565 7299; www.ltmuseum.co.uk. Open M-Th and Sa-Su 10am-6pm, F 11am-6pm; last admission 5:15pm. Wheelchair-accessible. £6, concessions £4.50, children under 16 free with adult.*)

BENJAMIN FRANKLIN HOUSE. Although this residence of American founding father Benjamin Franklin might be of great historical and archaeological importance, it does not provide its due for inquisitive tourists. The home is the stage for a "Historical Experience Tour" with short clips shown in the mostly empty home detailing the major events of Franklin's time in London as a representative from the American colonies. These short clips, though, are really all the tour has to offer and at the end of its 45min., you'll likely be left wanting more. (*36 Craven St.* ⊖*Charing Cross or Embankment.* ☎ *7839 2006; www.benjaminfranklinhouse.org. Open W-Su noon-5pm with tours at noon, 1, 2, 3:15, 4:15pm. £7.*)

COVENT GARDEN AND THE STRAND GALLERIES

▧ THE PHOTOGRAPHERS' GALLERY. This is one of London's only public galleries devoted entirely to photography. One large exhibit and one or two smaller ones run concurrently at the larger location (No. 5), which also boasts a cafe. Displays usually feature a single artist's work, ranging from classic landscape to socially conscious photography. The gallery and small bookshop at No. 8 house an equally exemplary show and also have a good selection of photographic monologues. Frequent gallery talks, book readings, and film screenings are free; occasional photographers' talks may charge admission. (*5 and 8 Great Newport St.* ⊖*Leicester Sq. or Covent Garden.* ☎ *7831 1772; www.photonet.org.uk. Open M-W and F-Sa 11am-6pm, Th 11am-8pm, Su noon-6pm. Free.*)

BLOOMSBURY

Bloomsbury is an ideal resting spot for national collections and small galleries. Students who are in a museum are probably there to read or write a paper, so abide by museum etiquette (unless, of course, you are in the Pollock's Toy Museum). Although it is one of the loveliest neighborhoods in London, with its bounty of squares and quiet side streets, Bloomsbury's allure is almost exclusively due to the British Museum; expect crowds.

SEE MAP, p. 362

▧ BRITISH MUSEUM

Great Russell St. ⊖*Tottenham Court Rd., Russell Sq., or Holborn.* ☎ *7323 8299; www.thebritishmuseum.ac.uk. Great Court open M-W and Su 9am-6pm, Th-Sa 9am-11pm*

(9pm in winter); galleries open daily 10am-5:30pm, selected galleries open Th-F 10am-8:30pm. Free 30-40min. tours daily starting at 11am from the Enlightenment Desk. "Highlights Tour" daily 10:30am, 1, 3pm; advanced booking recommended. Wheelchair-accessible. Free; £3 suggested donation. Temporary exhibitions around £5, concessions £3.50. "Highlights Tour" £8, concessions £5. Audio tours £3.50, family audio tours for 2 adults and up to 3 children £10. MC/V.

The funny thing about the British Museum is that there's almost nothing British in it. The museum was founded in 1753 as the personal collection of Sir Hans Sloane. Work started on the current Neoclassical building in 1824, which ultimately took another 30 years to construct. The museum juxtaposes Victorian Anglocentrism with a more modern, multicultural acceptance. The building itself is magnificent, and a leisurely stroll through the less frequented galleries is well worth an afternoon visit. The many visitors who don't make it past the main floor miss out—the galleries upstairs and downstairs are some of the museum's best, if not the most famous.

 HIGHLIGHTS IN A HURRY: BRITISH MUSEUM. Gape at the grandness of the **Great Court,** then hit the closely packed stars of the **Egypt/Greece** wings (Rosetta Stone, Elgin Marbles). Take more time in the quieter **African** and **Islamic** galleries in the north wing. Head upstairs for actual British artifacts and for the **Clock Gallery.** If you plan on spending the day in the museum, bring a book to the **Enlightenment Gallery** or the **Reading Room.**

GREAT COURT. This is the largest covered square in Europe. Used as the British Library stacks for the past 150 years, the courtyard is still dominated by a gigantic **Reading Room.** The blue chairs and desks, set inside a towering dome of books, have shouldered the weight of research by Marx, Lenin, and Trotsky, as well as almost every major British writer and intellectual. Remember to respect the readers in the room with quiet.

WEST GALLERIES. From the main entrance, the large double doors to the left of the Reading Room lead to the Museum's most popular wing. The star of the **Egyptian Sculpture** rooms is the **Rosetta Stone.** Less iconic but enduringly huge are the monumental friezes and reliefs of the Assyrian, Hittite, and other **Ancient Near Eastern** civilizations. Most famous (and controversial) of the massive array of **Greek sculpture** on show are the **Elgin Marbles** from the Parthenon, statues carved under the direction of Athens's greatest sculptor, Phidias (Room 18). The Greek government has been asking for the Marbles back for years, but to no avail—technically, the British government bought the Marbles (although for a measly price). Other Hellenic highlights include remnants of two of the seven Wonders of the Ancient World, the **Temple of Artemis** at Ephesus and the **Mausoleum of Halikarnassos** (Rooms 21-22). Upstairs, the **Portland Vase** presides over Roman ceramics and housewares (Room 70). When discovered in 1582, the vase had already been broken and reconstructed. In 1845, it was shattered by a drunk museum-goer. When it was put back together, 37 small chips were left over. Since then, the vase has been reconstructed twice, with more leftover chips being reincorporated each time.

NORTH GALLERIES. More Egyptian sarcophagi and mummies await you in Rooms 61-66 of the North Galleries. The newer **African Galleries** are perhaps the best presented in the museum, with a fabulous collection accompanied by soft chanting, video displays, and abundant documentation (Room 25, lower floor). More overflow from the west wing continues the Near Eastern theme. Musical instruments and board games from the world's first city, **Ur,** show that leisure time is a historical constant (Rooms 51-59). Nearby, the **Americas** collection is dominated by **Mexico,** featuring extraordinary Aztec artifacts (Rooms 26-27). Just off the Montague

Place entrance is a collection of **Islamic** art (Room 34). Immediately above it, the largest room in the museum is dedicated to **China, South Asia,** and **Southeast Asia,** with some particularly impressive Hindu sculpture (Room 33). Upstairs, the highlight of the **Korean** display is a *sarangbang* house built on-site (Room 67). A tea house, meanwhile, is the centerpiece of the **Japanese** galleries (Rooms 92-94).

SOUTH AND EAST GALLERIES. The King's Library gallery holds artifacts gathered from throughout the world by English explorers during the **Enlightenment.** While the labeling is poor (and in some places non-existent), the collection itself is spectacular. The upper level of the museum's southeast corner is dedicated to ancient and medieval Europe, including most of the museum's British artifacts. A highlight of the collection is the treasure excavated from the **Sutton Hoo Burial Ship;** the magnificent inlaid helmet is the most famous example of Anglo-Saxon craftsmanship. Along with the ship is the **Mildenhall Treasure,** a trove of brilliantly preserved Roman artifacts (Room 41). Next door are the enigmatic and beautiful **Lewis Chessmen,** an 800-year-old Scandinavian chess set mysteriously abandoned on Scotland's Outer Hebrides (Room 42). Collectors and enthusiasts will also enjoy the comprehensive **Clock Gallery** (Room 44) and **Money Gallery** (Room 68).

OTHER BLOOMSBURY MUSEUMS

▧ BRITISH LIBRARY GALLERIES. Housed within the British Library (p. 179) is an appropriately stunning display of books, manuscripts, and related artifacts from around the world and throughout the ages. Displays are arranged by theme, and a rundown of highlights reads like some fantastic list of the most precious pages in history. The **Literature Corner** includes Shakespeare's first folio, as well as Lewis Carroll's handwritten first copy of *Alice in Wonderland,* personally donated by the author's young muse. The *Lindisfarne Gospels,* history's best-surviving Anglo-Saxon gospel and, perhaps, the most beautiful item on display, is part of the **Illuminated Manuscripts** section. **Music** showcases handwritten treats, from Handel's *Messiah* to an entire area devoted to the Beatles. Check out the original copy of the Magna Carta in **Historical Documents,** the fascinating pages of Leonardo da Vinci's notebook in **Science,** and the 4th-century Codex Sinaiticus in Bibles—the earliest manuscript of the complete New Testament. Witness the **Dawn of Printing,** European-style, with one of 50 known original Gutenberg Bibles (1454), then see how Eastern printers had perfected the technique 700 years earlier on the **Million Charms of Empress Shôtoku.** In **Sacred Texts,** go for Sultan Baybar's ornate 1304 Qur'an. Throughout the gallery, sound archive jukeboxes allow visitors to hear snippets of the texts and music on display, and to the rear of the exhibition, the **Turning the Page** computer enables anyone to (electronically) peruse the ancient tomes. Downstairs, the **Workshop of Sounds and Images** is aimed at a younger audience, with interactive displays charting the history of recording, from parchment to TV. *(96 Euston Rd. ↔ King's Cross St. Pancras. ☎ 7412 7332; www.bl.uk. Grab a free map at the main info desk. Open M and W-F 9:30am-6pm, Tu 9:30am-8pm, Sa 9:30am-5pm, Su 11am-5pm. Wheelchair-accessible. Free. Audio tours £3.50, concessions £2.50.)*

POLLOCK'S TOY MUSEUM. A maze of tiny rooms and passageways, the museum is congested with antique playthings of high kitsch value. It's neither comprehensive nor remotely interactive, but the atmosphere of old-time creakiness goes well with the glass-framed treasures on display. Highlights include the oldest known teddy bear ("Eric," born 1905), "Saucy Frauleins" who expose themselves at the tug of a string, and a room of elaborately furnished dollhouses. None of the toys on display can be touched, limiting the museum's appeal for children; however, curious grown-ups will appreciate the detailed labels and informative asides. It all leads back to Pollock's own old-fashioned toy shop by the entrance, with traditional playthings at good prices. *(1 Scala St., entrance on Whitfield St.* ⊖*Goodge St.* ☎ *7636 3452; www.pollockstoymuseum.com. Open M-Sa 10am-5pm; last admission 4:30pm. £3, concessions £2, children under 18 £1.50. AmEx/MC/V.)*

PERCIVAL DAVID FOUNDATION OF CHINESE ART. Heaven for lovers of Chinese porcelain; not worth the trip for others. This Georgian townhouse, part of the School of Oriental and African Studies (SOAS), boasts the finest collection of china outside of, well, China. On the ground floor, temporary exhibits, often including pieces from the 1700-item collection, illustrate trends and themes in Chinese art. The first floor houses superb early examples of imperial porcelain, including 13 pieces of extremely rare Ru wares collected by Sir Percival himself. The second floor features later examples of blue-and-white Ming and painted Qing work. *(53 Gordon Sq.* ⊖*Euston Sq. or Euston.* ☎ *7387 3909; www.pdfmuseum.org.uk. Open M-F 10am-12:30pm and 1:30-5pm. Wheelchair-accessible with 24hr. notice. Free.)*

BLOOMSBURY GALLERIES

BRUNEI GALLERY. Also affiliated with the SOAS, this beautiful three-story space is devoted to carefully and elaborately crafted exhibitions of African and Asian art and culture. Since its patron is the Sultan of Brunei, you'd expect nothing less. "Secrets of the River," an exhibit on the architectural site Sungai Limau Manis, will run from January through March 2008. April through June 2008 brings the "Illustrated Book in China" to the Gallery. "Retracing Heinrich Barth," based on Barth's travels and discoveries in North and Central Africa from 1849-55, will run from July through September 2008. Finally, the year will finish with "Keepers of the Fire," an exhibit on the story of Parsis, the Zorastrians of India, running from October through December 2008. *(10 Thornhaugh St., opposite the main SOAS entrance.* ⊖*Russell Sq.* ☎ *7898 4915; www.soas.ac.uk/gallery. Open Tu-Sa 10:30am-5pm when exhibits are running; visit website or call for schedule. Wheelchair-accessible. Group tours can be arranged on request. Free.)*

NORTH LONDON

North London's small collection of museums is diverse in their subject matter, and even though many tourists stay away, the savvy traveler will enjoy exploring the many hidden treasures, from RAF fighters to Rembrandts.

CAMDEN TOWN, KING'S CROSS, AND ISLINGTON

ROYAL AIR FORCE MUSEUM. Though a bit out of the way, the RAF Museum will delight plane fans and awe everyone else. This enormous museum contains three huge hangars, featuring planes from the first plane built in Europe to 1980s Harriers. Details of each plane's combat missions add to the realism. Galleries are divided into jets, fighter planes, helicopters, bombers, and aquatic machines. Torpedoes, engines, and missiles are on display, too. Complementing the planes are portraits, timelines, medallions, and memorabilia. "Our Finest Hour," a 15min. laser light show on the hour, is only worth it if there is no wait. *(Grahame Park Way. 10min. walk from* ⊖*Colindale (Zone 4); follow signs. Bus #303 goes from the station right to the museum's door.* ☎ *8205 2266; www.rafmuseum.org. Open daily 10am-6pm; last admission 5:30pm. Free 30min. tours throughout the day. Partially wheelchair-accessible. Free.)*

ESTORICK COLLECTION. This collection, started by an American sociologist who loved Italian art, focuses on lesser-known **Futurist art.** The Futurists' bizarre manifesto included destroying old buildings, abolishing museums (go figure), reinventing food (recipes included sausage cooked in black coffee and perfume), and making the universe affordable for everyone. Ninety years after their heyday, their paintings, drawings, etchings, and sculptures are tastefully displayed in an 18th-century Georgian mansion beside a secluded courtyard cafe that serves great food. There are also works from the Metaphysical school. Temporary exhibits change about every three months and have included works by Marcello Levi and Italian photographers. *(39a Canonbury Sq. ⊖Highbury and Islington. ☎ 7704 9522; www.estorickcollection.com. Open W-Sa 11am-6pm, Su noon-5pm. Partially wheelchair-accessible. £3.50, concessions £2.50, students and children under 16 free.)*

THE JEWISH MUSEUM. The Jewish Museum is actually composed of two complementary museums with different focuses. The first, **Camden,** focuses on the history of Jews in Britain, including a torah with the coat of arms of the first Jewish MP. The upstairs gallery houses regalia and artifacts relating to Jewish festivals and holidays. The Camden's crowning achievement is a magnificent 16th-century Venetian synagogue ark discovered by accident while being used as a lord's wardrobe. Special programs are offered, including workshops for children to learn about Jewish holidays and genealogy workshops. *(129-131 Albert St. ⊖Camden Town. ☎ 7284 1997; www.jewishmuseum.org.uk. Open M-Th 10am-4pm, Su 10am-5pm; last admission 30min. prior to close; closed Jewish holidays. Wheelchair-accessible. £3.50, seniors £2.50, students and children £1.50, families £8.)* The smaller Jewish Museum, **Finchley,** focuses on Jewish social history and 19th- and early 20th-century life in London's East End. The small Holocaust Education gallery is particularly moving, detailing the life of London-born Auschwitz survivor Leon Greenman. *(80 East End Rd. 10min. walk from Finchley Central (Zone 4); take the "Regent's Park Rd." Exit from the Tube, turn left on Station Rd., and then right on Manor View, which runs into East End Rd. by the museum. ☎ 8349 1143. Open M-Th 10:30am-5pm, Su 10:30am-4:30pm; closed Su in Aug. and Jewish holidays. Partially wheelchair-accessible. £2, children free.)*

> **TIP** **DON'T ZONE OUT.** When traveling to Islington, remember that ⊖Angel lies within Zone 1, while ⊖Highbury and Islington is in Zone 2. If your destination is anywhere near Upper St., it would be more sensible to save the extra fare price, do a bit of walking, and spend the money on a coffee instead.

ST. JOHN'S WOOD AND MAIDA VALE

FREUD MUSEUM. The comfortable home in which Sigmund Freud spent the last year of his life after fleeing the Nazis packs a bit more of a punch than most celebrity houses. In his later years, Freud delved into cultural analysis, evidenced by the anthropological collection of masks and random artifacts. He didn't drop his patients, however, and the infamous Persian rug-covered couch in his dark study stands ready for the next session. Upstairs hangs Dalí's cranially exaggerated portrait of Freud alongside the room of Anna Freud, Sigmund's youngest daughter, who was an eminent psychoanalyst in her own right. *(20 Maresfield Gardens. ⊖Swiss Cottage or ⊖Finchley Rd. ☎ 7435 2002; www.freud.org.uk. Open W-Su noon-5pm. Wheelchair-accessible. £5, concessions £3, children under 12 free.)*

HAMPSTEAD, HIGHGATE, AND GOLDERS GREEN

 THE IVEAGH BEQUEST. The impressive Iveagh collection in Kenwood House was bequeathed to the nation by the Earl of Iveagh, who purchased the estate in 1922. Everything on the estate is a work of art, from the ponds and paths to the rooms in the house, especially the library. A free booklet guides you through highlights including *The Guitar Player*—one of 35 known Vermeers in the world—Rembrandt's compelling self-portraits, and a beautiful Botticelli. Georgian society portraits by Reynolds, Gainsborough, Hogarth, and Romney fill the walls with faces of people who look as though they might have called Kenwood home. *(Kenwood House. Road access from Hampstead Ln. Walk or take Bus #210 from North End Way or Spaniards Rd. or from ⊖Archway or Golders Green. ☎ 8348 1286. Wheelchair-accessible. Open daily Apr.-Oct. 11am-5pm.; Nov.-Mar. 11am-4pm. Free.)*

MARYLEBONE AND REGENT'S PARK

Marylebone's museums, like its sights, display the best and the worst of London attractions: the classic and classy Wallace Collection as well as the cheesy Sherlock Holmes Museum.

SEE MAP, p. 369

■ **THE WALLACE COLLECTION.** Housed in palatial Hertford House, this stunning array of paintings, porcelain, and armor was bequeathed to the nation by the widow of Sir Richard Wallace in 1897. The impressive collection is rendered even more dazzling by its grand, gilded setting; the mansion has been restored to much of its 19th-century glory. Two minor drawbacks: poor labeling requires some sifting through long information sheets to learn more about a piece, and rotating gallery closings mean that you might miss out on what you came to see (call in advance). However, excellent daily gallery tours will ensure that you see a good overview of the collection. On the ground floor, the most popular display is just through the gift shop: four **Armoury Galleries** threaten and enthrall visitors with scads of richly decorated weapons and burnished suits of armor. Don't miss the imposing 15th-century German Gothic horse model, with a complete, terrifying suit of armor for horse and rider. Through the hall, the **Front State Room** retains its original appearance, with sumptuous furnishings and society portraits, and china buffs will swoon at the collection of Sèvres porcelain in the **Back State Room** next door. Italian and Flemish works dominate the 16th-century **Galleries** and **Smoking Room.** The first floor is home to a world-renowned array of 18th-century French art, announced on the staircase by Boucher's works, including the *Rising and Setting of the Sun*, all billowing clouds and trembling pink flesh. More Bouchers accompany Fragonards and Watteaus in the **West Room** and **West Gallery.** The **Small Drawing Room** displays a series of Venice views by Canaletto and Guardi. The **Great Gallery,** once called "the greatest picture gallery in Europe" by Lord Clark, has a varied collection of 17th-century work, with scenes by Van Dyck, Rembrandt, Rubens, and Velázquez, as well as the collection's most celebrated piece, Frans Hals's *Laughing Cavalier.* Hungry art appreciators can plop down in the swanky, gorgeous sculpture-garden restaurant **Café Bagatelle.** *(Hertford House, Manchester Sq. ⊖Bond St. or Marble Arch. ☎ 7563 9500; www.wallacecollection.org. Open daily 9am-5pm. Wheelchair-accessible. 1 hr. tours M-Tu and Th-F 1pm; W and Sa 11:30am, 1, 3pm; Su 1, 3pm; free. Talks M-F 1pm and occasional Sa 11:30am; free. Admission free (£2 suggested donation). Audio tours £3. Cafe: mains £12.50-18; call for reservations ☎ 7563 9505.)*

SHERLOCK HOLMES MUSEUM. Four floors of accurate decor culled meticulously from Sir Arthur Conan Doyle's literary descriptions, this museum claims to be the real 19th-century residence of fictional characters Sherlock Holmes and Dr. Watson. Fans unafraid of the corny may find it worth the six quid for a photo op in Mr. Holmes's cap. *(239 Baker St. ⊖Baker St. ☎ 7935 8866; www.sherlock-holmes.co.uk. Open daily 9:30am-6pm. £6, children 7-16 £4.)*

KENSINGTON AND EARL'S COURT

South Kensington's "Albertopolis" is home to three of London's biggest and best museums: the Victoria and Albert Museum, the Natural History Museum, and the Science Museum. While it's tempting to try and "do" them in a day, visiting more than two is a feat of superhuman stamina (not to mention a waste of at least one perfectly good museum). A traveling note: while most people just take the sign-posted "Subway" feeder tunnels from the Tube to the museums, it's just as quick (and far more pleasant in good weather) to use the above-ground route.

SEE MAP, pp. 366-367

▓ VICTORIA AND ALBERT MUSEUM

Main entrance on Cromwell Rd., wheelchair-accessible entrance on Exhibition Rd. ♻*South Kensington.* ☎ *7942 2000; www.vam.ac.uk. Open M-Th and Sa-Su 10am-5:45pm, F 10am-10pm. Wheelchair-accessible. Free tours meet at rear of main entrance. Introductory tours daily 10:30, 11:30am, 1:30, 3:30pm, plus W 4:30pm. British gallery tours daily 12:30 and 2:30pm. Subjects change regularly. Talks and events meet at rear of main entrance. Free gallery talks Th 1pm and Su 3pm, 45-60min. Admission free; additional charge for some special exhibits.*

When the V&A was founded in 1852 as the Museum of Manufactures, the curators were deluged with objects from around the globe. Today, as the largest museum of decorative (and not so decorative) arts in the world, the V&A rivals the British Museum for the sheer size and diversity of its holdings—befitting an institution dedicated to displaying "the fine and applied arts of all countries, all styles, all periods." Unlike the British Museum, the V&A's documentation is consistently excellent and thorough. Its five million sq. m of galleries house the "world's greatest collection" of miniature portraits, including Holbein's *Anne of Cleves;* newly refurbished glass and architecture galleries; and an exhaustive showcase of fashion from the 16th century through today. Interactive displays, high-tech touchpoints, and engaging activities ensure that the goodies won't become boring. Staff shortages can lead to the temporary closure of less popular galleries without notice; it's best to call in advance on the day of your visit if you want to see a specific gallery. Themed itineraries available at the desk can help streamline your visit, and **Family Trail** cards suggest routes through the museum with kids.

 HIGHLIGHTS IN A HURRY: VICTORIA AND ALBERT MUSEUM. Make a tour of the **Fashion Gallery** before heading over to see **Tippoo's Tiger,** the **Cast Courts,** and the collection of **Oriental Rugs.** Finish up with a trip through the **20th-Century** galleries or go further back in time in the **British Galleries.**

BRITISH GALLERIES. The subject of a £31 million refit, the vast British Galleries sprawl over three floors of reconstructed rooms documenting the progression of British taste and fashion from 1500 to 1900. From clothing to furniture to innumerable fascinating gadgets, exhibits all begin with the question "Who led taste?" (The answer, of course, is always British.)

FASHION GALLERY. Don't expect to find everyday clothing in the V&A's world-famous costume collection: nothing but the finest resides in this gallery. Men's suits and women's gowns are displayed on mannequins, with panels describing the major designers of the 20th century, from Jean-Paul Gaultier (French) to Issey Miyake (Japanese).

ASIAN GALLERIES. If the choice of objects in the V&A's Asian collections seems to rely on national clichés (Indian temple carvings, Chinese porcelain), the objects themselves are still spectacular. The choice piece here is **Tippoo's Tiger,** a graphically fascinating 1799 model of a tiger eating a man—complete with organ sounds and crunching noises. In addition to the requisite swords, armor, and paintings, the excellent **Japanese Gallery** displays an array of contemporary ceramic sculpture and kimonos.

UPPER FLOORS. The upper levels are arranged by material, with specialist galleries devoted to everything from musical instruments to stained glass. In the **textile** collection, where you can try on kimonos and tweed jackets, long cabinets contain swatches of thousands of different fabrics. Two exceptions to the materially themed galleries are the **Leighton Gallery,** with a fresco by the essential Victorian painter, and the sprawling **20th-Century** collections, a trippy highlight. Here, arranged by period and style, are illustration and design classics from Salvador Dalí's 1936 sofa modeled on Mae West's lips to a pair of 1990s latex hotpants.

HENRY COLE WING. The six-level Henry Cole wing is home to the V&A's collection of **British paintings,** including some 350 works by Constable and numerous Turners. Also here is a display of Rodin bronzes, donated by the artist in 1914. In the library-like **print room,** anyone can ask to see original works from the prodigious collection. *(Print room open Tu-Sa 10am-5pm.)*

OTHER KENSINGTON AND EARL'S COURT MUSEUMS

■ SCIENCE MUSEUM. Dedicated to the Victorian ideal of progress, the Science Museum focuses on the transformative power of technology in all its guises. There's something for everyone in this mix of state-of-the-art interactive displays and priceless historical artifacts. The gigantic **Making of the Modern World** entrance hall houses a collection of pioneering contraptions, including the Apollo 10 command module. To continue indulging your inner inventor, head down to the basement for the **Secret Life of the Home,** showcasing 100 years of household gadgets, including Sir Thomas Crapper's famed "valveless waste preventer" and a 1970s VCR the size of a large microwave. Then head to the newer **Welcome Wing** at the back, six stories of beeping, buzzing, futuristic diversions. It begins with the basement Launch Pad, a hands-on introduction to do-it-yourself science—communicate across the room using giant sound dishes, try building an arch, or solve the "hangover problem." The first floor offers **"Who am I?,"** a series of (potentially demoralizing) games and tests that lets you figure out how smart, attractive, successful, and happy you are. The third-floor **Flight Gallery** tells the story of air travel from Victorian attempts at steam-powered flight to modern jumbo jets, assisted by a supporting cast of dozens of airplanes and the interactive Flight Lab. Children will love the **Exploring Space** exhibit on the ground floor. **Science and Art of Medicine,** on the top floor, chronicles in impressive detail the history of medicine in its modern and cross-cultural incarnations. Alternatively, forsake modern medicine and take a **SimEx** simulator ride through Dino Island. *(Exhibition Rd. ❺South Kensington. ☎08708 704 868, IMAX 08708 704 771; www.sciencemuseum.org.uk. Open daily 10am-6pm; closed Dec. 24-26. Wheelchair-accessible. Free. Audio tours: "Soundbytes" cover Power, Space, and Making the Modern World; £3.50 each. IMAX shows usually daily every 1¼hr., 10:45am-5pm; £7.50, concessions £6. Call to confirm showtimes and for bookings. Online booking available. Daily demonstrations and workshops in the basement galleries and theatre. SimEx £4, concessions £3. MC/V.)*

 HIGHLIGHTS IN A HURRY: SCIENCE MUSEUM. Breeze through the entrance hall on your way to the **Welcome Wing.** Enjoy "**Who am I?,**" shoot up to the **Flight Lab,** and then check out the **Science of Art and Medicine.** With time to spare, discover the **Secret Life of the Home.**

■ NATURAL HISTORY MUSEUM. Architecturally the most impressive of the South Kensington trio, this cathedral-like Romanesque museum has been a favorite with Londoners since 1880. The entrance hall is dedicated to the **Wonders of the Natural History Museum,** a series of prehistorically important skeletons including a Diplodocus and a moa (a giant, flightless bird once native to New Zealand, extinct since the early 16th century). The **Dinosaur Galleries** will not disappoint the Jurassic Park generation: the animatronic T-rex is so popular that he's secured an exhibit entirely for himself. Don't miss the spine-chilling fun of **Creepy Crawlies,** with vomiting fly models right alongside a live webcast of the museum's ant colony.

The enormous **Human Biology** exhibit keeps adults and children busy with an endless succession of interactive and high-tech displays, not to mention an extremely detailed reproduction gallery. The adjacent stuffed and mounted **bird, reptile, and mammal** exhibits are decidedly less engaging, but the massive blue whale suspended from the ceiling is an uncontested crowd favorite. The **Origin of Species** display on the first floor offers a detailed explanation of evolution, from Darwin's finches to genetic engineering.

Less comprehensive but a bit more dynamic, the **Earth Galleries** are reached via a long escalator that journeys through the center of a model Earth on its way to **The Power Within,** an exposition of the awesome volcanic and tectonic forces beneath our planet's surface. A walk-through model of a Japanese supermarket provides a recreation of the 1995 Kobe earthquake, and, on the same floor, **Restless Surface** explores the gentler action of wind and water in reshaping the world. The history of the Earth itself, from the Big Bang to the ways humans have shaped the environment, is the subject of **From the Beginning,** located on the first floor. The **Earth's Treasury** presents an enormous array of minerals, from sandstone to diamonds. *(Cromwell Rd. ⊖South Kensington. ☎7942 5000; www.nhm.ac.uk. Open daily 10am-5:50pm; last admission 5:30pm. Closed Dec. 24-26. Wheelchair-accessible. Free; special exhibits usually £7, concessions £4.50. MC/V.)*

> **HIGHLIGHTS IN A HURRY: NATURAL HISTORY MUSEUM.**
> Shudder from **Creepy Crawlies** to the **Dinosaur** galleries, making sure to swing by the **blue whale** at some point. Then gape at the gems in the **Earth's Treasury** on your way to the **Kobe earthquake** upstairs.

SERPENTINE GALLERY. This tiny 1934 tea pavilion in the middle of Kensington Gardens is the unlikely venue for some of London's top contemporary art shows. Summer nights in the park also include architecture talks, live readings, and open-air film screenings. *(Off West Carriage Dr., Kensington Gardens ⊖South Kensington or Lancaster Gate. ☎7402 6075; www.serpentinegallery.org. Open daily 10am-6pm. Wheelchair-accessible. Free.)*

CHELSEA

Chelsea is more of a fresh, avant-garde neighborhood than a historic museum destination. That being said, there is one museum in Chelsea with an intriguing collection: those interested in the military may not initially think to visit Chelsea, but the National Army Museum is worth checking out.

SEE MAP, p. 363

NATIONAL ARMY MUSEUM. With weapons pointing at visitors around every turn, the museum has five floors of militaristic mayhem. Starting with the Battle of Agincourt in 1415 and ending with "The Modern Army," the chronological displays feature life-size recreations, videos, and memorabilia of combat through the ages. The wax figures occasionally border on the ridiculous, but engaging interactive opportunities abound; you can feel the weight of a cannonball or hopscotch through the progression of a battle. Naturally, there's also a permanent Waterloo display, complete with the skeleton of Napoleon's favorite horse, Marengo. *(Royal Hospital Rd. ⊖Sloane Sq., then Bus #137 or 360. ☎7881 2455; www.national-army-museum.ac.uk. Open daily 10am-5:30pm. Wheelchair-accessible. Free.)*

SAATCHI GALLERY. London's leading gallery for contemporary art moved to a new location in November 2007. Along with its renowned collection and always-fresh exhibits, the new building includes a bookshop and a cafe. *(⊖Sloane Sq. www.saatchi-gallery.co.uk. Check website for hours and information.)*

RSC in
LONDON'S
LONGEST RUNNING
COMEDY HIT
CRITERION
'A delight'
CRITERION
AMERICA
LONDON'S BEST COMEDY
Tonight at 8pm

ENTERTAINMENT

With West End ticket prices through the roof and the quality of some shows highly questionable (not that we don't enjoy a good song-and-dance routine), it may seem that the city that brought the world Shakespeare, the Sex Pistols, and even Andrew Lloyd Webber and Tim Rice has lost its originality and theatrical edge. But, forgetting the new wave of mega-musicals—where Hollywood B-listers come to revive careers, or to at least go down with a yelp—London is at its heart a city of immense talent: it is a classroom for student up-and-comers, proteges of London-based Rolling Stones, David Bowie, and The Police, who were themselves small fish at one time; it is the city of undergrounders who prefer to hear their names shouted by fans rather than showcased in neon lights; and a city of writers who experiment and constantly push the limits. Fringe venues in North, South, and East London still produce the cutting-edge, where smart and challenging performances shine particularly bright in comparison to lackluster actors who may fall over from boredom if they sing "Fame" just one more time.

We do not want to give you the impression that the West End is dead: although long-running, *Les Misérables* is one of the best shows around, while, new to the 2004-05 season, *Billy Elliot* and a dark and edgy *Mary Poppins* have gotten rave reviews. The Globe continues to put on Elizabethan classics, and famed British wit makes audiences belly-laugh in the same comedy clubs where *Whose Line Is It, Anyway?* got its start; the Royal Ballet is as notable as when Dame Margot Fonteyn headlined, while fans of punk rock still dance to their own beat. And, oh yeah, there's that whole sports phenomenon. Whatever your fancy, London is sure to keep you entertained.

 METRO IN THE TUBE. You don't have to buy the newspaper every morning to find the day's exciting entertainment and nightlife listings. Free in most Tube stations is *The Metro*, a small newspaper with headlines and event information, so read for free as you ride.

CINEMA

The heart of the celluloid monster is Leicester Square, where the dominant chains like **Odeon** take hold. Tickets to West End cinemas cost £5-10; weekday screenings before 5pm (and all day Monday) are usually cheaper and many offer regular student discounts (except on the weekends). *Time Out* publishes reviews and schedules for films, as do many other newspapers. Online, www.viewlondon.com also posts schedules. For listings of **film festivals**, see **Life and Times** (p. 78).

 CHOOSING A CINEMA. Unless you've booked early for a premiere, it's best to avoid the megaplex cinemas directly on Leicester Square—they all charge a few pounds more than those on the surrounding streets. There is another Odeon right down the road on Tottenham Court Rd. in Bloomsbury.

■ **Electric Cinema,** 191 Portobello Rd. (☎ 7908 9696; www.the-electric.co.uk), in **Notting Hill.** ⊖Notting Hill Gate or Ladbroke Grove. The improved version of London's oldest cinema (built in 1910). The Baroque splendor of a stage theatre paired with a sleek big screen and an in-theatre bar. Leather armchairs and loveseats make for a luxurious cinematic experience. Independent and international films, including docu-dramas, classics,

THE LOCAL STORY

HARRY POTTER'S LONDON

Few people have managed to escape Potter-mania, especially in London, which is host to numerous scenes of Harry's life in the books. Get your camera, books, and wand at the ready to rediscover Harry Potter's London.

First off, perhaps the most famous of all London stops for Potter fans is platform 9¾ in **King's Cross Station**. Have your picture taken trying to run through the wall with a trolley, but don't hit it too hard!

Next up is a trip to the **Australia House** building on the Strand, in the movies shown as Gringotts Bank. Due to it being a working embassy, access is limited, so don't think you'll be withdrawing any magical money (or seeing any treasure-hoarding goblins) while you're there.

Following Gringotts take a trip to **Leadenhall Market** (p. 121), in the heart of the city, where Harry and Hagrid once walked on their way to the Leaky Cauldron. BYOB—the Leaky Cauldron will not be serving refreshments.

Finally, visit the place where it all began, where Harry realized he was not a normal Muggle—in front of the Boa Constrictor tank in **London Zoo's** (p. 184) Reptile Houses. It's probably better if the snakes stay in their tanks, though, so keep the Parseltongue at home.

and recent hits. Wheelchair-accessible. Tickets M £7.50, Tu-Su £12.50. Front 3 rows M £5, Tu-Su £10, 2-seat sofa M £20, Tu-Su £30. Twinbills Su 2pm £5/7.50/20. Book online at least 2 weeks in advance. MC/V.

■ **National Film Theatre,** Belvedere Rd. (☎ 7928 3232; www.bfi.org.uk/nft), in the **South Bank.** ⊖Waterloo, Embankment, or Temple. Underneath Waterloo Bridge. This is a 1-stop shop for alternatives to the summer blockbusters: European art-house retrospectives, old American flicks, and special directors' series fill the program. 6 different shows hit 3 screens every evening (9 shows on weekends), starting around 6pm (2pm on weekends). The sprawling, super-popular cafe and bar on the ground floor serve up goodies to the masses. Annual membership (£22, concessions £14) gives £1 off movies, priority booking, and a free ticket when you join. All films £7.50, concessions £5.70. Wheelchair-accessible.

■ **Riverside Studios,** Crisp Rd. (☎ 8237 1111; www.riversidestudios.co.uk), in **West London.** ⊖Hammersmith. From the Tube, take Queen Caroline St. under the motorway and follow it past the Apollo (10min.) toward the Thames. Crisp Rd. is on the left, 1 block before the river. One of the best entertainment venues in London, Riverside is not well-known outside of West London—probably due to its less-than-aggressive marketing scheme and slightly hidden location—but its productions are very popular with locals. 2 theatres feature well-reviewed dramas, as well as homegrown fringe productions and comedy. The ■ **cinema** plays international art-house films, with an excellent film festival program featuring new international work and many classics (some with live piano) entirely in double bills. It also has an espresso cafe and cafeteria-style restaurant, convenient for mealtime shows. Plays £10-20, student prices vary with performance. Films £6.50; students, elderly, disabled, and unemployed £5.50. Wheelchair-accessible. Box office open daily noon-9pm. Schedules online. MC/V.

BFI London IMAX Cinema, 1 Charlie Chaplin Walk (☎ 0870 787 2525; www.bfi.org.uk/imax), in the **South Bank.** ⊖Waterloo. At the south end of Waterloo bridge, accessible via underground walkways from the South Bank and the Tube station. This theatre sticks out like a glass-enclosed sore thumb, rising in the center of a traffic roundabout. It houses the UK's biggest screen, at 20m high and 26m wide—taller than 5 double-decker buses stacked on top of each other. Blockbusters and educational movies shown. Shows start every 1½hr.; last show 8:15 or 8:45pm daily. £8.50, concessions (M-F only) £6.25, children under 16 £5. MC/V.

Curzon Soho, 93-107 Shaftesbury Ave. (☎ 7734 2255; www.curzoncinemas.com), in **Soho.** ⊖Leicester Sq. Retains good taste in films—watch the latest hot inde-

CINEMA SEATING. It pays to buy tickets in advance (or at least show up early to purchase); seating in most cinemas is assigned on a first-come, first-choice basis.

pendent and international films from plush, high-backed seats. Sleek cafe on the ground fl., and bar on the lower level. Frequent talks and Q&A sessions from big-name indie directors. 3 screens. Su classic and repertory double bills. M-F before 5pm £7, all other times £10; Su £6.50. Concessions £7. Wheelchair-accessible. AmEx/MC/V.

Everyman Cinema, 5 Holly Bush Vale (☎08700 664 777; www.everymancinema.com), in **North London.** ⊖Hampstead. One of London's oldest movie theatres, this 1930s picture house was recently revamped and is now hipper and more comfortable than ever. Lean back on the pillowed leather sofas on the "luxury" balcony or snuggle into one of the velvet stall seats. Mostly new independent films. Bars and lounges offer pre- or post-show drinks. Gallery with drink £15, standard £12, M-F concessions and Sa-Su matinees £7.50. Wheelchair-accessible. Box office open daily noon-11pm. Bar open daily 2-11pm. MC/V.

Gate Cinema, 87 Notting Hill Gate (☎08707 550 063; www.picturehouses.co.uk), in **Notting Hill.** ⊖Notting Hill Gate. Opened in 1911, Gate's drab exterior is a result of post-war reconstruction. Fortunately, the lovely Victorian interior remains intact, with comfortable leather chairs a welcome addition. Admire the ceiling details while waiting for the film to start. Arthouse, international, and select Hollywood flicks on daily rotation. Wheelchair-accessible. M £7, concessions £4.75; Tu-F before 5pm £8/5; Tu-Th and Su after 5pm £10/8; F-Sa after 6pm £11/9. MC/V.

Odeon (☎08712 241 999; www.odeon.co.uk). 11 locations in central London. See website for showtimes and contact information for a specific theatre.

MTR Studio 23, 23 Charlotte St. (☎7729 2323; www.mouththatroars.com), in **Westminster.** ⊖Old St. Founded to promote and develop independent film-making, this small studio offers free viewings and a snack bar serving cookies, coffee, and juice boxes (£1.20-1.80). Theatre seats arranged in pods of 3-4 and flat screen TVs make for a unique experience. Free film workshops year-round for those under 19. Check website for screenings.

Prince Charles Cinema, 7 Leicester Pl. (film info ☎09012 727 007, booking 0878 112 559; www.princecharlescinema.com), in **Soho.** ⊖Leicester Sq. Just off blockbuster-ridden Leicester Sq., the Prince Charles couldn't offer more of a contrast. It features 2nd-run Hollywood films and recent independents for unbelievably low prices. For a truly unique experience, perfect your do-re-mis at monthly sing-along screenings of *The Sound of Music* (generally last F of month; £14), complete with a costumed host and dress competitions. Tickets £3-4. MC/V.

Renoir, Brunswick Sq. (☎7837 8402), in **Bloomsbury.** ⊖Russell Sq. This independent movie house emphasizes current European (especially French) cinema. Only 2 screens, but the regular turnover makes this a standout. Doors and bar-cafe open 30min. before each screening. Wheelchair-accessible. £9, 1st performance of the day M-F £6, students £6. AmEx/MC/V.

Ritzy Picturehouse, Brixton Oval, Coldharbour Ln. (☎0871 704 2065; www.ritzycinema.co.uk), in **South London.** ⊖Brixton. Dating from the 1920s, the Picturehouse shows new Hollywood and independent films in well-preserved Art Deco screening rooms. For a pre-show snack, head to the cafe upstairs. Special events include several summer film series, like the African Film Festival. Tickets £8.50, matinees £6.50; concessions £7.25/5.25. MC/V.

Tricycle Cinema, 269 Kilburn High Rd. (box office ☎7328 1000; film info 7328 1900; www.tricycle.co.uk), entrance on Buckley Rd.; in **North London.** ⊖Kilburn. Showing independent and foreign films as well as Hollywood blockbusters. Films stay for 1-2 weeks; buy tickets in advance for popular movies. Recline on the plush pink seats and

ENTERTAINMENT

enjoy the show. Tricycle-print rugs and decor complete the picture. Tu pay-what-you-can tickets available to seniors, children, and students. Regular features £8, bargain M and Tu-F before 5pm £4.50; concessions M-F before 8pm and Sa-Su before 5pm £1 off. Wheelchair-accessible. MC/V.

TRICYCLE FOR POCKET CHANGE. The Tricycle Theatre (see p. 235) and Cinema offers occasional "pay-what-you-can" entry to films and plays. Although not to be taken advantage of, this system makes top-quality entertainment much more affordable to the budget-conscious.

COMEDY

Capital of a nation famed for its sophisticated sense of humor, London takes its comedy seriously. **Standup** is the mainstay, but **improvisation** fares well. Most clubs only run once a week or once a month, so call, or check listings in *Time Out* or a newspaper to keep up to speed. Summertime comedy seekers should note that London empties of comedians in **August,** when most head to Edinburgh to take part in the annual festival (trying to win an award); but **June** and **July** are full of feverish comic activity as performers test out new material prior to heading north.

■ **Canal Cafe Theatre,** Delamere Terr. (☎ 7289 6054; www.canalcafetheatre.com), above the Bridge House pub; in **North London.** ✪Warwick Ave. One of the few comedy venues to specialize in sketch comedy (as opposed to standup). Cozy red velvet chairs and a raised rear balcony means that everyone gets a good view. Grab dinner below and enjoy your drinks around the small tables. Box office opens 30min. before performance. Weekly changing shows W-Sa 7:30 and 9:30pm (£5, concessions £4). "Newsrevue," Th-Sa 9:30pm and Su 9pm, is London's longest-running comedy sketch show, a hilarious satire of weekly current events (£9, concessions £7). Both shows £14. £1.50 membership included in ticket price.

■ **Comedy Store,** 1a Oxendon St. (club inquiries ☎ 7839 6642, tickets 08700 602 340; www.thecomedystore.biz), in **Soho.** ✪Piccadilly Circus. The UK's top comedy club (founded in a former strip club) sowed the seeds that gave rise to *Absolutely Fabulous* and *Whose Line is it Anyway?* All 400 seats have decent views of stage. Grab food at the bar before the show and during the intermission (burgers £6). Tu Cutting Edge (contemporary news-based satire); W and Su London's well-reviewed ■ **Comedy Store Players Improv;** Th-Sa standup. Shows Tu-Th and Su 8pm; F-Sa 8pm, midnight. Book in advance. 18+. Tu-W and F midnight shows and all Su shows £16; concessions £8; Th-F early show and all Sa shows £15. Happy hour 6:30-7:30pm. Box office open M-Th and Su 6:30-9:30pm, F-Sa 6:30pm-1:15am. AmEx/MC/V.

Chuckle Club, at the Three Tuns Bar, Houghton St. (☎7476 1672; www.chuckleclub.com), in **Holborn.** ✪Holborn. From Holborn, walk south on Kingsway, turn left onto Aldwych, and then turn left onto Houghton St. It is in LSE's Clare Market Building on the right. Laid-back and unpretentious, this is not one of those "comedy is hip" clubs. A changing lineup of at least 3 headline acts and many tryouts guarantees more belly laughs than chuckles. Expect quality heckling from student-heavy audience. Every show opens with a rendition of the Chuckle Club Song. Policy of representing non-racist, non-sexist, and non-homophobic acts. 18+. Shows Sa 8:30pm; doors open at 7:45pm. Ticket admits you to the club that follows the show (until 3am). £10, students £8.

Downstairs at the King's Head, 2 Crouch End Hill (☎8340 1028; www.downstairsatthekingshead.com), in **North London.** ✪Finsbury Park; take the Wells Terr. Exit, then Bus #W7; get off after the bus turns right. One of London's oldest comedy clubs, in a cozy space under a pub. Shows 8 or 8:30pm; doors open 30min. before performance. M salsa class and dancing; Th tryouts bring up to 16 new acts; Sa-Su "comedy cabarets" mix up to 5 acts, from standup to songs to ventriloquism; Su 2-5pm jazz. Cover M £7, concessions £4; Th £4/3; Sa £9/7; Su £7/5.

DANCE

While the West End rivals Broadway any day, London cannot compete with the sheer number of New York City dance companies. But, what it does do with dance, it does well. The **Barbican Theatre** (p. 231) also hosts touring contemporary companies. For listings of dance classes, see **Practical Information** (p. 99).

Peacock Theatre, Portugal St. (☎0894 412 4322; www.sadlerswells.com), in **Holborn.** ⊖Holborn. Program leans toward contemporary dance, ballet, popular dance-troupe shows, and children- and family-geared productions. Some wheelchair-accessible seats (£9) can be booked 24hr. in advance. Box office open M-F 10am-6:30pm, 10am-8:30pm on performance days. £10-35; cheaper rates M-Th and Sa matinee. Standbys (1hr. before show) £15 and other discounts for students, seniors, under 16. Cheapest tickets at Box Office; fees for telephone and online booking. AmEx/MC/V.

The Place, 17 Duke's Rd. (☎7121 1000; www.theplace.org.uk), in **Bloomsbury.** ⊖Euston or King's Cross St. Pancras. A top venue for contemporary dance, attracting companies from the UK and abroad. Wheelchair-accessible. Online booking. Performances £5-15, depending on seats and advance booking; students £7. Day-of standbys (£15) available from 6pm. Box office and phone bookings open M-Sa noon-6pm, on performance nights noon-8pm. MC/V.

The Royal Opera House, Bow St. (☎7304 4000; www.roh.org.uk), in **Covent Garden.** ⊖Covent Garden. Containing both the Royal Opera and the Royal Ballet, the recently redesigned Royal Opera House is a glamorous venue. The Royal Ballet is considered one of the world's premier companies and performs top-notch classical pieces—*Swan Lake* and *The Nutcracker* are perennial favorites—as well as contemporary works. Royal Opera productions tend to be conservative but lavish, although recent contemporary works have been successful. Prices for the best seats (orchestra stalls) top £75 for the ballet and £100 for the opera, but standing room and restricted-view seating in the upper balconies run for as little as £5.67. Seats available from 10am on day of performance, limit 1 per person. For student standby tickets (£10), register online at www.roh.org.uk/studentstandby. Box office open M-Sa 10am-8pm. AmEx/MC/V.

Sadler's Wells, Rosebery Ave. (☎7863 8000; www.sadlerswells.com), in **Clerkenwell.** ⊖Angel. Exit left from the Tube, cross the road, and take the 2nd right on Rosebery Ave. Recently rebuilt, historic Sadler's Wells remains London's premier dance theatre, carrying everything from classical ballet to contemporary tap to the occasional opera. Matthew Bourne is the choreographer-in-residence, and recent performances include his version of *The Nutcracker* as well as visits from dance troupes from Argentina and China. 2 smaller stages within the complex also offer nightly performances. Sadler's Wells Express (SWX) bus to ⊖Waterloo via Farringdon and Victoria leaves 8min. after the end of each evening show (£2). Wheelchair-accessible. Box office open M-Sa 9am-8:30pm. £10-50; students and seniors £15; under-16 standbys £15 1hr. before curtain (cash only). AmEx/MC/V.

MUSIC

CLASSICAL AND OPERA

London boasts four world-class orchestras, three major concert halls, two opera houses, and more chamber ensembles than Simon Rattle could shake his baton at—and, even for the biggest names, there's no need to break the bank. Most venues have scads of cheap seats, and when music is the attraction, bad views of the stage are less important. To hear some of the world's top choirs, head to churches

NO WORK, ALL PLAY

THE PROMS

London's summer classical music season has been held at the Royal Albert Hall every year since 1895, with concerts every night from mid-July to mid-September. The term **"Promenade"** refers to the tradition of selling dirt-cheap standing tickets, and it's the presence of up to 1400 dedicated prommers that gives the concerts their unique, informal atmosphere—that and the lack of A/C.

Seats for popular concerts sell out months in advance, while lines for standing-room often start mid-afternoon. If you plan on standing, the **arena,** immediately in front of the orchestra is most popular. The nosebleed-inducing **gallery** has more space. The famous **Last Night** is an unabashedly jingoistic celebration complete with flag-waving and mass sing-a-longs of "Rule Britannia." Regarded with horror by "serious" music lovers, it's so popular that you have to have attended at least six other summer concerts before you can take part in a lottery for these tickets.

☎ 7589 8212; www.bbc.co.uk/ proms. Tickets go on sale in mid-June (£6-80; occasional discounts for under 16); 500 standing places sold 1½hr. before the concert (£5; cash only). All concerts are transmitted live on BBC Radio 3, 91.3FM, and broadcast on BBC 4. The Last Night is broadcast on a big screen in Hyde Park. Advance booking with MC/V.

throughout the city, including Westminster Abbey (see p. 164) or St. Paul's Cathedral (see p. 145); as a double bonus, you'll also get into the cathedral for free. For listings of **festivals,** particularly in summer, see **Life and Times** (p. 78).

Barbican Centre, see p. 231.

English National Opera, London Coliseum, St. Martin's Ln. (☎ 7632 8300; www.eno.org), in **Covent Garden.** ⊖Charing Cross or Leicester Sq. The Coliseum is staggering—huge, ornate, and complete with 500 balcony seats (£15-18) for sale every performance—and the ENO has proven it can fill the venue with its innovative, updated productions of classics as well as contemporary work. Wheelchair-accessible. Purchase best-available, standby student tickets (£12.50) and balcony tickets (£10) at box office 3hr. before show. Call to verify availability. Half-price tickets for children under 17. Box office open M-Sa 10am-8pm. AmEx/MC/V.

Holland Park Theatre, Holland Park (box office ☎ 0845 223 097; www.rbkc.gov.uk/hollandpark), in **Kensington and Earl's Court.** ⊖High St. Kensington or Holland Park. Open-air performance space in the atmospheric grounds of a Jacobean mansion. Sitting outside is generally the most adventurous part of the program. No need to fear the rain—everything is held under a huge white canopy. Performances June to early Aug. Tu-Sa 7:30pm, occasional matinees Sa 2:30pm. Box office in the Old Stable Block just to the west of the opera open late Mar. to early Aug. M-Sa 10am-6pm or 30min. after curtain. Tickets £20-46. Special allocation of tickets for wheelchair users. AmEx/MC/V.

Royal Albert Hall, Kensington Gore (☎ 7589 8212; www.royalalberthall.com), in **Kensington and Earl's Court.** ⊖High St. Kensington. Best known for the ▨ **Proms** (p. 222). Box office at Door 12 open daily 9am-9pm. MC/V.

Royal Opera, Bow St. (☎ 7304 4000; www.royaloperahouse.org), in **Covent Garden.** ⊖Covent Garden. Productions in this recently refurbished, sparkling venue tend to be conservative but lavish, although recent experiments with contemporary works have proven successful as well. Prices for the best seats (orchestra stalls) regularly top £100, but standing room and restricted-view seating in the upper balconies (if you're not afraid of heights) runs for as little as £5. For some performances, 100 of the very best seats available for £10; apply a minimum of 2 weeks in advance at www.travelex.royaloperahouse.org.uk. 67 seats available from 10am on day of performance, limit 1 per person. Box office open M-Sa 10am-8pm. AmEx/MC/V.

The South Bank Centre, Belvadere Rd. (☎ 0871 663 2501; www.rfh.org.uk), in the **South Bank.** ⊖Waterloo or Embankment. This megaplex of concert halls features all kinds of music. The main venue is the **Royal Festival Hall**—home to the Philharmonia and the London Philharmonic. **Queen Elizabeth Hall** features smaller, more varied programs. The **Purcell Room** is an intimate space for chamber music, soloists, and world music groups. Tickets can be purchased at Queen Elizabeth Hall (daily 10am-8pm) or by telephone (☎0871 663 2500). Some discounts for concessions and children under 16. Some £5-10 standby tickets available 2hr. before performance.

St. John's, Smith Square, Smith Sq. (☎ 7222 1061; www.sjss.org.uk), in **Westminster.** ⊖Westminster or St. James's Park. A former church that's now a full-time concert venue with a program heavy on chamber and classical music; rarely sold out but highly regarded by critics. Excellent acoustics. Restaurant in the undercroft serves concert suppers, including "quicker" options that are prepared in under 30min. Concerts Sept. to mid-July daily, mid-July to Aug. once to twice per week. Performances generally start 7:30pm. £8-15; student discounts at discretion of promoter. Box office open M-F 10am-5pm, on performance nights 10am-6pm. Internet booking also available. MC/V.

St. Martin-in-the-Fields, Trafalgar Sq. (☎ 7839 8362; www.smitf.org), in **Covent Garden.** ⊖Charing Cross. Frequent concerts and recitals are given in this ornate 18th-century church, which underwent a £36 million renovation project in the summer of 2007. Music includes solo and group baroque and chamber recitals. Call box office or visit website for show details.

Wigmore Hall, 36 Wigmore St. (☎ 7935 2141; www.wigmore-hall.org.uk), in **Marylebone.** ⊖Oxford Circus. London's premier chamber-music venue, in a beautiful setting with excellent acoustics; occasional jazz recitals. Wheelchair-accessible. Season Sept.-July; concerts most nights 7:30pm. Prices vary greatly with event (£2-35). Online booking free. Phone booking (£1.50 extra) M-Sa 10am-7pm, Su 10:30am-4pm. In-person booking M-Sa 10am-8:30pm, Su 10:30am-5pm. Student and senior standby tickets available 1hr. before (£10). Sales stop 30min. prior to performance. AmEx/MC/V.

JAZZ

London's jazz scene is small but serious; this ain't Chicago but hallowed clubs pull in big-name performers from across the world. **Pizza Express** restaurants often features jazz in its swankier branches, in addition to the one operating full-time club.

▨ **Jazz Café,** 5 Parkway (☎ 7534 6955; www.jazzcafe.co.uk), in **North London.** ⊖Camden Town. Famous and popular. Crowded front bar and balcony restaurant overlook the dance floor and stage, both of which are just the right size. Shows can be pricey at this nightspot, but the top roster of jazz, hip-hop, funk, and Latin performers (£10-30) explains Jazz Café's popularity. Jazzy DJs spin F-Sa following the show. Partially wheelchair-accessible. Cover £5-10. Open daily 7pm-2am. MC/V.

▨ **Ronnie Scott's,** 47 Frith St. (☎ 7439 0747; www.ronniescotts.co.uk), in **Soho.** ⊖Tottenham Court Rd. or Leicester Sq. London's oldest and most famous jazz club, having hosted everyone from Dizzy Gillespie to Jimi Hendrix. A change in ownership means the club isn't pulling in the legends it used to, but in-the-know folks are expecting a comeback. Support and main acts switch back and forth throughout the night. Table reservations essential for big-name acts, though there's limited unreserved standing room at the bar; if it's sold out, try coming back at the end of the main act's first set, around midnight. Chicken, pasta, and traditional English dishes £7-28; mixed drinks £7-9. Box office open M-F 11am-6pm, Sa noon-6pm. Club open M-Sa 6pm-3am, Su 6pm-midnight. Tickets generally £26. AmEx/MC/V.

▨ **Spitz,** 109 Commercial St. (☎ 7392 9032; www.spitz.co.uk), in **East London.** ⊖Liverpool St. The eclectic Spitz features an upstairs bar and a bistro downstairs. Crowds spill onto the Spitalfields market area during busy hours. Fresh range of live music including klezmer, jazz, world music, indie, pop, and rap. All profits support worthy causes through the Dandelion Trust, including global refugee health and tsunami relief.

Free music in the bistro 4 nights per week. For ticketed shows, check the website for details or book online at www.wegottickets.com. A small art gallery holds free exhibits from local artists. Occasional cover up to £15. Upstairs doors open at 7pm most nights, when evening acts usually begin. Open M-W 10:30am-midnight, Th-Sa 10:30am-1am, Su 4-10:30pm. MC/V.

100 Club, 100 Oxford St. (☎ 7636 0933; www.the100club.co.uk), in **Soho.** ⊖Tottenham Court Rd. Stage, audience, and bar are all bathed in sallow orange light in this jazz venue that makes frequent excursions into indie rock. Weekdays offer serious indie and jazz, while weekends tend to become more "date friendly" and mellow. Punk burst on the scene at a legendary gig here in 1976, when The Sex Pistols, the Clash, and Siouxsie and the Banshees all shared the stage in 1 evening. Featured nights: M "Stompin'" (swing and big band), Sa swing. Open F-Su 7:30pm, closing time varies; other nights vary. Cover £7-15, students with ID £5-10. AmEx/MC/V.

606 Club, 90 Lots Rd. (☎ 7352 5953; www.606club.co.uk), in **Chelsea.** ⊖Sloane Sq., then Bus #11 or 22. Look for the brick arch labeled 606 opposite the "Fire Access" garage; ring the doorbell to be let in downstairs. The intrepid will be rewarded with live jazz music in a candlelit basement venue. Entrance F-Su is with a meal only; M-Th you can choose to order just soft drinks. Mains £9-16. Cover (added to the bill): M-Th £8, F-Sa £12, Su £10. M-W doors open 7:30pm, 1st band 8-10:30pm, 2nd 10:45pm-1am; Th-Sa doors open 8pm, music 9:30pm-1:30am; Su doors open 8pm, music 9pm-midnight. Reservations recommended F-Su. MC/V.

Pizza Express Jazz Club, 10 Dean St. (☎ 7439 8722; www.pizzaexpress.co.uk/jazz.htm), in **Soho.** ⊖Tottenham Court Rd. Underneath a branch of the popular chain, sophisticated diners dig into pizzas and salads (£5-8) while feasting their ears on music. Surprisingly one of the better places to hear innovative contemporary jazz in an open and airy space. Big names have included Van Morrison and Diana Krall, along with more on-topic headliners. Table reservations recommended, especially F-Sa. Doors open 7:30pm, music 9-11:30pm; some F-Sa have 2 shows, with doors opening at 6 and 10pm. Per-person cover £15-20 added to the food bill. AmEx/MC/V.

ROCK, POP, AND FOLK

London is a town steeped in rock 'n' roll history; every major band and singer in the world has played at least one of its major venues. Dates for the biggest acts are usually booked months in advance and often sell out within days of tickets being released, so you need to start planning well before arriving in London to have a chance at bagging a seat. **Folk** (which in London usually means Irish) and world music usually keep a low profile. In general, outings are restricted to pubs and community centers.

The Water Rats, 328 Grays Inn Rd. (☎ 7813 1079; www.themonto.com), in **Bloomsbury.** ⊖King's Cross St. Pancras. A hip pub-cafe by day, a stomping venue for top new talent by night—this is where young indie rock bands come in search of a record deal. Oasis was signed here after their first London gig, although the place has been spiffed up since. Cover from £4. Open for coffee M-F 8:30am-midnight. Excellent, generous gastropub lunches (fish 'n' chips and baguettes £5-6) M-F noon-3pm. Music M-Sa 8pm-late (headliner 9:45pm). MC/V.

Borderline, Orange Yard (box office ☎ 7534 6970, 24hr. ticket line 08700 603 777), off Manette St. in **Soho.** ⊖Tottenham Court Rd. Warm basement space with 175 seats set around a small stage. Well-known groups with strong folk-rock flavor. Past luminaries include Oasis, Pearl Jam, and Spinal Tap. W rock, Th emo or heavy metal, F indie, Sa "Christmas Club." Special acts other nights. Cover for theme nights from £5-7. Box office open M-F 10am-6pm, Sa 10am-5pm. £2.20 fee for online booking. £6-25 in advance. AmEx/MC/V.

Carling Academy, Brixton, 211 Stockwell Rd. (☎ 7771 3000; www.brixton-acad-emy.co.uk), in **South London.** ⊖Brixton. Art Deco ex-cinema with a sloping floor ensures even those at the back have a chance to see the band. Named *Time Out's* "Live Venue of the Year" in 2004 and *New Music Express's* "Best Live Venue" in 2007. Recent perform-ers include Lenny Kravitz, Pink, and Basement Jaxx. Box office open only on performance evenings; order online or by telephone or go to the Carling Academy, Islington box office (16 Parkfield Street, Islington). Box office open M-Sa noon-4pm. Tickets £20-40.

Apollo Hammersmith, Queen Caroline St. (☎ 8563 3800, 24hr. ticketmaster 0870 606 3400; www.hammersmith-apollo.com, www.ticketmaster.co.uk), in **West Lon-don.** ⊖Hammersmith. In the shadow of the Hammersmith Flyover, this utilitarian venue, with a capacity of up to 5000, hosts a huge array of musical and theatrical diversions, from the Beach Boys to Wu-Tang Clan. Box office open 4-8pm on perfor-mance days. £18.50 and up. AmEx/MC/V.

Forum, 9-17 Highgate Rd. (☎ 7284 1001, box office 0871 230 1093; www.kentish-townforum.com), in **North London.** ⊖Kentish Town. Turn right out of the Tube, go over the crest of the hill, and bear left—you'll see the marquee. The outside may not be beautiful, but inside is a lavish Art Deco theatre. The great sound system and clear stage view has attracted some big names in the past: Van Morrison, Björk, Oasis, and Jamiroquai, among others. Many shows feature random smaller groups, but famous bands still play relatively often. Tickets from £15. MC/V.

The Garage, 20-22 Highbury Corner (box office ☎ 7607 1818, upstairs 08701 500 044; www.meanfiddler.com), enter on Holloway Rd.; in **North London.** ⊖Highbury and Islington. Hardcore and indie rock groups play F-Sa and often weeknights. Occasional smattering of American punk and emo bands. Lesser acts play the upstairs room. Music 8-11pm, F-Sa followed by an indie club night until 3am, included in gig ticket. F "Don't Stop Me Now" (pop music hits); Sa "International Hi-Fi." Punk Rock Karaoke, 1st and 3rd Sa of month (8:30pm, £6). Gigs £5-20. Cover F-Sa £7. MC/V.

Hammersmith Irish Centre, Black's Rd. (info ☎ 8563 8232; www.lbhf.gov.uk/irishcen-tre), in **West London.** ⊖Hammersmith. From the District and Piccadilly Tube exit, head west on King St. Take your first left on Angel Walk and your first left again on Black's Rd. Centre is on the right. Run by the local council, this claims to be London's foremost Irish center. Houses a small Irish lending library and frequently screens Irish films. Hosts Irish bands, dance sessions, comedians, and literary readings. Wheelchair-accessible. Library open W 6pm-7pm, Sa 10am-2pm. Most performances F-Sa 8:15pm. Free-£10.

The Koko Club, 1a Camden High St. (☎ 0870 432 5527; www.koko.uk.com), in **North London.** ⊖Mornington Crescent. The newly reincarnated face of the old landmark Cam-den Palace, the Koko Club hosts a variety of acts. In a converted Victorian theatre, now with space for 1600, it's an indie and rock venue that doubles as a dance club. Reuben and Slint are 2 groups that have played here recently. Cover £3-15. Opening times vary.

London Astoria (LA1), 157 Charing Cross Rd. (info ☎ 8963 0940, 24hr. ticket line ☎ 08701 500 044), in **Soho.** ⊖Tottenham Court Rd. Formerly a pickle factory, strip club, and music hall before becoming a full-time rock venue in the late 1980s. Now basking in an air of somewhat faded glory, the 2000-person venue occasionally hosts big names (recently, the Red Hot Chili Peppers and Blink 182). The venue is more famous for the popular "G-A-Y" M and Th-Sa club night (p. 273). Box office open M-F 10am-6pm, Sa 10am-5pm. AmEx/MC/V.

Mean Fiddler, 165 Charing Cross Rd. (box office ☎ 7434 9592, 24hr. ticket line 08705 344 444; www.meanfiddler.com), in **Soho.** ⊖Tottenham Court Rd. This 2-story music venue is more intimate and boasts a better sound system than its down-stairs neighbor, the Astoria. Popular rock nights F 11pm-3:30am. Alternative party nights with secret live band and DJ Sa 11pm-4am. Tickets £10-12. Check website for other shows. Box office open M-Sa 10am-6pm. MC/V on ticket line only.

ENTERTAINMENT

THE HIDDEN DEAL

WIMBLEDON WITHOUT THE WAIT

Londoners don't seem to care much about tennis until two weeks in early summer when the whole city turns up to watch Wimbledon. Getting in on the fair-weather-fan frenzy may be tougher than you think. While there are ways to skirt the system, finding tickets for high-profile matches generally requires planning (advance tickets sell out in December), a good-sized bank roll, or waiting in an overnight queue.

For the broke or impatient, the **Stella Artois Championships** offers an excellent alternative to the mayhem. A men's warm-up competition in the weeks leading up to Wimbledon, Stella Artois features many of the same players as its more famous counterpart, but without the long lines and sometimes exorbitant prices. Early in the tournament, high-level players duke it out on lower courts accessible to the masses.

Queen's Club, Palliser Rd. ⊖Baron's Court. ☎7385 3421; www.queensclub.co.uk, for tickets to the tournament www.stellartoistennis.com. While tickets are best booked in advance, a limited number of same-day tickets for unreserved seats on the lower courts are released each morning. Arriving a bit before the ticket office opens generally ensures admission.

Shepherd's Bush Empire, Shepherd's Bush Green (☎09050 203 999, ticket bookings 08707 712 000; www.shepherds-bush-empire.co.uk), in **West London.** ⊖Shepherd's Bush. This turn-of-the-century theatre right on the Green, once famous for hosting BBC game shows, is now a major music venue with a capacity of 2000. A host of popular musicians from Maroon 5 to Blondie has played here. £12.50-37.50. Box office open on performance days 4-6pm and 6:30-9:30pm. AmEx/MC/V.

Underground, 174 Camden High St. (☎7482 1932), in **North London.** ⊖Camden Town. Under the World's End; enter through the purple storefront. Showcases hardcore, punk, and indie bands, both local and from throughout the UK. Convenient location with gastropub downstairs. Box office upstairs open M-Sa 11am-11pm, Su noon-10:30pm. Tickets from £10. MC/V.

SPECTATOR SPORTS

FOOTBALL

Almost a million people attend professional matches, most dressed with fierce loyalty in team colors. The vast majority of game takes place on Saturdays, although there is the occasional Sunday or mid-week match. The most popular way to watch matches is on TV in a local bar or pub, where you get the benefit of multiple cameras and commentators. Most of these fans attend the matches of one of five London teams in England's **F.A. Premier League;** the big three London teams are **Arsenal, Chelsea,** and **Tottenham Hotspur.**

Arsenal, Emirates Stadium, 75 Drayton Park (box office ☎7704 4242; www.arsenal.com), in **North London.** ⊖Arsenal. £35-55. Box office open M-F 9:30am-5pm, Sa 9:30am-noon.

Charlton, The Valley (box office ☎8333 4010; www.cafc.co.uk), in **East London.** Rail: Charlton. DLR: North Greenwich (Zone 3), then Bus #53, 54, 161.

Chelsea, Stamford Bridge, Fulham Rd. (main switchboard ☎08703 001 212, box office 0870 300 2322; www.chelsea.afc.com), in **West London.** ⊖Fulham Broadway. £48.

Crystal Palace, Selhurst Park, Whitehorse Ln. (☎08712 000 071; www.cpfc.co.uk), in **South London.** Rail: Selhurst. Box office open M-F 9am-6pm, Sa 9:30am-12:30pm.

Fulham, Loftus Rd. (box office ☎08704 421 234; www.fulhamfc.com), in **West London.** ⊖White City. £10-15, concessions £5-10. Box office open M-F 9am-5pm.

Tottenham Hotspur, White Hart Lane Stadium, 748 High Rd. (ticket office ☎08704 205 000; www.spurs.co.uk), in **North London.** ⊖Seven Sisters (Zone 3). Tickets £27-71; half-price tickets (senior citizens, children under 16) subject to availability. Box office open M-F 10am-6pm.

West Ham United, Boleyn Ground, Green St. (box office ☎08701 122 700; www.whufc.com), in **East London.** ⊖Upton Park (Zone 3). Box office open M-F 9am-5pm, Sa 9am-1pm.

RUGBY

An excellent rowdy sport, rugby comes in a distant second to football in London, although it is much more popular to the north and to the west of the city. Still, locals turn out loyally to support the four big London teams, which play from August to May on weekend afternoons:

London Wasps, Twyford Ave. Sports Ground, Twyford Ave. (☎8993 8298, box office 0870 414 1515; www.wasps.co.uk), in **West London.** ⊖Ealing Common. £15-25, concessions £10-18.

NEC Harlequins, Stoop Memorial Ground, Langhorn Dr. (☎8410 6000, box office 08718 718 877; www.quins.co.uk), in **West London.** Rail: Twickenham.

Saracens, Vicarage Rd. Station (box office ☎01923 475 222; www.saracens.com), in **North London.** ⊖Watford. Tickets £17-40, concessions £9-35. Box office open M-F 9am-5:30pm.

CRICKET

Middlesex and **Surrey** are the main London teams; their grounds at Lord's and the Oval, respectively, are also used to host international test matches in which England traditionally loses abysmally.

Lord's Cricket Ground, St. John's Wood Rd. (☎7432 1000; www.lords.org), in **North London.** ⊖St. John's Wood. (See p. 180.)

Oval, Brit Oval, Surey County Cricket Club (☎08712 461 100, box office 7582 7764; www.surreycricket.com), in **South London.** ⊖Oval.

TENNIS

Demand for tickets at "The Championships" (Wimbledon) so exceeds supply that pre-sold tickets are lotteried in December; only 500 Centre, No. 1, and No. 2 Court tickets are saved for each day (except during the Final Four, when none are). To be assured one of these seats, overnight queuing is recommended.

Stella Artois, Queen's Club, Palliser Rd. (☎7385 3421; www.queensclub.co.uk; for tickets to the tournament www.artoischampionship.com), in **West London.** ⊖Barons Crt. Stella Artois tournament precedes Wimbledon in June.

Wimbledon, All England Lawn Tennis and Croquet Club (☎8971 2473; www.wimbledon.org), in **West London.** ⊖Southfields (Zone 3). 15min. walk along Wimbledon Park Rd. Wimbledon championship late June-early July. Box office open M-F 9am-5pm.

WIMBLEDON. The Wimbledon finals are broadcast on a big screen in Covent Garden Piazza. Pack your own strawberries and cream and head there for an affordable afternoon of tennis.

THEATRE

LONG-RUNNING SHOWS (THE WEST END)

London's West End is dominated by musicals and plays that run for years, if not decades. Below we list shows that have proved their staying power, as well as recent arrivals that look set to settle down for the long haul. Most long-running shows are in venues located in the West End; see the **Theatreland** map, p. 228.

ENTERTAINMENT

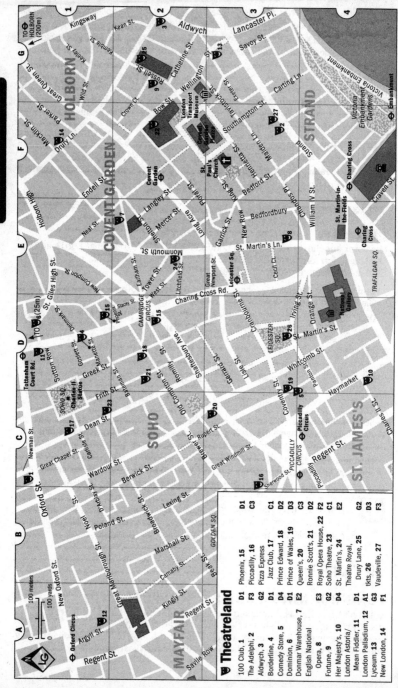

tkts, on the south side of Leicester Sq. (www.tkts.co.uk). ⊖Leicester Sq. (2nd location at Canary Wharf DLR Station, Platforms 4 and 5). Run by the Society of London Theatre, tkts is the only place where you can be sure your discounted tickets are genuine. The catch is that theatres only release the most expensive tickets to the booth, which means that it's a good deal for the best seats in the house, but they are rarely under £15 (most musicals around £23, plays £20-22). In addition, you can only buy day-of tickets in person, with little seating choice. Notice boards display which shows are available; £2.50 booking fee per ticket. Open M-Sa 10am-7pm, Su noon-3pm. MC/V.

 Many "discount" ticket booths will claim to offer you a reduced rate on tickets when in fact they are charging you more than the face value! Look for the logo of a white circle with a check mark on a ticket booth before purchasing—it denotes compliance with a set of rules and standards that ensures legitimate discounts.

MUSICALS

Billy Elliot: The Musical, Victoria Palace Theatre, Victoria St. (☎08708 955 577). ⊖Victoria. Local boy makes good—in tights. A thoroughly crowd-pleasing movie-to-musical adaptation, boasting some distinguished talent: new songs by Elton John and direction by the Oscar-nominated director of the film, Stephen Daldry. Shows M-W and F 7:30pm; Th and Sa 2:30, 7:30pm. £17.50-50. Call about limited day-of student standby tickets. AmEx/MC/V.

Blood Brothers, Phoenix Theatre, Charing Cross Rd. (☎08700 606 629; www.theambassadors.com/phoenix). ⊖Tottenham Court Rd. Nearing 20 years old, it's the British mega-hit that most foreigners have never heard of. Twins separated at birth, passionate melodrama, and a dash of 1980s social commentary—Willy Russell's songs are fantastic. Shows M-W and F 7:45pm; Th and Sa 3, 4, 7:45pm. £11.50-48.50; student and senior standby £15 1hr. before curtain. AmEx/MC/V.

Chicago, The Adelphi, The Strand (☎08704 030 303; www.chicagothemusical.com). ⊖Charing Cross. The musical that inspired the movie that inspired the Oscars. Merry murderesses want their name in lights. Plenty of slinky costumes, fantastic Fosse, and fabulous show stoppers. Shows M-Th 8pm; F 4:30pm; Sa 3, 8pm. £20-75. £2.75 additional fee for phone booking. AmEx/MC/V.

Dirty Dancing, Aldwych Theatre, Aldwych St. (☎08704 000 805; www.aldwychtheatre.com). ⊖Charing Cross. Based on the 80s hit movie, this version includes all of the dance-offs and drama and could not be considered complete without the recurring quote, "Nobody puts Baby in a corner." Shows M-Th 7:30pm; F-Sa 3, 7:30pm. £25-60. AmEx/MC/V.

Grease, Piccadilly Theatre, Denman St. (☎0844 412 6666). ⊖Piccadilly Circus. Everyone's favorite high-school musical takes its turn in the West End. A young and energetic cast makes the singing and dancing come alive. Shows M-Th 7:30pm; F-Sa 5, 8:30pm; Su 3, 7:30pm. £15-55. AmEx/MC/V.

Joseph and the Amazing Technicolor Dreamcoat, New London Theatre, Drury Ln. (☎08708 900 141). ⊖Holborn. Andrew Lloyd Webber's 2nd most famous biblical extravaganza (*Jesus Christ Superstar* being the 1st). All your favorite songs, plus the eye-catching overcoat. Shows M and Th-F 7:30pm; Tu 7pm; W and Sa 3, 7:30pm. £15-50. All tickets ½-price Tu 7:30pm. Student standby day of performance; call to check availability. AmEx/MC/V.

The Lion King, Lyceum Theatre, Wellington St. (☎08702 439 000; www.thelionking.co.uk). ⊖Covent Garden. Same script as the film, gorgeous new puppets. Disney has adapted its movie into an innovative and aesthetically pleasing show while still retaining the Disney pop appeal. Shows Tu and Th-F 7:30pm; W and Sa 2, 7:30pm; Su 3pm. £20-50. Limited day-of seats and standing-room tickets released at noon. Ask

TAKE YOUR SEATS

The terminology of English theatre can be difficult for anyone but native experts to understand. Here's a brief overview: **stalls** are what Americans call orchestra seats, and are nearest the stage. The **dress circle** (mezzanine) is the first tier of balcony above the stalls. This section often has better views of the stage; stalls and dress circle are usually the most expensive seats. Above the dress circle comes the **upper circle,** while the cheapest seats at the top of the theatre are **slips** or in the **balcony** (also known as the gallery). Patrons usually refer to these as **the gods,** a reference to their closeness to heaven and the impulse to scream "Oh God!" when looking down.

The **interval** (intermission) is the time for gin or the loo; audiences head to the **crush bar.** Instead of joining the undignified scramble, you can order interval drinks before the show and find them waiting for you—usually on an unguarded side table marked with your name. Fortunately, London theatre-goers do not seem to be of the drink-snatching variety.

Also remember **programmes** usually cost £1-3 and that **return line** is set up on the day of a performance to sell those seats that have been returned before use. **House seats** are saved for important people. If no one shows up, they often go on sale just before curtain. Many theatres offer day-of **student** tickets.

about student discounts. Purchase 2 tickets max. in person at box office. AmEx/MC/V.

Mamma Mia!, Prince of Wales Theatre, Coventry St. (box office ☎0870 950 0902, agents 0870 264 3333; www.mamma-mia.com). ⊖Leicester Sq. A revue of ABBA's music strung together with a simple plot; it's by far the best of the "pop's greatest hits" megashows. Nearly always sold out. Shows M-Th 7:30pm; F 5, 8:30pm; Sa 3, 7:30pm. £25-49. Check the box office daily for returns. AmEx/MC/V.

Mary Poppins, Prince Edward Theatre, Old Compton St. (☎08708 509 191; www.marypoppinsthemusical.co.uk). ⊖Leicester Sq. A different take on Britain's favorite nanny, based on the book by PL Travers and the classic Disney movie. There's much more than just a "spoonful of sugar" to be had in this well-reviewed musical. Shows M-W and F 7:30pm; Th and Sa 2:30, 7:30pm. £15-55. Same-day tickets released at noon; limit 2 per person. AmEx/MC/V.

Les Misérables, Queen's Theatre, Shaftesbury Ave. (☎08708 901 110; www.lesmis.com). ⊖Piccadilly Circus. One of the best renditions of an all-time great. If you don't recognize "I Dreamed a Dream," "On My Own," or "Master of the House," you've missed a few decades. Learning about the French Revolution has never been better. Intimate theatre perfect for tear-jerking plot and belted operetta. Shows M-Tu and Th-F 7:30pm; W and Sa 2:30, 7:30pm. £15-55. Day-of student discounts. AmEx/MC/V.

Phantom of the Opera, Her Majesty's Theatre, Haymarket (☎0870 534 4444; www.thephantomoftheopera.com). ⊖Piccadilly Circus. Andrew Lloyd Webber's famously romantic take on love and deformity at the Paris Opera. The chandelier still falls and the crowds still flock—this musical is timeless. Shows M and W-F 7:30pm; Tu and Sa 2:30, 7:30pm. £20-55. AmEx/MC/V.

Lord of the Rings, Theatre Royal, Drury Ln. (☎08708 901 109). ⊖Covent Garden. J.R.R. Tolkien's trilogy has opened to mixed reviews, but there is no denying the exquisite costumes and sets. The musical aims to cover all 3 books in 1 show—an imposing task. Shows M-Tu and Th-F 7:30pm; W and Sa 2:30, 7:30pm. £30-66. AmEx/MC/V.

Wicked, Apollo Victoria, 17 Wilton Rd. (☎08701 611 977). ⊖Victoria. The bestselling book is now a musical, detailing the story from the Wicked Witch of the West's perspective. Perhaps Dorothy wasn't the innocent victim we all thought? Shows M-Tu and Th-F 7:30pm; W and Sa 2:30, 7:30pm. £15-60. AmEx/MC/V.

We Will Rock You, Dominion Theatre, Tottenham Court Rd. (☎08701 690 116). ⊖Tottenham Court Rd. Adapted from Ben Elton's book and incorporating the popular chart-toppers of Queen, this futuristic tale pits a rock rebel against a globalized, conformist world. Another pop-rock-musical theatre bash. Shows M-F 7:30pm, Sa 2:30pm. £27.50-60. AmEx/MC/V.

TIX FOR POCKET CHANGE. Always ask at the box office for student discounts. Even if a theatre does not advertise such discounts, they may give them (usually 1hr. before curtain). Most theatres will give the best seats available for standby. It's best to go in the middle of the week.

NON-MUSICALS

The Mousetrap, St. Martin's Theatre, West St. (☎0870 162 8787). ⊖Leicester Sq. An Agatha Christie play. After 50 years on the stage, is there anyone left in London who doesn't know who did it in the Mousetrap, the world's longest-running play? Shows M and W-F 8pm; Tu 2:45 and 8pm; Sa 5 and 8pm. £13.50-37.50. AmEx/MC/V.

STOMP, Vaudeville Theatre, The Strand (☎08708 900 511; www.stomp.co.uk). ⊖Charing Cross. 8 performers pound out catchy rhythms with everything from brooms to kitchen sinks. A bold mix of theatre, dance, comedy, and percussion. Shows Tu-W and F 8pm; Th and Sa-Su 3, 8pm. £16-38.50. Su children ½ price Su. AmEx/MC/V.

The Woman in Black, Fortune Theatre, Russell St. (☎08700 606 626; www.thewomaninblack.com). ⊖Covent Garden. Proving that good writing is scarier than any amount of cinematic gore, an aging detective recalls the ghost of a dead woman. Shows M and W-F 8pm; Tu 3, 8pm; Sa 4, 8pm. £12.50-36. AmEx/MC/V.

REPERTORY

This is where the best of the best reside; these are the stages that make London the world's theatre capital.

▨ **Barbican Hall,** Silk St. (☎7638 4141; www.barbican.org.uk), in the **City of London.** ⊖Barbican or Moorgate. Recently refurbished, Barbican Hall is one of Europe's leading concert halls, with excellent acoustics and a nightly performance program. The resident **London Symphony Orchestra** plays here frequently. The hall also hosts concerts by international orchestras, jazz artists, and world musicians. Barbican is also the place to go for information on **festivals** and **season-specific events.** As many summer events sell out, it's worth checking what's going on early. Call in advance for tickets, especially for popular events. Otherwise, the online and phone box offices sometimes have good last-minute options. £10-35. Also includes the 2 venues below:

Barbican Centre. Equally famous for the quality of its very diverse offerings and 'for its mildly confusing layout, the Barbican is a 1-stop cultural powerhouse. The main **Theatre** is a futuristic auditorium that hosts touring companies and short-run shows as well as frequent short-run multicultural and contemporary dance performances. Prices vary considerably by seat, day, and production: £10-35, cheapest M-F evening and Sa matinee; student and senior standbys from 9am day of performance. **The Pit** is a smaller, intimate theatre used primarily for new and experimental productions. £10-15.

Barbican Cinema. Part of the Barbican Centre conglomerate. 2 smallish screens offering a rotation of the latest blockbusters with art-house, international, and classic movies. £8.50, seniors and students £6, under 15 £4.50.

▨ **Royal Court Theatre,** Sloane Sq. (☎7565 5000; www.royalcourttheatre.com), in **Chelsea.** ⊖Sloane Sq. Recognized by *The New York Times* as a standout theatre in Europe, the Court is dedicated to challenging new writing and innovative interpretations of classics. Their 1956 production of John Osborne's *Look Back in Anger* is universally acknowledged as the starting point of modern British drama. Tackles politically thorny issues like AIDS and the Middle East. Main auditorium £10-25, concessions £10, standing room 10p 1hr. before curtain. 2nd venue upstairs £15, concessions £10. M all seats £10, with some advance tickets and some released 10am on day of performance. Wheelchair-accessible. Box office open M-Sa 10am-7:45pm, closes 6pm non-performance weeks. AmEx/MC/V.

 Shakespeare's Globe Theatre, 21 New Globe Walk (☎ 7401 9919; www.shakespeares-globe.org), in the **South Bank.** ⊖ Southwark or London Bridge. Innovative, top-notch performances at this faithful reproduction of Shakespeare's original 16th-century playhouse. Choose among 3 covered tiers of hard, backless wooden benches (cushions £1 extra) or stand through a performance as a "groundling"; come 30min. before the show to get as close as you can. Should it rain, the show must go on, and umbrellas are prohibited. For tours of the Globe, see p. 158. Wheelchair-accessible. Performances mid-May to late Sept. Tu-Sa 7:30pm, Su 6:30pm; June-Sept. also Tu-Sa 2pm, Su 1pm. Box office open M-Sa 10am-6pm, 8pm on performance days. Seats from £12, concessions from £10, yard (i.e., standing) £5. Rain gear £2.50.

National Theatre, South Bank (info ☎ 7452 3400, box office 7452 3000; www.nationaltheatre.org.uk), in the **South Bank.** ⊖ Waterloo or Embankment. Founded by Laurence Olivier, the National Theatre opened in 1976 and has been at the forefront of British theatre ever since. The schedule often includes Shakespearian classics and hard-hitting new works from Britain's brightest playwrights. Bigger shows are mostly staged on the **Olivier,** seating 1160. The 890-seat **Lyttleton** is a proscenium theatre, while the **Cottesloe** offers flexible staging for new works. Tickets typically start at £10. Complicated pricing scheme, which is liable to change from show to show; contact box office for details. Wheelchair-accessible. Box office open M-Sa 9:30am-8pm. MC/V.

NATIONAL THEATRE FOR POCKET CHANGE. Almost every day in the summer, the courtyard at the National Theatre holds a free concert, film, or performance art exhibition. From magic shows to physical comedy, the Theatre will satisfy anyone looking for live entertainment.

Open-Air Theatre, Inner Circle, Regent's Park (☎ 08700 601 811; www.openairtheatre.org), in **Marylebone.** ⊖ Baker St. Charming venue in the middle of Regent's Park. Bring blankets and rain gear to this open-air stage; performances are cancelled only in extreme weather conditions. Program runs June-early Sept. and includes 2 Shakespeare plays, a musical, and a children's performance. Occasional Su night jazz and comedy shows. Bring your own picnic supplies or purchase barbecue or buffet dinner inside the venue. Wheelchair-accessible. Performances M-Sa 8pm; matinees every Th and Sa 2:30pm. £10-38; discounts for groups and under 16 (with adult); student and senior standby £10 from 1hr. before curtain. Box office open Mar.-May M-Sa 10am-6pm; June-Sept. M-Sa 10am-8pm, Su (performance days only) 10am-8pm. AmEx/MC/V.

"OFF-WEST END"

"Off-West End" is one of the best titles a theatre can have. Venues showcase new and raw talent from writers and actors who then go on to run the National Theatre or win an Academy Award. For reassurance, the Globe and the National Theatre, both situated on the South Bank, are both technically "off," but as older and larger venues, are listed separately.

The Almeida, Almeida St. (☎ 7359 4404; www.almeida.co.uk), in **North London.** ⊖ Angel. The top fringe theatre in London, the Almeida always comes up with novel scripts and quality shows, both dramatic and opera; also puts on classics from the likes of Shakespeare and Molière. Big-name stars such as Stockard Channing often take the stage. Renovations to the lobby and central areas have brought in more light and space. Shows M-Sa 7:30pm, Sa matinees 3pm. Tickets from £10. Wheelchair-accessible. MC/V.

Battersea Arts Centre (BAC), Old Town Hall, 176 Lavender Hill (☎ 7223 2223; www.bac.org.uk), in **South London.** ⊖Clapham Common, Clapham Junction, or Stockwell, then a 15min. ride on Bus #345 to the Old Battersea Town Hall. Buses #345, 77, 77a, 156, and G1 all stop at the door. From ⊖Clapham Junction, take the Shopping Center exit, turn left, and walk 10min. up Lavender Hill, just past the intersection with Latchmere Rd. Despite the long-winded directions, the BAC is worth a visit. One of London's top off-West End venues, best known for experimental theatre. Also hosts comedy, opera, and "mainstream works" (generally radical reinterpretations of canonical texts). On occasional "Scratch Nights," brave viewers can see works in progress for free (only with advance booking). Box office open M 10:30am-6pm, Tu-F 10am-9pm, Sa-Su 4-9pm. Tickets from £10, concessions from £5. MC/V.

The Bush Theatre, Shepherd's Bush Green (☎ 7610 4224; www.bushtheatre.co.uk), in **West London.** ⊖Shepherd's Bush or Goldhawk Rd. This theatre's offbeat and cutting-edge shows derive from a policy of encouraging submissions from new writers. Telephone booking M-Sa 10am-7pm. Box office open M-Sa 5-8pm. £13.50, students £9. AmEx/MC/V.

Donmar Warehouse, 41 Earlham St. (☎ 08700 606 624; www.donmarwarehouse.com), in **Covent Garden.** ⊖Covent Garden. In the mid-90s, artistic director Sam Mendes (later of *American Beauty* fame) transformed this gritty space into one of the most excellent theatres in the country, featuring highly regarded contemporary shows with an edge. This is the infamous stage where Nicole Kidman bared all in *The Blue Room* in 1998, so it's not surprising that this nondescript warehouse rarely has difficulty filling its 251 seats. Tickets £13-29; under 18 and students standby 30min. before curtain £12; £7.50 standing room tickets available once performance sells out. 10 tickets available on the day of a performance from 10:30am, limit 2 per person. Wheelchair-accessible. Box office open M-Sa 10am-7:30pm. AmEx/MC/V.

Etcetera Theatre, 265 Camden High St. (☎ 7482 4857; www.etceteratheatre.com), upstairs at the Oxford Arms, in **North London.** ⊖Camden Town. Aptly nicknamed "the smallest theatre in the capital," it's got only 42 seats leading straight to a good-sized stage. 2 plays per night of anything from drama to comedy. Mostly experimental works from new writers and unsolicited scripts, though there have been some famous directors and pieces featured here. Box office opens 30min. before curtain. Shows M-Sa 7 or

NO, NOT BLOOD ALCOHOL CONTENT

To be a visitor to the West End, all you need is a Tube pass and the patience to wait in line for a ticket. Through the classes offered at the **Battersea Arts Centre (BAC),** however, you just may become a West End star.

Offered over the course of a single weekend and open to aspiring thespians of all ages and abilities, the BAC's acting and directing classes are a wonderful way to experience the theatricality of London in a hands-on environment. Classes are taught by professional actors and directors, and give beginners insight into the inner-workings of theatre. Single classes on everything from costumes to song-writing are also offered on Tuesday nights.

For those ready for the spotlight, the BAC offers the unique experience, "Make a Show," in which students collaborate for three days and then present their piece at the BAC in front of a live audience. (Lessons on abating stage fright not included.) No previous experience is necessary. Now there's no reason to let the professionals have all of the fun and take all the credit.

☎ 7223 6557; www.bac.org.uk. "Make A Show" £45, concessions £30. Usually runs all day M and Sa-Su, with performances Tu-W.

7:30pm and 9 or 9:30pm, Su 6:30 and 8:30pm. £8-10, concessions £5-8. MC/V.

The Gate, 11 Pembridge Rd. (☎ 7229 0706; www.gatetheatre.co.uk), in **Notting Hill.** ⊖Notting Hill Gate. In a tiny room above the Prince Albert pub. Famous for supporting fledgling international writers, the Gate's aim is to "discover the hidden riches of international drama"—they often showcase new foreign works (in English translation) before they've been performed in their home countries. Recent productions have included *Tejas Verdes* and the more mainstream *Hair*. Wheelchair-accessible. Performances typically M-F 7:30pm. £15, concessions £10. MC/V.

 THE GATE FOR POCKET CHANGE. Happy Monday at The Gate means that the first 20 customers "pay what they can" at the door.

Hackney Empire, 291 Mare St. (☎ 8985 2424; www.hackneyempire.co.uk), in **East London.** ⊖Bethnal Green or DLR: Hackney Central, then Bus #D6, 106, 25. An unfortunately out-of-the-way site for such an ornate and beautiful theatre that has pulled in the stars for years: Charlie Chaplin performed here early in his career. Features a wide range of performing arts: comedy, musicals, opera, and drama. Recently completed a multi-million-pound overhaul. Call or check website for shows and prices. AmEx/MC/V.

Hampstead Theatre, Eton Ave. (☎ 7722 9301; www.hampsteadtheatre.com), in **North London.** ⊖Swiss Cottage; take the Eton Ave. Exit. This 40-year-old theatre features works selected from hundreds of scripts by budding unknowns from around UK, as well as more established works. Leans toward socially conscious plays and writings. Acting alums include John Malkovich and Jude Law. Shows M-F 7:45pm, Sa 3 and 7:45pm. M £13; Tu-F £19; Sa 1st show £19, 2nd show £22. Limited concessions. Day-of and student tickets £10. MC/V.

The King's Head, 115 Upper St. (☎ 7226 1916), in **North London.** ⊖Angel or Highbury and Islington. Above a pub, this theatre focuses on new writing and rediscovered works. The King's Head has enjoyed good reviews in the press, and successful productions often transfer to the West End. Alums, whose many pictures grace the wall of the pub, include Hugh Grant, Gary Oldman, and Anthony Minghella. 3-course meal (£14) is available to ticket holders 1hr. before the show. Shows Tu-Sa 8pm, Sa 3:30pm. £10-20, concessions M-Th and matinees £5 off. Occasional lunchtime shows and M night short-run shows might be playing; call for exact schedule. MC/V.

Lyric Hammersmith, Lyric Sq. (☎ 08700 500 511; www.lyric.co.uk), in **West London.** ⊖Hammersmith. Behind a concrete facade, this recently renovated, ornate 1895 theatre is known for classy yet controversial productions. Above the main theatre, the small **Lyric Studio** stages experimental drama. The Lyric invests heavily in art education and development programs for the surrounding community. Wheelchair-accessible. Box office open 9:30am-8pm on performance days. Telephone booking 9:30am-7pm. Theatre £10-20; students and concessions £6-10. Studio £12, concessions £7. MC/V.

New End Theatre, 27 New End (☎ 0870 033 2733; www.newendtheatre.co.uk), in **North London.** ⊖Hampstead. New work skillfully produced by local and touring companies tends to have a historically or socially conscious bent. Shows Tu-F 7:30pm, Sa 3:30 and 7:30pm, Su 3:30pm. Box office open M-Sa 10am-8pm, Su 10am-6pm. £15-23, concessions £14-20. MC/V.

The Old Red Lion, 418 St. John St. (☎ 7837 7816; www.oldredliontheatre.co.uk), in **North London.** ⊖Angel. Experimental plays and quirky adaptations of older works. Occasional film screenings and readings from new scripts. Shows change monthly or bimonthly. Performances Tu-Su 7:45 or 8pm; occasional M events. £12, Tu-Th and Su concessions £10. MC/V.

Old Vic, Waterloo Rd. (☎ 7369 1722; www.oldvictheatre.com), in the **South Bank.** ⊖Waterloo. Still in its original 1818 hall (the oldest theatre in London), the Old Vic is one of

London's most historic and beautiful theatres. These days, it hosts touring companies like the Royal Shakespeare Company, which set their own prices and show schedules. Contact box office or check website for listings. Box office M-Sa 10am-7:30pm. MC/V.

Royal Academy of Dramatic Arts (RADA), 62-64 Gower St. (☎7636 7076; www.rada.org), entrance on Malet St., in **Bloomsbury.** ⊖Goodge St. A cheaper alternative to the West End, Britain's most famous drama school has 3 on-site theatres, with productions throughout the year. Call in advance for event details. Wheelchair-accessible. £3-10, concessions £2-7.50. Regular Foyer events during the academic year, including plays, music, and readings M-Th 7 or 7:30pm (some free, others up to £4). Box office open M-F 10am-6pm, on performance nights 10am-7:30pm. AmEx/MC/V.

Soho Theatre, 21 Dean St. (☎0870 429 6883; www.sohotheatre.com), in **Soho.** ⊖Tottenham Court Rd. With a focus on new writers and plenty of low-priced tickets, this populist, modern "off-West End" theatre intends to introduce people of all ages to theatre. These aren't generally well-known plays, but that's what the excitement of new writers' theatre is all about. The associated writers' center will read any script you send them and provide comments. Matinees £5; M-Sa evening general admission £15, 10-20% student discount. Late-night stand-up comedy £8-15. Box office open M-Sa 10am-last performance. MC/V.

Tricycle Theatre, 269 Kilburn High Rd. (☎7328 1000; www.tricycle.co.uk), in **North London.** ⊖Kilburn or Rail: Brondesbury Park. A marvelous 3-in-1, with cinema (p. 219), art gallery, and a theatre known for cutting-edge work and new minority playwrights. One of the most fun places to see a show. Box office open M-Sa 10am-9pm, Su 2-9pm. Performances M-F 8pm, Sa 4 and 8pm. Tickets from £10. Wheelchair-accessible. MC/V.

Young Vic, 66 The Cut (☎7928 6363; www.youngvic.org), in the **South Bank.** ⊖Waterloo. Close to the Old Vic but completely independent, the Young Vic is conducive to experimental theatre. Closed for renovations and set to open in autumn 2006.

SHOPPING

London has long been considered one of the fashion capitals of the world, up there with such greats as New York City, Paris, and Milan. Where else could seven-story department stores (Harrods and Selfridges) bring in tourists and locals for all-day extravaganzas? Unfortunately, in today's globalized economy, London features as many underwhelming chain stores as it does one-of-a-kind boutiques. Oxford St. is the place for a quick club-wear fix but is often overrun with teenagers and tourists who consider Topshop the new vogue simply because it's from London (don't get us wrong, it's still a good store). Unfortunately, price tags are ever-rising; the truly budget-conscious should forgo buying and stick to window shopping in Knightsbridge and Regent St. boutiques for ideas on how to mimic the fashion greats like Vivienne Westwood. Vintage shopping in Notting Hill and wares farther up Portobello Rd. (as well as Camden Town and Spitalfields) are a viable alternative for fashionistas who need to return from a trip with something to show off. Previous decades' trends come back in style sooner or later, and you can usually get a good deal on 1970s go-gos or 80s pumps; beware of obvious fakes and steer clear, once again, of Oxford St., where so-called "vintage" clothing was probably made in 2002 and sells for twice as much as the regular line.

Let's Go understands that shopping is a part of tourism, particularly in London, but that top-notch shopping is not readily available to budget travelers; we therefore include a Notable Chains section (p. 238) for the best of the overrun. For the most part, though, shopping listings include quirks and perks that you may not otherwise find at home or in the West End.

SHOPPING BY TYPE

ALCOHOL		▦ Apple Tree(247)	WEND
▦ Gerry's(246)	WEND	▦ The Laden Showroom(240)	EL
		Oscar Milo(243)	WEND
ANTIQUES		Whistles(255)	CHEL
Hirst Antiques(252)	NH	World's End(255)	CHEL
BOOKS		CLOTHES: SALE	
▦ Books for Cooks(252)	NH	Browns Labels for Less(244)	WEND
Blackwell's(246)	WEND	Paul Smith Sale Shop(244)	WEND
Fosters Bookshop(255)	WL		
Foyles(246)	WEND	CLOTHES: VINTAGE	
Gay's the Word(249)	BLOOM	▦ Annie's(250)	NL
Hatchard's(243)	WEND	Dolly Diamond(252)	NH
Mega City Comics(250)	NL	▦ Pandora(253)	K/B
Oxfam Books(249)	BLOOM	Sam Greenberg(243)	WEND
▦ Shipley(247)	WEND	▦ Steinberg & Tolkein(254)	CHEL
▦ Sotheran's of Sackville Street(243)	WEND		
Stanfords(247)	WEND	DEPARTMENT STORES	
Ulysses(249)	BLOOM	Fortnum & Mason(244)	WEND
World's End Bookshop(254)	CHEL	Harrods(253)	K/B
		Harvey Nichols(254)	K/B
CLOTHES: NEW		▦ Liberty(244)	WEND
Ad Hoc(255)	CHEL	▦ Selfridges(244)	WEND

GIFTS AND MISCELLANY

Daisy & Tom(255)	CHEL
Hamley's(244)	WEND
Hats Etcetera(253)	KEN/EC
James Smith & Sons(249)	BLOOM
L. Cornelissen & Son(249)	BLOOM
■ Neal's Yard Dairy(248)	WEND
Neal's Yard Remedies(248)	WEND
Penhaligon's(248)	WEND
■ Sh! Women's Erotic Emporium(240)	EL
Twining's(242)	HOL

MARKETS

Apple and Jubilee(248)	WEND
Bayswater(251)	BAY
Berwick Street(246)	WEND
Brick Lane(241)	EL
■ Brixton(242)	SL
Camden Markets(250)	NL
■ Camden Passage(250)	NL
■ Greenwich Markets(241)	EL
Leather Lane(242)	HOL
Petticoat Lane(241)	EL
Portobello Road Markets(252)	NH
■ Spitalfields(240)	EL
Sunday (Up)(241)	EL

MUSIC

Black Market(246)	WEND
Honest Jon's(253)	NH
Out on the Floor(251)	NL
Sister Ray(246)	WEND
Revival Records(247)	WEND
Rough Trade(252)	NH
Turnkey(247)	WEND
Uptown Records(247)	WEND

SHOES

Egoshego(248)	WEND
Office(248)	WEND
Sukie's(255)	CHEL

NEIGHBORHOOD ABBREVIATIONS: BAY Bayswater **BLOOM** Bloomsbury **CHEL** Chelsea **CITY** The City of London **CLERK** Clerkenwell **HOL** Holborn **KEN/EC** Kensington and Earl's Court **K/B** Knightsbridge and Belgravia **M/RP** Marylebone and Regent's Park **NH** Notting Hill **SB** The South Bank **WEND** The West End **WEMIN** Westminster **NL** North London **SL** South London **EL** East London **WL** West London

NOTABLE CHAINS

As in almost any major city, London's retail scene is dominated by chains. Fortunately, local shoppers are picky enough that buying from a chain doesn't mean abandoning the flair and quirky stylishness for which Londoners are famed. Plus, in such an expensive city, chain stores are often a great place for deals. Most chains have a flagship store on or near Oxford St., usually with a second branch in Covent Garden. The branches will have slightly different hours, but almost all the stores listed below are open daily 10am-7pm, starting later (noon) on Sunday and staying open an hour later one night of the week (usually Thursday).

BOOKS

Waterstone's (www.waterstones.co.uk). More than a dozen branches, including 203-206 Piccadilly (☎7851 2400; ⊖Piccadilly Circus) and 82 Gower St. (☎7636 1577; ⊖Goodge St.). Europe's largest bookstore, with specialty sections in just about everything. Comprehensive map and travel guide section for London and Britain, including ■ **Let's Go.** Many branches have cafe or restaurant. Frequent special events, including book signings by big-name authors (£2-4). Wheelchair-accessible. AmEx/MC/V.

CLOTHES AND ACCESSORIES

FCUK, flagship 396 Oxford St. (☎7629 7766; www.fcuk.com). ⊖Bond St. 17 branches, including 249-251 Regent St. (☎7493 3124; ⊖Oxford Circus) and 168-170 Kensington High St. (☎7937 4665; ⊖High St. Kensington). The home of the 90s advertising coup has extensive men's and women's clothing collections sporting their vaguely offensive, subversive moniker. Somehow they manage to keep coming up with new ways to exploit those four letters. Very popular with well-off young professionals. Many designs have UK-specific references. AmEx/MC/V.

Jigsaw, flagship 126-127 New Bond St. (☎7491 4484; www.jigsaw-online.com). ⊖Bond St. 22 branches, including 449 Strand (☎7497 8663; ⊖Charing Cross) and 65 Kensington High St. (☎7937 3573; ⊖High St. Kensington). High-quality, mid-priced women's wear in feminine, classic cuts. Designs prize elegance over fad-based fashions, though there has been a move toward edgier designs. AmEx/MC/V.

Karen Millen (☎08701 601 830; www.karenmillen.co.uk). 17 branches including 247 Regent St. (⊖Oxford Circus), 22-23 James St. (⊖Covent Garden), 33 Kings Rd. (⊖Sloane Sq.), Jubilee Place (⊖Canary Wharf), and Barker's Arcade (⊖High St. Kensington). Best known for richly embroidered brocade suits and evening gowns, but recently edging toward a more casual line. Starting to expand their classic look to encompass a younger market. AmEx/MC/V.

Lush (☎01202 668 545; www.lush.co.uk). 13 London branches including Covent Garden Piazza Unit 11 (⊖ Covent Garden), 40 Carnaby St. (⊖Oxford Circus), 123 King's Rd. (⊖Sloane Sq.), and Unit 55, Broadgate Link, Liverpool St. Station (⊖Liverpool St.). All-natural cosmetics look good enough to eat: soap is hand-cut from blocks to look like cakes and cheeses (£2-5). Vegan cosmetics are marked with a green dot. New products come out every season. AmEx/MC/V.

Mango, flagship 106-112 Regent St. (☎7434 1384; www.mango.com). ⊖Piccadilly Circus. 2 other locations at 233 Oxford St. (☎7534 3505; ⊖Oxford Circus) and 8-12 Neal St. (☎7240 6099; ⊖Covent Garden). A UK foothold for a Spanish fashion empire that is quickly becoming a London mainstay, Mango carries a female line cut with classy, sensible designs appropriate for all occasions. Most casual tops and bottoms go for under £40, some as low as £10 during the summer sales. AmEx/MC/V.

Monsoon, flagship 5-7 James St. (☎7379 3623; www.monsoon.co.uk). ⊖Covent Garden. Over 20 branches, including 48 Brompton Rd. (☎7581 3972; ⊖Knightsbridge) and 264 Oxford St. (☎7499 2578; ⊖Oxford Circus). A haven for affordable, ethnic-inspired clothing for all shapes and sizes. Also sells a variety of shoes, and evening and bridal wear. AmEx/MC/V.

Muji (www.muji.co.uk). 8 branches including 187 Oxford St. (☎7437 7503; ⊖Oxford Circus), 135 Long Acre (☎7379 0820; ⊖Covent Garden), 118 King's Rd. (☎7823 8688; ⊖Sloane Sq.), 157 Kensington High St. (☎7376 2484; ⊖High St. Kensington), and 6-17 Tottenham Court Rd., Unit 5 (☎7436 1779; ⊖Tottenham Court Rd.). Escape the high-street frenzy. Minimalist lifestyle stores, with a sleek zen take on everything from outdoor gear to futons to home office accessories. AmEx/MC/V.

Oasis, flagship Unit 12-14 Argyll St. (☎7434 1799; www.oasis-stores.com). ⊖Oxford Circus. 22 branches, including 13 James St. (☎7240 7445; ⊖Covent Garden) and 28a Kensington Church St. (☎7938 4019; ⊖High St. Kensington). Colorful, sexy clothes for work and play, plus shoes and accessories. A favorite with students and 20-somethings. AmEx/MC/V.

Topshop, flagship 36-38 Great Castle St. (☎7636 7700; www.topshop.co.uk). ⊖Oxford Circus. 2nd main location at 60-64 Strand (☎7839 4144; ⊖Charing Cross). Dozens of locations in central London. Cheap, popular fashions for young people; over-25s will feel middle-aged. Boasts a huge range of casual clothes, strappy shoes, and skimpy women's clubwear. Free Style Advisor personal shopping service. Many locations have adjoining **Topman,** for men. AmEx/MC/V.

Zara, flagship 118 Regent St. (☎7534 9500; www.zara.com). ⊖Piccadilly Circus. 9 branches including 215-219 Oxford St. (☎7534 2900; ⊖Oxford Circus). Yet another stylish Spanish brand that has taken Europe by storm with its sleek, relatively inexpensive clothing. Prices similar to its neighbor Mango, but with brighter and younger designs. AmEx/MC/V.

MUSIC

HMV, 150 Oxford St. (☎0845 602 7800; www.hmv.co.uk). ⊖Oxford Circus. Also at 40 King St. (⊖Covent Garden). 3 massive floors with a huge range of new vinyl, especially dance music. Music madness done right. Games department has playable consoles from every game maker. Wheelchair-accessible. Hours vary by store.

Virgin Megastore, flagship 1 Piccadilly (☎7439 2500). ✪Piccadilly Circus. 13 branches including 213-219 Camden High St. (☎7482 5307; ✪Camden Town) and 62-64 Kensington High St. (☎7938 3511; ✪High St. Kensington). Covers the entire musical spectrum, including related books, magazines, and posters, DVDs, videos, and computer games. Internet cafe on ground fl. (£1 per 50min. before noon, £1 per min. after noon). Wheelchair-accessible. Hours vary by store.

SALES. Many boutiques and department stores hold seasonal sales, offering extraordinary discounts in January and July.

SHOPPING BY NEIGHBORHOOD

SHOPPING

EAST LONDON

WHITECHAPEL AND THE EAST END

In East London, street markets are lively and widespread, providing some of the most unique shopping in the area. **Spitalfields,** widely recognized as London's best market, offers a tasty weekend display of organic fruits and vegetables, along with trendy artwork, clothing, and jewelry. Just two blocks away, the new **Sunday (Up)** Market is a lesser-known alternative to the claustrophobia-inducing crowds of its neighbor. Petticoat Lane and Brick Lane Market, both popular tourist destinations, are unfortunately past their prime. In **Hoxton** and **Shoreditch,** as well as in the stretch of Brick Ln. just north of the Truman Brewery, independent young designers have opened up boutiques frequented by local artists and artsy pretenders. These places are great for clubbing gear, second-hand clothing, and ideas on how to modify your wardrobe.

CLOTHES

▨ **The Laden Showroom,** 103 Brick Ln. (☎7247 2431; www.laden.co.uk). ✪Aldgate East or Liverpool St. At this trendy spot, over 40 local designers have their own space, organized by white canvas hung to create small, cube-like displays. This hip shop is a fitting favorite of celebs like Posh Spice, who calls it one of London's hidden finds. Up-to-the-minute dressy and casual pieces, mostly for women, share space with choice accessories. Dedicated staff are highly knowledgeable. New and recently used items, most under £70. Open M noon-6pm, Tu-F 11am-6:30pm, Sa 11am-7pm, Su 10:30am-6pm. AmEx/MC/V.

GIFTS AND MISCELLANY

▨ **Sh! Women's Erotic Emporium,** 57 Hoxton Sq. (☎7613 5458; www.sh-women-store.com). ✪Old St. Just off Hoxton Square. Founded as a "fresh alternative to Soho sleaze," this sex shop catering to women has all the expected gadgets and gizmos with a female-friendly feel. Recently voted the "Best Sex Shop in London," the bubble gum-pink walls, comfy lounge chairs, and hot tea make customers feel comfortable, and friendly staff are eager to provide advice. Men allowed inside only when accompanied by a female. Open daily noon-8pm. MC/V.

MARKETS

▨ **Spitalfields Market,** Commercial St. ✪Shoreditch (during rush hour), Liverpool St., or Aldgate East. Formerly one of London's main wholesale vegetable markets, Spitalfields has matured to be the best of the East End markets. It's now a dizzying array of crafts and food stalls selling goods from organic fruits to baked goods to freshly cooked ethnic dishes. Su food shares space with rows of clothing by local independent designers. Crowds can be overwhelming; many head to the Sunday (Up) Market, but those in the know simply wait until late in the day for the scene to thin out. Crafts market open M-F 11am-3:30pm, Su 10am-5pm. Antiques market open Th 9am-5pm. Organic market open F and Su 10am-5pm.

Sunday (Up) Market, ⊖Shoreditch or Aldgate East. Housed in a portion of the old Truman Brewery just off Hanbury St., this Spitalfields neighbor offers more space but slightly less inspiring goods. The market showcases jewelry, handbags, art, housewares, clothing, and greeting cards by local designers. Excellent food options. Held outdoors in good weather, indoors in winter. Open Su 10am-5pm.

Brick Lane Market, ⊖Shoreditch or Aldgate East. At the heart of Whitechapel's sizable Bangladeshi community, Brick Lane hosts a large Su market. Most of the stands sell bargain household goods and trinkets, along with annoying offers for cell-phone unlocking and pirated DVDs. It's a challenge to get out of the crowd once you're in the thick of it. Go for the experience but don't expect to find many treasures. Open Su 8am-2pm.

Petticoat Lane Market, ⊖Liverpool St., Aldgate, or Aldgate East. Unless you're hunting for British flag socks, nightgowns, or clock radios, this shopping experience will likely disappoint. Once the height of the street-market scene, Petticoat now plays 2nd fiddle to its more popular sister markets mentioned above. Hectic shopping begins around 9:30am and is in full swing by 11am. Open Su 9am-2pm.

DOCKLANDS

Corporate Docklands has gone its own way from the rest of East London with huge **Cabot Place** and **Canada Place** malls. The newest addition, the **Jubilee Place** shopping center, sits a mere 2min. walk across the plaza. Sleek, modern, and at times utterly confusing to navigate, the three contain close to 200 different shops and restaurants, although they're mostly middle-range chain stores catering to the power-lunch crowd. (⊖/DLR: Canary Wharf.)

GREENWICH

While Greenwich's markets may not rival those of the East End, the longer trek tends to weed out the casual from the hard-core shoppers. Numerous weekend markets converge on Greenwich, and on Sundays it is blanketed with stalls and shoppers looking for deals among the multitudes of goods. You can expect Sundays to be less crowded here than at Spitalfields.

▨ **Greenwich Market,** in the block surrounded by King William Walk, Greenwich Church St., College Approach,

and Romney Rd. DLR: Cutty Sark. A worthwhile stop on the market crawl. Th antiques and collectibles 7:30am-5:30pm; F arts and crafts and collectibles 9am-5pm; Sa-Su arts and crafts with food court 9:30am-5:30pm.

Antiques Market, Greenwich High Rd. Rail: Greenwich or DLR: Cutty Sark. Mostly 20th-century goods, many affordable. Open Sa-Su 10am-5pm.

Village Market, Stockwell St. (☎8858 0808). DLR: Cutty Sark. The international food court is the best part here, but there are also second-hand clothes and bric-a-brac in this indoor market. Everything from gramophones to used books. Open Sa-Su 8am-late afternoon.

HOLBORN

With Covent Garden so close, Holborn is not a top shopping destination in comparison. **High Holborn** is a busy road with a few common chains, while **Fleet Street** has a number of indistinguishable clothing shops. Leather Lane Market is a local favorite, though, with jewelry and flower stands lining the street.

SEE MAP, p. 364

Leather Lane Market, between Gray's Inn Rd. and Hatton Garden. Confusingly enough, the name of the street actually has nothing to do with leather (it's a corruption of the 13th-century "Le Vrunelane"); but you can still buy yourself some shoes or a handbag at this 300-year-old market. Not well-known to tourists, this free-for-all tucked up above High Holborn serves the local and business communities, which come to browse the clothes, food, electrical goods, and cheap CDs/DVDs on display. Open M-F 10:30am-2:30pm.

Twining's, 216 Strand (☎7353 3511). ⊖Temple. London's narrowest shop, slightly out of place wedged between the many-storied office buildings. Twining's is the oldest family-run business in Britain to stay on the same premises (since founding the Golden Lyon tea house in 1717) and takes its legacy seriously. In addition to a small tea museum in the back, Twining's has its own epic lay, including the stirring: "Note, by the way, it was not *Twining's* tea the Boston rebels tossed into the sea." The real draw is, of course, the tea: Lady Grey (from £1.80 per 125g), Prince of Wales (from £1.60 per 100g), and other noble blends. Individual tea bags available from 15p. Tea services and tea boxes are also for sale. Open M-F 9:30am-5pm. AmEx/MC/V.

 BOOKWORMS REJOICE! The South Bank Book Market is the only established second-hand book market in Southern England. Situated just outside the BFI Theatre, the market is open daily for those who need more in front of their eyes than just a view.

SOUTH LONDON

Brixton is the place to go for fresh fruits and vegetables as well as for meats from animals common and exotic. The assortment of foods at the Brixton Market is dizzying, as is the smoke coming from some of the stalls. Shops along **Brixton Road** and **Coldharbour Lane** blast hip hop and reggae and peddle skimpy tops, tight pants, and gaudy accessories for a night out on the town.

▨ **Brixton Market,** along Electric Ave., Pope's Rd., and Brixton Station Rd., and inside markets in Granville Arcade and Market Row. ⊖Brixton. To experience Brixton fully in the daytime, stroll through the crowded streets of the market, where stalls hawk everything from cheap household items to bootlegged films. The market carries London's best selection of Afro-Caribbean fruits, vegetables, spices, and fish. Negotiate with the vendors for some unbelievable deals on meat and produce. Open M-Tu and Th-Su 8am-6pm; W 8am-3pm.

CASH MONEY. When visiting local markets, it's always wise to bring cash, especially in lower denominations. While many vendors have begun accepting plastic, there is often a transaction fee incurred which can either be a fixed amount or a percentage of your total.

THE WEST END

MAYFAIR AND ST. JAMES'S

Shopping in London is concentrated around a number of the poshest high streets in the world, many of which call Mayfair home. The bona-fide shopping nirvana, **Oxford Street**—appealing to chain-store aficionados and those who enjoy a great crowd—betrays Mayfair's real character. **Regent Street** is slightly more in line with the refined affairs of the neighborhood. Off Regent St., swingin' **Carnaby Street** has a decent selection of youth fashions from famous brands.

SEE MAP, p. 356

Near Piccadilly, a number of Regency and Victorian **arcades** are lined with boutiques whose less interesting wares have changed little in the last hundred years. The oldest is the **Royal Opera Arcade,** between Pall Mall and Charles II St.; the most prestigious is the **Royal Arcade,** patronized by Queen Victoria and home of palace chocolatiers Charbonnel and Walker. The most famous, and longest, is the **Burlington Arcade,** next to the Royal Academy of the Arts, which houses several leather and jewelry shops. Shoppers take note: these and the other arcades have a bit of a stuffed-shirt feel; they're filled with upmarket clothing shops specializing in tweed and top hats. (Shops inside keep their own hours, but most are open M-Sa about 10am-7pm, Su noon-6pm.)

BOOKS

⧉ **Sotheran's of Sackville Street,** 2-5 Sackville St. (☎ 7439 6151; www.sotherans.co.uk). ⊖Piccadilly Circus. Founded in 1761 in York, Sotheran's moved to London in 1815, when Charles Dickens began to frequent these stacks; the selection of collectible and rare books hasn't changed much since. And while the atmosphere of hushed voices and locked shelves might give the impression of a library, there are some newer books on shelf for sale (£10-35). Antique prints available downstairs. Open M-F 9:30am-6pm, Sa 10am-4pm. AmEx/MC/V.

Hatchard's, 187 Piccadilly (☎ 7439 9921; www.hatchards.co.uk). ⊖Green Park or Piccadilly Circus. Although London's oldest bookshop (est. 1797) has been bought by Waterstone's, it still has the respect of locals. Renowned for its selection of signed bestsellers. As you'd expect from Prince Charles's official bookseller, the fiction and royalty sections are particularly strong. Open M-Sa 9:30am-7pm, Su noon-6pm. AmEx/MC/V.

CLOTHES

Sam Greenberg, Unit 1.7 Kingly Court, Carnaby St. (☎ 7287 8474). ⊖Oxford Circus. Specializing in 80s T-shirts and old coats and jackets, this true vintage store caters to all post-punk throwbacks. Small collection of designer jeans from £50. T-shirts start at £10, and leather jackets (£40) are a real steal. Open M-W and F-Sa 11am-7pm, Th 11am-8pm, Su noon-6pm. MC/V.

Oscar Milo, 19 Avery Row (☎ 7495 5846). ⊖Bond St. Particularly good menswear boutique with clothes that may not be cheap but are a good value. The 3 small floors are neatly organized and stacked with well-cut jeans, shirts, and seriously smooth footwear (separates and shoes £50-110), and the staff is friendly yet professional. Open M-W and F-Sa 10:30am-6:30pm, Th 10:30am-7pm, Su 1-5pm. AmEx/MC/V.

THE REAL DEAL. The areas around **Oxford Street** and **Regent Street** are dominated by enormous chain stores. If you are interested in buying anything from music to clothing, veer off this well-beaten path to find independently owned stores. They may have smaller collections, but the quality of goods and services are likely to be better and uniquely English.

CLOTHES: SALE SHOPS

Paul Smith Sale Shop, 23 Avery Row (☎ 7493 1287; www.paulsmith.co.uk). ⊖Bond St. Small range of last-season and clearance items from the acknowledged master of modern British menswear. Decent-sized stock of casual and formal wear at least 30% off original prices: grab a shirt or a pair of jeans for £45. Open M-W 10am-6pm, Th 10am-7pm, F-Sa 10am-6pm, Su 1-5pm. AmEx/MC/V.

Browns Labels for Less, 50 South Molton St. (☎ 7514 0052; www.brownsfashion.com). ⊖Bond St. Remainders from the Browns mini-empire that's taking over South Molton St. The range is small, and the stock can be out of season, but high fashion brands are reduced to bearable prices—Missoni and Jil Sander tops drop to under £45. Open M-W 10am-6:30pm, Th 10am-7pm, F-Sa 10am-6:30pm. AmEx/MC/V.

DEPARTMENT STORES

▨ **Selfridges,** 400 Oxford St. (☎ 0870 837 7377; www.selfridges.com). ⊖Bond St. The total department store—tourists may flock to Harrods, but Londoners head to Selfridges. Fashion departments are not cheap but run the gamut from traditional tweeds to space age clubwear. They also include small selections from many chain stores, such as Oasis and Topshop. Departments specialize in every product imaginable, from antiques to scented candles (not to mention key cutting and theatre tickets). With 18 cafes and restaurants, a hair salon, an exchange bureau, and even a hotel, shopaholics need never leave. Massive Jan. and July sales. Wheelchair-accessible. Open M-F 10am-8pm, Sa 9:30am-8pm, Su noon-6pm. AmEx/MC/V.

▨ **Liberty,** 210-220 Regent St. (☎ 7734 1234; www.liberty.co.uk), main entrance on Marlborough St. ⊖Oxford Circus. Liberty's timbered, Tudor chalet (built in 1922) sets the regal tone for this unique department store. The focus on top-quality design and handcrafts makes it more like a giant boutique than a full-blown department store. Liberty is famous for custom fabric prints—with 10,000 Liberty prints now archived—sewn into everything from shirts to pillows. It also has a wide array of other high-end contemporary designer lines, home accessories, and hard-to-find beauty lines. Wheelchair-accessible. Open M-W and F-Sa 10am-7pm, Th 10am-8pm, Su noon-6pm. AmEx/MC/V.

Fortnum & Mason, 181 Piccadilly (☎ 7734 8040; www.fortnumandmason.co.uk). ⊖Green Park or Piccadilly Circus. As the official grocer of the royal family, this gourmet department store provides quality foodstuffs that are fit for a queen. From *foie gras* to preserves and tea, the price tags are hefty, but the quality is top-notch. Don't come here to do your weekly shopping—prices aside, the focus is very much on gifts and luxury items. A complete renovation in 2007 added a basement wine bar to the existing 3 restaurants. The fancy St. James Restaurant serves a lovely formal afternoon tea M-Sa 3-7:30pm. Classic set tea £24, rare set tea £27. Wheelchair-accessible. Fountain Restaurant open M-Sa 8:30am-8pm. Fortnum & Mason open M-Sa 10am-6:30pm, Su noon-6pm (food hall and patio restaurant only). AmEx/MC/V.

GIFTS AND MISCELLANY

Hamley's, 188-189 Regent St. (☎ 7734 3161; www.hamleys.co.uk). ⊖Oxford Circus. Quite simply one of the best toy shops in the world. Opened in 1760, Hamley's has 7 floors filled with every conceivable toy and game, plus dozens of strategically placed product demonstrations tempting the young (and not-so-young) with flying airplanes

SHOPPING

■ **West End Shopping**

ALCOHOL/FOOD

Gerry's, **1** — E2

BOOKS

Blackwell's, **2** — D2
Foyles, **3** — A2
Hatchard's, **4** — B2
Shipley, **5** — F2
Sotheran's of
Sackville, **6** — D3
Stanfords, **7** — B1
Waterstone's, **8** — B2, D3, G2

CLOTHES

Apple Tree, **9** — F1
Charles Tyrwhitt, **10** — D3
FCUK, **11** — A2
Karen Millen, **12** — B1, C2, G2
Lush, **13** — E1
Mango, **14** — D3
Oasis, **15** — F2
Oscar Milo, **16** — B2
Sam Greenberg, **17** — D2
Ted Baker, **18** — D2
Topshop/Topman, **19** — C1, C2
Zara, **20** — E3

CLOTHES: SALE SHOP

Brown's Labels for
Less, **21** — D2
Paul Smith
Sale Shop, **22** — A2

DEPARTMENT STORES

Fortnum and
Mason, **23** — B2
John Lewis, **24** — B2

Liberty, **25** — D3
Selfridges, **26** — B1

GIFTS AND MISCELLANY

Butler and Wilson, **27** — D2
Hamley's, **28** — A2
Neal's Yard Dairy, **29** — B2
Neal's Yard
Remedies, **30** — F2
Penhaligon's, **31** — G2

MARKETS

Apple and
Jubilee Markets, **32** — G2
Berwick St.
Market, **33** — E2

MUSIC

Black Market, **34** — F2
HMV, **35** — C1, D1
Music Zone, **36** — D1
Reckless Records, **37** — E2
Selectadisc, **38** — D2

Turnkey, **39** — F1
Uptown Records, **40** — D1
Virgin Megastore, **41** — D3

SHOES

Egoshego, **42** — F1
Office, **43** — F1

Office Sale
Shop, **44** — F2

SPORTING GOODS

Lilywhite's, **45** — E3

and rubber bugs that stick to the walls. Complete with a Build-a-Bear boutique and an overwhelmingly pink and glittery Barbie floor, even grown-ups may find themselves waxing nostalgic about childhood toys. The 4th fl. has enough model cars, planes, and trains for the most die-hard enthusiast; the basement has Lego stations, video game consoles, and, of course, an in-house candy shop. Wheelchair-accessible. Open M-F 10am-8pm, Sa 9:30am-8pm, Su noon-6pm. AmEx/MC/V.

SOHO

Soho's eternal trendiness has made it one of the world's top shopping destinations. The record stores of **D'Arblay** and **Berwick Street** will satisfy any music fan's needs. **Denmark Street,** on the eastern fringe of Soho, has been dubbed London's "Tin Pan Alley" due to its many musical instrument and equipment shops, while **Charing Cross Road** remains London's bookshop center.

ALCOHOL

Gerry's, 74 Old Compton St. (☎7734 2053). ⊖Piccadilly Circus or Leicester Sq. Gerry's stocks a staggering selection of beer and hard liquor in all sizes, from miniatures to magnums. With 80 different tequilas, 170 vodkas, a revolving bottle display, and an incendiary Italian absinthe that's 89.9% alcohol by volume (half-liter £40), you can get drunk just looking. Other popular choices include a Polish apple pie-flavored vodka and Brazilian spirits. Open M-F 9am-6:30pm, Sa 8am-10pm. MC/V.

MARKETS

Berwick Street Market. ⊖Leicester Sq. or Piccadilly Circus. Southernmost strip of Berwick St. One of central London's most well-known fresh fruit and vegetable markets since the 1840s. Small but with fresh, high quality merchandise. Also sells selections of chocolates and sweets. Especially lively at lunchtime. Open M-Sa 9am-5pm. Cash only.

BOOKS

Blackwell's, 100 Charing Cross Rd. (☎7292 5100; www.blackwell.co.uk). ⊖Tottenham Court Rd. or Leicester Sq. Get blissfully lost in the London flagship store of Oxford's top academic bookshop, with everything on 1 enormous fl. Go for the postmodern theory, stay for the huge selection of fiction. Wheelchair-accessible. Open M-Sa 9:30am-8pm, Su noon-6pm. AmEx/MC/V.

Foyles, 113-119 Charing Cross Rd. (☎7437 5660; www.foyles.co.uk). ⊖Tottenham Court Rd. or Leicester Sq. With over 30 mi. of recently renovated shelving, this labyrinthine bookshop spread over 5 floors is a good place to lose yourself in a book—or to lose a small child. A never-ending fiction department and a small art gallery top off an already overwhelming selection. Relax with a new book in the cafe or bring your laptop and take advantage of free Wi-Fi. Wheelchair-accessible. Open M-Sa 9:30am-9pm, Su noon-6pm. AmEx/MC/V.

MUSIC

Black Market, 25 D'Arblay St. (☎7437 0478; www.bm-soho.com). ⊖Oxford Circus. Metal-clad walls and massive speakers dominate the all-vinyl dance emporium, along with turntables ready for amateur or professional scratching. House and garage upstairs, phenomenal drum and bass section below with more underground garage. Also sells club tickets and own-label merchandise (£12-30). Open M-W and Sa 11am-7pm, Th-F 11am-8pm. AmEx/MC/V.

Sister Ray, 34-35 Berwick St. (☎7734 3297; www.sisterray.co.uk). ⊖Tottenham Court Rd. or Oxford Circus. The big daddy of the Berwick St. music shops emphasizes selection. Spacious compared to its competitors and packed with everything from hip hop to drum and bass to soul and beyond. The selections are often cheaper than other independent shops in the area (new releases £8-11). Strong vinyl and DVD offerings. Open M-Sa 9:30am-8pm, Su noon-6pm. MC/V.

Revival Records, 30 Berwick St. (☎ 7437 4271). ⊖Tottenham Court Rd. or Oxford Circus. Small secondhand shop has a varied collection of used CDs and vinyl. Recently revived under a new name and new ownership. Popular CDs around £9. Eclectic selection of used DVDs. Open M-Sa 10am-7pm. AmEx/MC/V.

Uptown Records, 3 D'Arblay St. (☎ 7434 3639; www.uptownrecords.com). ⊖Tottenham Court Rd. or Oxford Circus. DJs' daytime habitat. Descend the spiral staircase in this small all-vinyl store to hear them trying out new mixes and advising shoppers on the latest house, garage, and hip-hop happenings. DJ equipment £50-100. Open M-W and Sa 10:30am-7pm, Th-F 10:30am-8pm. AmEx/MC/V.

Turnkey, 114-116 Charing Cross Rd. (☎ 7419 9999; www.turnkey.co.uk). ⊖Tottenham Court Rd. A creative dance DJ's paradise, with a basement crammed with synthesizers, turntables, PA machines, amps, and a mix station. Packed with customers trying out the merchandise. Upstairs, play to your heart's content on dozens of dedicated analyzers, processors, and PCs. Massive range of guitars and keyboards on the 1st fl. Open M-W and F-Sa 10am-6pm, Th 10am-7pm. AmEx/MC/V.

 SHOP TILL YOU DROP. Most shops in London stay open late one night per week. To continue your consumerism into the early evening, head to Chelsea and Knightsbridge on Wednesday night and to Oxford St. and Covent Garden on Thursday night.

COVENT GARDEN AND THE STRAND

Once the hottest proving ground for new designers, Covent Garden is gradually being overtaken by large clothing chains: almost every store with an eye on the youth market has more than one shop in the area, with a main branch on Oxford St. or Regent St. Mid-priced chains and tacky souvenir shops fill the piazza, though there are still enough quirky specialty shops left to make it worth a quick wander. Still a top destination for funky footwear and mid-priced clubwear, **Neal Street** led the regeneration of Covent Garden back in the 90s, though it is now indistinguishable from Carnaby St. (p. 243). The fashion focus has shifted to nearby streets such as **Short's Gardens** to the east for chic menswear and **Earlham** and **Monmouth Street** to the west for a similarly stylish selection of women's clothing. *(⊖Covent Garden unless otherwise noted.)*

BOOKS

▨ **Shipley,** 70 and 72 Charing Cross Rd. (☎ 7836 4872; www.artbook.co.uk). ⊖Leicester Sq. Formerly Zwemmer, this art-specialist behemoth spreads its media over 2 stores. A wide selection of books on photography, film, and fashion, along with graphic design, typography, and painting sections makes this a key stop for any art buff. Staff is more than happy to suggest selections. Both stores open M-Sa 10am-6:30pm. AmEx/MC/V.

Stanfords, 12-14 Long Acre (☎ 7836 1321; www.stanfords.co.uk). Another location at 1 Regent St. A map superstore, Stanfords covers every corner, nook, and cranny of the universe. With a sweeping range of hiking maps, city maps, road maps, flight maps, star maps, wall maps, and globes, you'll never be lost again. Carries a massive selection of travel books (including ▨ **Let's Go**) covering the entire 1st fl. Store open M, W, F 9am-7:30pm, Tu 9:30am-7:30pm, Th 9am-8pm, Sa 10am-7pm, Su noon-6pm. MC/V.

CLOTHES

▨ **Apple Tree,** 62 Neal St. (☎ 7379 5944; www.finiki.co.uk). Small boutique that specializes in upcoming and independent clothing designers. Almost everything in the store is hand-sewn, and many items are exclusive to this store and one-of-a-kind. Selection ranges from beautiful eyelet dresses (£60) to printed tunics (£35) and ballet flats (£30). Many staff are designers as well. Open M-Sa 10:30am-7:30pm, Su 11am-6:30pm. AmEx/MC/V.

GIFTS AND MISCELLANY

Neal's Yard Dairy, 17 Short's Gardens (☎ 7240 5700; www.nealsyarddairy.co.uk). You'll smell it from a mile off—and that's a good thing. The enormous array of mostly British and Irish cheeses is entirely produced in small farms by traditional methods; massive wheels of stilton and cheddar line the shelves and countertops. The staff is eager to slice off samples and compare types. Also sells preserves, organic milk, and yogurts. Drop in to escape the summer heat—the chilly shop is essentially a walk-in refrigerator, in order to keep the cheese fresh. Call ☎ 7645 3555 for info on tutored cheese tastings (£38). Open M-Th 11am-6:30pm, F-Sa 10am-6:30pm. MC/V.

Neal's Yard Remedies, 15 Neal's Yard (☎ 7379 7222; www.nealsyardremedies.com). An alternative to more mainstream bath and body stores, Neal's offers soaps, lotions, and fragrances incorporating everything from lavender to some of nature's lesser-known treasures (like bladder wrack and pilewort). What started as a little yard shop has grown into a national chain, complete with books and pamphlets on natural health care. Most of the employees are licensed herbalists, homeopaths, and aromatherapists. Each Neal's has rooms for private therapeutic sessions; call ☎ 7379 7662 to reserve. Open M-Sa 10am-7pm, Su 11am-6pm. AmEx/MC/V.

Penhaligon's, 41 Wellington St. (☎ 7836 2150; www.penhaligons.com). Branches on Bond St. and in Piccadilly Circus. Founded by former palace barber William Henry Penhaligon in 1870, Penhaligon's still provides elite men and women with scents and grooming products. Winston Churchill never left home without a dab of the English classic Blenheim Bouquet. Wide selection of scented candles and *eau de toilettes* from £20. Call in to make a personal scent-layering appointment. Wheelchair-accessible. Open M-W and F-Sa 10am-6pm, Th 10am-7pm, Su noon-6pm. AmEx/MC/V.

MARKETS

Apple Market, inside the Covent Garden Piazza. Sells handcrafts, jewelry, and knick-knacks from artists and designers. Excellent finds, but expect to pay tourist prices. Unusually large selection of cufflinks. Wheelchair-accessible. Open daily 10:30am-6pm. Some vendors accept AmEx/MC/V.

Jubilee Market, Jubilee Hall on the corner of Covent Garden and Southampton. Clothing and accessories, along with quality arts and crafts Tu-Su. Antiques M. Paintings, drawings, and sketches also common finds. Wheelchair-accessible. Open daily 10:30am-6pm. Some vendors accept AmEx/MC/V.

SHOES

Office, 57 Neal St. (☎ 7379 1896). One of London's foremost fashion footwear retailers, with a larger selection than most of the shoe stores on the street. Carries its own stylish, wearable brand as well as other brands like Camper and LaCoste. Women's shoes £20-145 (average £50-80), men's £60-130. The **sale shop** at 61 St. Martin's Ln. (☎ 7497 0390; ⊖Leicester Sq. or Covent Garden) has good deals on all styles and includes mid-season reductions. Wheelchair-accessible. Neal St. store open M-W and F-Sa 10:30am-7:30pm, Th 10:30am-8pm, Su noon-6pm. Sale shop open M-Sa 10am-7pm, Su noon-6pm. 10% discount at Neal St. store with student ID. AmEx/MC/V.

Egoshego, 76 Neal St. (☎ 7836 9260). Carries both women's and men's shoes—most are not cheap, but at least there is a wide selection. Shoes range from spiky and sparkly to ultra-comfy. Everything is sufficiently up-to-the-moment trendy. The staff is helpful but not pushy. Open M-W 10:30am-7pm, Th 10:30am-8pm, F-Sa 10:30am-7pm, Su noon-6pm. AmEx/MC/V.

BLOOMSBURY

Not surprisingly, Bloomsbury's main commodity (other than A-level acumen) is books; the streets around the British Museum are crammed with specialist and cut-price book-shops, while the Waterstone's on Gower St. (p. 238) is one of London's largest. If you're after electronic equipment, head to **Tottenham Court Road** and haggle away—it's commonplace.

SEE MAP, p. 362

BOOKS

Oxfam Books, 12 Bloomsbury St. (☎ 7637 4610). ⊖Tottenham Court Rd. Up to 90% off publishers' prices on a wide range of fictional and academic books, with the proceeds going to charity. Large stock of scholarly and literary books on the humanities. An excellent used selection upstairs. Open M-Sa 10am-6pm, Su noon-5pm. MC/V.

Gay's the Word, 66 Marchmont St. (☎ 7278 7654; www.gaystheword.co.uk). ⊖Russell Sq. As the UK's largest gay and lesbian bookstore, GTW boasts a well-informed staff and an inventory large enough to devote entire sections to queer detective fiction. Erotic postcards, secondhand fiction, serious movies, and free magazines. Weekly events and discussion groups. Notice board with accommodations listings. Open M-Sa 10am-6:30pm, Su 2-6pm. AmEx/MC/V.

Ulysses, 40 Museum St. (☎ 7831 1600; ulyssesbooks@fsbdial.co.uk). ⊖Tottenham Court Rd. Carries a large stock of modern 1st editions and illustrated books (generally £35-100), with bargains in the basement. A perfect store for exploring, with stacks of unique finds. Open M-Sa 10:30am-6pm. AmEx/MC/V.

GIFTS AND MISCELLANY

James Smith & Sons, 53 New Oxford St. (☎ 7836 4731; www.james-smith.co.uk). ⊖Tottenham Court Rd. Groucho Marx once quipped that he hated London when it wasn't raining. The Smith family, in the umbrella business since 1830, must agree. There's a lovely time-warp feel about the ornate shop: signature handmade brollies (from £85) and walking sticks (from £20) share shelf space with the newest rain-repelling models. Open M-F 9:30am-5:15pm, Sa 10am-5:15pm. AmEx/MC/V.

L. Cornelissen & Son, 105 Great Russell St. (☎ 7636 1045; www.cornelissen.com). ⊖Tottenham Court Rd. With its original 1855 interior, Cornelissen's looks more like an apothecary than an art store. Jars of raw pigment, crystals, and lumps of foul-smelling "dragon's blood" reach to the ceilings, while mahogany drawers hide a fantastic array of brushes, nibs, paints, and crayons. An artist's dream. Open M-F 9:30am-5:30pm, Sa 9:30am-5pm. MC/V.

TIP **SAY CHEESE!** If you've run out of batteries for your camera or just feel like buying a new one, then Tottenham Court Rd. in Bloomsbury is the place to go. Electronics stores line the road, especially toward the Soho end of the street.

NORTH LONDON

CAMDEN TOWN, KING'S CROSS, AND ISLINGTON

Although you will be surrounded by a large percentage of London's (and the surrounding area's) under-25 population, North London is a much-needed alternative to Oxford St. with inexpensive and independent shopping. Most of the stores in **Camden Town** and its local **markets** are alternative, concentrating on cheap clothes and accessories. Even if studded belts and leather wristbands are not your style, you're bound to find something of interest. Serious music shop-

BOOKS FOR COOKS

Even from the outside, you can almost smell the treats that lie within. An ordinary looking bookshop, **Books for Cooks** is actually a laboratory that lives on the gastronomic cutting edge. Besides providing a wide range of books on food, nutrition, and cooking, Rosie Kindersley and Eric Treuille oversee an experimental kitchen where, every day, chefs from all over London come to try out new and exciting recipes. Salivating visitors are encouraged to sample the recipes and provide feedback. In operation since 1995, the laboratory has compiled well-received recipes into the *Books for Cooks Cookbook*, available at the shop (£5).

But, as the saying goes, give a person free food, and they eat for a day; give them a cookbook and cooking lessons, and they eat for a lifetime—a mantra with which Rosie and Eric comply. One-day courses range from the general, like "Salads and Dressings," to the more focused, like "Southern Spain." Whether you're browsing the shelves, tasting the treats, or learning how to create your own culinary masterpiece, Books for Cooks is the headquarters for any food-loving tourist.

4 Blenheim Crescent. ⊖Ladbroke Grove. ☎7221 1992. Classes are typically £30, and start at 11am. Open Tu-Sa 10am-6pm. Food available, usually after 10am.

pers will also revel here, particularly those interested in vinyl. There are a number of specialized DJ shops on **Inverness Street** in Islington.

BOOKS

Mega City Comics, 18 Inverness St. (☎7485 9320; www.megacitycomics.co.uk). ⊖Camden Town. New series and comics in mint condition, from collector's items to the latest imports, starting at 50p. Covers the entire spectrum from Tintin to erotic manga; most books are American and Japanese. Animated videos, DVDs, posters, and T-shirts also available. Open M-W and F-Sa 10am-6pm, Th 10am-7pm. MC/V.

CLOTHES

▨ **Annie's,** 12 Camden Passage (☎7359 0796), in Camden Passage Market. ⊖Angel. *Vogue* and *Elle* regularly use these vintage frocks in their photo shoots; movie costume designers often drop by, too. 1920s dresses are too expensive to buy at £300-600—or even try on lest you break a strap—but the less flashy 1930s pieces are more affordable (£60-150). Bags, shoes, and hats start at £30. Open M-Tu and Th-F 11am-6pm, W and Sa 8am-6pm, Su 11am-3pm. MC/V.

MARKETS

▨ **Camden Passage Market,** Islington High St. ⊖Angel. Turn right from the Tube; it's the alleyway that starts behind "The Mall" antiques gallery on Upper St. Not to be confused with Camden Market. More for looking than for buying, London's premier antique shops line these quaint alleyways. Smaller items may dip into the realm of the affordable, especially old prints, drawings, or small trinkets. Stalls are only open W and Sa 8:30am-6pm; some stores are open daily, but W is by far the best day to go.

Camden Markets, ⊖Camden Town. Make a sharp right out of the Tube station to reach Camden High St., where most of the markets start. Not what they used to be, many of the booths hawk unoriginal wares ("Mind the Gap" T-shirts). Crafts at Stables Market are worth it, but avoid the canal area.

Stables Market, farthest from the Tube station and the best of the bunch. No matter which entrance you pick, you'll find yourself lost among the myriad stalls, shops, and food peddlers. Stables manages to avoid the tacky trap so many markets fall into. Toward the back, at the horse hospital, you'll find some remaining independent artists as well as a 2-story antique market. Wheelchair-accessible. Open daily 9:30am-5:30pm.

Camden Lock Market, from the railway bridge to Regent's Canal. The main draw of the Lock is the food; stalls and restaurants perfume the air with everything from Caribbean plantains to chocolate strawberry waffles to Japanese dumplings. Open daily 10am-6pm.

Camden Canal Market, opposite Camden Lock. Follow it down past the 1st shops, which sell little more than cheap club gear and tourist trinkets. At the bottom, the more independent stores and restaurant stalls are open, but most of the stuff here can be found on High St. or at another market. Wheelchair-accessible. Open daily 9am-6:30pm.

The Camden Market, the nearest to ⊖Camden Town and the most crowded and least innovative. Oriented toward teenagers. Less emphasis on creative clothing and more on designer imitations, with jeans and sweaters at average prices. You can, however, find jewelry and some unique items if you head to the back. Wheelchair-accessible. Open daily 10am-late.

Inverness Street Market, off Camden High St. opposite the Tube. What was once just a daily fruit and vegetable market has become a small extension of Camden Market, although it's less crowded and still has cheap and fresh produce. Wheelchair-accessible. Open daily 8:30am-late.

 CAMDEN TOWN TUBE. Due to the hustle of the Sunday market crawl in Camden Town, ⊖Camden Town is only open to passengers disembarking, or changing from one train to another (1-5:30pm). No one can enter the station at that time from the street. You may have to take the bus back, or walk to ⊖Chalk Hill or Mornington Crescent.

MUSIC

Out on the Floor, 10 Inverness St. (☎7267 5989). ⊖Camden Town. 2 tiny but full floors of used records and CDs, specializing in 60-70s rock, soul, reggae, and funk on vinyl, as well as some tapes and CDs, all for around £5-10. Vintage posters for sale line the walls. Open daily 10am-6pm. MC/V.

BAYSWATER

Catering more to chain stores, Bayswater offers little of London's unique shopping experience. One exception: the weekly artists' market.

SEE MAP, p. 361

Bayswater Market (www.bayswater-road-artists.com). ⊖Queensway. Along Bayswater Rd. from Clarendon Pl. to Queensway. Every Su for the past 50 years, this open-air art show—the largest weekly expo of its kind in the world—has been packed along the gates of Kensington Gardens. The location and atmosphere are beautiful, even if the artwork may seem repetitive; over 250 painters, photographers, and various others ply their trade, sometimes with an overly firm eye on the tourist market. Despite this, surprises and delights abound. Shipping is often available. Open Su 10am-6pm in any weather.

 QUID IT. The slang for "pounds" is "quid," a more popular term in smaller shops or between locals while browsing.

NOTTING HILL

One of the most famous niches of Notting Hill life is **Porto-bello Road Market,** with both its street market and its local boutiques. **Golborne Road** has its own colorful street scene, with Moroccan and Portuguese shops and cafes. Book and antique lovers will enjoy the little shops lining **Blenheim Crescent.** Spread throughout the neighborhood are a number of excellent (and affordable) vintage and second-hand stores, particularly at **Notting Hill Gate.**

SEE MAP, p. 361

THE HIDDEN DEAL

DRESSING UP WITHOUT PAYING UP

With the names of Italian designers plastered all over the city, it's difficult to find a place in London to buy a decent pair of jeans without giving up a chunk of change. But Londoners always manage to look good, and if you want to party with the locals, dressing stylishly is a must.

Other than the yearly sales in January and July—when prices usually dip to seriously low levels—there are a number of hidden options for buying designer threads at bargain prices. **Pandora**, for instance, resells clothes and accessories on behalf of wealthy women and celebrities whose designer garments have become too voluminous to house. That leaves their Chanel suits, their Gucci handbags, and their Gaultier sunglasses available to the woefully underprivileged folks who generally get their high-fashion fix courtesy of Joan Rivers and her catty friends on E!

The good stuff is all "seasonally correct"—under two years old, and often barely worn. And the best part: prices are about a quarter of what they would be a few blocks over on Sloane St. You'll have to work for a deal—dig around to find your size and maybe elbow a few other shoppers out of the way—but the payoff can be great.

16-22 Cheval Pl. ☎ *7589 5289.* ⊖ *Knightsbridge. Open M-Sa 10am-7pm. MC/V.*

ANTIQUES

Hirst Antiques, 59 Pembridge Rd. (☎7727 9364; www.hirstantiques.co.uk). ⊖Notting Hill Gate. This shop, with its peacock-blue walls and ceiling strung with glass chandeliers, lives up to its reputation as "Aladdin's cave" with its ornate and stunning displays. Specializes in vintage costume jewelry. Earrings start from £20, bracelets from £25. Open M-Sa 11am-6pm. MC/V.

BOOKS

🏬 **Books for Cooks,** 4 Blenheim Crescent (☎7221 1992; www.booksforcooks.com). ⊖Ladbroke Grove. An entire store devoted to cookbooks and reads for cooks of all ages and abilities. Recipes from almost every world cuisine are available, and the knowledgeable staff is eager to help. Recipes are tested daily—grab a sample. MC/V.

CLOTHES

Dolly Diamond, 51 Pembridge Rd. (☎7792 2479; www.dollydiamond.com). ⊖Notting Hill Gate. This nostalgic shop specializes in men's and women's vintage clothing. Choose your look from classic 1950s to 70s casual wear and elegant 20s to 40s evening gowns. Dresses start at around £65, but an upstairs sale room (open F-Sa) features pieces from £5. Also sells shoes, bags, and swimwear. Open M-F 10:30am-6:30pm, Sa 9:30am-6:30pm, Su noon-6pm. MC/V.

MARKETS

Portobello Road Markets. Home to a number of markets that occupy different parts of the street and operate on different days. In order to see it all, come Friday or Saturday when everything is sure to be open. Stalls set their own times; hours below are general.

General Market. ⊖Westbourne Park or Ladbroke Grove. Farther north, from Elgin Crescent to Lancaster Rd. Sells food, flowers, and household essentials. Gourmet stalls with breads and organic produce compete with local eateries. Open M-W and F-Sa 8am-6:30pm, Th 8am-1pm.

Antiques Market. ⊖Notting Hill Gate. What most people associate with Portobello Rd. Stretches north from Chepstow Villas to Elgin Crescent. Most of what's on display is cheap bric-a-brac. Open Sa 7am-5pm.

Golborne Road Market. ⊖Ladbroke Grove. North of the Westway. Moroccan-influenced stalls selling gourmet olives, steaming couscous, and Berber handicrafts. Open F-Sa 9am-5pm.

Clothes Market. ⊖Ladbroke Grove. North of Lancaster Rd., with arms stretching along the Westway. A wide selection of secondhand clothes, ethnic gear, and jewelry, oddly interspersed with used electronics. Open F-Sa 8am-3pm.

MUSIC

Rough Trade, 130 Talbot Rd. (☎7229 8541). ⊖Ladbroke Grove. Don't be overwhelmed by the large selection—small reviews tacked to most CDs and records (from £5) make choosing a buy much easier. Try the in-store turntables, test CDs at the listening station, or take time to peruse the many posters and leaflets advertising local bands and concerts. Staff is knowledgeable and welcomes questions. Open M-Sa 10am-6:30pm, Su 1-5pm. AmEx/MC/V.

Honest Jon's, 276-278 Portobello Rd. (☎8969 9822). ⊖Ladbroke Grove. Boasting an impressive jazz, Latin, and "outernational" collection, the store also carries a wide selection of reggae, hip hop, house, and garage on vinyl and CD. Some soul and funk. You'll be drawn in by the cool selections audible a block away. Also buys and trades used discs. LPs start at £5. Wide range of CDs available around £10. Open M-Sa 10am-6pm, Su 11am-5pm. AmEx/MC/V.

KENSINGTON AND EARL'S COURT

Compared with Oxford St., **Kensington High Street** offers a similar, albeit more limited, range of mid-priced UK and international chains. Fortunately, it draws a smaller crowd than its West End rival (although Saturdays here can certainly approach sardine-tin crowding as well). **Kensington Church Street** provides an alternative, if pricey, experience: the south houses mostly clothing stores, the middle holds crafts and specialty shops, and the north is home to antiques and oriental art as it toward Notting Hill Gate.

SEE MAP, pp. 366-367

Hats Etcetera, 36b Kensington Church St. (☎7361 0000). ⊖High St. Kensington. As soon as wearing a sizable floral bouquet on your head becomes trendy, this store will be the height of style. A wide range of feather-adorned, seriously impractical, and wildly colorful "occasion-wear" hats (a la *Four Weddings and a Funeral*) will keep you entertained, but a glance at the price tags (£39-300) will prevent entertainment from turning into purchase. Open M-Sa 11am-6pm. AmEx/MC/V.

KNIGHTSBRIDGE AND BELGRAVIA

Brompton Road dominates Knightsbridge's shopping arteries, with representatives of most upmarket chains between Harvey Nichols and Harrods. Explore the side streets for spectacular deals on designer clothing or blow a cool £1000 on ultra-exclusive **Sloane Street,** which rivals Bond St. for designer boutiques. Window-shop Armani, Chanel, Dior, Gucci, Hermès, Kenzo, Versace, and Yves St. Laurent.

SEE MAP, p. 365

CLOTHES

▨ **Pandora,** 16-22 Cheval Pl. (☎7589 5289). ⊖Knightsbridge, take Harrods Exit. Second-hand designer clothes at affordable prices. All of the items on display at Pandora are seasonally correct. Sales Jan. and late July-late Aug. Open M-Sa 10am-7pm, Su noon-6pm. MC/V.

DEPARTMENT STORES

Harrods, 87-135 Brompton Rd. (☎7730 1234; www.harrods.com). ⊖Knightsbridge. In the Victorian era, this was the place for the wealthy to shop. Over a century later, it is less a provider of goods and more a tourist extravaganza. Given the sky-high prices, it's no wonder that only tourists and oil sheiks actually shop here. (Near-reasonable prices occur during sales in Jan. and July, when hours are extended.) Do go, though; it's an iconic bit of London that even the cynical tourist shouldn't miss. If nothing else, ride the Egyptian escalator in the middle, which leads down to the eerie "Diana and Dodi" memorial, with Diana's engagement ring and a wine glass she drank out of on her last night alive. Open M-Sa 10am-8pm, Su noon-6pm. Wheelchair-accessible. AmEx/MC/V.

LIGHT 'EM UP

Britain's famous Bonfire Night may seem like an uncharacteristic homage to the hippie movement, but its roots run historically deeper. At the turn of the 17th century, Guy Fawkes and 12 companions were angered by James 's religious intolerance and fostered a plan to assassinate him and his Parliamentary allies. Unfortunately for them, their plan was not of the professional, precise variety, but involved 36 barrels of gunpowder and some big explosions-to-be. Some of the plotters realized many innocents would be harmed due to their plan and exposed it to the authorities. Fawkes was caught with 36 barrels of gunpowder in the basement of the House of Lords early on November 5th, 1605. That night, aware of the assassination attempt on their rulers, Brits lit bonfires all over England in support of their king and government.

The night's events started an annual tradition, and Bonfire 'ight is now an anticipated festive celebration. Fireworks and bonfires, often elaborately assembled, are lit every November 5 throughout the UK. Many times, he bonfires include straw effigies of Guy Fawkes. While celebrations are widespread, even in former territories such as Canada and New Zealand, London boasts the best vantage point along the banks of the Thames between Waterloo and Blackfriars, where many pubs offer drink specials to mark the occasion.

Harvey Nichols, 109-125 Knightsbridge (☎ 7235 5000; www.harveynichols.com). ⊖ Knightsbridge. Imagine Bond St., Rue St. Honoré, and 5th Ave. all rolled up into one store. 5 of its 7 floors are devoted to the sleekest, sharpest fashion, from the biggest names to the hippest unknowns. Food hall on the 5th fl. has a swanky restaurant, a YO!Sushi, and the chic 5th Floor Cafe; there's a juice bar on the main fl. and a Wagamama in the basement. Sales late June-late July and late Dec.-late Jan. Open M-F 10am-8pm, Sa 10am-8pm, Su noon-6pm. Wheelchair-accessible. AmEx/MC/V.

CHELSEA

No serious shopper can come to London and ignore Chelsea, even if it has lost much of its punk-rock edge in recent years. The abundance of quirky one-off boutiques and the relative dearth of large chain stores

SEE MAP, p. 363

give the area a vitality and diversity absent from London's other shopping meccas. On the east side, **Sloane Square** is extremely "Sloaney" (the London equivalent of American "preppy"). To the west, **King's Road** gave us both the miniskirt and the Sex Pistols. Alternative styles have given way mostly to more mainstream trendy cuts, but the notorious Vivienne Westwood hasn't fled yet (see **World's End**, p. 255)—so hope remains for wannabe rebels.

BOOKS

World's End Bookshop, 357 King's Rd. (☎ 7352 9376). ⊖ Sloane Sq., then Bus #11 or 22. All the charm a closet-sized used bookstore can offer (which is a lot), with an especially good selection of architecture, art, biography, cinema, and cooking reads. Bargain bins are perfect for finding that 50p diversion for the plane ride home. Open daily 10am-6:30pm. AmEx/MC/V.

CLOTHES

▨ **Steinberg & Tolkien,** 193 King's Rd. (☎ 7376 3660). ⊖ Sloane Sq., then Bus #11, 19, 22, 319. London's largest collection of vintage American and European clothing. The place has a fantastic museum feel: touching, trying on, and buying the displays is encouraged. The inventory includes everything from early 1990s jean shorts (£15) to a 1920's champagne showgirl outfit (£2500) designed by Erte, to one of Jackie Kennedy's Givenchy classics. Check out the 75% discount on items in the rooms downstairs. Open Tu-Sa 11am-6:30pm, Su noon-6pm. AmEx/MC/V.

Ad Hoc, 153 King's Rd. (☎7376 8829). ⊖Sloane Sq., then Bus #11, 19, 22, 211, 319. This store is a pre-costume party must. Ad Hoc's scantily clad window mannequins display everything from candy bikinis to bling-heavy costume jewelry. Inside, a rainbow collection of wigs dominates the cluttered neon space. Check out the retro plastic jewelry (£5-10). Clothing £15-60. Open M-Tu and Th-Sa 10am-6:30pm, W 10am-7pm, Su noon-6pm. AmEx/MC/V.

World's End, 430 King's Rd. (☎7352 6551). ⊖Sloane Sq., then Bus #11 or 22. This small store's past legendary incarnations include SEX and Let it Rock, but not much remains of the punk store that launched the careers of the Sex Pistols. Owned by the notorious Vivienne Westwood (who recently got an entire special exhibit devoted to her at the Victoria and Albert Museum), the shop is now a pricey, slightly funky showplace for her latest designs (most items £100-300). Open M-Sa 10am-6pm. AmEx/MC/V.

Whistles, 31 Kings Rd. (☎7730 2006; www.whistles.co.uk). ⊖Sloane Sq., then Bus #11, 19, 22, 319. Other locations in Jubilee Place (⊖Canary Wharf) and The Market (⊖Covent Garden). This trendy women's clothing boutique transforms antique and bohemian fabrics into quirky, up-to-date work and casual wear. Incredibly popular with young working professionals. Open M-F 10am-7pm, Sa 10am-6:30pm, Su noon-6pm. AmEx/MC/V.

GIFTS AND MISCELLANY

Daisy & Tom, 181 King's Rd. (☎7352 5000; www.daisyandtom.com). ⊖Sloane Sq., then Bus #11, 19, 22, 211, 319. This multi-level kiddie paradise stocks toys, books, nursery goods, and clothing. It even boasts a hairdressing salon. The in-store carousel (every hr.) and marionette shows (every 30min. in the clothing department) are bound to please the under-5 set. Open M-Tu and Th-F 9:30am-6pm, W 10am-7pm, Sa 9:30am-6:30pm, Su 11am-5pm. AmEx/MC/V.

SHOES

Sukie's, 285 King's Rd. (☎7352 3431). ⊖Sloane Sq., then Bus #19 or 319. Sukie's carries a unique selection of Italian footwear in both classic and contemporary styles with unusual colors, materials, and textures. Many designed specifically for the store, with just a few pairs per size. Shoes starting from £30. Wheelchair-accessible. Open M-Sa 10am-6pm, Su noon-6pm. MC/V.

WEST LONDON

There is not much more than chain-store shopping (p. 238) in West London. It may be the place to beat the crowds of Oxford St., but not necessarily the place for the best bargains.

Fosters Bookshop, 183 Chiswick High Rd. (☎8995 2768). ⊖Turnham Green. One of the most charming used bookshops in London, marked from the street with a simple sign advertising "Books." This small, family-run business is a treasure trove for readers of all ages. Originally specializing in children's literature, the shop now sets itself apart from big chains with collector's editions of classics and out-of-print books. The selection includes everything from vintage fairy tale compilations to old religious texts. Open Th-Sa 10:30am-5pm. MC/V

NIGHTLIFE

Get ready to go crazy—you're in one of the best cities in the world for nocturnal celebrations. London's student population and fashionable in-crowd fuels the incredible array of destinations, and there's something for everybody. Partake in a London tradition by enjoying a pint in a historical pub; sample the freshest blends at a trendy bar; or dance until you're sore at an ear-splitting nightclub.

In a city where almost everyone enjoys a drink now and again, it is almost impossible to distinguish drinking from dancing. Even typical lounging "bars" that close around 11pm during the week open up with dancing and later hours during the weekend. *Let's Go* includes four categories of nightlife: pubs, bars, clubs, and gay, lesbian, bisexual, and transgender (GLBT). With so much to do, you may find yourself singing "God Save the Queen" well before midnight—at the very least you'll come home with some great stories for your friends. Remember to plan your Night Bus or (licensed) taxi trip home before you go out; Night Buses are listed with each establishment below.

GETTING HOME. The Tube closes around midnight, so planning transportation home is important. *Let's Go* includes local Night Bus routes for most nightlife listings—excluding pubs, which mostly close around 11pm. Coordinate the best Night Bus route by matching route numbers in nightlife listings with route numbers in accommodation listings. If you don't find a perfect fit, head toward a major transportation hub (Trafalgar Sq., Oxford Circus, Liverpool St., or Victoria) for a transfer.

NIGHTLIFE BY TYPE

PUBS

Arthur Baker's Harlem Soul Food(280)	BAY
Bar Room Bar(279)	NL
The Black Friar(259)	CITY
Cat and Canary(261)	EL
The Castle(277)	NL
The Chelsea Potter(283)	CHEL
Compton Arms(277)	NL
The Cross Keys(274)	WEND
Dog and Duck(270)	WEND
The Drayton Arms(282)	KEN/EC
Dublin Castle(277)	NL
Duke of Cambridge(277)	NL
The Duke of York(268)	WEND
The Eagle(262)	CLERK
Filthy MacNasty's Whiskey Café(277)	NL
Fitzroy Tavern(276)	BLOOM
The Freemason's Arms(279)	NL
French House(270)	WEND
The George Inn(264)	SB
The Golden Eagle(279)	M/RP
The Jeremy Bentham(276)	BLOOM
The Jerusalem Tavern(262)	CLERK
Lamb and Flag(274)	WEND
The Lord Nelson(265)	SB
The Market(280)	NH
Mitre(280)	BAYS
Nags Head(283)	K/B
O'Conor Don(280)	M/RP
The Old Bank of England(264)	HOL
Old Coffee House(270)	WEND
Pig's Ear Pub(283)	CHEL
Portobello Gold(281)	NH
Prince Albert Pub(281)	NH
Prospect of Whitby(261)	EL
The Queen's Larder(276)	BLOOM
Red Lion(267)	WEMIN
The Royal Oak(264)	SB
The Scarsdale(282)	KEN/EC
The Shepherds Tavern(268)	WEND
Sherlock Holmes(267)	WEMIN
Silver Cross(267)	WEMIN
Simpson's(259)	CITY
The Swan(280)	BAYS
Talbot(282)	K/B
The Three Kings(262)	CLERK

The Toucan(270)	WEND
The Troubador(281)	KEN/EC
The Walrus and the Carpenter(259)	CITY
Wilton Arms(282)	K/B
Ye Olde Cheshire Cheese(263)	HOL
Ye Olde Mitre Tavern(264)	HOL

BARS

22 Below(268)	WEND
Absolut Icebar(268)	WEND
Alphabet(271)	WEND
Amber(271)	WEND
Apartment 195(283)	CHEL
Babushka(263)	CLERK
Bar Kick(260)	EL
Bar Polski(264)	HOL
Bar Vinyl(277)	NL
Big Chill Bar(260)	EL
Bierodrome(266)	SL
Blue Bar(283)	K/B
Café Kick(262)	CLERK
Cantaloupe(260)	EL
Cocomo(260)	EL
Comedy Cafe(260)	EL
Detroit(275)	WEND
Dogstar(265)	SL
Floridita(271)	WEND
Fluid(263)	CLERK
Freud(275)	WEND
Fridge Bar(265)	SL
Gordon's Wine Bar(274)	WEND
Hobgoblin(265)	SL
Hoxton Square Bar & Kitchen(260)	EL
Janet's Bar(282)	KEN/EC
Karaoke Box(272)	WEND
Lab(270)	WEND
The Langley(275)	WEND
Living(265)	SL
Low Life(280)	M/RP
Match EC1(262)	CLERK
Mau Mau(281)	NH
Millbank Lounge(267)	WEMIN
O Bar(272)	WEND
Polka(271)	WEND
The Purple Turtle(278)	NL
Railway(266)	SL
Rinky Dink Bar(266)	SL
The Social(270)	WEND
Thirst(271)	WEND

Turnmills(263)	CLERK
Vats(276)	BLOOM
Vibe Bar(259)	EL
Visible(281)	NH

CLUBS

93 Feet East(261)	EL
AKA(275)	WEND
Aquarium(260)	EL
Bar Rumba(272)	WEND
Cargo(261)	EL
Electric Ballroom(278)	NL
The End(275)	WEND
Fabric(263)	CLERK
Fridge(266)	SL
Ghetto(272)	WEND
Herbal(261)	EL
Infernos(267)	SL
Madame Jojo's(272)	WEND
Mass(266)	SL
Ministry of Sound(265)	SB
Notting Hill Arts Club(281)	NH
Scala(278)	NL
Tongue&Groove(266)	SL
Turnmills(263)	CLERK
The White House(266)	SL

GLBT

Admiral Duncan(274)	WEND
BarCode(274)	WEND
The Black Cap(278)	NL
The Box(275)	WEND
Candy Bar(273)	WEND
"The Cock" (at Ghetto)(272)	WEND
The Colherne(282)	KEN/EC
Comptons of Soho(274)	WEND
"Discotec" (at The End)(275)	WEND
"DTPM" (at Fabric)(263)	CLERK
The Edge(273)	WEND
Escape Dance Bar(274)	WEND
G-A-Y(273)	WEND
G-A-Y Bar(273)	WEND
The George and Dragon(261)	EL
Heaven(276)	WEND
Ku Bar(273)	WEND
"Popstarz" (at Scala)(278)	NL
Profile(273)	WEND
Royal Vauxhall Tavern(267)	SL
Village Soho(274)	WEND

NEIGHBORHOOD ABBREVIATIONS: BAY Bayswater **BLOOM** Bloomsbury **CHEL** Chelsea **CITY** The City of London **CLERK** Clerkenwell **HOL** Holborn **KEN/EC** Kensington and Earl's Court **K/B** Knightsbridge and Belgravia **M/RP** Marylebone and Regent's Park **NH** Notting Hill **SB** The South Bank **WEND** The West End **WEMIN** Westminster **NL** North London **SL** South London **EL** East London **WL** West London

NIGHTLIFE

NIGHTLIFE BY NEIGHBORHOOD

THE CITY OF LONDON

The City is a nice place to enjoy a pint, although it doesn't offer the club scene of some of London's other hopping neighborhoods. Even if establishments are open past 6pm, you may feel a little lonely in otherwise deserted streets on your walk out of the City.

SEE MAP, p. 349

PUBS

🖼 **The Walrus and the Carpenter,** 45 Monument St. (☎7621 1647), at Lovat Ln. ⊖Monument. Outside picnic tables and bright hanging plants ensure that patrons will spill over into the cobblestone alleyway. Afternoons are the busiest; the post-lunch hour is the ideal time to visit. Solid selection of beers, wines, and mixed drinks draw a varied crowd; families often eat on the benches. Traditional pub food ranges from Oxford sausages (£7) to the traditional hamburger (£8). Wheelchair-accessible. Open M-F 11am-11pm. AmEx/MC/V.

Simpson's, Ball Court (☎7626 9985; www.simpsonstavern.co.uk), off 38½ Cornhill. ⊖Bank. "Established 1757" says the sign on the alley leading to this pub; it remains so traditional that an employee stands in the door to greet you. The open space outside the entrance fills with people after 3pm; inside, different rooms divide the patrons. Socialites populate the basement wine bar and snack on sandwiches (from £2.50), beer lovers frequent the standing-only bar on the ground fl., and diners relax in the downstairs and upstairs restaurants munching on traditional mains like steak-and-kidney pie (£7.95). Wheelchair-accessible. Open M-F 11:30am-3:30pm. MC/V.

The Black Friar, 174 Queen Victoria St. (☎7236 5474). ⊖Blackfriars. The Black Friar's claim to being one of London's truly unique pubs rests upon its Art Deco imitation of the 12th-century Dominican friary that once occupied this spot. Shaped like a wedge with mosaics on the walls, it was almost razed in the 1960s. An open-front room and a warm back dining area welcome visitors inside. Outside, cafe tables and umbrellas beckon, especially in sunny weather. Mains from £6. Wheelchair-accessible. Open daily 11am-11pm. Kitchen open 11:30am-10pm. AmEx/MC/V.

EAST LONDON

WHITECHAPEL AND THE EAST END

While Soho is considered by many to be London's nightlife capital, the neighborhoods of **Hoxton** and **Shoreditch** hold their own, and these much less touristy venues are fast encroaching on Soho's grasp. London's second hottest spot for dancing and drinking offers something for everybody. (*Night Bus transportation at Liverpool St. hub: #N8, N11, 23, N26, N35, N76, N133, 149, 214, 242, 271, unless otherwise indicated; additional Night Bus routes listed.*)

BARS

🖼 **Vibe Bar,** 91-95 Brick Ln. (☎7426 0491; www.vibe-bar.co.uk). ⊖Aldgate East or Liverpool St. Night Bus: see information on p. 259. Once the home of the Truman Brewery, this funky bar is loaded with style and is light on pretension. Vibe prides itself on promoting new artists and combining music with displays of visual arts. Dim lighting, brick interior, and mural-covered walls give the place an artsy, casual feel. Relax on a sofa in the all-red lounge or arrive early for an outside table. Free Internet access. The youngish crowd grooves to hip hop, garage, techno, and more. DJs spin M-Sa 7:30-11:30pm, Su 7-11:30pm. Cover F-Sa after 8pm £4. Open M-Th and Su 11am-11:30pm, F-Sa 11am-1am, Su 11:30am-11:30pm.

■ **Big Chill Bar,** Dray Walk (☎ 7392 9180; www.bigchill.net), off Brick Ln. ⊖Liverpool St. or Aldgate East. Night Bus: see information on p. 259. Despite its lack of an address, no one seems to have trouble finding this chill drinking spot off Brick Lane. DJs spin an eclectic mix nightly while famously friendly crowds chat it up on big leather couches and on the outdoor patio. Stay all day during perennially popular "Big Chill Sundae," with board games, brunch, and prime people-watching with the surrounding market crowds. Mixed drinks from £4. A menu of shareable foods such as pizza (£7-9) ensures no one goes hungry. Su brunch noon-9pm. Open M-Th noon-midnight, F-Sa noon-1am, Su 11am-midnight. MC/V.

■ **Bar Kick,** 127 Shoreditch High St. (☎ 7739 8700). ⊖Old St. Night Bus: see information on p. 259 as well as #N55, N243. A dream come true for "table football" aficionados, this bar doesn't take itself too seriously. World flags and football paraphernalia adorn the beamed ceiling and walls while upbeat music favorites and 4 foosball tables keep crowds happy and wrists sore. More bar than pub, despite sports influence. Tasty mixed drinks (mojitos and martinis £6.50) and a heavy continental European influence. Food such as nachos and burgers (£4-5) served M-F noon-3:30pm and 6-10pm, Sa-Su all day. Open M-W 10am-11pm, Th-F 10am-midnight, Sa noon-midnight, Su noon-10:30pm. AmEx/MC/V.

■ **Cantaloupe,** 35 Charlotte Rd. (☎ 7729 5566; www.cantaloupe.co.uk). ⊖Old St. Night Bus: see information on p. 259 as well as #N55, N243. A hip hangout with dim lighting, red walls, and aging wooden stools, Cantaloupe manages to be trendy and homey at the same time. Mismatched leather sofas in the back and 2 spacious skylit bar areas fill with 20- and 30-somethings starting their nights. Creative cocktails £6. Spanish tapas and street food £3-5. Free Wi-Fi. DJs spin F-Sa 9pm-midnight. Open M-F 11am-midnight, Sa 12:30pm-midnight, Su noon-11:30pm. AmEx/MC/V.

■ **Comedy Cafe,** 66 Rivington St. (☎ 7739 5706; www.comedycafe.co.uk). ⊖Old St. Night Bus: see information on p. 259. One of London's best venues for stand-up, featuring established stars and young talent alike. The outside is painted in comically bright oranges and reds while the inside holds a bar and music space as well as the comedy stage. Skip the food and stick to beers (£1.50-3). Tu cabaret night; W auditions; Sa disco and dancing. Cover W £4, Th £8, F-Sa £15. Group packages W-Sa £14-30. Happy hour F-Sa 6-7pm. Doors open Tu-Th 7pm, F-Sa 6pm; show 9pm; dancing until 1am. Reserve F-Sa. Book online or over the phone. MC/V.

Cocomo, 323 Old St. (☎ 7613 0315). ⊖Old St. Night Bus: see information on p. 259 as well as #N55, N243. A North African-inspired bar full of vintage furnishings and cushion-lined benches. Chill hangout before the clubs heat up. Friendly door staff and bartenders cater to a creative and chill crowd. DJs play rock, country, and rave. Open M-Sa 4:30pm-midnight. MC/V.

Hoxton Square Bar & Kitchen, 2-4 Hoxton Sq. (☎ 7613 0709). ⊖Old St. Night Bus: see information on p. 259. This spacious bar manages to be a lounge, restaurant, and drinking destination all in one. Incredibly popular at night. Relax in retro swivel chairs and low-slung leather couches. The pleasant outdoor patio is packed with funkified, art-chic drinkers every evening. 2 fully stocked and staffed bars and a long list of drinks make it a good spot for an unhurried drink. Wheelchair-accessible. No admission F-Sa after midnight. Open M 11am-midnight, Tu-Th 11am-1am, F-Sa 11am-2am, Su 11am-12:30am. MC/V.

CLUBS

■ **Aquarium,** 256 Old St. (☎ 7253 3558; www.clubaquarium.co.uk). ⊖Old St.; Exit 3. Night Bus: see information on p. 259. The only club in London where bringing your bathing suit is par for the course, this club boasts a huge pool and hot tub open to revelers. The 4 bars and 2 sofa-laden chill out rooms keep the dry occupied. Events here are hilarious, campy affairs: F "Creme de la Kremlin" (Russian pop and funky house; dress is smart casual; 10pm-

4am). Sa "Carwash" (funky/retro-glam-funk fashion fest)—one of the most awe-inspiring clubbing experiences in London; join stilt walkers, performers, and dancers in your finest 70s, 80s, and 90s gear. (Tickets ☎08702 461 966; www.carwash.co.uk. 10pm-3:30am.) Cover F men £15, women £10; Sa online £12, at door £15.

Herbal, 12-14 Kingsland Rd. (☎7613 4462; www.herbaluk.com). ⊖Old St. Night Bus: see information on p. 259. In a rather unglamorous building, Herbal is less flagrantly trendy than most of its neighbors—and often more fun. The action is divided into 2 floors—the smaller, loft-like upstairs room fills first (around midnight); downstairs has more space to dance. Most weekdays, guest DJs spin a range of urban music from hip hop to Latin to disco. Cover rarely over £8; check website or call. Open M-Th and Su 9pm-2am, F-Sa 9pm-3am or 9pm-6am, depending on act or night.

Cargo, Kingsland Viaduct, 83 Rivington St. (☎7739 3440; www.cargo-london.com). ⊖Old St. Night Bus: see information on p. 259 as well as #N55, N243. With great acoustics, an intimate candlelit lounge, a front restaurant (global tapas around £5), and 2 enormous arched rooms, Cargo remains a favorite among Londoners. A mix of DJs and live music manages to drag almost every lounger onto the dance floor at some point. A large garden with sunken benches and canopies adds a touch of ambience. Wheelchair-accessible. Occasional cover up to £10. Bar open M-Th noon-1am, F noon-3am, Sa 1pm-3am, Su 1pm-midnight.

93 Feet East, 150 Brick Ln. (☎7247 3293; www.93feeteast.com). ⊖Aldgate East or Liverpool St. Night Bus: see information on p. 259. Part of the old Truman Brewery complex, 93 rocks the post-*tandoori* Brick Lane night scene. Bar area with DJ; main dance fl. is sparsely decorated but has cool fluorescent lights. A separate room often hosts live music. Outside, there's plenty of space to dance or to set up camp at the patio tables. Music style changes virtually every night; call or check website for details. Cover after 9pm F £7, Sa £8. Open M-Th 5-11pm, F 5pm-1am, Sa noon-1am, Su noon-10:30pm.

GLBT

The George and Dragon, 2 Hackney Rd. (☎7012 1100). ⊖Old St. Night Bus: see information on p. 259. This creatively remodeled pub proudly caters to an eclectic crowd, with a gay-friendly feel, occasional drag parties, and lesbian nights. Small bar on the ground fl. fills up quickly; patrons take over the surrounding sidewalks on warm evenings. Decor pulled from the attic, with everything from old nautical paintings to oriental fans and tissue-paper lamps backing up the bar. A favorite with local artists and designers. Eclectic jukebox with every type of music imaginable gets the place moving. Wheelchair-accessible. Open M-Sa 5pm-midnight, Su noon-10:30pm.

DOCKLANDS

Even businesspeople need sustenance and relaxation, and those pubs in the midst of office buildings cater to an after-work crowd. Pubs and bars line the Promenades by Canary Wharf offering Happy hour specials and outdoor seating.

PUBS

🎖 **Prospect of Whitby,** 57 Wapping Wall (☎7481 1095). ⊖Wapping. From Tube exit, turn right, follow the street left around the bend, turn right onto Wapping Wall, and walk about 3 blocks down. Use caution if walking at night. This pub, built in 1520, is a little out of the way, but the spectacular river view is worth it. With 2 indoor dining rooms and an outdoor balcony and patio, you shouldn't have trouble finding a seat; a perch near the windows is a hotter commodity. Drink and food menus are average, yet the authenticity and traditional feel of the pub along with the sweeping views of the Thames are worth the trip. Sandwiches and burgers £5-6; mains £7-9. Open M-Th and Su noon-11pm, F-Sa noon-midnight. Kitchen open daily until 9pm. AmEx/MC/V.

Cat and Canary, 1-24 Fisherman's Walk (☎7512 9187). ⊖/DLR: Canary Wharf. Exiting the station, follow signs to Canada Sq. and walk through toward the river. Take the stairs down to the Promenade and walk left. It's at the far end, near the out-of-place pontoon pedestrian bridge. A fairly standard Fuller's Brewery pub, the Cat and Canary has an expansive river view, plenty of outdoor tables, and a spacious interior. The patrons are mixed, with a healthy dose of suit-clad businesspeople relaxing after a day at the Docklands' towers. The food is a step beyond fish 'n' chips, with specials like spinach and gruyere cheese quiche or curried chicken (£6-7.50). Wheelchair-accessible. Open M-Sa 11am-11pm, Su noon-8pm. Kitchen open M-F noon-9pm, Sa noon-8pm, Su noon-6pm. AmEx/MC/V.

CLERKENWELL

So trendy at times that it's almost painful, Clerkenwell provides a varied selection of nightlife. The many restaurants on Exmouth Market have bars that stay open late, and Charterhouse St. has numerous clubs and bars that cater to the young office workers in the surrounding area.

PUBS

SEE MAP, p. 364

🌟 **The Jerusalem Tavern,** 55 Britton St. (☎ 7490 4281; www.stpetersbrewery.co.uk). ⊖Farringdon. Tiny and wonderfully ancient, this showcase pub for the beers of the St. Peter's Brewery has many nooks and crannies, making it ideal for an evening of intense conversation. Popular with locals, the quirky spaces fill up at night. The availability of brews changes with the seasons and is advertised on a chalkboard outside. The broad selection of ales rewards the adventuresome. Specialty ales (£2.40) like grapefruit or cinnamon, several organic ales, Honey Porter, Summer Ale, and Suffolk Gold are available in season. Bring home a case of their speciality beer (£26). Pub grub £6.50-8.50. Open M-F 11am-11pm. Lunch served daily noon-3pm, dinner served Tu-Th 5-9:30pm. MC/V.

The Three Kings, 7 Clerkenwell Close (☎7253 0483). ⊖Farringdon. A bright exterior and large figurines over the door capture the merry atmosphere of this local favorite just off Clerkenwell Green. Eccentrically decorated with Christmas lights, a metal rhino head over the mantle, and a 1940s jukebox upstairs, the Three Kings serves traditional food (£6-9), including Cumberland sausages. Loud and crowded around the bar area at night; look for more privacy in the 2 smaller upper-level rooms. Open M-Th noon-11pm, F-Sa 7-11pm. Cash only.

The Eagle, 159 Farringdon Rd. (☎7837 1353). ⊖Farringdon. Down-to-earth atmosphere appeals to both lunching businessmen and lingering locals. This traditional pub serves anything but traditional food, with a surprising menu of tasty dishes like penne, proscuitto and nutmeg pasta, or roast lamb with vegetables and cumin (£7-8). Open M-F 12:30-3pm and 6:30-10:30pm, Sa 12:30-3:30pm and 6:30-10:30pm, Su 12:30-3:30pm. Bar open M-Sa noon-11pm, Su noon-5pm. MC/V.

 CHOWING DOWN. If you walk into a pub and plop down at the nearest table, you'll be waiting all night for a drink or a meal. Most pubs don't have wait staffs; order at the bar. The menu is usually posted on a chalkboard nearby.

BARS

Café Kick, 43 Exmouth Market (☎7837 8077; www.cafekick.co.uk). ⊖Farringdon or Angel. Night Bus #N19, N38, N43. Chill out with Spanish flair or try your hand at an intense game of foosball. Comfortably worn-in bar with paintings of world flags on the floor. With Caribbean music and a crowd that spills onto the street, dinner here can often turn into a long and fulfilling night. Beer and mixed drinks from £2.60. Happy hour daily 4-7pm (beer of the day £2, mixed drinks £4.50). Open M-F noon-11pm, Sa 1pm-midnight, Su 3-10:30pm. MC/V.

Match EC1, 45-47 Clerkenwell Rd. (☎7250 4002; www.matchbar.com). ⊖Farringdon or Barbican. Night Bus #N35, N55, N243. Swanky surroundings, pretty people, and exclusive drink concoctions create an intriguing atmosphere. Terribly expensive drink menu ("Nicola," punch with vodkas and berries £14). Other quality mixed drinks £6-10. New menu offers many small plates from £4-7, good for groups or sharing. Sunken bar and plush setting make Match an ideal spot for lounging. Open M-F 11am-midnight, Sa-Su 5pm-midnight. AmEx/MC/V.

Babushka, 25-27 Farringdon Rd. (☎ 7405 6214). ✪Farringdon. Night Bus #N63. This restaurant-bar has dim lighting and quiet corners, perfect for a more talkative crowd. The white bar and fab furniture provide a unique environment for chilling out to DJ-spun music (W-F). Main dishes from £6. Mixed drinks £5.50. Open M-W 4pm-midnight, Th 4pm-1am, F-Sa noon-1am, Su noon-12:30am. MC/V.

Fluid, 40 Charterhouse St. (☎ 7253 3444). ✪Farringdon or Barbican. Night Bus #242. Advertising itself as "an excellent lubricant for social intercourse," this sushi bar by day and intimate night club by night is the perfect antidote to mega-club madness. The basement dance floor, adorned with a Tokyo cityscape at one end and a glowing bar at the other, is too small for serious dancing. Chill upstairs on the leather couches under the ambient lighting. DJs throughout the week spinning a variety of styles; call for details. Cover F-Sa 9-10pm £3, 10pm-4am £5. Open Tu-W noon-midnight, Th noon-2am, F-Sa 7pm-4am. MC/V.

CLUBS

▨ **Fabric,** 77a Charterhouse St. (☎ 7336 8898; www.fabriclondon.com). ✪Farringdon. Night Bus #242. One of London's most-hyped clubbing venues; expect lines. Fabric is large and loud, boasting Europe's first vibrating "bodysonic" dance floor that is actually one giant speaker (a unique experience that will hammer some rhythm into even your most uptight friends). Beds (for *relaxing*), multiple bars, and 3 dance floors crammed with close to 2000 hopping Londoners and curious tourists complete the scene. The rather young crowd is generally dressed down. F "Fabric Live" (hip hop, breakbeat, bass and drum); Sa DJs and live acts; Su "DTPM Polysexual Night" (☎ 7749 1199; www.blue-cube.net). Wheelchair-accessible. Cover F £12; Sa in advance £12, at the door £15. Open F 9:30pm-5am, Sa 10pm-7am, Su 10pm-5am. MC/V.

Turnmills, 63b Clerkenwell Rd. (☎ 7250 3409; www.turnmills.co.uk). ✪Farringdon. Night Bus #N35, N55, N243. Enter through a Spanish restaurant into a subterranean maze of themed zones, from post-industrial jungle to French bistro. The glammed-up crowd is more intent on eyeing up than getting down. Upstairs at Turnmills Top Floor, posh decor, candlelight and jazz surround an older crowd. F "The Gallery" (mainstream house; 10:30pm-7:30am). Dress code calls for smart-casual (no sportswear). Cover F before midnight £12, after midnight £15; Sa £12-20. MC/V only at bar.

HOLBORN

Holborn is one of the best neighborhoods for pubs, but that's about the extent of its nightlife. Spend an early evening chatting with friends over a pint and then head elsewhere.

PUBS

▨ **Ye Olde Cheshire Cheese,** Wine Office Court. (☎ 7353 6170; www.yeoldecheshirecheese.com). By 145 Fleet St., not to be

SEE MAP, p. 364

confused with The Cheshire Cheese on the other side of Fleet St. Entrance in alleyway. ✪Blackfriars or St. Paul's. Dating from 1667, the Cheese was once a haunt of Samuel Johnson, Charles Dickens, Mark Twain, and Theodore Roosevelt. A dark labyrinth of oak-paneled, low-ceilinged rooms on 3 fl. Each room offers a different menu and style of food. Enjoy salads or sandwiches (£3-4) in the Cheshire at the back; order meaty traditional dishes and pies in the Chop Room (mains from £10); eat daily hot specials (£5) on the long wooden benches of the downstairs Cellar; or savor fancier cuisine upstairs in the Johnson Room (£7-13). Front open M-Sa 11am-11pm, Su noon-6pm.

Cellar Bar open M-Th noon-2:30pm and 5:30-11pm, F noon-2:30pm. Chop Room open M-F noon-9:30pm, Sa noon-2:30pm and 6-9:30pm, Su noon-5pm. Johnson Room open M-F noon-2:30pm and 7-9:30pm. AmEx/MC/V.

■ **The Old Bank of England,** 194 Fleet St. (☎7430 2255). ⊖Temple. Next to the Royal Courts of Justice and directly across from the entrance to the Temple. Opened on the premises of the 19th-century Bank of England, this pub takes full advantage of its predecessor's towering ceilings, massive oil paintings, impressive chandeliers, and walled-in garden in the back. Sweeney Todd, "the Demon Barber of Fleet St.," killed his victims in the tunnels beneath the modern pub; his mistress turned them into meat pies sold to the unsuspecting public next door. The Old Bank of England is "extremely proud" of its own meat pies (£8-9). Afternoon tea M-F 2:30-5:30pm. Mains £5-10, sandwiches £3-5. Reservations recommended for lunch. Open M-F 11am-11pm. Kitchen open M-Th 11am-9pm, F 11am-8pm. AmEx/MC/V.

Ye Olde Mitre Tavern, 1 Ely Court (☎7405 4751), off #8 Hatton Garden. ⊖Chancery Ln. To find the alley where this pub hides, look for the street lamp on Hatton Garden bearing a sign of a mitre. This classic pub fully merits the "ye olde"—it was built in 1546 by the Bishop of Ely. With oak beams and spun glass, the 2 rooms are perfect for nestling up to a bitter, and the winding courtyard outside is ideal in nice weather. Popular in the evenings, the pub and its tiny Ely Court generally fill with merriment and people during the summer. Hot meals subject to availability (about £4), with bar snacks and superior sandwiches (£1.50) served until 9:30pm. Open M-F 11am-11pm. AmEx/MC/V.

BARS

■ **Bar Polski,** 11 Little Turnstile (☎7831 9679). ⊖Holborn. Night Bus #N1, N68, N91, N171, N243. Hidden in the pub-filled alleyways behind the Holborn Tube station—when you see Pu's Brasserie, look to the left. Recently renovated, the slick, modern interior is not that of a traditional Polish bar. The food is, however, offering dishes like kielbasa and pierogi (£7-8). Decent-sized salad and sandwich menu starts at £3.50. Best of all are the over 65 types of vodka from £2.10 a shot (add a mixer for 60p). Popular at night—but come any time and you'll enjoy this unusual Eastern experience. Wheelchair-accessible. Open M 4-11pm, Tu-F 12:30-11pm, Sa 6-11pm. MC/V.

 HOW MUCH TO DRINK? Know your wine metrics! 175mL equals one small "pub" glass, 375mL is a half-bottle, and 750mL means one bottle.

THE SOUTH BANK

Nightlife to most South Bankers means dinner and the theatre, or possibly even a late night at the Tate. Strangely enough, though, the South Bank is also home to one of the largest club venues in London.

SEE MAP, pp. 370-371

PUBS

■ **The George Inn,** 77 Borough High St. (☎7407 2056). ⊖London Bridge. With a mention in Dickens's *Little Dorritt* and the honor of being the only remaining galleried inn in London, the George takes great pride in its historical tradition. A deceptively tiny interior leads out into a popular patio, full of migrants from the City across the river. The ale (from £2.50) is excellent and the atmosphere is relaxed. Open M-Sa 11am-11pm, Su noon-10:30pm. Wheelchair-accessible patio. AmEx/MC/V.

The Royal Oak, 44 Tabard St. (☎7357 7173). ⊖Borough. With classic Victorian decor and a loyal group of local patrons, this pub is a little out of the way, but it is a must for anyone in search of the perfect pint. Superior pub grub (from £4) served noon-2:45pm and 5-9:15pm. Open M-F 11:30am-11pm, Sa 6pm-11pm, Su noon-6pm. MC/V.

The Lord Nelson, 243 Union St. (☎ 7207 2701). ⊖Blackfriars. This quiet pub is tucked into the industrial building surroundings, but it has carved out space enough for a circular outdoor seating area and plenty of games and tables inside. Sports on the TVs. If it's sunny, you can't beat the patio. Traditional British tucker from £7. Food served M-F noon-8pm, Sa-Su noon-5pm. Open M-F 11am-11pm, Sa 1-11pm, Su noon-3pm and 7-10:30pm. Wheelchair-accessible.

CLUBS

▧ Ministry of Sound, 103 Gaunt St. (☎ 7378 6528; www.ministryofsound.co.uk). ⊖Elephant and Castle; take the exit for South Bank University. Night Bus #N35, N133, N343. Mecca for serious clubbers worldwide—arrive before it opens or queue all night. Emphasis on dancing rather than decor, with a massive main room, smaller 2nd dance floor, and perpetually packed overhead balcony bar. Dress code generally casual, but famously unsmiling door staff make it sensible to err on the side of smartness: no tracksuits or sneakers, especially on weekends. F "Smoove" R&B; 10:30pm-5am; Sa vocal house 11pm-7am. Cover: F £12, Sa £15.

SOUTH LONDON

Nightlife features prominently in Brixton and Clapham's renaissance, with an ever-increasing number of bars and clubs luring London's choosiest and largest concentration of under-40s. Since many clubs are small, lounging generally takes priority over dancing, though the recent proliferation of DJ bars signals a shift back to good old-fashioned booty-shaking. While some nightspots are little different from their Hoxton and Clerkenwell brethren, there are destinations that have escaped yuppification.

BRIXTON

BARS

Living, 443 Coldharbour Ln. (☎ 7326 4040; www.livingbar.co.uk). ⊖Brixton. Equally perfect for a cozy conversation among friends or cutting the floor to 80s pop. Comfy couches provide a good view of video screens. Warm and friendly atmosphere beckons loungers and dancers alike. M-Th and Su mixed drinks ½-price. Tu Latin. F-Sa house and 80s. Music starts pumping nightly around 9pm. Cover F-Sa after 10pm £5, after 11pm £7. Open M-Th and Su 5pm-2am, F-Sa 5pm-4am. MC/V.

Dogstar, 389 Coldharbour Ln. (☎ 7733 7515; www.thedogstar.co.uk). ⊖Brixton. Loud and boisterous, the crowd here runs the gamut from brooding artists to hardcore dancers. Large selection of beer and drinks and ample room to sit and people-watch make this bar a great spot to pass the night. Transitions from pub to club midway through the night. M "Afterglow" (funk, 80s, and indie fare); Tu "Souled Out" (funk and soul); W "Offshore" (breakbeats and world); Th "Brixton High" (old school 80s jams); F "Shoot from the Hip" (house classics); Sa "Latin Quarter" (Latin house and party); Su "Funk to Punk." Wheelchair-accessible. Cover F-Sa after 10pm £3, after 11pm £5. Open M-F 4pm-2am, Sa-Su noon-4am. MC/V.

Fridge Bar, 1 Town Hall Parade, Brixton Hill (☎ 7326 5100; www.fridge.co.uk). ⊖Brixton. Next to Fridge nightclub (p. 266). Brixtonians from both sides of the fence mingle in this bright, narrow bar. Groove downstairs on the dance floor or lounge with pals and locals upstairs. Beer from £3. DJs spin nightly from 9pm: M roots and reggae; Tu salsa; W 80s; Th soulful house and R&B; F-Sa hip hop, rap, and R&B (21+); Su 70s and 80s faves (22+). Dress code F-Sa: no sneakers or tracksuits. Cover F-Sa 10:30-11pm £5, 11pm-midnight £7, after midnight £10; Su after 10:30pm £5. Happy hour M-F 6-9pm (½-price drinks). Open M-Th 6pm-2am, F-Sa 6pm-4:30am, Su 6pm-3am. MC/V.

Hobgoblin, 95 Effra Rd. (☎ 7501 9671). ⊖Brixton. An all-purpose nightlife venue, with bar, music, karaoke, and comedy sets. Housed in an old brewery building with ample outdoor seating. This informal bar is a great alternative to the packed lounges in the center of Brixton. Play pool or take in the nightly live music. Su 8:30pm Brixton comedy club performance (£5.50). Open daily noon-2am. MC/V.

CLUBS

▨ **Tongue & Groove,** 50 Atlantic Rd. (☎7274 8600; www.tongueandgroove.org). ⊖Brixton. Humbly trendy club and bar so popular and narrow that people dance on the speakers. Arrive early to claim a seat. Soak up the red-light-district look and relax on huge black leather sofas lining one wall. Anticipate early-morning revelry. Don't underestimate the mixed drinks (doubles £5). Cover Th after 11pm £2; F-Sa after 10:30pm £3. Open M-W and Su 7pm-3am, Th-Sa 7pm-5am. MC/V.

Fridge, 1 Town Hall Parade, Brixton Hill (☎7326 5100; www.fridgelondon.com). ⊖Brixton. A revered institution that packs in good-looking, sweaty clubbers serious about dancing. This converted cinema was the 1st venue played by hallowed rockers Eurythmics and the Pet Shop Boys. The fully restored original Rococo features are complemented by luxurious lounge areas and a disco-ballin' dance floor. Popular theme nights rotate (check website and weekly listings). Wheelchair-accessible. Dress code relaxed, but less is always more. Cover £5-15.

Mass, St. Matthew's Church, Brixton Hill (☎7738 7875; www.mass-club.com). ⊖Brixton. Entrance to the left of Bug Bar. 3 dark, inviting rooms beckon to a happy crowd intent on gyrating the night away. The combination of being in a church and being underground gives the club an extra naughty feel. Try not to dance up on any pious women in black robes. F "Last Suppa" (R&B and slow jams); Sa hard dance and house. Cover F before midnight £6, after midnight £8; Sa £8. Open W 10pm-2am, Th 8:30pm-1am, F-Sa 10pm-6am.

CLAPHAM

BARS

Bierodrome, 44-48 Clapham High St. (☎7720 1118; www.belgo-restaurants.com). ⊖Clapham North. If beer is your thing, then Bierodrome is your place, where even the food has been marinated in it. More beers on offer than you can shake a stick at (from £3). Mixed drinks are also available for something a little sweeter (from £5.75). Open M-W noon-midnight, Th noon-1am, F-Sa noon-2am, Su noon-12:30am. MC/V.

Rinky Dink Bar, 38 Clapham High St. (☎7627 1036; www.rinkydinkbar.co.uk). ⊖Clapham North. This drinking establishment has a relaxed friendly vibe, ideal for both a quiet pint or the start of a big night out. Happy hour Th-F 5-10pm offers 2-for-1 mixed drinks, including their mojito, heralded as the best in South London (see their website for recipe). Rinky Dink also offers fresh pizzas for those who need to fill their stomachs before imbibing. Open M-Th 5pm-midnight, F-Sa 5pm-2am, Su 5-11pm. MC/V.

Railway, 18 Clapham High St. (☎7622 4077; www.helmshine.co.uk). ⊖Clapham North. The Railway has all the charm of a local British pub combined with events that would make a city pub jealous. 2nd Su of the month Comedy Night showcases high-quality comedians 8:30pm (£6); reservations recommended. Beers from £3. Mixed drinks from £4. Open daily noon-late. MC/V.

CLUBS

The White House, 65 Clapham Park Rd. (☎7498 3388; www.thewhitehouselondon-don.co.uk). ⊖Clapham Common. Despite its name, it's the New York clubbing scene the White House aims to bring to London. The club plays host to constantly changing events that make it one of the most popular dance haunts in the entire city. The roof terrace is perfect for long summer nights. Occasional cover £5-10. Open W-Th 5:30pm-2am, F-Sa 5:30pm-4am, Su 5pm-2am. MC/V.

Infernos, 146 Clapham High St. (☎7720 7633; www.infernos.co.uk). ❸Clapham Common. One of the most happening disco scenes in Clapham. Infernos offers various retro theme nights to get the party started—don't forget to bring your boogie shoes and Travolta hairdo. Open F-Sa 9pm-late. MC/V.

GLBT

Royal Vauxhall Tavern, 372 Kennington Ln. (☎7820 1222; www.theroyalvauxhalltavern.co.uk). ❸Vauxhall. Night Bus #N2, N36, N77. Just across the street from the Vauxhall station, this London icon has been around longer than many of the new developments in the neighborhood have. Friendly crowd. Tu "Jazz Club" 7pm-midnight, £5; Th "Cabaret" 7pm-midnight (£5); Sa "Duckie" 9pm-2am. Cover Sa £5. Open daily; call for events and hours. MC/V.

WESTMINSTER

Split between the historic Whitehall and residential Pimlico, Westminster is a destination for the early-evening crowd rather than all-night clubbers. Relax with a pint in a pub.

SEE MAP, p. 368

PUBS

■ **Red Lion,** 48 Parliament St. (☎7930 5826). ❸Westminster. TVs carrying the Parliament cable channel and portraits of politicians on the walls remind you that this is still the original politico's pub. MPs listen to the debates over a warm pint while a "division bell" alerts them to drink up when a vote is about to be taken. Very chill, despite the distinguished clientele. The food (sandwiches £3-4, fish 'n' chips £6) may not be fancy but is dependable. Downstairs cellar bar offers more space during crowded hours. Wheelchair-accessible. Open M-Sa 11am-11pm, Su noon-7pm. Kitchen open daily noon-2:30pm; snacks noon-3pm. MC/V.

Silver Cross, 33 Whitehall (☎7930 8359). ❸Charing Cross. Copper pots, odd bits of china, and the occasional barrel decorate this homey and spacious drinking destination. Stone flooring and wood accents add to the relaxed feel. Popular with young locals. Excellent and slightly upscale pub grub includes mushroom risotto (£6.50), roasted lamb (£8.50), and chicken Kiev (£7.50). Open M-Sa 11am-midnight, Su noon-11pm. MC/V.

Sherlock Holmes, 10-11 Northumberland St. (☎7930 2644). ❸Charing Cross. Numerous Holmesian "artifacts" are displayed in the pub, acquired with help from Sir Arthur Conan Doyle's family. There's no mystery to the excellent upstairs restaurant, just fine British food (mains £9-13), and patrons can even view a replica of Holmes's study, complete with a wooden statue of the famous fictional detective. Cheaper sandwiches (£4-5) and British mains (shepherd's pie £7) served downstairs. Sherlock Holmes Ale £2.30. Ground fl. is wheelchair-accessible. Open M-Th 11am-11pm, F-Sa 11am-midnight, Su noon-10:30pm. Restaurant open M-Th noon-3pm and 5:30-10pm, F-Su noon-10pm. MC/V.

BARS

Millbank Lounge, 30 John Islip St. (☎7630 1000). ❸Pimlico. Night Bus #88; hub at Victoria Station. On the 1st fl. of the City Inn. A swanky red interior and even swankier guests make this the hotel bar of the moment. Friendly bartenders mix a range of creative concoctions (£6.75-9) with theatrics straight from the movie *Cocktail*. The "Midnight Kiss" mixes apricot, chocolate, vanilla, and espresso for a unique taste. DJs spin Th-Sa. Beers £3.50-3.80. Wine by the glass from £3.75. Wheelchair-accessible. Open daily 11am-midnight. AmEx/MC/V.

THE BIG SPLURGE

ABSOLUTELY ICED

London's nightlife is among the most exciting in the world, with more than its share of high-concept bars. One especially chill spot might take the cake, however. In 2005 the vodka company Absolut brought the United Kingdom its very first Icebar. No, that's not a bar with ice sculptures or extra cold drinks. It's a bar made entirely out of solid ice. From the walls to the tables to the bar to the stools and even to the glasses, the **Absolut Icebar** is composed completely of ice imported directly from the Torne River in Sweden.

Admission includes entrance to the bar for 45min. and one drink. Patrons are provided with a cloak and optional gloves and shoes. The bundled-up boozers enter a decompression chamber, and finally the bar, where the temperature is kept at a constant -5° C and nothing but Absolut vodka cocktails are served. After time is up, patrons proceed into the Below Zero bar and restaurant where they can enjoy a full menu of dishes and snacks. But the unique upstairs experience is why most wannabe Eskimos show up at the Icebar, so button up and get ready for the big chill!

31-33 Heddon St. ☎7478 8910 ⊖Piccadilly Circus and ⊖Oxford Circus. Cover M and Su £12, Th-Sa £15. Open M-W 3:30-11pm, Th 3:30-11:45pm, F 3:30pm-12:30am, Sa 12:30pm-12:30am, Su 3:30pm-10:15pm.

THE WEST END

MAYFAIR AND ST. JAMES'S

While Mayfair and St. James's may not pack the nightlife punch that nearby Soho and Covent Garden and the Strand do, the area maintains a solid collection of libatory options.

SEE MAP, p. 356

PUBS

The Shepherds Tavern, 50 Hertford St. (☎7499 3017). ⊖Green Park. With worn leather couches and antique chandeliers, this traditional tavern probably has the same feel now as it did when it opened in 1735. Local businessmen stop by for lunchtime pints. Linger by the downstairs bar with a pint or enjoy English fare (rump steak; £8) in the lounge upstairs. Wheelchair-accessible. Open M-Sa 11am-11pm, Su noon-10:30pm. AmEx/MC/V.

The Duke of York, 7 Dering St. (☎7629 0319). ⊖Bond St. This recently remodeled pub gives you plenty of choices for the perfect pint (£3). The 3 floors are connected by a spiral staircase right in the middle of the room—the ground fl. has old-fashioned arcade games and a big bar. 1st fl. serves as a restaurant, and the "comfort zone" basement is perfect for some lazy lounging or a game of darts. Of course, pubbers are welcome to just lounge outside, with windowsills on which to rest glasses. Open M-Sa 11am-11pm, Su noon-10:30pm. MC/V.

BARS

▨ **22 Below,** 22 Great Marlborough St. (☎0871 223 5531; www.22below.co.uk). ⊖Oxford Circus. In a basement next to Cafe Libre and opposite Carnaby St. This hidden, amber-hued night spot is worth searching for. Entertaining comedy nights, over-sized fresh fruit martinis (£6-7), and a friendly, casual crowd will make it hard to pull yourself off the comfy leather couches. Bartenders test drinks with tiny straws while mixing to ensure quality. DJs Th-Sa night. Tu comedy (£3). Open M-F 5pm-midnight, Sa 8pm-midnight. £10 min. for MC/V.

▨ **Absolut Icebar,** 31-33 Heddon St. (☎7894 208 848; www.belowzerolondon.com). ⊖Oxford Circus. Because it's everyone's dream to see what it's like to get tipsy in the Arctic. Absolut Icebar is kept just below freezing year-round, and guests are escorted in wearing special silver capes and hoods for their pre-booked 40min. time slot. The entire bar and its contents are constructed completely of Swedish-imported ice and undergo a complete renovation every 6 months. Entrance fee includes use of cape and hood, a personalized ice mug, and vodka cocktail; M-W and Su £12, Th-Sa £15. Open M-W 3:30-11pm, Th 3:30-11:45pm, F 3:30pm-12:30am, Sa 12:30pm-12:30am, Su 3:30-10:15pm.

NIGHTLIFE

West End Nightlife

PUBS

The Cross Keys, 1	E2
Dog and Duck, 2	C2
The Duke of York, 3	A2
French House, AA	D2
Lamb And Flag, 4	E3
Old Coffee House, BB	B3
The Shepherds	
Tavern, 5	A4
The Toucan, 6	C2

GLBT NIGHTLIFE

Admiral Duncan, 7	C2
BarCode, 8	C3
The Box, 9	D2
Candy Bar, 10	C2
Comptons of Soho, 11	C2
The Edge, 12	C1
Escape, 13	C2
G-A-Y, 14	D1
G-A-Y Bar, 15	D2
Heaven, 16	E4
Ku Bar, 17	D2
Profile, a	C2
The Village Soho, 19	C3

BARS

22 Below, 20	B2
Absolut Icebar, A	B3
Alphabet, 21	C2
Amber, B	E2
Detroit, 22	C3
Floridita, C	C3
Freud, 23	E4
Gordon's Wine Bar, 24	D2
Karaoke Box, 25	D2
Lab, 26	C2
The Langley, 27	C3

O Bar, 28	C3
The Social, 29	B1
Strawberry Moons, 30	B3
Thirst, 31	D2
Trap, 32	C2

CLUBS

AKA, 33	E1
Bar Rumba, 34	C3
The End, 35	E1
Ghetto, 36	D1
Madame Jojo's, 37	C2

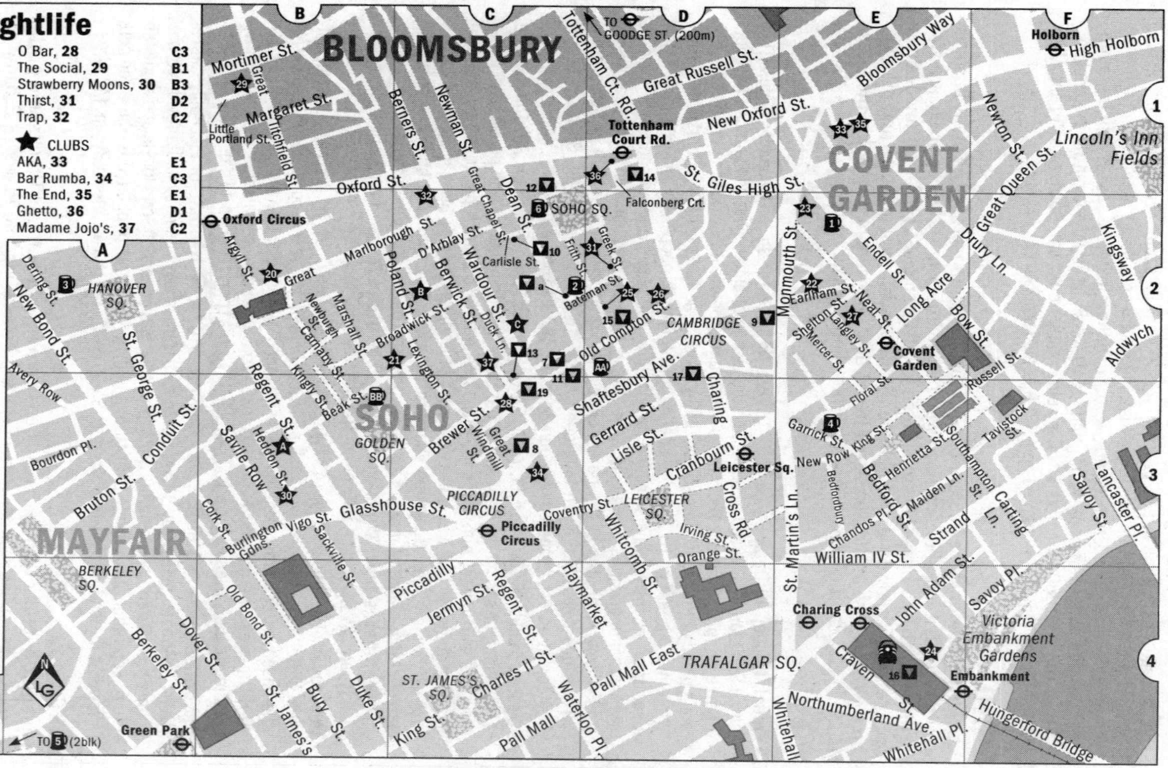

Map areas/labels: BLOOMSBURY, COVENT GARDEN, SOHO, MAYFAIR

0   200 meters
0   200 yards

The Social, 5 Little Portland St. (☎ 7636 4992; www.thesocial.com). ✪Oxford Circus. One of 3 UK Socials, this small, labyrinthine DJ-driven bar has a packed schedule of musical guests and DJs. Upstairs, wood paneling fosters a low-key dining atmosphere complete with booths for grubbing. Downstairs is edgier but more spacious. Mixed drinks £5.80, shooters £3. DJs spin nightly from 7pm. Cover after 11pm, M-Th £3, F-Sa £5. Open M-W noon-11pm, Th-F noon-1am, Sa 1pm-1am.

SOHO

Popularly considered the heart of London nightlife, Soho has just as many busts as bustling clubs. Avoid the tourist crowds by staying clear of Leicester Square and the places with tour buses out front. Head to **Old Compton Street** for gay and lesbian nightlife; mixed crowds also mingle on the streets and in many bars and pre-club joints. Whatever your pleasure—feathered boas and sequins, karaoke, the latest Madonna hit, or some good ol' rock 'n' roll—Soho has it.

PUBS

■ **French House,** 49 Dean St. (☎ 7437 2799). ✪Leicester Sq. or Piccadilly Circus. This small Soho landmark used to be frequented by personalities such as Maurice Chevalier, Charlie Chaplin, Salvador Dali, and Dylan Thomas before it became the unofficial gathering place of the French Resistance during World War II. It's said that Charles de Gaulle wrote his "Appeal of 18 June," a speech to the French people, in this very pub. Enjoy beer or an extensive wine selection (available by the glass) and hob-nob with some of the most interesting characters in Soho. Come early so that you can get a seat inside and a look at photos of the personalities who have graced this pub in times past. Wheelchair-accessible. Open M-W noon-11pm, Th-Sa noon-midnight, Su noon-11pm. Restaurant on 1st fl. open daily noon-3pm and 5:30-11pm. AmEx/MC/V.

■ **Dog and Duck,** 18 Bateman St. (☎ 7494 0697). ✪Tottenham Court Rd. This historic establishment sits on the past site of the Duke of Monmouth's Soho house, and is the smallest and oldest pub in Soho. The name refers to Soho's previous role as royal hunting grounds. This was a regular haunt of George Orwell's; the bar on the 1st fl. is named in his honor. Gorgeous Victorian tile interior surrounds a little hearth and 4 tables. More standing room is available near the bar or outside on the sidewalk when the weather is nice. Wheelchair-accessible. Open M-Sa noon-11pm, Su noon-10:30pm. Kitchen open daily noon-3pm and 5-9pm. MC/V.

The Toucan, 19 Carlisle St. (☎ 7437 4123). ✪Tottenham Court Rd. A small pub right outside of Soho Sq., bursting with Irish pride and named for the mascot of Guinness beer. In the basement bar, order from the extensive menu of classic or rare Irish whiskeys (£2.50-50). Beer can be ordered to go and taken to Soho Park, just outside the door. Arrive before the early evening crowds. Open M-F 11am-11pm, Sa noon-11pm. MC/V.

Old Coffee House, 49 Beak Street. (☎ 7437 2197). ✪Oxford St. or Piccadilly Circus. Don't let the name fool you: this down-to-earth pub is no coffee house. It provides a welcome break from Soho's trendy atmosphere. A regular cast of Soho locals and some fab flair keeps this pub a lively spot throughout the day and popular with the after-work crowd at the end of the week. Open M-Sa 11am-11pm, Su 12pm-10:30pm. MC/V.

BARS

When bar-hopping through Soho's busy streets keep in mind that some of the swankiest and most popular bars in the area, including The Player (8 Broadwich St.) become members-only after 11pm. Others, like Milk & Honey (61 Poland St.), have special members-only areas. You can enjoy their hip ambience—just make sure to call ahead or be prepared to leave when the clock strikes 11.

■ **Lab,** 12 Old Compton St. (☎ 7437 7820; www.lab-townhouse.com). ✪Leicester Sq. or Tottenham Court Rd. With restroom signs for "bitches" and "bastards," the only thing this funky cocktail bar takes seriously is its stellar drink menu. Licensed mixologists serve up their own award-winning concoctions (£6-7), while hip 20-somethings lounge in the orange-and-purple retro atmosphere. DJs spin house and funk nightly from 8pm. Open M-Sa 4pm-midnight, Su 4pm-10:30pm. AmEx/MC/V.

▨ **Floridita,** 100 Wardour St. (☎ 7314 4000). ⊖Oxford St. or Piccadilly Circus. One of Soho's largest and swankiest bars, Floridita's 2 fl. appeal to the classy set. The vibe, though, is decidedly Cuban. Try their popular signature daiquiris (£7.50). A new house band every month provides live salsa music 6 nights a week for dancing in the ultra-hip basement bar. There is a hefty cover charge on the weekends: Th-Sa after 7pm £15. Open M-W 5:30pm-2am, Th-Sa 5:30pm-3am. AmEx/MC/V.

▨ **Alphabet,** 61-63 Beak St. (☎ 7439 2190). ⊖Oxford St. or Piccadilly Circus. You don't need a firm grasp on your ABCs to figure out that this lounge bar is the in-spot for the Soho in-crowd. Each weekend, the turquoise-tinged interior is filled with people sipping wine (£4.50-7 per glass) or tasty fruit and champagne mixed drinks (£6-7). Buy a piece of modern artwork off the upstairs walls, or head downstairs to plot your stumble home on the jumbo Soho street map beneath your feet. DJs spin eclectic tunes Th-Sa. Open M-F noon-11:30pm, Sa 5-11:30pm. AmEx/MC/V.

▨ **Thirst,** 53 Greek St. (☎ 7437 1977; www.thirst-bar.com). ⊖Oxford St. On the corner of Greek and Bateman. With all the drink specials at this trendy DJ bar, you'll come away anything but thirsty. This popular early evening drinking spot turns into a late night dance scene downstairs, with DJs spinning funky house music every night from 9pm to 3am. The bar is small, so put your name on the online guestlist, or show up early. "Stupid Hour" daily 5-7pm (½-price mixed drinks, beers and house spirits £2.50, bottles of wine £10). Happy hour M-W 7pm-3am, Th-Sa 7-9pm (mixed drinks £3). Cover M-Th after 10pm £3, F-Sa after 10pm £5. Open M-Sa 5pm-3am. AmEx/MC/V.

Amber, 6 Poland St. (☎ 7343 3029). ⊖Oxford St. or Piccadilly Circus. Amber, Alphabet's sister bar, is located around the corner and attracts a younger, less professional crowd. The food, drinks, and decor are South American- and Spanish-inspired. Downstairs bar open Th-Sa, live DJs after 8pm. Open M-Sa noon-1am. AmEx/MC/V.

Polka, 58-59 Poland St. (☎ 7287 7500). ⊖Oxford St. or Piccadilly Circus. Polka feels like a grown-up bar with a contemporary vibe. Nothing quirky—just classic cocktails, a clean design, and a crowd made mostly of young professionals from the area. This is the place to come after a hard day at work, or if you're looking pol-

IN RECENT NEWS

SMOKING BAN

Got a light? Head outside... enclosed public spaces and workplaces in England became smoke free on July 1, 2007. England became the 29th country in the world to have some form of smoking ban in place. London is now in the company of such smoke-free cities as Boston, New York City, and Quebec.

The smoking ban has its fair share of both supporters and detractors. Supporters, of course, are glad that the air inside pubs and other public places will be clean of second-hand smoke. Those against the smoking ban include pubs who believe they will lose many of their regular customers, as well as the tobacco industry and smokers themselves. However, studies show that non-smokers will be far more likely to go out to pubs with the ban in place. Most pubs have outdoor seating areas already—the ban will just make these areas more crowded (and increase awning sales for a while). A small decline in pub sales is predicted, as has happened in other countries with the smoking ban, but all cases have shown a recovery to pre-ban levels after a brief period.

The ban's effect on London nightlife remains to be seen. What is certain is that bar and club patrons will now be able to breathe easy, without the lasting smell of smoke on their clothes after a night out on the town.

ished and neat and want a laid-back place to hang out. DJs spin Th-Sa 8pm-midnight. Open M-Sa noon-midnight, Su 1pm-midnight. AmEx/MC/V.

O Bar, 83-85 Wardour St. (☎ 7437 3490; www.the-obar.co.uk). ✚Piccadilly Circus. or Leicester Sq. Popular with tourists or those with a taste for the dramatic, O Bar features 3 fl. of candlelit elegance, comfy leather couches, and friendly staff members. Enjoy a glass of wine on the intimate 1st fl., mingle with a continental clientele on the ground fl., and get your groove on downstairs in the basement. Affordable cocktails into the wee hours. Daily drink specials 4-8pm. DJs spin nightly. Dancing Th-Sa. Open M-Th 5pm-3am, F 4pm-3am, Sa 3pm-3am, Su 4-10pm. AmEx/MC/V.

Karaoke Box, 18 Frith St. (☎ 7494 3878). ✚Oxford St., Piccadilly Circus, or Leicester Sq. Across the street from legendary jazz venue Ronnie Scott's, make your own music at this Japanese-style karaoke bar. Private rooms for 5-12 people, with TV, sound system, and all the ABBA lyrics you'll ever need. 5-bed rooms £12 per hr. noon-5pm, £18 per hr. 5-9pm, £28 per hr. 9pm-close; 7-bed rooms £15/25/34; 9-bed rooms £19/30/45; 12-bed rooms £24/40/55. Cover F-Sa after 6pm £3. Open M-Th noon-2am, F-Sa noon-3am. AmEx/MC/V.

CLUBS

Bar Rumba, 36 Shaftesbury Ave. (☎ 7287 6933; www.barrumba.co.uk). ✚Piccadilly Circus. Despite the fact that Bar Rumba is located next to the London Trocadero, a family entertainment complex, it draws a young crowd that makes good use of the industrial-strength interior for dancing. Many of the best DJs spin here. Excellent sound system is often blasted at full volume—pick up earplugs from employees. M Leaders of the True Skool (hip-hop, reggae, house); Tu "Barrio Latino" (salsa-rap and techno-merengue; salsa dance class 7:30-9pm; club and class £7); W Flavaz (hip-hop, R&B, reggaeton); Th "Movement" (drum and bass); F "GetDown" (hip hop, 21+); Sa "Flip'd" (urban eclectic; no sportswear); Su "Bubbling Over" (street soul and R&B). Cover: M after 10pm £5, students £3; Tu 9-11pm £4, 11pm-3am £5, students £3 all night; W £7; Th before 10pm £4, after 10pm £7, students £6, women free before 11pm; F 9-11pm £8, after 11pm £10, students £6; Sa 10-11pm £5, after 11pm £10; Su £5, women free before 10pm. Open M 9pm-3am, Tu 6pm-3am, W hours vary, Th 8pm-3:30am, F 6pm-3:30am, Sa 9pm-4am, Su 9pm-2am. MC/V.

Ghetto, Falconberg Court (☎ 7287 3726; www.ghetto-london.co.uk). ✚Tottenham Court Rd. Behind the Astoria. Crusading against "lack of originality," Ghetto squeezes alternative nightlife into Soho's trendy culture. Mixed crowd. M Rockstarz (rock, indie); Tu "Don't Call Me Babe" (bubblegum pop); W "NagNagNag" (alternative pop and rock); Th "Miss Shapes" (pop and indie); F "The Cock" (gay night); Sa "Top Secret" (kitsch and trashy tunes); Su "Detox" (funky house). Cover: M £3; Tu after 11:30pm £3; W after 11:30pm £5; Th £2, after 11:40pm £4; F £7, students £5; Sa £7 students before 11:30pm £5; Su £6, with flyer £5. Open M-W 10:30pm-3am, Th-Sa 10:30pm-5am, Su 10pm-3am.

Madame Jojo's, 8-10 Brewer St. (☎ 7734 3040; www.madamejojos.com). ✚Piccadilly Circus or Leicester Sq. Jojo's does it all: comedy, disco, jazz, and the famous deep funk. Tu "White Heat" (punk and New Wave 8pm-3am; bands play from 10:30pm); F "Deep Funk" (10pm-3am); Sa "Lost and Found" (music from the 1950s, 60s, and 70s); Su "Groove Sanctuary" (soulful house, disco, Latin 9:30pm-2am). Cover: Tu £5, with flyer £4; F before 11pm £6, after 11pm £8; Sa £8; Su £5, free with flyer. Open Tu 8pm-3am, F-Sa 10pm-3am, Su 9:30pm-2am. AmEx/MC/V.

DRESSING THE PART. Clubbing in London is an earnest endeavor, and some clubs take dress seriously. Although many will allow jeans, sneakers and baseball caps are usually not permitted. More upscale lounges may even turn you away with your best Diesels. Dress codes are far stricter on weekends.

GLBT

Check out Boy Magazine, available at many bars and clubs in Soho, for listings of GLBT events for the coming week—and for debaucherous photos of the past week's events.

■ **The Edge,** 11 Soho Sq. (☎7439 1313; www.edge.uk.com). ⊖Oxford Circus or Tottenham Court Rd. A friendly gay and lesbian drinking spot just off Soho Sq. offers several types of venues, complete with Häagen Dazs ice cream and £14 bottles of wine. 4 fl. of stylish brick, silver, and hot pink interior feature a lounge bar on the 1st fl., a piano bar on the 2nd, and a newly refurbished disco dance bar on the top fl. Piano bar Tu-Sa, DJs and dancing Th-Sa. Cover Th-Sa after 10pm £2. Open M-Sa noon-1am, Su noon-11pm. MC/V.

■ **Profile,** 56 Frith St. (☎7734 8300; www.profilesoho.com). ⊖ Tottenham Court Rd. One of Soho's newest and most popular night spots, Profile opened as a joint venture with gay personals website www.gaydar.co.uk. Featuring 3 bars on 3 fl. as well as 2 of the most stylish Internet cafes you're likely to encounter in London, this is definitely a place to see and be seen in Soho. Enjoy the main bar, the dance bar on the 1st fl., or the lounge on the top fl. Happy hour M-Th 4-9pm. DJs spin Th-Sa 8pm-1am. Open M-F 4pm-1am, Sa-Su noon-1am. AmEx/MC/V.

■ **Candy Bar,** 4 Carlisle St. (☎7494 4041; www.thecandybar.co.uk). ⊖Tottenham Court Rd. or Oxford Circus. This estrogen-packed, pink-hued drinking spot is a one-stop shop for lesbian entertainment. Karaoke, striptease performances, DJs, and popular dance nights keep the young crowds happy 7 days a week. There's a pool bar on the 1st fl. and dance bar in the basement. Guys allowed in only with a female escort. M "Set it Off" (alternative); Tu "Indie Girl" (indie); W "Opportunity Knockers" (karaoke); Th "First Class" professional pole-dancing (house and R&B); F "Grind" (house, urban); Sa funky house and R&B; Su funk, soul, and R&B. Cover F-Sa after 9pm £5. Open M-Th 5-10:30pm, F-Sa 3pm-2am, Su 3-10:30pm. MC/V.

■ **G-A-Y,** 157 Charing Cross Rd. (☎7434 9592; www.g-a-y.co.uk). ⊖Tottenham Court Rd. Frequently besieged by teenage girls on weekends. Madonna previewed 6 songs from her newest album here. G-A-Y (you spell it out when you say it) has become a Soho institution. M "Pink Pounder" (90s classics with 70s and 80s faves in the bar); Th "Music Factory" (house, dance, and a little pop); F "Camp Attack" (attitude-free 70s and 80s cheese with a 2nd room devoted to 90s music); Sa G-A-Y big night out, rocking the capacity crowd with commercial-dance DJs and live pop performances. Wheelchair-accessible. Cover M and Th with flyer or ad (available at most gay bars) £1, students 50p; F with flyer or ad £2, after midnight £3; Sa depending on performer £8-15. Open M and Th-F 11pm-4am, Sa 10:30pm-5am. Cash only.

Ku Bar, 30 Lilse St. (☎7600 4353; www.ku-bar.co.uk). ⊖Leicester Sq. This fashionable gay hangout has recently relocated and upgraded. Ku Bar boasts a dance space in the basement, a bar on the ground fl. and a lounge on the top fl. It attracts a mixed crowd, with the ages of the clientele generally increasing with the fl. number. Drink specials Su-Th. M "Karaoke" (a live band followed by open mic); Tu "Ruby Tuesdays" (for girls and their guy friends); W "Cabaret"; Th "Silk" (screenings of gay films from around the world); Su "Gay Tea Dance" (dance party). Main bar open M-Sa noon-11pm, Su 1-10:30pm. Downstairs Dance Bar open M-Sa 8pm-3am. AmEx/MC/V.

G-A-Y Bar, 30 Old Compton St. (☎7494 2756; www.g-a-y.co.uk). ⊖Leicester Sq. or Piccadilly Circus. A gay-and-lesbian feeder bar for the perennially popular G-A-Y Club, with the same fluorescent pop appeal. Music videos of 80s classics and contemporary pop play on video screens make way for as much dancing as drinking. Cheap drink specials attract a younger, more budget-conscious set. Lesbian-dominated bar downstairs opens after 7pm. Plenty of straight folks tag along for the fluffy scene full of boas, hot pants, and the occasional bachelorette party. M-Th and Su mixed drinks and beers £1.60. Open M-Sa noon-midnight, Su noon-10:30pm. AmEx/MC/V.

NIGHTLIFE

Village Soho, 81 Wardour St. (☎ 7434 2124; www.village-soho.co.uk). ⊖Piccadilly Circus. Enter at the main door on Wardour St. or the slightly less-polished back door around the corner on Berwick St. This Soho institution has been around for 15 years and attracts a young crowd. Speedo-sporting superhero dancers along with cruising tourists make this bar consistently packed and always over the top. Come for their famous Karaoke Night Tu after 7pm. Daily drink specials 5-8pm. Cover F-Sa after 10pm £3. Open M-Sa 3pm-1am, Su 3pm-11:30pm. AmEx/MC/V.

Comptons of Soho, 53 Old Compton St. (☎ 7479 7961). ⊖Leicester Sq. or Piccadilly Circus. Soho's oldest gay pub. Fills up early with a friendly, predominantly older male crowd. Horseshoe-shaped bar is open all the time, while upstairs, the Soho Club Lounge (opens 6:30pm) has a more mellow scene and a break from the noise. Open M-Sa noon-11pm, Su noon-10:30pm. MC/V.

Escape Dance Bar, 10a Brewer St. (☎ 7731 2626; www.kudosgroup.com). ⊖Leicester Sq. A small gay and lesbian dance bar with something for everyone—including those with a fetish for scantily clad, costumed doormen. Dance with young, friendly folks to the latest pop hits in an enjoyably cramped and sweaty space. A video DJ plays tunes with big, bright screens from 8pm to 3am daily. Open Tu-Sa 4pm-3am. AmEx/MC/V.

BarCode, 3-4 Archer St. (☎ 7734 3342). ⊖Piccadilly Circus. A bustling, male-dominated bar in the seedier side of Soho. Mostly older, grittier crowd and techno music. F-Sa the action shifts to the downstairs dance fl., open 9:30pm. Comedy club Tu evenings after 7:30pm. Wheelchair-accessible. Open M-Sa 4pm-1am, Su 4-10:30pm. AmEx/MC/V.

Admiral Duncan, 54 Old Compton St. (☎ 7437 5300). ⊖Leicester Sq. or Piccadilly Circus. A cornerstone of the Soho gay pub scene, this bar is still going strong after a bombing attack in 1999. Loyal local men hang out at the long, funky narrow bar in the center and sip a pint or two. A relaxed crowd comes early, but the place doesn't fill up until evening. Mostly standing room, with space to dance in the back. Wheelchair-accessible. Open M-Th noon-11pm, F-Sa noon-midnight, Su noon-10:30pm.

COVENT GARDEN AND THE STRAND

While serious partiers and wise locals head to Soho or over to Clerkenwell for a night out, the northern section of Covent Garden, close to Seven Dials, has several quality bars and clubs off Earlham St.

PUBS

▨ **Lamb and Flag,** 33 Rose St. (☎ 7497 9504). ⊖Leicester Sq. A neighborhood mainstay since the 1700s. Nestled on a small, cobblestone street, you'd never know this neighborhood used to be for "persons of meane quallite." Patrons go outside and order beer from the open front window. Regularly packed, but everyone's too happy to notice. Live jazz upstairs Su from 7:30pm. Wheelchair-accessible. Open M-Th 11am-11pm, F-Sa 11am-11:45pm, Su noon-10:30pm. Kitchen open daily noon-3pm. MC/V.

▨ **The Cross Keys,** 31 Endell St. (☎ 7836 5185). ⊖Covent Garden. It's all about ambience at Cross Keys. Deep red lighting inside makes it the darkest pub around. Check out the collection of paintings, antiques, and Beatles memorabilia. Copper kettles and pots hang from the ceiling. Outside, the flowers and vines surround picnic tables, ideal for a beer in the sun. Bitters start around £3. Wheelchair-accessible. Open M-Sa 11am-11pm, Su noon-10:30pm. Kitchen open daily noon-2:30pm. AmEx/MC/V.

BARS

▨ **Gordon's Wine Bar,** 47 Villiers St. (☎ 7930 1408; www.gordonswinebar.co.uk). ⊖Embankment or Charing Cross. Once the home of Rudyard Kipling, this basement wine bar is the oldest in London. A honeycomb of low, candlelit vaults and aged brick walls will take you straight back to 1890. Sherry and port from wood barrels around £3.50 per glass, wide selection of wine (average £3.75 per glass, £14 per bottle). Also serves traditional English fare (meat pies, stuffed potatoes) with all-you-can-eat salad bar for £6-10. Open M-Sa 11am-11pm, Su noon-10pm. £10 min. for AmEx/MC/V.

The Langley, 5 Langley St. (☎7836 5005). ♻Covent Garden. This all-purpose basement party bar draws the crowds in early and keeps them there. Friendly 20-somethings file in for Happy hour deals (daily 5-7pm; mixed drinks £3.25, margaritas and martinis £4.25) and then head to the Geneva Bar, a cavernous dance floor and bar out back with DJs playing old-school dance and pop music. Exposed brick and piping and chain-link chairs make for a sleek but jeans-appropriate experience. Bar food (chicken satay, sandwiches, and the like) served until midnight. DJs Th-Sa from 9pm. Cover Th after 10pm £3, F-Sa after 10pm £7. Open M-Sa 4:30pm-1am, Su 4-10:30pm. AmEx/MC/V.

Detroit, 35 Earlham St. (☎7240 2662; www.detroit-bar.com). ♻Covent Garden. Imposing double doors swing open to reveal a subterranean den full of cave-like enclaves. Low ceilings, orange lighting, and cushy, curtained-off booths add to the experience. Top-notch mixed drinks £7. Bar snacks available (£2-5). Happy hour 2-for-1 drinks (£7) until 7pm. Open M-Sa 5pm-midnight. £10 min. for AmEx/MC/V.

Freud, 198 Shaftesbury Ave. (☎7240 9933). ♻Covent Garden. Not to be confused with the metalworks store on the ground fl. Occasional live jazz Su 5pm. The few tables, surrounded by sand-blasted walls, are always packed. Drink a toast to Freud and invigorate your psyche with cheap mixed drinks (from £6). Most bottled beers less than £3.50. Salads, sandwiches, and soups noon-4:30pm £3-6.25. Open M-W 11am-11pm, Th 11am-1am, F-Sa 11am-2am, Su noon-11:30pm. MC/V.

CLUBS

AKA, 18 W. Central St. (☎7836 0110; www.akalondon.com), next to The End (p. 275). ♻Tottenham Court Rd. or Holborn. From Holborn, walk west along High Holborn and turn right onto Museum St.; look for the lavender building. A sleek DJ bar full of attractive 20-somethings. The loungy decor makes for a decidedly chill dance floor. Musical focus on quality underground electronic, with themes changing regularly: check the website for most recent updates. Pizza through neighboring Pizza Express. Mixed drinks £5-10. Th occasional comedy nights. 1st Tu of month quiz night. Sa joins with The End for **As One** (£15 for both clubs). Wheelchair-accessible. Casual dress. Cover Th after 10pm £6; F 9-10pm £6, after 10pm £8; Sa after 9pm £10. Open Tu 10pm-4am; W opening time varies from 6-9pm, with closing at 2am; Th 6pm-4am; F-Sa 6pm-5am; Su 10pm-4am. £10 min. for AmEx/MC/V.

The End, 16a West Central St. (☎7419 9199; www.endclub.com), next to AKA. ♻Tottenham Court Rd. or Holborn. With speaker walls capable of earth-shaking bass, a huge dance floor, and a lounge bar, The End is a cutting-edge clubber's paradise, full of hard house and pumping dancing. M "Trash" (glam rock to disco); Th "Discotec" (mixed/gay clubbing with cosmopolitan crowd); Sa **As One** joins up with AKA (p. 275). Wheelchair-accessible. Cover M £6; W before 11:30pm £5, after 11:30pm £6; Th before midnight £8, after midnight £9; F £10-15; Sa £15. Open M 10pm-3am, W 10:30pm-3am, Th-F 10pm-4am, Sa 6pm-7am. £10 min. for AmEx/MC/V.

> **TIP**
> **LIVIN' THE DREAM.** If you have your heart set on getting into an exclusive club, try asking your hotel concierge to call for a reservation or pick up the phone yourself; it's surprising what a bit of advanced planning can procure.

GLBT

The Box, 32-34 Monmouth St. (☎7240 5828). ♻Covent Garden. Bright, friendly, and—despite the name—quite spacious, this gay/mixed bar and *brasserie* has an airy charm that keeps its hip clientele loyal. Fresh flowers and candles decorate each table. Food specials, including soups, pastas, and mains (£8-9), change daily. Also sells club tickets to gay nightclub venues. Outdoor seating in good weather. Open M-Sa 11am-11pm, Su noon-10:30pm. Kitchen open daily until 5pm; select menu afterward. MC/V.

Heaven, The Arches, Craven Terr. (☎7930 2020; www.heaven-london.com). ⊖Charing Cross or Embankment. The self-proclaimed "most famous gay nightclub in the world." Intricate interior rewards explorers—try unguarded doors to find the fantastically lit main fl., 5 additional bars/dance fl., and a coffee bar. M "Popcorn" (mixed crowd; chart-toppers, 70s-80s disco hits, and commercial house; £2 drinks); F "Bang" (pop; drinks from £3). Cover M before midnight £5, after midnight £8; W before 11:30pm £2, after 11:30pm £4; F before midnight £5, after midnight £7; Sa £12, with flyer £10. Open M 10pm-5am, W 10:30pm-3:30am, F varies, Sa 10:30pm-5am.

BLOOMSBURY

Bloomsbury may be London's premier pub neighborhood—Clerkenwell and Holborn come close, but both are deserted by their population when work gets out. Students in the classroom and library all day tend to hit the pubs hard every night of the week, which makes for an always exciting student evening scene. The pubs and bars listed below have a fair mix of drinking and eating.

SEE MAP, p. 362

PUBS

▨ **Fitzroy Tavern,** 16 Charlotte St. (☎7580 3714). ⊖Goodge St. Popular with artists and writers (Dylan Thomas was known to frequent Fitzroy), this pub now oozes with good-looking students. Good luck getting within 20 ft. of the pub on summer evenings, thanks to the crowds spilling out from all sides. The center of Bloomsbury's "Fitzrovia" neighborhood (guess where the area's name came from). Traditional British lunches include bangers 'n' mash and baked pork chop. Umbrella-covered outdoor seating in summer. W 8:30pm comedy night (£5). Open M-Sa 11am-11pm, Su noon-10:30pm. MC/V.

The Queen's Larder, 1 Queen's Sq. (☎7837 5627). ⊖Russell Sq. A pub has stood here since 1710. The present incarnation dates to the late 1700s, when Queen Charlotte rented out the cellar to store food for her ailing husband, King George III. Traditional English fare, including a popular roast with Yorkshire pudding, available in the tiny upstairs restaurant (mains £6.25-8.25). Candlelit outdoor picnic tables perfect for warm nights. Open M-Sa noon-11pm, Su noon-10:30pm. MC/V.

The Jeremy Bentham, 31 University St. (☎7387 3033). ⊖Euston Sq. 2 floors packed with students from nearby UCL, a friendly staff, superior food, and a broad ale selection make this is an extremely popular pub. Sandwiches and burgers from £4. Open M-Sa noon-11pm. MC/V.

BARS

▨ **Vats,** 51 Lambs Conduit St. (☎7242 8963). ⊖Russell Sq. Move through the wooden foyer to the classic main bar, flanked by an antique reading desk piled high with wine-related volumes. Friendly staff is happy to let you taste before you commit. Food is a bit pricey (starters £4-8, meat mains £10-16) but delicious and innovative. Vats has too many wines to fit them all on the list, so if you have something particular in mind, don't be afraid to ask. "Good ordinary claret" £3.50 per glass, £14.50 per bottle. Burgundy from £15 per bottle. Lunch served noon-2:30pm, dinner 6-9:30pm. Open M-F noon-11pm. AmEx/MC/V.

NORTH LONDON

CAMDEN TOWN, KING'S CROSS, AND ISLINGTON

With swarms of young people in the area, it comes as a surprise that **Camden Town's** nightlife scene is centered on a handful of clubs and bars. The local council doesn't like handing out late licenses; the burgeoning bar scene is abruptly cut short at 11pm, so grab a few drinks here before heading to adjacent neighborhoods for your late-night fun. Music is the main reason to be in Camden at night. Nightlife in **Islington** is good for loungers and drinkers who bar hop around Upper St. **Clerkenwell's** mega-clubs are just a short jaunt away. In recent years, however, the area on the Islington side of **King's Cross** has developed some popular nightlife of its own.

PUBS

▓ **Compton Arms,** 4 Compton Ave. (☎ 7359 6883). ⊖Highbury or Islington. Removed enough from Upper St. to escape the hectic crowds. Low ceilings and multicolored barstools enhance the amiable atmosphere of this 17th-century pub. The big draw is the "beer garden," a picturesque outdoor patio where locals enjoy their bangers 'n' mash. Su comedy video night. Open M-Sa noon-11pm, Su noon-10:30pm. Kitchen open M-F noon-2:30pm and 6-8:30pm, Sa-Su noon-4pm. MC, V.

▓ **Duke of Cambridge,** 30 St. Peter's St. (☎ 7359 3066; www.dukeorganic.co.uk). ⊖Angel. Runner-up in the 2006 *Observer Food Magazine* "Best Pub in the UK" competition, the Duke is dedicated to environmentally responsible dining, from the sophisticated, exclusively organic menu to the must-try organic beer selection. Specializes in fresh dishes with surprise ingredients; the kitchen changes the menu twice per day. Game pie (venison, pigeon, and partridge) £13.50. More delicate mains like haddock (£14). Open M-Sa noon-11pm, Su noon-10:30pm. Kitchen open M-F 12:30-3pm and 6:30-10:30pm, Sa 12:30-3:30pm and 6:30-10:30pm, Su 12:30-3:30pm and 6:30-10pm. AmEx/MC/V.

▓ **The Castle,** 54 Pentonville Rd. (☎ 7713 1858). ⊖Angel. With the mentality of a neighborhood pub and the decor and style of a trendy bar, The Castle is an eclectic experience. Striped wallpaper and sofas make for a lounge-like atmosphere. Upstairs, the roof terrace is a wonderful place to drink away the afternoon. Sandwiches from £4. Mains from £6. Open M-Th 11am-midnight, F-Sa 11am-1am, Su noon-10pm. MC/V.

▓ **Filthy MacNasty's Whiskey Café,** 68 Amwell St. (☎ 7837 6067; www.filthymacnastys.com). ⊖Angel or King's Cross. Night Bus #N10, N63, N73, N91, 390. Shane MacGowan, U2, and the Libertines have all played in this laid-back Irish pub. Recently renovated, it has become a trendy neighborhood destination. Outside, red picnic benches support the rowdy overflow. It's actually 2 spaces with separate entrances, linked by the passage marked "toilets." Live music and occasional literary readings add to the hipster-intellectual atmosphere. 14 varieties of whiskey from £2. Pub grub £5-6. Open M-Sa noon-11pm, Su noon-10:30pm.

Dublin Castle, 94 Parkway (☎ 7485 1773). ⊖Camden Town. Night Bus #N5, N28, N31. Good up-and-coming acts perform in the back room every night, and record execs and talent scouts often descend looking for the next big thing. After the bands finish, the pub turns into a dance club. On weekends it gets crowded; get there early to avoid a queue. 3 bands nightly 8:45-11pm; doors open 8:30pm. Wheelchair-accessible. Cover varies. Open M-Sa 11am-1am, Su 11am-midnight.

BARS

Bar Vinyl, 6 Inverness St. (☎ 7681 7898). ⊖Camden Town. Night Bus #N5, N28, N31. One of the only bars in London with its own decks. DJs spin loud music in a narrow space

HEY, MR. DJ

Eric Miller has been DJing in the UK for over 20 years. He founded "nu funky people," a group that encourages experimental musicians.

LG: What are your favorite venues in London?
EM: Among others, I enjoy the Tongue&Groove, because it's a very intimate venue, and it feels like you're dancing with the crowd in there, which is very unusual. It reminds you that you're there having fun and it's great—though not when people spill drinks on you, of course.

LG: Why do you think the clubbing scene is so big in London?
EM: In London, everything is extremely fast-paced and cosmopolitan, and I think it's reflected in the music. You go to a techno night, and you could have a Brazilian techno DJ who puts Latin sounds in his music. The eclecticism here really makes a difference.

LG: What do you think of pop music?
EM: I tend to go for good song writing and musicianship. I've got nothing against pop music; I just don't like the churned-out, conveyor-belt, boy/girl band crap. My favorite genre is jazz, as well as drum and bass—anything funky. That's one of the beauties of dance music today: people are a lot more open-minded about these different genres.

dominated by a blue bar running down one wall. Tiny dance space always has a few takers; the rest of the crowd hangs out toward the quieter front of the room. During the day, it's a relaxed spot for coffee or lunch, with an open kitchen at the rear (most food £5-8). Most drinks under £5. DJs W-F night and Sa-Su from 3pm. Open daily 11am-11pm. Kitchen open 11am-9pm.

The Purple Turtle, 61-65 Crowndale Rd. (☎7383 4976; www.purpleturtlebar.com). ⊖Mornington Crescent. Night Bus #24, 27, N29. A young, eclectic crowd frequents this purple drinking haven, which turns into a packed dance space on weekend nights. Upstairs is a chill place. Downstairs, clubbers shake it to the music. Close to 50 shooters to choose from at the bar. For a relaxed Turtle experience forgo the sweaty crowds and come during the week or earlier on weekends for drinks. Cover daily after 10pm £3. Open M-Th 3pm-1am, F 3pm-3am, Sa 1pm-3am, Su 1pm-1am. MC/V.

> **MIND YOUR DRINK.** A "pint" in England is 20 fl. oz. and generally contains 4-5% alcohol by volume. A "pint" in the US is 16 fl. oz. and tends to be less alcoholic.

CLUBS

Scala, 275 Pentonville Rd. (☎7833 2022, box office 0870 060 0100; www.scala-london.co.uk). Night Bus #N10, N63, N73, N91, 390. ⊖King's Cross. Booze and house beats fill the nights on the huge main floor and the bar that overlooks the dance floor. So much space means that sometimes it seems empty but also that there's always room to dance. F "Popstarz" (musical eclectica devoted to sexual diversity and to house beats; pop on top floor); Sa constantly changing DJs and promotions bring a blend of hip hop and R&B. Occasional live events during the week. Dress code: Sa no caps, sneakers, or sportswear. Cover varies. Open F 10pm-4am, Sa varying hours (open late). MC/V.

Electric Ballroom, 184 Camden High St. (☎7485 9006; www.electric-ballroom.co.uk). ⊖Camden Town. Night Bus #N5, N28, N31. Clubbers here are just out for a good time. You won't find the latest sound systems or a particularly stylish decor, but foosball and pinball help make up for it. 2 large floors of dancing and 1 floor for relaxing with an expensive drink. F "Sincity" (alternatively styled patrons); Sa "Shake" (generic 70s and 80s night) often doubles as a raucous singalong. Occasional live events during the week. Cover £7-10. Open F-Sa 10:30pm-3am. MC/V.

GLBT

▧ **The Black Cap,** 171 Camden High St. (☎7428 2721; www.theblackcap.com). ⊖Camden Town. North London's most popular gay bar and cabaret is always buzzing and tends to draw an eclectic male and female crowd. The rooftop patio is the highlight of the place, with plenty of tables for outside pint-nursing. Live shows and club scene downstairs F-Su nights and some weeknights (times vary; call for details). Partially wheelchair-accessible. Cover for downstairs M-Th and Su before 11pm £2, 11pm-close £3; F-Sa before 11pm £3, 11pm-close £4. Open M-Th noon-2am, F-Sa noon-3am, Su noon-1am. Kitchen open noon-10pm.

HAMPSTEAD, HIGHGATE, AND GOLDERS GREEN

PUBS

Bar Room Bar, 48 Rossyln Hill (☎ 7431 8802). ⊖Hampstead. This hip, laid-back bar and art gallery fills up in the afternoon and stays busy into the evening. Ponder the bizarrely cool teacup chandelier or head out to the rear garden when it's sunny. Live art exhibitions of local artists line the walls. Pizzas from £2.65. Tu 2-for-1 pizza special. Th 2-for-1 drink special. Bottles of wine £7 daily from 5-7pm. Su live jazz from 8pm. Wheelchair-accessible. Open M-F 11am-11pm, Sa 11am-midnight, Su noon-10:30pm. MC/V. ❷

The Freemason's Arms, 32 Downshire Hill (☎ 7433 6811). ⊖Hampstead. Large pub on the corner across from the Heath. Vast stone patio out front is perfect for people-watching. A spacious, bright bar and a series of high-ceilinged dining rooms inside. Recently rebuilt beer garden in the back is one of the largest in London and a favorite of David and Posh Beckham when they're in town. Seasonal menu has pizzas (£7-8.50) and starters from £4. Wheelchair-accessible. Open M-F noon-11pm, Sa 11am-11pm, Su 10:30am-11pm. MC/V. ❷

MARYLEBONE AND REGENT'S PARK

Like many West End neighbors, Marylebone doesn't boast a strong nightlife scene. Pubs abound, but all close by 11pm—too early to be considered true London nightlife. Only a few places meet patrons halfway between pub

SEE MAP, p. 369

and club, with a real bar, music, and dancing.

PUBS

▩ **The Golden Eagle,** 59 Marylebone Ln. (☎ 7935 3228). ⊖Bond St. The quintessence of "olde worlde"—both in clientele and in charm—this is one of the friendliest pubs around. Sidle up to this local-filled bar and enjoy authen-

LG: What do you think of the Ministry of Sound [London's biggest and most famous dance club, p. 265]?
EM: I would like to do it just for the sound system. They were one of the pioneers of bringing the dance floor to the masses. They were quite businesslike about their approach, so what they did was introduce the whole club culture to the masses, which I think is a good thing. In a way, it's like a popular culture that's an alternative to pop music.

LG: Do you get a lot of chicks as a DJ?
EM: Well, yes. You are approached by lots of girls—you're on stage, you're like a mini-god for a while, and it's very exciting. But they don't do that when I'm not working.

LG: Why London?
EM: There's this sense here that anything goes; that you're free to do what you want to do. There's no set way of living here. I've lived in Hoxton, Islington, Notting Hill—and then I fell in love with South London when I first came. There's a real sense of community here, even if everyone's from different parts of the world; that's why I came to London in the first place.

tic pub sing-alongs (Tu 8:30-10:30pm, Th-F 8:30-11pm) around the piano in the corner. Limited menu—sausage rolls (£1.50) and pasties (£2.20). Sandwiches (£3.50) available M-F noon-3pm. Open M-Sa 11am-11pm, Su noon-7pm. MC/V.

O'Conor Don, 88 Marylebone Ln. (☎7935 9311; www.oconordon.com). ⊖Bond St. Well-known and well-loved authentic Irish pub, with Guinness ads plastered across the walls. See if they stand up to their claim of the "Best Guinness in London." Restaurant open M-F noon-2:30pm and 6-10pm. Bar open M-F noon-midnight. Bar kitchen open noon-10pm. MC/V.

BARS

Low Life, 34a Paddington St. (☎7935 1272). ⊖Baker St. or Regent's Park. Proudly advertising its "football-free zone," this DJ bar is a quirky and popular alternative to the neighborhood's pubs. Comic book menus, graffiti decor, velvet stools, and an assortment of fruit-flavored mixed drinks (£6-8) don't quite fit together, but that's part of the fun. Book a spot on the open decks M night, or dance the (early) night away to hip hop, funk, and 80s music. Open M-Sa 5-11pm, Su 5-10:30pm. Bar snacks (£2-6.50) end 30min. before closing. AmEx/MC/V.

BAYSWATER

While Bayswater's nightlife scene offers a few pubs and bars, most people head elsewhere for a night out.

SEE MAP, p. 361

PUBS

Mitre, 24 Craven Terr. (☎7262 5240). ⊖Lancaster Gate. This comfortable, sprawling Victorian pub is perfect for a lazy afternoon. Perched on a quiet corner, this large mansion has dining areas with restored fireplaces, stained-glass skylights, and picnic tables outside for nice weather. Hearty pub grub £5-8. Beer from £3. Free Wi-Fi. Open M-Sa 11am-11pm, Su noon-10:30pm. Kitchen open noon-3pm and 6-10pm. AmEx/MC/V.

Arthur Baker's Harlem Soul Food, 78 Westbourne Grove (☎7985 0900; www.harlem-soulfood.com). ⊖Bayswater. Recently opened bar and club that aims for a fashionable blend of comfort and style. The restaurant and bar serve an eclectic mix of drinks and comfort food (such as old fashioned mac 'n' cheese, £5) while the small club below, with candles and leather booths cut into the walls, features live DJs spinning until 2am most nights. M all-you-can-eat soul food buffet. Open M-F noon-2:30am, Sa 10am-2:30am, Su 10am-midnight. AmEx/MC/V.

The Swan, 66 Bayswater Rd. (☎7262 5204). ⊖Lancaster Gate. This pub claims to have been the final drinking place for victims of the gallows that once stood nearby, but now welcomes a slightly more upbeat crowd. A large patio and upstairs balcony offer great places to sit and relax with a pint (£3) and a view of Kensington Gardens directly across the street. Burgers and sandwiches £5-7. F-Su nights live acoustic music. Open M-Sa 10am-11:30pm, Su 10am-11pm. AmEx/MC/V.

NOTTING HILL

Dominated by young, artsy bohemians, Notting Hill stands in contrast to the clubs of West End side streets as the center of "alternative" nightlife culture. Even pubs in the area have their own distinct flavor.

SEE MAP, p. 361

PUBS

The Market, 240a Portobello Rd. (☎7229 6472). ⊖Ladbroke Grove. Night Bus #N52. Look for the iron-like sculpture above the door. This is consistently the loudest spot on Portobello, and that's saying a lot. Huge mirrors, dripping candles, and plenty of space make it a fine place to appreciate the West Indian atmosphere. Make some friends while downing a cool Cuban punch, *caipirinha*, or mojito (£4.50). M-F noon-3pm Thai food upstairs. F-Sa DJs. Open M-W and Su 11am-11pm, Th-Sa noon-midnight.

Portobello Gold, 95-97 Portobello Rd. (☎7460 4900; www.portobellogold.com). ⊖Notting Hill Gate. Classic pub with a healthy selection of draughts and ales (£3-4) and 20 varieties of whiskey. Picturesque restaurant area in back serves lunch and dinner as well as a generous set tea for £2.50, beneath a glass ceiling. Ploughman's Lunch £6. Oyster shooters from £2.50. Internet £1 per 30min. Wheelchair-accessible. Open daily 9:45am-midnight. MC/V.

Prince Albert Pub, 11 Pembridge Rd. (☎7727 5244). ⊖Notting Hill Gate. Solid wood floors and an assortment of comfy leather couches and booths make this a great spot for an afternoon pint and some traditional pub grub. Try one of the 21 beers on tap (from £2.75) or choose from an ample selection of bottles. Open M-Sa noon-11pm, Su noon-10pm. MC/V.

BARS

Visible, 299 Portobello Rd. (☎8969 0333). ⊖Ladbroke Grove. Night Bus #N52. None of the reggae madness of the other area bars, but equally appealing. Hip red and blue interior and some of the softest couches around. A variety of interesting drinks (from £6.50) such as the Black Velvet (Guinness and champagne) and Applesinthe (absinthe, schnapps, and juice) fill the menu. Open Tu-Th 4-11pm, F-Sa 10am-1am, Su 10am-10:30pm. MC/V.

Mau Mau, 265 Portobello Rd. (☎7229 8528; www.maumaubar.com). ⊖Ladbroke Grove. Night Bus #N52. Known for its Bohemian vibe and live music, particularly the Th jazz nights, Mau Mau pulls in a strong crowd of local devotees. The bar in the front serves standard cocktails (£6) and a decent selection of beer (from £2.80). A small stage and performance area occupies the back, and getting there early may provide a better chance at securing a spot on one of the worn-in couches. 18+. Open M-Th noon-11:30pm, F-Sa noon-2am, Su noon-10:30pm. Cash only.

CLUBS

Notting Hill Arts Club, 21 Notting Hill Gate (☎7598 5226; www.nottinghil-lartsclub.com). ⊖Notting Hill Gate. Night Bus #N94, 148, 207, 390. Excellent place for relaxed grooving. Turntables, a dance floor, and minimal decoration make the club very chill. A friendly, casual venue to sip mixed drinks (from £5) and move to a range of eclectic music. Cheap drinks like house beer and wine (£2.10) until 9pm. Acts vary daily, check website for details. Capacity is 218 people, strictly enforced with a 1-in, 1-out policy. Get there early to claim some space and avoid a wait. Cover Th-Sa after 8pm £5-7. Open M-F 6pm-2am, Sa 4pm-2am, Su 4pm-1am. MC/V.

KENSINGTON AND EARL'S COURT

After a day of hard-core shopping or museum visiting, most people in the area prefer to go to sleep rather than to head out for the night, but there are a few places to relax with a drink.

SEE MAP, pp. 366-367

PUBS

▨ **The Troubadour,** 265 Old Brompton Rd. (☎7370 1434; www.troubadour.co.uk). ⊖Earl's Court. A pub, cafe, and deli all under 1 roof; each wing is uniquely fantastic. Once upon a time, the likes of Bob Dylan and Paul Simon played in the basement club, which retains a bohemian appeal. The quirky decor is equally suited for morning espresso shots and evening vodka shots. Live music or poetry most nights. Breakfast served 9am-3pm £3-9, lunch and dinner £7-14. Open daily 9am-midnight. MC/V.

The Scarsdale, 23a Edwardes Sq. (☎7937 1811). ⊖High St. Kensington. Hidden down an alleyway off Earl's Court Rd.: turn onto Earl's Walk (right next to the police stations), follow it to the end, and turn right; it's on the corner. Built during a bout of wishful thinking, this picture-perfect pub was initially intended to house Napoleon's officers after they "conquered" Britain. Now its elaborate decor and great food make it fantastically popular with locals of all ages. Dinner reservations are essential, even during the week. Mains (£7.75-16) served noon-3pm and 6-9pm; bar food (salads and sandwiches; £5-10) served M-Sa noon-10pm, Su noon-9:30pm. Open daily noon-11pm. AmEx/MC/V.

The Drayton Arms, 153 Old Brompton Rd. (☎7835 2301). ⊖Gloucester Rd. or South Kensington. A local favorite on a quiet stretch of tree-lined Old Brompton Rd. This large and airy pub has comfortable, mismatched furniture, and a hefty wine list. Traditional mains like pork sausage and mash (£7.50-10) are a mouthful. Su live music 3-6pm. Open M-Sa noon-11pm, Su noon-10:30pm. Kitchen open M-F noon-4pm and 6-10pm, Sa noon-10pm, Su noon-9pm. MC/V.

BARS

Janet's Bar, 30 Old Brompton Rd. (☎7581 3160). ⊖South Kensington. Night Bus #14, N74, N97. Adorned with pink flamingoes, random retro relics, and plenty of pictures of Janet herself, this local hole in the wall is a welcome alternative to the pubs and glamor bars in the area. Mixed drinks are a steep £8.50, so stick to the house wine (£5.25 per glass) or beer (£4). Hungry visitors can order basic pastas (£6.65) and pizzas (£5-16), along with more adventurous sushi (£7-8.75). Live music most nights from 9:30pm. Open M-Th and Su 11:45am-1am, F-Sa noon-2am. MC/V.

GLBT

The Coleherne, 261 Old Brompton Rd. (☎7244 5951). ⊖Earl's Court or West Brompton. An older and quieter gay men's hangout. Women welcome but will stand out in the testosterone-heavy crowd. An outside seating area perfect for Old Brompton people-watching. Pool table and occasional cabarets keep locals entertained. Su night karaoke 8:30pm. Open M-Sa noon-11pm, Su noon-10:30pm. AmEx/MC/V.

KNIGHTSBRIDGE AND BELGRAVIA

Knightsbridge is not the place to go for a low-key night of inexpensive drinking, so if you're going to go out on the town here, you might as well splurge and take your liquor with the celebrity and jet-set crowds.

SEE MAP, p. 365

PUBS

Talbot, Little Chester St. (☎7235 1639). ⊖Knightsbridge or Sloane Sq. This pub's outdoor patio beckons many a London professional for lunch and after-work drinks. Cheerful, bright, and airy setting topped off with a superior wine list. Sandwiches £4-5; traditional British mains £6.50-8.50. On a hot afternoon, go for a pitcher of Pimm's and lemonade for £10. Takeaway available. Open M-F 10am-11pm. AmEx/MC/V.

Wilton Arms, 71 Kinnerton St. (☎7235 4854). ⊖Knightsbridge or Hyde Park Corner. Reading is actually encouraged at this traditional pub, with bookshelves full of classic novels lining the walls. Boozers and socializers won't feel out of place, though, thanks to a good selection of lagers and bitters (from £2.60) and a friendly crowd. Sit outside on the quiet street in nice weather. Shepherd's pie, curry dishes, vegetarian dishes, and steak-

and-kidney pie £5. Toasted sandwiches £3.25. Burgers £5.25. Open M-Sa 11am-11pm, Su noon-10:30pm. Kitchen open M-F noon-10pm, Sa noon-3pm; closed Su. MC/V.

Nags Head, 53 Kinnerton St. (☎7235 1135). ⊖Hyde Park Corner or Knightsbridge. Head in through cascading flowers to this outstanding traditional pub. Model airplanes, Boston Red Sox gear, miniature tables, and an antique fireplace make this an eccentric and endearing drinking spot. Have a seat at the bar so that the bartender isn't talking to your shins—the serving area is actually lower than the seats around it. Sandwiches from £4.50. Open M-Sa 11am-11pm, Su noon-10:30pm. Cash only.

BARS

Blue Bar, Berkeley Hotel, Wilton Pl. (☎7201 1680). ⊖Knightsbridge. Night Bus #N9, N10, 14, N19, N22, N52, N74, N97, N137. Blue Bar is suitably marine-hued for its moniker, with a sumptuous decor that can best be described as eclectic expensive. With a mixed drink list including over 50 types of finely aged whiskey, this is swanky London at its best. Wheelchair-accessible. Dress code smart casual. Open M-Sa 4pm-1am, Su 3pm-midnight. MC/V.

CHELSEA

Chelsea was once the spot for nightlife. Today, with one of the highest concentrations of prams (strollers) in London, Chelsea's raging parties generally involve birthday cakes and brightly-colored balloons. A few pubs serve up dependable pints to a younger crowd, but the options are slim after reasonable bedtime hours.

SEE MAP, p. 363

PUBS

Pig's Ear Pub, 35 Old Church St. (☎7352 2908; www.thepigsear.co.uk). ⊖Sloane Sq., then Bus #19 or 319. Funky background music and a shiny new decor lend the Pig's Ear a bit of yuppified smartness to complement its generally young crowd. Play board games on the ground floor, or head upstairs to the restaurant for well-reviewed fine dining. The pub serves dishes like roast plaice and mashed potatoes (£16.50) and steak tartare with fries (£18.75). Wide selection of drinks. Bar open M-Sa noon-11pm, Su noon-10:30pm. Restaurant open M-Sa 7pm-midnight, Su noon-4pm. AmEx/MC/V.

The Chelsea Potter, 119 King's Rd. (☎7352 9479). ⊖Sloane Sq., then Bus #11, 19, 22, 211, 319. This potter's studio-turned-pub is friendly and flowery. Try your luck at one of the video gambling machines or join the locals for a round of pints. Serves dependable fare, including fish 'n' chips (£7), burgers (£6.39), and sandwiches (£4-4.75). Open M-Th and Su 11am-11pm, F-Sa 11am-midnight. AmEx/MC/V.

BARS

Apartment 195, 195 Kings Rd. (☎7351 5195; www.apartment195.co.uk). ⊖Sloane Sq., then Bus #11, 19, 22, 319. Night Bus #N11, N19, N22. This über-posh bar, hidden behind a discreet doorway on King's Rd., won the *Evening Standard's* "Best Bar" award in 2003, and its popularity hasn't faded. Huge Victorian bay windows, an open fireplace, and a celestially themed bar make for a divine drinking ambience. Asian-themed bar food £7-8; mixed drinks £8. Dress is smart casual. Table reservations recommended Th-Sa. Open M-Sa 4-11pm. AmEx/MC/V.

DAYTRIPS

London offers enough intrigue, history, and excitement to satisfy any traveler, but we shouldn't forget that many of Britain's finest destinations fall within an easy jaunt of the city. If you're yearning for a break from the urban bustle, you can find country respite in Richmond, academic tradition in Oxford and Cambridge, or a literary legacy in Stratford-upon-Avon. With easy, convenient transport to all of the locations below, you'll be able to amply explore and return to your comfortable London base (or spend the night in your village of choice).

BATH   ☎ 01225

One of the world's first tourist towns, Bath has been a must-see for travelers since AD 43, when the Romans built an elaborate complex of baths to house the curative waters of the town they called Aquae Sulis. In the 18th and 19th centuries, Bath became a social capital second only to London, immortalized by Jane Austen and Charles Dickens. Today, hordes of tourists and backpackers admire the nationally recognized Georgian architecture by day and continue to create scandal by night.

▞ TRANSPORTATION

Trains: (☎ 08457 484 950). From **London Paddington** (1½hr., 2 per hr., £46); **London Waterloo** (2½hr., 2 per day, £34).

Buses: National Express (☎ 08705 808 080) from **London Victoria** (3½hr., every 1½hr., £17).

Taxis: Abbey Radio (☎ 444 444).

▞ ▞ ORIENTATION AND PRACTICAL INFORMATION

The **Roman Baths,** the **Pump Room,** and **Bath Abbey** cluster in the city center, bounded by York St. and Cheap St. The **River Avon** flows just east of them and wraps around the south part of town near the train and bus stations. Uphill to the northwest, historical buildings lie on **Royal Crescent** and **The Circus.**

Tourist Information Centre: Abbey Chambers (☎ 08704 446 442; www.visitbath.co.uk). Town map and mini-guide £1. The free *This Month in Bath* lists events. Books rooms for £5 plus a 10% deposit. Open May-Sept. M-Sa 9:30am-6pm, Su 10am-4pm; Oct.-Apr. M-Sa 9:30am-5pm, Su 10am-4pm.

Tours: Several companies run tours of the city and surrounding sights.

Bizarre Bath (☎ 335 124; www.bizarrebath.co.uk). The guides impart few historical facts on this comedic walk, but their tricks (including a bunny escape) prove entertaining. 1½hr. tours begin at the Huntsman Inn at N. Parade Passage. Tours daily Apr.-Sept. 8pm. £7, concessions £5.

The Great Bath Pub Crawl (☎ 310 364; www.greatbathpubcrawl.com). Meets at Lambretta's Bar on N. Parade Passage, delves into Bath's illicit past, and stops for a few rounds. Tours Apr.-Sept. M-W and Su 8pm. £5.

Ghost Walk (☎ 350 512; www.ghostwalksofbath.co.uk). Tours leave from the Nash Bar of Garrick's Head, near Theatre Royal. 2hr. tours Apr.-Oct. M-Sa 8pm; Nov.-Mar. F 8pm. £6, concessions £5.

Mad Max Tours (☎ 464 323; www.madmaxtours.com). Tours begin at the Abbey and spin through Stonehenge, Avebury, Castle Combe in the Cotswolds, and Lacock National Trust Village (the backdrop of the *Harry Potter* films). Full-day tours depart daily 8:45am, ½-day tours depart daily 1:30pm. Full-day tours £22.50, ½-day £12.50. Entrance to Stonehenge not included.

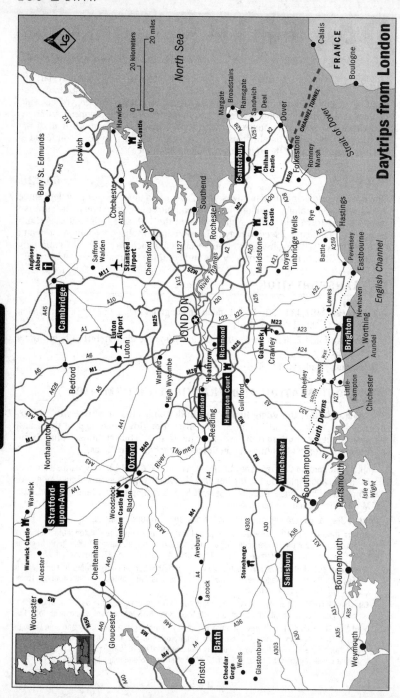

Daytrips from London

Banks: Banks are ubiquitous; most are open M-F 9:30am-5pm, Sa 9:30am-12:30pm. **Thomas Cook,** 20 New Bond St. (☎492 000). Open M-W and F-Sa 9am-5:30pm, Th 10am-5:30pm.

Police: Manvers St. (☎01275 818 181), near the train and bus stations.

Pharmacy: Boots, 33-35 Westgate St. (☎482 069.) Open daily 10am-6pm.

Hospital: Royal United Hospital, (☎428 331). Coombe Park, in Weston. Take bus #14.

Internet Access: Central Library, Podium Shopping Centre (☎394 041), above Waitrose. Free. Open M 10am-6pm, Tu-Th 9:30am-7pm, F-Sa 9:30am-5pm, Su 1-4pm. **Ret@iler Internet,** 12 Manvers St. (☎443 181). £1 per 20min. Open M-Sa 9am-9pm, Su 10am-9pm.

Post Office: 21-25 New Bond St. (☎08457 740 740), across from the Podium Shopping Centre. **Bureau de change** inside. Open M-Sa 9am-5:30pm. **Postal Code:** BA1 1AJ.

ACCOMMODATIONS

Well-to-do visitors drive up prices in Bath, but the city's location and popular sights bring in enough backpackers and passing travelers to sustain several budget accommodations. B&Bs cluster on **Pulteney Road** and **Pulteney Gardens. Marlborough Lane** and **Upper Bristol Road,** west of the city center, also offer options.

Bath Backpackers, 13 Pierrepont St. (☎446 787; www.hostels.co.uk/bath). This laid-back backpacker's lair with music-themed dorms is always full of fun-loving travelers. Hang out in the lounge with a big screen TV or have a few drinks in the "Dungeon." Kitchen. Luggage storage £2 per bag. Internet access £2 per hr., free Wi-Fi. Reception 8am-11pm. Check-out 10:30am. Dorms £15; doubles £35; triples £52.50. Book ahead in summer. MC/V. ❷

YMCA, International House, Broad St. Pl. (☎325 900; www.bathymca.co.uk). Up the stairs from High and Walcot St. Spacious rooms overlooking a courtyard garden. Rec room. Continental breakfast included. Internet access. Dorms £13-15; singles £24-28; doubles £36-44; triples £48-54; quads £60-68. MC/V. ❷

YHA Bath, Bathwick Hill (☎465 674). From N. Parade Rd., turn left on Pulteney Rd., right on Bathwick Hill, and climb the hill (40min.), or take Bus #18 or 418 (every 20min., 80p). Secluded, beautiful mansion is frequented mostly by families and school groups. Kitchen. Reception 7am-11pm. Dorms £12.50, under 18 £9; doubles £32, with bath £36. MC/V. ❷

St. Christopher's Inn, 16 Green St. (☎481 444; www.st-christophers.co.uk). Downstairs bar offers an ideal hangout area for young crowd. Simple and clean bunks, but not a lot of space to do much else but sleep. Free luggage storage. Internet access £1 per 20min. Dorms £14-22; 1 double £40-48. Online booking discounts. MC/V. ❷

Toad Hall Guest House, 6 Lime Grove (☎423 254). Make a left off Pulteney Rd. after the overpass. 3 spacious rooms. Hearty breakfast included. Singles £25; doubles £48. Cash only. ❸

FOOD

Although restaurants in Bath tend to be expensive, reasonably priced eateries dot the city. For fruits and vegetables, visit the **Bath Guildhall Market.** (☎477 945. Open M-Sa 9am-5:30pm.) Next door to Green Park Station, a **supermarket** will satisfy. (☎444 737. Open M-F 8am-10pm, Sa 7am-10pm, Su 10am-4pm.)

Cafe Retro, 18 York St. (☎339 347). Mismatched chairs and wooden floors give this cafe-bar a simultaneously hip and old-world feel. 2 floors and plenty of space to enjoy your sandwich (£4) or entree (£6). Breakfast served all day. Open M-W and Su 9am-5pm, Th-Sa 9am-11pm. MC/V. ❶

Riverside Cafe, (☎ 480 532). Below Pulteney Bridge. Serves up light dishes and coffee in a sheltered enclave overlooking the River Avon. If you can't get a table outside, take your food to the nearby park. Sandwiches and soups £3-8. Open daily in summer 9am-9:30pm; in winter 9am-4:30pm. MC/V. ❶

Mai Thai, 6 Pierrepont St. (☎445 557). Huge portions of Thai food at affordable prices. Ornate tables and authentic decorations make the atmosphere as rich as the food. Entrees £6.50-11. Open daily noon-2pm and 6-10:30pm. 10% discount on takeaway orders of £10 or more. Reserve ahead on weekends. AmEx/MC/V. ❷

Yak Yeti Yak, 12 Argyle St. (☎442 299), 2nd entrance under the arch of Pulteney Bridge. Dine on traditional floor cushions at this colorful Nepalese restaurant. Spices ground in-house create unique and delicious dishes. Entrees from £7. *Menu £11.50.* Open M-Th and Su noon-2pm and 6-10pm, F-Sa noon-2pm and 6-10:30pm. MC/V. ❸

Demuths Restaurant, 2 N. Parade Passage (☎446 059; www.demuths.co.uk), off Abbey Green. Exotic vegetarian and vegan dishes (£11-16) served in a small, purple-tinted dining room. Superb chocolate fudge cake £5.25. *Prix-fixe lunch £8.* Open M-F and Su 10am-5pm and 6-10pm, Sa 9:30am-5:30pm and 6-11pm. Reservations recommended in summer. MC/V. ❷

👁 SIGHTS

THE ROMAN BATHS. In 1880, sewer diggers inadvertently uncovered an extravagant feat of Roman engineering. For 400 years, the Romans harnessed Bath's bubbling springs, which spew 264,000 gallons of 115°F (46°C) water every day. After excavation, the city became a mecca for Britain's elite. The 🖼**museum** merits the entrance price with its displays on Roman excavation finds and building design. It's also the only way to get up close and personal with the ancient baths and to see the extensive Roman architecture. Make sure to see the Roman curses (politely referred to as offerings to Minerva), wishing eternal damnation upon naughty neighbors. Audio tours are a must. *(Stall St. ☎477 785; www.romanbaths.co.uk. Open daily July-Aug. 9am-9pm; Sept.-Oct. and Mar.-June 9am-6pm; Jan.-Feb. and Nov.-Dec. 9:30am-5:30pm. Last admission 1hr. before close. £10-11, concessions £8.75. Joint ticket with Museum of Costume £13.50/11.50.)*

BATH ABBEY. Occupying the site where King Edgar was crowned the first king of all England in AD 973, the 140 ft. abbey stands in the city center. England certainly has its fair share of beautiful cathedrals, and the Bath Abbey stands out among the competition. Bishop Oliver King commissioned the abbey to replace a Norman cathedral, and the crowned olive tree on the ceiling symbolizes the message he heard from God: "Let an Olive establish the Crown and a King restore the Church." A stunning stained-glass window contains 56 scenes from the life of Christ. Also note the church's extraordinarily high number of memorial plaques (including one for William Bingham, a 19th-century US Senator). The underlying **Heritage Vaults** contain an exhibit on the abbey's uses through the ages. *(Next to the baths. ☎422 462; www.bathabbey.org. Open Apr.-Oct. M-Sa 9am-6:30pm, Su 8am-6pm; Nov.-Mar. M-Sa 9am-4pm, Su between services. Requested donation £2.50. Heritage Vaults open M-Sa 10am-4pm. Last admission 3:30pm. Requested donation £1.)*

MUSEUM OF FASHION AND ASSEMBLY ROOMS. The museum hosts a dazzling parade of 400 years of catwalk fashions, from 17th-century silver tissue garments to Jennifer Lopez's racy Versace jungle-print ensemble. Thematic displays show how fashion has changed through the years in everything from pockets to gloves, and interactive displays let visitors try on a corset and hoop skirt. *(Bennett St. ☎477 785; www.museumofcostume.co.uk. Open daily Mar.-Oct. 11am-6pm, Nov.-Feb. 11am-5pm. Last admission 1hr. before close. £6.50, concessions £5.50.)* The museum is in the basement

DAYTRIPS

Bath

▲ ACCOMMODATIONS
Bath Backpackers, **13**
St. Christopher's Inn, **5**
Toad Hall Guest House, **15**
YHA Bath, **12**
YMCA, **3**

🍺 PUBS
The Bell, **1**
Pig and Fiddle, **4**
The Lamb and Lion, **14**

🍴 FOOD
Cafe Retro, **9**
Demuths Restaurant, **10**
Mai Thai, **16**
Riverside Cafe, **7**
Yak Yeti Yak, **6**

★ CLUBS
Delfter Krug, **8**
Moles, **2**
PoNaNa, **11**

THE BIG SPLURGE

SO FRESH AND SO CLEAN

he waters that have drawn people to Bath since ancient times ave once again opened their varm arms to the public. Ironically, for over 30 years, the spa own of Bath had no public baths o call their own. **Thermae Bath Spa** has corrected this egregious crime—channeling the natural, hermal spas into three glorious oools and a one-of-a-kind bath- ouse worth every penny.

The £20-50 admission grants ccess to the peaceful pools and he four intoxicating aroma steam ooms, waterfall showers, and oot baths that occupy the Geor- jian buildings. The *pièce de résis- ance* is the open-air rooftop pool, vhere bathers relax in natural pring water and enjoy beautiful iews of the city and surrounding ills. For a smaller splurge, try the maller Cross Bath, a secluded, oval pool where waters cascade rom a fountain.

Whatever you choose, bathing n the waters of Thermae Bath Spa is guaranteed to leave you eeling relaxed, rejuvenated, and ike the Roman royalty who took o the waters before you.

he Hetling Pump Room, Hot Bath St. ☎335 678; www.thermaebath- pa.com. Open daily 9am-10pm. hr. £20, 4hr. £30, full day £50; ½hr. in Cross Bath £12. No reser- ations required.

of the Assembly Rooms, which once held *fin-de-siè- cle* balls and concerts. Today's visitors, dressed some- what less elegantly, can still take tea. Bombing during WWII ravaged the rooms, but a renovation has dupli- cated the originals. (*☎477 785. Open daily 11am-5pm. Free. Rooms are sometimes booked for private functions.*)

OTHER MUSEUMS AND GALLERIES. Next to Pulteney Bridge, the **Victoria Art Gallery,** Bridge St., holds a diverse collection of oil paintings from the mid-18th century to today, with a study in changing British perspective. It houses Thomas Barker's "The Bride of Death"—Victorian melodrama at its sappi- est. Rotating exhibits take place on the ground floor. (*☎477 233; www.victoriagal.org.uk. Open Tu-F 10am- 5:30pm, Sa 10am-5pm, Su 2-5pm. Free.*) The **Jane Austen Centre** depicts Austen's time in Bath, where she vis- ited her family and lived briefly. Ironically, she dis- liked living in Bath and wrote nothing while living here, but she frequently wrote about the city in her novels—most notably in *Persuasion* and *Northanger Abbey*. Tours of Bath sights mentioned in Austen's books and her family's homes are also available. (*40 Gay St. ☎443 000; www.janeausten.co.uk. Open daily in summer 10am-5:30pm, in winter 11am-4:30pm. Last entrance 1hr. before close. Tours Oct.-Sept. Sa-Su 11am. £6, students £4.50. Tours £4.50, concessions £3.50.*) Architecture buffs will enjoy the **Building of Bath Museum,** which explains the extensive planning and building of Bath as well as the history of the city's famous Gregorian buildings. Check out the model of the city—it took 10,000 hours to perfect its layout at a 1:500 scale. (*Countess of Huntingdon's Chapel, the Par- agon. ☎338 727; www.bath-preservation-trust.org.uk. Open Tu-Su 10:30am-5pm. £4, concessions £3.50.*) The **Museum of East Asian Art,** 12 Bennett St., displays objects dat- ing back to 5000 BC, with a large collection of jade and ceramics, as well as metalwork and amulets from various cultures. (*☎464 640; www.meaa.org.uk. Open Tu-Sa 10am-5pm, Su noon-5pm. Last admission 4:30pm. £4, families £9, concessions £3-3.50.*) The **American Museum,** Claverton Manor, has enough colonial relics to make any Yank feel at home. Check out the folk art building nestled among the well-man- icured grounds. (*☎460 503; www.americanmuseum.org. Open late Mar.-Oct. Tu-Su 2-5:30pm. Last admission 5pm. Gardens and tearoom open Tu-Su noon-5:30pm. £6.35, concessions £3.50. Grounds admission £4/2.50.*)

HISTORIC BUILDINGS. The city's oldest house in Bath is **Sally Lunn's,** 4 North Passage Parade. Built on the sight of an old monastery, you can check out the ancient "faggot" oven used to bake her world- famous buns and buy a giant bun to take home. (*☎461 634. Museum free. Hot buns £1.54. Open daily from*

10am.) In the city's residential northwest corner are the **Georgian rowhouses,** built by famed architects John Wood the elder and John Wood the younger. **The Circus,** which has the same circumference as Stonehenge, has attracted illustrious inhabitants for two centuries; former residents include Thomas Gainsborough and William Pitt. Proceed up Brock St. to the **Royal Crescent,** a half-moon of 18th-century townhouses. The interior of **1 Royal Crescent** has been painstakingly restored to the way it was in 1770, down to the last butter knife. (*☎428 126. Open from mid-Feb. to Oct. Tu-Su 10:30am-5pm; Nov. Tu-Su 10:30am-4pm. Last admission 30min. before close. £5, concessions £3.50.*) For stupendous views, climb the 154 steps of **Beckford's Tower,** Lansdown Rd., 2 mi. north of town. Take bus #2 or 702 to Ensleigh; otherwise, it's a 45min. walk. (*☎460 705. Open Easter-Oct. Sa-Su 10:30am-5pm. £3, families £7, concessions £2.*)

GARDENS AND PARKS. Consult a map or the TIC's *Borders, Beds, and Shrubberies* brochure to locate the city's many stretches of cultivated green. Next to the Royal Crescent, **Royal Victoria Park** contains dozens of rare trees. For bird aficionados, there's also an aviary. (*Always open. Free.*) **Henrietta Park,** laid in 1897 to celebrate Queen Victoria's Diamond Jubilee, was redesigned as a garden for the blind—only the most fragrant plants were chosen for its grounds. The **Parade Gardens,** at the base of N. Parade Bridge, have lawn chairs, flower beds, and a pleasant green on the River Avon. The gardens won the Britain in Bloom competition so often that they were asked not to enter again. (*☎391 041. Open daily June-Aug. 10am-8pm; Apr. and Sept. 10am-7pm; Nov.-Mar. 10am-4pm. Apr.-Sept. £1; Oct.-Mar. free.*)

🎵 NIGHTLIFE

Tourists and two universities keep this otherwise small town full of nightlife. Most pubs close around 11pm, and late-night clubs almost always charge a cover, so be prepared to spend some serious money when you go out.

Pig and Fiddle, 2 Saracen St. (☎460 868), off Broad St. The first stop for many pub crawlers. The cozy interior and huge heated patio are always full of backpackers enjoying cider and local ales. Can't get enough of the Pig? Join their Facebook group for updates on live music. Open M-Sa 11am-11pm, Su noon-10:30pm.

The Lamb and Lion, 15 Lower Borough Walls (☎474 931). Cheap pints make this a popular pre-club pub with students and locals on the weekends. Beer garden out back is fabulous in the summer, as is the perfectly crafted, fruit-filled Pimm's. Open M-Sa 11am-11pm, Su noon-10:30pm. MC/V.

Moles, 14 George St. (☎404 445; www.moles.co.uk). Pounds out soul, funk, and house with frequent live acts in an underground setting. M and Th up-and-coming live bands. Tu, F, and Sa dance club night. Cover £3-5. Open M-Th 9pm-2am, F-Sa 9pm-4am.

The Bell, 103 Walcot St. (☎460 426), challenges its clientele to talk over (or sing along with) the live folk, jazz, blues, funk, salsa, and reggae playing most nights. Pizza served in the garden on weekend evenings. Live music M and W evenings, Su lunch. Free Wi-Fi. Open M-Sa 11:30am-midnight, Su noon-10:30pm.

Delfter Krug, Saw Close (☎443 352; www.delfterkrug.com). Draws a large weekend crowd with its outdoor seating and lively 2-story club. Comfy couches offer a break from the crowded dance floor. Jams hip hop and pop with drink specials almost every night. Cover £2-5. Open M-Sa noon-2am, Su noon-10:30pm.

PoNaNa, N. Parade and Pierrepont St. (☎401 115; www.barclub.com/ponana). Descend the staircase into a subterranean lair to find tons of beats and sweaty dancers. W drum and bass nights. F "Squeeze the Cheese." Cover £3-5. Open M and W 9:30pm-2am, Tu and Th 10pm-2am, F-Sa 10:30pm-2:30am.

🎵 🎆 ENTERTAINMENT AND FESTIVALS

In summer, buskers (street musicians) fill the streets with music, and a brass band often graces the Parade Gardens. Keep an eye open for the singing Jamaican who is sure to put a smile on your face. The magnificent **Theatre Royal,** Saw Close, showcases opera and theatre. (At the south end of Barton St. ☎448 844. Box office open M-Sa 10am-8pm, Su noon-8pm. Tickets £5-27.) The **Little Theatre Cinema,** St. Michael's Place, Bath St., is Bath's local arthouse cinema, showing mostly independent and foreign films with a smattering of select blockbusters. (☎330 817. Box office open daily 1-8pm. Tickets £6, concessions £4-5.) Bath hosts several festivals; for information or reservations, call the Bath Festivals Box Office, 2 Church St., Abbey Green. (☎463 362; www.bathfestivals.org.uk. Open M-Sa 9:30am-5:30pm.) The renowned **Bath International Music Festival** (typically May-June, check www.bathmusicfest.org.uk for updates) features world-class symphony orchestras, choruses, and jazz bands. The overlapping **Fringe Festival** (☎480 079; www.bathfringearts.co.uk) celebrates the arts with over 200 live performances (May-June). The **Jane Austen Festival,** at the end of September, features Austen-themed walks, meals, and movies (contact the Jane Austen Centre at ☎443 000; www.janeausten.co.uk). The **Literature Festival** is held in March, the **Balloon Fiesta** in mid-May, and the **Film Festival** in late October. Pick up the weekly *Venue* (£1.30), available at bookstores.

BRIGHTON ☎01273

Brighton (pop. 250,000) is one of Britain's largest seaside resorts. King George IV came to Brighton in 1783, and enjoyed the anything-goes atmosphere so much that he transformed a farmhouse into his headquarters for debauchery (the Royal Pavilion). A regal rumpus ensued. Since then, Brighton continues to turn a blind eye to some of the more scandalous activities that occur along its shores, as holiday-goers and locals alike peel it off—all off—at England's first bathing beach. Kemp Town has a thriving gay and lesbian population. The huge student crowd, flocks of foreign youth, and frequent hen and stag partiers feed the notorious clubbing scene of this "London-by-the-Sea."

▐ TRANSPORTATION

Trains: From **London Victoria** (☎08457 484 950; 1hr., 2 per hr., £18.40).

Buses: National Express (☎08705 808 080) leaves from **London Victoria** (2-2½hr., every hr., £10.30).

Public Transportation: Local buses operated by **Brighton** and **Hove** (☎886 200; www.buses.co.uk) congregate around Old Steine. The TIC can give route and price information for most buses; all carriers charge £1.50 in the central area. Frequent local buses serve Brighton's town center and Marina. **Day Super Saver** tickets available for £3.

Taxis: Brighton Taxis (☎202 020). 24hr.

✳ 🛈 ORIENTATION AND PRACTICAL INFORMATION

Brighton is easily explored on foot. **Queen's Road** connects the train station to the English Channel, becoming **West Street** halfway down the slope at the intersection with Western Rd. Funky stores and restaurants cluster around **Trafalgar Street,** which runs east from the train station. From Queen's Rd., head east onto North St. to reach the narrow streets of the **Lanes,** a pedestrian shopping area by day and nightlife center after dark. **Old Steine,** a road and a square, runs in front of the **Royal Pavilion,** while **King's Road** parallels the waterfront.

Brighton

ACCOMMODATIONS
Baggies Backpackers, 5
Christina Guest House, 20
Dorset Guest House, 8
Hotel Pelirocco, 6

✦ FOOD
Deli India Restaurant, 1
Food for Friends, 10
The Hop Poles, 9
The Mock Turtle, 14
Nia Restaurant and Cafe, 2
Queen Adelaide
  Tea Room, 7

📖 PUBS
The FishBowl, 13
Fortune of War, 16
The Mash Tun, 4
Three and Ten, 18
Ye Olde King and Queen, 3

★ CLUBS
Audio, 15
The Beach, 17
Candy Bar, 12
Casablanca Jazz Club, 11
Charles St., 19

DAYTRIPS

English Channel

500 yards
500 meters

Tourist Information Centre: Royal Pavillion Shop, 4-5 Pavilion Buildings (☎09067 112 255; www.visitbrighton.com). Staff sells guides and maps, books National Express tickets, and reserves rooms for £1.50 plus a 10% deposit. Open June-Sept. M-F 9:30am-5pm, Sa 10am-5pm, Su 10am-4pm; Oct.-May M-F 9:30am-5pm, Sa 10am-5pm.

Tours: CitySightseeing (☎01708 866000; www.city-sightseeing.com). 50min. bus tours leave from Brighton pier every 30min. Apr.-Oct., with stops at Royal Pavilion, the railway station, and Brighton Marina. £6.50, students £5.50, families £15.50.

Banks: Banks line North St., near Castle Sq. **ATMs** outside Lloyds, at the corner of North St. and East St. (☎08453 000 000. Open M-Tu and Th-F 9am-5pm, W 10am-5pm, Sa 9:30am-1pm.)

Special Concerns: Disability Advice Centre, 6 Hove Manor, Hove St., Hove (☎203 016). Open M and F 10am-4pm, Tu-Th 10am-1pm.

GLBT Resources: Lesbian and Gay Switchboard, (☎204 050). Open daily 5-11pm. The **TIC** also offers an extensive list of gay-friendly accommodations, clubs, and shops.

Police: John St. (☎0845 607 0999).

Pharmacy: Boots, 129 North St. (☎207 461). Open M-Sa 8am-7pm, Su 11am-5pm.

Hospital: Royal Sussex County, Eastern Rd. (☎696 955).

Internet Access: Internet cafes cluster in the town center, especially along West St. and St. James St. Try **Starnet,** 94 St. James St. (80p per 30min., £1.20 per hr.). **Riki-Tik,** 18a Bond St. (☎683 844) has free Wi-Fi. Open daily 10am-2am.

Post Office: 51 Ship St. (☎08457 223 344). **Bureau de change** inside. Open M and W-Sa 9am-5:30pm, Tu 9:30am-5:30pm. **Postal Code:** BN1 1BA.

ACCOMMODATIONS

On weekdays, accommodations in Brighton go for about half the price of their weekend markups. Brighton's best budget beds are in its hostels; the TIC has a complete list. The city's B&Bs and hotels begin at £25-30 and skyrocket from there. Many mid-range (£35-50) B&Bs line **Madeira Place;** cheaper establishments abound west of **West Pier** and east of **Palace Pier.** To the east, perpendicular to the shoreline, **Kemp Town** has a huge number of B&Bs. Frequent conventions and weekenders, especially in summer, make rooms scarce—book early or consult the TIC.

■ **Baggies Backpackers,** 33 Oriental Pl. (☎733 740). Join in the fun at this super social hostel, where spontaneous parties on Baggies Beach are common. Racecar sheets and welcoming staff. Book ahead, especially on weekends. Co-ed bathrooms. Kitchen. Laundry £1.40. Key deposit £5. Dorms £13; 1 double £35. Cash only. ❷

■ **Hotel Pelirocco,** 10 Regency Sq. (☎327 055; www.hotelpelirocco.co.uk). Wannabe rock stars will revel in the over-the-top, hip-to-be-different atmosphere of Pelirocco. Each of the 19 individually themed rooms (try leopard-print "Betty's Boudoir," or Jamie Reid's "Magic Room," decorated by the Sex Pistols artist himself) has video games and a private bath. Singles £50-65; doubles £100-145. AmEx/MC/V. ❹

Christina Guest House, 20 St. George's Terr. (☎690 862; www.christinaguesthouse-brighton.co.uk). Family-run house a short walk from the seafront, with rooms with bath. Full breakfast with vegetarian options included. £25-35 per person. MC/V. ❸

Dorset Guest House, 17 Dorset Gardens (☎571 750). On the lively streets of Kemp Town, this B&B offers small, pleasant rooms with all the amenities of home. Convenient location near the Lanes. Breakfast included. Singles £25, doubles £35. MC/V. ❸

FOOD

Over 400 restaurants in the city satisfy almost any craving. **Queen's Road** is lined with chain restaurants and fast food. Cheap ethnic eateries from Indian to Mediterranean to Morrocan can be found along **Preston Street. The Lanes** are full of trendy patisseries and cafes that offer over-priced but memorable meals and great people-watching. Get **groceries** at Somerfield, 6 St. James St. (☎570 363. Open M-Sa 8am-10pm, Su 11am-5pm.) Brighton's history as a health resort has not been forgotten—vegetarian options pervade the city. Satisfy sugar cravings with **Brighton rock candy** from any of the many shops claiming to have invented it.

■ **Food for Friends,** 17a-18a Prince Albert St. (☎202 310). This bright corner restaurant offers inventive vegetarian dishes and a decadent afternoon tea (£5.50). Elegant entrees (£8-11) draw from Indian and East Asian cuisines. Open M-Th and Su noon-10pm, F-Sa noon-10:30pm. AmEx/MC/V. ❷

Nia Restaurant and Cafe, 87 Trafalgar St. (☎671 371), east of the train station. Delicious dishes (£11-15) in a romantic cafe near the North Laine. Unique menu offers international flavors, influenced by Japanese, French, and Mediterranean cuisine. Open M-Sa 9am-11pm, Su 9am-6pm. MC/V. ❸

Deli India, 81 Trafalgar St. (☎ 699 985). A stand-out among the many Indian restaurants in Brighton. Delicatessen and tea shop with mouth-watering vegetarian and meat *thali* (£6.50-7.50). Open M-F 10am-7:30pm, Sa 10am-6pm, Su noon-3pm. MC/V. ❷

The Mock Turtle, 4 Pool Valley (☎327 380). With homemade pastries and lace decor, this tucked-away cafe is the perfect stop for afternoon tea with scones and a generous helping of clotted cream (£5.50). Open T-Su 9:30am-6:30pm. Cash only. ❶

The Hop Poles, 13 Middle St. (☎710 444). This popular hangout is also a bar with a heated garden. Menu offers unique entrees, like Thai vegetable green curry. Vegan options. Entrees £7. Food served M-Th and Su noon-9pm, F-Sa noon-7pm. MC/V. ❷

◉ ◪ SIGHTS AND BEACHES

In 1752, Dr. Richard Russell's treatise on the merits of drinking and bathing in seawater to treat glandular disease was published. Thus began the transformation of the sleepy village of Brighthelmstone into a free-spirited beach town.

◪ROYAL PAVILION. A touch of the Far East is in the heart of England. Much of Brighton's present extravagance can be traced to the construction of the unabashedly gaudy Royal Pavilion. In 1815, George IV enlisted architect John Nash to turn an ordinary farm villa into an ornate fantasy palace, with Taj Mahal-style architecture offset by Chinese interiors. After living there for several months, Queen Victoria was going to have it demolished until the town bought the royal playground and opened it to the public. The magnificent **Banquet Room** centers around a 30 ft. long chandelier held by the claws of a dragon. Smaller dragons hold lotus lamps that, when lit, give the impression of fire-breathing. After your tour, find a seat on the balcony of the **Queen Adelaide Tea Room** ❶ for a spot of tea and a scone. (☎292 880. Open daily Apr.-Sept. 9:30am-5:45pm; Oct.-Mar. 10am-5:15pm. Last admission 45min. before close. £7.50. Tours daily 11:30am and 2:30pm; £2. Free audio tours. Queen Adelaide Tea Room open daily Apr.-Sept. 10am-5pm; Oct.-Mar. 10:30am-4:30pm. Admission to the Pavilion required for Tea Room.)

◪DOWN BY THE SEA. Brighton's original attraction is, of course, the beach, but the closest things to sand are fist-sized rocks. Turquoise waters, bikini-clad beach bums, live bands, and umbrella-adorned drinks make the seaside a must-visit. A debaucherous Brighton weekend would not be complete without a visit to the **nude beach,** 20min. east of Brighton Pier, marked by green signs.

THE PIERS. The bright lights of the **Brighton Pier** give the oceanfront some kitsch and character. The pier houses slot machines, video games, and candy-colored condom dispensers, with a roller coaster and other mildly dizzying rides thrown in for good measure. Give weary legs a rest on **Volk's Railway,** the oldest electric railway in the world, which shuttles along the waterfront from the pier to the

marina. (☎ *292 718. Open Apr.-Sept. M-F 11am-5pm, Sa-Su 11am-6pm. Round-trip £2.50.)*
The **Grand Hotel,** King's Rd., has been rebuilt since a 1984 IRA bombing that killed
five but left target Margaret Thatcher unscathed.

BRIGHTON MUSEUM AND ART GALLERY. Adding a touch of class to the town's
attractions, this recently renovated gallery features English and international
paintings, pottery, and Art Deco collections as well as an extensive Brighton historical exhibit that fully explicates the phrase "dirty weekend." The fine **Willett Collection of Pottery** has postmodern porcelains and Neolithic relics. *(Church St., around
the corner from the Pavilion. ☎ 292 882. Open Tu 10am-7pm, W-Sa 10am-5pm, Su 2-5pm. Free.)*

LANES AND LAINES. Small fishermen's cottages once thrived in the **Lanes,** an
intricate maze of 17th-century streets (some no wider than 3 ft.) south of North St.
in the heart of Old Brighton. Replace those cottages with overpriced, touristy boutiques and a plethora of chic restaurants, and you have the Lanes today. For a less
commercialized foray into shopping, head to **North Laines,** off Trafalgar St., where
a variety of novelty shops crowd around colorful cafes and impromptu markets.

■ NIGHTLIFE

For info on hot-and-happening nightspots, check *Latest 7* or *The Source,* free at
pubs, news agents, and record stores, or *What's On,* a poster-sized flyer found at
record stores and pubs. **GLBT** friendly venues can be found in the free monthly
issues of *G Scene* and *3Sixty,* available at newsstands; *What's On* also highlights
gay-friendly events. The City Council spent £5 million installing surveillance
equipment on the seafront and major streets to ensure safety during late-night par-
tying, but still exercise caution. The Lanes, in particular, can be too deserted for
comfort, and don't be surprised to stumble across a drunk (or 20) along the beach.
Night buses N69, 85, and 98-99 run infrequently but reliably in the early morning,
picking up at Old Steine, West St., Clock Tower, North St., the train station, and in
front of many clubs, usually hitting each spot twice between 1 and 2:30am (£1-4).

PUBS AND BARS

J.B. Priestley once noted that Brighton was "a fine place either to restore your
health...or to ruin it again." The waterfront between West Pier and Brighton Pier is
a good party spot, and there is a pub or bar on practically every corner of the city
center. Many pubs also offer specials and long Happy hours during the week.

■ **The Fish Bowl,** 73 East St. (☎ 777 505). Crowded by hip 20-somethings and students,
   this bar is a chilled-out hot spot that's cool without trying to be. You can't miss the
   bright turquoise exterior. Open M-Sa 11am-11pm, Su noon-10:30pm.

■ **Fortune of War,** 157 King's Road Arches (☎ 205 065), beneath King's Rd. Popular
   beachfront bar shaped like the hull of a 19th-century ship. Patrons sip their beverage of
   choice (pints £3.10) and watch the sun set over the Channel, and night owls keep the
   place packed until it rises again. Open daily from noon until they feel like closing.

   The Mash Tun, 1 Church St. (☎ 684 951). Lounging in plush leather sofas and on
   wooden church pews, a laid-back student crowd parties until the wee hours. Good food,
   graffiti-adorned walls, and music ranging from hip hop to rock to country keep the scene
   lively. Happy hour M-Th and Su 3-9pm; £4 for a "double spirit and splash." Open M-Th
   noon-midnight, F noon-1am, Sa 11am-1am. Kitchen open daily noon-7pm.

   Three and Ten, 10 Steine St. (☎ 609 777). Fills early and stays busy with a mellow
   crowd of locals and tourists in the know. Cheap beer £2. Mixed drinks £3. Open M-Th
   and Su noon-1am, F-Sa noon-3am.

Ye Olde King and Queen, Marlborough Pl. (☎607 207). This 1779 farmhouse offers TV, a beer garden, and multiple bars. Packed during football matches. Open M-Th noon-11pm, F-Sa noon-midnight, Su noon-10:30pm. Kitchen open M-Sa noon-6pm, Su noon-5pm.

CLUBS

The clubbing capital of the South, Brighton is also the hometown of Fatboy Slim and major dance label Skint Records—it's no surprise that Brightonians know their dance music. Most clubs are open Monday through Saturday 10pm-2am; after 2am the party moves to bonfires and revelry on the waterfront. Many clubs have student discounts on weeknights and higher covers ($5-10) on weekends.

Audio, 10 Marine Dr., (☎606 906). This nightlife fixture is the place to be in Brighton. 2 floors of debauchery and a mix of music. Always packed to the brim. Cover M-Th £3-4, F £5, Sa £7. Open M-Sa 10pm-2am.

The Beach, 171-181 King's Road Arches (☎722 272). Big beats right on the shore. Packed with weekenders dancing to an eclectic mix of hits. Snacks served noon-2pm. Cover £10, students £8. Open M and W-Th 10pm-2am, F-Sa 10pm-3am.

Charles St., 8-9 Marine Parade (☎624 091). Gay-friendly party with DJs spinning dance tracks. Anything-goes atmosphere breeds anything-goes dancing. Cover M £1.50, Th £3, F no cover, Sa £5-8. Open M 10:30pm-2am, Th-Sa 10:30pm-3am.

Casablanca Jazz Club, 3 Middle St. (☎321 817; www.casablancajazzclub.com). One of few clubs in Brighton that regularly offers live bands playing jazz, funk, disco, and Latin tunes for a mix of students and 20-somethings. Dance floor, DJ, and bar upstairs. Bands in the basement. Cover W after 11pm £2, F-Sa £5-7. Student discount £1. Open M and Th-Sa 9:30pm-3am, Tu-W 9:30pm-2am.

Candy Bar, 129 St. James St. (☎622 424; www.thecandybar.co.uk). This venue caters mainly to lesbian clubbers with always entertaining, often risqué theme nights. Check signs outside for the week's events. Tu karaoke night. Cover M £3; F-Sa free before 10pm, £4 from 10-11pm, £5 from 11pm-midnight, £6 after midnight. Open M-Th 9pm-2am, F-Su 9pm until manager's discretion.

🎵 ENTERTAINMENT

Pick up free *Events Guide* and *Theatre Royal Brighton* brochures at the TIC for the latest info on dates and locations. **Brighton Centre,** King's Rd. (☎0870 900 9100; www.brightoncentre.co.uk; box office open M-Sa 10am-5:30pm), and **The Dome,** 29 New Rd. (☎709 709; www.brighton-dome.org.uk; box office open 10am-6pm), host Brighton's biggest events, from Chippendales shows to concerts. Local plays and London productions take the stage at the **Theatre Royal** on New Rd., a Victorian beauty with a plush interior. (☎328 488; www.theatreroyalbrighton.co.uk. Tickets $10-25. Open M-Sa 10am-8pm.) **Komedia,** on Gardner St., houses a cafe with Wi-Fi, bar, comedy club, and cabaret. (☎647 100; www.komedia.co.uk. Tickets $5-12; discounts available. Standby tickets 15min. before curtain. Box office open M-F 10am-10pm, Sa 10am-10:30pm, Su 1-10pm.) The **Brighton Festival** (box office ☎709 709), held each May, is one of the largest arts festivals in England, celebrating music, film, and other art forms. The **Brighton Pride Festival** in early August is the largest Pride Festival in the UK (☎730 562; www.brightonpride.org).

CAMBRIDGE ☎01223

Unlike museum-oriented, metropolitan Oxford, Cambridge is a town for students before tourists. It was here that Newton's gravity, Watson and Crick's model of DNA, the poetry of Byron and Milton, and Winnie the Pooh were born. No longer the exclusive academy of upper-class sons, the university feeds the minds of women, foreigners, and state-school pupils alike. At exams' end, Cambridge explodes in Pimm's-soaked glee, and May Week is a swirl of parties and balls.

▊ TRANSPORTATION

Bicycles are the primary mode of transportation in Cambridge, a city which claims more bikes per person than any other place in Britain. If you are prepared to face the maze of one-way streets by driving to Cambridge, take advantage of its efficient park-and-ride bus system (www.parkandride.net/cambridge/cambridge_frameset.shtml).

Trains: (☎08457 484 950) from **London King's Cross** (45min., 3 per hr., £18).

Buses: National Express (☎08705 808 080) from **London Victoria** (3hr., every hr., £10).

Public Transportation: Stagecoach (☎423 578) runs **CitiBus** from the train station to the city center and around town (£1-2).

Taxis: Cabco (☎312 444) and **Camtax** (☎313 131). Both 24hr.

Bike Rental: Mike's Bikes, 28 Mill Rd. (☎312 591). £10 per day. £35 deposit. Lock and light included. Open M-Sa 9am-6pm, Su 10am-4pm. MC/V.

▊▊ ORIENTATION AND PRACTICAL INFORMATION

Cambridge has two main avenues; the main shopping street starts at **Magdalene Bridge** and becomes **Bridge Street, Sidney Street, Saint Andrew's Street, Regent Street,** and **Hills Road.** The other main thoroughfare starts as **Saint John's Street,** becoming **Trinity Street, King's Parade,** and **Trumpington Street.** From the **Drummer Street** bus station, **Emmanuel Street** leads to the shopping district near the TIC. To get to the center from the train station, turn right onto Hills Rd. and follow it for ¾ mi.

Tourist Information Centre: Wheeler St. (☎09065 862 526; www.visitcambridge.org), 1 block south of Market Sq. Books rooms for £3 plus a 10% deposit. Cambridge Visitors Card gives city-wide discounts (£2.50). Sells National Express tickets. Open Easter-Oct. M-F 10am-5:30pm, Sa 10am-5pm, Su 11am-4pm; Nov.-Easter M-F 10am-5:30pm, Sa 10am-5pm.

Tours: 2hr. walking tours leave from the TIC daily (July-Aug. 4 per day). Tours including King's College £9, children £4.50; St. John's College £7, children £4.50. Call for times and tickets (☎457 574). **City Sightseeing** (☎01353 663 659) runs 1hr. hop-on, hop-off bus tours every 15-30min. Apr.-Oct. £9, concessions £7, children £3.50.

Banks: Banks and **ATMs** on Market Sq. **Thomas Cook,** 8 St. Andrew's St. (☎543 100). Open M-Tu and Th-Sa 9am-5pm, W 10am-5pm. **American Express,** 25 Sidney St. (☎08706 001 060). Open M-F 9am-5:30pm, Sa 9am-5pm.

Police: Parkside (☎358 966).

Pharmacy: Boots, 65-67 Sidney St. (☎350 213). Open M 9am-6pm, Tu 8:30am-6pm, W 8:30am-7pm, Th-Sa 8:30am-6pm, Su 11am-5pm.

Hospital: Addenbrookes, Long Rd. (☎245 151). Take Cambus C1 or C2 from Emmanuel St. (£1), and get off where Hills Rd. intersects Long Rd.

Internet Access: Jaffa Net Cafe, 22 Mill Rd. (☎308 380). From £1 per hr. 10% student discount. Open daily 10am-10pm. **Budget Internet Cafe,** 30 Hills Rd. (☎464 625). 3p per min. Open daily 9am-11pm.

Post Office: 9-11 St. Andrew's St. (☎08457 223 344). **Bureau de change** inside. Open M and W-Sa 9am-5:30pm, Tu 9:30am-5:30pm. **Postal Code:** CB2 3AA.

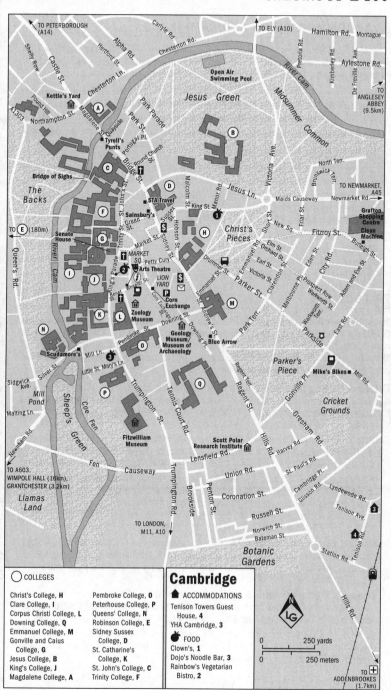

TO PETERBOROUGH (A14)
TO ELY (A10)
Hamilton Rd. Montague
Carlyle Rd.
Alpha Rd.
Shelly Row
Castle St.
Hertford St.
Chesterton Rd.
Chesterton Ln.
Aylestone Rd.
De Freville Ave.
Pretoria Rd.
Kimberley Rd.
River Cam
Midsummer Common
TO ANGLESEY ABBEY (9.5km)
Open Air Swimming Pool
Jesus Green
Kettle's Yard
Northampton St.
A1303
Pound Hill
Magdalene St.
Quayside
Park St.
Park Parade
A
Tyrell's Punts
Portugal Pl.
Round Church
B
North Terr.
Brunswick Terr.
Victoria Ave.
Bridge of Sighs
The Backs
C
Bridge St.
St. John's St.
Malcolm St.
King St.
Jesus Ln.
Maids Causeway
TO NEWMARKET, A45
Newmarket Rd.
D
STA Travel
Sainsbury's
Senate House
Trinity St.
Green St.
Sidney St.
Christ's Pieces
Short St.
New Sq.
Friar St.
Fitzroy St.
Grafton Shopping Centre
Clean Machine
Eden St.
City Rd.
TO E (180m)
River Cam
F
G
Market St.
MARKET SQ.
Petty Cury
Hobson St.
H
Elm St.
Orchard St.
Drummer St.
Emmanuel St.
Earl St.
Victoria St.
Clarendon St.
Melbourne Pl.
Prospect Row
Warkworth St.
Adam and Eve St.
East Rd.
Queen's Rd.
I
King's Parade
Bene't St.
Wheeler St.
J
Arts Theatre
LION YARD
Corn Exchange
Coin Exchange
St. Andrew's St.
M
Parker St.
Park Terr.
Warkworth Terr.
Parkside
Zoology Museum
Downing St.
Downing Pl.
K
L
Geology Museum
Museum of Archaeology
Blue Arrow
Pembroke St.
O
Regent Terr.
Parker's Piece
Mike's Bikes
Mill Rd.
N
Scudamore's
Mill Ln.
3
Little St. Mary's Ln.
Gonville Pl.
Cricket Grounds
Sidgwick Ave.
Silver St.
P
Trumpington St.
Tennis Court Rd.
Q
Regent St.
Gresham Rd.
Mill Pond
Sheep's Green
Coe Fen
Malting Ln.
TO A603, WIMPOLE HALL (16km), GRANTCHESTER (3.2km)
Newman Rd.
Llamas Land
Fitzwilliam Museum
Fen
Causeway
Scott Polar Research Institute
Lensfield Rd.
Hills Rd.
Harvey Rd.
St. Paul's Rd.
Cambridge Pl.
Glisson Rd.
Lyndewode Rd.
Tenison Ave.
TO LONDON, M11, A10
Brookside
Penton St.
Union Rd.
Coronation St.
Russell St.
Norwich St.
Bateman St.
Tenison Rd.
3
4
Botanic Gardens
Station Rd.
Hills Rd.
TO ADDENBROOKES (1.7km)

○ COLLEGES

Christ's College, **H**
Clare College, **I**
Corpus Christi College, **L**
Downing College, **Q**
Emmanuel College, **M**
Gonville and Caius College, **G**
Jesus College, **B**
King's College, **J**
Magdalene College, **A**

Pembroke College, **O**
Peterhouse College, **P**
Queens' College, **N**
Robinson College, **E**
Sidney Sussex College, **D**
St. Catharine's College, **K**
St. John's College, **C**
Trinity College, **F**

Cambridge

▲ ACCOMMODATIONS
Tenison Towers Guest House, **4**
YHA Cambridge, **3**

🍎 FOOD
Clown's, **1**
Dojo's Noodle Bar, **3**
Rainbow's Vegetarian Bistro, **2**

N

0   250 yards
0   250 meters

■ ACCOMMODATIONS AND CAMPING

John Maynard Keynes, who studied and taught at Cambridge, tells us that low supply and high demand usually means one thing: high prices. B&Bs gather around **Portugal Street** and **Tenison Road** outside the city center. Book ahead in summer.

Tenison Towers Guest House, 148 Tenison Rd. (☎363 924; www.cambridgecitytenisontowers.com), 2 blocks from the train station. Freshly baked muffins and impeccable rooms in a Victorian house. No smoking. Singles £35; doubles £55. Cash only. ❹

YHA Cambridge, 97 Tenison Rd. (☎354 601), close to the train station. Relaxed, welcoming atmosphere draws a diverse clientele. Always crowded. 103 beds. Well-equipped kitchen, laundry, luggage storage (£1-2), 2 TV lounges, and bureau de change. English breakfast included; other meals available. Lockers £1. Internet access 50p per 7min. Reception 24hr. Dorms £18.50, under 18 £14.50. MC/V. ❷

Warkworth Guest House, Warkworth Terr. (☎363 682). Sunny, spacious rooms with bath near the bus station in a family-run Victorian mansion. Free Wi-Fi in lounge. Breakfast included. Singles £50; doubles £70; family suites £90. MC/V. ❹

Highfield Farm Camping Park, Long Rd., Comberton (☎262 308; www.highfieldfarmtouringpark.co.uk). Take Cambus #18 to Comberton (every 45min.) from Drummer St. Showers and laundry. July-Aug. £9.50; May-June and Sept. £10.75; Apr. and Oct. £7.25-8.50. Closed Jan.-Mar. and Nov.-Dec. Electricity £2. Cash only. ❶

■ FOOD

Market Square has bright pyramids of cheap fruit and vegetables. (Open M-Sa 9:30am-4:30pm.) Get **groceries** at Sainsbury's, 44 Sidney St. (☎366 891. Open M-Sa 8am-10pm, Su 11am-5pm.) Cheap Indian and Mediterranean fare on the edges of the city center satisfies hearty appetites. South of town, **Hills Road** and **Mill Road** are full of budget restaurants popular with the college crowd.

▨ Clown's, 54 King St. (☎355 711). The staff at this cozy Italian eatery will remember your name if you come more than once. Children's artwork plasters the orange walls. Huge portions of pasta and dessert (£2.50-6.50). Set menu includes a drink, salad, small pasta, and cake (£6.50). Open M-Sa 8am-midnight, Su 8am-11pm. Cash only. ❶

▨ CB1, 32 Mill Rd. (☎576 306). A student hangout coffee shop with piping hot drinks (£1-1.50) and walls crammed with books. Enjoy free Wi-Fi and the decidedly chill atmosphere while lounging on couches. Open M-F 8am-8pm, Sa-Su 10am-8pm. ❶

Dojo's Noodle Bar, 1-2 Mill Ln. (☎363 471; www.dojonoodlebar.co.uk). Rave reviews bring long lines, but the enormous plates of wok-fried, soup-based, and sauce-based noodles are served quickly from the counter. Wide selection of vegetarian options and rice dishes. Everything under £7. Open M-Th noon-2:30pm and 5:30-11pm, F noon-4pm and 5:30-11pm, Sa-Su noon-11pm. MC/V. ❶

Mai Thai Restaurant, Park Terr. (☎367 480; www.mai-thai-restaurant.com). Location, location, location. This stylish, colorful restaurant with great views across Parker's Piece serves authentic Thai food with fresh ingredients. Popular lunch menu £10. Entrees £7-16. Open daily noon-3pm and 6-11pm. AmEx/MC/V. ❸

Rainbow's Vegetarian Bistro, 9a King's Parade (☎321 551; www.rainbowcafe.co.uk). Even carnivores enjoy this tiny basement spot in the city center. Asian-inspired vegetarian fare (£8). Open Tu-Sa 10am-10pm. Kitchen open 10am-9:30pm. Cash only. ❷

La Raza, 4 Rose Crescent (☎464 550). Live music every night and an affordable tapas menu (£3-8). Stays busy with a bar crowd well into the night. Open M-Th 9am-1am, F-Sa 9am-2am, Su 9am-midnight. MC/V. ❷

Choice, 11 St. John's St. (☎568 336). Branch at 16 Silver St. A quick, cheap stop popular with students. Make a picnic of the flapjacks (£1.20 each) and ample sandwiches (£2-2.60). 20% student discount. Open daily 8am-5pm. Cash only. ❶

🎵 NIGHTLIFE

King Street has a diverse collection of pubs. Most stay open 11am-11pm (Su noon-10:30pm). The local brewery, **Greene King,** supplies many of them. Pubs are the core of Cambridge nightlife, but clubs are also in the curriculum. The city is small enough that a quick stroll will reveal popular venues.

PUBS

The Anchor, Silver St. (☎353 554). Have a beer in the same spot that Pink Floyd's Syd Barrett drew his inspiration. Crowded undergrad watering hole. Savor a pint on an outdoor table and scoff at amateur punters colliding under Silver St. Bridge. Open M-Sa 10am-11pm, Su 11am-10:30pm. Kitchen open M-Sa noon-9:30pm, Su noon-9pm.

The Mill, 14 Mill Ln. (☎357 026), off Silver St. Bridge. Low ceilings, wood interior, and great beer. Patrons relax outside for punt- and people-watching. Features a rotating selection of ales. Open M-Th noon-11pm, F noon-midnight, Sa 11am-midnight, Su 11am-11pm. Food served M-Th noon-3pm and 5-9pm, F-Sa noon-7pm, Su noon-9pm.

The Free Press, Prospect Row (☎368 337), behind the police station. Named after an abolitionist rag and popular with locals. No pool table, no cell phones, no overwhelming music. Just good beer and entertaining conversation. Open M-F noon-2:30pm and 6-11pm, Sa noon-3pm and 6-11pm, Su noon-3pm and 7-10:30pm.

The Eagle, 8 Benet St. (☎505 020). Cambridge's oldest pub located in the heart of town. Packed with boisterous tourists. When Watson and Crick rushed in to announce their discovery of DNA, the barmaid insisted they settle their 4-shilling tab before she'd serve them. Check out the RAF room, where WWII pilots stood on each other's shoulders to burn their initials into the ceiling. Open M-Sa 11am-11pm, Su noon-10:30pm.

CLUBS

The Fez Club, 15 Market Passage (☎519 224). Moroccan setting complete with floor cushions. Students dance to everything from Latin to trance. Cover M-Th £2-5, F-Sa £6-8; M and W students ½-price. Open daily 9pm-3am.

The Kambar Club, 1 Wheeler St. (☎842 725), opposite the Corn Exchange box office. Small and dim, with a mix of indie and electronica tunes. Drinks can be expensive, but the energy is great on weekends. Cover £5, students £3. Open M-Sa 10pm-2:30am.

🏛 SIGHTS

Cambridge is an architect's utopia, packing some of England's most impressive monuments into less than a single square mile. The soaring **King's College Chapel** and St. John's postcard-familiar **Bridge of Sighs** are sightseeing staples, while more obscure college quads open onto ornate courtyards and gardens. Most historic buildings are on the **east bank** of the Cam between Magdalene Bridge and Silver St. The gardens, meadows, and cows of the **Backs** lend a pastoral air to the **west bank.** The **University of Cambridge** has three eight-week terms: Michaelmas (Oct.-Dec.), Lent (Jan.-Mar.), and Easter (Apr.-June). Visitors can access most of the 31 colleges daily, although times vary; consult the TIC for hours. Many are closed to sightseers during Easter term, virtually all are closed during exams (from mid-May to mid-June), and visiting hours are limited during May Week festivities. A visit to **King's, Trinity,** and **Saint John's Colleges** should top your to-do list, as should a stroll or punt along the Cam. Porters (bowler-wearing ex-servicemen) maintain security. The fastest way to blow your tourist cover is to trample the **grass** of the courtyards, a privilege reserved for the elite. In July and August, most undergrads skip town, leaving it to Ph.D. students, international students, and mobs of tourists.

COLLEGES

KING'S COLLEGE. King's College was founded by Henry VI in 1441 as a partner school to Eton; it was not until 1873 that students from schools other than Eton were admitted. King's is now the most socially liberal of the Cambridge colleges, drawing more of its students from state schools than any other. Its most stunning attraction is the gothic **Chapel**. From the southwest corner of the courtyard, you can see where Henry's master mason left off and the Tudors began work—the earlier stone is off-white. The wall that separates the college grounds from **King's Parade** was a 19th-century addition; the chapel and grounds were originally hidden behind a row of shops and houses. Inside, painted angels hover against the world's largest fan-vaulted ceiling. Behind the altar hangs Rubens's *Adoration of the Magi* (1639). John Maynard Keynes, E. M. Forster, and Salman Rushdie lived in King's College. In mid-June, university degree ceremonies are held in the Georgian Senate House. *(King's Parade.* ☎*331 100. Chapel and grounds open M-Sa 9:30am-5pm, Su 10am-5pm. Last admission 4:30pm. Contact TIC for tours. Listing of services and musical events available at porter's lodge. Choral services 10:30am and 5:30pm most nights. £4.50, students £3; with audio tours £7, students £5.50.)*

TRINITY COLLEGE. Henry VIII intended the College of the Holy and Undivided Trinity (founded 1546) to be the largest and richest in Cambridge. Currently Britain's third largest landowner (after the Queen and the Church of England), the college has amply fulfilled his wish. The alma mater of Sir Isaac Newton, who lived in E staircase for 30 years, the college has many illustrious alumni: literati John Dryden, Lord Byron, Alfred Tennyson, and Vladimir Nabokov; atom-splitter Ernest Rutherford; philosopher Ludwig Wittgenstein; and Indian statesman Jawaharlal Nehru. The **Great Court,** the world's largest enclosed courtyard, is reached from Trinity St. through **Great Gate.** The castle-like gateway is fronted by a statue of Henry VIII grasping a wooden chair leg—the original scepter was stolen so frequently that the college administration removed it. The apple tree near the gate supposedly descended from the tree that inspired Newton's theory of gravity, while in the north cloister of **Nevile's Court,** Newton calculated the speed of sound by stamping his foot and timing the echo. On the west side of the court stand the dour **chapel** and **King's Gate tower.** Lord Byron used to bathe nude in the **fountain,** the only one in Cambridge. The poet also kept a bear as a pet (college rules only forbade cats and dogs). The south side of the court is home to the **Master's Lodge** and the **Great Hall.** The building houses alumnus **A. A. Milne's** handwritten copies of *Winnie the Pooh* and Newton's personal copy of his *Principia.* Pass through the drab **New Court** (Prince Charles's former residence), adjacent to Neville's Court, to get to the Backs, where you can enjoy the view from **Trinity Bridge.** *(Trinity St.* ☎*338 400. Chapel and courtyard open daily 10am-5pm. Easter-Oct. £2.20, families £4.40, concessions £1.30; Nov.-Easter free.)*

SAINT JOHN'S COLLEGE. Established in 1511 by Lady Margaret Beaufort, mother of Henry VIII, St. John's centers around a paved plaza rather than a grassy courtyard. The **Bridge of Sighs,** named after the Venetian original, connects the older part of the college with the towering Neo-Gothic extravagance of **New Court.** The **School of Pythagoras,** a 12th-century pile of wood and stone thought to be the oldest complete building in Cambridge, hides in St. John's Gardens. The college also boasts the longest room in the city—the **Fellows' Room** in Second Court spans 93 ft. and was the site of D-Day planning. *(St. John's St.* ☎*338 600. Open daily 10am-5:30pm. Evensong Tu-Su 6:30pm. £2.50, families £5, concessions £1.50.)*

QUEENS' COLLEGE. Queens' College has the only unaltered Tudor courtyard in Cambridge, but the main attraction is the **Mathematical Bridge.** The structure is rumored to be built on geometric principles alone, which is perhaps why the 1749 original no longer stands. *(Silver St. ☎ 335 511. Open Mar.-Oct. M-F 10am-5pm, Sa-Su 9:30am-5pm. £1.30.)*

CLARE COLLEGE. Clare's coat of arms—golden teardrops ringing a black border—recalls the college's founding in 1326 by thrice-widowed, 29-year-old Lady Elizabeth de Clare. The college has some of the most cheerful **gardens** in Cambridge, and elegant **Clare Bridge**, dating from 1638, is the oldest surviving college bridge. Walk through Wren's **Old Court** for a view of the University Library, where 82 mi. of shelves hold books arranged by size rather than subject. *(Trinity Ln. ☎ 333 200. Open daily 10am-4:30pm. £3, children under 10 free.)*

CHRIST'S COLLEGE. Founded as "God's house" in 1448 and renamed in 1505, Christ's has since won fame for its **gardens** and its association with John Milton and Charles Darwin. Darwin's rooms (unmarked and closed to visitors) were on G staircase in First Court. **New Court,** on King St., is one of Cambridge's most modern structures, with symmetrical concrete walls and dark windows. Bowing to pressure from aesthetically offended Cantabrigians, a wall was built to block the view of the building from all sides except the inner courtyard. *(St. Andrews St. ☎ 334 900. Gardens open daily in summer 9:30am-noon; term-time 9am-4:30pm. Fellows' garden open M-F in summer 9:30am-noon; term-time M-F 9:30am-noon and 2-4pm. Free.)*

JESUS COLLEGE. Jesus College has preserved an enormous amount of medieval work on its grounds. Beyond the walled walk called the "Chimney" lies a three-sided courtyard fringed with flowers. Through the arch on the right sit the remains of a gloomy medieval nunnery. *(Jesus Ln. ☎ 339 339. Courtyard open daily 9am-8pm.)*

MAGDALENE COLLEGE. Located within a 15th-century Benedictine hostel, Magdalene (MAUD-lin), was the occasional home of Christian allegorist and Oxford man C. S. Lewis. **Pepys Library,** in the second court, displays the noted statesman and prolific diarist's collections. The college did not accept women until 1988. *(Magdalene St. ☎ 332 100. Library open M-Sa Easter-Aug. 11:30am-12:30pm and 2:30-3:30pm; Sept.- Easter 2:30-3:30pm. Free.)*

SMALLER COLLEGES. Thomas Gray wrote his *Elegy in a Country Churchyard* while staying in **Peterhouse College,** the smallest college, founded in 1294. *(Trumpington St. ☎ 338 200.)* The modern brick pastiche of **Robinson College** is the newest. In 1977, local self-made man David Robinson founded it for the bargain price of £17 million, the largest single gift ever received by the university. *(Across the river on Grange Rd. ☎ 339 100.)* **Corpus Christi College,** founded in 1352 by the townspeople, contains the oldest courtyard in Cambridge, aptly named Old Court and unaltered since its enclosure. The library has a huge collection of Anglo-Saxon manuscripts. Alums include Sir Francis Drake and Christopher Marlowe. *(Trumpington St. ☎ 338 000.)* The 1347 **Pembroke College** holds the earliest work of Sir Christopher Wren and counts Edmund Spenser, Ted Hughes, and Eric Idle among its grads. *(Next to Corpus Christi. ☎ 338 100.)* A chapel designed by Wren dominates the front court of **Emmanuel College,** known as "Emma." John Harvard, benefactor of a different university, studied here and is commemorated in a stained-glass window in the chapel. *(St. Andrews St. ☎ 334 200.)* **Gonville and Caius** (KEYS) **College** was founded twice, once in 1348 by Edmund Gonville and again in 1557 by John Keys, who chose to use the Latin form of his name. *(Trinity St. ☎ 332 400.)*

MUSEUMS AND CHURCHES

■ **FITZWILLIAM MUSEUM.** The museum fills an immense Neoclassical building, built in 1875 to house Viscount Fitzwilliam's impressive collections. Egyptian, Chinese, Japanese, Middle Eastern, and Greek antiquities are joined by 16th-century German armor. Upstairs, galleries feature works by Rubens, Monet, Van Gogh, Picasso, and Brueghel. *(Trumpington St.* ☎ *332 900. Open Tu-Sa 10am-5pm, Su noon-5pm. Call about lunchtime and evening concerts. Suggested donation £3.)*

OTHER MUSEUMS. For those with a green thumb, the Botanic Garden displays over 8000 plant species and was opened in 1846 by Professor John Henslow, Darwin's mentor. *(*☎*336 265. Open daily Apr.-Sept. 10am-6pm, Feb.-Mar. and Oct. 10am-5pm, Jan. and Nov.-Dec. 10am-4pm. £3, concessions £2.50.)* **Kettle's Yard,** at the corner of Castle and Northampton St., was founded by former Tate curator Jim Ede and displays extensive early 20th-century art in an intimate space. *(*☎*352 124; www.kettlesyard.org.uk. House open Apr.-Sept. Tu-Su 1:30-4:30pm; Oct.-Mar. Tu-Su 2-4pm. Gallery open Tu-Su 11:30am-5pm. Free.)* The **Scott Polar Research Institute,** Lensfield Rd., commemorates arctic expeditions with photos and artistic memorabilia. *(*☎*336 540; www.spri.cam.ac.uk. Open Tu-Sa 2:30-4pm. Free.)*

CHURCHES. The **Round Church (Holy Sepulchre),** where Bridge St. meets St. John's St., is one of five surviving circular churches in England and the second oldest building in Cambridge, predating even the university. Built in 1130, it is based on the pattern of the Holy Sepulchre in Jerusalem. *(*☎*311 602. Open M and Su 1-5pm, Tu-Sa 10am-5pm. Tours W 11am, Su 2:30pm. £1.50, students and children free. Tours £3.50.)* The only building older than the Round Church is **St. Benet's,** a rough Saxon church on Benet St., built in 1025. *(*☎*353 903. Open daily 8am-6pm. Free.)* The tower of **Great St. Mary's Church,** off King's Parade, gives views of the broad greens and the colleges. Pray that the 12 bells don't ring while you're ascending the 123 tightly packed spiral steps. *(Tower open M-Sa 9:30am-5:30pm, Su 12:30-5pm. £2.30, children £1, families £5. Church free.)*

🎵 🎆 ENTERTAINMENT AND FESTIVALS

🎆 **PUNTING.** Punting on the Cam is as traditional and obligatory as afternoon tea. Touristy and overrated? Maybe, but it's a still a blast. Punters take two routes—from Magdalene Bridge to Silver St. or from Silver St. to Grantchester. The shorter, busier, and more interesting first route passes the colleges and the Backs. To propel your boat, thrust the pole behind the boat into the riverbed and rotate the pole in your hands as you push forward. Punt-bombing—jumping from bridges into the river alongside a punt, thereby tipping it—is an art form. Some ambitious punters climb out midstream, scale a bridge while their boat passes underneath, and jump back down from the other side. Be careful of bridge-top pole-stealers. You can rent at **Scudamore's,** Silver St. Bridge. *(*☎*359 750; www.scudamores.com. M-F £14 per hr., Sa-Su £16 per hr. £70 deposit. MC/V).* Student-punted tours (about £12) are another option.

THEATRE AND CINEMA. The **Arts Box Office** *(*☎*503 333; open M-Sa noon-8pm),* around the corner from the TIC on Pea's Hill, handles ticket sales for the **Arts Theatre,** which shows musicals, dramas, and pantomime. The **ADC Theatre** (Amateur Dramatic Club), Park St. *(*☎*359 547),* offers student-produced plays, term-time movies, and a folk festival during the summer months. The **Corn Exchange,** at the corner of Wheeler St. and Corn Exchange St. across from the TIC, is a popular venue for concerts. *(*☎*357 851. Box office open M-Sa 10am-6pm, until 9pm on performance days; Su 6-9pm on performance days only. £10-30, concessions available.)* Independent and foreign-language films play at the **Arts Picture House,** 38-39 St. Andrews St. *(*☎*551 242; www.picturehouse.co.uk. £6, £5 students.)*

FESTIVALS. Midsummer Fair, dating from the 16th century, fills the Midsummer Common with carnival rides and wholesome fun for five days during the 3rd week of June (call ☎457 555 for specific dates and hours; www.cambridge-summer.co.uk). The **Cambridge Shakespeare Festival** (www.cambridgeshakespeare.com), in association with the festival at Oxford, features plays throughout July and August. Tickets (£12, concessions £9) are available at the door and from the City Centre Box Office at the Corn Exchange. The free **Strawberry Fair** (www.strawberry-fair.org), on the 1st Saturday in June, attracts a crowd with food, music, and body piercing. **Summer in the City** (www.cambridge-summer.co.uk) keeps Cambridge buzzing with a series of concerts and special exhibits. The festival culminates in a huge weekend celebration known as the **Cambridge Folk Festival** on the last weekend of July. World renowned musicians—with past performers such as James Taylor and Elvis Costello—gather for folk, jazz, and blues in Cherry Hinton Hall. Book tickets well in advance. (☎357 851; www.cambridgefolkfestival.co.uk. Tickets about £43. Camping on the grounds is an additional £5-18.)

MAY WEEK. May Week is actually in June—you would think that all those bright Cambridge students would understand a calendar. An elaborate celebration of the end of the term, the week is crammed with concerts, plays, and balls followed by recuperative riverside breakfasts and 5am punting. The boat clubs compete in races known as the **bumps.** Crews line up along the river and attempt to ram the boat in front before being bumped from behind. The celebration includes **Footlights Revue,** a series of comedy skits by undergrads. Past performers have included future *Monty Python* stars John Cleese, Eric Idle, and Graham Chapman. Guests can partake in the festivities for a mere £250.

CANTERBURY ☎01227

In 1170, four knights left Henry II's court in France and traveled to Canterbury to murder Archbishop Thomas à Becket beneath the massive columns of his own cathedral. Three centuries of innumerable pilgrims in search of miracles flowed to St. Thomas's shrine, creating a great medieval road between London and Canterbury. Chaucer caricatured the pilgrimage in *The Canterbury Tales,* which have done more to enshrine the cathedral than the saint's now-vanished bones. In summer, hordes of tourists descend upon the cobbled city center, while for the rest of the year, Canterbury remains a lively college town.

▐ TRANSPORTATION

Trains: Canterbury has 2 central stations.
> **East Station** receives trains from **London Victoria** (1¾hr.; 2 per hr.; £19.50 before 10am, after 10am £15.40).
> **West Station** receives trains from **Central London** (1½hr., every hr., £16.10).

Buses: National Express (☎08705 808 080; 2hr., 2 per hr., £13.10).

Taxis: Longport Cars Ltd. (☎458 885). 24hr.

Bike Rental: Downland Cycle Hire, West Station (☎479 643; www.downlandcycles.co.uk). £10 per day. Bike trailers £7 per day; £25 deposit. Open Tu-Sa 10am-6pm, Su 11am-5pm.

◤ ◢ ORIENTATION AND PRACTICAL INFORMATION

Canterbury's center is roughly circular, defined by the eroding medieval city wall. The main street crosses the city northwest to southeast, changing names from **Saint Peter's Street** to **High Street** to **The Parade** to **Saint George's Street.** Butchery Ln. and Mercery Ln., each only a block long, run north to the **Cathedral Gates,** while numerous other side streets lead to hidden pubs and chocolatiers.

DAYTRIPS

Tourist Information Centre: The Buttermarket, 12-13 Sun St. (☎378 100; www.visit-canterbury.co.uk). Books accommodations for £2.50 plus a 10% deposit. Open Easter-Christmas M-Sa 9:30am-5pm, Su 10am-4pm; Christmas-Easter M-Sa 10am-4pm. Offers 1½hr. **guided tours** of the city Apr.-Oct. daily 2pm; July-Sept. M-Sa 11:30am and 2pm. £4.25, concessions £3.75, families £12.50.

Banks: Banks and **ATMs** are on High St. **Thomas Cook,** 9 High St. (☎597 800). Open M-W and F-Sa 9am-5:30pm, Th 10am-5:30pm, Su 11am-4pm.

Police: Old Dover Rd. (☎762 055), outside the eastern city wall.

Pharmacy: Boots, 12 Gravel Walk (☎470 944). Open M-W and F 9am-6pm, Th and Sa 8am-7pm, Su 11am-5pm.

Hospital: Kent and Canterbury Hospital, 28 Ethelbert Rd. (☎766 877).

Internet Access: Dot Cafe (☎478 778; www.ukdotcafe.com), at the corner of St. Dunstan's St. and Station Rd. £3 per hr. Wi-Fi £2 per hr. Open daily 9am-9pm. Canterbury **Library,** in the Beaney Institute on High St. (☎463 608). Free. Open M-W and Sa 9am-6pm, Th 9am-8pm, Su 9am-5pm).

Post Office: 29 High St. (☎473 810). **Bureau de change** inside. Open M and W-Sa 9am-9:30pm, Tu 9:30am-5:30pm. **Postal Code:** CT1 2BA.

▐ ACCOMMODATIONS AND CAMPING

Canterbury attracts visitors throughout the year, and single rooms are scarce; always reserve ahead. B&Bs cluster around **High Street** and near **West Station.** The less expensive options (£18-20) on **New Dover Road,** half a mile from East Station, fill fast; turn right from the station and continue to Upper Bridge St. At the second roundabout, turn right onto St. George's Pl., which becomes New Dover Rd.

Kipps Independent Hostel, 40 Nunnery Fields (☎786 121), 10min. from the city center. Century-old townhouse with modern amenities. Kitchen and TV lounge. Laundry £3. Internet access £1 per 30min. If there are no vacancies, ask to set up a tent in the garden. Key deposit £10. Dorms £14; singles £19; doubles £33. MC/V. ❷

YHA Canterbury, 54 New Dover Rd. (☎462 911), located 1 mi. from East Station and town center. The trek through town is rewarded by quiet rooms and an all-you-can-eat breakfast buffet. Game room, TV lounge, and kitchen. Lockers £1. Laundry £1.50. Internet access 7p per min. Reception 7:30-10am and 3-11pm. Reserve ahead in summer. Dorms £17.50, under 18 £13.50. MC/V. ❷

Camping & Caravanning Club Site, Bekesbourne Ln. (☎463 216), off the A257, 1½ mi. east of the city center on a large plot of land near the golf course. Laundry (£3). Wheelchair-accessible. £5 per person. MC/V. ❶

◖ FOOD

The Safeway **supermarket,** St. George's Center, St. George's Pl., is a 4min. walk from the town center. (☎769 335. Open M-F 8am-9pm, Sa 8am-8pm, Su 11am-5pm.) A **farmers' market** fills the streets near the cathedral on Wednesday afternoons.

Cafe des Amis du Mexique, St. Dunstan's St. (☎464 390; www.cafedez.co.uk), just outside the West Gate. Share a plate of the sizzling steak fajitas (£22) and grab your own margarita (£6). Inspired Mexican dishes in a funky cantina setting. Open M-Sa noon-10:30pm, Su noon-9:30pm. AmEx/MC/V. ❷

Marlowe's, 55 St. Peter's St. (☎462 194; www.marlowesrestaurant.co.uk). The walls, covered with black-and-white photos from New York's Broadway, are as busy as the restaurant. Manages to add some pizzazz to traditional English food. Choose from 7 toppings for 8 oz. burgers (£7). Open M-Sa 9am-10:30pm, Su 10am-10:30pm. MC/V. ❷

Azouma, 4 Church St. (☎ 760 076; www.azouma.co.uk). Arabic music, pillow seating, and belly dancers every Th night. The Moroccan and Lebanese lunch buffet (£7) is a great deal, and dinner brings generous portions of Middle Eastern and Mediterranean cuisine (£11-14). Open M-Sa noon-midnight, Su noon-11pm. AmEx/MC/V. ❸

C'est la Vie, 17b Burgate (☎ 457 525). Grab an inventive takeaway sandwich and head to the nearby cathedral. Stuff a baguette with any of the 30-plus fillings. 10% student discount. Open M-Sa 9:30am-3:30pm. Cash only. ❶

🔵 SIGHTS

▓**CANTERBURY CATHEDRAL.** The massive gate and stony facade of Canterbury Cathedral command attention and advertise opulence. Pilgrims' contributions funded most of the cathedral's architectural wonders, including the early Gothic **nave,** constructed mostly between the 13th and 15th centuries on a site allegedly consecrated by St. Augustine 700 years earlier. The shrine to **Saint Thomas à Becket,** destroyed by Henry VIII in 1538, is marked by a single candle. The **Martyrdom** stands where Becket fell—the fatal strike was supposedly so forceful that the blade's tip shattered as it sliced Becket's skull. Henry IV, possibly uneasy after having usurped the throne, had Becket's body entombed near his sacred shrine instead of in Westminster Abbey. Across from Henry lies Edward, the Black Prince, and the decorative armor he wore at his funeral adorns the wall. The **treasury** houses a 1200-year-old Saxon pocket sundial among other excavated objects. The **Corona Tower** rises above the eastern apse but is closed to visitors. Stand under the **Bell Harry Tower,** at the crossing of the nave and transepts, to see the perpendicular arches supporting the 15th-century fan vaulting. *(☎ 762 862; www.canterbury-cathedral.org. Cathedral open Easter-Sept. M-Sa 9am-6:30pm, Su 12:30-2:30pm and 4:30-5:30pm; Oct.-Easter M-Sa 9am-5pm, Su 12:30-2:30pm and 4:30-5:30pm. 1¼hr. tours, M-Sa 3 per day; check nave for times. Evensong M-F 5:30pm, Sa-Su 3:15pm. £6.50, concessions £5. Tours £4, concessions £3. Audio tours £3.50, concessions £2.50.)*

SAINT AUGUSTINE'S ABBEY. The skeletons of once-magnificent arches and walls are all that remain of one of the most significant abbeys in Europe, built in AD 598 to house Augustine and 40 monks sent from Rome to convert England. Indoor exhibits and a free audio tour reveal the abbey's history as a burial place, royal palace, and pleasure garden. Don't miss St. Augustine's humble tomb under a pile of rocks. *(Outside the city wall near the cathedral. ☎ 767 345. Open Apr.-Sept. daily 10am-6pm; Oct.-Mar. W-Su 10am-4pm. £4, concessions £3.)* Just beyond the abbey, the **Church of Saint Martin,** the oldest parish church in England, witnessed the marriage of pagan King Æthelbert and the French Christian Princess Bertha in AD 562, which paved the way for England's conversion to Christianity. The church also holds the final resting place of author Joseph Conrad. *(North Holmes St. ☎ 463 469. Open Jul.-Aug. daily 10am-6pm; Apr.-Jun. W-Su 10am-5pm; Sept.-Mar. Su 11am-5pm. £4, concessions £2.)*

MUSEUM OF CANTERBURY. Housed in the medieval Poor Priests' Hospital, the museum spans Canterbury's history from St. Thomas to WWII bombings to children's book character Rupert the Bear. Browse displays to learn about Roman foundations and Becket's unsanitary undergarments. *(20 Stour St. ☎ 475 202. Open June-Sept. M-Sa 10:30am-5pm, Su 1:30-5pm; Nov.-May M-Sa 10:30am-5pm. Last admission 4pm. £3.30, concessions £2.20. The Museum Passport grants admission to the Museum of Canterbury, the Westgate Museum, and the nearby Roman Museum. £6, concessions £3.60.)*

THE CANTERBURY TALES. Interested in literature but not in reading? Chaucer's medieval England is recreated in scenes complete with ambient lighting and moving wax characters. The smell isn't the guy standing next you—the facility actually pipes in the "authentic" stench of sweat, hay, and grime to help bring you back in time. Headphone narrations take you through the scenes in a 45min. abbreviation of Chaucer's bawdy masterpiece. *(St. Margaret's St. ☎ 479 227; www.canterburytales.org.uk. Open daily July-Aug. 9:30am-5pm; Mar.-June and Sept.-Oct. 10am-5pm; Nov.-Feb. 10am-4:30pm. £7.50, students £6.50.)*

GREYFRIARS. England's first Franciscan friary, Greyfriars was built over the River Stour in 1267. It was used as a prison in the 19th century, and prisoners' etchings still mark the cell walls. Now the building has a chapel and a museum about the local order. For a quiet break, walk through the riverside gardens. *(6a Stour St. ☎ 462 395. Chapel open Easter-Sept. M-Sa 2-4pm. Gardens open daily 10am-5pm. Free.)*

WESTGATE TOWERS MUSEUM. The Westgate Towers have guarded the road to London for centuries and are one of the few medieval fortifications to survive wartime blitzing. Built in 1380 as an English defense against France in the Hundred Years War, the structure was a town prison before it was converted into a museum for armor and old weapons. Up a steep, winding staircase sits James, the perennially incarcerated wax figure, enjoying commanding views and plotting his escape from his cell atop the gates. *(☎ 789 576; www.canterburymuseum.co.uk. Open M-Sa 11am-12:30pm and 1:30-3:30pm. Last admission 15min. before close. £1.25, families £2.70, concessions 70p. Westgate gardens free.)*

BEST OF THE REST. Canterbury Historic River Tours runs 30min. cruises several times per day. *(1 St. Peter's St. ☎ 07790 534 744; www.canterburyrivertours.co.uk. £6.)* In the city library, the **Royal Museum and Art Gallery** showcases paintings by locally born artists of earlier centuries and recounts the history of the "Buffs," one of the oldest regiments of the British Army. Don't miss the newly acquired Van Dyck and collections by T. S. Cooper. *(18 High St. ☎ 475 221. Open M-Sa 10am-4:45pm. Free.)* Near the city walls to the southwest lie the remnants of **Canterbury Castle.** *(☎ 378 100. Open daily 8:30am-dusk. Free.)* The vaults of **Saint Dunstan's Church** contain a buried relic said to be the head of Thomas More. However, legend claims that his daughter bribed the executioner for it. *(St. Dunstan's St. ☎ 463 654. Open daily 8am-4pm; call to confirm. Free.)*

 PUBS

Coffee & Corks, 13 Palace St. (☎ 457 707). Cafe-bar with a cool, bohemian feel. Mixed drinks (£4), wines by the bottle (£10), and a wide selection of teas (£1.50). Scrabble, occasional live music, and Wi-Fi. Open daily noon-midnight. MC/V.

Alberry's, 38 St. Margaret's St. (☎ 452 378). Cuddle on leather couches in the corners of this stylish wine bar that pours late into the evenings. Free Wi-Fi. M live music, Tu-Th DJ. Happy hour 5:30-7pm. Open M 11am-1am, Tu-Sa 11am-2am.

Simple Simon's, 3-9 Radigunds Ln. (☎ 762 355). Any local can direct you to this 14th-century alehouse. Settle down with a hand-pulled Kent brew on the terraced garden for live jazz, folk, and blues music. The restaurant upstairs serves entrees (£8-11) daily 6-9pm. Open M-Sa 11am-11pm, Su noon-10:30pm. AmEx/MC/V.

Casey's, Butchery Ln. (☎ 463 252). Centrally located near the cathedral, Casey's offers quasi-Irish ambience and traditional food (£6), all in the company of Harry the cat. Schedule of live Irish music (Th-Sa) posted outside. Open M-Th noon-11pm, F-Sa 11am-midnight, Su noon-10:30pm. Kitchen open daily until 4pm.

The White Hart, Worthgate Pl. (☎ 765 091), near East Station. Walk off the train and into this congenial pub. Lunches (£6-8), sweets (£3.50), and some of Canterbury's best bitters (£2.30-2.80). Home of the city's largest beer garden. Open M-Sa noon-11pm, Su noon-4pm. Kitchen open W-F noon-2:30pm, Sa noon-11pm, Su noon-4pm.

♪ ✿ ENTERTAINMENT AND FESTIVALS

The TIC distributes brochures on up-to-date entertainment listings. **Buskers,** especially along St. Peter's St. and High St., play streetside Vivaldi while bands of impromptu players ramble from corner to corner, acting out the more absurd of Chaucer's scenes. **Marlowe Theatre,** The Friars, across from the Pilgrim Hotel, puts on touring productions in the largest theatre in Kent. (☎787 787; www.marlowetheatre.com. Box office open M and Sa 10am-9pm, Tu 10:30am-9pm, Su 2hr. before curtain. Tickets £10-35, concessions available. £5 student standbys available from 30min. before most performances.) The **Gulbenkian Theatre** at the University of Kent shows films in Cinema 3 and stages dance, drama, music, and comedy performances. (University Rd., west of town on St. Dunstan's St. ☎769 075; www.gulbenkiantheatre.co.uk. Box office open M-F 11am-5pm, Sa-Su 5:30-9pm. Tickets £7-25; £7 rush available from 7pm on performance nights.)

In the fall, the **Canterbury Festival** fills two weeks in mid-October with drama, opera, cabaret, chamber music, dance, talks, walks, and exhibitions. (☎452 853, box office 378 188; www.canterburyfestival.co.uk.) In Ashford, 5 mi. southwest of Canterbury, the popular **Stour Music Festival** celebrates Renaissance and Baroque music for seven days in mid-June. The festival takes place at All Saint's Boughton Aluph Church, on the A28 and accessible by rail from West Station. Call the bookings office a month in advance. (☎812 740. Tickets £5-14.)

THE COTSWOLDS

The Cotswolds have deviated little from their etymological roots: "Cotswolds" means "sheep enclosures in rolling hillsides." Despite the rather sleepy moniker, the Cotswolds are filled with rich history and traditions (like cheese-rolling) that date back to Roman and Saxon times. The country here offers the perfect break from the concrete and crowds of London.

▛ TRANSPORTATION

Trains run from **London** (1½hr., every 1-2hr., £30) via Oxford (30min., £9.50) to **Moreton-in-Marsh Station** (open M-Sa 5:45am-7:15pm, Su 5:45am-12:30pm). Trains also run from **London Paddington** (2½hr., every hr., £20) to **Cam and Dursley Station** (3 mi. from Slimbridge, unstaffed) in the Southern Cotswolds. It's easier to reach the Cotswolds by **bus.** The Cheltenham TIC's free *Getting There* details service between the town and 27 destinations. The free *Explore the Cotswolds by Public Transport*, available at most TICs, lists routes for major services between villages and provides basic information on frequency. Consult the TIC for departure times, and note that schedules vary depending on the day of the week. Traveline (☎0870 608 2608) is a true lifeline for those traveling by public transport, especially in the Cotswolds, where a journey from one small village to another may require a few transfers.

GOOD MORNING, SUNSHINE. It is possible to see 3 or even 4 small villages in 1 day by public transport, but travelers should be mindful that many buses run on a 9am-6pm schedule. To avoid getting stuck, make the 1st morning bus out to your destination (typically between 8:45 and 9:30am).

The easiest way to explore is by car, but the best way to experience the Cotswolds is on foot or by bike. The Toy Shop, on High St. in Moreton-in-Marsh, offers **bike rentals** with a lock, map, and route suggestions. (☎01608 650 756. £12 per half day, £14 per full day. Credit card deposit. Open M and W-Sa 9am-1pm and

2-5pm.) The **YHA** in Stow-on-the-Wold (p. 310) also rents bikes with a lock and helmet. (☎01451 830 497. Open daily 8-10am and 5-10pm. £6 per half day, £9.50 per full day.) **Taxis** are a convenient, if expensive, way of getting to areas inaccessible by public transportation. TICs have lists of companies serving their area: **"K" Cars** (☎01451 822 578 or 07929 360 712) is based in Bourton-on-the-Water, and **Cotswold Taxis** (☎07710 117 471) operates from Moreton-in-Marsh.

▚ 〽 ORIENTATION AND PRACTICAL INFORMATION

The Cotswolds lie mostly in Gloucestershire, bound by Stratford-upon-Avon in the north, Oxford in the east, Cheltenham in the west, and Bath in the south. The northern Cotswolds house more postcard-worthy villages and impressive hills, hence more visitors and higher B&B prices. The range is not grandiose—the average Cotswold hill reaches only 600 ft.—but the rolling hills make hiking and biking tough. The best bases, transport- and provision-wise, from which to explore are Cirencester, Gloucester, Moreton-in-Marsh, and Stow-on-the-Wold.

Tourist Information Centres: All provide maps, bus schedules, and pamphlets on area walks. They also book beds, usually for a £2 charge plus a 10% deposit.

Bath: See p. 305.

Bourton-on-the-Water: Victoria St. (☎01451 820 211). Open Apr.-Oct. M-F 9:30am-5pm, Sa 9:30am-5:30pm; Nov.-Mar. M-F 9:30am-4pm, Sa 9:30am-4:30pm.

Broadway: 1 Cotswold Ct. (☎01386 852 937). Open M-Sa 10am-1pm and 2-5pm.

Chipping Campden: Old Police Station, High St. (☎01386 841 206). Open daily Apr.-Oct. 10am-5:30pm; Nov.-Mar. 10am-5pm.

Cirencester: Corn Hall, Market Pl. (☎01285 654 180). Open Apr.-Dec. M 9:45am-5:30pm, Tu-Sa 9:30am-5:30pm; Jan.-Mar. M 9:45am-5pm, Tu-Sa 9:30am-5pm.

Gloucester: 28 Southgate St. (☎01452 396 572). Open July-Aug. M-Sa 10am-5pm, Su 11am-3pm; Sept.-June M-Sa 10am-5pm.

Moreton-in-Marsh: District Council Building, High St. (☎01608 650 881). Open in summer M 8:45am-4pm, Tu-Th 8:45am-5:15pm, F 8:45am-4:45pm, Sa 10am-1pm; in winter M 8:45am-4pm, Tu-Th 8:45am-5:15pm, F 8:45am-4:45pm, Sa 10am-12:30pm.

Stow-on-the-Wold: Hollis House, The Square (☎01451 831 082). Open Easter-Oct. M-Sa 9:30am-5:30pm; Nov.-Easter M-Sa 9:30am-4:30pm.

Winchcombe: High St. (☎01242 602 925), next to Town Hall. Open Apr.-Oct. M-Sa 10am-1pm and 2-5pm, Su 10am-1pm and 2-4pm; Nov.-Mar. Sa-Su 10am-4pm.

⛺ ACCOMMODATIONS AND CAMPING

The *Cotswold Way Handbook and Accommodation List* (£2) details B&Bs, which usually lie on convenient roads a short walk from small villages. The *Cotswolds Accommodation Guide* (50p) lists B&Bs in or near larger towns. Expect to pay £30-55 per night for a single room unless you stay at one of the YHA hostels. **YHA Stow-on-the-Wold ❷**, The Square, is a 16th-century building beside the TIC. The hostel offers ensuite rooms with wood bunks and village views. (☎01451 830 497. Family room with toys, kitchen, and lounge. Laundry available. Reception daily 8-10am and 5-10pm. Lockout 10am-5pm. Curfew 11pm. Book in advance, especially in the summer. Dorms £15, under 18 £12. Add £3 for nonmembers. MC/V.) The 56-bed **YHA Slimbridge ❶**, Shepherd's Patch, off the A38 and the M5, has spacious common areas and a large duck pond behind the building. The nearest train station (Cam and Dursley) is 3 mi. away. It's easier to take Bus #91 from Gloucester to the Slimbridge Crossroads roundabout and walk 2 mi. (☎08707 706 036. Laundry £2.60. Reception daily 7:15-10am and 5-11pm. Curfew 11pm. Open daily mid-July to early Sept.; F-Sa Oct.-Nov. and Jan. to mid-July. Dorms £11, under 18 £8; twins £26; families £38-69. MC/V.) There are several campsites close to Cheltenham, but there are also convenient places to rough it within the Cotswolds. Try **Fosseway Farm ❶** (p. 312). *Camping and Caravanning in Gloucestershire and the Cotswolds,* free at local TICs, lists more options.

◤ HIKING AND BIKING

For centuries, travelers have walked the well-worn Cotswolds footpaths from village to village. Tranquil hillsides and the allure of pubs with local brews make moving at a pace beyond three or four villages per day inadvisable. The free *Cotswold Events* booklet, available at TICs, lists music festivals, antique markets, woolsack races, and cheese-rolling events.

The TIC stocks a variety of **walking** and **cycling guides.** The *Cotswold Map and Guidebook in One* (£5) is good for planning bike routes and short hikes. Hikers planning more than a short stroll should use the Ordinance Survey Outdoor Leisure Map #45 (1:25,000; £7), which provides topographic information and highlights nearly all public footpaths. The Cotswolds Voluntary Warden Service (☎01451 862 000) leads free **guided walks,** some with themes (1½-7½hr.). All walks are listed on its website (www.cotswoldsaonb.com) and in the Programme Guide section of the biannual *Cotswold LION* (free at the TIC).

Long-distance hikers can choose from a handful of trails. The extensive **Cotswold Way** spans just over 100 mi. from Bath to Chipping Campden, has few steep climbs, and can be done in a week. The trail passes through pastures and the remains of ancient settlements. Pockmarks and gravel make certain sections unsuitable for biking or horseback riding. Consult the **Cotswold Way National Trail Office** (☎01453 827 004) for details. The **Oxfordshire Way** (65 mi.) runs between the popular Bourton-on-the-Water and Henley-on-Thames, site of the famed Henley Royal Regatta. Amble through pastures on your way from Bourton-on-the-Water to Lower and Upper Slaughter along the **Warden's Way,** a half-day hike. Adventurous souls can continue to Winchcombe. The **Thames Path Walk** starts on the western edge of the Cotswolds in Lechlade and follows the Thames 184 mi. to Kingston, near London. The section from the Cotswolds to Oxford is low-impact and particularly peaceful. The **Severn Way** runs for 210 mi. from Plynlimon in Wales to Bristol along the River Severn and runs along the western border of the Cotswolds. Contact the **National Trails Office** (☎01865 810 224) for details. Local roads are perfect for **biking**—rolling hills welcome both casual and hardy cyclers. Even though the routes are slightly rut-riddled, parts of the Oxfordshire Way are hospitable to cyclists. TICs in all towns have a Cotswolds cycling route packet (£3) that outlines five different routes between villages. They also have free cycling guides detailing trails from 16-30 mi.

WINCHCOMBE. A tiny village 7 mi. north of Cheltenham, Winchcombe is home to the secluded **Sudeley Castle,** a 10min. walk from the town center. Lord and Lady Ashcombe have filled the castle with Tudor memorabilia. The castle also has 14 acres of prize-winning gardens, all of which offer stunning views of the surrounding hills. The chapel contains the tomb of Henry VIII's Queen number six, Katherine Parr. In summer, Sudeley also holds jousting tournaments and Shakespeare under the stars. (☎01242 602 308; www.sudeleycastle.co.uk. Castle open daily Mar.-Oct. 11am-5pm. Last admission 4:30pm. Gardens open daily Mar.-Oct. 10:30am-5:30pm. Castle and gardens £7.20, children £4.20, concessions £6.20. Gardens only £5.50/3.25/4.50. £1 surcharge Su May-Aug.) **Belas Knap,** a 4000-year-old burial mound, stands 1½ mi. southwest of Sudeley Castle. It is accessible from the Cotswold Way or via a scenic 2½hr. walk from Winchcombe. The Winchcombe TIC has a free pamphlet with directions.

BOURTON-ON-THE-WATER. Known as the most beautiful village in the Cotswolds, Bourton-on-the-Water feels like an old-fashioned town. The footbridge-straddled

River Windrush runs along the main street, giving Bourton the moniker "Venice of the Cotswolds." The beauty and location of Bourton has made it a popular destination, so expect more tourist traps here than in other villages. The Oxford Way trailhead is here, along with a handful of other trails, including the Warden's, Heart of England, Windrush, and Gloucestershire Ways. For a taste of life as a giant, follow signs to **The Model Village,** a scale model of Bourton built in 1937. (Open daily in summer 10am-5:45pm; in winter 10am-4pm. £2.75, concessions £2.25-2.50.) **Birdland,** on Rissington Rd., has a motley crew of winged creatures from neon pink flamingoes to penguins. (☎820 480; www.birdland.co.uk. Open daily Apr.-Oct. 10am-6pm; Nov.-Mar. 10am-4pm. Last admission 1hr. before close. £5.20, seniors £4.20, children £3, families £15.) Next door, the **Dragonfly maze** is the best place to get lost in the Cotswolds. An intricate hedge maze contains a hidden chamber where you must solve a puzzle—we know the answer, but telling you would ruin the fun, wouldn't it? (Open daily 10am-5:30pm, weather permitting. £2.50.)

STOW-ON-THE-WOLD. Inns and taverns crowd Market Sq. of this self-proclaimed "Heart of the Cotswolds." A traditional **farmers' market** takes place on the second Thursday of every month in the Market Square. (☎01453 758 060. Open 9am-2pm.) Three miles downhill, off the A424, **Donnington Trout Farm** lets visitors fish, feed, and eat the trout. (☎01451 830 873. Open Apr.-Oct. daily 10am-5:30pm; Nov.-Mar. Tu-Su 10am-5pm.) The **YHA hostel ❷** (p. 310) is in the center of town. (☎0870 770 6050. £15.50, under 18 £11.) Ensuite rooms are a perk at the **Pear Tree Cottage ❹,** a stone house on High St. (☎01451 831 210. Singles £32-35; doubles £45-50. Cash only.)

MORETON-IN-MARSH. With a train station, frequent bus service, and a bike shop, Moreton is a convenient base from which to explore the north. The village has typical Cotswolds charm but holds few attractions. Two miles west on A44 is **Batsford Arboretum,** with 56 acres of waterfalls, a Japanese rest house, and more than 1600 species of trees. (☎01386 701 441; www.batsarb.co.uk. Open Feb. to mid-Nov. daily 10am-5pm; mid-Nov. to Jan. Sa-Su 10am-4pm. £6, children £2, concessions £5.) Every Tuesday, High St. plays host to the largest **open-air market** in the region. **Warwick House B&B ❸,** London Rd., has an energetic owner and a host of perks, including four-poster beds, Wi-Fi, and an ample breakfast. Follow A44 east out of town toward Oxford for 10min.; the hostel is on the left. (☎01608 650 773; www.snoozeandsizzle.com. Free pickup from station. £30-35 per person. Cash only.) **Blue Cedar House ❸,** Stow Rd., a 5min. walk on High St. toward Stow Rd., has welcoming rooms and an airy breakfast area. (☎01608 650 299. Book ahead. From £26 per person. Cash only.) Try **Fosseway Farm ❶,** Stow Rd., 5min. out of Moreton-in-Marsh toward Stow-on-the-Wold. (☎01608 650 503. Camper's breakfast £3.50. Caravans and tents £12. Electricity available. MC/V.) Enjoy tea and lunch at **Tilly's Tea Room ❶,** High St., which has a host of homemade cakes and jams to enjoy in their garden. (☎01608 650 000. Tea and scone £4.35. Cash only.)

BROADWAY. Broadway lives up to its name, with a long, wide High St. bordered by pubs and specialty shops. **Broadway Tower,** a 30-40min. uphill hike, inspired the likes of poet Dante Gabriel Rossetti and affords an excellent view of 12 counties. Take Johnson Bus #21/22 from the High St. to Broadway Tower Park (M-Sa 4 per day, 10min.). Alternatively, from High St., follow the Cotswold Way uphill out of town. (☎01386 852 390. Open Apr.-Oct. daily 10:30am-5pm; Nov.-Mar. Sa-Su 11am-3pm, weather permitting. £3.80, children £2.50, families £10, concessions £3.) **Snowshill Manor,** 2½ mi. southwest of Broadway, was once home to a collector of everything and anything. It now houses about 20,000 knick-knacks. (☎01386 852 410. Open late Mar.-Apr. M-Th and Su noon-5pm; May-Oct. M-W and Su noon-5pm. £7.30, children £3.65.) Past Snowshill Manor, **Snowshill Lavender Farm** lets you wander through the sweet-smelling lavender fields and watch the distillation process. (☎01386 854 821; www.snowshill-lavender.co.uk. Open from Good Friday through summer W-Su 11am-5pm. £2.50.)

CHIPPING CAMPDEN. Years ago, quiet Chipping Campden was the capital of the Cotswolds' wool trade ("chipping" means "market"). Market Hall, in the middle of the main street, attests to 400 years of commerce. The gothic **St. James Church,** a 5min. walk from High St., houses England's only full set of 15th-century altar hangings. From the TIC entrance, turn right onto High St. and take the right fork up the hill to the church. (☎01386 840 671; www.stjameschurchcampden.co.uk. Open Mar.-Oct. M-Sa 10am-5pm, Su 2-6pm; Nov. and Feb. M-Sa 11am-4pm, Su 2-4pm; Dec.-Jan. M-Sa 11am-5pm. Suggested donation £1.) Currently, the town is famous for its **Cotswold Olympic Games,** held in the first week of June. The games take place on Dovers Hill. From St. Catherine's on High St., turn right onto West End Terr., take the first left, and follow the public footpath 1 mi. uphill. The 2012 Olympic Games in London will coincide with the 400th anniversary of the Cotswold Games. The town has scheduled a massive celebration.

CIRENCESTER. One of the larger towns and regarded as the capital of the region, Cirencester (SI-ruhn-ses-ter) is the site of Corinium, a Roman town founded in AD 49. Although only scraps of the amphitheater remain, the **Corinium Museum,** Park St., has a formidable collection of Roman mosaics and relics from the town's past as well as exhibits on the region's Anglo-Saxon and wool-producing history. (☎01285 655 611. Open M-Sa 10am-5pm, Su 2-5pm. £4, concessions £2-3.) Cirencester's **Parish Church of St. John the Baptist** is Gloucestershire's largest "wool church." The church is home to a cup made for Anne Boleyn in 1535. (☎01285 659 317. Open M-Sa 9:30am-5pm, Su 2:15-5pm. 3 services per day. Grounds close 9pm. Donation requested.) The world's highest evergreen bounds Lord Bathurst's mansion at the top of Park St. Bear right and make a left on Cecily Hill to enter the 3000-acre **Cirencester Park,** whose stately central aisle was designed by Alexander Pope. Alexcars (☎01285 653 985) Bus A1 runs to the arboretum from Cirencester on Saturdays in summer (40min., Apr.-Sept. Sa 2 per day, £3 round-trip). Otherwise, take Bus A1 to Tetbury (45min., M-F 7 per day, £1.70) and transfer to Stagecoach Bus #620 or 628 (7min., M-Sa 5 per day, £1.30). An **antique market** occurs on Fridays in Corn Hall, near the TIC. (☎0171 263 6010. Open 10am-4:30pm.) A **cattle market** takes place every Tuesday on Tetbury Rd., and a **country market** every Friday at Brewery Arts, off Castle St. (Open 8:30-11:30am.) A short walk south of town center, **Apsley Villa Guest House ❸,** 16 Victoria Rd., offers affordable rooms and elegance. (☎01285 653 489. Singles £30; doubles and twins £45. Cash only.)

DOVER ☎01304

From the days of Celtic invaders to the age of the Chunnel, the white chalk cliffs of Dover have been many a traveler's first glimpse of England. They have also been witness to some serious wartime bombardment, from Napoleon's cross-Channel threats to heavy bombing in both World Wars. In July and August, adventurous swimmers make the 21 mi. doggy-paddle across the Channel to France. On land, walk along the cliffs or through the formidable castle.

▐ TRANSPORTATION

Trains: (☎08457 484 950), from **London.** 2hr., 4 per hr., £22.

Buses: National Express (☎08705 808 080) buses run from London (2½hr., every hr., £11.80) to **Pencester Road Station** between York St. and Maison Dieu Rd.

Taxis: Central Taxi Service (☎240 0441). 24hr.

⚡ PRACTICAL INFORMATION

Tourist Information Centre: The Old Town Gaol (☎205 108; www.whitecliffscountry.org.uk), off High St. where it divides into Priory Rd. and Biggin St. Helpful staff sells ferry, bus, and hoverspeed tickets and books accommodations for 10% deposit; after hours call ☎01271 336 093 for accommodations list. Open June-Aug. daily 9am-5:30pm; Apr.-May and Sept. M-F 9am-5:30pm, Sa-Su 10am-4pm; Oct.-Mar. M-F 9am-5:30pm, Sa 10am-4pm.

Tours: White Cliffs Boat Tours, at the Marina (☎01303 271 388; www.whitecliffsboat-tours.co.uk). 4 per day. £5.

Banks: Several banks and **ATMs** are in Market Sq., including **Barclays** in the northwest corner. Open M-F 9:30am-4:30pm.

Police: Ladywell St. (☎240 055), off High St.

Pharmacy: Superdrug, 33-34 Biggin St. (☎211 477). Open M-Sa 8:30am-5:30pm, Su 10am-4pm.

Internet: Miles & Barr Coffee Barr, 7 Canon St. (☎202 111). Internet access £2 per hr., Wi-Fi £1.50 per hr. Open Tu-F 9:30am-5:30pm, Sa 9:30am-5pm.

Hospital: Buckland Hospital, Coomb Valley Rd. (☎201 624), northwest of town. Take bus #67 or 67A from the post office.

Post Office: 68-72 Pencester Rd. (☎241 747). Open M-F 8:30am-5:30pm, Sa 8:30am-2pm. **Postal Code:** CT16 1PW.

🏠 ACCOMMODATIONS AND CAMPING

Rooms are scarce in summer; book well ahead. July and August are especially busy due to the influx of distance swimmers eager to try the Channel. Cheaper **B&Bs** gather on **Folkestone Road,** a hike past the train station. Pricier B&Bs lie near the city center on **Castle Street,** and more can be found on **Maison Dieu Road.**

Churchill Guest House, 6 Castle Hill Rd. (☎208 365). Enormous, tidy rooms near the castle base. Breakfast included. Singles £35; doubles £55-70. Cash only. ❹

Victoria Guest House, 1 Laureston Pl. (☎205 140). Cheerful ensuite rooms and talkative owners in a large mansion with views of Dover. Doubles £48-58. AmEx/MC/V. ❸

YHA Charlton House, 306 London Rd. (☎201 314), half a mile from Priory station; turn left on Folkestone Rd., then left at the roundabout on High St., which becomes London Rd. Lounge, pool table, kitchen, lockers, and Internet. Sells ferry tickets. Breakfast included. Lockout 10am-1pm. Curfew 11pm. Dorms £17.50, under 18 £14. MC/V. ❷

Linden Bed & Breakfast, 231 Folkestone Rd. (☎205 449). A bit far from the town center, but this plush B&B makes every effort to accommodate—ask about pickup from the train station or docks as well as breakfasts for special dietary concerns. Discount vouchers for local sights. Satellite TV. Singles £30; doubles and twins £45-60. MC/V. ❸

Hawthorn Farm (☎852 658), at Martin Mill Station off the A258 between Dover and Deal. 2min. walk from the train station; follow the signs. Set among 28 acres of gardens. Hot showers and laundry facilities available. Closed Nov.-Feb. June-Aug. 2-person tent and car £14, with electricity £17; Mar.-May and Sept.-Oct. £12/14. Hikers and bikers £4; Mar.-May and Sept.-Oct. £3.50. Cash only. ❶

FOOD AND PUBS

Despite Dover's proximity to the Continent, its cuisine remains staunchly English. Most of the restaurants in the city are unimpressive, but diligent travelers will find a few worthwhile options. Chip shops line **London Road** and **Biggin Street**. Visit Holland & Barrett, 35 Biggin St., for **groceries**. (☎241 426. Open M-Sa 9am-5:30pm.)

La Salle Verte, 14-15 Cannon St. (☎201 547). A relative newcomer to the city center, this modern cafe has old-fashioned charm. Specialty coffees (£1.50-2) and a selection of pastries (£2-4) served on a garden patio or comfortable leather love seats. Wi-Fi £1.50 per hr. Open M-Su 9am-5pm. Cash only. ❶

Dickens Corner, 7 Market Sq. (☎206 692). The ground floor bustles with channelers downing baguettes and cakes (£2-3.50) or hot lunches (£4-5.50) in a sun-filled room. Upstairs, avoid the wait and have a more leisurely meal. Additional outdoor seating faces the water fountain in Market Sq. Open M-Sa 9am-4:30pm. MC/V. ❶

Chaplins, 2 Church St., (☎204 870), off Market Sq. Huge portions of traditional English food. Sandwiches (£2.75), savory pies (£6), and heavenly apple pie with cinnamon cream (£2.75). Su roast served noon-3pm. Open daily 8am-5pm. MC/V. ❷

Louis Armstrong Pub, 58 Maison Dieu Rd. (☎204 759), on the outskirts of town, marked by a picture of Satchmo himself. Su live jazz music. Excellent selection of ales. Open M-Sa 11am-11pm, Su noon-2pm and 7-11pm. Cash only. ❶

The Lighthouse Cafe and Tea Room, at the end of Prince of Wales Pier. View emerald waters and chalky cliffs from half a mile offshore in the closest cafe to France. Mediocre food, but worth it for the view. Open in summer daily 10am-5:30pm. Cash only. ❶

◎ SIGHTS

▓ **DOVER CASTLE.** More fortress than fairy tale, Dover Castle, Castle Hill Rd. on the east side of town, is imposing and magnificent. The safeguard of England since Roman times, the castle was a focus of conflict from the Hundred Years' War to WWII, during which its guns were pointed toward German-occupied France. Watch the introductory video in the **Keep** before entering simulations of the castle under siege and in preparation for a king's visit. Hitler's missiles destroyed the **Church of St. James,** leaving the ruins crumbling at the base of the hill. The **Pharos lighthouse**—the only extant Roman lighthouse and the tallest remaining Roman edifice in Britain—towers over **St. Mary-in-Castro,** a tiled Saxon church. Climb to the platform of the **Admiralty Lookout** for views of the cliffs and harbor. For 20p, you can spy on France through binoculars. The (not so) ▓**Secret Wartime Tunnels,** a 3½ mi. labyrinth deep within the white rock, were only recently declassified. Begun in 1803, when Britain was under the threat of attack by Napoleon, the underground burrows doubled as the base for the WWII evacuation of Allied troops from Dunkirk and a shelter for Dover citizens during air raids. The lowest of the five levels, not open to the public, was intended to house the government should the Cuban Missile Crisis have gone sour. Tours fill quickly, and there is often a long wait; check in at the tunnels first. Give yourself at least 3hr. to tour the entire castle and grounds. *(Buses from the town center run daily Apr.-Sept. (every hr., 55p). Otherwise, scale Castle Hill using the pedestrian ramp and stairs to the left of Castle St. Open Apr., June-July, and Sept. daily 10am-6pm; Aug. daily 9:30am-6pm; Oct. daily 10am-5pm; Nov.-Jan. M and Th-Su 10am-4pm; Feb.-Mar. daily 10am-4pm. £9.80, concessions £7.40.)*

THE WHITE CLIFFS. Lining the most famous strip of England's coastline, the white cliffs are a beautiful backdrop for a stroll along the pebbly beach. A few miles west of Dover, the whitest, steepest, and most famous of them all is **Shakespeare Cliff,** traditionally identified as the site of blind Gloucester's battle with the brink in *King Lear*. *(25min. by foot along Snargate St. and Archcliffe Rd.)* To the east of Dover, past Dover Castle, the **Gateway to the White Cliffs** overlooks the Strait of Dover and is an informative starting point. *(Buses go from the town center to Langdon Cliff at least once per hr. ☎202 756. Open daily Mar.-Oct. 10am-5pm; Nov.-Feb. 11am-4pm.)* Dozens of **cliff walks**

lie a short distance from Dover; consult the TIC or the visitor center at the Gateway to the White Cliffs for trail information. Dover White Cliffs Boat tours, at the Clock Tower in Dover Marina, offers 40min. trips around the coastline. (☎01303 271 388; www.whitecliffsboattours.co.uk. £6, children £3, families £16.) **The Grand Shaft,** a 140 ft. triple-spiral staircase, was blasted through the rock in Napoleonic times to link the army on the Western Heights with the city center. (Snargate St. ☎201 066. Open select days throughout year; call for dates. The cliffs to the east and west of Dover can be viewed and photographed at a distance from the tip of Prince of Wales Pier.)

DOVER MUSEUM. This museum depicts Dover's Roman days as the colonial outpost Dubras. The **Bronze Age Boat Gallery** houses the remnants of the oldest ship yet discovered—it's 3550 years old. (Market Sq. ☎201 066. Open Apr.-Sept. M-Sa 10am-5:30pm, Su noon-5pm; Oct.-Mar. M-Sa 10am-5:30pm. £2.50, families £6, concessions £1.50.)

OTHER SIGHTS. Recent excavations unearthed a remarkably well-preserved **Roman painted house.** It's the oldest Roman house in Britain, with central heating and indoor plumbing. It also holds the best-preserved Roman wall painting in Britain, more than 1800 years old. (New St., off York St. and Cannon near Market Sq. ☎203 279. Open Apr.-Sept. Tu-Su 10am-5pm. Last admission 4:30pm. £2, concessions 80p.) For striking views, take Bus A20 toward Folkestone to **Samphire Hoe,** a park planted in the summer of 1997 with material dug from the Channel Tunnel. The D2 bus to Aycliffe (£1) stops about a 10min. walk from the park, or follow the North Downs Way along the clifftop. (Open daily 7am-dusk.) Climb the 73 steps of the **South Foreland Lighthouse** for 360° views of Kent and the channel. (2 mi. from the Gateway to the White Cliffs Visitor Centre. Open daily 11am-5:30pm. Visits by guided tours only. £4.)

HAMPTON COURT

Only 12 mi. upriver of central London, Hampton Court is considered part of Greater London, in the London borough of Richmond-upon-Thames. There isn't much else in the area besides the Hampton Court Palace itself, but the palace and surrounding gardens are definitely worth a visit—give up that day on Oxford St. and head to Hampton Court instead.

TRANSPORTATION

The fastest way to reach Hampton Court is to take the **train** from **Waterloo** (30min., every 30min.; same-day return £4.90, big discount with Travelcard). The palace is a 5min. walk from the train station. More relaxing, scenic, and slower, **boats** led by the **Westminster Passenger Association** (Westminster Pier; ⊖Westminster; ☎7930 2062; www.wpsa.co.uk) run from April through October (4hr.; daily 10:30, 11:15am, noon, 2pm; £13.50, round-trip £19.50; children £6.75/9.75; concessions £9/13). Tides may affect schedules; call to confirm. As the trip is long, think about taking a boat one-way and returning by train; or, board at Kew or Richmond instead.

SIGHTS

HAMPTON COURT PALACE. Although a monarch hasn't lived here for 250 years, Hampton Court still exudes regal charm. Cardinal Wolsey built the first palace here in 1514, showing the young Henry VIII how to act the part of a powerful ruler. Henry learned the lesson all too well, confiscating Hampton in 1528 (because Wolsey's palace was nicer than his) and embarking on a massive building program. In 1689, William and Mary employed Christopher Wren to bring the Court up to date, but less than 50 years later George II abandoned it for good. The **palace** is divided into six 20min. to 1hr. tour routes, all starting at **Clock Court,** where you can pick up a program of the day's events and an audio tour. In ▓**Henry VIII's State Apartments,** only the massive Great Hall and exquisite Chapel Royal hint at past magnificence. A costumed guide leads the Henry VIII tour. Below, the **Tudor Kitchens** offer insight into how Henry ate himself to a 54 in. waist. Predating Henry's additions, the 16th-century **Wolsey Rooms** are complemented by Renaissance masterpieces. Wren's **King's Apartments** were restored to their original appearance after a 1986 fire. The **Queen's Apartments** weren't completed until 1734, postponed by Mary II's death. The **Georgian Rooms** were created by William Kent for George II's family. No less impressive are the **gardens,** with Mantegna's *Triumphs of Caesar* paintings tucked away in the Lower Orangery. North of the palace, the **Wilderness,** a pseudo-natural area earmarked for picnickers, holds the ever-popular **maze,** planted in 1714. Its small size belies a devilish design. *(45min. from Waterloo by train, round-trip £5.60. 3-4hr. by boat; daily 10:30, 11am, noon, 2pm; £13.50, round-trip £19.50; children £6.75/9.75; concessions £9/13. Westminster Passenger Cruises ☎ 7930 4721; www.thamesriverboats.co.uk. Palace ☎ 08707 527 777; www.hamptoncourtpalace.org.uk. Open daily late Mar.-late Oct. 10am-6pm; late Oct.-late Mar. 10am-4:30pm. Last admission 45min. before close. Palace and gardens £13, concessions £10.50, children 5-15 free. Admission free for worshippers at Chapel Royal; services Su 11am and 3:30pm. Audio and guided tours included.)*

HAMPTON COURT GARDENS. In the sunshine (or in the light drizzle), the palace has to compete with the equally lavish gardens. Palace tickets are required for entry to the flower-rich South Gardens, the first of which is the ornate **Privy Garden,** built for the private enjoyment of William III and now available for public enjoyment. The stunning **Pond Gardens** are off-limits to visitors, but you can stand at the rail and stare longingly at the posies. Nearby, the giant **Great Vine** is housed in its own terrace; it is the world's oldest vine, planted by Lancelot "Capability" Brown sometime between 1768 and 1774. It still produces 500-700 lb. of grapes every year, sold in the shop in late summer and early fall. Down in the neighboring **Lower Orangery** you'll find Andrea Mantegna's series *The Triumphs of Caesar* (1484-1505). Among the most important works of the Italian Renaissance, the nine paintings are displayed in almost total darkness to protect the fragile colors. The rest of the gardens are open to all. The **Home Park** stretches beyond the impeccably manicured trees, paths, and fountains of the East Front Gardens. Another popular area here is the **Tiltyard Tearoom,** where jousting matches used to take place—it's really a sandwich cafeteria with beautiful seating by the gardens. The palace also hosts the annual **Hampton Court Palace Flower Show** every July. *(Admission to Maze and South Gardens £3.50, children £2.50; other gardens free. Flower show: contact the Royal Horticultural Society. ☎ 7834 4333; www.rhs.org.uk/hamptoncourt. Call or visit website for ticket details.)*

OXFORD ☎ 01865

Oxford has been home to nearly a millennium of scholarship—25 British prime ministers and numerous other world leaders have been educated here. In 1167, Henry II founded Britain's first university, and its distinguished spires have since captured the imaginations of luminaries such as Lewis Carroll and C. S. Lewis. The city's legendary scholarship and enthralling architecture also make Oxford a must-see for tourists and a popular place to study abroad. For a true sense of this enclave of academia, avoid the hordes choking Broad St. and roam the alleyways to find ancient bookshops, serene college quads, and, of course, history-laden pubs inviting you to sample their brew.

▐ TRANSPORTATION

Trains: From **London Paddington** (1hr., 2-4 per hr., £9.50-18.10).

Buses: Stagecoach (☎772 250; www.stagecoachbus.com) operates the **Oxford Tube** from London (1¾hr.; 3-5 per hr.; £12, students £10, children under 16 £6). The **Oxford Bus Company** (☎785 400; www.oxfordbus.co.uk) also runs buses from the city (1¾hr.; 3-5 per hr.; £12, students £10).

Public Transportation: The **Oxford Bus Company Cityline** (☎785 400) and **Stagecoach Oxford** (☎772 250) offer swift and frequent service to: **Iffley Road** (Stagecoach #3, Oxford Bus #4, 4A, 4B, 4C); **Banbury Road** (Stagecoach #2, 2A, 2B, 2D); **Abingdon Road** (Stagecoach #32, 33; Oxford Bus X3, X4); **Cowley Road** (Stagecoach #1, 5A, 5B, 10; Oxford Bus #5). Fares are low (most 60p-£1.40). Stagecoach offers a **DayRider ticket** while the Oxford Bus Company offers a **Freedom ticket,** which give unlimited travel on the respective company's local routes (£3.30-5.50 for 24hr., £10-17 for 5 days). A **Plus Pass** grants unlimited travel on all Oxford Bus Company, Stagecoach, and Thames Travel buses and can be purchased onboard (☎785 410; 1 day £5, 1 week £14).

Taxis: Radio Taxis (☎242 424). **ABC** (☎770 077). **City Taxis** (☎201 201). All 24hr.

▐▐ ORIENTATION AND PRACTICAL INFORMATION

Oxford's colleges gather around **St. Mary's Church,** which is the spiritual heart of both the university and the greater city. The city's center is bounded by **George Street** and connecting **Broad Street** to the north, and **Cornmarket** and **High Street** in the center. To the northwest, the district of **Jericho** is less touristed and is the unofficial hub of student life.

Tourist Information Centre: 15-16 Broad St. (☎726 871; www.visitoxford.org). The busy staff books rooms for £4 plus a 10% deposit. Expect to pay for information (or just use your handy *Let's Go* guide): visitors guide and map £1.25, accommodations list £1. Look for the free restaurant list and *In Oxford* monthly guide. Job listings, long-term accommodations listings, and entertainment news posted daily at the TIC and at www.dailyinfo.co.uk. Open Nov.-Easter M-Sa 9:30am-5pm; Easter-June and Aug.-Oct. M-Sa 9:30am-5pm, Su 10am-3:30pm; June-July M-Sa 9:30am-5pm, Su 10am-4pm. Last room booking 4:30pm.

Tours: The 2hr. official Oxford University **walking tour** (☎726 871) leaves from the TIC and provides access to some colleges otherwise closed to visitors. Tours allow only up to 19 people and are booked on a first come, first served basis, so get tickets early in the day. (Daily in summer 10:30, 11am, 1, 2pm; in winter 11am and 2pm. £6.50, children £3.) **Blackwell's walking tours** (☎333 606) leave from Canterbury Gate at Christ Church. (General tours Tu 2pm, Th 11am, Sa noon. £6, concessions £5.50. Literary tour of Oxford Tu 2pm, Th 11am; "Inklings" tours about C. S. Lewis, J. R. R. Tolkien, and their circle of friends W 11:45am; Historic Oxford Tour F 2pm. All tours 1½hr. £6, concessions £5.) **Guided Tours** (☎07810 402 757) depart from outside Trinity College on Broad St. and offer access to some colleges and other university buildings. (1½hr., daily every hr. 11am-4pm. £6, children £3.) The same company runs evening **Ghost Tours.** (1¼hr, in summer daily 8pm. £5, children £3.) **City Sightseeing** (☎790 522) offers hop-on, hop-off bus tours of the city with over 20 stops. (Every 10-15min. from Bay 14 of the bus station. Pick up tickets from bus drivers or stands around the city. £9.50, students £8.50.)

Banks: Banks line Cornmarket St. **Marks & Spencer,** 13-18 Queen St. (☎248 075), has a **bureau de change** with no commission. Open M-W and F 8:30am-6:30pm, Th 8:30am-7:30pm, Sa 8:30am-6:30pm, Su 11am-4:30pm. **Thomas Cook,** 5 Queen St. (☎447 000). Open M-Sa 9am-5:30pm. The **TIC** also has a **bureau de change** with no commission.

Police: (☎505 505) St. Aldates and Speedwell St.

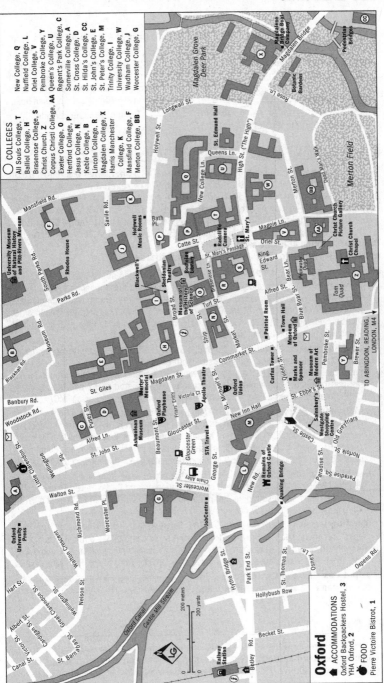

COLLEGES

All Souls College, **T**
Balliol College, **H**
Brasenose College, **S**
Christ Church, **Z**
Corpus Christi College, **AA**
Exeter College, **O**
Hertford College, **P**
Jesus College, **N**
Keble College, **B**
Lincoln College, **R**
Magdalen College, **X**
Harris Manchester College, **K**
Mansfield College, **F**
Merton College, **BB**
New College, **Q**
Nuffield College, **L**
Oriel College, **V**
Pembroke College, **Y**
Queen's College, **U**
Regent's Park College, **C**
Somerville College, **A**
St. Cross College, **D**
St. Hilda's College, **CC**
St. John's College, **E**
St. Peter's College, **M**
Trinity College, **I**
University College, **W**
Wadham College, **J**
Worcester College, **G**

Oxford

🛏 ACCOMMODATIONS
Oxford Backpackers Hostel, **3**
YHA Oxford, **2**

🍴 FOOD
Pierre Victoire Bistrot, **1**

DAYTRIPS

Hospital: John Radcliffe Hospital, Headley Way (☎741 166). Take bus #13 or 14.

Pharmacy: Boswell's, 1-4 Broad St. (☎241 244). Open M-F 9:30am-6pm, Sa 9am-6pm, Su 11am-5pm.

Internet Access: Oxford Central Library, Queen St. (☎815 549), near Westgate Shopping Centre. Free. Open M-Th 9:15am-7pm, F-Sa 9:15am-5pm. **Link Communications,** 33 High St. (☎204 207). £1 per 45min. Open M-F 9:30am-10pm, Sa 10am-10pm, Su 11am-8pm. **The Letting Shop,** 60 High St. (☎790 609). £1 per hr. Open M-F 10am-8pm, Sa 10am-5pm.

Post Office: 102-104 St. Aldates (☎08457 223 344). **Bureau de change** inside. Open M-Sa 9am-5:30pm. **Postal Code:** OX1 1ZZ.

▐ ACCOMMODATIONS AND CAMPING

Book at least a week ahead from June to September, especially for singles. **B&Bs** (from £25) line the main roads out of town and are reachable by bus or a 15-45min. walk. Try www.stayoxford.com for affordable options. The 300s on **Banbury Road,** north of town, are accessible by Bus #2, 2A, 2B, and 2D. Cheaper B&Bs lie in the 200s and 300s on **Iffley Road** (Bus #4, 4A, 4B, 4C, and 16B to Rose Hill) and on **Abingdon Road** in South Oxford (Bus #16 and 16A). If it's late, call the **Oxford Association of Hotels and Guest Houses** (East Oxford ☎721 561, West Oxford ☎862 138, North Oxford ☎244 691, South Oxford ☎244 268).

▓ **Central Backpackers,** 13 Park End St. (☎242 288). Located above Thirst Bar. The newest hostel in Oxford has spacious rooms and a downright fun atmosphere. Have a few drinks with the Aussie owners on the rooftop terrace—a frequent spot for summertime barbecues. Reception 8am-11pm. Check-out 11am. Free luggage storage. Free Internet access. Self-service kitchen. 4-bed mixed dorms £18; 6-bed female or 8-bed mixed dorms £16; 12-bed mixed dorms £14. MC/V. ❷

Oxford Backpackers Hostel, 9a Hythe Bridge St. (☎721 761), between the bus and train stations. A self-proclaimed "funky hostel" with colorful murals adorning the walls and music constantly playing in the hallway. Inexpensive bar and pool table in common area. Passport required. Female-only dorm available. Luggage storage £2 per item. Laundry £2.50. Internet access £1 per 30min. Dorms £14; quads £16 per person. MC/V. ❷

YHA Oxford, 2a Botley Rd. (☎727 275). From the train station, turn right onto Botley Rd. and go under the bridge. Photos of famous Oxfordians line the walls. The quietest of Oxford's 3 hostels. TV room, kitchen, library, and ensuite bathrooms. Full English breakfast included. Lockers £1. Towels 50p. Laundry £3. Internet access 7p per min. 4- and 6-bed dorms £21, under 18 £16; doubles £46. Add £3 for non-YHA-members. £3 student discount. MC/V. ❷

Heather House, 192 Iffley Rd. (☎249 757). A 5-10min. walk from Magdalen Bridge, or take the "Rose Hill" bus from the bus or train station or from Carfax Tower. The charming proprietor keeps spotless rooms complete with bath, small flat screen TVs, and Wi-Fi. Soft carpet. Singles £35-45; doubles £65-75. MC/V. ❹

Old Mitre Rooms, 4b Turl St. (☎279 976), between Mahogany Hair Salon and Past Times Stationery. Look for the blue door. Owned by Lincoln College and used as a dorm term-time. Packed on weekends; book ahead. Bookings and check-in at Lincoln College. Open July-Sept. Singles £30; doubles £55, ensuite £60; triples £72. MC/V. ❸

Oxford Camping and Caravanning, 426 Abingdon Rd. (☎244 088), behind Touchwoods camping store. Communal bath. Laundry facilities. £4.10-5.80 per person. Electricity £2.30. MC/V. ❶

▐ FOOD

A bevy of budget options seduce tourists and students fed up with college food. ▓**Gloucester Green Market,** behind the bus station, abounds with tasty treats. (Open W 8am-3:30pm). The **Covered Market,** between Market St. and Carfax, has produce and deli goods. (Open M-Sa 8am-5pm). Get **groceries** at Sainsbury's, in the Westgate Shopping Centre. (Open M-Sa 7am-8pm, Su 11am-5pm). Across Magdalen Bridge, cheap restaurants along the first four blocks of **Cowley Road** serve Chinese, Lebanese, Indian, and Polish food in addition to the standard fish 'n' chips. For a truly on-the-go meal, try a sandwich from the **kebab vans,** usually found on Broad St., High St., Queen St., and St. Aldates.

▨ **The Alternative Tuck Shop,** 24 Holywell St. (☎792 054). Behind an unassuming veneer lies Oxford's most popular sandwich shop. Students and residents alike line up for a slew of delicious made-to-order sandwiches (under £3) and famous panini (£2.80). There will more than likely be a line, but the staff moves quickly. Open daily 8:30am-6pm. Cash only. ❶

▨ **Vaults & Garden,** Radcliffe Sq., under St. Mary's Church (☎279 112; www.vaultsand-garden.co.uk). Follow your nose to the delectable homemade soups and organic entrees (£6). Choose to sit in the cozy booths inside or the outdoor tables in the garden overlooking the iconic Radcliffe Camera. Open daily 9am-5:30pm. Cash only. ❷

Kazbar, 25-27 Cowley Rd. (☎202 920). Mediterranean tapas bar just outside of town. Posh atmosphere, with Spanish-style decor and sexy lighting. Tasty tapas (£2.20-4.75) like *patatas con chorizo*. Free tapas with drink M-F 4-7pm. Open M-F 4-11pm, Sa-Su noon-midnight. AmEx/MC/V. ❶

G&D's Cafe, 55 Little Clarendon St. (☎516 652). Additional location on St. Aldates. Superb homemade ice cream (£1.75-4), pizza bagels (£3.45-4.15), and a boisterous student atmosphere. The great food and outdoor patio make it a favorite in the Jericho area. Open daily 8am-midnight. Cash only. ❶

The Nosebag, 6-8 St. Michael's St. (☎721 033). Cafeteria-style service on the 2nd fl. of a 15th-century stone building. Eclectic menu includes great vegan and vegetarian entrees and tasty homemade soups for under £8. Indulge in a scrumptious dessert (£1.35-2.75) such as the double fudge cake. Lunch specials under £3. Open M-Th 9:30am-10pm, F-Sa 9:30am-10:30pm, Su 9:30am-9pm. AmEx/MC/V. ❷

Pierre Victoire Bistrot, 9 Little Clarendon St. (☎316 616). French cuisine with daily specials. M-Th and Su 3-course *menu*, wine, and coffee £17.50. M-Th and Su 7-9pm pre-theatre 2-course *menu* and coffee £10. Lunch £5-7, dinner £9-14. Open M-Sa noon-2:30pm and 7-11pm, Su noon-3:30pm and 6-10pm. MC/V. ❸

Queen's Lane Coffee House, 40 High St. (☎240 082). Opened in 1654, the Queen's Lane is supposedly the first place where coffee was sold in Europe. You can still get a good cup of java as well as delicious sandwiches and desserts (£3-6). ½-price sandwiches after 5:30pm on busy nights. Open daily 7:30am-8pm. Cash only. ❶

St. Giles Cafe, 52 St. Giles St. (☎552 110). Grab all-day breakfast (£4.50) and a big cup of coffee in this much-adored greasy spoon. Students nurse hangovers and locals meet for coffee. Open M-F 8am-3pm, Sa-Su 9am-3pm. Cash only. ❶

◎ SIGHTS

The TIC sells a map ($1.25) and the *Welcome to Oxford* guide ($1), which lists the colleges' visiting hours. Hours can also be accessed online at www.ox.ac.uk/visitors/colls.shtml. Note that hours can be changed without explanation or notice. Some colleges charge admission, while others are accessible only through blue badge tours, booked at the TIC. Don't bother trying to sneak into Christ Church outside open hours, even after hiding your backpack and copy of *Let's Go*—bouncers, affectionately known as "bulldogs," in bowler hats and stationed 50 ft. apart, will squint their eyes and kick you out.

CHRIST CHURCH

THE COLLEGE. "The House" has Oxford's grandest quad and its most distinguished students, counting 13 past prime ministers among its alumni. Charles I made Christ Church his headquarters for 3½ years during the Civil Wars and escaped dressed as a servant when the city was besieged. Lewis Carroll first met Alice, the dean's daughter, here. The dining hall and Tom Quad serve as shooting locations for *Harry Potter* films. In June, be respectful of irritable students prepping for exams as you navigate the narrow strip open to tourists.

Through an archway to your left as you face the cathedral lies **Peckwater Quad.** Look for rowing standings chalked on the walls and for the beautiful exterior of Christ Church's library—the most elegant Palladian building in Oxford—which is closed to visitors. Spreading east and south from the main entrance, **Christ Church Meadow** compensates for Oxford's lack of "backs" (the riverside gardens in Cambridge). The meadows themselves are beautiful and offer great views of Christ Church College if you don't want to pay to go inside the buildings. *(Down St. Aldates from Carfax. ☎ 286 573; www.chch.ox.ac.uk. Open M-Sa 9am-5:30pm, Su 1-5:30pm; last admission 4pm. Chapel services M-F 6pm; Su 8, 10, 11:15am, and 6pm. £4.70, families £9.40, concessions £3.70.)*

CHRIST CHURCH CHAPEL. The only church in England to serve as both a cathedral and college chapel, it was founded in AD 730 by Oxford's patron saint, St. Frideswide, who built a nunnery here in honor of two miracles: the blinding of her persistent suitor and his subsequent recovery. A stained-glass window (c. 1320) depicts Thomas à Becket kneeling moments before his death in Canterbury Cathedral. Look for the floating toilet in the bottom right of a window showing St. Frideswide's death and the White Rabbit fretting in the windows in the hall.

TOM QUAD. The site of undergraduate lily-pond dunking, Tom Quad adjoins the chapel grounds. The quad takes its name from Great Tom, the seven-ton bell that has rung 101 (the original number of students) times at 9:05pm (the original undergraduate curfew) every evening since 1682. The bell rings specifically at 9:05pm because, technically, Oxford should be 5min. past Greenwich Mean Time. Christ Church keeps this time within its gates. Nearby, the college hall displays portraits of some of Christ Church's famous alums—Sir Philip Sidney, William Penn, John Ruskin, John Locke, and a bored-looking W.H. Auden in a corner by the kitchen.

CHRIST CHURCH PICTURE GALLERY. Generous alumni gifts have established a small but noteworthy collection of works by Tintoretto, Vermeer, and da Vinci, among others. *(In the Canterbury quad. Entrances on Oriel Sq. and at Canterbury Gate; visitors to the gallery should enter through Canterbury Gate. ☎ 276 172. Open Apr.-Sept. M-Sa 10:30am-1pm and 2-5:30pm, Su 2-5pm; Oct.-Mar. M-Sa 10:30am-1pm and 2-4:30pm, Su 2-4:30pm. £2, concessions £1.)*

OTHER COLLEGES

Oxford's extensive college system (totalling 39 official Colleges of the University) means that there are plenty of beautiful grounds to stroll year-round. The following is a selection of the most popular colleges. For information on others, check one of the many guides found at the TIC.

ALL SOULS COLLEGE. Candidates who survive the admission exams to All Souls are invited to a dinner, where the dons confirm that they are "well-born, well-bred, and only moderately learned." All Souls is also reported to have the most heavenly wine cellar in the city. The Great Quad, with its carefully manicured lawn and two spires, may be Oxford's most serene, as hardly a living soul passes over it. *(Corner of High and Catte St. ☎ 279 379; www.all-souls.ox.ac.uk. Open Sept.-July M-F 2-4pm. Free.)*

BALLIOL COLLEGE. Students at Balliol preserve tradition by hurling abuse over the wall at their Trinity College rivals. Matthew Arnold, Gerard Manley Hopkins, Aldous Huxley, and Adam Smith were all sons of Balliol's mismatched spires. The interior gates of the college bear lingering scorch marks from the executions of 16th-century Protestants, and a mulberry tree planted by Elizabeth I still shades slumbering students. *(Broad St. ☎ 277 777; www.balliol.ox.ac.uk. Open daily 2-5pm. £1, students and children free.)*

MAGDALEN COLLEGE. With extensive grounds and flower-laced quads, Magdalen (MAUD-lin) is considered Oxford's handsomest college. The college has a deer park flanked by the river Cherwell and Addison's Walk, a circular path that touches the river's opposite bank. Though Dudley Moore attended, the college's most brilliant wit is alumnus Oscar Wilde. *(On High St., near the Cherwell. ☎ 276 000; www.magd.ox.ac.uk. Open daily Apr.-June 1-6pm; July-Sept. noon-6pm; Oct.-Mar. 1pm-dusk. £3, concessions £2.)*

MERTON COLLEGE. Merton's library houses the first printed Welsh Bible. J. R. R. Tolkien lectured here, inventing the Elven language in his spare time. The college's 14th-century **Mob Quad** is Oxford's oldest and least impressive, but nearby **St. Alban's Quad** has some of the university's best gargoyles. Japanese Crown Prince Narahito lived here during his university days. *(Merton St. ☎ 276 310; www.merton.ox.ac.uk. Open M-F 2-4pm, Sa-Su 10am-4pm. Library tours £2. Free.)*

NEW COLLEGE. This is the self-proclaimed first real college of Oxford. It was here, in 1379, that William of Wykeham dreamed up an institution that would offer a comprehensive undergraduate education under one roof. The bell tower has gargoyles of the Seven Deadly Sins on one side and the Seven Virtues on the other—all equally grotesque. New College claims Kate Beckinsale and Hugh Grant as two attractive alums. *(New College Ln. Use the Holywell St. Gate. ☎ 279 555; www.new.ox.ac.uk. Open daily from Easter to mid-Oct. 11am-5pm; Nov.-Easter 2-4pm. £2, students and children £1.)*

QUEEN'S COLLEGE. Though the college dates back to 1341, Queen's was rebuilt by Wren and Hawksmoor in the 17th and 18th centuries in the distinctive Queen Anne style. A trumpet call summons students to dinner, where a boar's head graces the table at Christmas. That tradition supposedly commemorates a student who, attacked by a boar on the outskirts of Oxford, choked the animal to death with a volume of Aristotle—probably the nerdiest slaughter ever. *(High St. ☎ 279 120; www.queens.ox.ac.uk. Open to blue badge tours only.)*

TRINITY COLLEGE. Founded in 1555, Trinity has a Baroque chapel with a limewood altarpiece, cedar latticework, and cherubim-spotted pediments. The college's series of eccentric presidents includes Ralph Kettell, who would come to dinner with a pair of scissors to chop anyone's hair that he deemed too long. *(Broad St. ☎ 279 900; www.trinity.ox.ac.uk. Open M-F 10am-noon and 2-4pm, Sa-Su 2-4pm; during holidays also Sa-Su 10am-noon. £1.50, concessions 75p.)*

UNIVERSITY COLLEGE. Built in 1249, this soot-blackened college vies with Merton for the title of oldest, claiming Alfred the Great as its founder. Percy Bysshe Shelley was expelled for writing the pamphlet *The Necessity of Atheism* but was later immortalized in a prominent monument, on the right as you enter. Bill Clinton spent his Rhodes Scholar days here. *(High St. ☎ 276 602; www.univ.ox.ac.uk. Open to blue badge tours only.)*

OTHER SIGHTS

ASHMOLEAN MUSEUM. The grand Ashmolean, Britain's finest collection of arts and antiquities outside London and the country's oldest public museum, opened in 1683. The museum is undergoing extensive renovations until 2009 but continues to show an exhibit of "treasures"—more than 200 artifacts from its galleries—including the lantern carried by Guy Fawkes in the Gunpowder Plot of 1605 and the deerskin mantle of Powhatan, father of Pocahontas. *(Beaumont St. ☎ 278 000. Open Tu-Sa 10am-5pm, Su noon-5pm; in summer open Th until 7pm. Tours £2. Free.)*

BODLEIAN LIBRARY. Oxford's principal reading and research library has over five million books and 50,000 manuscripts. It receives a copy of every book printed in Great Britain. Sir Thomas Bodley endowed the library's first wing in 1602—the institution has since grown to fill the immense **Old Library** complex, the **Radcliffe Camera** next door, and two newer buildings on Broad St. Admission to the reading rooms is by ticket only. The Admissions Office will issue you a two-day pass ($3) if you are able to prove your research requires the use of the library's books and present a letter of recommendation and ID. No one has ever been permitted to take out a book, not even Cromwell. Well, especially not Cromwell. *(Broad St. ☎ 277 000. Library open in summer M-F 9am-7pm, Sa 9am-1pm, in winter M-F 9am-10pm, Sa 9am-1pm. Tours leave from the Divinity School in the main quad; in summer M-Sa 4 per day, in winter 2 per day, in the afternoon. Audio tours £2. Tours £4.)*

BOTANIC GARDEN. Plant life has flourished for three centuries in the oldest botanic garden in the British Isles, owned and used by Oxford University. The path connecting the garden to Christ Church Meadow provides a view of the Thames and the cricket grounds on the opposite bank. *(At the intersection of High St. and Rose Ln. From Carfax, head down High St. ☎ 286 690. Open daily May-Sept. 9am-6pm, last admission 5:15pm; Mar.-Apr. and Oct. 9am-5pm, last admission 4:15pm; Nov.-Feb. 9am-4:30pm, last admission 4:15pm. Greenhouses open daily 10am-4pm. Mar.-Sept. £2.70, concessions £2, children free; Nov.-Feb. donation suggested.)*

CARFAX TOWER. The tower marks the center of the pre-modern city. A climb up its 99 (very narrow) spiral stairs affords a superb view from the only remnant of medieval St. Martin's Church. Carfax gets its name from the French *carrefour* (crossroads), referring to the intersection of the North, South, East, and West Gates. *(Corner of Queen St. and Cornmarket St. ☎ 792 653. Open daily Apr.-Oct. 10am-5pm; Oct.-Mar. 10am-3:30pm, weather permitting. £1.90, under 16 90p.)*

MUSEUM OF OXFORD. From hands-on exhibits to a murderer's skeleton, the museum provides an in-depth look at Oxford's 800-year history. *(St. Aldates. Enter at corner of St. Aldates and Blue Boar St. ☎ 252 761. Open Tu-F 10am-4:30pm, Sa 10am-5pm, Su noon-4pm. Last admission 30min. before close. £2, children 50p, children under 5 free, families £4, concessions £1.50.)*

OXFORD CASTLE. Oxford's newest attraction, the castle has been an Anglo-Saxon church, a Norman castle commissioned by William the Conqueror, a courthouse, and (until 1996) a prison. Now the complex houses restaurants, an open-air theatre, and a luxury hotel. Visitors are issued personal video tours outlining life as an inmate and the gory details of 17th-century executions. Climb to the top of St. George's tower for a view of the city formerly enjoyed only by prison guards. *(44-46 Oxford Castle on New Rd. ☎ 293 679, tour bookings 411 414. Open daily 10am-5pm, last tour at 4:20pm. £7.25, children £5.25, concessions £6.)*

SHELDONIAN THEATRE.. This Roman-style auditorium was designed by a teenage Christopher Wren. Graduation ceremonies, conducted in Latin, take place in the Sheldonian, as does everything from student recitals to world-class opera performances. *The Red Violin* and *Quills*, as well as numerous other movies, were filmed here. Climb up to the cupola for an excellent view of Oxford's scattered quads. *(Broad St. ☎ 277 299. Open July-Aug. M-Sa 10am-12:30pm and 2-4:30pm, Su 11am-4pm; Jan.-June and Sept.-Dec. M-Sa 10am-12:30pm and 2-3:30pm. Occasionally closed for university ceremonies. £2, concessions £1. Purchase tickets for shows from Oxford Playhouse, ☎ 305 305. Box office open M-Tu and Th-Sa 9:30am-6:30pm or until 30min. before last show, W 10am-6:30pm. Shows £15.)*

BEST OF THE REST. At **The Oxford Story**, 6 Broad St., a slow-moving but informative ride hauls visitors through dioramas that chronicle Oxford's past. *(☎ 728 822. Open July-Aug. daily 9:30am-5pm; Sept.-June M-Sa 10am-4:30pm, Su 11am-4:30pm. 45min.*

ride. £7.25, students and seniors £6, children £5.25.) Oxford's oldest building, a Saxon tower built in 1040, stands as part of **St. Michael at the North Gate.** Climb the steps for a brief history of the tower and the church as well as a birds-eye view of the city. (☎ *240 940. Open daily Apr.-Oct. 10:30am-5pm; Nov.-Mar. 10:30am-4pm. £1.80, concessions £1.20.)* With 6 mi. of bookshelves, **Blackwell's bookstore,** 53 Broad St., is by far the largest bookshop in Oxford and is famous for letting patrons read undisturbed. (☎ *792 792. Open M and W-Sa 9am-6pm, Tu 9:30am-6pm, Su 11am-5pm.)*

Behind the University Museum of Natural History, the **Pitt-Rivers Museum** has an eclectic archaeological and anthropological collection, including shrunken heads, rare butterflies, and magical amulets. (☎ *270 927; www.prm.ox.ac.uk. Open daily noon-4:30pm. Free.)* The **Museum of the History of Science** features clocks, astrolabes, and Einstein's blackboard, preserved as he left it after an Oxford lecture in the 1930s. *(Broad St.,* ☎ *277 280. Open Tu-Sa noon-4pm, Su 2-5pm. Tours £1.50. Free.)* The **Modern Art Oxford,** 30 Pembroke St., hosts international shows. (☎ *722 733. Tu-Sa 10am-5pm, Su noon-5pm. Free.)*

NIGHTLIFE

PUBS
In Oxford, pubs far outnumber colleges—some even consider them the city's prime attraction. Most open by noon, begin to fill around 5pm, and close at 11pm (10:30pm on Su). Recent legislation has allowed pubs to stay open later, but there may be conditions, including an earlier door-closing time or a small cover charge. Be ready to pub crawl—many pubs are so small that a single band of celebrating students will squeeze out other patrons, while just around the corner others will have several spacious rooms.

Turf's Tavern, 4 Bath Pl. (☎ 243 235), hidden off Holywell St. Arguably the most popular student bar in Oxford, this 13th-century pub is tucked in an alley off an alley, but that doesn't stop just about everybody in Oxford from partaking in its 11 different ales. Bob Hawke, former prime minister of Australia, downed a yard of ale (over 2½ pints) in a record 11 seconds here while at the university. Open M-Sa 11am-11pm, Su noon-10:30pm. Kitchen open daily noon-7:30pm.

The King's Arms, 40 Holywell St. (☎ 242 369). Oxford's unofficial student union (locally known as "the KA"). Lots of space and large tables make getting a seat possible even when it's busy. Merry masses head to the back rooms, and locals sip tea and coffee in the bright tearoom. Open M-Sa 10:30am-11pm, Su 10:30am-10:30pm.

The Bear, 6 Alfred St. (☎ 728 164). Patrons once exchanged their club neckties for a free pint at this oldest and tiniest of Oxford's many pubs, established in 1242. Now over 4500 neckties, arranged in frames by category, adorn the walls and ceiling of the pub, established in 1242. Unfortunately, the deal no longer applies. During the day, the clients are older than the neckwear, and the young sit out back with 2-pint pitchers of Pimm's (£9). Open M-Sa noon-11pm, Su noon-10:30pm.

The White Horse, 52 Broad St. (☎ 722 393). Squished between the 2 entrances of Blackwell's, this tiny pub is favored by locals for lively conversation. Relatively late closing time means students head here at the end of the night. Open daily noon-midnight. Kitchen open noon-7pm.

The Eagle and Child, 49 St. Giles (☎ 302 925). A historic pub, the dark-paneled back room once hosted "The Inklings," a group of 20th-century writers including C. S. Lewis and J. R. R. Tolkien, who referred to it as the "Bird and Baby." *The Chronicles of Narnia* and *The Hobbit* were first read aloud here. Open M-Sa 11am-11pm, Su noon-10:30pm. Kitchen open M-F noon-10pm, Sa-Su noon-9pm.

The Head of the River, Folly Bridge, St. Aldates (☎ 721 600). This aptly named pub has the best location in Oxford to view the Thames, known locally as the Isis. Much bigger than the pubs closer to town, at least you can be sure to find a seat. The large beer garden fills up quickly in the early evening. Open M-Sa 11:30am-11pm, Su noon-10:30pm. Kitchen open daily noon-2:30pm and 5-9pm.

St. Aldates Tavern, 108 St. Aldates (☎250 201). Local charm and regional ales make this a classic Oxford pub. Student discounts keep the crowds coming back for more. Open M-Sa 11am-11pm, Su noon-10:30pm.

Chequers Inn, 131 High St. (☎727 463). Numerous pool tables and a heated beer garden make this a great place to kick off a pub crawl. Rustic decor and energetic atmosphere. Open M-Th and Su 11am-11:30pm, F-Sa 11am-midnight.

The Grapes, 7 George St. (☎793 380). This Victorian pub hasn't changed much since the 19th century. A veritable Oxford institution frequented by professors and students alike. Open M-W and Su 11am-11pm, Th-Sa 11am-midnight.

BARS

After Happy hour at the pubs, head up Walton Street or down Cowley Road for late-night drinking.

✪ Jericho Tavern, 56 Walton St. (☎311 775). Recently renovated, this pub has an upstairs venue where Radiohead had their debut gig in 1984 and Britpop group Supergrass was discovered. Downstairs, patrons enjoy the sleek new decor and specialty draft beer. Open M-Sa noon-midnight, Su noon-11pm.

✪ Thirst, 7-8 Park End St. (☎242 044). Lounge bar with a DJ and back-door garden. Thirst serves up cheap mixed drinks (from £1.50). Budget drinks served during "stupid hour" (5-8pm) and Happy hour (8-10pm). Open M-Sa 5pm-2am, Su 6pm-12:30am.

Freud, 119 Walton St. (☎311 171). Formerly St. Paul's Church. Impressive, bizarre decoration: part cathedral, part circus, part modern art installation gone wrong. Cafe by day, collegiate cocktail bar by night. Open M-Tu and Su 11am-midnight, W 11am-1am, Th-Sa 11am-2am.

The Bridge, 6-9 Hythe Bridge St. (☎242 526; www.bridgeoxford.co.uk). Dance to R&B, hip hop, house, and pop on 2 floors. Erratically frequented by big student crowds. Cover £3-7. Open M-Sa 9pm-2am.

Anuba, 11-13 Park End St. (☎242 526; www.bridgeoxford.co.uk). Sister club to The Bridge. Offers a smaller, more intimate pre-club atmosphere. Dance floor in the back is small but a nice alternative to the huge clubs throughout the city. Open M-Sa 6:30pm-11pm, Su 6:30pm-12:30pm.

KISS, 36-39 Park End St. (☎200 555; www.kissbar.co.uk). Intimate bar conveniently located near several clubs for some pre-dancing drinks. 40 flavors of vodka and a special vodka cocktail menu. 2-for-1 drink specials during daily Happy hour (7-9:30pm). Open M-Sa 7:30pm-2am.

🎵 ENTERTAINMENT

Check *This Month in Oxford*, free at the TIC, or *Daily Information*, posted all over town and online (www.dailyinfo.co.uk), for event listings.

MUSIC. Centuries of tradition give Oxford a solid music scene. Colleges offer concerts and Evensong services; **New College** has an excellent boys' choir. Performances at the **Holywell Music Rooms,** on Holywell St., are worth checking out; **Oxford Coffee Concerts** feature famous musicians and ensembles every Sunday at 11:15am. (☎305 305. Tickets £9.) The **City of Oxford Orchestra,** a professional symphony orchestra, plays a subscription series at the Sheldonian and in college chapels during the summer. (☎744 457. Tickets £16-18.) The **New Theatre,** George St., features performances from jazz to musicals to the Welsh National Opera. (☎320 760. Tickets £10-50. Student, senior, and child discounts available.) With a large student population and its proximity to Manchester and London, Oxford is on an excellent circuit for smaller bands at clubs and large venues.

THEATRE. The **Oxford Playhouse,** 11-12 Beaumont St., hosts amateur and professional musicians and dance performances. The playhouse also sells discounted tickets for venues city-wide. (☎305 305; www.oxfordplayhouse.com. Box office open M-Tu and Th-F 9:30am-6:30pm, W 10am-6:30pm.) College theatre groups often stage productions in gardens or cloisters.

FESTIVALS. The university celebrates **Eights Week** at the end of May, when the colleges enter crews in bumping races and beautiful people sip Pimm's on the banks. In early September, **St. Giles Fair** invades one of Oxford's main streets with an old-fashioned English fun fair. Daybreak on **May Day** (May 1) cues one of Oxford's most inspiring moments: the Magdalen College Choir sings madrigals from the top of the tower beginning at 6am, and the town indulges in Morris dancing, beating the bounds, and other age-old rituals of merry men. Pubs open at 7am.

RICHMOND

Richmond is where London ends and the countryside begins. Although accessible by Tube, it is a town in its own right. Edward III built the first royal palace here in 1358, but a major fire in 1497 burned it down. The rebuilt palace was called the Shene until 1501, when Henry VII named it after his earldom in Yorkshire. Later destroyed by Cromwell, only the gateway of that palace still remains, but many durable attractions linger. Countless artists set up their easels on the 17th-century terrace to paint the picturesque gardens. Neighboring Twickenham, just across the river, is the well-loved and oft-pummelled home of English rugby.

▐ TRANSPORTATION

Richmond is at the end of one of the branches of the District line; the quickest route there is by **Tube** or **Silverlink train** (25min.). For a more leisurely, scenic journey, **boats** make the 2hr. cruise upriver from Westminster. Travelcard holders receive a 33% discount on most riverboat fares—be sure to ask. (Westminster Passenger Association, Westminster Pier. ☎7930 2062; www.wpsa.co.uk. ↔Westminster. Departures mid-Apr. to Sept. daily 10, 10:30am; returning 4, 6pm. Tides may affect schedules; call to confirm. £10.50, round-trip £16.50; children £5.25/8.25; concessions £7/11. MC/V.)

■ ▐ ORIENTATION AND PRACTICAL INFORMATION

Richmond is considered part of Greater London. From **Richmond** station, turn left on **The Quadrant,** which becomes **George Street** and then **Hill Street.** Turning right from Hill St. on **Bridge Road** takes you across **Richmond Bridge** into **Twickenham,** while bearing left on **Hill Rise** leads to **Richmond Hill** and **Richmond Park.** Running from Hill St. to the river, **Whittaker Avenue** is home to the **Tourist Information Centre,** where you can pick up a free map of the town and the surrounding sites. (Old Town Hall, Whittaker Ave. ☎8940 9125; www.visitrichmond.co.uk. Open May-Sept. M-Sa 10am-5pm, Su 10:30am-1:30pm; Oct.-Apr. M-Sa 10am-5pm. Audio tours £4, concessions £2.50.) The **post office** is on 6a Finkle St. (**Postal Code:** DL10 4QB.)

▐ SIGHTS

■**RICHMOND PARK.** Along with Hampstead Heath, this is the closest to nature you'll get while still within the capital. Now the largest city park in Europe, Richmond's lush and beautiful 2500 acres were first enclosed by Charles I, who in 1637 built a wall around other people's property and declared it his hunting ground. Large herds of **deer** still wander about. Heading right along the main footpath from Richmond Gate will bring you to **Henry VIII's Mound,** actually a Bronze Age barrow. This is the highest point in the park, and offers a great view: look through a small hole cut in the foliage at the top of the mound for a glimpse of St. Paul's in the distance. Bertrand Russell grew up in **Pembroke Lodge,** an 18th-century conversion job by the versatile Sir John Soane that's now a popular cafe. Deeper in the park, the **Isabella Plantation** bursts with color in the spring. Make sure to explore some of the smaller footpaths—not only do you have a better chance of spotting the deer, you're less likely to be run over by cyclists and joggers. *(Main gate at the top of Richmond Hill. Bus #371 from Richmond. Park office ☎ 8948 3209; www.royalparks.org.uk/parks/ richmond_park. Open daily Mar.-Sept. 7am-dusk, Oct.-Feb. 7:30am-dusk. Free.)*

■ **ROYAL BOTANICAL GARDENS, KEW.** In the summer of 2003, UNESCO named the Royal Botanical Gardens a World Heritage site—a privilege shared by many of the historic sights in London. The 250-year-old Royal Botanical Gardens, about an hour's Tube ride outside of central London, extend with a green English placidity in a 300-acre swath along the Thames. The three conservatories are at the center of the collection. The steamy Victorian Palm House boasts *Encephalartos Altensteinii,* "The Oldest Pot Plant In The World." The Princess of Wales Conservatory houses 10 different climate zones, from rainforest to desert, including two devoted entirely to orchids. Low-season visitors will not be disappointed—the Woodland Glade is renowned for displays of autumn color. Close to the Thames in the northern part of the gardens, newly renovated Kew Palace is a modest red-brick affair used by royalty, and which is now open to the public for the first time in 200 years. On the hill behind and to the right of the palace, 17th-century medicinal plants flourish in the stunning Queen's Garden. *(Kew, on the south bank of the Thames. Main entrance and Visitors Centre are at Victoria Gate, nearest the Tube. Go up the white stairs that go above the station tracks, and walk straight down the road. ⊖ Kew Gardens. ☎ 8332 5000; www.kew.org. Open Apr.-Aug. M-F 9:30am-6:30pm, Sa-Su 9:30am-7:30pm; Sept.-Oct. daily 9:30am-6pm; Nov.-Jan. daily 9:30am-4:15pm. Last admission 30min. before close. Glasshouses close Apr.-Oct. 5:30pm; Nov.-Feb. 3:45pm. £12.25, concessions £10.25, under 17 free; £10.25 45min. before close. Free 1hr. walking tours daily 11am and 2pm start at Victoria Gate Visitors Centre. "Explorer" hop-on, hop-off shuttle makes 40min. rounds of the gardens; 1st shuttle daily 11am, last 4pm; £3.50, under 17 £1. Free 1hr. "Discovery Bus" tours for mobility-impaired daily 11am and 2pm; booking required; free.)*

HAM HOUSE. Some way down river of Richmond, Ham House sits in resplendent gardens. William Murray received the house as a reward for being Charles I's "whipping boy"—he took the punishment whenever the king-to-be misbehaved. Later, it was occupied by the famously extravagant Duchess of Lauderdale, renowned as a dazzling beauty and a ruthless political schemer. Today, the house has been restored to the height of its glory, filled with 17th-century portraits, furniture, and tapestries, though the gardens are the main attraction. The formal **Cherry Garden** is actually a diamond-shaped lattice of lavender, santolina, and hedges with not a cherry tree in sight. **The Wilderness** is even less aptly named, an orderly array of trimmed hedges surrounding nooks of roses and wildflowers, with a 17th-century statuary standing guard. And for those who love the practical-gone-extravagant, the **Kitchen Garden** offers endless rows of fresh fruit and vegetables. *(At the bottom of Sandy Ln., Ham. Bus #65 (then a 15min. walk) or 371 (then a 10min. walk) from Richmond station; or a beautiful 30min. walk along the Thames. A ferry crosses the river from Marble Hill, Twickenham Sa-Su 10am-6:30pm/dusk; Feb.-Oct. M-F 10am-6pm, Sa-Su 10am-6:30pm or dusk. 70p, children 35p. Ham House: ☎ 8940 1950; www.nationaltrust.org.uk/ hamhouse. Open Apr.-Oct. M-W and Sa-Su 1-5pm. Gardens open year-round M-W and Sa-Su 11am-6pm/dusk. Gardens £3, children £2, families £7; house and gardens £9/5/22. MC/V.)*

RICHMOND THEATRE. A popular and well-lauded regional theatre, Richmond Theatre is a pre-West End proving ground for a number of popular shows. Recent shows include *Swan Lake* and an adaptation of Henry James's *Daisy Miller*. *(On Richmond Green, just above George St. ☎8939 9277, box office 0870 060 6651; www.richmondtheatre.net. Performances M-Tu and Th-F 7:45pm, W and Su 2:30pm and 7:45pm. Tickets start at £10, concessions £2 off M-Th and Sa matinee; students £8 from 1hr. before curtain. £2.50 online or phone booking fee. Box office open M-Sa 10am-8pm.)*

OTHER SIGHTS. Quite the hidden treasure, the ▓**Museum of Richmond** has a small but fascinating array of exhibits on the history of Richmond, from the days of Queen Elizabeth I to its Blitz legacy. *(Whittaker Ave. ☎8332 1141; www.museumofrichmond.com. Open 11am-5pm. Free.)* Across the river from Ham House, **Marble Hill** was built in 1724 by Henrietta Howard, using an allowance from her former lover, George II. *(Marble Hill Park, Richmond Rd. Bus #33, H22, R68, R70, 490 from Richmond; or via ferry which crosses from Ham House, Richmond; see above. Alternatively, a 15min. walk from the town center—turn right on Richmond Bridge from Hill St., then left on Richmond Rd. House: ☎8892 5115; www.english-heritage.org.uk/server/show/nav.12809. Open Apr.-Oct. Sa 10am-2pm, Su and bank holidays 10am-5pm. £4.20, concessions £3.20, children £2.10.)* Only James Gibbs's richly decorated Octagon Room survives the 18th-century **Orleans House.** Louis Philippe, Duc d'Orleans, rode out the French Revolution here before becoming king in 1830. *(Riverside, Twickenham. Transportation same as for Marble Hill. House: ☎8831 6000; www.richmond.gov.uk/home/leisure_and_culture/arts/orleans_house_gallery.htm. Open Apr.-Sept. Tu-Sa 1-5:30pm, Su and bank holidays 2-5:30pm; Oct.-Mar. Tu-Sa 1-4:30pm, Su and bank holidays 2-4:30pm. Grounds open daily 9am-dusk. Free.)*

SALISBURY ☎01722

Salisbury's winding alleyways and old-fashioned cinema are a step back in time. Despite its tourist popularity, Salisbury retains its small-town charm. Market Square's pavement cafes and tea shops are lively, and a quick glance down any street reveals facades dating from the Middle Ages to the industrial era. Town life spirals outward from the market, overlooked by the towering cathedral spire.

DAYTRIPS

▆ TRANSPORTATION

Trains: Trains (☎08457 484 950) from **London Waterloo** (1½hr., 2 per hr., £26.30).

Taxis: Cabs cruise by the train station. **505050 Value Cars** (☎505 050) runs 24hr.

Bike Rental: Hayball Cycles Sport, 26-30 Winchester St. (☎07909 883 006), across from Coaches and Horses. £10 per day, £5 overnight, £65 per week; deposit £25 per bike. Open M-Sa 9am-5pm; bikes due back at 5pm. TIC has suggested routes.

▐ PRACTICAL INFORMATION

Tourist Information Centre: Fish Row (☎334 956, accommodations booking 01271 336 066; www.visitsalisbury.com), the Guildhall, in Market Sq. Free maps. Books rooms for a 10% deposit. Open June-Sept. M-Sa 9:30am-6pm, Su 10:30am-4:30pm; Oct.-May M-Sa 9:30am-5pm. 1½hr. **guided walks** leave Apr.-Oct. M-Th and Sa-Su 11am, F 11am and 8pm; Nov.-Mar. Sa-Su 11am. £3.50-4, children £1.50-2.

Banks: Banks are everywhere. **Thomas Cook,** 18-19 Queen St. (☎08701 111 111). Open M-W and F-Sa 9am-5:30pm, Th 10am-5:30pm. **HSBC,** corner of Market Pl. and Minster St., has a **24hr. ATM.**

Police: Wilton Rd. (☎411 444).

Pharmacy: Boots, 51 Silver St. (☎333 233). Open M-Tu and Th-Sa 8:30am-5:30pm, W 9am-5:30pm, Su 10:30am-4:30pm.

Hospital: Central Health Clinic, Avon Approach (☎328 595).

Internet Access: Salisbury Library, Market Pl. (☎324 145). Open M 10am-7pm, Tu-W and F 9am-7pm, Th and Sa 9am-5pm. 30min. free Internet with photo ID. **Internet Cafe,** 14 Endless St. (☎421 328). Open M-Sa 10am-7pm.

Post Office: 24 Castle St. (☎08457 223 344), at Chipper Ln. **Bureau de change** inside. Open M-F 8:30am-5:30pm. **Postal Code:** SP1 1AB.

ACCOMMODATIONS AND CAMPING

Salisbury's proximity to Stonehenge breeds numerous guest houses and B&Bs, most of them starting at around £35 per person. Ask for an accommodations guide or free booking assistance from the TIC. Book ahead in summer.

Farthings B&B, 9 Swaynes Close (☎330 749; www.farthingsbandb.co.uk), 10min. from the city center. Comfortable retreat with large, floral rooms and subtle touches of home. Smaller rooms share a bath. Continental breakfast included. May-Sept. singles £32; doubles £56. Oct.-Apr. singles £25; doubles £46. Cash only. ❸

YHA Salisbury, Milford Hill House, Milford Hill (☎327 572), on the edge of town. 70 beds. Kitchen and TV lounge. Breakfast included. Laundry £3. Internet access 7p per min. Book in advance, especially Easter-Oct. Dorms £17.50, under 18 £14. MC/V. ❷

78 Belle Vue Rd., (☎329 477), on a residential road near the cathedral. Victorian terrace house offers 2 rooms with shared bath. Single £23, double £45. Cash only. ❷

Hudson's Field, Castle Rd. (☎320 713). Between Salisbury and Stonehenge, 30min. from city center. Clean, modern camping facilities. Vehicle curfew 11pm. Open Mar.-Oct. Tents £5.40, adults £5.30, children £2.50. Electricity £2.60. MC/V. ❶

FOOD AND PUBS

Even jaded pub-dwellers can find a pleasant surprise among Salisbury's 60-odd watering holes. Most pubs serve food (£4-6) and many have live music. **Market Square,** in the town center, fills from May to December on Tuesdays and Saturdays for the **charter market** and on Wednesdays for the **farmers' market** (open 7am-4pm). The TIC has the market schedule for each summer. A Sainsbury's **supermarket** is at The Maltings. (☎332 282. Open M-Sa 7am-10pm, Su 10am-4pm.)

▧ Harper's "Upstairs Restaurant," 6-7 Ox Rd., Market Sq. (☎333 118). Inventive English and international dishes (£7-10). 2-course early-bird dinner before 8pm £7.50. Open June-Sept. M-F noon-2pm and 6-9:30pm, Sa noon-2pm and 6-10pm, Su 6-9pm; Oct.-May closed Su. AmEx/MC/V. ❷

Alchemy @ the Chough, Blue Boar Row (☎330 032). Find a couch in one of the many nooks and crannies. Original art and signs still hang on the walls. The Alchemy mix (£10) is a platter of finger foods. Entrees £8-10. Open M and W noon-11pm, Tu 11am-11pm, Th-F noon-midnight, Sa 11am-midnight, Su noon-10:30pm. MC/V. ❷

Coach and Horses, 39 Winchester St. (☎414 319). Traditional pub food (£8-14) and generously poured drinks (pints £2.70) flow nonstop, drawing families during the day and a louder crowd at night. Salisbury's oldest pub, open since 1382. For extra room, check out the beer garden in the back. Open M-Sa 11:30am-11pm, Su noon-10:30pm. Kitchen open M-Sa 11:30am-9:30pm, Su noon-9pm. MC/V. ❶

Salisbury Chocolate Bar & Patisserie, 33 High St. (☎327 422). Indulge your sweet tooth with luscious hot chocolate (£2) or scrumptious pastries (£3-4), like the decadent ganache-filled Fudgey cake. Open daily 9:30am-5pm. MC/V. ❶

The Old Mill Hotel, Town Path (☎327 517). At the end of a 10min. walk along Town Path through the Harnem Water Meadow, in a 12th-century mill. Entrees can be pricey (£13-17), but the pub food is just as delicious and more reasonably priced (£6-8). Open M-Sa 11am-11pm, Su noon-10:30pm. Kitchen open M-Th noon-2pm and 7-9pm, F-Sa 11am-11pm, Su noon-10:30pm. AmEx/MC/V. ❸

👁 SIGHTS

█ SALISBURY CATHEDRAL. Salisbury Cathedral, built between 1220 and 1258, rises from its grassy close to a neck-breaking height of 404 ft., making it medieval England's highest spire and one of Britain's most impressive displays of Gothic architecture. The bases of the marble pillars bend inward under the strain of 6400 tons of limestone. Nearly 700 years have left the building in need of repair, and scaffolding shrouds parts of the outer walls that are under extensive renovation expected to be completed by 2015. A tiny stone figure rests in the nave—legend has it that either a boy bishop is entombed on the spot or that it covers the heart of Richard Poore, founder of the cathedral. The adjoining **Chapter House** holds the best preserved of the four surviving copies of the Magna Carta. The text is still legible, which is great for people who can read medieval Latin. Spot the punctures at the bottom of the vellum where King John's seal was once attached—the priceless artifact was inadvertently chucked with the weekly trash. Ask a guide for a list of the relief figures in the detailed friezes. (☎555 120. Cathedral open daily 7:15am-6:15pm. Limited hours in winter. Free tours every 30min.: May-Oct. M-Sa 9:30am-4:45pm, Su 4-6:15pm; Nov.-Feb. M-Sa 10am-4pm. 1½hr. roof and tower tours: May-Sept. M-Sa 11:15am, 2:15, 3:15, and 5pm; Su 4:30pm. June-Aug. M-Sa 11am, 2, 3, and 6:30pm; Su 4:30pm. Requested donation £4, concessions £3.50. Roof and tower tour £4.50, concessions £3.50.)

SALISBURY AND SOUTH WILTSHIRE MUSEUM. The museum, in the Salisbury Cathedral's close, is home to a mixture of artwork ranging from Turner's watercolors to period clothing and doll houses. The worthwhile Stonehenge exhibit gives extensive history, and displays the bones of the mysterious archer buried at Stonehenge around the time the first stones were raised. (65 The Close, along the West Walk. ☎332 151. Open July-Aug. M-Sa 10am-5pm, Su 2-5pm; Sept.-June M-Sa 10am-5pm. £5, under 16 £1.50, families £9.50, concessions £3.50.)

🔲 🌿 NIGHTLIFE AND FESTIVALS

Read the sign outside **The Chapel,** 30 Milford St., carefully before trying to enter. It states, in clear mathematical terms: "no effort=no entry." Loosely translated—dress to impress. With three dance floors and hot music mixes, this club advertises itself as one of the UK's best. Without much competition in Salisbury, it can surely claim to be the best in town. (☎504 255; www.thechapelnightclub.co.uk. Cover W £2; Th £4, ladies free until 11:30pm; F £8; Sa £10. Open W-Th 10:30pm-2:30am, F-Sa 10:30pm-3am.) **MOLOKO,** 5 Bridge St., is a chain bar, but still one of the most popular hangouts in town. There's an endless list of vodkas (£2.50-4.50) and a stylish crowd. (☎507 050. F special £1 house vodkas 7-9pm. M-Th noon-midnight, F-Sa noon-2am, Su 3-10:30pm.)

Salisbury's repertory theatre company puts on shows at the **Playhouse,** Malthouse Ln., over the bridge off Fisherton St. (☎320 333; www.salisburyplayhouse.com. Box office open M-Sa 10am-6pm, until 8pm on performance days. Tickets £8.50-17. ½-price tickets available same day.) The **Salisbury Arts Centre,** Bedwin St., hosts music and theatre events year-round. (☎321 744. Box office open Tu-Sa 10am-4pm. Tickets from £5.) During the summer, enjoy free Sunday **concerts** in various parks; call the TIC for info. The **Salisbury International Arts Festival** features dance exhibitions, music, and wine tasting for two weeks in late May

HERE COMES THE SUN

Perhaps no man-made structure evokes more mystical associations than Stonehenge. Ties to Arthurian legend, Celts, druids, aliens, giants, and witches bring tourists to the mysterious stones year-round. For 364 days of the year they are roped off—almost regal in their standoffishness. But every June, the summer solstice arrives, the ropes are pulled back, admission is free, and visitors enter the circle to worship as they like.

In droves they come: druids with staffs waiting for the sun, hippies with magical plants caressing the stones, and curious bystanders unsure of what will happen next. In a matter of hours, the vacant field is transformed into a drum-filled festival complete with glow sticks and champagne.

As the crowd swells to an impenetrable mob, the drumming thunders and the sun finally rises, casting a shadow perfectly across the center of the stones. Suddenly, elation erupts from the milling masses—an unforgettable energy that validates the mystical qualities of Stonehenge.

The 2008 summer solstice occurs on June 21. There is no admission fee the night before or morning of the solstice, but make plans to get a bus early as crowds form fast.

and early June. Contact the Festival Box Office at the Playhouse or the TIC for a program. (☎ 320 333; www.salisburyfestival.co.uk. Tickets from £2.50.)

STONEHENGE

A half-ruined ring of colossal stones amid swaying grass and indifferent sheep has become a world-famous attraction. Curious tourists visit Stonehenge in droves to see the 22 ft. high stones, pockmarked by the wind that whips across the flat Salisbury plains. The current ring is actually the fifth temple constructed on the site—Stonehenge was already ancient in ancient times. The first arrangement probably consisted of an arch and circular earthwork furrowed in 3050 BC. Its relics are the **Aubrey Holes** (white patches in the earth) and the **Heel Stone** (the rough block standing outside the circle). The present shape, once a complete circle, dates from about 1500 BC. The tremendous workforce—estimated at tens of millions of man-hours—and innovation required to transport and erect the 45-ton stones make Stonehenge an impressive monument to human (alien?) effort. Sensationalized religious and scientific explanations for Stonehenge's purpose add to its intrigue. Some believe the stones are oriented as a calendar, with the position of the sun on the stones indicating the time of year. Celtic druids, whose ceremonies took place in forests, did not actually worship here, but modern druids are permitted to enter Stonehenge on the summer solstice to perform ceremonial exercises. Admission to Stonehenge includes a helpful 30min. audio tour, including legends about the stones and the surrounding landscape. **English Heritage** also offers free guided tours (30min.). From the roadside or from Amesbury Hill, 1½ mi. up the A303, you can get a free, if distant, view of the stones. There are also many walks and trails that pass by; ask at the Salisbury TIC. *(All Stonehenge transportation is through Salisbury. Wilts and Dorset runs daily service from the Salisbury train station and bus station (☎ 336 855. #3, 40min., round-trip £7.50). The first bus leaves Salisbury at 9:45am, and the last leaves Stonehenge at 4:05pm. Check a schedule before you leave; intervals between dropoffs and pickups are at least 1hr. A £6.50 Explorer ticket allows travel all day on any bus, including those to Avebury, Stonehenge's less-crowded cousin, and Old Sarum. Wilts and Dorset runs a tour bus from Salisbury, 3 per day, £7.50-15. ☎ 01980 624 715. Open daily June-Aug. 9am-7pm; from mid-Mar. to May and from Sept. to mid-Oct. 9:30am-6pm; from mid-Oct. to mid-Mar. 9:30am-4pm. £6, concessions £4.40.)*

STRATFORD-UPON-AVON ☎ 01789

While the Globe on the South Bank gives visitors to London a glimpse into Shakespeare's life and times, diehard fans and the merely curious alike will enjoy visiting Stratford, his place of birth. Proprietors tout the dozen-odd properties linked, however remotely, to the Bard and his extended family: shops and restaurants devotedly stencil his prose and poetry on their windows and walls. Beyond the sound and fury of rumbling tour buses and chaotic swarms of daytrippers, there lies a town worth seeing for the beauty of the River Avon and for the riveting performances in the Royal Shakespeare Theatre.

┏ HENCE, AWAY!

Trains: From **London Paddington** (2¼hr., 2 per hr., £41.50).

Public Transportation: Stagecoach #1618 services **Coventry** (2hr., every hr., £3.50) via **Warwick** (20-40min., every hr., £3).

⁈ WHO IS'T THAT CAN INFORM ME?

Tourist Information Centre: Bridgefoot (☎0870 160 7930). Provides maps (£1.20), guidebooks, tickets, and accommodations lists. Books accommodations for £3 and a 10% deposit. Open Apr.-Oct. M-Sa 9am-5:30pm, Su 10am-4pm; Nov.-Mar. M-Sa 9am-5pm.

Tours: 2hr. **walking tours** led by Shakespearean actors start at the Royal Shakespeare Theatre (☎412 617). Sa 10:30am. £8, concessions £6. **City Sightseeing Bus Tours,** Civic Hall, 14 Rother St. (☎412 680; www.stagecoachbus.com/warwickshire), heads to Bard-related houses every 15-20min. from the front of the Pen and Parchment, next to the TIC. £10, children £5, concessions £8. Offers bus ticket and discounted admission to any of the Shakespeare Houses. Office open daily 9am-5:30pm. **Stratford Town Walk** (☎292 478) arranges various walking tours throughout the city, including the popular **Ghost Walks.** All walks depart from the Swan fountain, near the Royal Shakespeare Theatre, Th 7:30pm. £5. Town walk M-W 11am, Th-Su 2pm. Advanced booking required for Ghost Walk.

Banks: Barclays, (☎08457 555 555), at the intersection of Henley and Wood St. Open M-Tu and Th-F 9am-5pm, W 10am-4:30pm. **Thomas Cook,** 37 Wood St. (☎293 582). Open M and W-Sa 9am-5:30pm, Tu 10am-5:30pm.

Police: Rother St. (☎414 111).

Pharmacy: Boots, 11 Bridge St. (☎292 173). Open M-Sa 8:30am-5:30pm, Su 10:30am-4:30pm.

Hospital: Stratford-upon-Avon Hospital, Arden St. (☎205 831), off Alcester Rd.

Internet Access: Central Library, 12 Henley St. (☎292 209). Free. Open M and W-F 9am-5:30pm, Tu 10am-5:30pm, Sa 9:30am-5pm, Su noon-4pm. **Cyber Junction,** 28 Greenhill St. (☎263 400). £2.50 per 30min., £4 per hr.; concessions £2-3.50. Open M-F 10am-6pm, Sa 10:30am-5:30pm.

Post Office: 2-3 Henley St. (☎08457 223 344). **Bureau de change** inside. Open M-Sa 8:30am-6pm. **Postal Code:** CV37 6PU.

┏ TO SLEEP, PERCHANCE TO DREAM

B&Bs abound, but singles are rare. Accommodations in the £25-35 range line **Evesham Place, Evesham Road,** and **Grove Road.** Try **Shipston Road** across the river, a 15-20min. walk from the station.

Carlton Guest House, 22 Evesham Pl. (☎293 548). Spacious rooms and spectacular service make this B&B a great value. Book early, as it hosts groups in the summer. Singles £20-26; doubles £40-52; triples £60-78. Cash only. ❸

The Marlyn Hotel, 3 Chestnut Walk (☎293 752). Classy new B&B near the RSC Theatre. The pristine white linens and pastel walls will make you feel like you've been whisked away to the seaside. Full English breakfast included. Singles £30; doubles £45. AmEx/MC/V. ❸

YHA Stratford, Wellesbourne Rd., Alveston (☎297 093), 2 mi. from Clopton Bridge. Follow B4086 from town center (35min.), or take bus X18 or 77 from Bridge St. (10min., every hr., £2). Isolated hostel catering mostly to school groups and families. A solid, inexpensive option for longer stays. Breakfast included. Internet access 7p per min. Dorms £21, under 18 £14.50. Add £3 for non-YHA-members. MC/V. ❷

Melita Hotel, 37 Shipston Rd. (☎292 432). Upscale B&B with gorgeous garden, retreat-like atmosphere, and excellent breakfasts. Guests relax on the sunny patio with less-than-intimidating guard dog Harvey and his accomplice, Daisy. Singles from £52; doubles £79; triples £106; quads £125. AmEx/MC/V. ❹

Penshurst Guest House, 34 Evesham Pl. (☎205 259; www.penshurst.net). 4 distinctly decorated rooms. Access to a large kitchen. Double and triple with bath £30-45; family room with bath £40-57. Prices vary; call ahead. Cash only. ❸

Riverside Caravan Park, Tiddington Rd. (☎292 312), 30min. east of town on the B4086. Sunset views on the Avon, but often crowded. A 3-4min. walk to the village pub. Open Easter-Oct. Tent sites for up to 4 people £11. AmEx/MC/V. ❶

■ IN THE CAULDRON BOIL AND BAKE

Baguette stores and bakeries are scattered throughout the town center; a Somerfield **supermarket** is in Town Sq. (☎292 604. Open M-W 8am-7pm, Th-Sa 8am-8pm, Su 10am-4pm.) The 1st and 3rd Saturdays of every month, the River Avon's banks welcome a **farmers' market.**

The Oppo, 13 Sheep St. (☎269 980). Receives rave reviews from locals. Low 16th-century-style ceilings and candles make for a classy ambience. Try the lasagna (£9) or grilled goat cheese and tomato salad (£10). Open M-Th noon-2pm and 5:30-9:30pm, F-Sa noon-2pm and 5-11pm, and Su noon-2pm and 6-9:30pm. MC/V. ❸

Hussain's, 6a Chapel St. (☎267 506). Stratford's best Indian menu and a favorite of Ben Kingsley. Tandoori prepared with homemade spices and served in an elegant red dining room. 3-course lunch *menu* £6. Entrees from £6.75, but they don't include rice or naan, so be prepared to shell out an extra £2 for sides. 10% discount for takeaway and pre-theatre dining. Open daily 12:30-2:30pm and 5pm-midnight. AmEx/MC/V. ❷

Cafe Bar (☎403 415). Inside the Courtyard Theatre. Serves homemade sandwiches and pastries by the river. A perfect spot for a drink during matinee intermission. Summer specials £3.50-8.50. Open M-Sa 10:30am-8:30pm. ❷

Must Go, 21 Windsor St. (☎293 679). This Asian restaurant is unabashedly straightforward. After perusing the 4 ft. long menu outside, enter the "Out" doorway for takeaway or the "In" door for a meal in surprisingly comfortable quarters. "Meal deals" £5-7. Open Apr.-Oct. M-Th and Su noon-midnight, F-Sa noon-12:30am; Sept.-Mar. M-Th and Su noon-2pm and 5pm-midnight, F-Sa noon-12:30am. MC/V. ❷

■ THE GILDED MONUMENTS

TO BARD...

Stratford's Will-centered sights are best seen before 11am, when the daytrippers arrive, or after 4pm, when the crowds disperse. The five official **Shakespeare prop-**

erties are Shakespeare's Birthplace, Mary Arden's House, Nash's House and New Place, Hall's Croft, and Anne Hathaway's Cottage. Opening hours are listed by season: summer (June-Aug.); mid-season (Apr.-May and Sept.-Oct.); and winter (Nov.-Mar.). Diehards should get the **All Five Houses** ticket, which also includes entrance to Harvard House. (☎204 016. £14, children £6.50, families £29, concessions £12.) Those who don't want to visit every house can get a **Three In-Town Houses** pass, covering the Birthplace, Hall's Croft, and Nash's House and New Place (£11/23/5.50/9).

SHAKESPEARE'S BIRTHPLACE. The only in-town sight directly associated with Him includes an exhibit on his father's glove-making business, a peaceful garden, and the requisite walkthrough on the Bard's documented life, including a First Folio and records of his father's illegal refuse dumping. Join such distinguished pilgrims as Charles Dickens in signing the guestbook. *(Henley St. ☎201 822. Open in summer M-Sa 9am-5pm, Su 9:30am-5pm; mid-season daily 10am-5pm; winter M-Sa 10am-4pm, Su 10:30am-4pm. £7, children £2.75, families £17, concessions £5.50.)*

SHAKESPEARE'S GRAVE. The least-crowded and most authentic way to pay homage to the Bard is to visit his grave inside the quiet Holy Trinity Church—though groups pack the arched door at peak hours. Rumor has it that Shakespeare was buried 17 ft. underground by request, so that he would sleep undisturbed. A curse on the epitaph (said to be written by the man himself)

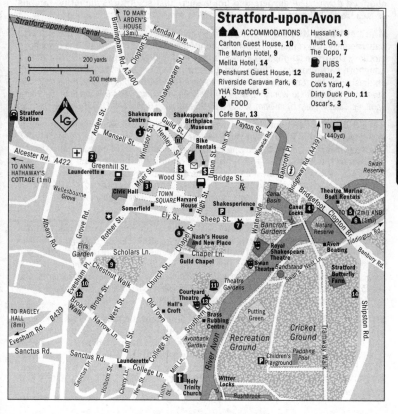

Stratford-upon-Avon

🏠🏠 ACCOMMODATIONS
Carlton Guest House, **10**
The Marlyn Hotel, **9**
Melita Hotel, **14**
Penshurst Guest House, **12**
Riverside Caravan Park, **6**
YHA Stratford, **5**

🍴 FOOD
Cafe Bar, **13**

Hussain's, **8**
Must Go, **1**
The Oppo, **7**

🍺 PUBS
Bureau, **2**
Cox's Yard, **4**
Dirty Duck Pub, **11**
Oscar's, **3**

DAYTRIPS

anticipates the curiosity of prying archaeologists. To the left is a large memorial bust of Shakespeare and his birth and death records. The church also harbors the graves of wife Anne and daughter Susanna. *(Trinity St. ☎266 316. Entrance to church free; almost forced donation to see grave £1, students and children 50p. Open Apr.-Sept. M-Sa 8:30am-6pm, Su noon-5pm; Mar. and Oct. M-Sa 9am-5pm, Su noon-5pm; Nov.-Feb. M-Sa 9am-4pm, Su noon-5pm. Last admission 20min. before close.)*

NASH'S HOUSE AND NEW PLACE. Tourists flock to the home of the first husband of Shakespeare's granddaughter Elizabeth, William's last descendant. **Nash's House** has been restored to its Elizabethan grandeur and holds temporary exhibits on the Bard, but most want to see **New Place**, Shakespeare's retirement home and, at the time, Stratford's finest house. Today only the foundations and a garden remain due to a disgruntled 19th-century owner named Gastrell who razed the building and cut down Shakespeare's mulberry tree in order to spite Bard tourists (jealous much?). Gastrell was run out of town, and to this day Gastrells are not allowed in Stratford. Knowledgeable guides hang out to answer questions. *(Chapel St. ☎292 325. Open in summer M-Sa 9:30am-5pm and Su 10am-5pm; mid-season daily 11am-5pm; winter M-Sa 11am-4pm. £3.75, children £1.75, families £9, concessions £3.)* Down Chapel St. from Nash's House, the sculpted hedges, manicured lawn, and abundant flowers of the **Great Garden of New Place** offer a respite from the mobbed streets and contain a mulberry tree said to be grown from the one Gastrell chopped down. The garden also holds surrealist sculptures depicting famous scenes from Shakespeare's plays. *(Open M-Sa 9am-dusk, Su 10am-5pm. Free.)*

MARY ARDEN'S HOUSE. This farmhouse in Wilmcote, 3 mi. from Stratford, was only recently determined to be the childhood home of Mary Arden (Shakespeare's mother). Historians thought she grew up in the stately building next door. She didn't. Longhorn cattle roam the farm, and a history recounts how Mary fell in love with Shakespeare, Sr. *(Connected by footpath to Anne Hathaway's Cottage, or take the train from Stratford 1 stop north to Wilmcote. ☎293 455. Open in summer M-Sa 9:30am-5pm, Su 10am-5pm; mid-season daily 10am-5pm; winter daily 10am-4pm. £6, children £2.50, concessions £5.)*

HALL'S CROFT. Dr. John Hall married Shakespeare's oldest daughter, Susanna, and garnered fame in his own right as one of the first doctors to keep detailed records of his patients. Shakespearean quotes about medicine loosely tie the exhibits to the Bard. The Croft features an exhibit on Hall, a grand garden with flowers mentioned in Shakespeare's works, and artifacts from Shakespeare's time, when spiderwebs were used to guard against scurvy. *(Old Town. ☎292 107. Open in summer M-Sa 9:30am-5pm, Su 10am-5pm; mid-season daily 11am-5pm; in winter daily 11am-4pm. £3.75, children £1.75, families £10, concessions £3.)*

ANNE HATHAWAY'S COTTAGE. The birthplace of Shakespeare's wife, about a mile from Stratford in **Shottery,** is a fairy-tale, thatched-roof cottage. It boasts (very old) original Hathaway furniture and a hedge maze. Entrance entitles you to sit on a bench Bill may or may not also have sat on. *(Take the hop-on, hop-off Guide Friday tour bus or brave the poorly marked footpaths north. ☎292 100. Open in summer M-Sa 9am-5pm, Su 9:30am-5pm; mid-season M-Sa 9:30am-5pm, Su 10am-5pm; winter daily 10am-4pm. £5.50, children £2, families £13, concessions £4.50.)*

SHAKESPEARIENCE. This extravaganza is definitely the most unique exhibit in town. A two-act show starting with a visual tour of Shakespeare's life and times and featuring a holographic summary of his most famous works. The blasting winds and surround sound may seem a bit over the top, but it's actually a fun way to chill with Will. Have a drink at the bar upstairs after the show to help wash down the cheese. *(Waterside, across from the Bancroft gardens and carousel. ☎293 678. Shows daily every hr. 10am-5pm. £7.95, concession £6.95.)*

...OR NOT TO BARD

Believe it or not, there are some non-Shakespearean sights to visit.

STRATFORD BUTTERFLY FARM. Europe's largest collection of butterflies flutters through tropical surroundings. Less appealing creepy-crawlies—like the Goliath bird-eating spider—dwell in glass boxes nearby. *(Off Swan's Nest Ln. at Tramway Walk, across the river from the TIC. ☎ 299 288. Open daily in summer 10am-6pm, in winter 10am-5pm. Last admission 30min. before close. £5.25, children £4.25, concessions £4.75.)*

HARVARD HOUSE. Once inhabited by the mother of the founder of that university in the Cambridge across the pond, the house is now owned by the Shakespeare Birthright Trust. It houses more pewter than crimson, but son Johnny gets a small exhibit on the second floor. *(High St. ☎ 204 507. Open May-July and Sept.-Oct. F-Su noon-5pm; July-Sept. W-Su noon-5pm. £2.75, children free.)*

RAGLEY HALL. Eight miles from Stratford on Evesham Rd. (A435), Ragley Hall houses the Earl and Countess of Yarmouth. Set in a stunning 400-acre park, the estate has an art collection and a sculpture park. *(Bus #246, M-Sa 5 per day, runs to Alcester Police Station. Walk 1 mi. to the gates, then ½ mi. up the drive. ☎ 762 090. House open Apr.-Sept. M-Th and Su 10am-6pm; last entry 4:30pm. £8, concessions £6.50.)*

🍷 DRINK DEEP ERE YOU DEPART

Oscar's, 14 Meer St. (☎ 292 202). Cafe by day, bar by night. Feels like a tree house for adults. Red walls, bubble machine, and seats by upstairs windows. Tu live music, "International Wednesdays," and Th-Sa DJs. Try the 10-shot "Bullseye" (£20) if you dare. Open M-Sa 8pm-3am.

Bureau, 1 Arden St. (☎ 297 641). Silver staircase leading to a huge dance area. Various promotions, like M "£1-ish drinks" and Th 2-for-1 drink specials. Heats up late. Cover M and W-Sa £2-5. Open M and Th-F 9pm-2am, Tu-W 8pm-midnight, Su 11pm-2am.

Dirty Duck Pub, 66 Waterside (☎ 297 312). Originally called "The Black Swan" and rechristened by alliterative Americans during WWII. River view outside, huge bust of Shakespeare within. Actors make entrances almost nightly. Dame Judy Dench got engaged here and has her own table in the back room. Open M-Sa 11am-11pm, Su noon-10:30pm.

Cox's Yard, Bridgefoot (☎ 404 600; www.coxsyard.co.uk), next to Bancroft Gardens. Have a pint outdoors on the banks of the Avon. Upstairs bar with tribute bands. Call for performance times and tickets. Pub and beer garden open in summer M-Tu and Su noon-11pm, W-Th noon-12:30am, F-Sa noon-1:30am.

🎭 ALL THE WORLD'S A STAGE

THE ROYAL SHAKESPEARE COMPANY

The box office in the Courtyard Theatre handles the ticketing for all theatres. Ticket hotline ☎ 0844 800 1110; www.rsc.org.uk. Open M and W-Sa 9:30am-8pm, Tu 10am-8pm. Tickets £5-40. Students and those under 25 receive advance ½-price tickets for M-W evening performances, otherwise by availability on performance days. Standby tickets in summer £15; in winter £12. Disabled travelers should call in advance to advise the box office of their needs; some performances feature sign language interpretation or audio description.

One of the world's most acclaimed repertories, the Royal Shakespeare Company (RSC) sells well over 1 million tickets each year and claims Kenneth Branagh and Ralph Fiennes as recent members. The Royal Shakespeare Theatre is currently undergoing a £100 million renovation and will re-open in 2010 with a 1000-seat thrust stage, bringing the whole audience within 50 ft. of the action. The construc-

DAYTRIPS

tion will also close the Swan Theatre, the RSC's more intimate neighbor, until 2010. The company will continue to perform shows down the road at The Courtyard Theatre. Visitors can get backstage tours and a glimpse at the high-tech stage to be installed at the Royal Shakespeare Theatre. The RSC has also planned an extensive touring campaign throughout England and the US while the theatres are renovated; inquire at the box office for details.

OUR RUSTIC REVELRY

A **traditional town market** is held on Rother St. in Market Pl. on the 2nd and 4th Saturdays of every month. On Sundays from June to August, a **craft market** takes place along the river. (☎267 000. Both open 9am-5pm.) Stratford's biggest festival begins on the weekend nearest April 23, **Shakespeare's birthday.** The modern, well-respected **Shakespeare Birthplace Trust,** Henley St., hosts a **Poetry Festival** every Sunday evening in July and August. Past participants include Seamus Heaney, Ted Hughes, and Derek Walcott. (☎292 176. Tickets £7-10.)

WINCHESTER ☎01962

This ancient capital of medieval England is now a modern hot spot best known for its massive cathedral. Home to Jane Austen and John Keats, Winchester was the center of the kingdoms of both Alfred the Great and William the Conqueror. During the Great Plague of 1665, the town was also a place of escape for Charles II. Winchester's royal history continues to draw visitors during its floral summer.

TRANSPORTATION

Trains: From **London Waterloo** (1hr., 3-4 per hr., £22).

Buses: National Express (☎08705 808 080) runs from **Victoria Station** (2hr., 12 per day, £13).

Taxis: Francis Taxis (☎884 343), by the market. **WinTaxi** (☎866 208) and **Wessex Cars** (☎877 749) are also available.

ORIENTATION AND PRACTICAL INFORMATION

Winchester's main commercial axis, **High Street,** stretches from the statue of Alfred the Great at its east end to the arch of **Westgate** opposite. The city's bigger roads stem off High St., which becomes **Broadway** as you approach Alfred.

Tourist Information Centre: The Guildhall, Broadway (☎840 500; www.visitwinchester.co.uk), across from the bus station. Stocks free maps, helpful brochures, seasonal *What's On* guides, and other city guides. **Walking tours** £3, children free. Books accommodations for £3 plus 10% deposit. Open May-Sept. M-Sa 9:30am-5pm, Su 11am-3:30pm; Oct.-Apr. M-Sa 10am-4:30pm.

Banks: Major **banks** and **ATMs** cluster at the junction of Jewry St. and High St. Farther down is the **Royal Bank of Scotland,** 67-68 High St. (☎863 322). Open M-Tu and Th-F 9:15am-4:45pm, W 10am-4:45pm.

Police: North Walls (☎08450 454 545), near the intersection with Middle Brook St.

Hospital: Royal Hampshire County, Romsey Rd. (☎863 535), at St. James Ln.

Pharmacy: Boots, 35-39 High St. (☎852 2020). Open M-Sa 8:30am-6pm, Su 10:30am-4:30pm.

Internet Access: Winchester Library, Jewry St. (☎853 909). Open M-Tu and F 9:30am-7pm, W-Th and Sa 9:30am-5pm.

Post Office: Middlebrook St. Open M and W-Sa 9am-5:30pm, Tu 9:30am-5:30pm. **Postal Code:** SO23 8UT.

ACCOMMODATIONS AND CAMPING

B&Bs are the best option in Winchester but are difficult to find and book. For last-minute bookings, the TIC is your best bet. Buses #29 and 47 (2 per hr.) make the journey from the town center to the corner of **Ranelagh Road** and **Christchurch Road,** where many B&Bs are located.

Mrs. P. Patton, 12 Christchurch Rd. (☎854 272), down the road from the train station. Elegant Victorian mansion on beautifully landscaped property. Homemade bread and preserves with breakfast. Singles £35-40; doubles £45-50. Cash only. ❸

29 Christchurch Rd., 29 Christchurch Rd. (☎868 661), 10min. from the city center. Well-kept rooms with TV and soft beds. 2 blocks from Mrs. P. Patton. Singles from £35; doubles from £65. Cash only. ❸

RJ and VJ Weller, 63 Upper Brook St. (☎416 560). Victorian cottage in the city center with big rooms and large English breakfast. Singles £30; doubles £55. Cash only. ❸

Morn Hill Caravan Club Site, Morn Hill (☎869 877), 3 mi. east of Winchester off A31, toward New Forest. Mainly for RVs. Limited facilities for campers. Open Mar.-Oct. RVs £8.50-20.60. Tents (at warden's discretion) £3-6 plus £3-4 per adult, £1-2 per child; call ahead. Cash only. ❶

FOOD AND PUBS

High Street and **Saint George's Street** are crowded with markets, fast-food chains, and tea houses. Restaurants serve more substantial fare on **Jewry Street,** where you'll find Winchester Health Food Centre, 41 Jewry St. (☎851 113. Open M-F 9:30am-5:45pm, Sa 9am-5:30pm.) For **groceries,** head to Sainsbury's, on Middle Brook St. off High St. (☎861 792. Open M-Sa 7am-8pm, Su 11am-5pm.) For a fresher option, try the **open-air market** (open W-Sa 8am-6pm) and **farmers' market**—the largest in the UK with everything from ostrich meat to locally grown water-cress (2nd and last Su of every month; open early morning until 3pm).

The Bishop on the Bridge, 1 High St. (☎855 111), on the river. Enjoy a leisurely meal on the heated terrace or lounge inside on leather chairs. Students flock here and stay late. Most entrees £7-9. Open M-Th noon-11pm, F-Sa noon-midnight, Su noon-10:30pm. Kitchen open M-Sa noon-9pm, Su noon-8pm. MC/V. ❷

The Eclipse Inn, The Square (☎865 676). Winchester's smallest pub is also one of its most popular. The 16th-century rectory has decent food (£3-7) that attracts regulars and, according to legend, ghosts. Open M-Sa 11am-11pm, Su noon-11pm. Kitchen open daily noon-3pm. MC/V. ❶

Wykeham Arms, 175 Kingsgate St. (☎854 411). A Winchester institution, this pub draws a large crowd day and night. Sit in an old school desk and check the blackboard for daily specials. Try the Wyke cottage pie (£6) or bangers at the bar for 40p each. Open M-Sa 11am-11pm, Su noon-10:30pm. MC/V. ❷

Royal Oak, Royal Oak Passage (☎842 701). Yet another pub that claims to be the kingdom's oldest, tracing its origins back to 1390. Squeeze into the alley by God Begot House and descend underground to enjoy the locally brewed cask ale (£2.35) and pub food (£4-7). Open daily 11am-11pm. Kitchen open daily 11am-9pm. MC/V. ❶

The Exchange, 9 Southgate St. (☎854 718). Sports pub with a variety of burgers (the "gourmet" has goat cheese and red onion jam), sandwiches, and jacket potatoes (all £2-5). Tables fill quickly with students and locals, but the multi-level beer garden provides additional space. Open M-Sa 11am-11pm, Su noon-10:30pm. MC/V. ❷

ⓖ SIGHTS

WINCHESTER CATHEDRAL. Winchester and Canterbury, housing the respective shrines of St. Swithun and St. Thomas à Becket, were the two spiritual capitals of medieval England. Winchester Cathedral's placement atop peat bogs has forced several reconstructions, rendering the modern structure a stylistic hybrid. The Norman transept, crypt, and tower are juxtaposed with the Gothic nave (the longest medieval nave in Europe at 556 ft.), while the oddly Cubist stained glass offsets the older architecture. Jane Austen is entombed beneath a humble stone slab in the northern aisle in the company of several English kings. *(5 The Close. ☎857 200; www.winchester-cathedral.org.uk. Free 1hr. tours depart from the west end of the nave daily 10am-3pm on the hr. 1¼hr. tower tours also available W 2:15pm, Sa 11:30am and 2:15pm; £3. Open M-Sa 8:30am-6pm, Su 8:30am-5:30pm. East End closes at 5pm. £4, concessions £3.50, students £2. Photography permit £2.)* At the south transept, the illuminated 12th-century Winchester Bible resides in the **Library,** and the **Triforium Gallery** contains several relics, including a Saxon bowl said to have held King Canute's heart. *(Open in summer M 2-4:30pm, Tu-F 11am-4:30pm, Sa 10:30am-4:30pm; in winter W and Sa 11am-3:30pm. £1.)* Outside, to the south of the cathedral, tiny **St. Swithun's Chapel** sits above **Kingsgate.** *(Free.)*

GREAT HALL. William the Conquerer built Winchester Castle in 1067, but unyielding forces (time and Cromwell) have all but destroyed the fortress. The Great Hall remains, a gloriously intact medieval structure containing an imitation (or, according to locals, legendary) Arthurian Round Table. Henry VIII tried to pass the table off as authentic to Holy Roman Emperor Charles V, but the repainted "Arthur," resembling Henry himself, fooled no one. *(At the end of High St. atop Castle Hill. Open daily Mar.-Oct. 10am-5pm, Nov.-Feb. 10am-4pm. Free.)*

MILITARY MUSEUMS. From the Great Hall, cut through Queen Eleanor's Garden to the Peninsula Barracks. Five military museums (the **Royal Hampshire Regiment Museum,** the **Light Infantry Museum,** the **Royal Greenjackets Museum,** the **Royal Hussars Museum,** and the **Gurkha Museum**) celebrate the city's military might. The Royal Greenjackets Museum is the best of the bunch. The highlight is a 276 sq. ft. diorama of the Battle of Waterloo containing 21,500 tiny soldiers and 9600 tiny steeds. Arrive at noon at the **Royal Armouries,** near Fort Nelson, for the firing of the guns. *(Between St. James Terr. and Southgate St. ☎828 549. Open M-Sa 10am-1pm and 2-5pm, Su noon-4pm. Hours for the other 4 museums are similar. Royal Greenjackets admission £2, families £6, concessions £1. Gurkha admission £1.50, concessions 75p. All others free.)*

CITY MUSEUM. The city's history is displayed through archaeological finds, photographs, and interactive exhibits. The Roman gallery includes a complete floor mosaic from the local ruins of a Roman villa, and the Anglo-Saxon room holds a 10th-century tomb. *(At Great Minster St. and The Square. ☎848 269. Open Apr.-Oct. M-Sa 10am-5pm, Su noon-5pm; Nov.-Mar. Tu-Sa 10am-4pm, Su noon-4pm. Free. Audio tours £2.)*

WOLVESEY CASTLE. Some may find the walk along the River Itchen to Wolvesey Castle, a previous home to the Norman bishop, more enjoyable than the site itself. Only the walls of the once magnificent castle remain. Check out the mansion next door, where the current bishop resides. *(The Close. Walk down The Weir on the river or to the end of College St. ☎252 000. Open daily Apr.-Sept. 9am-5pm. Free.)*

WALKS. At 12 High St., **the Buttercross** is a good starting point for several walking routes through town. This statue, portraying St. John, William of Wykeham, and King Alfred, derives its name from the shadow it cast over the 15th-century market, keeping the butter cool. A beautiful walk runs along the **River Itchen,** the same route taken by poet John Keats; directions and his "Ode To Autumn" are available at the TIC (50p). For a panoramic view of the city, including the Wolvesey ruins, climb to **Saint Giles's Hill Viewpoint** at sunset. Pass the mill and take Bridge St. to the gate marked Magdalen Hill; follow the path from there. *The Winchester Walk*, detailing various walking tours of Winchester, is available at the TIC.

🎵 🌺 ENTERTAINMENT AND FESTIVALS

Weekends attract revelers to bars along **Broadway** and **High Street.** The **Theatre Royal,** Jewry St., hosts regional companies and concerts. (☎840 440; www.theatre-royal-winchester.co.uk. Box office open M-F 10am-6pm, Sa 10am-5pm.) The **Homelands Music Festival** takes place the last weekend of May. (Buy tickets from the TIC.) In early July, the **Hat Fair** (☎849 841; www.hatfair.co.uk), the longest-running street theatre festival in Britain, fills a weekend with free theatre and unusually outgoing bald people.

WINDSOR AND ETON ☎01753

The town of Windsor and the attached village of Eton center entirely on Windsor Castle and Eton College, two famed symbols of the British upper crust. Windsor is thick with specialty shops, tea houses, and pubs, but not budget accommodations—leave enough time to return to the city for the evening.

▐ TRANSPORTATION

Trains depart from **London Paddington** to Windsor and Eton Central and Windsor and Eton Riverside (45min., 2 per hr., round-trip £9.30). Trains also travel from **London Waterloo** to Windsor and Eton Riverside (40min., 4 per hr., round-trip £8). **Green Line bus** #702 departs from **London Victoria** (1¼hr., every hr., round-trip £5-10). Bus #77 departs from **London Heathrow** (45min., every hr., round-trip 4.20).

✳ 🛈 ORIENTATION AND PRACTICAL INFORMATION

Windsor village slopes from the foot of the castle. **High Street** spans the hilltop, then becomes **Thames Street** at the statue of Queen Victoria and continues to the river, at which point it reverts to High St. as it enters Eton. The main shopping area, **Peascod Street,** meets High St. at the statue. The **Tourist Information Centre,** Old Booking Hall, Windsor Royal Shopping Center, has free brochures, great maps, and an accommodations guide. (☎743 900; www.windsor.gov.uk. Open Apr.-June daily 10am-5pm; July-Aug. M-Sa 10am-5:30pm, Su 10am-5pm; Sept.-Mar. M-Sa 10am-5pm, Su 10am-4pm.) Other services include: **police,** on the corner of St. Mark's Rd. and Alma Rd. (☎08458 505 505; M-Sa 8am-10pm, Su 9am-5pm); **Internet** access at the **library** on Bachelors Acre (☎743 940; free 30min. guest pass; open M and Th 9:30am-5pm, Tu 9:30am-8pm, W 2-5pm, F 9:30am-7pm, Sa 9:30am-3pm) or **McDonald's,** 13-14 Thames St. (£2 per hr.; open daily 6:30am-10pm); **banks** with **ATMs** along Peascod St.; **Boots pharmacy,** 113 Peasod St. (☎863 595; open M-Sa 8:20am-6pm, Su 10:30am-4:30pm); and the **post office,** 38-39 Peascod St. (open M and W-F 9:30am-5:30pm, Tu 9:30am-5:30pm, Sa 9am-4pm). **Postal Code:** SL4 1LH.

TOP TEN LIST

ETON-SPEAK

The elite prep school Eton College has educated philosophers, princes, and prime ministers. Eton has a vernacular to describe the school's many ranks, quirks, and rituals. Common words (with example sentences) include:

1. Stick-ups: collars worn with the school's black morning suit. "Tom's had a pink **stick-up** because he washed a red sock with his white laundry."

2. Beak: a schoolmaster. "Barnaby passed a note to Allister while the **beak** wasn't looking."

3. Absence: roll call. "Jacob ran into the classroom just on time for **absence.**"

4. Wet bob: a boy who rows crew in summer. "David, a **wet bob,** suffered from bad tan lines."

5. Dry bob: a boy who plays cricket in summer. "Daniel, a **dry bob,** suffered from shin splints."

6. Half: a school term. "At Eton, three **halves** make a year."

7. Tap: the school's bar. "Jeremy counted down the days until his birthday celebration at the **tap.**"

8. Division: a class, or grade. "Tipsy Tim spent too much time at the tap and failed sixth **division.**"

9. The Block: a stool where students were flogged. "Michael, and his buttocks, quivered as he passed **The Block.**"

10. Pop, popper: one of the 25 self-elected student prefects. "Peter Piper picked a peck of pickled **poppers.**"

◎ SIGHTS

WINDSOR CASTLE

☎ *831 118. Open daily Mar.-Oct. 9:45am-5:15pm; Nov.-Feb. 9:45am-4:15pm. Last admission 1¼hr. before close. £13.50, students £12, under 17 £7.50. Tours free.*

The largest and oldest continuously inhabited castle in the world, Windsor features some of the most sumptuous rooms in Europe and some of the rarest artwork in the Western tradition. Windsor Castle was built high above the Thames by William the Conqueror as a fortress rather than as a residence, and 40 reigning monarchs have since left their marks. In 1992, a fire devastated over 100 rooms, including nine state rooms, but a massive project has restored the apartments to their original glory. Windsor is the official residence of the Queen, who spends the month of April and many of her private weekends here. During royal stays, large areas of the castle are unavailable to visitors. The admission prices are lowered on these occasions, but it is wise to call ahead or check out the flagpole—when the Queen is in residence, the castle flies the light blue flag of the monarchy. Visitors can watch the **Changing of the Guard** in front of the Guard Room at 11am (Apr.-July M-Sa; Aug.-Mar. alternate days M-Sa). The Guards can also be seen at 10:50 and 11:30am as they march to and from the ceremony.

UPPER WARD. You can reach the upper ward through the Norman tower and gate. The line on the far left enters ▨**Queen Mary's Doll House,** a replica of a grand home on a 1:12 scale, with tiny, handwritten classics in its library, miniature crown jewels, and functional plumbing and electrical systems. Velvet ropes lead to the opulent **state apartments,** used for ceremonial events and official entertainment for world leaders and heads of state. The rooms are ornamented with art from the prodigious **Royal Collection,** including works by Holbein, Reubens, Rembrandt, van Dyck, and Queen Victoria herself. The **Queen's Drawing Room** features portraits of Henry VIII, Elizabeth I, and Mary I, but don't miss smaller embellishments, like the silver dragon doorknobs. The fully restored **Lantern Room,** the **Grand Reception Room,** and **St. George's Hall** are stunning.

MIDDLE AND LOWER WARD. The **Round Tower** dominates the middle ward. A stroll downhill to the lower ward brings you to **St. George's Chapel,** a 15th-century structure with delicate vaulting and a wall of stained glass dedicated to the Order of the Garter, England's most elite knighthood. Used for the marriage of Sophie and Prince Edward in 1999, the chapel also holds the tombs of the Queen Mother, George III, and Queen Mary. Ask a guide to explain how the bones of Charles I and Henry VIII were accidentally placed under the same stone.

OTHER SIGHTS

ETON COLLEGE. Eton College is best known as one of England's most elite public—which is to say, private—schools. Ironically, it was founded by Henry VI in 1440 as a college for paupers. Despite its current position at the apex of the British class system, Eton has shaped some notable dissident thinkers, including Aldous Huxley, George Orwell, and former Liberal Party leader Jeremy Thorpe. The male students still stay true to many of the old traditions, including wearing tailcoats to class. The 25 houses that surround the quad act as residences for the approximately 1250 students. The **Museum of Eton Life** displays relics and stories of the school's extensive past. *(A 10-15min. walk down Thames St., across Windsor Bridge, and along Eton High St. ☎ 671 177. Open daily from late Mar. to mid-Apr. and July-Aug. 10:30am-4:30pm; Sept.-June 2-4:30pm; schedule depends on academic calendar. Tours daily 2:15 and 3:15pm. £4, under 16 and seniors £3.25. Tours £5, under 16 £4.20.)*

LEGOLAND WINDSOR. A whimsical addition to the town, this imaginative amusement park boasts an impressive 50 rides, playgrounds, and circuses. Its Miniland took 100 workers, three years, and 25 million Lego bricks to craft. The replica of the City of London includes a 6 ft. tall St. Paul's Cathedral and dozens of other city landmarks. *(Tickets available at the Windsor TIC. ☎ 08705 040 404; www.legoland.co.uk. Open daily Apr.-June and Sept.-Oct. 10am-5pm or 6pm; from mid-July to Aug. 10am-7pm. £30, children and seniors £23. Shuttle from town center £3, children £1.50.)*

DAYTRIPS

APPENDIX

CLIMATE

Although considered one of the dreariest cities in the world, London's weather can actually be quite pleasant. In the city's temperate climate, summers are warm, but seldom hot; winters are cool, but seldom bitter or severe. The highest temperature ever recorded was 38.1°C (100.6°F); the lowest was -10°C (14°F). Snow does not fall often, but rain does; definitely keep an umbrella handy.

Month	Low Temperature		High Temperature		Avg. Rainfall
	°C	°F	°C	°F	mm
Dec.–Feb.	2	36	8	46	49
Mar.–May	4	39	17	63	49
June–Aug.	12	53	22	72	48
Sept.–Nov.	5	41	19	66	56

MEASUREMENTS

London uses the metric system. The basic unit of length is the **meter (m),** which is divided into 100 **centimeters (cm),** or 1000 **millimeters (mm).** One thousand meters make up one **kilometer (km).** Fluids are measured in **liters (L),** each divided into 1000 **milliliters (ml).** A liter of pure water weighs one **kilogram (kg),** divided into 1000 **grams (g),** while 1000kg make up one metric **ton.** Pub aficionados will note that an Imperial pint (20 oz.) is larger than its US counterpart (16 oz.).

MEASUREMENT CONVERSIONS	MEASUREMENT CONVERSIONS
1 in. = 25.4mm	1mm = 0.039 in.
1 ft. = 0.30m	1m = 3.28 ft.
1 yd. = 0.914m	1m = 1.09 yd.
1 mi. = 1.609km	1km = 0.62 mi.
1 oz. = 28.35g	1g = 0.035 oz.
1 lb. = 0.454kg	1kg = 2.205 lbs.
1 fl. oz. = 29.57ml	1ml = 0.034 fl. oz.
1 gal. = 3.785L	1L = 0.264 gal.

LANGUAGE

PHRASEBOOK

American English may derive from British English, but there are many British words that may seem completely foreign to a US citizen. Also, some American phrases will certainly get you into trouble in the UK. If your host dad says, "Hey, go knock up my daughter," they aren't looking for a grandchild—they just want you to wake her up.

BRITISH ENGLISH	AMERICAN ENGLISH	BRITISH ENGLISH	AMERICAN ENGLISH
bathroom	room with bathtub	fag	cigarette
bank holiday	public holiday	fanny	vagina
barmy	insane, erratic	first floor	second floor
bed-sit or bed-sitter	studio apartment	flat	apartment
beer mat	coaster	fortnight	two weeks
bird	girl	full stop	period (punctuation)
biro	ballpoint pen	geezer	adult male
bit of all right	attractive (for females)	gob	mouth
bloke	guy	grotty	grungy
bobby	police officer	give a bollocking to	shout at
bonkers	crazy	hi-fi	stereo system
bonnet	car hood	handbag	purse
boot	car trunk	hash	pound sign
braces	suspenders	high street	main street
brilliant	great	hire	rental, to rent
brolly	umbrella	holiday	vacation
bum bag	fanny pack	hoover	vacuum cleaner
busker	street musician	interval	intermission
caravan	trailer, mobile home	in a street	on a street
car park	parking lot	jumper	sweater
cheeky	mischievous	kip	sleep
cheers, cheerio	thank you, goodbye	kit	sports team uniform
chemist/chemist's	pharmacist/pharmacy	knackered	tired, worn out (usually from sex)
chuffed	pleased	lavatory, "lav"	restroom
cinema	movie theatre	lay-by	roadside turnout
coach	intercity bus	legless	intoxicated
concession	discount on admission	to let	to rent (property)
dear	expensive	lift	elevator
dicey, dodgy	sketchy	loo	restroom
dim	unintelligent	lorry	truck
the dog's bollocks	the best	mac (macintosh)	raincoat
dual carriageway	divided highway	mad	crazy
dustbin	trash can	mate	pal
ensuite	with attached bathroom	mingin'	gross
motorway	highway	single ticket	one-way ticket
mobile	cell phone	single carriageway	non-divided highway
naff	cheap, in poor taste	sod it	forget it
nappy	diaper	snogging	making out
nutter	crazy person	suspenders	garters
pants	underwear	subway	underpass
petrol	gasoline	ta	thanks
phone box, call box	telephone booth	takeaway	takeout
piss off	screw you	ta-ta	goodbye
take the piss	make fun	thick	stupid
pissed	drunk	tights	pantyhose
plaster	Band-Aid	torch	flashlight

BRITISH ENGLISH	AMERICAN ENGLISH	BRITISH ENGLISH	AMERICAN ENGLISH
pram	unpleasant person	Tory	Conservative Party
prat	stupid person	trainers	sneakers
pull	to seduce	trousers	pants
public school	private school	trunk call	long-distance call
punter	average person	vest	undershirt
purse	change purse	waistcoat	men's vest
queue	line	wanker	masturbator; see prat
quay	river bank	way out	exit
quid	pound (in money)	W.C. (water closet)	toilet, restroom
return ticket	round-trip ticket	wicked	cool
roundabout	rotary road intersection	yob	delinquent
rubber	eraser	"zed"	the letter Z
self-catering	with kitchen facilities	zip	zipper
a shag, to shag	sex, to have sex		

BRITISH PRONUNCIATION

All right, cowboy. So your decidedly foreign accent is drawing stares from that group of Manchester United fans with surly demeanors and slightly crooked teeth. Not to worry! Here are some common pronunciations that will make you, too, a bona-fide Londoner.

Berkeley	BAHK-lee	gaol	jail
Berkshire	BAHK-sher	Islington	IHZ-ling-tun
Birmingham	BERM-ing-um	Leicester	LES-ter
Cholmondely	CHUM-lee	Marylebone	MAR-lee-bun
Derby	DAR-bee	Magdalen	MAUD-lin
Dulwich	DULL-ich	quay	key
Edinburgh	ED-in-bur-ra	Norwich	NOR-ich
Featherstonehaw	FAN-shaw	Salisbury	SAULS-bree
Gloucester	GLOS-ter	Southwark	SUTH-uk
Greenwich	GREN-ich	Thames	tems
Grosvenor	GRO-vna	Worcester	WOO-ster

MAP APPENDIX

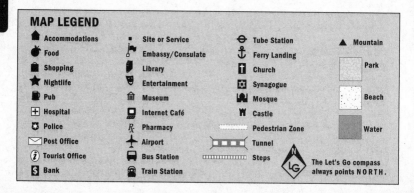

MAP LEGEND

Accommodations	Site or Service	Tube Station	Mountain
Food	Embassy/Consulate	Ferry Landing	
Shopping	Library	Church	Park
Nightlife	Entertainment	Synagogue	
Pub	Museum	Mosque	Beach
Hospital	Internet Café	Castle	
Police	Pharmacy	Pedestrian Zone	Water
Post Office	Airport	Tunnel	
Tourist Office	Bus Station	Steps	The Let's Go compass
Bank	Train Station		always points NORTH.

The City of London

🍎 **FOOD**

Café Spice Namaste, **1**	D4
Futures, **2**	C5
Leadenhall Market, **3**	C4
The Place Below, **4**	B4
Spianata & Co., **5**	B4

🔴 **SIGHTS**

All Hallows-By-The-Tower, **6**	D5
Bank of England, **7**	C4
Guildhall, **8**	B3
Lloyd's of London, **9**	D4
Monument, **10**	C4

St. Dunstan-in-the-East, **11**	D5
St. Margaret Lothbury, **12**	C3
St. Mary-le-Bow, **13**	B4
St. Mary Woolnoth, **14**	C4
St. Paul's Cathedral, **15**	A4
St. Stephen Walbrook, **16**	C4
Tower Bridge, **17**	D5
Tower of London, **18**	D5

🏛 **MUSEUMS**

Barbican Art Gallery, **19**	B2
The Clockmaker's Museum and Guildhall Library, **20**	B3

Bank of England Museum, **21**	C4
Guildhall Art Gallery, **22**	B3
Museum of London, **23**	B3

🎭 **ENTERTAINMENT**

Barbican Centre, **24**	B2

🍺 **PUBS**

The Black Friar, **25**	A4
Simpson's, **26**	C4
The Walrus and the Carpenter, **27**	C5

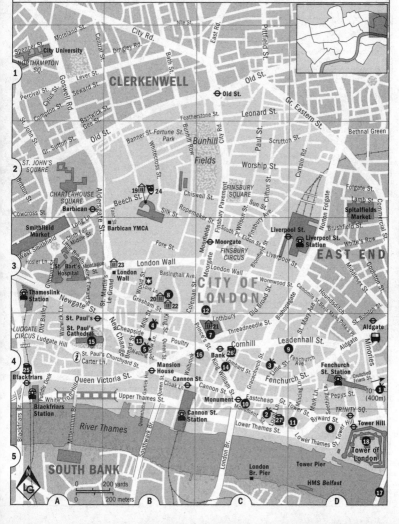

APPENDIX

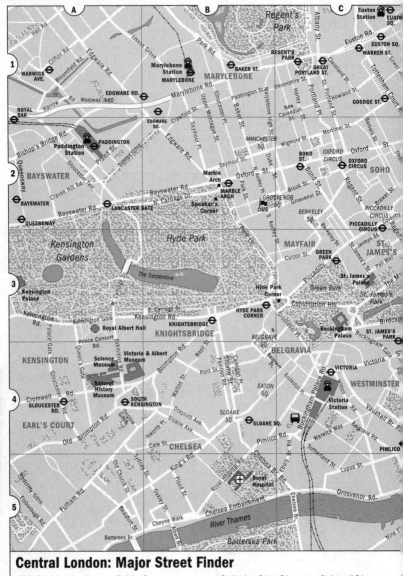

Central London: Major Street Finder

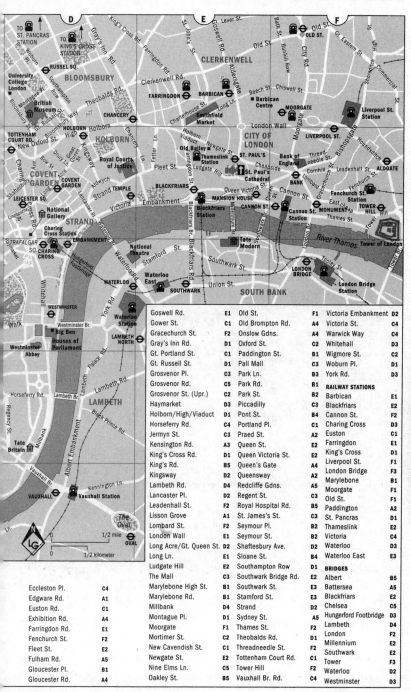

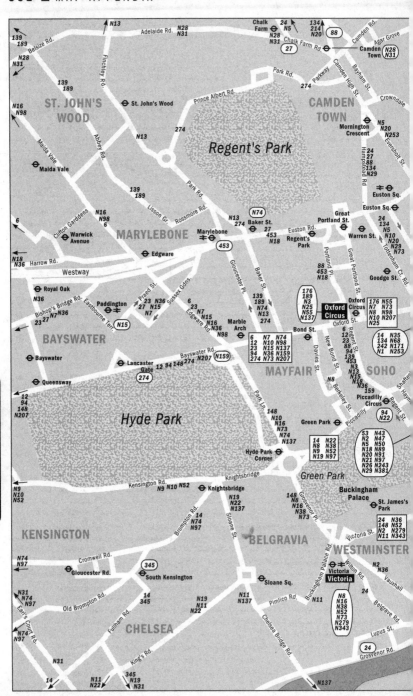

Night Buses

N76 Bus Route
⊖ Underground
⇌ National Rail

| 12 / 94 | Multiple Routes |
| (274) | Route Terminus |

ISLINGTON

KING'S CROSS

BLOOMSBURY

CLERKENWELL

HOLBORN

CITY OF LONDON

SOUTH BANK

LAMBETH

274 N10 274 N91 N19 N43 N91

N279 214

N63 King's Cross

St. Pancras

Angel

271 N76

149 242 N243

Pentonville Rd. 214 N73

City Rd. 214

274

Goswell Rd.

N26 N55

Rosebury Ave. 341 N19 N38 N43

N63

N35 N55 N243

Hackney Rd.

N8

Russell Square

N7

N91

N35 N55 Old St. Old Street

N243

Bethnal

149 242 N8 N26 N35

Clerkenwell Rd.

N63

Farringdon

214 271 N76

23 214 271 N11 N133

N19 N43 N35 N55 N38 N243

N98 N207

341

High Holborn

242 N8 N25

Barbican

London Wall

Moorgate Moorgate Liverpool Liverpool St.

Holborn Chancery Lane

Holborn Viaduct

N76 N133

Old Broad St.

N15 N25 N50 N106 N253

242 N43 N1 N55 N8 N68 N19 N91 N25 N98 N35 N171 N38 N207

Tottenham Court Rd.

New Oxford St.

N1 N68 N171 N243

Bishopsgate

Aldgate

N106 N253

23 N26 341 N47 N11 N76 N15 N89 N21

St. Paul's

242 N8

Bank

Ludgate Hill

Leadenhall St.

N25 N50

Minories

Covent Garden

23 N26 341 N47 N11 N76 N15 N89 N21

Fleet Street

Blackfriars

Queen Victoria St.

Victoria St.

N50

149 N35

Tower Hill Tower N15 Hill

6 N13 N77 N5 N15 N89 139 N21 N91 179 N26 N155 N9 N44 N243 N11 N47 N343

N13 N77 N15 N89 N21 N91 N26 N155 N44 N243 N47 N343

Aldwych Temple N50

6 N9 N77 N13 N155

Mansion House

Cannon St. Cannon St.

Monument

Leicester Sq.

139 N68 176 N76 341 N171 N1 N343

Charing Cross

Embankment

149 N21 N35 N47 N133

London Bridge

N2 N55 N343 N381

N50

Trafalgar Sq.

Stamford St. N343 N381

N381 N343 Southwark St.

149

Tooley St. N47

Trafalgar Square

12 N44 24 N52 53 N77 88 N155 453 N159 N2 N279 N3 N343 N11 N381 N36

Embankment

139

Waterloo

SOUTH BANK

Southwark

London Bridge (149)

St. Thomas St.

N21 N35 N133 N343

N47 N381

Westminster

341 N76 N381

176

N68 N171

N63 N89

Borough

12 N44 53 N155 148 N159 453 N381

76 Lambeth North

Westminster Bridge Rd.

Lambeth Bridge Rd.

N35 N133 N343

Great Dover St.

N21

N1

N159

Grange Rd.

88

N3 N77

N44

Lambeth Rd.

Lambeth Palace Rd.

12 53 148 453 N155

St. George's Rd.

London Rd.

53 453 N1 N63 New Kent Rd.

Elephant and Castle

N1

N3

Millbank

Marsham St.

N44

Kennington Rd.

Rodney Rd.

Old Kent Rd.

Pimlico

88 N2

N36 N77

Vauxhall

Kennington Park Rd.

Kennington

N133 N155

Walworth Rd.

N343

Thurlow St.

53 453 N21 N63

LAMBETH

N3 N159

Bridge Rd.

Kennington Lane

Albany Rd.

12 148 176 N35 N68 N89

N44 88 N2 N36

N77

Harleyford Rd.

N3 N133 N155 N159

N343

Wandsworth Rd.

0 — 1 kilometer
0 — 1000 yards

APPENDIX

APPENDIX

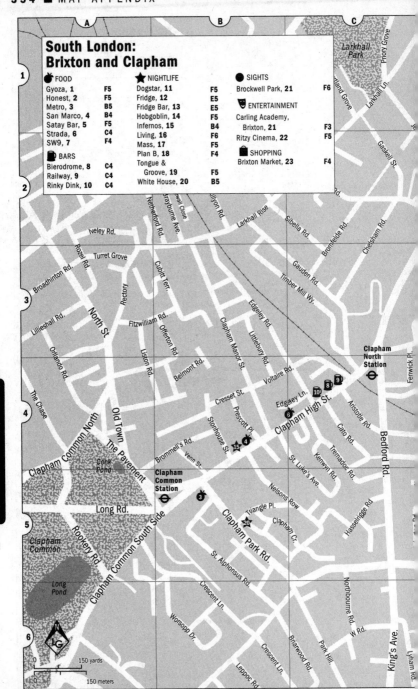

**South London:
Brixton and Clapham**

🍴 **FOOD**

Gyoza, 1	F5
Honest, 2	F5
Metro, 3	B5
San Marco, 4	B4
Satay Bar, 5	F5
Strada, 6	C4
SW9, 7	F4

🍸 **BARS**

Bierodrome, 8	C4
Railway, 9	C4
Rinky Dink, 10	C4

⭐ **NIGHTLIFE**

Dogstar, 11	F5
Fridge, 12	E5
Fridge Bar, 13	E5
Hobgoblin, 14	F5
Infernos, 15	B4
Living, 16	F6
Mass, 17	F5
Plan B, 18	F4
Tongue & Groove, 19	F5
White House, 20	B5

● **SIGHTS**

Brockwell Park, 21	F6

🎭 **ENTERTAINMENT**

Carling Academy, Brixton, 21	F3
Ritzy Cinema, 22	F5

🛍 **SHOPPING**

Brixton Market, 23	F4

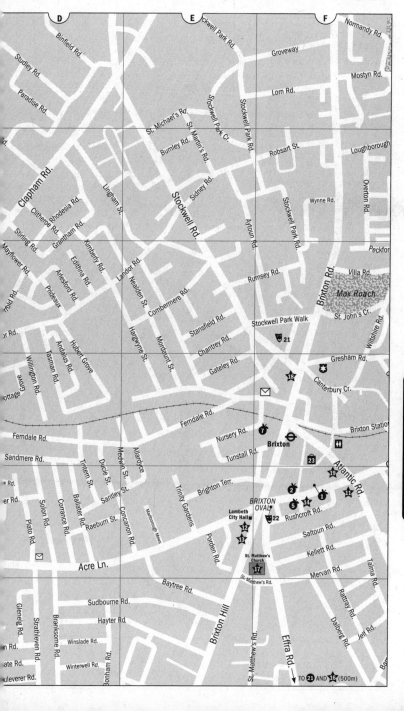

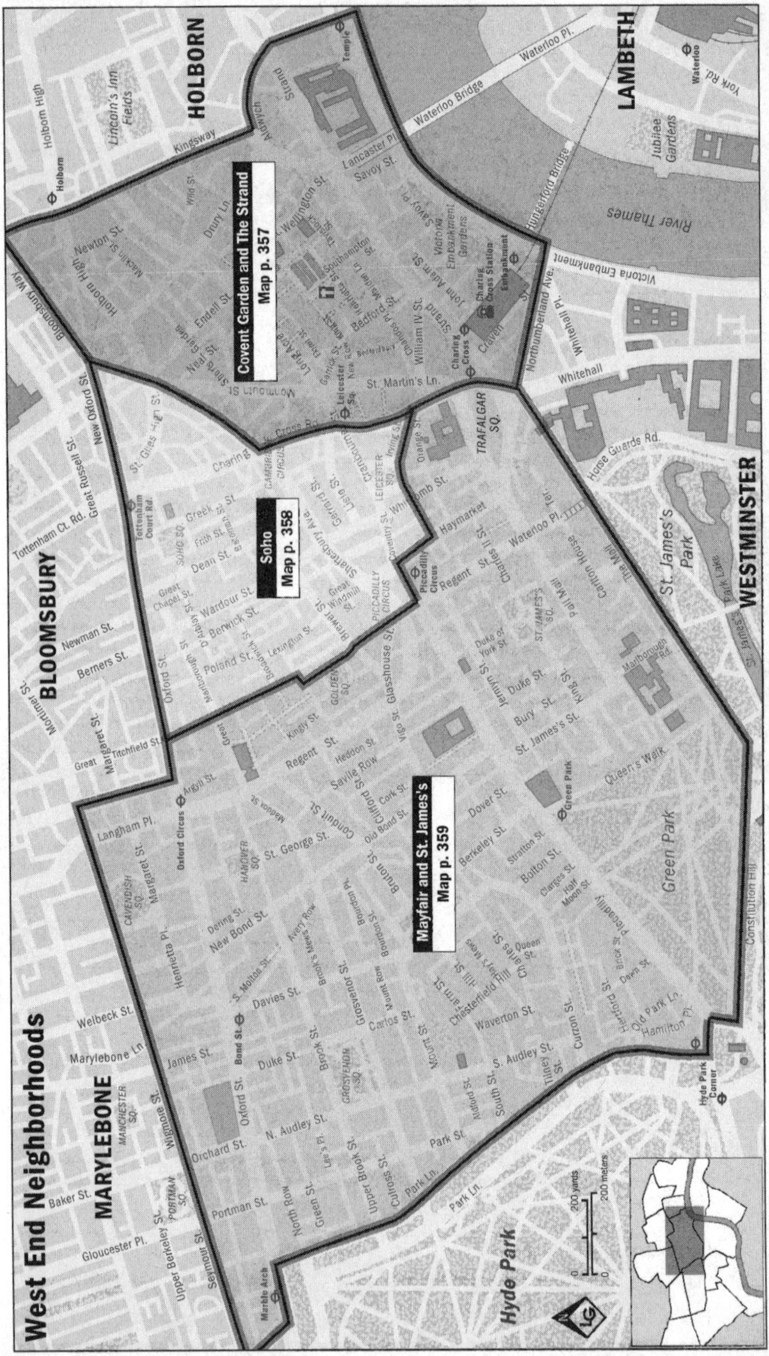

West End Neighborhoods

HOLBORN

LAMBETH

Covent Garden and The Strand
Map p. 357

Soho
Map p. 358

BLOOMSBURY

MARYLEBONE

Mayfair and St. James's
Map p. 359

WESTMINSTER

Hyde Park

Green Park

St. James's Park

TRAFALGAR SQ.

River Thames

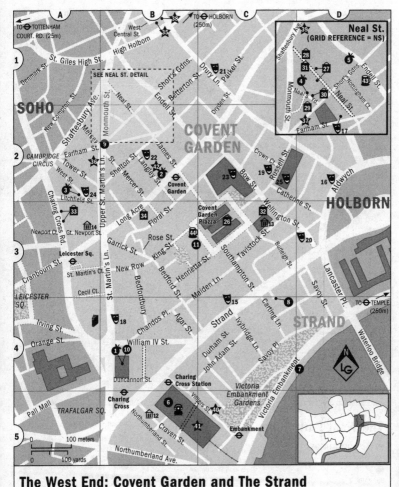

The West End: Covent Garden and The Strand
(NS = NEAL ST. DETAIL)

🍴 FOOD

Cafe in the Crypt, **1**	B4
Café Pacifico, **2**	B2
The Ivy, **3**	A2
Neal's Yard Salad Bar, **4**	NS
Rock and Sole Plaice, **5**	B1

● SIGHTS

Charing Cross, **6**	B5
Cleopatra's Needle, **7**	D4
The Savoy, **8**	C4
Seven Dials, **9**	B2
St. Martin-in-the-Fields, **10**	B4
St. Paul's, **11**	B3

🏛 MUSEUMS

Benjamin Franklin House, **12**	B5
London's Transport Museum, **13**	C3
The Photographers' Gallery, **14**	A3

🎭 ENTERTAINMENT

The Adelphi, **15**	C4
Aldwych Theatre, **16**	D2
Donmar Warehouse, **17**	NS
English National Opera, **18**	B4
Fortune Theatre, **19**	C2
Lyceum, **20**	D3
New London Theatre, **21**	C1
Pineapple Dance Studio, **22**	B2
Royal Opera House, **23**	C2
St. Martin's Theatre, **24**	A2
Theatre Royal, Drury Lane, **25**	C2

🛍 SHOPPING

Apple and Jubilee Markets, **26**	C3
Apple Tree, **27**	NS
Egoshego, **28**	NS
Neal's Yard Dairy, **29**	NS
Neal's Yard Remedies, **30**	NS

Office, **31**	NS
Penhaligon's, **32**	C3
Shipley, **33**	A3
Stanfords, **34**	B3

★ NIGHTLIFE

AKA, **35**	B1
The Box, **36**	A2
Detroit, **37**	NS
The End, **38**	B1
Freud, **39**	NS
Gordon's Wine Bar, **40**	C5
Heaven, **41**	B5
The Langley, **42**	B2

🍺 PUBS

The Cross Keys, **43**	NS
Lamb and Flag, **44**	B3

APPENDIX

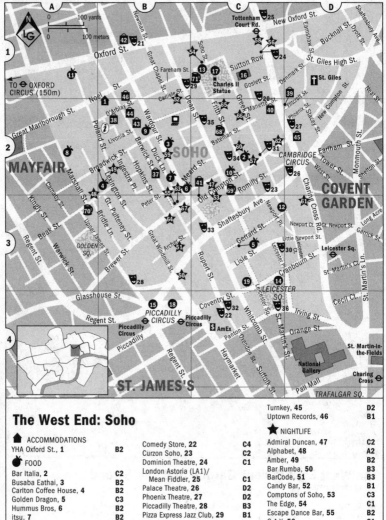

APPENDIX

The West End: Soho

🏠 **ACCOMMODATIONS**

YHA Oxford St., **1**	B2

🍴 **FOOD**

Bar Italia, **2**	C2
Busaba Eathai, **3**	B2
Carlton Coffee House, **4**	B2
Golden Dragon, **5**	C3
Hummus Bros, **6**	B2
itsu, **7**	B2
Masala Zone, **8**	A2
Mr. Jerk, **9**	B2
Patisserie Valerie, **10**	C2
Soba Noodle Bar, **11**	A1

⬤ **SIGHTS**

Chinatown, **12**	C3
French Protestant Church, **13**	C1
Leicester Square, **14**	C3
Piccadilly Circus, **15**	B4
St. Patrick's Catholic Church, **16**	C1
Soho Square, **17**	C1
Statue of Eros, **18**	B4
Swiss Centre, **19**	C3

🎭 **ENTERTAINMENT**

100 Club, **20**	C1
Borderline, **21**	B1

Comedy Store, **22**	C4
Curzon Soho, **23**	C2
Dominion Theatre, **24**	C1
London Astoria (LA1)/ Mean Fiddler, **25**	C1
Palace Theatre, **26**	D2
Phoenix Theatre, **27**	D2
Piccadilly Theatre, **28**	B3
Pizza Express Jazz Club, **29**	B1
Prince Charles Cinema, **30**	C3
Prince Edward Theatre, **31**	C2
Prince of Wales Theatre, **32**	C4
Queen's Theatre, **33**	C3
Ronnie Scott's, **34**	C2
Soho Theatre, **35**	C2
tkts, **36**	C4

🛍️ **SHOPPING**

Berkwick St. Market, **37**	B2
Black Market, **38**	B2
Blackwell's, **39**	D1
Foyles, **40**	C2
Gerry's, **41**	C2
Music Zone, **42**	B1
Revival Records, **43**	B2
Sister Ray, **44**	B2

Turnkey, **45**	D2
Uptown Records, **46**	B1

⭐ **NIGHTLIFE**

Admiral Duncan, **47**	C2
Alphabet, **48**	A2
Amber, **49**	B2
Bar Rumba, **50**	B3
BarCode, **51**	B3
Candy Bar, **52**	B1
Comptons of Soho, **53**	C3
The Edge, **54**	C1
Escape Dance Bar, **55**	B2
G-A-Y, **56**	C1
G-A-Y Bar, **57**	C2
Ghetto, **58**	C1
Floridita, **59**	B2
Karaoke Box, **60**	C2
Ku Bar, **61**	D3
Lab, **62**	C2
Madame Jojo's, **63**	B2
O Bar, **64**	B3
Profile, **65**	C2
Thirst, **66**	C2
Village Soho, **67**	B3

🍺 **PUBS**

Dog and Duck, **68**	C2
French House, **69**	C2
Old Coffee House, **70**	A3
The Toucan, **71**	C1

MARYLEBONE

SOHO

MAYFAIR

ST. JAMES'S

WESTMINSTER

Hyde Park

Green Park

The West End:
St. James's and Mayfair
SEE MAP KEY, p. 360

TO BAKER ST.
(200m)

TO HYDE
PARK CORNER
(500m)

Lawnchair
Rentals

Easy
Internet
Cafe

Speaker's
Corner

Marble Arch

Trafalgar
Sq.

Charing Cross Station

Charing
Cross

Leicester
Sq.

Piccadilly
Circus

Oxford
Circus

Green
Park

The Ritz

Admiralty
Arch

New Zealand

Horse Guards Rd.

Whitehall

Northumberland Ave.

The Mall

Marlborough Rd.

Cleveland Row

Queen's Walk

Stratton St.

Bolton St.

Clarges St.

Half Moon St.

White
Horse St.

Down St.

Curzon St.

Tinley St.

S. Audley St.

Mount St.

Adam's Row

Reeves Mew

Aldford St.

Park St.

Upper Brook St.

Curzon St.

Carlos St.

Waverton St.

Chesterfield Hill

Hill St.

Farm St.

Charles St.

Queen St.

Shepherd St.

Hertford St.

Brick St.

Berkeley
Sq.

Davies St.

Gilbert St.

Binney St.

Duke St.

Balderton St.

N. Audley St.

Lee's Pl.

Orchard St.

Welbeck St.

Marylebone Ln.

Wigmore St.

Oxford St.

Henrietta Pl.

Cavendish
Sq.

Margaret St.

Holles St.

Dering St.

New Bond St.

St. Christopher's Pl.

James St.

Hanover
Sq.

Grosvenor
Sq.

US

Canada

Bourdon Pl.

Brook's Mews

Avery Row

Maddox St.

Regent St.

Conduit St.

St. George St.

St. George's St.

Savile Row

Old Bond St.

Albemarle St.

Dover St.

Berkeley St.

Cork St.

Clifford St.

Burlington
Gdns.

Sackville St.

Glasshouse St.

Regent St.

Air St.

Vigo St.

Heddon St.

Beak St.

Bridle Ln.

Golden
Sq.

Kingly St.

Carnaby St.

Foubert's Pl.

Newburgh St.

Great
Marlborough St.

Marshall St.

Broadwick St.

Lexington St.

Poland St.

Berwick St.

Wardour St.

D'Arblay St.

Bateman St.

Dean St.

Frith St.

Greek St.

Old Compton St.

Brewer St.

Glasshouse St.

Piccadilly

Haymarket

Whitcomb St.

Coventry St.

Orange St.

St. Martin's St.

Irving St.

Charing Cross Rd.

Cranbourn St.

Lisle St.

Gerrard St.

Shaftesbury Ave.

Cambridge
Circus

Moor St.

Greek St.

Soho
Sq.

Oxford St.

Newman St.

Berners St.

Eastcastle St.

Great
Titchfield St.

Mortimer St.

Margaret St.

Little Portland St.

Langham Pl.

Gr. Castle St.

Argyll St.

Regent St.

Carburton St.

Tottenham
Court Rd.

Charing
Cross Rd.

St. Giles

St. Martin's Ln.

Monmouth St.

Earlham St.

Shelton St.

Neal St.

Long Acre

Garrick St.

New Row

Bedfordbury

Bedford St.

Chandos Pl.

William IV St.

Strand

Duncannon St.

Craven St.

John Adam St.

Covent
Garden

Endell St.

Shorts Gdns.

Cross Rd.

Floral St.

Tavistock St.

Maiden Ln.

St. Paul's
Church

Cockspur St.

Pall Mall East

Pall Mall

St. James's
Sq.

Charles II St.

Waterloo Pl.

Jermyn St.

Duke of
York St.

Prince's
Arcade

Piccadilly
Arcade

King St.

Duke St.

Bury St.

St. James's St.

Ryder St.

Portman
Sq.

Manchester
Sq.

Montagu
Sq.

Portman St.

Baker St.

George St.

Seymour St.

Bryanston St.

Upper Berkeley St.

Gloucester Pl.

Great Cumberland Pl.

North Carriage Dr.

Park Ln.

North Row

Green St.

Upper Brook St.

Brook St.

Grosvenor
Sq.

Mount Row

Culross St.

Park St.

St. Barnabas

St. Giles

MARBLE ARCH

200 meters
200 yards

N

TRAFALGAR
SQ.

The West End: Mayfair and St. James's

SEE MAP, p. 359

🍓 FOOD

Carluccio's, **1**	B1
L'Autre, **2**	C4
Mo Tearoom, **3**	D3
Prezzo, **4**	C4
Richoux, **5**	B3
Sofra, **6**	C4
Tamarind, **7**	C4

⬤ SIGHTS

Burlington Arcade, **8**	D2
Carlton House Terrace and Waterloo Place, **9**	F4
Carnaby Street, **10**	D3
Grosvenor Square, **11**	B3
Royal Arcade, **12**	D3
Royal Opera Arcade, **13**	F3
Shepherd Market, **14**	C4
Spencer House, **15**	D4
St. James's Church, Piccadilly, **16**	E3
St. James's Palace, **17**	E4
Trafalgar Square, **18**	G3

🏛 MUSEUMS

Christie's, **19**	E4
Gagosian Gallery, **20**	C2
Institute of Contemporary Art, **21**	F3
Marlborough Fine Arts, **22**	D3
National Gallery, **23**	F3
National Portrait Gallery, **24**	F4
Robert Sandelson, **25**	D3
Royal Academy of Art, **26**	D3
Sotheby's, **27**	D2

🎭 ENTERTAINMENT

Danceworks, **28**	B2
Her Majesty's Theatre, **29**	C2
London Palladium, **30**	D1
Theatre Royal Haymarket, **31**	F3

🛍 SHOPPING

Brown's Labels for Less, **32**	C2
Fortnum & Mason, **33**	E3
Hamley's, **34**	D2
Hatchard's, **35**	E3
House of Fraser, **36**	C1
John Lewis, **37**	C1
Liberty, **38**	D2
Lillywhite's, **39**	E3
Oscar Milo, **40**	C2
Paul Smith Sale Shop, **41**	C2
Sam Greenberg, **42**	E2
Selfridges, **43**	B2
Sotheran's of Sackville Street, **44**	E3

⭐ NIGHTLIFE

22 Below, **45**	D2
Absolut Ice Bar, **46**	D2
The Social, **47**	D1

🍺 PUBS

The Duke of York, **48**	C2
The Shepherds Tavern, **49**	C4

Bayswater and Notting Hill

SEE MAP, p. 361

🏨 ACCOMMODATIONS

Admiral Hotel, **1**	G2
Balmoral House Hotel, **2**	G2
Garden Court Hotel, **3**	D2
The Gate Hotel, **4**	C3
Hyde Park Hostel, **5**	E3
Kensington Gardens Hotel, **6**	D3
Portabello Gold, **7**	B3
Quest Hostel, **8**	E3

🍓 FOOD

Aphrodite Taverna, **9**	D2
Arthur Baker's Soul Food, **10**	D2
La Bottega del Gelato, **11**	D3
Durbar Tandoori, **12**	D2
George's Portobello Fish Bar, **13**	A1
The Grain Shop, **14**	B2
Hummingbird Bakery, **15**	B2
Khan's Restaurant, **16**	D2
Kitchen & Pantry, **17**	B2
Lazy Daisy Café, **18**	C3
Levantine, **19**	G2
Lisboa Patisserie, **20**	A1
Manzara, **21**	C3
The Tea and Coffee Plant, **22**	B2
Tom's Delicatessen, **23**	B2

🛍 SHOPPING

Bayswater Market, **24**	E3
Books for Cooks, **25**	B2
Dolly Diamond, **26**	C3
Hirst Antiques, **27**	C3
Honest Jon's, **28**	A1
Rough Trade, **29**	B2
Teaze, **30**	C3
The Travel Bookshop, **31**	B2

🎭 ENTERTAINMENT

Electric Cinema, **32**	B2
The Gate, **33**	C4
Gate Cinema, **34**	C4

⭐ NIGHTLIFE

Notting Hill Arts Club, **35**	C4
Visible, **36**	A1

🍺 PUBS

The Market, **37**	B2
Mau Mau, **38**	B2
Mitre, **39**	F3
Portobello Gold, **40**	B2
Prince Albert Pub, **41**	C3
The Shakespeare, **42**	B2
The Swan, **43**	F3

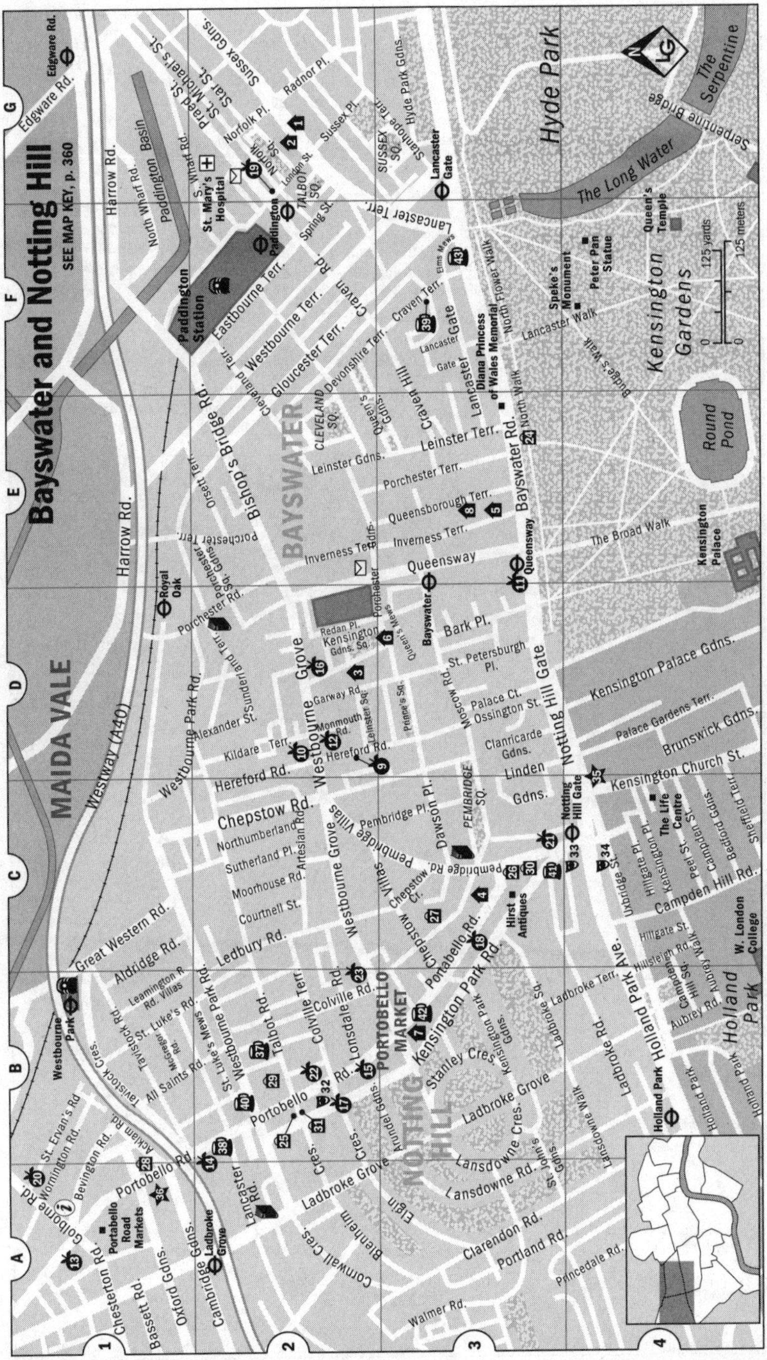

Bayswater and Notting Hill
SEE MAP KEY, p. 360
MAIDA VALE
BAYSWATER
NOTTING HILL
PORTOBELLO MARKET
Hyde Park
Kensington Gardens
Holland Park
Paddington Station
St. Mary's Hospital
Paddington Basin
The Serpentine
Serpentine Bridge
The Long Water
Round Pond
Kensington Palace
Queen's Temple
Peter Pan Statue
Speke's Monument
Diana Princess of Wales Memorial
The Life Centre
Hirst Antiques
Portabello Road Markets
W. London College
Westway (A40)
Harrow Rd.
Edgware Rd.
Praed St.
Sussex Gdns.
Bishop's Bridge Rd.
Westbourne Terr.
Gloucester Terr.
Eastbourne Terr.
Craven Rd.
Craven Hill
Lancaster Terr.
Lancaster Gate
Leinster Terr.
Leinster Gdns.
Porchester Terr.
Queensborough Terr.
Inverness Terr.
Queensway
Bayswater Rd.
The Broad Walk
Lancaster Walk
Budge's Walk
North Flower Walk
Kensington Palace Gdns.
Palace Gardens Terr.
Brunswick Gdns.
Kensington Church St.
Notting Hill Gate
Pembridge Rd.
Pembridge Villas
Pembridge Pl.
Westbourne Grove
Westbourne Park Rd.
Hereford Rd.
Chepstow Rd.
Chepstow Villas
Portobello Rd.
Kensington Park Rd.
Ladbroke Grove
Ledbury Rd.
Great Western Rd.
Talbot Rd.
Lonsdale Rd.
Colville Terr.
Elgin Cres.
Lansdowne Rd.
Lansdowne Cres.
Clarendon Rd.
Portland Rd.
Holland Park Ave.
Campden Hill Rd.
Ladbroke Rd.
Cornwall Cres.
Blenheim Cres.
Golborne Rd.
Chesterton Rd.
Oxford Gdns.
Cambridge Gdns.
Walmer Rd.
Princedale Rd.
Westbourne Park
Ladbroke Grove
Royal Oak
Bayswater
Queensway
Notting Hill Gate
Holland Park
Lancaster Gate
Paddington
Edgware Rd.
125 yards
125 meters

Bloomsbury

🏠 **ACCOMMODATIONS**

Ashlee House, **1**	D1
Astor's Museum Hostel, **2**	C3
Carr-Saunders Hall, **3**	A3
Commonwealth Hall, **4**	C2
The Generator, **5**	C2
George Hotel, **6**	C2
Jenkins Hotel, **7**	C2
The Langland Hotel, **8**	B3
Pickwick Hall International Backpackers, **9**	C3
Thanet Hotel, **10**	C3
YHA St. Pancras International, **11**	C1

🍎 **FOOD**

Diwana Bhel Poori House, **12**	B2
ICCo, **13**	B4
Navarro's Tapas Bar, **14**	B4

Newman Arms, **15**	B4
North Sea Fish Restaurant, **16**	C2
Savoir Faire, **17**	C4
Wagamama, **18**	C4

● **SIGHTS**

British Library, **19**	C1
Coram's Fields, **20**	D3
Senate House, **21**	C3
St. George's Bloomsbury, **22**	C4
St. Pancras Station, **23**	C1
University College London, **24**	B2

🏛 **MUSEUMS**

British Library Galleries, **25**	C1
British Museum, **26**	C4
Brunei Gallery, **27**	C3
Percival David Foundation of Chinese Art, **28**	C2
Pollock's Toy Museum, **29**	B3

🎭 **ENTERTAINMENT**

The Place, **30**	C2
RADA, **31**	B3
Renoir, **32**	C3
The Water Rats, **33**	D1

🛍 **SHOPPING**

Gay's the Word, **34**	C2
James Smith & Sons, **35**	C4
L. Cornelissen & Son, **36**	C4
Ulysses, **37**	C4
Oxfam Books, **38**	C4

⭐ **NIGHTLIFE**

Vats, **39**	D3

🍺 **PUBS**

Fitzroy Tavern, **40**	B4
The Jeremy Beutham, **41**	B3
The Queen's Larder, **42**	C3

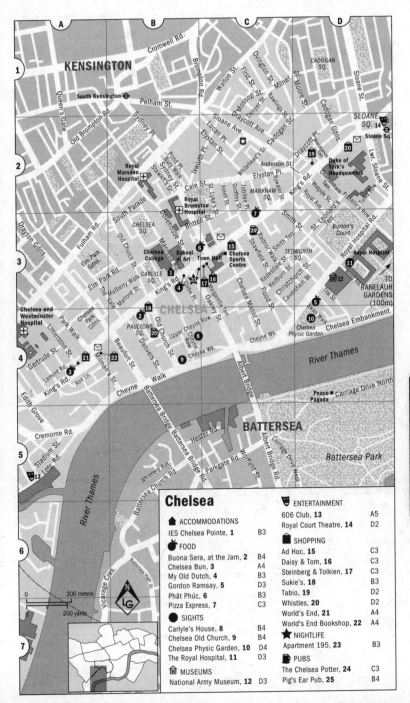

Chelsea

🏠 ACCOMMODATIONS
IES Chelsea Pointe, **1**	B3

🍴 FOOD
Buona Sera, at the Jam, **2**	B4
Chelsea Bun, **3**	A4
My Old Dutch, **4**	B3
Gordon Ramsay, **5**	D3
Phât Phúc, **6**	B3
Pizza Express, **7**	C3

● SIGHTS
Carlyle's House, **8**	B4
Chelsea Old Church, **9**	B4
Chelsea Physic Garden, **10**	D4
The Royal Hospital, **11**	D3

🏛 MUSEUMS
National Army Museum, **12**	D3

🎭 ENTERTAINMENT
606 Club, **13**	A5
Royal Court Theatre, **14**	D2

🛍 SHOPPING
Ad Hoc, **15**	C3
Daisy & Tom, **16**	C3
Steinberg & Tolkien, **17**	C3
Sukie's, **18**	B3
Tabio, **19**	D2
Whistles, **20**	D2
World's End, **21**	A4
World's End Bookshop, **22**	A4

⭐ NIGHTLIFE
Apartment 195, **23**	B3

🍺 PUBS
The Chelsea Potter, **24**	C3
Pig's Ear Pub, **25**	B4

Holborn and Clerkenwell

ACCOMMODATIONS

City University Finsbury Residences, 1	D2
Grenville House Hotel, 2	A2
Guilford House Hotel, 3	A2
Rosebery Hall, 4	C1

FOOD

3 Things Coffee Room, 5	C2
Al's Café/Bar, 6	B2
Aki, 7	B2
Anexo, 8	C2
Bleeding Heart Bistro and Restaurant, 9	C3
Bleeding Heart Tavern, 10	C3
Cafe 180, 11	B2
Carrot Cafe, 12	A2
Chutney Raj, 13	A3
Clerkenwell Kitchen, 14	C2
Curved Angel, 15	C2
The Greenery, 16	C3
Sofra, 17	B1
St. John, 18	C3
Woolley's, 19	A3

SIGHTS

The Charterhouse, 20	D3
Clerkenwell Green, 21	C2
Elm Court, 22	C2
Ely Place, 23	C3
Gray's Inn, 24	B3
Hatton Garden, 25	B3
Marx Memorial Library, 26	B5
Middle Temple, 27	B5
Old Sessions House, 28	C2
Priory of St. John, 29	C2
Royal Courts of Justice, 30	B4
St. Bartholomew The Great, 31	D3
St. Bride's Church, 32	C5
St. Clement Danes, 33	B5
St. Dunstan-in-the-West, 34	B4
St. Etheldreda's, 35	C3
St. John's Gate, 36	C2
St. John's Square, 37	C2
The Temple, 38	B5
Temple Church, 39	B5

MUSEUMS

Hunterian Museum, 40	A4
Somerset House, 41	B4
Sir John Soane's Museum, 42	A4

ENTERTAINMENT

Chuckle Club, 43	A4
Peacock Theatre, 44	A4
Sadler's Wells, 45	B1

SHOPPING

Twining's, 46	B5
Leather Lane Market, 47	B3

NIGHTLIFE

Babushka, 48	C3
Bar Polski, 49	A3
Café Kick, 50	B1
Fabric, 51	C3
Fluid, 52	D3
Match EC1, 53	C2
Na Zdrowie, 54	A4
Turnmills, 55	C2

PUBS

The Eagle, 56	B2
The Jerusalem Tavern, 57	C2
The Old Bank of England, 58	B4
The Three Kings, 59	C2
Ye Olde Cheshire Cheese, 60	C4
Ye Olde Mitre Tavern, 61	C3

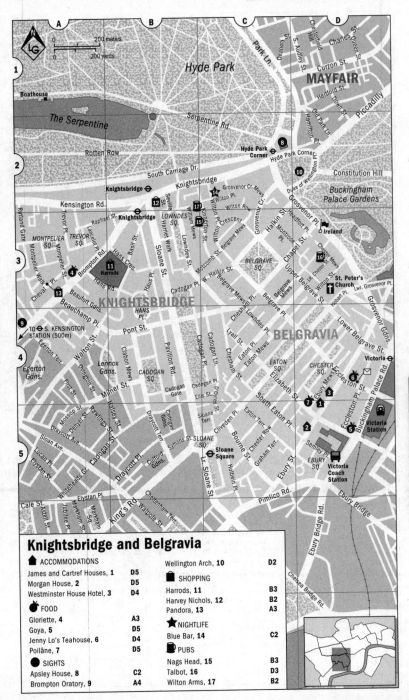

Knightsbridge and Belgravia

🏠 **ACCOMMODATIONS**

James and Cartref Houses, **1**	D5
Morgan House, **2**	D5
Westminster House Hotel, **3**	D4

🍴 **FOOD**

Gloriette, **4**	A3
Goya, **5**	D5
Jenny Lo's Teahouse, **6**	D4
Poilâne, **7**	D5

⬤ **SIGHTS**

Apsley House, **8**	C2
Brompton Oratory, **9**	A4

Wellington Arch, **10**	D2

🛍 **SHOPPING**

Harrods, **11**	B3
Harvey Nichols, **12**	B2
Pandora, **13**	A3

⭐ **NIGHTLIFE**

Blue Bar, **14**	C2

🍺 **PUBS**

Nags Head, **15**	B3
Talbot, **16**	D3
Wilton Arms, **17**	B2

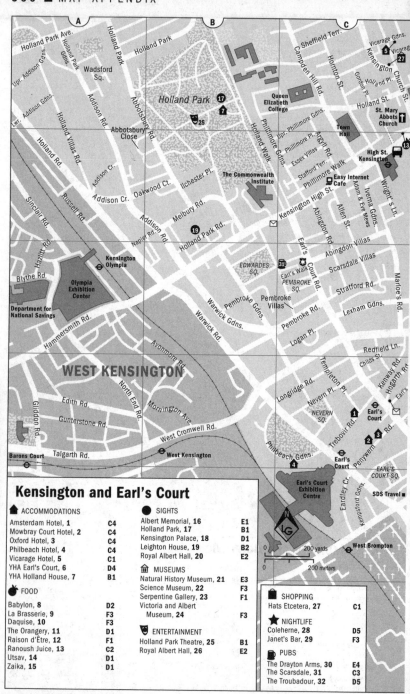

Kensington and Earl's Court

🏠 ACCOMMODATIONS

Amsterdam Hotel, 1	C4
Mowbray Court Hotel, 2	C4
Oxford Hotel, 3	C4
Philbeach Hotel, 4	C4
Vicarage Hotel, 5	C1
YHA Earl's Court, 6	D4
YHA Holland House, 7	B1

🍴 FOOD

Babylon, 8	D2
La Brasserie, 9	F3
Daquise, 10	F3
The Orangery, 11	D1
Raison d'Être, 12	F1
Ranoush Juice, 13	C2
Utsav, 14	D1
Zaika, 15	D1

● SIGHTS

Albert Memorial, 16	E1
Holland Park, 17	B1
Kensington Palace, 18	D1
Leighton House, 19	B2
Royal Albert Hall, 20	E2

🏛 MUSEUMS

Natural History Museum, 21	E3
Science Museum, 22	F3
Serpentine Gallery, 23	F1
Victoria and Albert	
Museum, 24	F3

🎭 ENTERTAINMENT

Holland Park Theatre, 25	B1
Royal Albert Hall, 26	E2

🛍 SHOPPING

Hats Etcetera, 27	C1

★ NIGHTLIFE

Coleherne, 28	D5
Janet's Bar, 29	F3

🍺 PUBS

The Drayton Arms, 30	E4
The Scarsdale, 31	C3
The Troubadour, 32	D5

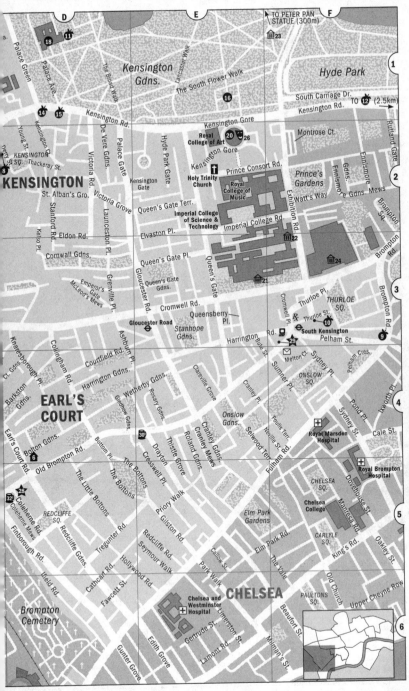

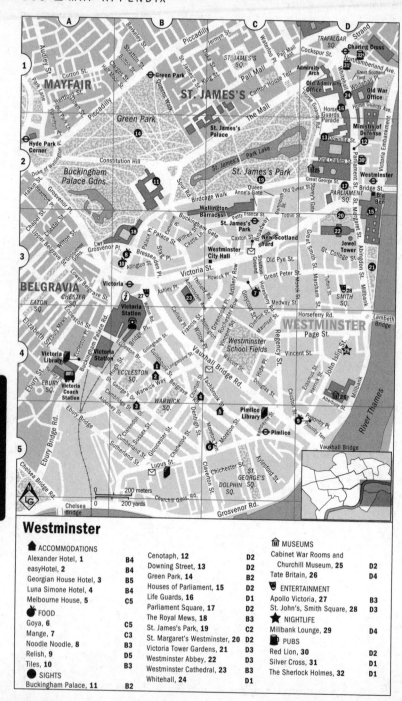

Westminster

ACCOMMODATIONS

Alexander Hotel, **1**	B4
easyHotel, **2**	B4
Georgian House Hotel, **3**	B5
Luna Simone Hotel, **4**	B4
Melbourne House, **5**	C5

FOOD

Goya, **6**	C5
Mange, **7**	C3
Noodle Noodle, **8**	B3
Relish, **9**	D5
Tiles, **10**	B3

SIGHTS

Buckingham Palace, **11**	B2
Cenotaph, **12**	D2
Downing Street, **13**	D2
Green Park, **14**	B2
Houses of Parliament, **15**	D2
Life Guards, **16**	D1
Parliament Square, **17**	D2
The Royal Mews, **18**	B3
St. James's Park, **19**	C2
St. Margaret's Westminster, **20**	D2
Victoria Tower Gardens, **21**	D3
Westminster Abbey, **22**	D3
Westminster Cathedral, **23**	B3
Whitehall, **24**	D1

MUSEUMS

Cabinet War Rooms and Churchill Museum, **25**	D2
Tate Britain, **26**	D4

ENTERTAINMENT

Apollo Victoria, **27**	B3
St. John's, Smith Square, **28**	D3

NIGHTLIFE

Millbank Lounge, **29**	D4

PUBS

Red Lion, **30**	D2
Silver Cross, **31**	D1
The Sherlock Holmes, **32**	D1

Marylebone and Regent's Park

ACCOMMODATIONS

Hart House Hotel, **1**	B4
Lincoln House Hotel, **2**	C4
International Student House, **3**	D3
University of Westminster Halls, **4**	C3

FOOD

Giraffe, **5**	C4
La Galette, **6**	C4
The Golden Hind, **7**	C4
Mandalay, **8**	A4
Patogh, **9**	A4
Ranoush Juice, **10**	B5
Royal China, **11**	C4
Spighetta, **12**	C4

SIGHTS

All Souls Langham Place, **13**	D4
Edgware Road, **14**	B5
Gardens of St. John's Lodge, **15**	C2
London Zoo, **16**	C1
Madame Tussaud's, **17**	C3
Portland Place, **18**	D3
Queen Mary's Gardens, **19**	C2
Regent's Park, **20**	C1
Royal Institute of British Architects, **21**	D4

MUSEUMS

Sherlock Holmes Museum, **22**	B3
The Wallace Collection, **23**	C4

ENTERTAINMENT

Marylebone Dance Studio, **24**	B4
Open-Air Theatre, **25**	C2
Wigmore Hall, **26**	D5

NIGHTLIFE

Low Life, **27**	C4

PUBS

The Golden Eagle, **28**	C4
O'Conor Don, **29**	D5

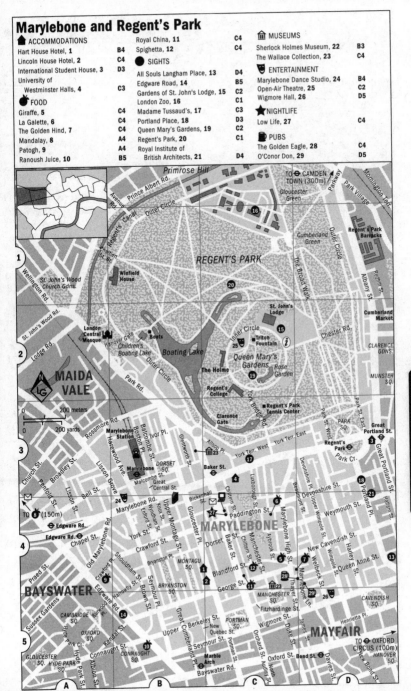

APPENDIX

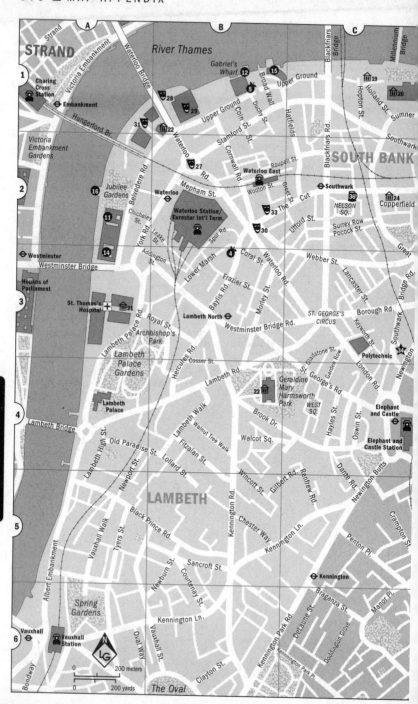

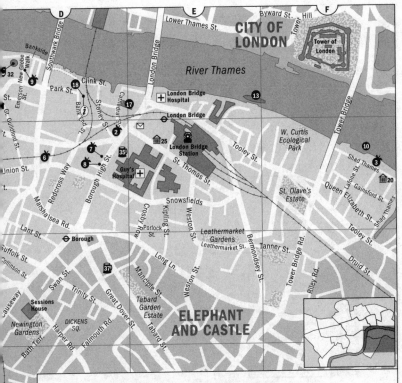

The South Bank and Lambeth

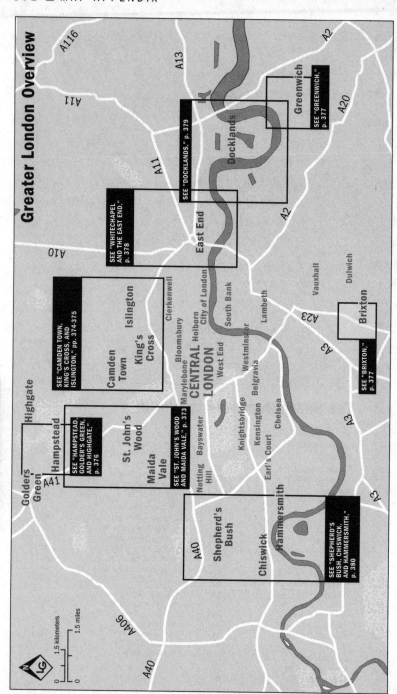

Greater London Overview

SEE "CAMDEN TOWN, KING'S CROSS, AND ISLINGTON," pp. 374-375

SEE "DOCKLANDS," p. 379

SEE "WHITECHAPEL AND THE EAST END," p. 378

SEE "GREENWICH," p. 377

SEE "BRIXTON," p. 377

SEE "HAMPSTEAD, GOLDER'S GREEN, AND HIGHGATE," p. 376

SEE "ST. JOHN'S WOOD AND MAIDA VALE," p. 373

SEE "SHEPHERD'S BUSH, CHISWICK, AND HAMMERSMITH," p. 380

Highgate

Golders Green

Hampstead

St. John's Wood

Maida Vale

Camden Town

King's Cross

Islington

Clerkenwell

Bloomsbury

Marylebone

Notting Hill

Bayswater

Holborn

City of London

CENTRAL LONDON

West End

South Bank

Westminster

Docklands

East End

Greenwich

Dulwich

Brixton

Vauxhall

Lambeth

Belgravia

Knightsbridge

Kensington

Chelsea

Earl's Court

Shepherd's Bush

Chiswick

Hammersmith

A116

A13

A2

A11

A11

A20

A11

A10

A2

A23

A3

A3

A3

A41

A40

A40

A406

1.5 kilometers

1.5 miles

0

0

North London:
St. John's Wood and Maida Vale

● SIGHTS
Abbey Rd., **4**
Lord's Cricket Ground, **5**

🏛 MUSEUMS
Freud Museum, **1**

🎭 ENTERTAINMENT
Canal Cafe Theatre, **6**
Hampstead Theatre, **2**
Tricycle / Tricycle Cinema, **3**

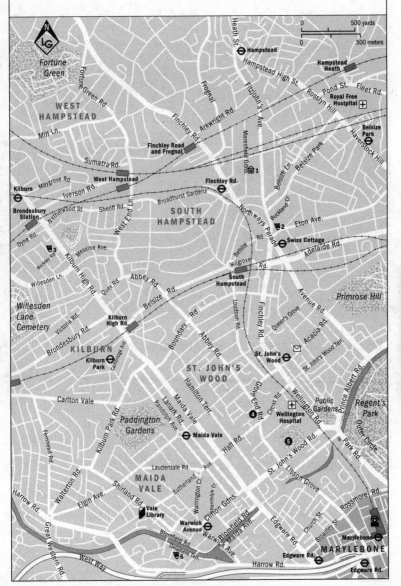

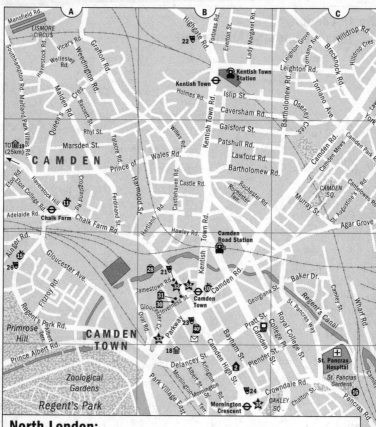

North London:
Camden Town, King's Cross, and Islington

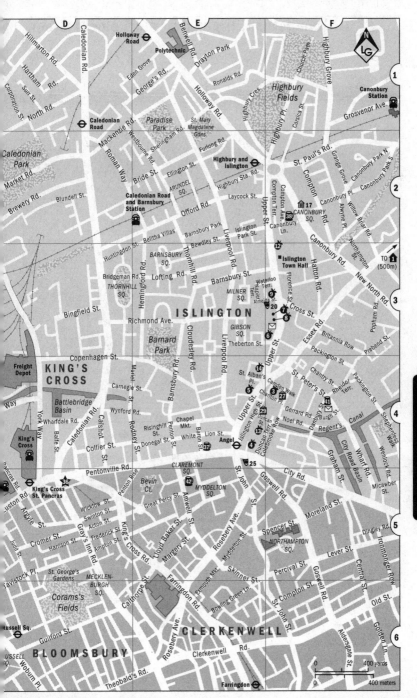

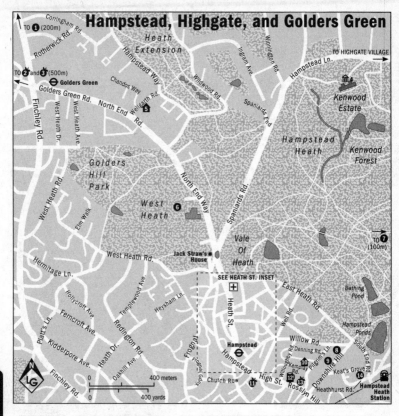

Hampstead, Highgate, and Golders Green

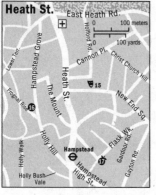

Heath St.

🏠 ACCOMMODATIONS
Hampstead Village
  Guest House, **10**
YHA Hampstead Heath, **5**

🍎 FOOD
Al Casbah, **17**
Bloom's, **3**
Carmelli Bakery, **2**
Giraffe, **13**
Le Crêperie de Hampstead, **11**

● SIGHTS
Fenton House, **14**
Golders Green Crematorium, **1**
Hill Garden, **6**
Keats House, **8**
Parliament Hill, **7**
Two Willow Road, **16**

🏛 MUSEUMS
The Iveagh Bequest, **4**

🎭 ENTERTAINMENT
New End Theatre, **15**

🍺 PUBS
Bar Room Bar, **12**
Freemason's Arms, **9**

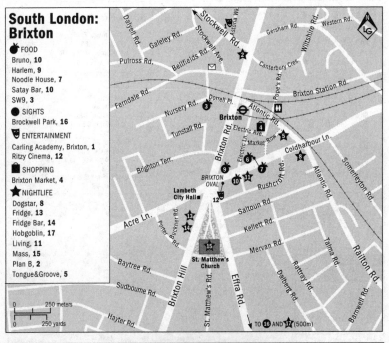

South London: Brixton

🍎 FOOD
Bruno, 10
Harlem, 9
Noodle House, 7
Satay Bar, 10
SW9, 3

● SIGHTS
Brockwell Park, 16

🎭 ENTERTAINMENT
Carling Academy, Brixton, 1
Ritzy Cinema, 12

🛍 SHOPPING
Brixton Market, 4

★ NIGHTLIFE
Dogstar, 8
Fridge, 13
Fridge Bar, 14
Hobgoblin, 17
Living, 11
Mass, 15
Plan B, 2
Tongue&Groove, 5

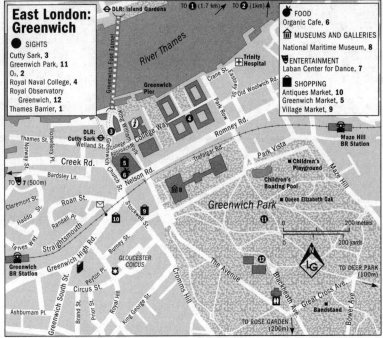

East London: Greenwich

● SIGHTS
Cutty Sark, 3
Greenwich Park, 11
O2, 2
Royal Naval College, 4
Royal Observatory
  Greenwich, 12
Thames Barrier, 1

🍎 FOOD
Organic Cafe, 6

🏛 MUSEUMS AND GALLERIES
National Maritime Museum, 8

🎭 ENTERTAINMENT
Laban Center for Dance, 7

🛍 SHOPPING
Antiques Market, 10
Greenwich Market, 5
Village Market, 9

East London: Whitechapel and The East End

(HS = HOXTON AND SHOREDITCH INSET, p. 379)

🍴 FOOD
Aladin, **1**	B2
Hoxton Apprentice, **2**	HS
Beigel Bake, **3**	B2
Café 1001, **4**	B2
Coffee@, **5**	HS
Drunken Monkey, **6**	A2
The Real Greek, **7**	HS
Shish, **8**	HS
Sweet and Spicy, **9**	B3
Yelo, **10**	HS

● SIGHTS
Bevis Marks Synagogue, **11**	A3
Brick Lane, **12**	B3
Christ Church Spitalfields, **13**	A3
East London Mosque, **14**	B3

🏛 MUSEUMS
Geffrye Museum, **15**	A1
Museum of Childhood, **16**	C1
Victoria Miro, **17**	HS
Whitechapel Art Gallery, **18**	B3
White Cube, **19**	HS

🎭 ENTERTAINMENT
Hackney Empire, **20**	C1
Spitz, **21**	A3

🛍 SHOPPING
Brick Lane Market, **22**	B2
The Laden Showroom, **23**	B2
Petticoat Lane Market, **24**	A3

Sh! Women's Erotic Emporium, **25**	HS
Spitalfields Market, **26**	A3
Sunday (Up) Market, **27**	A2

★ NIGHTLIFE
93 Feet East, **28**	B2
Aquarium, **29**	HS
Bar Kick, **30**	HS
Big Chill Bar, **31**	B2
Cantaloupe, **32**	HS
Cargo, **33**	HS
Cocomo, **34**	HS
Comedy Cafe, **35**	HS
The George and Dragon, **36**	HS
Herbal, **37**	HS
Hoxton Sq. Bar & Kitchen, **38**	HS
Vibe Bar, **39**	B2

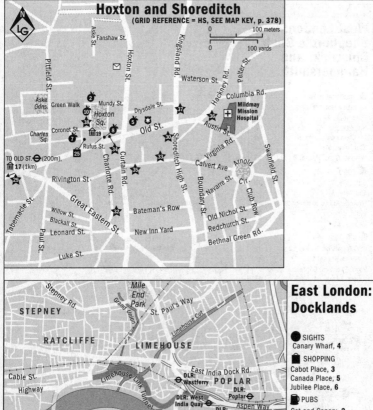

Hoxton and Shoreditch
(GRID REFERENCE = HS, SEE MAP KEY, p. 378)

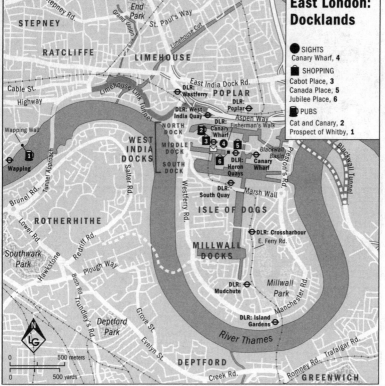

East London: Docklands

● SIGHTS
Canary Wharf, 4

🛍 SHOPPING
Cabot Place, 3
Canada Place, 5
Jubilee Place, 6

🍺 PUBS
Cat and Canary, 2
Prospect of Whitby, 1

APPENDIX

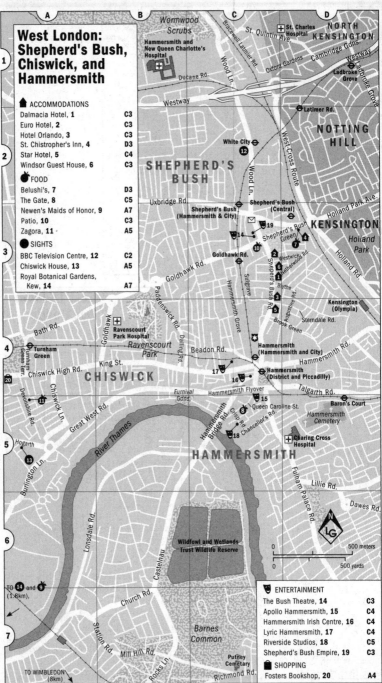

West London: Shepherd's Bush, Chiswick, and Hammersmith

🏠 ACCOMMODATIONS
Dalmacia Hotel, 1 — C3
Euro Hotel, 2 — C3
Hotel Orlando, 3 — C3
St. Chistropher's Inn, 4 — D3
Star Hotel, 5 — C4
Windsor Guest House, 6 — C3

🍎 FOOD
Belushi's, 7 — D3
The Gate, 8 — C5
Newen's Maids of Honor, 9 — A7
Patio, 10 — C3
Zagora, 11 — A5

● SIGHTS
BBC Television Centre, 12 — C2
Chiswick House, 13 — A5
Royal Botanical Gardens, Kew, 14 — A7

🎭 ENTERTAINMENT
The Bush Theatre, 14 — C3
Apollo Hammersmith, 15 — C4
Hammersmith Irish Centre, 16 — C4
Lyric Hammersmith, 17 — C4
Riverside Studios, 18 — C5
Shepherd's Bush Empire, 19 — C3

🛍 SHOPPING
Fosters Bookshop, 20 — A4

INDEX

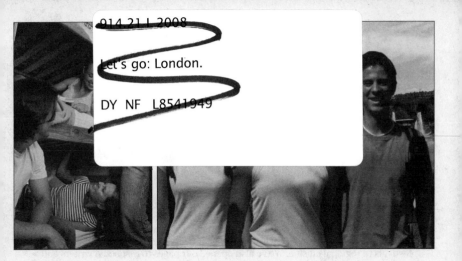

914.21 L 2008

Let's go: London.

DY NF L8541949

GET CONNECTED & SAVE WITH THE HI CARD

An HI card gives you access to friendly and affordable accommodations at over 4,000 hostels in over 60 countries, including across Britain and Ireland. Members also receive complementary travel insurance, members-only airfare deals, and thousands of discounts on everything from tours and dining to shopping, communications and transportation.

Join millions of HI members worldwide who save money and have more fun every time they travel.

Hostelling International USA

Get your card today!   **HIUSA.ORG**

ABOUT LET'S GO

NOT YOUR PARENTS' TRAVEL GUIDE

At Let's Go, we see every trip as the chance of a lifetime. If your dream is to grab a machete and forge through the jungles of Costa Rica, we can take you there. If you'd rather bask in the Riviera sun at a beachside cafe, we'll set you a table. We write for readers who know that there's more to travel than sharing double deckers with tourists and who believe that travel can change both themselves and the world—whether they plan to spend six days in Mexico City or six months in Europe. We'll show you just how far your money can go, and prove that the greatest limitation on your adventures is not your wallet, but your imagination.

BEYOND THE TOURIST EXPERIENCE

To help you gain a deeper connection with the places you travel, our fearless researchers scour the globe to give you the heads-up on both world-renowned and off-the-beaten-track attractions, sights, and destinations. They engage with the local culture only to emerge with the freshest insights on everything from local festivals to regional cuisine. We've also opened our pages to respected writers and scholars to hear their takes on the countries and regions we cover, and asked travelers who have worked, studied, or volunteered abroad to contribute first-person accounts of their experiences. In addition, we increased our coverage of responsible travel and expanded each guide's Beyond Tourism chapter to share more ideas about how to give back while on the road.

FORTY-EIGHT YEARS OF WISDOM

Let's Go got its start in 1960, when a group of creative and well-traveled students compiled their experience and advice into a 20-page mimeographed pamphlet, which they gave to travelers on charter flights to Europe. Four and a half decades later, we've expanded to cover six continents and all kinds of travel—while retaining our founders' adventurous attitude toward the world. Laced with witty prose and total candor, our guides are still researched and written entirely by students on shoestring budgets, experienced travelers who know that train strikes, stolen luggage, food poisoning, and marriage proposals are all part of a day's work.

THE LET'S GO COMMUNITY

More than just a travel guide company, Let's Go is a community. Our small staff comes together because of our shared passion for travel and our desire to help other travelers see the world the way it was meant to be seen. We love it when our readers become part of the Let's Go community as well—when you travel, drop us a postcard (67 Mt. Auburn St., Cambridge, MA 02138, USA), send us an e-mail (feedback@letsgo.com), or post on our forum (http://www.letsgo.com/connect/forum) to tell us about your adventures and discoveries.

For more information, visit us online: www.letsgo.com.